EUROPEAN UNION POLITICS

JOHN McCORMICK

SECOND EDITION

 macmillan education   palgrave

First edition 2011
Second edition 2015
Published by
PALGRAVE

Palgrave in the UK is an imprint of Macmillan Publishers Limited, registered in England, company number 785998, of 4 Crinan Street, London, N1 9XW.

Palgrave Macmillan in the US is a division of St Martin's Press LLC, 175 Fifth Avenue, New York, NY 10010.

Palgrave is a global imprint of the above companies and is represented throughout the world.

Palgrave® and Macmillan® are registered trademarks in the United States, the United Kingdom, Europe and other countries.

ISBN: 978–1–137–45339–6 hardback
ISBN: 978–1–137–45338–9 paperback

This book is printed on paper suitable for recycling and made from fully managed and sustained forest sources. Logging, pulping and manufacturing processes are expected to conform to the environmental regulations of the country of origin.

A catalogue record for this book is available from the British Library.

Library of Congress Cataloging-in-Publication Data
McCormick, John, 1954-
    European Union politics / John MCCormick. — Second edition.
                                pages cm. — (Palgrave foundations series)
    Includes bibliographical references and index.
    ISBN 978-1-137-45338-9
    1. European Union. 2.   European Union countries — Politics and government.   I. Title.
JN30.M375 2015
341.242'2 — dc23

                                2015012178

Typeset by Aardvark Editorial Limited, Metfield, Suffolk.

EUROPEAN UNION POLITICS

Palgrave Foundations Series

A series of introductory texts across a wide range of subject areas to meet the needs of today's lecturers and students

Foundations texts provide complete yet concise coverage of core topics and skills based on detailed research of course requirements suitable for both independent study and class use – the firm foundation for future study.

Published

A History of English Literature (third edition)

Biology

British Politics (second edition)

Chemistry (fourth edition)

Communication Studies

Contemporary Europe (third edition)

European Union Politics (second edition)

Foundations of Marketing

Global Politics (second edition)

Modern British History

Nineteenth-Century Britain

Philosophy

Physics (fourth edition)

Politics (fourth edition)

Theatre Studies

Brief Contents

Full Contents

Illustrations and Features

Figures

Tables

Maps

Illustrations

Documents

Debates

Understanding Integration

Focus on

Profiles

Timelines

About the Author

John McCormick is Jean Monnet Professor of European Union Politics at the Indianapolis campus of Indiana University, US. He has held visiting positions at the University of Exeter and the University of Sussex in Britain, has been Fulbright-Schuman Chair in EU-US Relations at the College of Europe in Belgium, and is involved with a multinational European consortium that offers a master's degree on European culture. His teaching and research interests lie in comparative politics and public policy, with particular interests in the politics of the EU, British politics, environmental policy and transatlantic relations. His other publications include *The European Superpower* (Palgrave Macmillan, 2007), *Europeanism* (Oxford University Press, 2010), *Why Europe Matters: The Case for the European Union* (Palgrave Macmillan, 2013) and *Understanding the European Union* (Palgrave Macmillan, 6th edn, 2014).

Preface to the Second Edition

The second edition of this book remains true to the goals and character of the first: to explain the politics and policies of the European Union as clearly and engagingly as possible, primarily for students taking courses or modules on the EU, but also for anyone who wants to find out more about how the EU works and what difference it makes. It starts with the premise that the EU is critically important for Europeans and non-Europeans alike, yet at times frustratingly opaque and peculiar. It has changed how we understand Europe, how Europeans relate to each other, how Europe fits into the global political and economic system, and even how we think about government and politics more generally. But its goals and structure are unique, its rules constantly change, and opinion on its value and significance is divided.

As with the first edition, this book is driven by two main goals. First, foremost and overwhelmingly, it sets out to be informative and challenging while being readable and relevant. The EU has long suffered from an unfortunate image of impenetrability, summed up in the reflections of the British journalist Emma Hartley (2006, pp. ix, 31). She recalls a university course she took on Europe, which she described with terms such as 'baffling', 'jargon-filled' and 'mind-numbing'. Later, as a journalist, she found that the media had a habit of making the EU seem technical and bureaucratic, and 'a special gift for making things seem boring'. With these concerns in mind, *European Union Politics* sets out to make the EU real, alive, relevant and approachable. It recognizes the importance of specialist vocabulary, but tries to cut through the jargon to bring out the drama, intrigue, crises, triumphs, heroes and villains that can be found sprinkled through the long and fascinating history of European integration.

Second, the book is written with the understanding that students will have different backgrounds and different levels of interest in the politics of the EU, and will come from different countries. For some, this will probably be their only formal exposure to the topic. Others, meanwhile, will want to take their studies to another level and will be looking for the foundation that helps make that possible. The comments provided by anonymous reviewers of the first and second editions have been helpful, but they also emphasize that everyone has their own ideas about how much attention should be paid to different topics, and following through on all the suggestions would have made the book much longer. The aim of the chapters that follow is to provide a survey of all the most important ideas, facts and principles of the EU, to place the EU within its broader political context, and offer a taste of the current debates about European integration, influenced by my own take on what it all means. My hope is that students who use the book will become well-informed observers of the EU, and that it will give them the tools they need to take their studies to a deeper level, if that is what they have in mind.

As with the first edition, the chapters that follow are divided into three parts, Part 1 dealing with the ideas and history that are essential to an understanding of the EU, Part 2 covering the major institutions and key political processes that drive EU politics and governance, and Part 3 covering the major policy areas in which the EU is active. At first glance this looks like a fairly conventional approach, but *European Union Politics* also includes material found in no other comparable texts: there are separate chapters, for example, on the defining qualities of Europe and the Europeans, and on public opinion in the EU and how it relates to European integration. There is also more detailed coverage of the specialized agencies of the EU (such as the European Central Bank), as well as environmental policy, justice and home affairs, trade policy, and the different facets of external relations.

In terms of presentation, the overall design follows that of others in the Palgrave Foundations series, but while I have borrowed some of their features, I have introduced many of my own, the overall goal being to present all the material as clearly and compellingly as possible.

Changes to the second edition

The second edition is unchanged in terms of its broad structure, approach and style, but includes many detailed revisions and updates, as well as being about three per cent shorter than the first edition. Most importantly, it addresses all the recent changes in the rules driving integration, integrates new scholarship on the EU, fine-tunes many of the core arguments, has tables and figures based on all the latest data, adds many new examples to illustrate broader points, includes new sources in the lists of further reading, and updates the story of the EU, with coverage of all key developments since the first edition went to press in late 2010. Publication has also been timed to allow for inclusion of the results of the 2014 European Parliament elections, and for changes at the helm of the European Commission, the European Council and the EU foreign affairs structure. In summary:

- Chapters 1–3 remain relatively unchanged, since there have been few developments in our approaches to understanding how the EU evolved and what it has become. But, in response to requests from users and reviewers, new Understanding Integration boxes have been added here and elsewhere in the book to give more coverage of important theoretical and conceptual debates. These boxes go beyond the standard theories of integration and look in detail at concepts that help us better understand the EU as a political system in its own right. At the same time, though, this is not a book about theory, and they are discussed only where it is important to know something about past and current scholarly debates.
- Chapters 4–7 on the history of the EU have been reformulated, reducing the coverage of the early years of European integration in Chapters 4–5 in order to make room for new and expanded coverage in Chapter 7 of recent developments, particularly the fallout from the euro zone crisis.

- Chapters 8–9 update the coverage of the treaties and the member states, with new material on treaty developments in the wake of the crisis in the euro zone, and the latest on prospects for further enlargement of the EU.
- Chapters 10–14 focus on EU institutions, with updates on organizational changes and new information on the most recent appointments to senior positions within the EU structure. Chapter 14 offers expanded coverage of the European Central Bank.
- Chapters 15–17 focus on popular participation in the work of the EU, with new analysis in light of the results of the 2014 European Parliament elections, and expanded coverage of changes in public opinion in the wake of the euro zone crisis.
- Chapters 18–25 look at policy processes and outcomes, the biggest changes coming in Chapter 20 (on the euro) and in Chapters 24 and 25, dealing with developments at the global level, notably with events in Ukraine and the Middle East.

All the supporting material used in the first edition has carried over into the second edition:

Chapter summaries Every chapter begins with a preview of what the chapter will be about and how it is structured, and ends with a summary that recaps the major topics covered and the major arguments made in each chapter.

Key issues Every chapter begins with a brief set of open-ended and occasionally provocative questions designed to help students think about some of the critical issues raised in the book, and to suggest subjects for further research.

Terms and concepts Key terms in the text (nearly 200 in all) are given short marginal definitions (which are then listed at the end of each chapter), while short paragraphs go into more depth on key concepts such as the state, enlargement, euroscepticism and power. Several new definitions and concepts have been added to the second edition.

Understanding integration Some 14 new boxes have been added, offering more detailed explanations of the key theoretical dimensions of understanding the EU. These include supranationalism, intergovernmentalism, Europeanization and multilevel governance.

Debates Several chapters include debates that put the case for and against a proposition, such as whether or not the EU needs a constitution and whether or not the euro will thrive. These are designed to encourage consideration of some of the more critical disagreements in the saga of European integration.

Focus on The debates are complemented by boxes that go into more depth on topics related to the material in the body of the text. New topics in the second edition include the troubled role of Britain in the EU and the compelling explanation of the euro crisis offered by financier George Soros.

Profiles Profiles of key European personalities – some from history and others holders of the key offices in today's EU institutions – are designed to put a human face on the EU, and offer insight into some of the characters who have taken their turn on the European stage.

Tables and figures The text is dotted with tables and figures that present key data on the EU or try to express some of the more complex ideas in visual form. Most are based on the latest data available from the websites of key EU and international organizations. Using the URLs to visit those websites will provide the most recent data.

Timelines and documents The history chapters include timelines that list key events and quotations from selected documents of key historical significance, such as treaties, speeches and declarations.

Further reading Every chapter ends with a short list of books chosen to provide useful further information, with a focus on the most recent, important and/or helpful sources.

Websites A companion website for this text can be found at www.palgrave.com/politics/mccormick. It contains links to key EU institutions and key sources of news and information on EU affairs, sites contained within figures and tables in the book, updates on key developments in the EU, a searchable glossary, chapter outlines, a full (and searchable) chronology, test banks and additional discussion questions.

Acknowledgements and Photo Credits

This was one of the two final projects I worked on with the incomparable Steven Kennedy before his retirement in 2014. Steven had been my publisher for the best part of 20 years, and consistently brought the kind of engagement, professionalism, encouragement and good humour to his job that we cloistered authors so often need. I will miss him, but the transition to Stephen Wenham (with whom I have worked for the best part of a decade) has been seamless, and builds on the good fortune that I have had in working with such an excellent publishing company as Palgrave Macmillan. My thanks also to Maddy Hamey-Thomas for her editorial assistance on this book, and to Maggie Lythgoe and Linda Norris for overseeing the copy-editing and production in such a smooth and efficient manner. And my love to Leanne, Ian and Stuart, as ever, for all the really important things.

The author and publisher would like to thank the following who have kindly given permission for the use of pictorial copyright material:

John McCormick, pp. 15, 287, 318, 387; European Union, pp. 19, 46, 65, 67, 69 (both photographs), 75, 76, 82, 84, 91, 94, 97, 107, 124, 131, 141, 165 (Walter Hallstein, Jean Rey, Franco Maria Malfatti, Sicco Mansholt, Francois-Xavier Ortoli, Roy Jenkins, Gaston Thorn, Jacques Delors, Jacques Santer and Romano Prodi), 194, 196, 201, 212, 215 (European judges), 223, 235, 242, 251, 305, 314, 328, 346, 368, 380, 385, 403, 411, 420; Peter Haas, p. 20; Photographic Service of the Council of the EU © European Union, pp. 23, 37, 115, 152, 165 (José Manuel Barroso), 178, 184, 187, 190, 398; Audiovisual Services for Media (European Parliament), pp. 49, 52, 161, 164, 198, 228, 265, 299, 353, 397; Picture Alliance, p. 59; Press Association, pp. 110, 132, 159, 226, 270, 277, 334, 361; Court of Justice of the European Union, pp. 215 (Vassilios Skouris), 220.

Acronyms and Abbreviations

ACP	African Caribbean Pacific programme
ALDE	Alliance of Liberals and Democrats for Europe
CAP	Common Agricultural Policy
CCP	Common Commercial Policy
CFP	Common Fisheries Policy
CFSP	Common Foreign and Security Policy
CoR	Committee of the Regions
Coreper	Committee of Permanent Representatives
DG	directorate-general
EADS	European Aeronautic Defence and Space Company
EAP	Environment Action Programme
EBRD	European Bank for Reconstruction and Development
EC	European Community
ECB	European Central Bank
ECHR	European Convention on Human Rights (Ch. 8)/European Court of Human Rights (Ch. 13)
ECJ	European Court of Justice
ECSC	European Coal and Steel Community
ECTS	European Credit Transfer and Accumulation System
ECU	European Currency Unit
EDC	European Defence Community
EEA	European Economic Area
EEC	European Economic Community
EESC	European Economic and Social Committee
EFTA	European Free Trade Association
EIB	European Investment Bank
EMI	European Monetary Institute
EMS	European Monetary System
EMU	economic and monetary union
ENP	European Neighbourhood Policy
EP	European Parliament
EPC	European Political Community (Ch. 5)/European Political Cooperation (Ch. 6)
EPP	European People's Party
ERDF	European Regional Development Fund
ERM	Exchange Rate Mechanism
ESA	European Space Agency
ESDP	European Security and Defence Policy
ESF	European Social Fund

ESM	European Social Model
EU	European Union
EU-12	the 12 pre-1995 member states of the EU
EU-15	the 15 pre-2004 member states of the EU
EU-28	the existing 28 member states of the EU
Euratom	European Atomic Energy Community
Eurojust	Judicial Cooperation Unit
Europol	European Police Office
GDP	gross domestic product
GNI	gross national income
HR	High Representative (for foreign and security policy/foreign affairs and security policy)
IGC	intergovernmental conference
IGO	intergovernmental organization
IMF	International Monetary Fund
IO	international organization
IPE	international political economy
IR	international relations
JHA	justice and home affairs
MEP	Member of the European Parliament
NATO	North Atlantic Treaty Organization
NGO	nongovernmental organization
ODA	official development assistance
OECD	Organisation for Economic Co-operation and Development
OEEC	Organisation for European Economic Co-operation
PR	proportional representation
QMV	qualified majority vote
RIA	regional integration association
S&D	Progressive Alliance of Socialists and Democrats
SAA	Stabilization and Accession Agreement
SAP	Stabilization and Association Process
SEA	Single European Act
SMP	single-member plurality
TEC	Treaty Establishing the European Community
TEEC	Treaty Establishing the European Economic Community
TEU	Treaty on European Union
TFEU	Treaty on the Functioning of the European Union
UN	United Nations
VAT	value added tax
WEU	Western European Union
WTO	World Trade Organization

EU member states

AT	Austria
BE	Belgium
BG	Bulgaria
CY	Cyprus

CZ	Czech Republic
DE	Germany
DK	Denmark
EE	Estonia
EL	Greece
ES	Spain
FI	Finland
FR	France
HR	Croatia
HU	Hungary
IE	Ireland
IT	Italy
LT	Lithuania
LU	Luxembourg
LV	Latvia
MT	Malta
NL	Netherlands
PL	Poland
PT	Portugal
RO	Romania
SE	Sweden
SI	Slovenia
SK	Slovakia
UK	United Kingdom

Introduction

At a glittering ceremony in Oslo in December 2012, leaders of the European Union accepted the Nobel Peace Prize on behalf of the EU, which it had won in recognition of more than 60 years of contributions 'to the advancement of peace and reconciliation, democracy and human rights in Europe'. The award seemed to confirm the dream of the founders of the EU, that the countries of Europe needed to work harder and more closely together to avoid the kinds of conflicts and wars that had blighted the region for centuries. There have been no inter-state wars in Europe since 1945, and the EU has grown into the one major actor on the global stage that relies on opportunity rather than threats to advance its cause. Thus, it seemed to be a worthy Nobel laureate.

But even as the award was being accepted in Oslo, there were many who questioned how much the EU had contributed to regional peace, and who argued that the North Atlantic Treaty Organization (NATO) deserved at least a share of the credit. Others pointed to the irony of the EU winning the prize against a background of economic crisis; most EU states were mired in recession at the time, many of their governments had imposed harsh austerity measures, the single European currency – the euro – tottered on the verge of collapse, high unemployment made life miserable and unpredictable for millions, public opinion was turning against the EU (although it was even more harsh in its assessment of national government), and the future of European integration looked questionable at best.

This ongoing tension, between success and failure, between swagger and humility, and between optimism and pessimism, has been part of the story of European integration since the beginning, and is the core theme of this book. On the one hand, supporters credit the European experiment with bringing lasting peace to Europe, revitalizing the European marketplace, changing the definition of Europe, and altering the global balance of power. The personality of Europe has been transformed under the guidance of integration, they argue, and while the EU continues to wrestle with unemployment, problems with productivity, labour market restrictions, and a declining and ageing population, Europeans are far better off overall with the opportunities it has created. The EU has redefined the way Europeans see themselves and the way the world sees Europe, and the building of a common body of laws and policies has brought Europeans closer together. Some even look forward to the day when Europeans can become citizens of a 'United States of Europe'.

Not so fast, respond the critics. The European experiment has undermined the sovereignty of European states, sullied the quality of European democracy, been foisted on unwilling Europeans by political elites, takes too little account of national differences, and makes it more difficult for European states to address economic problems that could once be contained by national governments responding to local circumstances. The EU constitutes a new level of European 'government' that lacks adequate transparency or accountability, and its member states have suffered rather than benefited from the effects of integration, losing their identity and some of their freedoms as faceless bureaucrats in Brussels write new laws that seem to be driven by the goal of creating a bland and homogenized Europe.

Meanwhile, the EU continues to generate much bafflement. It is not a conventional state, and non-Europeans often scratch their heads over the distinction between the EU and its member states, undecided over whether to treat the EU as a single entity or simply as a club to which its member states happen to belong. As a global actor, the EU is routinely criticized for punching below its weight, while much of the speculation about the changing balance of power in the international system has bypassed the EU, leapfrogging instead to China, India and even Brazil. The euro quickly became the most recognized symbol of European integration after its launch as a physical currency in 2002, but in the wake of a debt crisis that broke in Greece in 2009 and had euro zone leaders scrambling to respond, it soon became a symbol of much that was wrong with the EU. There was speculation that some of its members would leave, and even that the EU itself might collapse, or at the very least shrink.

But whatever we think of the EU, and however we understand its core personality, it is hard to ignore. On the global stage, the EU is the world's wealthiest marketplace, the world's biggest trading power, the world's biggest market for corporate mergers and acquisitions, the world's biggest source of and target for foreign direct investment, and it plays a role in international relations (IR) unlike that of any other major actor in history, in the sense that it relies on civilian and peaceful means to project itself, rather than military means.

From the modest first step taken with the signature of the Treaty of Paris in April 1951, creating the European Coal and Steel Community, we now have today's European Union: 28 member states containing more than half a billion people, with almost every other European state actively seeking membership of the club, or certainly pondering the possibility. The Cold War political and economic divisions of Europe have all but disappeared, and it is now less realistic to think of European states in isolation than as partners in an ever closer European Union. It may not be a United States of Europe, but it is hard to imagine a future for Europe that does not involve continued deep political and economic cooperation.

In short, Europeans and non-Europeans alike need to better understand how the EU works and what difference it makes. Hence, this book, which sets out to provide a survey of the principles, history, politics, policies and effects of European integration. It asks six core questions:

1 What is the European Union?
2 Where did it come from and how has it evolved?
3 What is the context within which it works?
4 How is it governed?
5 What are the results of its work?
6 How has it changed Europe and Europeans?

Understanding Integration... *The role of theory*

Theory is best understood as an abstract or generalized approach to explaining or understanding a phenomenon, supported by a significant body of hard evidence. Theory and practice are often contrasted with one another, the implication in the case of the EU being that we need to be familiar with the work of the EU (the practical part of the equation) and with efforts to explain that work (the theoretical part of the equation).

In the natural sciences, numerous theories have come to be so well supported by the evidence that they are unlikely ever to be challenged, and they can even be used to make predictions about events and phenomena that have not yet been observed. We know, for example, that the earth rotates around the sun and that matter is made up of atoms. But the social sciences suffer much greater uncertainties (we cannot even agree on a definition of the term 'social science', or which subjects fit under the heading; see Trigg, 2001), with the result that they produce theories that are subject to stronger doubts, are routinely disputed, and tend to go in and out of fashion. Broadly speaking, the major division in the case of European integration is between those who see

the EU mainly in intergovernmental terms, and those who see it mainly in supranational terms, and the chapters that follow set out to address all the competing approaches equally, if often necessarily briefly.

Unfortunately, we have yet to develop a grand theory that explains the entirety of European (or even regional) integration. Much of the debate instead centres on middle-range theorizing, which tries to bridge the gap between the abstract and the empirical. It recognizes the dangers of grand theories that become so broad as to be impossible to test, and instead focuses on theorizing at a level that is both grounded in reality and sufficiently abstract as to allow generalization.

The difficulties of theorizing the EU are summarized by Michael Burgess (2006, p. 245), who describes the EU as a conceptual enigma and an intellectual puzzle, an outcome he ascribes to a combination of the novel manner in which European integration was originally planned and built, and the inadequacies of existing mainstream theories of IR and European integration. The result, he concludes, is that 'the EU works in practice but not in theory'.

This book addresses these questions by dividing the story of integration into three parts. **Part 1** (Chapters 1–9) sets the scene by reviewing the history and core principles of European integration. It begins with two chapters that look at the theoretical and conceptual debates over how and why the EU evolved, and then over what it has become. They are not intended to be capsule surveys of integration theory so much as an introduction to the key reference points that must form the basis of any analysis of the EU. They make clear that although many explanations have been proposed, there is almost no agreement among scholars of the EU on how best to understand it, and we have not yet even agreed an easy answer to the simple question 'What is the EU?' Chapter 1 reviews key theories coming out of the study of IR, including functionalism, intergovernmentalism, supranationalism, realism and constructivism. Chapter 2 switches the focus to comparative politics, considering the qualities of the EU as a political system, looking at the 'normal science' (that is, standard) approaches to understanding the EU, and comparing the explanatory value of federalism and confederalism.

Chapter 3 tries to come to grips with the parameters of Europe, reviews the troubling questions about identity in Europe, and then looks at some of its critical demographic trends. Chapters 4–7 provide a survey of the history of the EU, beginning with an explanation of the challenges facing postwar Europe and

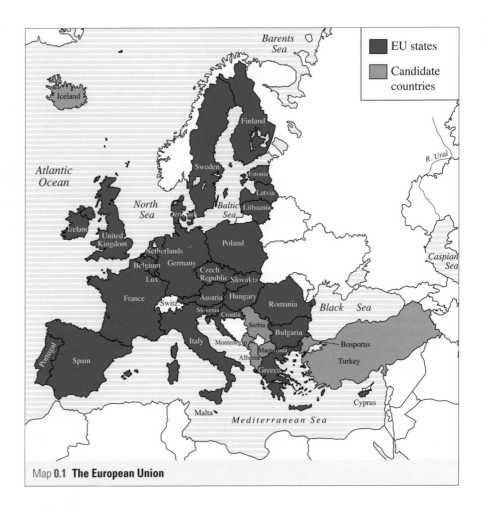

Map **0.1** **The European Union**

then tracing integration through the development of treaties, the different stages in enlargement, key policy developments, and the international context within which integration proceeded.

Today's European Union can be traced back to the signature of the 1951 Treaty of Paris, which created the European Coal and Steel Community (ECSC). Although a useful start, the ECSC was limited in its aims and in 1957 the Treaty of Rome was signed, creating the European Economic Community, the core goal of which was the creation of a European single market. Only six states initially took part, but the first of several waves of enlargement occurred in 1973, moving through stages to 2013 when the accession of Croatia took membership to 28. Along the way, new treaties expanded the reach of integration into new areas of policy, a landmark change coming with the creation of the European Union as a result of the 1992 Treaty on European Union, and another coming in 1999 with the launch of the euro. Chapters 8 and 9 round out Part 1 by looking in turn at the nature of the agreements reached among Europeans, and the impact these have had on the relations between EU institutions and the member states.

Part 2 (Chapters 10–17) focuses on politics and governance by looking at the work and structure of the major EU institutions:

- The *European Commission* is the administrative and executive arm of the EU, promoting European interests and responsible for drafting new laws and overseeing their execution once they have been adopted, managing the EU budget, and playing a key role in the EU's external relations, most notably its common trade interests. Headquartered in Brussels, it is overseen by an appointed president who chairs a 28-member College of Commissioners and about 24,000 career bureaucrats.
- The *Council of Ministers* is an intergovernmental body comprising ministers from each of the member states, and shares powers with the European Parliament over the adoption of new EU laws. Headquartered in Brussels, it is steered by a presidency, held in a rotation of six months each by the governments of the member states. It is closely related to the *European Council*, comprising the heads of government of the member states, chaired by an appointed president, and which is responsible for making key strategic decisions.
- The *European Parliament* is the only directly elected European institution, represents the interests of European voters, and shares powers with the Council of Ministers over the adoption of new EU laws. Split between Brussels, Luxembourg and Strasbourg in France, it has 751 members divided up among the member states on the basis of population, and elected for fixed five-year renewable terms. Members organize themselves into cross-national political groups, and it is chaired by a president elected from among its members.
- The *European Court of Justice* is the EU's constitutional court, charged with interpreting the treaties and issuing judgments on cases involving parties in a dispute over EU law, and for issuing rulings in cases in national courts where an EU law is at stake. Based in Luxembourg, it is headed by a president, has one judge for each member state, and is supported by a General Court (dealing mainly with less complex cases) and a Civil Service Tribunal (dealing with EU staff matters).
- A growing network of more specialized agencies deal with specific aspects of EU policy. They include financial bodies such as the European Central Bank, decentralized agencies such as the European Aviation Safety Agency and the European Police Office (Europol), temporary executive agencies that manage specific EU programmes, and advisory bodies such as the Committee of the Regions. Finally, independent bodies such as the European Space Agency cannot be ignored.

Each chapter begins with a brief historical background, then focuses on the structure and powers of the institutions, showing what each of them does and how they relate to the others. Part 2 ends with Chapters 15–17, which focus on the ways in which Europeans engage with these institutions through the work of political parties and interest groups, look at the mechanics and impact of European elections and national referendums, and review public opinion in the EU, about integration itself and a range of broader issues.

Part 3 (Chapters 18–25) asks what difference the EU has made by focusing on its policy outputs. Chapter 18 sets the scene with a survey of the policy process and the qualities of public policy in the EU, and is followed by separate chapters dealing with the key policy areas in which the EU has been most active:

Table **0.1** **The EU in figures**

	Area (000 sq. km)	Population (million)	Gross domestic product (billion $)	Per capita gross national income ($)
European Union (28)				
Germany	357	80.6	3,635	46,100
France	549	66.0	2,735	42,250
UK	244	64.1	2,522	39,110
Italy	301	59.8	2,071	34,400
Spain	505	46.6	1,358	29,180
Netherlands	42	16.8	800	47,440
Sweden	450	9.6	558	59,130
Poland	313	38.5	517	12,960
Belgium	31	11.2	508	45,210
Austria	84	8.5	416	48,590
Denmark	43	5.6	331	61,110
Finland	338	5.4	257	47,110
Greece	132	11.0	242	22,530
Portugal	92	10.5	220	20,670
Ireland	70	4.6	218	39,110
Czech Republic	79	10.5	198	18,060
Romania	238	20.0	190	9,060
Hungary	93	9.9	125	12,410
Slovakia	49	5.4	91	17,200
Luxembourg	3	0.5	60	71,810
Croatia	57	4.3	58	13,330
Bulgaria	111	7.3	53	7,030
Slovenia	20	2.0	45	22,830
Lithuania	65	3.0	42	13,820
Latvia	65	2.0	28	14,060
Estonia	45	1.3	24	17,370
Cyprus	9	1.1	23	26,390
Malta	0.3	0.4	9	19,730
TOTAL	**4,386**	**505.1**	**17,638**	**34,033**

Note: Countries in blue are part of the euro zone.

	Area (000 sq. km)	Population (million)	Gross domestic product (billion $)	Per capita gross national income ($)
Non-EU Europe (16)				
Turkey	784	74.9	820	10,950
Switzerland	41	8.1	651	80,950
Norway	324	5.0	513	102,610
Ukraine	604	45.5	177	3,960
Azerbaijan	87	9.4	74	7,350
Belarus	208	9.5	72	6,720
Serbia	88	7.2	43	5,730
Bosnia and Herzegovina	51	3.8	18	4,740
Georgia	70	4.5	16	3,570
Iceland	103	0.3	15	43,930
Albania	29	2.8	13	4,700
Armenia	30	3.0	10	3,790
Macedonia	26	2.1	10	4,800
Moldova	34	3.6	8	2,460
Kosovo	11	1.8	7	3,890
Montenegro	14	0.6	4	7,260
TOTAL	**2,504**	**182.1**	**2,346**	
Other				
United States	9,364	316.1	16,800	53,670
China	9,600	1,357.4	9,240	6,560
Japan	378	127.3	4,902	46,140
Brazil	8,515	200.3	2,246	11,690
Russia	17,098	143.5	2,097	13,860
India	3,287	1,252.1	1,877	1,570
Indonesia	1,919	249.9	868	3,580
WORLD	**134,593**	**7,125.0**	**74,900**	**10,564**

Note: States are ranked by GDP.

Source: Area figures from Food and Agriculture Organization of the UN, http://faostat.fao.org. Population and economic figures for 2013 from World Bank World Development Indicators database, www.worldbank.com (all figures retrieved July 2014).

economic, monetary, cohesion, agricultural, environmental, and justice and home affairs, ending with two chapters that look first at the underlying principles and general policies of the EU as a global actor, and then at the nature of its relationship with particular parts of the world, focusing on the US, its most immediate neighbours, China, and the developing world.

Throughout this survey of the EU, the tensions between success and failure are clearly on show. Advances are contrasted with retreats, achievements are reviewed along with failures, and the immensity of the task of moving independent states into the unexplored territory of integration is reviewed. At the same time, the chapters that follow will also ask why so many troubling existential questions are asked about European integration, when they are almost entirely missing from reviews of politics and policy in EU member states and other liberal democracies. What is it about the EU that invites so much scepticism and doubt? Is it that we do not fully understand the EU or where it is headed, or that we have not yet understood how it compares with conventional state political systems, or is it simply that the exercise is genuinely flawed? These and other questions will be addressed in the chapters that follow.

1 HISTORY AND IDEAS

Part 1 introduces the core concepts that have helped us better understand the European Union, reviews the history of the EU, and then looks at the legal effects of its binding treaties and the place of the member states within the EU. Chapters 1–2 look at the competing theories of how the EU evolved and what it has become, paving the way for an effort in Chapter 3 to answer the troubling question of how best to define and understand Europe and Europeans.

Chapters 4–7, covering the history of the EU, begin with an analysis of the circumstances under which efforts to integrate Europe were born, then examine the key stages and developments in the history of the EU, including the passage of the key treaties, the stages through which the EU expanded from 6 to 28 member states, the shaping of the single market and the euro, and the development of key policies, with an emphasis on economic and foreign policies. These developments are placed along the way within their wider international context.

Chapters 8–9 look in detail at how the EU treaties evolved, the features of the legal order that has emerged as a result, and the evolving relationship between the EU and its member states. Chapter 9 ends with some speculation regarding possible future changes in the membership of the EU.

1 Understanding Integration

Preview

The roots of today's European Union can be traced to the creation in 1952 of the European Coal and Steel Community (ECSC). With this event began a complex process by which national interests came to be overlaid with collective European interests, leading to today's EU. How and why this happened has been the subject of much debate. Multiple theories and approaches have been proposed, ranging from federalism to neofunctionalism and constructivism, but while they offer valuable insights, they have all been criticized in their own way, and no grand theory of European integration has yet won approval.

The earliest explanations came mainly out of the discipline of international relations (IR), and portrayed the European Community either as a process with its own internal logic or as an international organization with the governments of the member states as key actors. These theories are reviewed in this chapter. But as the reach of European integration expanded, so the focus switched to explanations coming out of comparative politics and public policy, which see the EU as a political system in its own right, and pay more attention to the character of its institutions, processes and policy dynamics. These approaches are reviewed in Chapter 2.

At the same time, how we think about the EU depends mainly on how we understand the changing role of states. Once the dominant actors on the European political stage, states have changed in the wake of the growing interstate cooperation brought on by political and economic pressures. Some argue that the EU has developed many of the features of a European superstate, or a new level of government and authority working above the level of the traditional state. Others, however, are not so sure. Either way, we need to be clear on the parameters of the debate, which is where this chapter begins.

Key issues

- What is happening to the international state system? Is it still strong, is it undergoing a transformation, or is it dying?
- How far can we still think of the EU as an international organization, and how far has it developed the features of a state?
- What role does theory play in understanding the EU, and should theories be primarily explanatory, predictive, or a combination of the two?
- How do realist, liberal and idealist approaches compare as a means of thinking about today's international system?
- Are intergovernmentalist arguments still helpful as a means for understanding the EU?

Concept

The Westphalian system

The international state system is often known as the Westphalian system after the 1648 Peace of Westphalia. States had, however, begun to emerge well before 1648, and the worldwide reach of the state system did not accelerate until the break-up of European empires after 1945. Some now question the health of the system, arguing that the state is dying, and pointing to the EU and other examples of regional integration as proof of how government and authority are being redefined.

States and nations

For the past 300–400 years, the state has been the usual means for organizing large-scale political communities. The modern state was born in Europe some time in the Middle Ages as competition for power and influence among empires, kingdoms, duchies and the Catholic Church changed territorial boundaries. By the seventeenth century, the outlines of today's European state system had become clearer, the defining event being the 1648 Peace of Westphalia. This brought an end to the Eighty Years' War and the Thirty Years' War, strengthened religious freedom, adjusted the boundaries of Sweden, France and the German states, and confirmed the independence of the Netherlands, Switzerland and the northern states of what is now Italy. Borders and sovereignty achieved a new prominence, and the term Westphalian system is often used today as shorthand for the resulting international order.

Although there is little agreement on the definition of the state, most scholars would agree that it is a legal and political entity that has four key qualities: territory, sovereignty, independence, and legitimacy (see Figure 1.1). None of these qualities has ever been static or absolute, because the boundaries of states change, the authority of state institutions is not equally recognized by everyone, no states are truly independent because none is self-sufficient, and there are many states whose international legal standing is either disputed (including Taiwan, Northern Cyprus and Kosovo) or ambiguous (including the micro-states of Europe, such as Andorra, Monaco and the Vatican City).

In 1800 there were barely 24 states in the world, and only 45 more had been created by the time of the outbreak of the Second World War. With decolonization and the break-up of European empires after the war, there was an explosion of newly independent states (80 emerged in the period 1950–79 alone, mainly in Africa), and more than 20 were added to the list in the 1990s with the break-up of the Soviet Union and Yugoslavia. Today there are nearly 200 states in the world, with more in the pipeline as pressures grow for independence, secession or

The state: A legal and political arrangement through which all large-scale political communities are organized, combining territory with sovereignty, independence and legitimacy.

Sovereignty: The authority to rule, control and/or make laws, usually associated with states and incorporating territorial integrity and political independence.

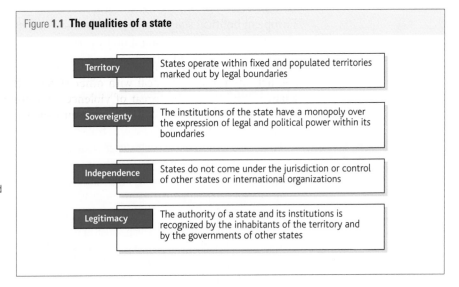

Figure **1.1 The qualities of a state**

Territory	States operate within fixed and populated territories marked out by legal boundaries
Sovereignty	The institutions of the state have a monopoly over the expression of legal and political power within its boundaries
Independence	States do not come under the jurisdiction or control of other states or international organizations
Legitimacy	The authority of a state and its institutions is recognized by the inhabitants of the territory and by the governments of other states

dissolution in Western Sahara, Kosovo, Palestine, Somalia, Belgium, Dagestan, Corsica and the Basque Country.

Alongside states, we must also understand – particularly in the European context – the sometimes competing claims of nations. If a state is a legal and political entity, then a nation is mainly a cultural entity: a group of people who identify with one another on the basis of a shared language, ancestry, history, culture, territory, religion, myths and symbols. National identity began to grow rapidly at about the time of the French Revolution, quickly becoming the main source of political legitimacy in Europe (Dunkerley et al., 2002, p. 44), and the glue that many governments used to extend and define their power. It was also used by minorities to claim their right to self-determination and independence. The nineteenth-century French philosopher Ernest Renan (1882) described nations as 'a soul, a spiritual principle' driven by a legacy of memories and sustained by the willingness of individuals to live together and value their heritage. More recently, Benedict Anderson (2006, p. 6) has described them as 'imagined communities'.

Pushed far enough, identification with nations may spawn nationalism, a belief in the value of preserving the identifying qualities of a nation and promoting its interests. Because few states coincide with nations, nationalism has often sparked intercommunity conflict and political instability. In extreme cases, it has spilled over into ethnocentrism, racism, genocide, civil war and interstate war. It was at the heart of many of the disputes that destabilized Europe during the nineteenth century, and was at the heart of the pressures that led to the outbreak of the First World War. In the interwar years, it plumbed new depths with the Nazi interpretation of history as a racial struggle and Hitler's belief in extending the *Lebensraum* (living space) of Germans and persecuting the Jews and the Roma. As late as the 1990s, nationalist violence tore apart Yugoslavia, and even today national minorities in several European states continue to campaign for self-government or even independence, and nationalism has come to be identified with the rise of right-wing anti-immigrant political parties.

Despite the number of national minorities who would like their own states, and in spite of the role of European states in running public programmes such as welfare and social security, there are many doubts today about the health of the state. It has always had its critics, who accuse states of creating unnecessary divisions among humans, often being the major protagonists in war and conflict, often failing to deal with other states without building antagonistic alliances and using the threat of violence, and doing a poor job of working with other states to address shared problems such as terrorism, transboundary pollution, illegal immigration, and the spread of disease. And in the globalized world of the twenty-first century, the lines that distinguish sovereignty, independence and legitimacy are becoming increasingly blurred. Some now argue that states have lost so much of their power and credibility that the Westphalian system may be on its way out (see Camilleri and Falk, 1992; Ohmae, 2005).

Others are not prepared to go so far, arguing instead that the state is not declining so much as being transformed. States still have a monopoly over the control and use of militaries, they are still the major players in the management of economic production and international trade networks, their citizens still identify mainly with states and are subject to the authority and rules of the

Nation: A community whose members identify with each other on the basis of a shared history, language and culture.

Nationalism: A belief in the primary interests of nations and the promotion of nation-states founded on self-determination.

state, and the ability of states to respond to new challenges has grown thanks to technological innovation. Rather than the state being on its way out, perhaps its role is simply changing, as globalization, trade, international law, changes in national identity and modernization have changed the nature of state power, the relationship among states, and the relationship between states and citizens. (For a survey of the debate, see Sørensen, 2004, 2006.)

These debates matter in the European context, where the focus of people's allegiance is now divided between states, nations and Europe. The implications are discussed in more depth in Chapter 3, but the rise of the EU must be seen not only as a reaction to the tensions created by states and nations, but also as a challenge to conventional ideas about political organization. Where once almost every European associated with a state or a nation, what may be happening today is the construction of the EU as a new kind of political organization, sitting alongside a revival of identification with nations and the relative decline of state power. Not everyone is pleased with the results.

International organizations

Just as we have seen a growth since the end of the Second World War in the number of states, so we have seen the growth of interstate cooperation. The underlying motives have varied: states cooperate in order to promote peace, encourage trade, share ideas and resources, reduce duplication, and address shared problems such as illegal immigration, environmental decline, cross-border crime, terrorism and financial regulation. Most of their efforts have been channelled through bilateral and multilateral contacts between and among governments, but states have also sometimes found it more efficient to create international organizations (IOs), within which their representatives can work together and which can employ staff to manage joint programmes, gather data, and monitor the progress of international agreements.

The oldest IOs predate the First World War, but the real era of growth in international cooperation has only been since the Second World War. By one estimate, there were less than 220 IOs in existence in 1909, about 1,000 in 1951, and still only about 4,000 as late as 1972. By 1989, the number had risen to nearly 25,000, and today there may be as many as 66,000 (Union of International Associations, www.uia.org). Most IOs fall into one of two major categories:

1 International nongovernmental organizations, whose members are individuals or the representatives of private associations. They include interest groups such as Amnesty International, Greenpeace and the International Red Cross, and multinational corporations such as HSBC, Royal Dutch Shell, Toyota, ING and Walmart.
2 Intergovernmental organizations (IGOs), whose members are states and whose goal is to promote cooperation among state governments. They include the United Nations, the World Trade Organization (WTO), NATO, the Council of Europe and Interpol.

International organization (IO): A body set up to promote cooperation between or among states, based on the principles of voluntary cooperation, communal management and shared interests.

Unlike states, IGOs do not have control over territory. Nor do they have much opportunity for independent action, since they are based on the voluntary cooperation of their members, who define what the IGOs can and cannot

Illustration **1.1**
The Council of Europe

The Council of Europe in Strasbourg is one of Europe's oldest international organizations, its achievements in fields such as human rights often overlooked in the attention focused on the EU.

do. Nor do they usually have much authority beyond the requirements of the terms of membership, which rarely provides them with independent powers or the ability to impose their rulings on their members. (The WTO is one notable exception; its dispute resolution procedure allows member states to use the WTO to help resolve trade disputes.) But they do have legitimacy, at least among their members, because they are created through the free will of their members (see Figure 1.2).

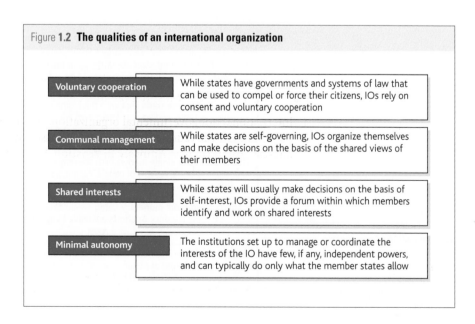

Figure **1.2 The qualities of an international organization**

Voluntary cooperation	While states have governments and systems of law that can be used to compel or force their citizens, IOs rely on consent and voluntary cooperation
Communal management	While states are self-governing, IOs organize themselves and make decisions on the basis of the shared views of their members
Shared interests	While states will usually make decisions on the basis of self-interest, IOs provide a forum within which members identify and work on shared interests
Minimal autonomy	The institutions set up to manage or coordinate the interests of the IO have few, if any, independent powers, and can typically do only what the member states allow

Regional integration

The promotion of cooperation and collective action among a group of states based on the identification of shared interests, common goals, the promotion of efficiency, the pooling of resources, and the creation of opportunity. Although states may be motivated by broad philosophical goals such as peace and unity, integration is usually focused on economic cooperation, including the promotion of trade and investment. The arrangements made to achieve this usually include treaties outlining goals and terms, and the creation of new regional institutions charged with working towards those goals.

Taken far enough, international cooperation can evolve into regional integration, a process summarized by Haas (1958, p. 16) as one in which 'political actors in several distinct national settings are persuaded to shift their loyalties, expectations, and political activities toward a new center, whose institutions possess or demand jurisdiction over the pre-existing national states'. This usually happens when a group of states forms a regional integration association (RIA) designed to encourage collective action and develop common rules on shared interests (usually economic cooperation). (This use of the term *regional* should not be confused with cooperation among local communities *within* states.) Regional integration involves the creation of institutions that have the authority (or 'competence', in EU terminology) to make new rules and policies in areas where their members have agreed to cooperate. But the institutions are set up in such a way that the governments of the member states have the key role in the adoption and execution of those rules and policies.

Regional integration is nothing new, and traces its roots back to the alliances that were once made among monarchs and imperial leaders. In the modern era, the first major exercises in integration date from the nineteenth century, and include the *Zollverein* (customs union) among German states dating from the 1820s that laid the foundations for the eventual unification of Germany, the Moldovian-Wallachian customs union of 1847 that was a key step on the road to the creation of Romania in 1878, and the 1848 constitution that formed the basis of the Swiss Confederation (Mattli, 1999, pp. 1–5).

The motives behind integration vary by time and place, but in most cases involve economic cooperation, which – depending on political and economic circumstances – can lead to progressively deeper degrees of integration (see Figure 1.3). Although today there are few countries in the world that are not members of one RIA or another (see Table 1.1), their prospects for success vary (see discussion later in this chapter about integrative potential), and the impli-

Figure 1.3 Stages in the process of integration

Regional integration is not necessarily a linear process, and different groups of states will have different ideas about the appropriate steps to take. But if there is a European model of integration, it would be as follows.

Agreement of **free trade area** with the easing of internal barriers to trade (such as tariffs and border restrictions) while maintaining a common external tariff against non-member states

The creation of a **single market** with the removal of internal barriers to the free movement of people, capital, goods and services

Efforts to promote **monetary union**, where smaller currencies are tied to a leading currency or efforts are made to agree a single currency

RIAs often talk in general terms about the value of peace and political cooperation, and even of political 'unity', but so far the idea of **political union** has been too controversial to be anything more than a theoretical goal

Regional integration association (RIA): An organization within which independent states work to encourage cooperation and the pooling of authority and resources for the mutual benefit of its members.

Concept

Federalism

Simply expressed, federalism means promotion of, or support for, the idea of federation. For European federalists, this means a belief in the merits of working towards replacing the European state system with a new European federation, or a United States of Europe. In conceptual terms, however, it is not really a theory, and falls victim to the confusion between its explanatory role in analysing the nature of today's EU and its prescriptive role in explaining what some would like the EU to become.

Table **1.1** **Selected regional integration associations**

Year of founding	Name	Membership in 2014
1952	European Union	28
1967	Association of Southeast Asian Nations	10
1967	East African Community (defunct 1977–99)	5
1973	Caribbean Community (Caricom)	15
1975	Economic Community of West African States	15
1980	Latin American Integration Association (ALADI)	13
1985	South Asian Association for Regional Cooperation	8
1989	Asia-Pacific Economic Cooperation	21
1991	Southern Common Market (Mercosur)	5
1992	Southern African Development Community	15
1994	North American Free Trade Agreement	3
2002	African Union	54
2011	Union of South American Nations	12

cations of states forming themselves into regional blocs are debatable. The study of regional integration is still dominated by the European case and by academics from Europe and the US (Breslin et al., 2002), and the broader implications of integration – and its sometimes different motives outside Europe – are not yet fully understood.

From federalism to neofunctionalism

In surveying the ruins left by the Second World War, many Europeans were prompted to argue that states had lost their credibility and their political rights because they could not guarantee the safety of their citizens (Spinelli, 1972). There was now a concern that elites would rebuild the state system, raising the danger of a revival of interstate tensions and so of renewed conflict and war. The answer to the problem – argued some – lay in federalism, or an effort to replace the European state system with a European federation. Hoping to build on this idea, and seeking particularly to address the perennial problem of tensions between France and Germany, members of the wartime resistance movements in 1946 created the European Union of Federalists, whose first congress met in The Hague in 1948.

Among the ranks of the federalists was a French bureaucrat named Jean Monnet. He saw federalism as an end-state that could only be reached gradually: a federal Europe would not be created as a result of 'some great political mutation', he later argued (Monnet, 1978, p. 367), but the creation of the European Coal and Steel Community (ECSC) in 1952 would be the first small step, and the ECSC experience would spread to other areas of policy, with the eventual achievement of a European federation. Looking beyond the state to solve common problems could encourage new cooperative links and new habits of

Understanding Integration... *International relations*

Theoretical debates about the EU have long been dominated by the academic discipline of **international relations** (IR). Born after the First World War as international cooperation entered its initial phase of growth, the study of IR accelerated after the Second World War as cooperation spawned the creation of many new international organizations and the signature of international agreements.

That studies of the European Economic Community (EEC) were long dominated by scholars of IR was hardly surprising, given that the early EEC was always – in spite of the dreams of European federalists – an international organization at heart. It may have had supranational qualities and aspirations, but integration was driven primarily by the decisions of governments negotiating with one another. As a result, theories of European integration were focused on decisions taken by governments, the dynamics of diplomacy and summitry, and the manner in which the governments of member states related to one another.

Realism has long been the foundational theory in the study of IR. With a heritage dating back to the ancient Greeks, this argues that because humans are by nature self-centred and competitive, rational self-interest and conflicting objectives encourage states to protect their interests relative to other states and not to trust long-term cooperation and alliances. Realists talk

of an anarchic global system in which there is no authority above the level of states that is capable of helping them manage their interactions with one another, and believe that states must use conflict and cooperation to ensure their security through a balance of power among states.

Alternative understandings are offered by liberalism, which also talks of an anarchic international system but believes in the possibility of cooperation to promote change, and by idealism, which emphasizes the role of ideas in shaping international relations. Where realism has been most actively promoted by American scholars, idealism has its strongest supporters in Europe, where – as Snyder (2003) puts it – the increasingly legalistic approach to international relations reflected in the process of forming the EU has provided fertile soil for idealist conceptions. See Chapter 24 for more details.

A response to the dominance of IR theory in integration studies began to emerge in the 1990s, when it was argued that the EU could be understood as a political system in its own right (see discussion in Chapter 2). But there have been recent attempts to return to IR approaches, prompted by the new significance of the EU as an actor on the world stage, and by suggestions that it can be studied as an example of the new regionalism that has emerged in response to globalization (Rosamond, 2013).

International relations (IR): The study of relations among states, focusing on alliances, diplomacy, and the dynamics of decisions reached by states working together or in competition with each other.

Realism: A theory which argues that we live in an anarchic global system (one without rules or an authority above the level of the state), and that international relations are driven by a struggle for power among self-interested states.

working together, the commitment to which would be strengthened as results started to be felt.

This so-called 'Monnet method' of 'federalism by instalments' was criticized by the Italian politician Altiero Spinelli, who argued that Monnet's proposal suffered from the lack of a political centre, or the leadership to push the process along. Strong and independent institutions were needed, otherwise the process of integration would be run by state governments (see Burgess, 2009). But the idea of transferring power to such institutions has always been anathema to many, and even today there remains much resistance to federalist ideas among Europeans. Even Monnet's idea of federalism by stages is widely regarded with suspicion.

Another critic of federalism was David Mitrany, a Romanian-born British social scientist whose treatise *A Working Peace System* became the basis of

Profile *Jean Monnet*

Jean Monnet (1888–1979) is often regarded as the founding father of Europe, his main contribution being the ideas that lay behind the ECSC. A committed internationalist, he was born in western France, working for his family's cognac business and picking up valuable skills in sales and languages, as well as travelling widely and learning the benefits of open borders and free trade. He became an adviser to the French government during the First World War, and was then named first secretary-general of the League of Nations. He later worked as a financier, advising eastern European governments and living and working in the US and China. He was behind a proposal for an Anglo-French union in 1940, then served as a representative for the British government in Washington DC. He headed France's postwar planning commission, and oversaw the discussions that led to the creation of the ECSC, becoming first president of its High Authority.

functionalism. Criticizing the 'fixation' with states that had become central to studies of IR (Rosamond, 2000, p. 34), Mitrany argued that the key challenge was 'to weld together the common interests of all without interfering unduly with the particular ways of each'. He claimed that federalism was too rigid in its framework, its constitution, and in the limits it placed on action, and that it would be difficult to maintain against a background of political nationalism (Mitrany, 1966, pp. 68, 155–6). The best way to bring about peace was not through alliances and agreements among governments, but by setting up a network of functionally specific international institutions dealing with relatively non-controversial matters such as postal services or the harmonization of weights and measures, and managed by bureaucrats.

Mitrany (1966, pp. 25, 27–31, 92, 163) argued that within their separate areas, these agencies would find themselves coordinating their functions across state lines, then coordinating with other groups of functional agencies, then working together with international planning agencies. Success in one area would encourage cooperation in others, building a network of cooperation that would result in the decline of national sovereignty and its replacement by a new international community. In time, the economic and functional ties built among states would

Functionalism: The theory that if states create functionally specific interstate institutions and agencies, regional integration will develop its own internal dynamic, and peace can be achieved through the creation of a web of interstate ties without the need for grand intergovernmental agreements.

Profile *David Mitrany*

David Mitrany (1888–1975) was a historian and political theorist best known today as the pioneer of integration theory. Born in Romania, he studied sociology at the London School of Economics before serving in British government intelligence during the First World War, and then working as a journalist on *The Guardian* and on the faculty of several British and American universities. He became a naturalized British citizen. At the core of his scholarly interests was the question of how states could work together to address transboundary problems, and the approach he adopted became known as functionalism. His best-known publication was *A Working Peace System*, first published in 1943.

lead to political ties, because governments would find themselves living in a web of international agencies, leaving them less capable of independent action. In short, peace was more likely to be achieved through stealth by 'doing things together in workshop and marketplace than by signing pacts in chancelleries', and this web of cooperation would result not in a 'protected peace' but in a 'working peace'.

Mitrany was interested in how to achieve world peace, not just European peace, and his arguments were not so much a theory as a suggested course of action, spelling out what should be done to achieve peace rather than explaining the conditions needed to make his scheme succeed (Mattli, 1999, p. 23). This perceived shortcoming was addressed in 1958 by the American political scientist Ernst Haas in his book *The Uniting of Europe*, which set out to develop a grand theory of regional integration using the case of the still new ECSC. Haas's work (which made no mention of Mitrany) tried to generalize 'the processes by which political communities are formed among sovereign States', and gave birth to the theory of neofunctionalism.

Haas was among the first to realize that reducing the barriers to the cross-border flow of money and people might transform the European state system. Questioning the core ideas of realism, he wanted to understand how and why states voluntarily cooperated with their neighbours while acquiring new techniques for resolving conflict (Haas, 1970). He concluded that in addition to the cooperation that would automatically arise from functional links, integration would need to be deliberately encouraged by political and economic actors pursuing self-interest. These actors worked mainly at the subnational level (including interest groups and political parties) and at the supranational level (the new regional institutions). The role of state governments was only to respond to these developments, by accepting, ignoring, sidestepping, or trying to sabotage the efforts of the regional institutions (Mattli, 1999, p. 24).

Haas (1958, p. 29) argued that if two or more states agreed to cooperate in a particular area of activity, and created a new regional organization to oversee that cooperation, the full benefits of integration would not be felt until there was cooperation in other, related areas of activity. Governments would soon find themselves subjected to growing regional pressures, and obliged to give more authority to regional organizations. The expectations of citizens would shift increasingly to the region, and satisfying those expectations would increase the

Grand theory: A theory that explains the entirety of a phenomenon, which has so far been lacking in efforts to explain and understand European integration.

Neofunctionalism: The theory that states are not the only important actors in efforts to integrate, and that supranational institutions, interest groups and political parties all play a key role.

Profile *Ernst Haas*

Ernst Haas (1924–2003) was the founder of the theory of neofunctionalism. Born in Germany, he emigrated to the US with his family in 1938, and studied at Columbia University before joining the faculty of the University of California at Berkeley in 1951. He has been credited with helping 'invent' the study of European integration, mainly through his development of neofunctionalism (which he insisted was not a theory). The best known of Haas's many publications was *The Uniting of Europe*, published in 1958 and later chosen by the journal *Foreign Affairs* as one of the 50 most important twentieth-century books on IR (see Ruggie et al., 2005).

likelihood of economic and social integration evolving into political integration (Ruggie et al., 2005). Integration would take on a life of its own (an 'expansive logic') through the phenomenon of spillover, described as a process by which 'a given action, related to a specific goal, creates a situation in which the original goal can be assured only by taking further actions, which in turn create a further condition and a need for more action' (Lindberg, 1963, p. 10). (For more discussion, see Chapter 18.)

Haas and Schmitter (1964) had begun to wonder how far theories of European integration could be applied elsewhere in the world. This encouraged Joseph Nye in 1970 to argue that attempts to understand neofunctionalism were too driven by the European case, and that it could stand to be used comparatively and also applied to non-European cases. Building on Haas, Nye (1970) argued that regional integration involved an integrative potential that determined the extent to which different groups of states were likely to succeed in their efforts, and that this depended on several conditions:

- The economic equality and compatibility of the states involved.
- The extent to which the elite groups that controlled economic policy in the member states thought alike and held the same values.
- The presence and the extent of interest group activity, the absence of which made integration more difficult.
- The capacity of the member states to adapt and respond to public demands, which depended in turn on levels of domestic stability and the capacity – or desire – of decision-makers to respond.

On almost all these counts, the EU has a relatively high integrative potential, in contrast, for example, to the African Union. The latter was created in 2002 to replace the Organization of African Unity, and is an almost exact copy – institutionally speaking – of the EU. But it has 54 members that vary enormously in their economic wealth and potential, are often divided by race and religion, include authoritarian regimes in which no formal opposition or independent group activity is allowed, and where levels of freedom of expression vary. Where western Europe had, early on, many of the necessary preconditions for successful integration, Africa faces a longer uphill struggle.

The spotlight moves to governments

Spillover: A key element in neofunctionalist theory, describing the pressures through which cooperation among states in one area of policy will lead to pressures to cooperate in other areas.

Integrative potential: A measure of the extent to which states will be able to integrate successfully, based on a combination of economic and political factors.

Neofunctionalism dominated early studies of European integration, but by the 1970s was beginning to fall out of favour, thanks in part to Haas's own loss of faith in his creation, which he felt lacked strong predictive abilities (Haas, 1975). Neofunctionalism did not adequately explain the role of governments in the process of integration, or show how the preferences of subnational and supranational actors would translate into political action. There also seemed to be little prospect of the western European experience being replicated anywhere else in the world, and the process of European integration itself – after early optimism – had entered stormy waters, including political disagreements among its members, economic difficulties, and the failure of early efforts to build a single currency, all of which seemed to suggest that the role of national governments in the process of integration had been underestimated.

Prompted by these developments, the political scientist Stanley Hoffmann argued that neofunctionalism concentrated too much on the process of integration without paying enough attention to the global context. Hoffmann also questioned the automatic nature of spillover, and argued that the importance of state actors and the persistence of nationalism had been overlooked by neofunctionalists. He argued that national interests still played an important role in European politics, and that while spillover had worked in some areas of 'low politics' (such as agriculture and trade), in areas of 'high politics' (such as foreign and security policy) it had slowed to a trickle. It had become easier for the EEC to agree negative measures (such as eliminating tariffs and quotas) than positive measures that required a more painful transformation of existing practices; the first integrative steps had been easiest, but as more vital interests began to be at stake, so the process became more difficult (Hoffmann, 1965). In a well-known article published in 1966, Hoffmann (1966) asked whether the states of western Europe should be regarded as obstinate rather than obsolete.

Hoffmann instead focused on the idea of intergovernmentalism. This is a theory and a model, is underpinned by realism, and sees the EU primarily as a meeting place in which representatives from the member states negotiate with each other in an attempt to achieve a consensus, but pursue state interests while paying less attention to the broader interests of the community of states. Hoffmann (1966) argued that while non-state actors played an important role in the process of integration, state governments alone had legal sovereignty, the political legitimacy that came from being elected, and the authority to decide the pace of integration. Alan Milward (1984) later agreed, his study of the early years of integration leading him to the conclusion that national governments and bureaucracies were the key actors in the process of integration, the extent of integration being determined by national self-interest.

Intergovernmental ideas stand in contrast to supranationalism, another combined theory and model in which the EU is still the meeting place of the representatives of the member states, but where governments compromise state interests in the common good, and transfer authority to institutions that work in the interests of the EU as a whole. But as we will see in Chapters 10–13, while European interests tend to dominate the work of the European Commission and the European Court of Justice, it has to be seen in the context of the defence of national interests, which dominates the work of the Council of Ministers and the European Council. Just how much the institutions work independently of the member states, or are still ultimately contained in their actions by the wishes of the member states, is debatable.

As with all theories of regional integration, intergovernmentalism has its critics. The main problem is that decisions among governments cannot be treated in isolation, and governments are subject to economic and social forces that either encourage them to cooperate or discourage them from cooperating. The motives behind cooperation also vary; governments may be responsible for making key decisions, but they are often forced into making those decisions by circumstances, a prime example being the start of the Greek debt crisis in 2009. The history of the EU offers numerous cases where governments have been pushed into cooperating by the external logic of economics and efficiency. Spillover, for example, has been at the core of the construction of the European single market, which generated many unanticipated hurdles. These include different

Intergovernmentalism: A theory/model based on the idea that key cooperative decisions are made as a result of negotiations among representatives of the states involved.

Supranationalism: A theory/model based on the idea that IGOs become the forum for the promotion of the joint interests of the states involved in cooperation, and that there is a transfer of authority to those IGOs.

Illustration **1.2**
Intergovernmentalism at work

With the help of their translators, German Chancellor Angela Merkel and French President François Hollande discuss policy on the sidelines of a European Council meeting in Brussels in October 2014.

environmental standards, different educational systems, different technical standards, and the pressures created by different levels of unemployment and different sets of working conditions. (This understanding has generated a revival of neofunctionalist ideas since the 1990s, although it is argued that they explain only some elements of European integration, and are not a grand theory.)

Logically, then, the key to understanding how the EU has evolved is probably to combine intergovernmentalism and supranationalism, seeing them not as two points on a spectrum of cooperation but as complementary aspects of the process of integration. Mitrany (1970, p. 103) argued that cooperation among governments was 'not a matter of surrendering sovereignty, but merely of pooling as much of it as may be needed for the joint performance of the particular task'. As outlined in the Schuman Declaration (see Chapter 4), the creation of the ECSC was all about the pooling of decisions over coal and steel production. Keohane and Hoffmann (1990, p. 277) agreed later that the European Community could be seen as 'an experiment in pooling sovereignty, not in transferring it from states to supranational institutions'. For his part, Haas (1964, p. 66) argued that supranationalism did not mean that Community institutions exercised authority over national governments but rather that it was a style of decision-making in which 'the participants refrain from unconditionally vetoing proposals and instead seek to attain agreement by means of compromises upgrading common interests'.

An attempt to combine the two approaches led to development of the theory of liberal intergovernmentalism, associated mainly with the American political scientist Andrew Moravcsik. Emerging in the 1980s and 90s, it combines the neofunctionalist view of the importance of domestic politics with the role of the governments of EU member states in making major political choices. Moravcsik (1993, 1998) talks of a two-level game, the first involving a combination of national preferences generated by the pressures of domestic politics in the member states. Governments want to keep themselves in office, which means

Liberal intergovernmentalism:
A theory combining elements of neofunctionalism and intergovernmentalism, arguing that intergovernmental bargains are driven by pressures coming from the domestic level.

they need the support of voters, parties, interest groups and bureaucracies at home. The pressures created show themselves at a second level, by determining the positions that governments take in international negotiations. Governments have the advantage of having more information available to them in EU-level negotiations, and they can use this information to reach agreements they can then sell to domestic audiences. In other words, the positions of member states' governments are decided at the domestic level, and European integration then moves forward as a result of bargains reached among those governments negotiating at the European level.

The final theory of note that comes out of IR is constructivism, which focuses on the historical and social origins of political structures, and argues that material interests (such as a focus on economic integration) are not enough to explain European integration. As Knutsen (1997, pp. 281–2) puts it, states are not static objects and state identities are not given, but they both evolve, and the distinctions between domestic politics and international relations become more tenuous as a result. People act not only on the basis of rational cost–benefit analysis, but because they live within social structures, they sometimes act against their own best interests and are guided by social norms shaped through a process of permanent interaction (Saurugger, 2013, p. 146). By focusing on the impact of social interaction on international relations, constructivism poses a challenge to intergovernmentalism with its emphasis on the state. Pinning down constructivism is not easy, however, because it is used and understood in many different ways, but it has been applied to understanding European integration by focusing on the role of socialization and learning in the construction of a European identity.

Constructivism: A theoretical approach that focuses on the social construction of interests and the manner in which they influence and shape institutions.

Summary

- Academic debates about the origins and history of the EU have been dominated by theories of international relations, which portray the EU mainly as an international organization driven by decisions taken by the governments of the member states.

- How we think about the EU depends in large part on how we think about states and their changing role and powers in the world since 1945.

- Our understanding of European states also demands an understanding of nations, which have played a key role in determining political and social relations among Europeans since at least the French Revolution.

- Since the Second World War there has been a marked growth in the number of international organizations, set up to promote cooperation among states, and based on the principles of communal management, shared interests and voluntary cooperation.

- Realists argue that humans are self-centred and competitive, that we live in an anarchic global system lacking an authority above the level of states that is capable of helping them manage their interactions, and that states must use conflict and cooperation to ensure their security.

- Liberals believe in the possibility of cooperation to promote change, view states and international organizations as key actors in the global system, and stress their mutual interdependence.

- Functionalists argue that the best way to achieve global peace is through the creation of functionally specific interstate institutions, which bind states into a web of cooperation.

- Neofunctionalists argue that states, supranational institutions, interest groups and political parties all play a role in integration, which is driven by a process of spillover through which governments find themselves cooperating in a growing range of policy areas.

- Intergovernmentalists take the focus back to the deliberate and conscious decisions of governments, and argue that the pace and nature of integration has been ultimately driven by state governments pursuing state interests.

Key terms and concepts

Constructivism

Federalism

Functionalism

Grand theory

Integrative potential

Intergovernmentalism

International organization

International relations

Liberal intergovernmentalism

Nation

Nationalism

Neofunctionalism

Realism

Regional integration

Regional integration association

Sovereignty

Spillover

The state

Supranationalism

Westphalian system

Further reading

Haas, Ernst B. (1958) *The Uniting of Europe: Political, Social, and Economic Forces, 1950–1957* (Stanford: Stanford University Press). First systematic study of the process of European integration.

Walt, Stephen M. (1998) 'One World, Many Theories', *Foreign Policy*, 110, pp. 29–32, 34–46. Snyder, Jack (2004) 'One World, Rival Theories', *Foreign Policy*, 145, pp. 53–62. Two excellent, brief surveys of the main strands of thinking in IR theory.

Wiener, Antje, and Thomas Diez (eds) (2009) *European Integration Theory*, 2nd edn (Oxford: Oxford University Press). Saurugger, Sabine (2013) *Theoretical Approaches to European Integration* (Basingstoke: Palgrave Macmillan). Two surveys of theories of European integration, outlining all the major theories and the responses to them.

2 What is the European Union?

The beginning of wisdom, runs a Chinese proverb, is to call things by their right names. But this is no easy task with the EU, which fits few of our conventional ideas about the way in which politics and government function. In our attempts to understand how large-scale political communities are organized, we have only two mainstream points of reference: states and international organizations. But while the EU has some of the qualities of both, it is not entirely either.

As we saw in Chapter 1, attempts to understand how the EU evolved have spawned lengthy theoretical debates, but few agreements. There has been a similar problem with the debates over what the EU has become. Scholars have suggested concepts such as *multilevel governance*, *consociationalism* and *quasi-federal polity*, but none has yet won general acclaim. Others have applied older and more well-worn terms such as *federal* and *confederal*, but the former is not a neutral idea for many Europeans, and (for reasons that are not entirely clear) few scholars or politicians are willing to think of the EU as a confederation. Yet others have opted for describing the EU vaguely as an actor, or as sui generis (unique), before quickly moving on. For Jacques Delors, former president of the European Commission, the EU was simply an 'unidentified political object'.

Chapter 1 focused on theories developed by international relations (IR) scholars, which focus on its intergovernmental qualities. This chapter, by contrast, focuses on the EU as a political system in its own right and its supranational qualities, and reviews the arguments made by scholars of comparative politics and public policy. After reviewing the main approaches to the discussion, it discusses the comparative approach, and then goes into detail on the contrasting features of federations and confederations.

- What are the relative strengths and weaknesses of using IR and comparative approaches to understanding the EU?
- What is the difference between multilevel governance and federalism?
- When some Europeans worry about a federal Europe, what exactly are they worrying about?
- Why have confederal ideas been so marginal to attempts to understand the character of today's EU?
- What is the EU?

Where to start?

There are at least five possible approaches to pinning down the character of the today's EU (see Figure 2.1), but each presents its own problems. The first option is to think of the EU as an international organization (IO), but while the European Economic Community in its early years was a fairly conventional IO, the EU today is much more. It has many supranational qualities, it has long had much bigger ambitions than any other IO, and it goes further than any other IO in terms of its reach, powers and obligations of membership. At the same time, Moravcsik (2007, p. 47) warns us that 'we learn far more by viewing the EU as the most advanced model for international cooperation ... rather than as a nation-state in the making, which encourages cycles of overambition and disappointment'.

Our second option is to understand the EU as a regional integration association (RIA), which allows us to apply theories developed by comparative studies of regionalism (see Fawcett and Hurrell, 1992; Laursen, 2003; Farrell et al., 2005; Rüland et al., 2008). But since RIAs have most of the same core features as IOs, the focus would still be on intergovernmentalism with its limitations as an explanatory theory. In terms of the reach of its institutions, policies and laws, the EU has moved far beyond most other examples of regional integration, which have more to learn from the EU than the EU has to learn from them. But just how far the EU has evolved is a matter of debate, and in recent years there has been a backlash against its authority, accompanied by growing demands for reform.

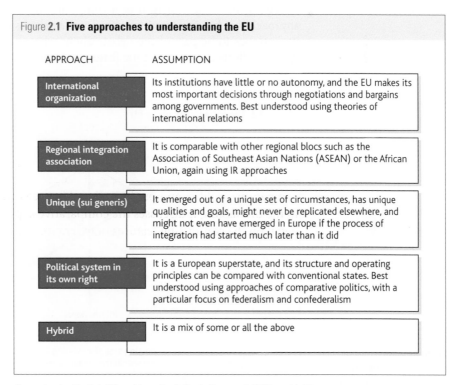

Figure **2.1 Five approaches to understanding the EU**

APPROACH	ASSUMPTION
International organization	Its institutions have little or no autonomy, and the EU makes its most important decisions through negotiations and bargains among governments. Best understood using theories of international relations
Regional integration association	It is comparable with other regional blocs such as the Association of Southeast Asian Nations (ASEAN) or the African Union, again using IR approaches
Unique (sui generis)	It emerged out of a unique set of circumstances, has unique qualities and goals, might never be replicated elsewhere, and might not even have emerged in Europe if the process of integration had started much later than it did
Political system in its own right	It is a European superstate, and its structure and operating principles can be compared with conventional states. Best understood using approaches of comparative politics, with a particular focus on federalism and confederalism
Hybrid	It is a mix of some or all the above

Source: Inspired by, but different from, the listing in Rosamond, 2000, pp. 14–16.

Our third option is simply to acknowledge that the EU is unique, but this is a rather lazy option, and how we can we have sensible and productive conversations about the EU unless we decide what it is? The terms *actor* and *entity* are often applied to the EU, but they are vague and clumsy, which leaves us with the more general term polity, referring to an organized system of government and administration. At the same time, enough scholars of the EU have identified enough points of comparison or similarity between the EU and other kinds of political organizations to suggest that the EU may not be all that unique, but just a reconfiguration of our conventional understandings about political structures and institutions. And, as we will see below, the term *government* is controversial when used in relation to the EU.

Our fourth option is to think of the EU as a political system in its own right, an idea that has gained traction since the 1990s as the impact of the EU has grown and its procedures have become more complex. It is also the approach taken in this book. One problem is that most of our understandings of political systems are based on how they work at the state level, and, as we saw in Chapter 1, the EU lacks many of the defining qualities of a state. At the same time, if the term *system* is understood to imply coordination, organization and order, there is no denying that the EU is a political system with institutions, laws, procedures, responsibilities, obligations and policies. It even, in some ways, looks much like a state: it encapsulates territory, and has a large degree of authority (if not necessarily sovereignty), and a lesser degree of independence and legitimacy.

Given the disputes among scholars about how the EU evolved, the final option is to combine elements of the first four of these explanations and to regard the EU as a hybrid or a compound of a state and an IO. This is the approach that has underwritten some of the debates reviewed in Chapter 1, and it continues to be part of the debate about what the EU has become. And yet the EU reflects ever fewer of the features of a conventional IO or RIA, and ever

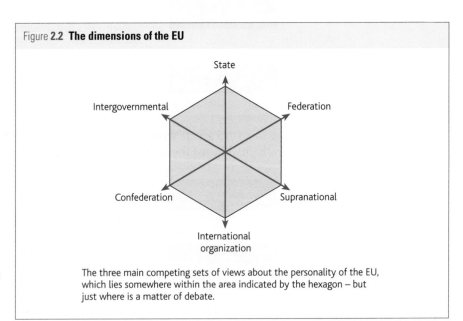

Figure **2.2 The dimensions of the EU**

The three main competing sets of views about the personality of the EU, which lies somewhere within the area indicated by the hexagon – but just where is a matter of debate.

Polity: An organized and structured system for the government and administration of a political unit, such as a state or a city.

more of the features of a state, raising questions even about the balance of its composite qualities. And then there is the problem of deciding which elements of the four approaches to adopt and which to ignore, and the danger that we will just find ourselves back at the noncommittal idea of thinking of the EU as unique. So, having argued that it is difficult to know where to start, what are the explanatory concepts available to us?

The comparative approach

As we saw in Chapter 1, the debates over how the EU evolved have been dominated by IR scholars, but the conclusions they have reached have been conditional at best. And while the European Economic Community (EEC) might reasonably have been studied as an IO until as late as the passage of the 1986 Single European Act, much has since changed: the process of integration has accelerated, the relationship between EU institutions and the member states has changed, the input of public opinion into the process of integration far exceeds that found with any other international organization, and the reach of EU institutions, law and policy has expanded. This has led some to conclude that we should consider the EU as a political system in its own right, using the methods and principles of comparative politics.

The oldest and the most elemental of all approaches to understanding politics and government, comparative politics involves the study of different political systems or different elements of those systems with the goal of using an understanding of each to shed light on the others. We can study political systems in isolation, but the picture we paint will always be incomplete until we appreciate their differences and similarities with others. The comparative method is based on using cases to draw broader conclusions, helps us describe political systems, gives us the context we need to decide what is important or unusual or missing in different systems, gives us points of reference to help us better understand the significance of what we are studying, and helps us draw up rules about politics and government by helping us develop and test hypotheses, explain trends, and better understand, explain and predict political change (see discussion in Landman, 2008, pp. 6–10).

Because the EEC began life as an international organization, it was long assessed – as we saw in Chapter 1 – using approaches that came out of the discipline of IR, and that focused on intergovernmentalism. An early hint of a shift came in a 1975 article written by Donald Puchala (1975), in which he noted how often he had heard the complaint from officials in the EEC that political scientists, in their search for models of the Community, were 'working at levels of theoretical abstraction too far removed from day-to-day political behaviour' and were painting 'elaborate and sophisticated pictures of phenomena that are simply not happening'. One official bluntly told him that when he read the results:

Comparative politics: The study of different political systems, often based on cases, and aimed at drawing up general rules about how those systems function.

Comparative method: One of the core methods for all research (the others being the experimental, the statistical, and the case study methods), based on drawing conclusions from the study of a small number of samples.

> You tell me that I am working to cause spillover, or that I am making a new nationality from old ones, or that I am challenging national sovereignty. This is nonsense. I and my colleagues are working to harmonize economic, social and legal practices in several countries so that the Common Market can function effectively for the benefit of all. (Puchala, 1975)

Understanding Integration... *Comparative politics*

Where the study of IR focuses on the relationships among or between states, comparative politics focuses on the study of those states in their own right, and on making comparisons among or between them. In other words, comparative politics is less interested in how states relate to each other horizontally than with how they function within themselves vertically, and how those functions compare and contrast from one state to another. At its heart is the comparative method, by which different cases or samples are systematically studied in order to establish empirical relationships among two or more variables while the others are held constant (Lijphart, 1971). It has been argued that to talk of an independent comparative method is redundant, because the scientific method is 'unavoidably comparative' (Lasswell, 1968), and that if political science is a science, then it goes without saying that it is comparative in its approach (Almond, 1966).

Most comparison is based on the study of a few carefully selected cases using a middle level of analysis, rather than the more intensive analysis possible with a few cases, or the more abstract analysis necessary with many cases (Landman, 2008, p. 29). The two most common approaches to comparative study are based on levels of similarity (see Lim, 2006, pp. 34–44):

1 The *most similar systems* (MSS) approach is based on the idea that the greater the similarities among cases, the easier it should be to isolate the factors responsible for their differences (Lipset, 1990, p. xiii). So, for example, we can look at levels of secularism in the otherwise generally similar cases of western Europe and the US and perhaps isolate the factors that explain why so many more Americans than Europeans participate in organized religion.

2 The *most different systems* (MDS) approach uses cases that are different in almost every respect except for the variable under investigation. So if we want to understand why people migrate within Europe, we can compare it with Asia, Africa and Latin America, which are different in many respects apart from the fact that they too have large numbers of migrants. By ignoring the differences as an explanatory factor, we can try to isolate the particular quality or factor that explains why Europeans move across borders.

One of the key benefits of thinking of the EU as more than an exercise in international cooperation is that it addresses the problem of trying to study the EU as a sample of one (Rosamond, 2000, pp. 17–18); regarding it as sui generis denies us the opportunity of comparing it to other systems and thus of making meaningful generalizations about its character and work.

A chastened Puchala decided to take a comparative case study approach in order to better understand the effects of the decisions taken at the Community level, a move that hinted at new thinking about the Community as an international regime within which member state governments cooperated on the basis of rules, norms and decision-making procedures (Hoffmann, 1982). Studying it as such meant that it could be compared with other exercises in economic integration, and even with federations such as the US, Canada or Germany. But then the passage of the 1986 Single European Act (SEA) paved the way for a transformation of scholarly perspectives:

Regime: The rules and norms that lie at the basis of a system of government. The term can also be used to describe (sometimes with negative implications) the holders of office within a government.

■ European integration entered a period of furious activity, with five more treaties signed after the SEA, membership of the Community (later EU) growing from 10 to 28, integration reaching into new policy areas, and the euro replacing national currencies in 18 countries. These changes dramatically altered perceptions about the personality of the EU.

■ It has become clear that the work of the EU has a greater reach – and has involved greater commitments on the part of its members – than any IO that has ever existed. This has made it a more likely candidate for comparison with federal states, and even to some extent with non-federal (that is, unitary) states such as France and Poland.

■ The growth in the number of RIAs has opened up new comparative possibilities. Even if the EU is clearly the most highly evolved of all RIAs, the experience of the others could be used with the MDS approach to argue that the EU is more like a conventional state than a conventional regional association.

More hints of a change in scholarly interest followed. In 1983, William Wallace – noting the disagreements that the governments of the member states were having over rules, powers and objectives – argued that the Community's capacity for handling complex issues and promoting discussion, bargaining and decision-making on them was 'extremely limited', and concluded that the Community was 'more than an international regime, but less than a fully-developed political system' (Wallace, 1983, p. 409). And yet with further enlargement, agreement of the SEA, and the first steps along the path to the euro, the Community's joint decision-making capacity was clearly growing.

In 1992, Alberta Sbragia (1992) identified two views of the Community among American scholars: one view held that it was mainly a free trade area whose institutions were marginal to economic forces, and whose dynamics were thus frequently overlooked, and another view held that the Community and its member states were governed in roughly the same way, and that the Community was an emerging superstate. Sbragia suggested that comparative federalism in particular had much to offer as a way of understanding the Community, and that perhaps the study of the Community could be incorporated into and contribute to the study of comparative politics rather than being isolated.

In 1994, Simon Hix (1994) argued that while the political system of the Community might only be part-formed, the practice of politics in the EC was not so different from that in any democratic system. While IR theories had been helpful to an understanding of European integration, he suggested, the Community was now more than an IO, and comparative politics approaches were more appropriate to understanding Community politics; they could help us understand how power was exercised in the Community, how Europeans related to Community institutions, and how European 'government' was influenced by political parties, elections and interest groups.

Acknowledging the EU as a political system in its own right gives us a wider array of new theories on which to draw, among which are the approaches related to institutionalism that have become popular since the 1990s. Where the old institutional approaches were concerned only with the formal aspects of government, new institutionalism looks more broadly at a combination of the formal rules and the whole array of social interactions that are involved in government. At the same time, there are many who do not like the idea of a European government, because use of the term *government* implies that the EU institutions constitute a level of authority above that of the member states, and that they have powers to make laws and drive the political agenda.

Although the EU clearly has a group of 'governing' institutions staffed by several thousand full-time employees, few scholars would argue that there is a

New institutionalism: A revival of traditional studies of the institutions of government that focuses as much on social interactions as on the formal rules of government.

Government: The institutions and officials that make up the formal structure by which states or other administrative units (counties, regions, provinces, cities, towns, and even universities) are managed and directed.

European government as there are national or local governments in the member states. Many instead prefer the looser term governance, describing an arrangement in which laws and policies are made and implemented not by a formally constituted set of governing institutions with the power to make and execute laws and policies, but as a result of interactions among a complex variety of actors, including member state governments, EU institutions, interest groups, and other sources of influence. Put another way, governance means that decisions are made and implemented without the existence of a government in the conventional sense of the term.

Taking this idea a step further, the term multilevel governance has become popular since the early 1990s as a way of explaining the character of the EU. This describes a system in which power is shared among the supranational, national, subnational and local levels of government, with a high degree of interaction among these levels (see Marks, 1993; Hooghe and Marks, 2001). Peters and Pierre (2004) describe the main features of multilevel governance as follows:

- It is about governance, not government.
- It 'refers to a particular kind of relationship (both vertically and horizontally, between several institutional levels') that is not hierarchically ordered.
- It applies to 'a negotiated order rather than an order defined by formalized legal frameworks'.
- It is often conceived as a political game.

Meanwhile, several other concepts have been developed or adopted that are of potential interest to understanding the EU, including the following:

- *Cooperative federalism* describes an arrangement in which national, state and local governments work together to address and solve common problems, rather then working separately on policy. No level has exclusive competence in any policy area, and decisions are made as a result of cooperation among the parts.
- *Consociationalism* is an idea associated with the political scientist Arend Lijphart (1977, 1999), and describes an arrangement in which power is shared among groups in divided societies, with representation based on the population of each group, government through a grand coalition of elites from each group, and the encouragement of consensus decision-making through mutual veto. While it has been proposed as a way of understanding the EU (McCormick, 1996; Gabel, 1998), it has failed to exert much of a grip on the mainstream debate.

Governance: An arrangement by which decisions, laws and policies are made without the existence of formal institutions of government.

Multilevel governance: An administrative system in which power is distributed and shared horizontally and vertically among many different levels of government, from the supranational to the local, with considerable interaction among the parts.

The invention and adoption of new conceptual terms reflects how little agreement there has been on how best to understand the EU. The failure to agree on any of them suggests, in turn, that the debate still has some way to go, with more terms being added to the lexicon before it runs its course. But as is so often true in life, the best options may be the simplest, and here we might focus on two older and better developed concepts to offer us guidance through the maze. One of these is *federalism,* which has already been discussed in relation to how the EU evolved. The other is *confederalism,* which languishes on the margins of the debate in spite of how much it promises as a path to understanding the EU.

Concept

Federation

An administrative system in which authority is divided between two or more levels of government, each with independent powers and responsibilities. Although there are about two dozen federations in the world, the relationship between national and local governments varies from one to another, and has evolved in each over time. In Switzerland, for example, the federal government is weaker relative to local government (the cantons) than is the case in Russia, where the federal government dominates Russia's local governments. As for the EU, it is considered quasi-federal at best.

Federalism

Federalist ideas have played a key role in the political and theoretical debates about how European integration has evolved, yet they have been given surprisingly short shrift as a possible means of understanding what the EU has become. Rosamond (2000, p. 23) points out that there are no famous names in the academic debate about federalism to compare with Mitrany and Haas, and that there is no clear-cut academic school of European federalism. Part of the explanation may lie in the political nature of the federalist debate; because it is not seen as a neutral concept, but is instead the dream of those who hope for a United States of Europe (and a nightmare for those who do not), it is widely avoided as a possible analytical tool.

The more technical part of the explanation lies in the difficulty of pinning down what federalism actually means (see Burgess, 2006, Ch. 1). At first glance it might appear fairly straightforward: a federation is a system of administration involving two or more levels of government with autonomous powers and responsibilities (see Figure 2.3), while the term *federalism* refers either to the principles involved in federal government, or to advocacy for the idea of federation. The federal approach contrasts with the unitary systems we find in states such as France and Sweden, where the balance and focus of power lies with the national government.

But as Birch (1966, p. 15) long ago remarked, federalism is a concept with 'no fixed meaning', and more recently Watts (2008, p. 1) has warned that 'there is no single pure model of federalism' and that we cannot 'just pick models off a shelf'. On the contrary, and even though there are less than two dozen formally declared federations in the world (see Table 2.1), they contain many differences, the specifics changing according to the relationship between the whole and the parts. This means that federalism runs the danger of being whatever we want it to be, and the definition and presence of federalism will be decided by the preferences of the observer rather than by objective measures of how power is divided and shared. This means, in turn, that the existence of federalism can be denied simply because we have no fixed agreement on how federations work. How, then,

Table **2.1** **The world's federations**

Federations		
Australia	Ethiopia	Pakistan
Austria	Germany	Palau
Belgium	India	St Kitts and Nevis
Bosnia and Herzegovina	Mexico	Switzerland
Brazil	Micronesia	United Arab Emirates
Canada	Nigeria	United States
Transitional or quasi-federations		
Argentina	Malaysia	Sudan
Comoros	Russia	Venezuela
Democratic Republic of Congo	South Africa	
Iraq	Spain	

Source: Based on Watts, 2008.

can anyone warn of the dangers of a federal Europe when no one can agree on what a federal system looks like (see discussion in Börzel, 2005)?

Even in the US – the benchmark for all federal systems because it was the world's first modern federation – there has been an ongoing debate about how federalism works in practice. The states were originally powerful, with their own independent arenas of power, but since the 1930s there has been a shift towards the federal government in Washington DC, as a result both of historical trends towards greater national unity and the growth of federal government programmes that have reduced state powers. Americans constantly debate the appropriate role of the federal government in national life and how the American federation works, with at least three possibilities offered:

1 Dual federalism (sometimes known as layer cake federalism), where national and local levels of government are distinct from each other, with separate responsibilities.
2 Cooperative federalism (or marble cake federalism), where the layers are intermingled and it is difficult to see who has ultimate responsibility.
3 Picket fence federalism, where national and local government share powers. (There is an extensive literature on American federalism; for surveys, see Morgan and Davies, 2008; Zimmerman, 2008.)

The waters of the debate about federalism have been muddied by developments in several other countries that have never formally described themselves as federations, but where the transfer of powers to local units of government has resulted in a process of federalization. In Britain, for example, the creation in the 1990s of regional assemblies in Scotland, Wales and Northern Ireland made all three more like states within a federal United Kingdom; all it would take to finish the job would be to create an English regional assembly. In Argentina, Spain and South Africa, too, powers have devolved to provinces and local communities without the formal creation of a federation, creating de facto federations or quasi-federations.

What of the EU as a federation? Unsurprisingly, opinion ranges widely. William Wallace (1983) described the European Community as 'less than a federation, more than a regime'. David McKay (2001, pp. 8–10) argues that we can think of the EU as 'a species of federal state', with some clear federal qualities and a trend over time to greater federalism. Andrew Moravcsik (2001, p. 186) has described the EU as 'an exceptionally weak federation' because of its modest budget and bureaucracy, its lack of coercive force, the constraints on its decision-making rules, and its powerful competitors; in fact, he argues, its federal qualities are so weak that the difference between the EU and national federations is not one of degree but one of kind.

Few have expended more effort on reviewing the EU's federal qualities than Michael Burgess (2006, p. 226), who argues that 'until recently it was possible to describe the EU as a classic example of federalism without federation'. In other words, it has always been a repository of federal ideas and influences without becoming a formal federation. But he goes on to argue that the main reason why it has been so hard to pin down is 'precisely because it is a new kind of federal model the like of which has never before been seen', which was born out of a slow, incremental and piecemeal metamorphosis (see also Burgess, 1996, 2000).

Although the EU is not a de jure federation with statehood, and its member states still have far more power and authority than the local units of government

Quasi-federation: An arrangement by which powers are divided between central and regional government, resulting in some of the features of federalism without the creation of a formal federal structure.

in a formal federation such as Australia or Canada, federalism is still very much a part of the analytical debate about the EU. That debate, however, has so far been limited to discussions about tendencies in the EU rather than absolutes. Burgess (2000, p. 273) sees a continuity of federal ideas, influences and strategies in the evolution of the European idea, argues that federal ideas have seeped into all the central institutions of the EU, and describes federalism as 'a constant reminder of a conception of Europe going well beyond mere intergovernmental cooperation'. But its application continues to be limited both by the dominance of IR theory in understanding the EU, and political resistance in Europe to the idea of a federal EU.

Confederalism

If the EU is not a federation, then perhaps it is a confederation. This is a conceptual cousin of federalism, describing a looser form of association among states. Where a federation is a unified state, within which power is divided between national and local levels of government, and where there is a direct link between government and citizens (government exercises authority over citizens, and is answerable directly to the citizens), a confederation is a group of sovereign states with a central authority deriving its authority from those states, and citizens linked to the central authority through the states in which they live (see Figure 2.3). Central government has few if any truly independent powers, the cooperating states retain most of the control over decision-making (and thus confederalism is a form of intergovernmentalism), and there is no confederal citizenship or tax. As Lister (1996, p. 106) puts it, if a federation is a union of peoples living within a single state, then a confederation is a union of states.

While the number of federations worldwide has grown, there have been few examples in history of confederations, and none have lasted:

- **Switzerland** was confederal from the medieval era until 1789, and then again from 1815 to 1848, when it tightened its internal political links and became a federation. But the Swiss brand of federalism emphasizes the parts at the expense of the whole; direct democracy through referendums is encouraged,

> ### Concept
>
> *Confederation*
>
> An administrative system in which independent states come together for reasons of security, efficiency, or mutual convenience, retaining the powers they consider best reserved to themselves, and working together through joint institutions on matters best dealt with together, such as foreign, trade and security policy. Put another way, a confederation is a looser form of a federation, a union of states with more powers left in the hands of the constituent members.

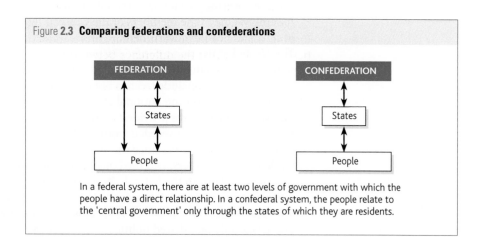

Figure **2.3 Comparing federations and confederations**

In a federal system, there are at least two levels of government with which the people have a direct relationship. In a confederal system, the people relate to the 'central government' only through the states of which they are residents.

CONFEDERATION

There is no European constitution capable of being amended and developed by proposals from the EU institutions. Instead, the EU is based on treaties designed and developed by intergovernmental conferences.

The EU is a union of states, not a United States of Europe. It has administrative institutions, but is a system of governance rather than a system of government.

The interests of the citizens of the EU member states are represented indirectly through their governments (with the notable exception of the elected European Parliament).

The EU member states are distinct political units, they have their own national defence forces and policies, they can sign bilateral treaties with non-EU states, and their governments can still argue that the EU institutions exist at their discretion.

The EU may have its own flag and anthem, but most of the citizens of the member states still have a higher sense of allegiance towards national flags, anthems and other symbols, and cannot surrender their state citizenships and become citizens of the EU.

The EU is a voluntary association, so its members are free to leave if they wish.

FEDERATION

The EU has treaties that are the functional equivalent of a constitution, that allow for administrative institutions that work above the level of the member states, and that distribute powers between the European institutions and the member states.

There are at least two systems of law in the EU: the European and the national (not forgetting subnational systems of law in federations such as Austria, Belgium and Germany).

The EU has a separate executive/bureaucracy (the European Commission), a separate legislature (the European Parliament), and a separate court (the European Court of Justice), which coexist with their national equivalents.

The existence of the European Parliament and the European Central Bank takes the EU beyond a confederation.

The EU institutions have a high level of authority over agricultural, environmental, competition and trade policy, and – in the euro zone – over monetary policy.

The EU member states are increasingly defined not by themselves but in relation to their EU partners, and although it is happening only slowly, Europeans increasingly identify with Europe and European priorities.

and the governing Federal Council is elected by the directly elected Federal Assembly. One of the members of the Council serves a one-year term as head of state and head of government.

■ **The United States** was a confederation from 1781 to 1789, operating under Articles of Confederation that created a 'league of friendship'. This could declare war and conclude treaties but could not levy taxes or regulate commerce, there was no national executive or judiciary, Congress met rarely, and defence was provided by state militias. How far the Confederate States of America that seceded from the United States in 1861–65 were truly confederate is debatable, since the states won new powers in some areas but lost them in others, and the constitution of the confederacy was copied almost directly from the federal US constitution.

■ **Germany** was a confederation from 1815 to 1866 when several central European states came together as successors to the Holy Roman Empire. There was only one shared political institution, a Federal Assembly made up of ambassadors from the different parts of the confederation, and it met rarely. The states agreed not to make war with one another, they were allowed to make external alliances, they contributed to a common army, and most were brought closer together in 1834 under the *Zollverein* (the customs union) (see Forsyth, 1981, pp. 43–53).

What of the EU as a confederation? Curiously, there has been almost no debate on the matter, for five possible reasons:

1 Confederalism has been all but ignored by modern scholars of politics – in general terms as well as in its application to the EU (for two of the few exceptions, see Forsyth, 1981; Lister, 1996). Any entity that looks like a confederation can simply be described as a weak form of federation, a concept that has attracted far more study and attention.
2 The EU has never formally been declared to be a confederation. But this does not mean that it is now.
3 Confederalism pleases neither European federalists, who want much more, nor eurosceptics, for whom history shows that confederations typically evolve into federations or new states.
4 As with federalism, there is no standard, uniform or simple model of confederalism. Indeed, while there are plenty of federations in existence today with which comparisons can be made, there are no formal confederations.
5 There is a strong statist tradition in Europe; Europeans have lived with states since Westphalia, a confederation is not a state (Majone, 2006), and thus it is rarely regarded as an option.

At the same time, the idea of thinking about the EU as a confederal system does have its small band of academic proponents. Forsyth (1981, p. 183) argued that the study of confederations in history revealed that the EEC was clearly an economic confederation in both content and form. Lister (1996, Ch. 2) later agreed, describ-

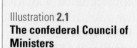

Illustration **2.1**
The confederal Council of Ministers

As a central institution deriving its powers from the EU member states, the Council of Ministers in Brussels fits the definition of a confederal institution.

ing the EU as a 'jumbo confederation' whose member states and governments continue to dominate the EU's institutions. For Moravcsik (2007, p. 25), quoted above as describing the EU as 'an exceptionally weak federation', the EU is, 'despite a few federal elements, essentially a confederation of member-states'. Majone (2006, p. 136) agrees, arguing that the confederal model describes 'precisely' the arrangement found in the EU, and bemoaning the fact that confederalism has been 'practically banned from the discourse about the future and finality of the Union'.

Just because confederalism is not in fashion as an explanatory tool does not mean that it is entirely without value, and perhaps it is time to consider lifting the ban to which Majone refers. At the very least, and returning to the point made earlier in this chapter about combining competing approaches to understanding what the EU has become, perhaps we should consider combining federal and confederal explanations. McKay (2001) argues that depending upon how we understand federalism, it may be best to think of the EU as quasi-federal or a hybrid. Burgess (2006, p. 239) concedes that the EU is not a federation in the conventional sense, but that it is 'a political union with strong federal and confederal elements ... [or] a new kind of federal-confederal union that we can classify as a "new confederation" or a new federal model'. Blankart (2007) argues that the EU is neither a confederation nor a federation, but is instead an 'association of compound states', some policies being dealt with in a federal manner and others in a confederal manner. And Watts (2008, pp. 56–8) describes the EU as a 'hybrid confederation-federation', and sees its confederal roots in the powers of the Council of Ministers, its small budget, its legal basis in a series of treaties, and the policy powers kept by the member states. He sees its federal qualities in the work of the European Commission and the European Court of Justice.

While the concept of confederalism has something to offer our understanding of what the EU has become, so do federalism, multilevel governance and – to a lesser degree – consociationalism. But just as there is no general agreement on how and why the EU evolved the way it did, so there is no general agreement on what it has become. When we ask 'What is the EU?', it would be helpful to have an answer. It would certainly save us a great deal of ultimately fruitless discussion about what the EU means to its residents and those who relate to it from outside, and about what it might or might not become. Unfortunately, in the absence of clear agreement on its personality and character, it is prone to being whatever we want it to be. For some, it is valuable exercise in cooperation that has helped sustain peace in Europe and opened up markets and opportunities, while for others, it has impinged upon the sovereignty of its member states and the people who live in those states.

Most of us are still locked in to the idea of states, and we look at the EU in terms of how far (or not) it has travelled along the road to becoming a European superstate. This is a loaded concept, though, because there are many Europeans who fear and resist such an outcome. Until we can think outside the box of the state, it is unlikely that we will be able to agree on the character of the EU. And there is no particular reason why we should continue to define politics and citizenship according to states; as we saw in Chapter 1, the state system is not all that old, and it has many imperfections. The model of regional integration also has its imperfections, to be sure, but it also has many advantages. The challenge, though, is to understand what it is and how it works. The EU, without doubt, has an identity problem.

Summary

- There are at least five possible approaches to understanding the EU today: we could think of it as an international organization, a regional integration association, a unique organization with unique qualities, a political system in its own right, or a hybrid.

- While the debates over how the EU evolved have been dominated by IR scholars, the debate over what the EU has become have been increasingly dominated by scholars of comparative politics, who approach the EU as a political system with its own institutions, processes, procedures and policies.

- There is a debate over whether we should approach the EU as a government, or use the looser term *governance* to understand its procedures. The term *multilevel governance* has won some support.

- Federalism has been given short shrift as a means of understanding the EU. This is partly because there is so much resistance to the idea of a federal Europe, and also because there is no standard model of federalism.

- Even less attention has been paid to confederalism as a means of understanding the EU, in part because there are few historical examples of confederalism at work (and no contemporary examples), and in part because it falls short of the hopes of European federalists.

- One compromise may be to think of the EU as a unique hybrid federal-confederal system of administration.

- When it comes to the question 'What is the EU?', there is no simple answer.

Key terms and concepts

Comparative method

Comparative politics

Confederation

Federation

Governance

Government

Multilevel governance

New institutionalism

Polity

Quasi-federation

Regime

Further reading

Burgess, Michael (2000, 2006) *Federalism and European Union: The Building of Europe, 1950–2000* (London: Routledge), *Comparative Federalism: Theory and Practice* (London: Routledge). Two books from the most prolific scholar of the EU as a federation, the former a revisionist history of the evolution of the EU.

Forsyth, Murray (1981) *Unions of States: The Theory and Practice of Confederation* (Leicester: Leicester University Press). Lister, Frederick K. (1996) *The European Union, the United Nations, and the Revival of Confederal Governance* (Westport, CT: Greenwood). Two of the few full-length studies of confederalism, both prompted by the case of the EU.

Hix, Simon, and Bjørn Hoyland (2011) *The Political System of the European Union*, 3rd edn (Basingstoke: Palgrave Macmillan). The paradigm text of the argument that the EU should be approached as a political system in its own right.

3 Who are the Europeans?

Preview

Understanding the European Union demands more than a review of its legal and political character. We must also understand its people: who they are, how they think of themselves in relation to others, and how they perceive the EU. Most Europeans still regard themselves mainly as citizens of the states in which they live, or as members of a national group, and only a few have taken to the idea that they are also Europeans.

Europe has a population of nearly 600 million, divided among 40 sovereign states (or nearly 690 million if we expand the definition of Europe to include Turkey and the Caucasus), speaking more than 60 major languages, and belonging to several hundred different national groups. Because the lines of states and nations do not always coincide, most European states are multinational, and many of the larger national groups are divided among two or more states. The exercise of European integration – although it was designed to help Europeans move past their historical suspicions of one another – has made only limited progress in helping build a sense of European identity, or community of the kind discussed by transactional theory.

This chapter begins with an attempt to pin down where Europe begins and ends. It then reviews questions of identity in Europe, touching on the constructivist ideas introduced in Chapter 1, and looking at what divides Europeans while also explaining how the sense of association with Europe and the EU is changing. It ends with a review of some of the key demographic trends in Europe, including its declining and ageing population, the impact of immigration, and changes in the European definition of the family. It argues that Europe is undergoing a fundamental change of identity, but that while current trends are becoming clearer, the long-term implications are still open to debate.

Key issues

- Where should the borders of Europe be drawn? Should Turkey or Russia be included?
- What does it mean to be European, and how does allegiance to Europe differ from allegiance to states or nations?
- What matters most in defining identity: culture, place, history, language, ethnicity, religion, ideology, philosophy, or aesthetics?
- Should citizens of EU member states be offered the alternative of citizenship of the EU? If so, what would that citizenship mean in practical terms?
- Is Europe's declining population the problem that many make it out to be, or an opportunity to rethink political, economic and social priorities?

Where is Europe?

Europe is often described as a continent, but geographers define continents as large, unbroken and discrete landmasses almost entirely surrounded by water. On that basis, only North and South America, Asia, Africa, Australia and Antarctica wholly fit the bill. Strictly speaking, Europe is part of the Asian continent (or the supercontinent of Eurasia, as it is sometimes called), and so is more properly described as a subcontinent. But Europeans are racially, culturally and linguistically distinct from Asians, and vice versa, and although they share the same landmass, geography is less a defining feature of Europe than culture and history. (The same is true of Africa, with its division between Arabs and non-Arabs.)

On three sides, Europe's limits are reasonably clear. To the south it ends with the Mediterranean, to the west it ends with the Atlantic, to the north it ends with the Arctic Ocean, and in all three directions it includes islands with political and cultural links to Europe, such as Greenland, Iceland, Svalbaard, Crete, Sicily and Malta. But to the east and the southeast there are many unanswered questions. The border with Asia is particularly problematic, the conventional view being that it is marked by the Ural Mountains in Russia. But this is convention only because of a decision by the eighteenth-century Russian historian Vasily Tatishchev, who thought that naming the Urals as the border would allow Russia to claim to be an Asian as well as a European power. All well and good, but the Urals are more than 1,000 km inside Russia, and they are a natural feature rather than a cultural or political boundary.

Russians themselves are undecided: some see themselves as part of Europe and the West, others distrust the West and see their state as distinct from both Europe and Asia, and yet others see Russia as a bridge between the two (Smith, 1999, p. 50). Ethnic Russians make up about 80 per cent of the population of Russia, and there are also large Russian minorities living in EU member states such as Estonia, Latvia and Lithuania. While the case could be made that they and the Slavic and Caucasian minorities of western Russia (including Ukrainians, Belarusians and Ossetians) are European, three-quarters of the land area of Russia lies east of the Urals (territory that is clearly in Asia, not Europe) and is home to numerous ethnic minorities – including Tatars, Kazakhs, Uzbeks and the Siberian minorities of Buryatia, Evenki, Khakassia and Selkup – that are unquestionably Asian. For practical political purposes, then, the border between Europe and Asia is best taken as the western frontier of Russia.

To the southeast, meanwhile, the lines are also fuzzy. The easy option is to connect the Russian–Ukrainian border to the Bosporus Strait between Turkey and the Balkans, but many of the 16 million residents of Armenia, Azerbaijan and Georgia might protest. Ethnographers consider them European, all three states have been members of the Council of Europe since 2001, and – as we will see in Chapter 9 – there have been hints in the cases of all three (as with Ukraine) of future EU and NATO membership. But all three also have close political and economic ties with Russia, and unless Turkey also joined, they would be physically isolated from the rest of the EU.

Without question the most troubling debate about the limits of Europe relates to Turkey. Geographically, only the four per cent of its land area that lies west of the Bosporus is European, but Turkey's historical ties with Europe are strong, not least because it is the successor to the Ottoman Empire that once covered most of the Balkans, including Bulgaria, Hungary and Romania. The question of Turkey's European credentials has been growing since 1963 when Turkey became an associate member of the European Community, which agreed at the time that eventual full membership was possible. Turkey has been a member of NATO since 1952, and has been lobbying for membership of the EU since 1987, but although it is now recognized as a candidate country, opinion on its prospects remains deeply divided (see Chapter 9), and questions about its claims to be European remain unanswered.

One final but much less seriously considered candidate for inclusion in Europe is Israel. Its creation was accelerated by a European event (the Holocaust), many of its Jewish residents have European roots, and its strained relations with many of its Middle Eastern neighbours have encouraged Israel to build stronger ties with Europe. Several Israeli government ministers have broached the idea of EU membership, as have the leaders of several eastern European states and former Italian Prime Minister Silvio Berlusconi. But the political relationship between Israel and the EU is a troubled one (see Chapter 25), Israel has a large Arab minority, and in geographical terms it is not a European state. Although

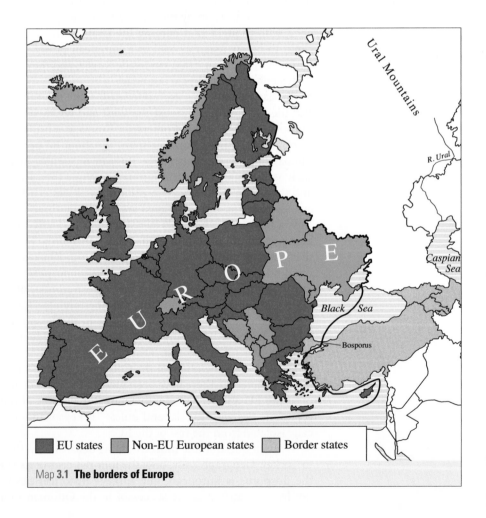

Map **3.1 The borders of Europe**

Identity

A term used in the social sciences to describe how people understand or see themselves, either as individuals or as part of a group. Individual identity is driven by psychological questions such as role, gender, image and self-esteem, but group identity is driven by a wider range of factors such as culture, place, history, language, ethnicity, religion, ideology, philosophy and aesthetics. Europeans today find themselves faced by the sometimes competing options of local, national, state and European identity.

Israel and the EU have agreements that establish limited free trade and allow for discussions on political and economic questions, the prospects of Israeli membership of the EU have never been seriously discussed.

Where, then, is Europe? If its eastern limits are its borders with Turkey and Russia, then today it comprises 40 states: the 28 members of the EU, 3 other western European states (Iceland, Norway and Switzerland), and 9 eastern/central European states. (Strictly speaking, there are also five micro-states that might be included in the list: Andorra, Liechtenstein, Monaco, San Marino and Vatican City. These are legally independent, and all except Vatican City are members of the Council of Europe and the United Nations, but none has separate membership of the EU, and none is conventionally listed among the major states of Europe.) If a broader definition of Europe is accepted, then it includes 4 more states (Armenia, Azerbaijan, Georgia and Turkey) for a total of 44 (or 49 if the micro-states are counted separately) (see Table 3.1).

Understanding European identity

If geography is inconclusive as an indicator of Europe, even more problematic is the question of identity, or how Europeans define themselves relative to others. This topic has been the subject of an increasingly lively debate, the questions about how identity is formed and changed typically outnumbering the answers (see Robyn, 2005; Fligstein, 2008; Cerutti and Lucarelli, 2008). It has also been behind the growth in constructivist ideas about integration, which focus on how the social norms of political actors shape their identities and their interests. The most immediate sense of identity comes from place, or the community to

Table 3.1 **The states of Europe**

Albania	(Georgia)	Netherlands
(Armenia)	Germany	Norway
(Azerbaijan)	Greece	Poland
Austria	Hungary	Portugal
Belarus	Iceland	Romania
Belgium	Ireland	Serbia
Bosnia and Herzegovina	Italy	Slovakia
Bulgaria	Kosovo	Slovenia
Croatia	Latvia	Spain
Cyprus	Lithuania	Sweden
Czech Republic	Luxembourg	Switzerland
Denmark	Macedonia	(Turkey)
Estonia	Malta	Ukraine
Finland	Moldova	United Kingdom
France	Montenegro	

Micro-states: Andorra, Liechtenstein, Monaco, San Marino, Vatican City (none is a member of the EU).

Blue: Member states of the EU. Parentheses: States whose European credentials are debated.

Note: All except Belarus, Kosovo and Vatican City were members of the Council of Europe in 2010, along with Russia.

which people feel the greatest sense of affinity. But this has different meanings for Europeans:

- It may be the village, town or city in which they live.
- It can be the local administrative unit under whose jurisdiction they fall, whether they are a county, a province, a department, or a region.
- It may be the part of the state in which they live. The English and the Italians, for example, make distinctions between northerners and southerners, and ascribe many different characteristics – whether real and mythical – to the two groups.
- National identity remains alive and well, such that – for example – many Scots feel more Scottish than British, and many Basques place national feelings above association with Spain or France.
- It may be the state of which they are a citizen or a legal resident.
- To all these sets of association, the notion of identity with the EU and Europe more generally has been added in the past few decades. And some consider themselves more broadly to be citizens of the world.

Attempts to pin down what it means to be European are most immediately complicated by cultural and political associations with nations. As noted in Chapter 1, a nation is a group of people who identify with one another on the basis of a mixture of language, history, culture and a variety of symbols and myths that tie them together. One of the most telling – and sometimes most troubling – of political and societal pressures in Europe since at least the late eighteenth century has been the push among nations to have their own states. But while the borders of nations and states have increasingly coincided, no European state is entirely homogeneous in national terms, and Europeans have long lived in states divided by culture, nation and language. In most, a workable balance has been achieved, but in others the nationalist tensions remain: Belgium, for example, is divided between the Dutch-speaking Flemish, French-speaking Walloons, and a small German-speaking minority in the east.

There are numerous national groups in Europe, although estimates of the number vary according to how a nation is defined: Minahan (2000) lists 143 nations, or 106 if European Russia is excluded, while Pan and Pfeil (2004) list 160 nations in the 28-member EU alone. They range in size from tens of millions to tens of thousands (see Table 3.2), with Germans, Italians, French, English, Polish and Spanish among them accounting for nearly two-thirds of the population of the EU-28. To further complicate the picture, few European states are culturally homogeneous; while almost all have a single dominant national group, all but the smallest have at least three indigenous national minorities, and in most cases many more (Pan and Pfeil, 2004; see also Panayi, 2000). This diversity is the heritage of the repeated reordering of territorial lines in Europe over the centuries, with new patterns of immigration since 1945 adding more variety. The result has been the creation of at least six groups of minorities within Europe:

1   National minorities related to national majorities in neighbouring states, such as Germans living in Romania, Albanians in Kosovo, Greeks in Cyprus, Poles in the Ukraine, Czechs in Slovakia, and Ukrainians in Poland. Talk in 2010 of offering Hungarian citizenship to the estimated 2.5 million Magyars

Table **3.2 Selected nations of Europe**

Largest (40–85 million)	Large (10–25 million)	Medium (5–10 million)	Small (1–5 million)	Smallest (less than 1 million)
German	Romanian	Catalan	Norwegian	Frisian
Italian	Dutch	Lombard	Walloon	Cornish
French	Magyar	Serb	Moldovan	Montenegrin
Ukrainian	Portuguese	Swede	Welsh	Corsican
English	Greek	Sicilian	Basque	Madeiran
Polish	Czech	Albanian	Slovene	Maltese
Spanish	Bavarian	Flemish	Ligurian	Icelander

Source: Based on Minahan, 2000.

living in Slovakia, Ukraine, Romania and Serbia raised the spectre of a revival of Hungarian nationalism and territorial claims on Slovakia.

2 Transnational minorities that live in two or more states but do not form a majority anywhere. These include the Basques and Catalans of Spain and France, and the Frisians of Germany and the Netherlands.

3 Indigenous minorities living within a single state, including the Scots and the Welsh of Britain, the Corsicans and Bretons of France, and the Galicians of Spain.

4 Foreigners legally resident in the EU, including citizens of one EU member state living in another. According to Eurostat, there were about 33 million foreign citizens legally resident in the EU-27 in 2011, accounting for nearly 7% of the population (Eurostat website). The biggest groups were in Germany, Spain and the UK.

5 New racial and religious minorities arriving from outside Europe. In spite of the attention drawn to them by the media, these minorities actually make up a small part of the bigger picture: only about 25 million of the EU's legal residents (5% of the population) belong to a racial minority, a proportion far smaller than the US (23%) or Canada (16%).

6 Foreigners illegally resident in Europe. It is impossible to know the exact number of 'irregular immigrants' (as the European Commission likes to call them), but the numbers probably run into the low millions. See Chapter 23 for more discussion.

The clearest indicator of national differences is language, the preservation of which has been at the heart of many struggles by minorities to assert their separate identity. Language is also the most effective barrier to the development of a true sense of European identity; in spite of the growth of language education, most Europeans speak only their native language, creating a barrier to cross-cultural communication and making it difficult for Europeans to better understand each other. Natives of the EU alone speak more than 40 different languages, of which 24 are currently recognized as official (see Table 3.3). This designation means that all EU documents must be translated into those languages, simultaneous translation must be offered if requested at EU meetings, and EU citizens have the right to be heard by EU institutions in those languages.

Table **3.3 Official languages of the EU**

Bulgarian	French	Maltese
Croat	German	Polish
Czech	Greek	Portuguese
Danish	Hungarian	Romanian
Dutch	Irish	Slovak
English	Italian	Slovene
Estonian	Latvian	Spanish
Finnish	Lithuanian	Swedish

But English, thanks in part to its growth as the international language of commerce, technology and diplomacy, and in part to the spread of Western (mainly American) culture, is rapidly becoming the common language of Europe, not to mention a global language (Crystal, 2003). The work of EU institutions is increasingly conducted in English (and to a lesser extent French), European corporate executives are increasingly expected to be able to speak English, it is used more often in higher education, and it has become the lingua franca of European tourism. Its spread worries the French in particular and other Europeans to some extent, but it offers the advantage of giving Europeans a way of talking to each other, thereby helping reduce the cultural differences that divide them.

Citizenship and patriotism

If cultural associations with nations complicate attempts to pin down what it means to be European, they are further complicated by legal associations with states. As noted in Chapter 1, a state is a legal and political entity marked by territory, with a government that has sovereignty within that territory, and whose independence and legitimacy is recognized in law. European state lines have changed often, with potential new states waiting in the wings, as pressures grow for the independence of Catalonia and Corsica, and the break-up of Belgium.

Illustration **3.1**
Multilingual Europe

The winning design by Polish graphic designer Szymon Skrzypczak for the logo commissioned to mark the 50th anniversary of the treaties of Rome in 2007, reproduced here in all official languages of the EU.

Concept

Citizenship

A complex notion tied to the idea of belonging to a political community (normally a state). Citizenship of a state means the right to live in that state, to hold a passport of that state, to take part in the political life of a state, and to enjoy freedom of speech and a minimum standard of economic and social welfare. But legal residents of a state of which they are not citizens have almost all the same rights and duties as citizens. Ultimately, an individual could declare that, like the Greek philosopher Diogenes, they were a citizen of the world, but this is a state of mind or a philosophy, not a legal reality.

Although many Europeans owe their cultural allegiance to nations, they owe their legal allegiance to states through the ties of citizenship.

The debate over the meaning of citizenship has ranged over the centuries across its social, moral, legal and political qualities, along the way touching on ideas about identity, and being divided by philosophical arguments about duties (the civic republican strain) and rights (the liberal strain). Although duties such as civic engagement and military service are still relevant to an understanding of citizenship, it is the liberal strain that is the most real and immediate to most people. Tracing its roots to the transition in Britain from a monarch–subject relationship to a state–citizen relationship, it ties citizenship to the right to vote, the right to just treatment under the law, and the right to own property (Heater, 2004).

For most of us, citizenship comes down to a series of legal qualities: being a citizen of a state means having the right to live and work in that state (although this right is also given to legal residents), to vote and run for elective office, to be protected against forcible removal from that state to another without the agreement of the governments involved, to hold (or claim) a passport of that state, and to receive protection from the home state when outside its borders. A citizen is regarded as a subject of their home state by other governments, and must usually obtain the permission of other governments to travel through or live in their territory. Reduced to its most basic, about the only difference between a citizen and a legal resident of a state is that the citizen has the right to vote and run for office, while the non-citizen does not, and a non-citizen can be expelled while a citizen cannot. Otherwise, the two have more or less the same rights and responsibilities.

The EU has developed its own concept of European citizenship, but it is less than it seems. While the Treaty of Lisbon (Article 20) says that 'every person holding the nationality of a Member State shall be a citizen of the Union', it also goes on to note that 'citizenship of the Union shall be additional to and not replace national citizenship'. Symbolically, all passports of EU member states are printed in the same burgundy colour and list 'European Union' alongside the name and symbol of the member state. Citizens of EU member states also have the additional benefit of going through the same lines when entering the EU from abroad, while travellers from non-EU states go through different and sometimes slower moving lines with sometimes different documentary requirements. Beyond that, citizens of the EU have the following rights:

- To move and live freely within the territory of member states, although this is not an unconditional right, and is also available to almost anyone who is a legal resident of an EU member state.
- To vote and stand as a candidate in local and European Parliament elections in whichever state they are legally resident.
- To seek the help of any EU embassy if they run into difficulties in a foreign country where their state has no representation.
- To address EU institutions in any of the 24 official languages of the EU, and receive a reply in the same language.

European citizenship: A concept developed by the EU in order to provide its citizens with more of a transnational sense of belonging, but falling short of conventional ideas of citizenship.

Ward (1996, p. 40) describes these qualities as 'a pleasant touch, but of limited practical value', while Guild (1997, p. 30) sees them as no more than 'some fancy words on a piece of paper'. What they ultimately fail to offer is an alternative to state citizenship; in other words, citizens of an EU state cannot turn in their national passports and have them replaced with EU passports, and EU citizens

Understanding Integration... *Transactionalism*

Integration is not just a political phenomenon, but also has a social element: there is only so much that governments can do to deepen their mutual ties without the citizens of the participating states thinking it is a good idea and being able to see the benefits in their own lives. Where many of the IR theories discussed in Chapter 1 revolve around promoting peace and cooperation through the actions of governments and the creation of institutions, the related theory of **transactionalism** focuses on achieving the same goal by improving the levels and quality of communication (the transactions) among people. The core idea is that encouraging trust and goodwill among communities in different countries will make conflict and war less likely (Eilstrup-Sangiovanni, 2006, p. 29). In other words, the quality of integration among states is a function of the level of community that exists among them.

The person most often associated with this concept is the Czech political scientist Karl Deutsch (1912–92), who argues that there are two levels of integration in this scenario (Deutsch et al., 1957). First, increased social integration among people – involving interaction, communication, movement and contact – will result in the creation of 'security communities' that are capable of resolving their differences peacefully. These security communities might involve the formal merger of states, or they might just involve integration without a political merger. Second, and based on the foundation of these communities, it would be possible to move on to political integration. In order for these security communities to develop, Deutsch felt that there needed to be a compatibility of major values among them, a shared ability to respond to each other's needs without a recourse to violence, and a mutual sense of predictability in regard to their political, economic and societal behaviour.

Transactionalism has been criticized for its failure to outline the processes and mechanisms through which communication is improved and transactions undertaken. At the same time, it is highly salient as a theory, given that one of the core problems faced by the EU today is the extent to which integration is elite driven rather than being driven by the wishes of ordinary Europeans. Leaders have put the cart before the horse, focusing on political cooperation rather than improved social interaction.

Transactionalism: A theory of integration that emphasizes the importance of building communication among people before moving on to political integration.

still do not have the option of what Maas (2007, p. 95) describes as 'supranational political membership', or what Balibar (2004) describes as 'transnational citizenship'. This has not happened for the simple reason that there is no European state, government or authority that would be responsible for protecting the rights of European citizens, and to which these citizens might appeal if they had problems with any of the member states of the EU.

Against the background of this discussion about the role of nations and states in identity, how do we approach the meaning of identity with Europe? Who are those people who take a European view of themselves and the world around them? Who are the 'Eurostars', as Favell (2008) labels them: the people who have taken up, physically or culturally, the new opportunities for mobility offered by integration? The results of opinion polls give us some sense of what is happening. For example, when respondents in the then EU-15 member states were asked by the Eurobarometer polling service in 2004 how they would conceive of themselves in the near future in terms of identity, only 4% considered themselves European. But 41% identified exclusively with their home states, meaning that a clear majority had at least some sense of identity with Europe (see Figure 3.1). (Unfortunately, no similar polls have been carried out since then, so we have little idea how views have changed.)

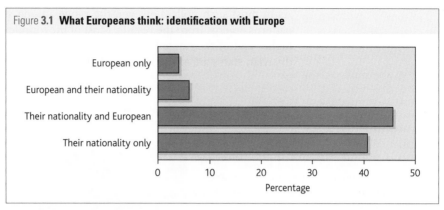

Figure **3.1 What Europeans think: identification with Europe**

Source: Eurobarometer 61, Spring 2004.

Fligstein (2008, p. 250) puts it slightly differently when he divides Europe into three camps: one (including 10–15% of the population) is connected by deep economic and social ties, and benefits materially and culturally from Europe; a second (40–50%) has a more shallow relationship with Europe, aware of what is going on across borders but still wedded to national language, culture and politics; the third (40–50%), which tends to be older, poorer and less educated, does not travel or consume culture from other societies, is more wedded to home, and is more fearful of European integration.

Eurobarometer also periodically asks Europeans if they feel a sense of attachment to the EU (but does not explain what 'attachment' means). The 2013 poll revealed that less than half of respondents had such a feeling (see Figure 3.2), a figure that correlates closely with the number of Europeans who agree that membership of the EU has been a good thing for their country (see Chapter 17).

Illustration **3.2 EU passports**

Efforts to build a sense of European citizenship have been exemplified in the largely symbolic replacement of national passports by burgundy 'European' passports in all the member states.

As in most such polls, however, the range among states is wide, and few clear patterns emerge from the results. Most of the founder states of the EEC are at the higher end of the range (the Netherlands being a notable exception), the Scandinavian states are at the lower end of the range, and Britain has its accustomed

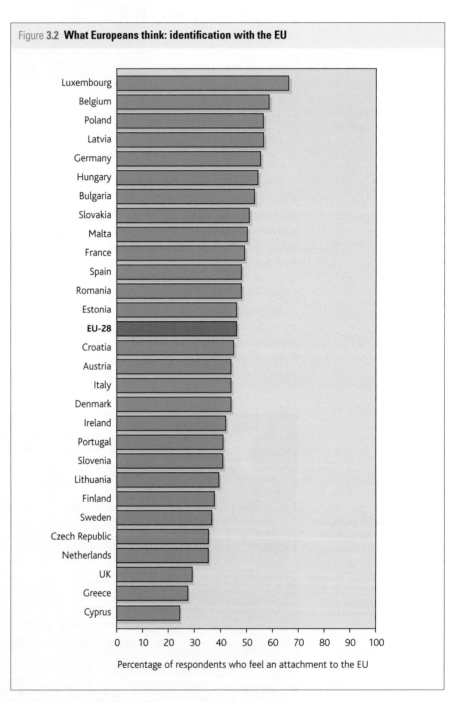

Figure **3.2** **What Europeans think: identification with the EU**

Percentage of respondents who feel an attachment to the EU

Source: Eurobarometer 80, Autumn 2013.

Concept

Patriotism

Pride in, love of, or devotion
to country, driven by a
sense of identification
with the history and
achievements of that
country. Although usually
associated with positive
support for a country, it can
spill over into hostility or
superiority towards other
countries, and the belief
that criticisms of the home
country are unpatriotic. For
some it can be conflated
with nationalism, which
may mean the pursuit of
the interests of a national
group over others that
stand in its way or pose a
real or imaginary threat.
While some Europeans take
pride in the achievements
of the EU, it has not yet
achieved a place in public
consciousness that makes it
the object of patriotism.

place at the lowest end of the range. Comparing polls in 2007 and 2013, we find
that identification with the EU has grown in several eastern European states –
notably Bulgaria, Estonia and Slovakia – as well as in Finland, Luxembourg and
Germany, while it has fallen most in Italy, Portugal, Greece and France (unsur-
prising, given the economic problems of these countries) as well as Sweden,
Belgium and Poland.

But what does 'attachment' or 'identification' mean? Most of us feel attached
to (or identify with) the states of which we are citizens either because we 'fit in'
and are comfortable and familiar with their character and customs, or because we
have a legal association through a passport or some other document that confirms
our citizenship, or because we know little else. Beyond that, identity is hard to
quantify. For many, that sense of association translates into patriotism, or a sense
of pride in the state or nation to which we belong. But this is another concept that
is hard to measure, and many Europeans are wary of patriotism, which has earned
a bad name through its long-time association with nationalism, conflict and war.

The idea that Europeans might identify more actively with Europe is further
complicated by the absence of all the usual factors that give people a sense of
belonging; there is no single European state, nation, language,
government, people, religion, citizenship, passport, army, police force, or culture.
The EU has worked to generate symbols of Europe – including a flag, an anthem,
a motto ('United in Diversity'), an annual Day of Europe (9 May), and there are
also claims that the euro and the burgundy EU passport are symbols of Europe –
but these have not yet attracted the same sense of association with Europe or the
EU as national and state symbols.

Icons are an important element of 'belonging', to be sure, but Europeans are
repeatedly reminded of their differences: language is the most telling reminder,
with culture and history also playing their part. The EU has tried to overcome
the divisions by promoting activities aimed at drawing attention to Europe's
common cultural heritage while preserving diversity. It provides funding and
other support for the arts, education and language training, selects one or two
cities each year as European capitals of culture (examples have included Florence, Madrid, Helsinki, Cork, Liverpool, Istanbul and Riga), and the Commission gives annual awards for the preservation of cultural heritage. But while
such projects have value, it is ultimately up to Europeans themselves to develop
a sense of European identity, which in turn means that they must better understand what they have in common (see discussion in Chapter 17).

Europe's changing demography

Europe has long been a dynamic centre of population growth, and is today one
of the most populous and most densely populated regions of the world: with
a population of 505 million if just the EU is counted, or nearly 690 million if
all 44 European states are included, it ranks third after China (1.3 billion) and
India (1.1 billion), and well ahead of the US (310 million), Russia (142 million)
or Japan (128 million). But current trends suggest that Europe faces some potentially damaging demographic problems: fewer Europeans are having children,
more of them are living longer, and the balance between workers and retirees
is changing. These trends promise, in turn, to lead to social and economic diffi-

Focus on... *The European flag*

Without question, the most ubiquitous and immediately recognizable symbol of European integration is the flag of the EU, its 12 gold stars on a blue background found everywhere from government buildings and hotels to vehicle licence plates, driving licences, identity cards, passports and euro banknotes. Yet, despite how common the flag has become, little is known about how it evolved or what its design represents. The story is a curious one.

Soon after its creation in 1949, the Council of Europe appointed a committee to design a flag. Although no public competition was announced, the Council received more than 120 prospective designs, ranging from the dull to the strange and the outright bizarre. Among the suggestions:

- the flag of the Pan-European Movement – a red cross on a yellow circle on a blue background
- the flag of the European Movement – a large green E on a white background
- a single yellow star on a blue background
- a constellation of 35 yellow stars on a blue background, laid out to indicate Europe's capital cities

- a leaping tiger
- a circle of 15 yellow stars on a blue background, each star representing a member state of the Council of Europe.

The design eventually chosen was the circle of stars, but with the number reduced to 12 because of various objections to the numbers 13, 14 and 15.

The flag was approved and unveiled in 1955, the Council encouraging other European organizations to adopt it so that it could become the symbol of Europe more generally. It was adopted by the European Parliament in 1983, and then by the European Council (for use by the European Community) in 1985, and finally for use by the European Union from 1993. It is now controlled jointly by the EU and the Council of Europe.

When membership of the Community was 12, many thought that the 12 stars each represented a Community member state, but the number was not increased after enlargement in 1995, leading to a number of entertaining suggestions about what the stars signified. These ranged from the months in the year to the number of apostles, the signs of the zodiac, the labours of Hercules, and the tribes of Israel. There has also been speculation, mainly in Catholic countries like Poland, that the stars were inspired by those sometimes found in the halo surrounding the head of the Madonna in church paintings and stained glass windows. But the 12 stars were chosen simply because all members of the design committee could live with that number. The number has no political, religious, social, or cultural significance or symbolism whatsoever. (Information in this box comes mainly from Kowalski, 2009.)

culties: rising costs for healthcare and social security that must be met out of a shrinking tax base, and concerns about everything from declining economic productivity to reduced standards of living, intergenerational tensions, changes to the way businesses operate and work is organized, and new approaches to the planning of urban development, transport and infrastructure.

An allied issue is that of immigration, which is a worldwide phenomenon but has been particularly important in Europe, where even countries that were long sources of emigration (such as Ireland and Italy) have been magnets for immigration (see Parsons and Smeeding, 2006a). While natural increase accounted for almost all population growth in Europe in the 1960s, growth in numbers is now almost entirely generated by net immigration. But this has not been big enough to make up for population decline, and even if it helps add to overall European population numbers, it brings with it the promise of increased social, economic and political tensions, since many of Europe's newcomers are Arabs, Africans, and/or Muslims. Immigration has grown since the 1950s and 60s, but efforts by European governments to protect jobs by limiting the entry of foreign workers have not only contributed to an influx of unskilled illegal workers, but these workers have long been marginalized, with few efforts made to integrate them into mainstream society. Racism and religious bigotry have worsened, and support for right-wing anti-immigrant parties has grown, while infrastructure and social institutions have come under greater pressure. (See Chapter 23 for more details.)

The numbers are clear. Where Europe in 1900 accounted for about a quarter of the world's population, today it accounts for one-ninth, and UN projections suggest that it could account for just one-fourteenth by 2050. This is due, in part, to rapidly growing populations in other parts of the world, but also to slowing growth in Europe. Fertility rates in the EU fell by 45% between 1960 and 2004 (Pearce and Bovagnet, 2005), and today stand at well below the replacement level of 2.1. No EU state has a rate higher than 1.7, while in Italy and Spain it is as low as 1.2, and the EU average is 1.5. As a result, the European population is projected to fall by 6% between 2015 and 2050, while that of India will grow by 25%, the US by 22%, and Brazil by 8%. China will grow by 5% by 2035, after which it will start to fall (see Figure 3.3). While numbers in most

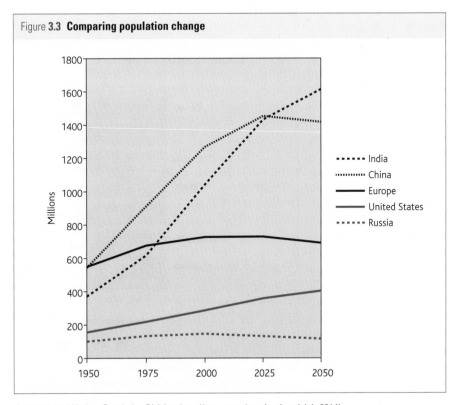

Figure **3.3 Comparing population change**

Source: United Nations Population Division, http://esa.un.org/wpp (retrieved July 2014).

smaller European countries are climbing, in the bigger states the story is quite different: the populations of Germany and Poland are already falling, that of Italy is expected to fall after 2020, and that of France will level out after 2045, leaving only Britain among the big EU states with a growing population, thanks mainly to immigration.

Meanwhile, there has been an ageing of the population. As of 2013, almost a quarter of Europeans were aged 60 and older (just under twice the figure for the world, and nearly five times the figure for Africa), leaving the region with more retirees than any other part of the world except Japan (see Figure 3.4). While the median age for the world's population in 2010 was just under 29, in Europe it was 40.3 and rising (UN Department of Economic and Social Affairs, 2103a). The ratio of pensionable people to people of working age in Europe is expected to rise, coming close to parity in some countries.

Some European governments have become so worried about these trends that they have adopted policies aimed at encouraging people to have more children, including increased job security, extended parental leave, expanded childcare and after-school programmes, free or subsidized education and healthcare, and flexible work schedules. But while the decision to have a child is a deeply personal one, it has long been influenced by economic pressures: where once children were a source of labour and then of support for ageing parents, today the decision to have children is delayed by the number of women pursuing careers and medical advances that make it possible to have children later in life. Government policies, no matter how generous, will not have much impact on these trends.

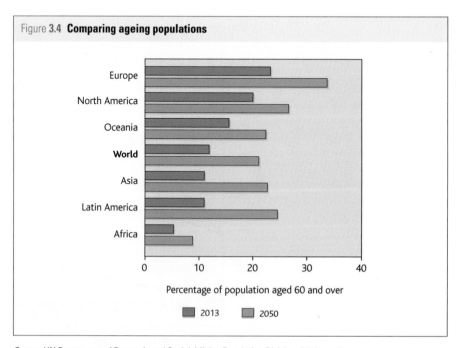

Figure **3.4 Comparing ageing populations**

Percentage of population aged 60 and over

■ 2013   ■ 2050

Source: UN Department of Economic and Social Affairs, Population Division, 2013a, p. 7.

Birth patterns in Europe have also been influenced by developments in the structure of the family. The notion of the 'standard' family unit (one in which a parent or two married parents live together with their children in what sociologists call a 'nuclear' or 'conjugal arrangement') has long been something of a myth, but certainly nowhere is this more true today than in Europe, where the nuclear family is becoming a rarity, impacted by three key trends:

1 Fewer Europeans are marrying, and they are delaying the age at which they marry. Where once it was usual for people to marry in their early twenties, and often even in their late teens, the average age for first marriages in the EU in 2008 ranged between 26 in Lithuania and 33 in Sweden (figures from OECD website). This is explained mainly by the desire of more women to start careers, but also by the decision of more Europeans not to marry.
2 More children are being born outside marriage, the figure in western Europe rising from 2–5% in 1960 to nearly 40% in 2011, and as high as 55–60% in Sweden, Slovenia, Bulgaria and Estonia (Eurostat website). Birth outside marriage, once associated mainly with poverty, is increasingly a deliberate choice for European parents.
3 Households without children have become more usual, accounting for a remarkable 72% of households in the EU-25 in 2010, while barely a quarter of households had two or more adults and children (Eurostat, 2010).

Although similar trends are underway in other industrialized countries, nowhere have they gone so far as in Europe, and nowhere has the debate about the possible implications been more vocal. Those who doubt the wisdom of European integration wonder if the EU can sustain its political influence and economic growth so long as its population is declining. But quality is arguably more important than quantity; it is not how many people we have, so much as how well they live. China and India may be the world's population superpowers, but many of their people live in abject poverty with minimal access to basic services. We have also been warned for decades of the dangers of a rising global population and its growing pressures on finite natural resources. While the changing balance between workers and retirees in Europe will inevitably force reforms of welfare and social security, declining population numbers will also mean less pressure on resources and less overcrowding. Is this a crisis, then, or an opportunity?

Summary

- The geographical, political and ethnic borders of Europe are debatable. To the south, west and north, they are marked by coastlines, but there is no obvious border to the east.

- If the external limits of Europe are contested, so is its internal identity. Nations offer Europeans the most obvious reminder of their differences, with language, culture, history and symbols preventing a broader sense of European identity.

- Europe is divided into at least 40 different states and 160 different nationalities, with natives of the EU speaking more than 40 different languages, of which 24 are currently recognized as official. English, though, is rapidly becoming the common language of Europe.

- Although the EU has promoted an EU 'citizenship' (giving EU citizens the right to live in different EU states, and to run and vote in local and European Parliament elections, for example), this is not the same as providing Europeans with the same rights and legal status as those who are citizens of a member state.

- Polls suggest that only about 4% of Europeans consider themselves as such, while about 41% identify exclusively with the states of which they are citizens, and about 55% have some mixture of European and state identity. Less than half of EU residents feel a sense of attachment to the EU.

- A combination of declining fertility and improved life expectancy means that the population of Europe is shrinking and becoming older. This is leading to concerns about the region's economic productivity and the growing costs of supporting an ageing population.

- Europe's population growth is now almost entirely accounted for by net immigration, which presents a host of troubling political and social challenges.

Key terms and concepts

Citizenship

European citizenship

Identity

Patriotism

Transactionalism

Further reading

Checkel, Jeffrey T. and Peter J. Katzenstein (eds) (2009) *European Identity* (Cambridge: Cambridge University Press). Study of the idea of European identities and how they might be better understood from political, historical, sociological and anthropological perspectives.

Favell, Adrian (2008) *Eurostars and Eurocities: Free Movement and Mobility in an Integrating Europe* (Oxford: Blackwell). Study of the human face of integration, looking at what mobility has meant to individual Europeans.

Fligstein, Neil (2008) *Euroclash: The EU, European Identity, and the Future of Europe* (Oxford: Oxford University Press). Argues that changes in European business, trade, popular culture and social interaction have helped promote a transnational European identity.

4 Organizing Postwar Europe

The roots of today's European Union date back centuries. War and conflict were long part of the fabric of Europe, inspiring philosophers to develop numerous plans for bringing peace to the region, but finding their suggestions falling mainly on deaf ears. The tensions among Europeans deepened during the nineteenth century as nationalism burgeoned and great power competition paved the way for two world wars. Those powers maintained empires that circled the globe, their corporations dominated global trade, and their banks, financial institutions, armies and navies faced few serious challenges. But the two world wars delivered a shattering blow to their power and influence, changing the way they saw themselves and the way they defined their security.

Europe embarked on peace in 1945 with most of its economies devastated, its political systems destabilized, its colonies agitating for independence, and its states distrustful of each other and divided by a new kind of Cold War between two external powers: the US and the Soviet Union. Europeans had tired of violence, and sought ways to make future conflict impossible, but while there was support for the idea of regional cooperation, governments and elites were divided over what this meant in practice and how to proceed.

A modest start was made with the creation in 1949 of the Council of Europe, but this was not enough for federalists, who focused instead on the development of supranational institutions; a new approach was taken in 1952 with the founding of the European Coal and Steel Community. Tracing the story from Bretton Woods to the Marshall Plan and the start of the Cold War, this chapter sets out to capture the spirit of the postwar debate, and understand the confluence of circumstances that came together to make the first steps in the process of integration possible.

- What were the major historical causes of European conflict and war?
- What had changed by 1945 to make Europeans more receptive to the idea of cooperation?
- Why were France and Germany so central to the interests of European integration?
- How important was the Marshall Plan to the postwar recovery of Europe?
- Was focusing on coal and steel a wise move, or a distraction?

Europe before the Second World War

The advent of the EU is just the latest (and perhaps most revolutionary) development in the search for an answer to the long-standing question of how politics and economies should be ordered in one of the world's most heavily populated, politically competitive and culturally complex regions. That Europeans have lived in relative harmony since 1945 is remarkable given the long history of violence in the region. The story of conflict runs from the wars of antiquity through to the invasions of the Early Middle Ages, the Crusades, wider European conflicts such as the Hundred Years' War (1337–1453) or the Eighty Years' War (1568–1648), attempts to fend off foreign invaders such as the Arabs and the Ottoman Turks, civil wars, wars of independence, and the two world wars of the twentieth century.

The causes of Europe's conflicts have shifted from wars over land and between competing dynastic houses to wars of religion in the Middle Ages as first the Latin and Orthodox churches struggled with each other, then Catholics and Protestants fought for influence, then monarchs challenged the authority of the papacy. Through the sixteenth and seventeenth centuries much of Europe was in a state of almost constant religious warfare. A milestone was reached in 1648 when the Peace of Westphalia brought an end to more than a century of war, and confirmed the emergence of the modern state system. Political boundaries in Europe began to achieve a new clarity, but so did the power and reach of governments, which established standing armies to protect their interests, creating new tensions and possibilities for conflict.

A new element was added to the mix by the mismatch between states and nations: people speaking different languages and with separate cultural and sometimes religious identities were brought together under common governments, whose rule they often resented. As Enlightenment ideas led to the rejection of claims by monarchs that their powers were based on God's authority, and growing support for the idea that sovereignty lay with the people, so the struggles for national self-determination grew. Another combustible element was added when European states began to build overseas empires, bringing a global dimension to competition for power within Europe.

Frustrated by what they saw, idealists explored ways in which Europeans might cooperate through regional associations. Suggestions ranged from assemblies of princes to courts that might adjudicate disputes, a European parliament, and a European federation (see de Rougemont, 1966; Heater, 1992; Urwin, 1995; Salmon and Nicoll, 1997). The philosophical benchmark for the debate was laid down in 1795 when the German philosopher Immanuel Kant published his thoughts on the conditions needed for mankind to achieve a state of perpetual peace, including the abolition of standing armies and a federation of free states (Kant, [1795] 2009). Europe's achievements in maintaining peace since 1945 have often earned the region the epithet *Kantian* (see Chapter 24).

The Napoleonic Wars (1803–15) were sparked at least in part by the resistance of nationalists to Napoleon's plans to build a European empire, and although Europe as a whole was mainly at peace between the 1815 Congress of Vienna and the outbreak of the Great War in 1914, nationalism introduced dangerous new pressures. Governments asserted their authority as minorities struggled for independence, the goal for many being the creation of nation-states: a state for every nation. This meant resistance to foreign rule in Belgium, Bulgaria, Greece, Hungary, Ireland, Italy, Poland and Romania, and efforts to unify Germany and Italy. Nationalism and imperialism came together in a volatile combination, and it took only one small spark – the assassination in June 1914 of the heir to the Austro-Hungarian throne by a Slav nationalist – to set off a series of events that would lead within two months to the outbreak of the Great War.

The war resolved little, and did so at staggering cost: an estimated 15 million people died, including unprecedented numbers of civilians. If there was anything positive to come out of the carnage, it was the birth of a new audience – particularly in smaller states tired of being caught in the crossfire of big power rivalry – that was more amenable to notions of interstate cooperation. But although several modest attempts were made to put ideas into practice (Belgium and Luxembourg, for example, created a limited economic union in 1922), most Europeans remained doggedly attached to their national and state identities.

In 1922, the Austrian diplomat Count Richard von Coudenhove-Kalergi wrote an article (turned into a book titled *Pan-Europa* in 1923) in which he warned that Europe was 'a powder keg of international conflicts' whose atmosphere was poisoned by 'the mutual hatred of Europeans for each other'. Its problems would be 'resolved only by the union of the peoples of Europe', to which the greatest obstacle, in his view, was the 'thousand-year rivalry' between Germany and France (von Coudenhove-Kalergi, 1926). His ideas found a receptive audience in several current and future political leaders, including French Prime Minister Édouard Herriot (in office 1924–25), who suggested the creation of a United States of Europe founded on the postwar cooperation being promoted by the new League of Nations. His colleague Aristide Briand followed up in 1930 by suggesting a European federation working within the League of Nations, using in his proposal such terms as *common market* and *European Union* (Briand, 1997).

But the 1919 Treaty of Versailles, by punishing Germany and demanding reparations, had already laid the foundations for more conflict. The rise of Nazism squashed all ideas of peaceful cooperation, and the outbreak of another

Profile Richard von Coudenhove-Kalergi

Richard von Coudenhove-Kalergi (1894–1972) was the son of an Austro-Hungarian diplomat and his Japanese wife. Born in Tokyo, he was raised mainly in what is now the Czech Republic, and educated in Vienna. He was author of the pamphlet *Pan-Europa*, creator in 1923 of the Pan-Europa Union, and editor of its journal *Paneuropa* until 1938. He proposed dividing the world into five power groups: Paneuropa (including all European states except Britain), the British Empire, a Pan-American Union in North and South America, the Soviet Union in Eurasia, and a Pan-Asian Union centred on Japan and China. He spent the Second World War in exile, mainly in the US, inspiring the character Victor Laszlo in the film *Casablanca*. He continued to promote his ideas of European unity after the war, and lived to see the creation of the European Economic Community. It was on the basis of suggestions from von Coudenhove-Kalergi that the Council of Europe, and then the EEC, adopted Beethoven's 'Ode to Joy' as its anthem and celebrated Europe Day in May.

Map **4.1** **Europe after the Second World War**

European war in 1939 suggested that the region was incapable of finding the formula for a lasting peace (Marks, 2003). The Second World War brought new levels of death and destruction, cost millions of civilian and military lives, left cities in ruins, cut agricultural production by half, left an estimated 13 million refugees at war's end, destroyed essential infrastructure, and brought political and economic dislocation to winners and losers alike.

The troubled state of postwar Europe

Relief at the end of the war was reflected in the rejoicing and celebration that broke out on VE Day, 8 May 1945. But it was also clear that Europeans now faced the sobering and monumental task of rebuilding not just the infrastructure destroyed by war but often entire political, economic and social systems. They had suffered physically and psychologically, and now cast anxious eyes at the challenges that lay ahead, some more apparent than others:

- **France** had suffered a wartime division between collaborators and the Resistance, and now worried about how to modernize its economy and extend welfare provisions, its international standing unclear. It acted like a great power, but the constitution of the Fourth Republic (adopted in 1946) was flawed, and France was to suffer blows to its military pride in Indochina in 1954 and again at Suez in 1956 (see Chapter 5). Charles de Gaulle would come out of retirement in 1958 to head the new Fifth Republic, and to reorder France's place in Europe and the world.

- **Britain** had seen its finest hour during the war, but while it was politically stable and enjoyed rapid economic recovery after the war, bolstered by nationalization and welfare reform, its international role had changed. The beginning of the end of its great power status came in August 1947 with independence for India and Pakistan, but many Britons still held on to their national pride and their interests outside Europe, valued close cooperation with the US, and paid little attention to developments on the continent. Suez was to force a reappraisal, but even today many Britons remain reluctant Europeans.

- **West Germany** was focused on economic reconstruction and dealing with a national sense of shame. Germany as a whole was under four-way foreign occupation, and by 1948 was divided into socialist eastern and capitalist western sectors. The Federal Republic of Germany (or West Germany) was founded in May 1949, and the Christian Democrats won the August elections. The popular Chancellor Konrad Adenauer (in office 1949–63) worked to side his new state with the new Atlantic Alliance (see later in this chapter) and to rebuild German respectability, goals that inevitably made it a champion of regional integration.

- **Italy** was less successful than West Germany in achieving postwar economic and political stability. Christian Democrats dominated the new Italian republic created in June 1946, but there were frequent changes of government, systematic corruption, and bureaucratic incompetence. For Prime Minister Alcide de Gasperi (in office 1945–53), integration with Europe was a means of encouraging peace while helping Italy deal with its economic problems. But the country has never lived up to its potential as a leading European power.

- The **Nordic states** had different wartime experiences: Sweden remained neutral, Finland became neutral after going to war with the USSR, Denmark and Norway were both invaded by Germany, and a newly independent Iceland was wary of international cooperation (there were street riots when it became a founding member of NATO in 1949). But the five had political stability, homogeneous populations, and few internal social problems. They harmonized national laws, agreed common foreign policy positions, and launched joint ventures such as the airline SAS (created in 1946). In 1952 the Nordic Council was formed to promote the abolition of passport controls, the free movement of workers, and more joint ventures.

- The **Benelux states** (Belgium, the Netherlands and Luxembourg) had all been occupied by the Germans, and were interested in economic cooperation. In 1948 the Benelux customs union was created, paving the way for the 1960 Benelux Economic Union, which proved to be a landmark experiment in European integration.

- In **Greece**, **Portugal** and **Spain**, the road to democracy and economic growth was rocky. Greece enjoyed postwar economic growth, but political tensions would lead to a military dictatorship in 1967–74. Portugal had been under the authoritarian government of Antonio Salazar since 1928, and Spain under the dictatorship of Francisco Franco since 1939. Surrounded by efforts to encourage postwar international cooperation, all three remained relatively isolated.

- **Ireland** had been officially neutral during the war but with its economy bound to that of Britain, its postwar approach to Europe was subject to the British lead. It joined the Community in 1973 with Britain, after which it maintained its neutrality while enjoying economic growth.

- **Austria** had been left relatively unscathed by war, and although it was divided like Germany into separate postwar zones of occupation, it returned quickly to its 1920 constitution and held democratic elections. It declared itself neutral in 1955, but economic ties pulled it into the western European orbit.

- Prospects of **eastern Europe** taking part in broader regional cooperation were trampled by its postwar absorption into the Soviet sphere, and its obligation to follow the Soviet lead on foreign policy, which meant no cooperative deals with the West. Only after the end of the Cold War in 1989–91 would eastern Europe emerge from its shell and begin working with the West.

The Second World War also resulted in a reordering of the international system. Until 1939, the world's great powers were mainly European, their influence based on their large militaries and economies, their strong positions in international trade, and their financial investments around the world (Levy, 1983, pp. 16–18). But while Britain and France continued to act like great powers after the war, it soon became clear that there was a new international order in place, dominated by the US and the Soviet Union. Their power was so great and their reach so far that they earned the new label *superpower* (Fox, 1944, pp. 20–1) (see Chapter 24 for further discussion). Europe's decline was soon confirmed by the region's division in an ideological Cold War between the superpowers in which Europeans were to play only a supporting role.

Three urgent priorities now faced European states:

1 Economic reconstruction was needed if Europe was to recover and regroup, but it was clear that the region was too tired and drained to be able to manage this alone.

2 Europeans not only continued to be suspicious of each other, but also faced the prospect of being the battlefield in a war between the Americans and the Soviets, and the danger of the ultimate form of destruction: nuclear annihilation.

3 Nationalism had been the main cause of both world wars, and Europeans could not hope to live in peace unless it was channelled in a more benign direction.

Cold War: A war of words, ideas and ideologies between the US and its surrogates, on the one hand, and the Soviet Union and its surrogates on the other. It lasted from the late 1940s to the late 1980s.

Timeline	*Organizing postwar Europe*	
1914–18		First World War
1919	June	Signature of Treaty of Versailles
1923		Creation of Pan-Europa Union
1939–45		Second World War
1944	July	Bretton Woods conference
1945	May	End of the war in Europe
1946	March	Churchill's 'iron curtain' speech
	June	Creation of Italian republic
	September	Churchill's 'United States of Europe' speech
	October	Creation of French Fourth Republic
1947	March	Announcement of Truman Doctrine
	June	George Marshall's speech at Harvard
	August	Independence of India and Pakistan
1948	January	Benelux customs union enters into force
	March	Brussels Treaty creates Western Union
1948	April	Launch of the Marshall Plan; first meeting of OEEC
	May	Congress of Europe meets in The Hague
	June	Start of Berlin blockade
	October	Creation of European Movement
1949	April	Signature of North Atlantic Treaty, and creation of NATO
	May	Creation of Council of Europe; end of Berlin blockade; creation of Federal Republic of Germany
1950	May	Schuman Declaration
	June	Negotiations begin on coal and steel agreement
1951	April	Signature of Treaty of Paris
1952	March	Creation of Nordic Council
	July	Treaty of Paris enters into force
	August	European Coal and Steel Community begins work
1955	May	Creation of Warsaw Pact

Looking back today with the benefit of hindsight, it is remarkable how much Europe has since been able to achieve: after centuries of bloodshed, the region has become the poster child for peace, diplomacy and the resolution of conflict, to the extent that the EU was awarded the 2012 Nobel Peace Prize. But achieving this has not been easy, and it happened only because of a fortuitous coincidence of circumstances, without which the history of postwar Europe might have taken a very different turn.

Concept

Bretton Woods system

The arrangement agreed at Bretton Woods in 1944, by which it was hoped that the economic and financial mistakes of the mid-war years would be avoided, and a new and more sustainable international commercial and financial system created. The key goal of the system was exchange rate stability, using gold as the reference point, and a free convertibility of currencies that would encourage trade. The system ended in August 1971 when the US unilaterally ended the convertibility of gold and the US dollar, sparking exchange rate volatility and helping encourage western Europe to take the first steps in what would eventually lead to the creation of the euro.

Marshall Plan: A programme under which the US offered financial assistance to encourage postwar recovery in Europe. Often credited with providing the investments needed to pave the way for regional integration.

Rebuilding economies (1945–51)

The postwar international economic system was mapped out at a landmark meeting in July 1944, when economists and government leaders from both sides of the Atlantic gathered at the Mount Washington Hotel, set in the forested hills of Bretton Woods, New Hampshire. There they laid down the principles of what became known as the Bretton Woods system: the convertibility of currencies, free trade, non-discrimination, and stable rates of exchange. These would be underpinned by the new strength of the US dollar and the creation of two new international organizations: the International Monetary Fund would encourage exchange rate stability in the interests of promoting international trade, and the World Bank would lend to European countries affected by war (van Dormael, 1978). A third body, the International Trade Organization, failed to win support in the US Congress and it was instead agreed to set up the General Agreement on Tariffs and Trade as a temporary measure to oversee negotiations aimed at the progressive reduction of barriers to trade.

Noble as these goals may have been, it soon became clear that the economic costs of conflict had been underestimated: there was a brief postwar boom in western Europe, but growth was not sustained, food was still being rationed, and governments were using up their dollar reserves buying essential imports. Large amounts of capital investment were needed, and the only ready source was the US. Its wartime economy had prospered, and although it had provided more than $10 billion in loans and aid to Europe between 1945 and 1947 (Milward, 1984, pp. 46–8), a more structured approach was needed.

In a speech at Harvard University in June 1947, US Secretary of State George Marshall announced that the US would do whatever it could to help encourage Europe's economic revival. His motives were clearly political (a strong Europe would help prevent Soviet expansionism and create a new market for US exports), but he couched his arguments in humanitarian terms, arguing that US policy was directed 'against hunger, poverty, desperation and chaos' and that 'its purpose should be the revival of a working economy in the world so as to permit the emergence of political and social conditions in which free institutions can exist' (Marshall, 1947).

Within weeks, representatives of 16 western European governments had met in Paris to begin listing needs. (The Soviets also attended, but left when they decided that US goals were incompatible with their own.) Between 1948 and 1951 the European Recovery Programme, otherwise known as the Marshall Plan, was to provide $12.5 billion in aid (Milward, 1984, p. 94) (about $125 billion in 2015 terms, adjusted for inflation). But while Marshall was awarded the 1953 Nobel Peace Prize for his efforts, the long-term role and significance of Marshall aid remains contested. Hitchcock (2004, pp. 134–8) points out that economic recovery was already underway before the aid arrived, with most western European countries already back up to, or close to, prewar levels of production. Furthermore, the aid itself was only a small fraction of the gross national product of the recipient states. On the other hand, it had psychological value: it reassured an economically nervous western Europe, helped bind together transatlantic economic interests, and helped offset communist influence in western Europe. In short, contends Judt (2005, p. 97), it 'helped Europeans feel better about themselves'.

Illustration **4.1**
The Marshall Plan
Marshall Plan assistance begins to arrive in Europe, providing devastated postwar economies with an essential boost to their plans for reconstruction.

The Marshall Plan also helped lay critical foundations for European integration. The US insisted on the creation of a new international body, the Organisation for European Economic Co-operation (OEEC), to coordinate the distribution of aid. Meeting for the first time in April 1948, its goals included reduced tariffs and other barriers to trade, and a free trade area or customs union among its members (Articles 4–6 of the Convention for European Economic Cooperation, quoted in Palmer and Lambert, 1968, p. 81). Critics have dismissed the OEEC as clumsy and inadequate, and as nothing more than a clearinghouse for economic information (Wexler, 1983, p. 209; Milward, 1984, p. 208; Dinan, 2014, p. 30). But it was western Europe's first permanent organization for economic cooperation, it encouraged interstate cooperation, and it helped reveal the degree of economic interdependence among its members (Urwin, 1995, pp. 20–2). (In December 1960 the OEEC was reorganized as the Organisation for Economic Co-operation and Development.)

Addressing external threats (1946–49)

Organisation for European Economic Co-operation (OEEC): An international body set up to coordinate and manage Marshall aid, which some see as the first significant step in the process of postwar European integration.

Economic reconstruction was their most immediate priority, but western Europeans also worried about threats to their security, now more external than internal. The US had pulled most of its military out of Europe soon after the war, encouraged by public opinion at home that favoured leaving future peacekeeping efforts to the new United Nations. But it soon became clear that Stalin had plans to spread Soviet influence in Europe, replacing the old Nazi threat with a new communist threat. Winston Churchill drew public attention to the dilemma with his famous March 1946 speech in Fulton, Missouri, in which he warned of the descent of an 'iron curtain' across Europe. He also observed that from what he had seen of the Russians during the war, there was nothing they admired so much as strength, 'and there is nothing for which they have less respect than … weakness, especially military weakness' (Churchill, 1946).

The Americans expected that responsibility for European security would be shared with the British and the French, but neither had the resources to meet their end of the bargain. Britain had provided financial aid and military security in Greece (which Churchill had established as a British sphere of influence in return for giving the Soviets control over Romania), but it soon had to withdraw, raising concerns about communist influence in the region. In March 1947, US President Harry S. Truman concluded that the US should step into the breach, and announced what was to become known as the Truman Doctrine: it would now be US policy, he declared, 'to support free peoples who are resisting attempted subjugation by armed minorities or by outside pressures' (Truman, 1947). The new insecurities of Europe were quickly illustrated by events in Germany.

While the western Allies favoured German self-sufficiency, the Soviets first wanted reparations and a guarantee of security from German aggression. Prompted by Soviet belligerence, in March 1948 Britain, France and the Benelux states signed the Brussels Treaty, creating a Western Union (renamed Western European Union in 1954; see Chapter 5), whose members pledged to provide 'all the military and other aid and assistance in their power' in the event of attack. The Allies also began discussions aimed at building a new West German government and tying West Germany into the Atlantic Alliance. When they announced their plans in June 1948 (which included the creation of a new currency, the deutschmark), the Soviets responded by setting up a blockade of West Berlin, obliging the British and the Americans to organize an 11-month airlift of supplies to the beleaguered city.

With the twin need of protecting western Europe and also sharing the burden, the Americans and their western European allies signed the North Atlantic Treaty in April 1949, under which the idea of mutual protection was expanded to include the US, Britain, France, Canada, Italy, the Benelux countries, Denmark, Iceland, Norway and Portugal. The treaty was given institutional substance with the creation of the North Atlantic Treaty Organization (NATO).

As with the Marshall Plan, opinion on the significance of NATO has been divided. On the one hand, the treaty stated that 'an armed attack against one or more of [the members]… shall be considered an attack against them all', but it obliged each member to respond only with 'such action as it deems necessary, including the use of armed force'. In other words, there was no firm commitment to a combined military response. On the other hand, the creation of NATO sent a telling message to the Soviets, who countered in 1955 with the creation of their own defensive agreement, the Warsaw Pact. NATO also represented the first peacetime military agreement ever made by the US, and set up the first ever peacetime integrated military command.

North Atlantic Treaty Organization (NATO): A defensive alliance created in 1949 among the US, Canada and most major western European states, designed in part to send a hands-off warning to the Soviet Union. More broadly known as the Atlantic Alliance.

The Council of Europe (1946–49)

Within a few years of the end of the Second World War, then, and encouraged mainly by the US, there was a new atmosphere of receptivity to cooperation in

Profile Winston Churchill

Winston Churchill (1874–1965) (*second from right*) was prime minister of Britain between 1940 and 1945, and again between 1951 and 1955. Although he was the great symbol of British resistance to the Nazi threat during the Second World War, he is a controversial figure in the gallery of Europeanists. On the one hand, he inspired many of the ideas that set the tone for discussions about cooperation, including his suggestion for a United States of Europe, his role in the creation of the Council of Europe, and his warning of the 'iron curtain' that had descended across the continent. On the other hand, he was clearly a champion of Britain's association with the English-speaking peoples of the world, and equivocated on the precise role that Britain might play in Europe. He has never quite been elevated to the same ranks in the European debate as the other 'founding fathers', such as Paul-Henri Spaak of Belgium (*left*) and Robert Schuman (*right*).

European Movement: An organization created in 1948 to champion the cause of European integration. It was behind the setting up of the Council of Europe and continues today to lobby for a federal Europe.

Council of Europe: An organization founded in 1949 at the suggestion of Winston Churchill, which has gone on to promote European unity with a focus on issues relating to democracy and human rights.

western Europe. Several pro-European groups were founded or revived, but what was lacking was a strong political lead, which could come only from Britain, still the major power in Europe. During the war, Winston Churchill had suggested the creation of 'a United States of Europe' operating under 'a Council of Europe', with reduced trade barriers, free movement of people, a common military, and a High Court to adjudicate disputes (Palmer and Lambert, 1968, p. 111). He repeated the suggestion in a speech co-drafted by von Coudenhove-Kalergi (Salmon and Nicoll, 1997, p. 6) and given in Zurich in September 1946 (see Document 4.1). But Britain had too many interests outside Europe, including its empire and its links with the US, and Churchill neatly summed up British attitudes when he proclaimed that Britain was 'with Europe but not of it. We are interested and associated, but not absorbed' (Zurcher, 1958, p. 6).

Undeterred, pro-European groups organized the Congress of Europe in The Hague in May 1948, presided over by Churchill and attended by more than 600 delegates from 16 states and observers from Canada and the US. But opinion differed on the meaning of European unity (Dinan, 2014, p. 26). While federalists hoped for a wholesale redrawing of the map of Europe, with the replacement of individual states by a United States of Europe, others still believed in the superiority of the state and were interested only in cooperation. In October, the European Movement was created with a view to moving the debate along, and there was talk of creating a European Assembly. The eventual compromise was the signing on 5 May 1949 of a statute in London creating the Council of Europe.

The goal of the new body was to achieve 'a greater unity between its Members … by discussion of questions of common concern and by agreements and common action in economic, social, cultural, scientific, legal and administrative matters'. Its most lasting contribution was the drafting in 1950 and the subsequent management of the European Convention on Human Rights, which today plays a key role in the European legal structure (see Chapter 8). But as for the broader issue of European integration, the Council was too limited in its goals for the tastes of federalists. Jean Monnet described it as 'entirely useless', and later French President Charles de Gaulle regarded it as 'simply ridiculous' (Simpson, 2001, p. 646).

Document 4.1 *Churchill's Zurich speech, 19 September 1946 (excerpts)*

I wish to speak to you today about the tragedy of Europe. This noble continent ... is the home of all the great parent races of the western world. It is the fountain of Christian faith and Christian ethics. It is the origin of most of the culture, arts, philosophy and science both of ancient and modern times.

If Europe were once united in the sharing of its common inheritance, there would be no limit to the happiness, to the prosperity and glory which its ... people would enjoy. Yet it is from Europe that have sprung that series of frightful nationalistic quarrels, originated by the Teutonic nations, which we have seen even in this twentieth century and in our own lifetime, wreck the peace and mar the prospects of all mankind. ...

Some of the smaller States have indeed made a good recovery, but over wide areas a vast quivering mass of tormented, hungry, care-worn and bewildered human beings gape at the ruins of their cities and homes, and scan the dark horizons for the approach of some new peril, tyranny or terror. Among the victors there is a babel of jarring voices; among the vanquished a sullen silence of despair. ...

Yet all the while there is a remedy. ... It is to re-create the European Family, or as much of it as we can, and provide it with a structure under which it can dwell in peace, in safety and in freedom. We must build a kind of United States of Europe. ...

If Europe is to be saved from infinite misery, and indeed from final doom, there must be an act of faith in the European family and an act of oblivion against all the crimes and follies of the past. ... The first step in the re-creation of the European family must be a partnership between France and Germany. ...

If we are to form the United States of Europe or whatever name or form it may take, we must begin now. ... The first step is to form a Council of Europe. If at first all the states of Europe are not willing or able to join the Union, we must nevertheless proceed to assemble and combine those who will and those who can.

Source: James, 1974.

With more practical goals in mind, Monnet recruited to his cause Robert Schuman, the incumbent foreign minister of France. Both were committed integrationists, both felt that the noble statements of the unity lobby needed to be translated into practical action, and both agreed with Churchill that the logical focus should be on the Franco-German problem. Schuman was instinctively suspicious of Germany, but was encouraged by US Secretary of State Dean Acheson to give it political credit, and provide French leadership on the tricky question of bringing West Germany back into the western community. (The division of Germany had been confirmed by the founding in May 1949 of the western Federal Republic of Germany, followed three months later by the eastern German Democratic Republic.) An opportunity was created by US and British interest in West German rearmament; this ran the danger of tilting the European balance of power (Hitchcock, 2004, pp. 151–2), but not if West Germany was allowed to rebuild under the auspices of a new supranational organization that would bind it into the wider process of European reconstruction.

The European Coal and Steel Community (1949–52)

At early meetings of the European Movement, the suggestion had been made that coal and steel offered strong potential for cooperation. They were the building blocks of industry, the raw materials for weapons of war, and cooperation might eliminate waste and duplication, boost industrial development, and ensure that

Profile *Robert Schuman*

Robert Schuman (1886–1963) was the quintessential European: born to French parents in Luxembourg, he was brought up in then German-ruled Lorraine, attended university in Germany, and served in the German army during the First World War. Elected after the war to the French parliament, he refused to serve in the French Vichy government during the Second World War, and was imprisoned by the Gestapo for his criticism of German policy. He escaped, joined the French Resistance, and was re-elected to the French legislature in 1945. He served as France's finance minister and briefly as prime minister before serving as foreign minister from 1948 to 1952. Although the May 1950 declaration of the ECSC bears his name, it was the brainchild of Jean Monnet, and Monnet later claimed that Schuman 'didn't really understand' the plan (Jenkins, 1989, p. 220). Nonetheless, Schuman has won a permanent place in the pantheon of the pioneers of integration.

West Germany became reliant on trade with the rest of western Europe (Milward, 1984, p. 394). It would also allow France to exert some control over production in the German industrial heartland of the Ruhr. As to how to proceed, Monnet's experience as a bureaucrat told him that a new supranational organization with powers and a life of its own was needed. He discussed this with Schuman and West German Chancellor Konrad Adenauer, and they agreed on the creation of a new body within which responsibility for coal and steel production could be pooled so as to lay the foundations for what might eventually become a European federation. Their proposal was announced by Schuman at a press conference at the French Foreign Ministry in Paris on 9 May 1950 – almost five years to day after the end of the war in Europe (see Document 4.2).

Illustration **4.2**
The Schuman Declaration
Robert Schuman addresses a press conference in the Salon de l'Horloge at the Quai d'Orsay in Paris on 9 May 1950, and announces the plan to set up a European Coal and Steel Community.

Document 4.2 *The Schuman Declaration, 9 May 1950 (excerpts)*

World peace cannot be safeguarded without the making of creative efforts proportionate to the dangers which threaten it. The contribution which an organized and living Europe can bring to civilization is indispensable to the maintenance of peaceful relations. …

Europe will not be made all at once, or according to a single plan. It will be built through concrete achievements which first create a de facto solidarity. The coming together of the nations of Europe requires the elimination of the age-old opposition of France and Germany. …

With this aim in view, the French Government proposes that action be taken immediately on one limited but decisive point. It proposes that Franco-German production of coal and steel as a whole be placed under a common High Authority, within the framework of an organization open to the participation of the other countries of Europe. The pooling of coal and steel production should immediately provide for the setting up of common foundations for economic development as a first step in the federation of Europe, and will change the destinies of those regions which have long been devoted to the manufacture of munitions of war, of which they have been the most constant victims.

The solidarity in production thus established will make it plain that any war between France and Germany becomes not merely unthinkable, but materially impossible. The setting up of this powerful productive unit, open to all countries willing to take part and bound ultimately to provide all the member countries with the basic elements of industrial production on the same terms, will lay a true foundation for their economic unification.

Source: Europa website, http://europa.eu/abc/symbols/9-may/decl_en.htm (retrieved June 2014).

The Schuman Plan was revolutionary in the sense that France was offering to surrender a measure of national sovereignty in the interests of building a new supranational authority that might help build a new European peace (Gillingham, 1991, p. 231). But few other governments shared Monnet's enthusiasm, and only four agreed to sign up: Italy sought respectability and stability, and the three Benelux countries were small and vulnerable, had twice been invaded by Germany, were heavily reliant on exports, and felt that the only way they could have a voice in world affairs and guarantee their security was to be part of a bigger unit. As for the others:

- Britain trusted neither the French nor the Germans, still had too many political and economic interests outside Europe, exported little of its steel to Europe (Milward, 1984, p. 402), and had recently nationalized its coal and steel industries. Prime Minister Clement Attlee argued that he was 'not prepared to accept the principle that the most vital economic forces of this country should be handed over to an authority that is utterly undemocratic and is responsible to nobody' (Black, 2000, p. 303). He, like his social democratic peers in the Scandinavian countries, was also wary of the role being played by continental Christian democrats in early initiatives on integration.
- Because Ireland's economy was predominantly agricultural, it had little to gain from the proposal. It also had to follow the British lead because of its economic ties with Britain.
- For Denmark and Norway, memories of the German occupation were still too fresh, while Austria, Finland and Sweden valued their neutrality.
- Portugal and Spain were dictatorships with only limited interest in international cooperation.
- Eastern Europe was out of the picture thanks to Soviet control.

Against this less than encouraging background, the governments of the Six opened negotiations in June 1950. There was resistance to Monnet's plans to break down coal and steel cartels, and Gillingham (2003, p. 25) notes that the negotiations were 'often tough and even brutal', several times standing on the brink of collapse. Disagreement centred on the break-up of the German coal and steel industries, the role of the ECSC High Authority, the weighting of votes in its Council of Ministers, and even which languages should be used and where the ECSC institutions should be based (Dinan, 2014, pp. 53–7). But Monnet prevailed and on 18 April 1951 the Treaty of Paris was signed, creating the European Coal and Steel Community (ECSC). It was charged with building a common market in coal and steel by eliminating import and export duties, discriminatory measures among producers and consumers, subsidies and state assistance, and restrictive practices. The treaty entered into force in July 1952 and the new organization began work in August, managed by four institutions (see Figure 4.1).

Opinion on the long-term significance of the ECSC is divided. For Dinan (2014, pp. 58, 67), it was 'politically important and institutionally innovative but economically insignificant', and he doubts that it contributed much to Europe's economic growth. And although it initially benefited from rising demand for coal and steel on the back of the Korean War, it ultimately failed to achieve its core goal of a single market for coal and steel (Gillingham, 1991, p. 319). But like the Marshall Plan and NATO, it had an important psychological effect, obliging the governments of the Six to work together and learn new ways of doing business. It functioned independently until 1965, when the High Authority and the Special Council of Ministers were merged with their counterparts in the EEC and Euratom (see Chapter 5). The Treaty of Paris expired in July 2002, 50 years after it came into force.

European Coal and Steel Community (ECSC): The first organization set up to encourage regional integration in Europe, with qualities that were both supranational and intergovernmental.

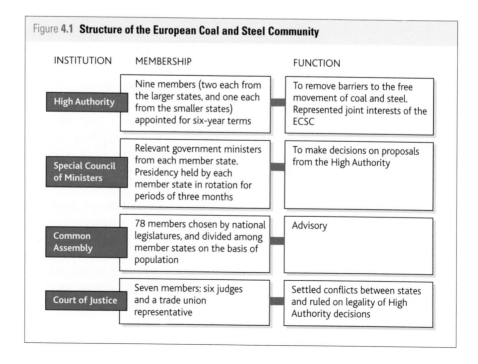

Figure **4.1 Structure of the European Coal and Steel Community**

INSTITUTION	MEMBERSHIP	FUNCTION
High Authority	Nine members (two each from the larger states, and one each from the smaller states) appointed for six-year terms	To remove barriers to the free movement of coal and steel. Represented joint interests of the ECSC
Special Council of Ministers	Relevant government ministers from each member state. Presidency held by each member state in rotation for periods of three months	To make decisions on proposals from the High Authority
Common Assembly	78 members chosen by national legislatures, and divided among member states on the basis of population	Advisory
Court of Justice	Seven members: six judges and a trade union representative	Settled conflicts between states and ruled on legality of High Authority decisions

Summary

- Europe had long been divided by conflict as one power invaded or tried to dominate another, or as religious disputes spilled over into violence, and then as states began to emerge and national minorities struggled for independence.

- Numerous suggestions had been made for ways in which Europeans might cooperate, but it took the traumas of two world wars to bring these ideas to a wider audience.

- The Franco-German question dominated many of the discussions, but while Italy and the Benelux countries were keen on cooperation, Britain kept its distance, others were wary of international efforts, and eastern Europe was under Soviet control.

- Western Europe in 1945 had three critical needs: to rebuild war-ravaged economies, ensure security from one another and from external threats, and limit the dangers of nationalism.

- Economic reconstruction was given a boost by the US, which provided assistance through the Marshall Plan. Security assurances were also provided by the US through the new North Atlantic Treaty Organization.

- The problem of nationalism was addressed by new initiatives to promote regional unity, beginning in 1949 with the creation of the Council of Europe. But its goals were too limited for the tastes of Europeanists such as Jean Monnet and Robert Schuman.

- The signature of the 1951 Treaty of Paris led to the creation in 1952 of the European Coal and Steel Community, a first step in the process of building European economic ties. But only France, West Germany, Italy and the three Benelux countries joined.

Key terms and concepts

Bretton Woods system

Cold War

Council of Europe

European Coal and Steel Community

European Movement

Marshall Plan

North Atlantic Treaty Organization

Organisation for European Economic Co-operation

Further reading

Dinan, Desmond (2014) *Europe Recast: A History of European Union*, 2nd edn (Basingstoke: Palgrave Macmillan). Best general history of European integration, essential reading before moving on to more detailed or revisionist studies.

Gilbert, Mark (2003) *Surpassing Realism: The Politics of European Integration since 1945* (Lanham, MD: Rowman & Littlefield). Gillingham, John (2003) *European Integration, 1950–2003: Superstate or New Market Economy?* (Cambridge: Cambridge University Press). Two more opinionated histories of European integration; Gillingham is particularly critical, writing of missed opportunities and bad decisions.

Hitchcock, William I. (2004) *The Struggle for Europe: The Turbulent History of a Divided Continent* (New York: Anchor Books). Does for Europe what Dinan does for the EU: a readable survey of postwar European history that helps place more detailed studies in perspective. For a more detailed treatment, see Judt, Tony (2005) *Postwar: A History of Europe since 1945* (New York: Penguin).

5 The European Economic Community

Preview

The creation of the European Coal and Steel Community (ECSC) was a critical first step along the path to European integration, but its possibilities were always bound to be limited. So, after failing with ambitious attempts to launch defence and political communities, the six ECSC members switched their focus to the building of a single market. The 1957 Treaty of Rome created the European Economic Community (EEC) with the goal of creating a western European market within which there would be free movement of people, money, goods and services. But the EEC would see only mixed progress during the 1960s as its member states failed to exploit its possibilities.

This was also a troubling time on the global stage, with the Berlin crisis and the Cuban missile crisis, escalation of the war in Vietnam, and the Soviet crackdown on reform in Czechoslovakia, in all of which the key decisions were made by American and Soviet leaders. Meanwhile, the EEC was to be troubled by political disagreements over the powers and reach of its institutions and over enlargement, with French President Charles de Gaulle twice vetoing British applications for membership.

In 1973 the Community welcomed its first new members – Britain, Ireland and Denmark, followed in the 1980s by Greece, Spain and Portugal. The main effect of enlargement was to change the political balance of integration as France and Germany found their previously dominant roles challenged, and the economic and social disparities among EEC member grew. Efforts to achieve exchange rate stability pushed monetary union up the agenda, leading to the launch in 1979 of the European Monetary System. But it would be many more years before the circumstances were right for a single currency.

Key issues

- How important was the Suez crisis to the history of European integration?
- What does de Gaulle's role in the early years of the EEC say about the problems and possibilities of strong leadership in European affairs?
- What impact did Vietnam have on European integration?
- How did enlargement add to, or detract from, early efforts to integrate western Europe?
- What were the pressures that pushed economic and monetary union up the agenda of integration?

Internal and external shocks (1950–58)

The achievements of the ECSC were more symbolic than substantive, and it was soon clear that something more ambitious was needed if integration was to have the kind of reach and effects that its most committed supporters hoped for. In the search for bold initiatives, the focus now shifted from the modest to the patently overoptimistic.

The first project was the European Defence Community (EDC), which had first been proposed in 1949 by West German Chancellor Konrad Adenauer, seeking West German remilitarization in the interests of self-defence. It was given a decisive push by US support for rearming West Germany in the wake of the June 1950 outbreak of the Korean War (Dinan, 2014, pp. 59–61). A draft plan was published in October 1950, which, although named for incumbent French Prime Minister René Pleven, was mainly the work of Jean Monnet (Gillingham, 2003, p. 29). The Pleven Plan spoke of the need for a common defence and a European army made up of units from different countries coming under the control of a European minister of defence, responsible to a council of ministers and a European assembly (Stirk and Weigall, 1999, pp. 108–9).

A draft EDC Treaty was signed in May 1952 by the six members of the ECSC, but it immediately faced two critical handicaps: it lacked support from Britain, the only remaining large military power in Europe, and its core goal of building a Franco-German military force could not be achieved without the full remilitarization of West Germany, which was unlikely to happen for several more years. Then, in May 1954, came a humiliating blow to French national pride and global influence: the surrender of 12,000 French forces besieged by communists at Dien Bien Phu in French Indochina (for details, see Windrow, 2004). In a sombre mood, and following a debate in which concerns were expressed about the potential loss of national sovereignty, the French National Assembly rejected the EDC Treaty in August.

Eager to encourage military cooperation that went beyond the loose obligations of NATO, Britain now proposed transforming the Western Union into the Western European Union (WEU) (Urwin, 1995, pp. 68–71). This was to be intergovernmental (in contrast to the supranational EDC), and reiterated the commitment made in the 1948 Treaty of Brussels that, in the event of an attack on one of its members, the others would respond with 'all the military and other aid and assistance in their power' (a commitment that went beyond the NATO obligation on a member to respond only with 'such action as it deems necessary'). The WEU was also more than a security agreement: modifications to the Treaty of Brussels included agreement to 'promote the unity and to encourage the progressive integration of Europe.' The creation of the WEU in 1954 also helped give new clarity to the dynamics of the Cold War: it began work in May 1955, just as West Germany became a member of NATO, and within days the Soviet bloc had created its own defensive alliance in the form of the Warsaw Pact (the Treaty of Friendship, Cooperation and Mutual Assistance).

The second major initiative of the early 1950s was the European Political Community (EPC). Prompted mainly by the desire to create a political control mechanism to oversee the EDC and the ECSC (Gillingham, 2003, p. 30; Dinan, 2014, p. 65), a draft plan was agreed in 1953. Since described as Europe's 'first

European Defence Community (EDC): A stillborn plan to create a common European military as a means of binding a rearmed West Germany into western Europe.

Western European Union (WEU): A defensive alliance (created in 1948 as the Western Union) that was always to be overshadowed by NATO, and, in spite of being given a potential new role in EU defence in the 1990s, eventually became dormant.

European Political Community (EPC): An attempt to create a political community to oversee the ECSC and the European Defence Community, but collapsed with the demise of the latter.

constitution' (Griffiths, 2000), it included proposals for a European executive council, a council of ministers, a court of justice, and an elected bicameral parliament (anticipating much of today's EU). But it was too soon to be thinking so ambitiously, and the collapse of the EDC also meant the end of the EPC. The shockwaves were felt in the ECSC, where Monnet left the presidency of the High Authority in 1955, disillusioned by political resistance to its work (Monnet, 1978, pp. 398–404).

Another shock was to follow, with the unfolding of the 1956 Suez crisis. Seeking funds to build a new dam on the Nile, Egyptian leader Gamal Abdel Nasser nationalized the British- and French-run Suez Canal in July 1956. The canal's strategic value was declining, and the nationalization had no impact on British access, but because Nasser was considered a threat to western interests, the governments of Britain, France and Israel entered into an agreement by which Israel attacked Egypt in October, providing the British and the French with an excuse to step in and 'restore' peace in the canal zone. Coincidentally, the Soviets were cracking down on attempts by the Hungarian government to introduce democracy and withdraw from the Warsaw Pact, leaving the US in the invidious position of not being able to criticize the USSR without also criticizing British and French action at Suez. In the face of US demands, Britain and France withdrew from Suez with their tails between their legs.

The reverberations of Suez were to be felt for many years (see Hourani, 1989): the dominant role of the US in the Atlantic Alliance was confirmed, the French were left more doubtful than ever about American trustworthiness and more convinced of the importance of western European policy independence (Lundestad, 2003, p. 115), and Britain now began to realize that it was no longer a world power capable of significant independent action. Its leaders began to turn away from their traditional links with the empire, and started to look more towards Europe (Gorst and Johnman, 1997, pp. 151, 160). They concluded that they could never again so openly disagree with the US on matters of foreign policy, but while the US might have been an indispensable ally, Judt (2005, p. 302) notes that Britain's dependence on the US illustrated its weakness and isolation. It had shunned the ECSC, but within five years of Suez, it had applied for membership of the European Economic Community.

Suez crisis: An attempt made by Britain, France and Israel to reverse Egypt's nationalization of the Suez Canal, leading to an international outcry, the humiliation of Britain and France, and a change in British attitudes towards European integration.

Profile *Paul-Henri Spaak*

Paul-Henri Spaak (1899–1972) played a central role in the early years of European integration as a champion of a supranational Europe. He was prime minister of Belgium at the outbreak of the Second World War, and was part of the Belgian government-in-exile in London during the war. He served briefly as the first elected chair of the UN General Assembly in 1946, and then served three terms as Belgian foreign minister, two terms as prime minister (1946 and 1947–49), one term as president of the Common Assembly of the ECSC (1952–54), and one term as secretary-general of NATO (1957–61). He was involved in the creation of the Benelux customs union, and was chair of the committee whose report formed the basis of the discussions leading to the creation of the EEC.

Single market

A multi-state economic area, otherwise known as a common or internal market, in which there is free movement of people, money, goods and services – the so-called 'four freedoms'. Although the main goal of the EEC was the creation of a single market, progress was halting until the passage of the 1986 Single European Act. Even critics of European integration mainly agree that the single market was a noble goal, and complain that integration has since far overstepped this basic idea. But a truly open market does not yet exist in the EU, because there are still restrictions on the movement of workers and limits on trade in services.

The European Economic Community (1955–58)

Chastened by the failures of the European defence and political communities, ECSC foreign ministers met in June 1955 in Messina, Sicily to appoint a successor to Jean Monnet as president of the High Authority, and soon found their discussions turning to proposals for further economic integration. In the Messina Resolution, they agreed to consider working 'for the establishment of a united Europe by the development of common institutions, the progressive fusion of national economies, the creation of a single market, and the progressive harmonization of their social policies' (quoted in Weigall and Stirk, 1992, p. 94). A committee chaired by Belgian Foreign Minister Paul-Henri Spaak developed what Spaak himself admitted was a plan motivated less by economic cooperation than by a desire to take another step towards political union (Urwin, 1995, p. 76).

A new round of negotiations among the six ECSC members began in Venice in May 1956, paving the way for the signature on 25 March 1957 of the two Treaties of Rome, one creating the European Economic Community (EEC) and the other the European Atomic Energy Community (Euratom). Following ratification by member state parliaments during 1957, both treaties entered into force in January 1958. Euratom was of more interest to the French than to others and was quickly relegated to focusing on research. The EEC was by far the more substantial experiment, committing its six members to the following goals:

- The completion within 12 years of a single market in which there would be free movement of people, capital and services. Movement of workers was 'subject to limitations justified on grounds of public policy, public security or public health'.

European Economic Community (EEC): An international organization created in 1957 with the core goal of establishing a single (or common) market among its member states.

European Atomic Energy Community (Euratom): An international organization created in 1957 to coordinate research in its member states on the peaceful use of nuclear energy.

Illustration **5.1 The Treaty of Rome**

Delegates from six western European states gather in the Palazzo dei Conservatori on Capitoline Hill in Rome on 25 March 1957 to sign the Treaty of Rome.

- The elimination of customs duties between member states, and agreement of a common external customs tariff so that all goods coming into the EEC, wherever their point of entry, were subject to the same duties and quotas.
- The establishment of common policies on agriculture, trade, transport and competition.
- The creation of a European Social Fund and a European Investment Bank.
- The use of the same core institutional structure as the ECSC (see Figure 5.1), with some changes.

Timeline *The European Economic Community*

1952	May	Signature of the European Defence Community treaty
1953	March	Plans announced for European Political Community
1954	May	French defeat in Indochina
	August	Collapse of plans for European Defence Community and European Political Community
	October	Creation of Western European Union
1955	May	Creation of Warsaw Pact
	June	Opening of Messina Conference
1956	May	Opening of discussions on what would become the EEC
	Oct–Dec	Suez crisis
1957	March	Signature of Treaties of Rome
1958	January	Treaties of Rome enter into force
1960	January	Signature of Stockholm Convention creating European Free Trade Association
1961	August	Work begins on construction of the Berlin Wall; Britain applies for EEC membership
1962	October	Cuban missile crisis
1963	January	De Gaulle vetoes British membership of EEC
	July	Signature of Yaoundé Convention
1965	April	Signature of Merger treaty
	July	Empty chair crisis begins
1966	January	Empty chair crisis ends with Luxembourg Compromise
1967	May	Second British application for EEC membership
	November	Second veto by de Gaulle of British membership of EEC
1968	April	Beginning of Prague Spring
	July	Agreement of EEC's common external tariff
1969	December	EEC leaders agree principle of economic and monetary union
1971	August	US abandons dollar/gold convertibility; end of Bretton Woods system
1972	April	Launch of 'snake in the tunnel'
	September	Norwegian referendum goes against EEC membership
1973	January	Britain, Denmark and Ireland join EEC
	October	Yom Kippur War
1975	January	Launch of European Regional Development Fund
1979	March	Launch of the European Monetary System
1981	January	Greece joins Community
1986	January	Portugal and Spain join Community
1992	September 16	Black Wednesday

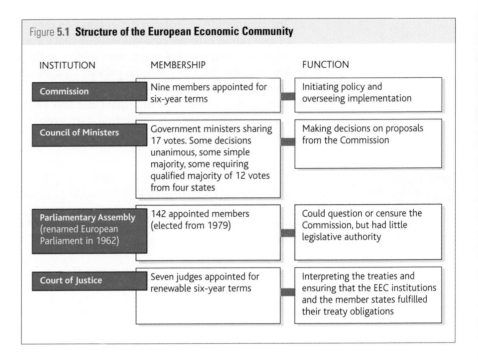

Figure **5.1 Structure of the European Economic Community**

INSTITUTION	MEMBERSHIP	FUNCTION
Commission	Nine members appointed for six-year terms	Initiating policy and overseeing implementation
Council of Ministers	Government ministers sharing 17 votes. Some decisions unanimous, some simple majority, some requiring qualified majority of 12 votes from four states	Making decisions on proposals from the Commission
Parliamentary Assembly (renamed European Parliament in 1962)	142 appointed members (elected from 1979)	Could question or censure the Commission, but had little legislative authority
Court of Justice	Seven judges appointed for renewable six-year terms	Interpreting the treaties and ensuring that the EEC institutions and the member states fulfilled their treaty obligations

The early record of the EEC was mixed, which was perhaps inevitable, given that it was sailing uncharted waters, making adjustments as it went along. Internal tariffs and trade quotas were brought down, clearing the way for agreement in July 1968 of a common external tariff and an industrial customs union. This helped encourage accelerated economic growth, a halving of the contribution of agriculture to economic output (Ionescu, 1975, pp. 150–4), and a growth in trade among the EEC partners at a rate three times faster between 1958 and 1965 than that with third countries (Urwin, 1995, p. 130). But non-tariff barriers to trade remained, mainly in the form of different national product standards. And while the Common Commercial Policy allowed the Six to work as one in international trade negotiations, exploiting the new power of the single market, there was slow progress on developing a common transport policy and addressing regional economic disparities.

After much debate, a Common Agricultural Policy (CAP) was agreed in 1968 with the acceptance of a watered-down version of a plan drawn up by agriculture commissioner Sicco Mansholt (Pinder, 1991, pp. 78–86; Urwin, 1995, pp. 132–5). Very much reflecting French national interests (specifically, how to manage its agricultural overproduction), the CAP created a single agricultural market and set guaranteed prices for almost everything produced by EEC farmers. But it did this at the expense of encouraging overproduction, benefiting large-scale commercial farmers at the expense of small farmers, ignoring the environmental consequences of greater use of chemical fertilizers and pesticides, and making the CAP the largest item in the Community budget, which in turn diverted spending from other areas.

Institutionally, the EEC was intergovernmental and elitist in character, key decisions being made by government ministers and the staff of the European institutions with little reference to public opinion. The identity of the European

Document 5.1 — *Opening articles of the Treaty of Rome, 25 March 1957*

Article 1

By this Treaty, the HIGH CONTRACTING PARTIES establish among themselves a EUROPEAN ECONOMIC COMMUNITY.

Article 2

The Community shall have as its task, by establishing a common market and progressively approximating the economic policies of Member States, to promote throughout the Community a harmonious development of economic activities, a continuous and balanced expansion, an increase in stability, an accelerated raising of the standard of living and closer relations between the States belonging to it.

Article 3

For the purposes set out in Article 2, the activities of the Community shall include ...

(a) the elimination ... of customs duties and of quantitative restrictions on the import and export of goods, and of all other measures having equivalent effect;

(b) the establishment of a common customs tariff and of a common commercial policy towards third countries;

(c) the abolition ... of obstacles to freedom of movement for persons, services and capital;

(d) the adoption of a common policy in the sphere of agriculture;

(e) the adoption of a common policy in the sphere of transport;

(f) the institution of a system ensuring that competition in the common market is not distorted;

(g) the application of procedures by which the economic policies of Member States can be co-ordinated and disequilibria in their balances of payments remedied;

(h) the approximation of the laws of Member States to the extent required for the proper functioning of the common market;

(i) the creation of a European Social Fund in order to improve employment opportunities for workers and to contribute to the raising of their standard of living;

(j) the establishment of a European Investment Bank to facilitate the economic expansion of the Community by opening up fresh resources;

(k) the association of the overseas countries and territories in order to increase trade and to promote jointly economic and social development.

Article 4

The tasks entrusted to the Community shall be carried out by the following institutions:
an ASSEMBLY [EUROPEAN PARLIAMENT],
a COUNCIL,
a COMMISSION,
a COURT OF JUSTICE.
Each institution shall act within the limits of the powers conferred upon it by this Treaty.

Source: www.epg.acp.int/fileadmin/user_upload/rometreaty2.pdf (retrieved July 2014).

Commission was fleshed out under the leadership of its first president, Walter Hallstein, and decision-making was streamlined in April 1965 with the signature of the Merger treaty, which created a single institutional structure for all three communities. The European Parliament shrewdly exploited its moral advantage as a 'representative' body to win more legislative authority, and the European Court of Justice contributed quietly but vitally by issuing judgments that changed the personality and the legal reach of the Community.

But then the young EEC was shaken by two major crises sparked by Charles de Gaulle's defence of French interests at the expense of moving along the debate on Europe. The first came in January 1963 when he unilaterally vetoed Britain's application to join the EEC (see details later in this chapter). The second came in July 1965 with the empty chair crisis, at the heart of which lay the question of the relative power of EEC institutions and EEC member states. Several factors came together to spark the crisis:

Empty chair crisis: A dispute in 1965 over the relative powers of EEC institutions and the governments of EEC member states, which encouraged France to boycott meetings of the Council of Ministers.

- Walter Hallstein was a federalist whose attempts to build the Commission were undermined by the fact that he had never been elected to office (he had spent much of his career as a law professor).
- Decision-making by qualified majority vote (a weighted voting system – see Chapter 11) was due to come into force in the Council of Ministers in January 1966 on several new issues, including agriculture and trade. This would restrict use of the national veto, even though it was understood that decision-making in the EEC was by consensus.
- During discussions over the CAP, Hallstein suggested that EEC funding should be changed from national contributions to 'own resources': an independent stream coming out of revenues from external tariffs and levies on agricultural imports.

Map **5.1 The European Economic Community, 1958**

This was all too much for de Gaulle, who faced a national election in late 1965 at which the Community for the first time became a central issue (Dinan, 2014, p. 111). Although Hallstein backed down in the face of pressure from West German Chancellor Ludwig Erhard, de Gaulle had already decided to express some of his frustrations with the direction being taken by the EEC, and instructed his representatives to boycott meetings of the Council of Ministers, making it impossible for decisions on new laws and policies to be taken. The crisis ended only with the January 1966 Luxembourg Compromise, by which it was agreed that the qualified majority vote would not be used when member states felt that 'important interests' were at stake, thereby preserving the national veto. Institutionally, the result was a deceleration in the growth of Commission powers and the placing of more authority into the hands of the Council of Ministers (see Palayret et al., 2006).

International developments: the nervous 1960s

Developments within the EEC took place within a troubled international context, where critical salvoes were being fired in the Cold War that would have long-term implications for the tripartite relationship between the US, the Soviet Union and Europe. In 1961 came the Berlin crisis, when – in order to stop the flow of easterners to the West – a barbed wire fence was built between East and West Berlin, followed by a concrete wall. When it was discovered in 1962 that the Soviets were building nuclear missile sites in Cuba, President John F. Kennedy, concerned that this was part of a Soviet ploy to get its way on Berlin (Judt, 2005, p. 254), put his foot down, and for 10 days in October the world teetered on the brink of nuclear war. Western Europeans were unsettled as much by the event as by how western European opinion seemed to have been marginalized in US calculations. For de Gaulle, it meant that Europeans might now face 'annihilation without representation' (quoted in Bernstein, 1980).

More transatlantic tensions were introduced by US policy in Vietnam, where the despatch of American military advisers in 1962–63 heralded an escalation into a fully fledged war in 1965. This was met with deep political misgivings and growing public hostility in western Europe, where the war revealed the extent to which views differed within the Atlantic Alliance on critical security problems. Anti-war demonstrations were held in many countries, and a 1967 poll found 80 per cent of western Europeans critical of US policy (Barnet, 1983, p. 264).

At the close of the 1960s, the focus shifted to a seeming thaw in relations between western and eastern Europe. First came the Prague Spring in Czechoslovakia, when the reformist Alexander Dubček came to power in 1968 and instituted a series of political and economic reforms that sparked an invasion by Soviet and other Warsaw Pact troops in August. Then came the initiative by Willy Brandt, elected West Germany's first social democratic chancellor in October 1969, to reach out to East Germany and then to Poland and other eastern European countries through his *Ostpolitik* (Eastern policy).

Although the Soviet crackdown on Czechoslovakia reminded western Europeans of the fragility of the international situation in which they found themselves, *Ostpolitik* showed what was possible in bringing east and west together.

Luxembourg Compromise: A 1966 agreement ending the empty chair crisis, and making consensus the informal norm in Council of Ministers decisions. The effect was to slow down the process of European integration.

Enlargement

The process of expanding membership of the European Community/Union. While it had many potential benefits, it also had political costs: France and Germany in particular have worried about how it has reduced their dominating role in European decision-making; and with more members, there has been a greater variety of interests to be heard, more political disagreements to be resolved, and greater economic and social disparities to address. With expansion from 6 to 9 to 12 to 15 to 28 members (with more waiting in the wings), the personality, goals, values and internal political and economic dynamics of the EU have continued to evolve.

But part of the bargain involved acknowledgment that the postwar division of Europe was permanent. Although Brandt's policies caused some initial divisions within western Europe, with France and Britain in particular worrying that it might result in West Germany being pulled into the Soviet orbit (Lundestad, 2003, pp. 172–3), Hitchcock (2004, p. 300) sees the changes as replacing the Cold War with a 'cold peace', and argues that by normalizing that division, 'Brandt may have been the first European statesman to swing a pickaxe at the Iron Curtain'.

Enlargement tops the agenda (1960–86)

There was only so much that the EEC could achieve with just six members. Together they had a population of about 180 million, or about 56 per cent of the western European total, along with a 56 per cent share of western Europe's economic wealth. But if regional peace and economic prosperity were the two underlying purposes of integration, then other European states had to be brought into the fold through enlargement. While the EEC Treaty (Article 237) stated that 'any European State may apply to become a member of the Community', the number of realistic potential new members was limited; all eastern Europe was excluded, the Scandinavians were wary of supranationalism and had their own internal ties, and Greece, Portugal and Spain were either too poor and/or not sufficiently democratic.

The most obvious absentee was Britain, still a large (if declining) economy and the largest military power in Europe, and a critical bridge between western Europe and the US. Until Suez, at least, Britain still saw itself as a great power, and one with global political and economic interests that might be compromised by closer association with the rest of Europe. For Dean Acheson (1969, p. 385), US secretary of state during the Truman administration, Britain's decision not to negotiate on membership of the ECSC had been its 'great mistake of the postwar period'. As for the EEC, few in the British government felt that it had much potential, the official view, according to Prime Minister Harold Macmillan (1971, p. 73), being 'a confident expectation that nothing would come out of Messina'.

Charles de Gaulle

Charles de Gaulle (1890–1970) was the pre-eminent statesman of France in the twentieth century, and a man known for his charisma, his defence of French interests, and his efforts to promote a global role for Europe in the face of US dominance. He served in the First World War and then in the opening battles of the Second World War, escaping after the fall of France in 1940 to Britain, from where he organized the Free French forces. Upon his return in 1944, he briefly became prime minister before retiring in 1946. Political crisis led to his return to power as the principal author of the new constitution of the Fifth Republic, and as the first president under the new constitution in 1958. De Gaulle's European policies focused on the Franco-German axis, resistance to the supranationalism of Community institutions, and efforts to reduce British influence (and, by extension, American influence). His heavy-handed leadership led to worker and student riots at home in 1968, and to his resignation as president in April 1969.

Britain's initial strategy was to champion the development of an alternative to the EEC, in the form of the looser and less ambitious European Free Trade Association (EFTA). This was founded in January 1960 with the signing of the Stockholm Convention by Austria, Britain, Denmark, Norway, Portugal, Sweden and Switzerland. It had the same core goal as the EEC of promoting free trade, but unlike the EEC, it involved no contractual arrangements, had no political objectives, and its only institutions were a Council of Ministers that met infrequently and a group of permanent representatives serviced by a small secretariat in Geneva. It helped cut tariffs and promoted trade among its members, but several of them did more trade with the EEC than with each other, and EFTA failed in its efforts to pull EEC states into a broader free trade area.

Even before the signing of the Stockholm Convention, Britain's attitude to the EEC had begun to change. Not only had Suez shattered the nostalgic idea of Britain as a great power, but it had become clear that political influence in Europe lay with the EEC, which was making strong economic progress, and Britain would risk political isolation and economic disadvantage if it stayed out. So, in August 1961, barely 15 months after the creation of EFTA, Britain applied to join the EEC. Denmark also applied, prompted by the importance of Britain as its main food export market, and by the view that the EEC was a big new market for Danish agricultural surpluses and a possible boost to Danish industrial development. Ireland also applied, obliged as it was to follow the British lead but also hoping that the EEC would reduce its reliance on agriculture and Britain. They were joined in 1962 by Norway, which saw the new importance of EEC markets. Britain was the giant at the negotiating table, however, accounting for about 85 per cent of the population and GDP of the four applicant countries.

All might have proceeded smoothly but for Charles de Gaulle, who resented Britain's lukewarm attitude towards integration and its role in creating EFTA, was concerned that Britain might want to redefine some of the goals of the Community at the expense of French interests (particularly on agriculture), and regarded Britain as a rival to French influence in the EEC and a back door for US influence in Europe. The smaller Community states disagreed, supporting British membership as a means of offsetting French influence, and the British application had the support of the US, West Germany and Jean Monnet.

De Gaulle's views prevailed, however, and in the space of just 10 days in January 1963, he vetoed the British application and signed a Franco-German friendship treaty (the Élysée Treaty). He referred his decision to none of his EEC partners except West Germany, showing, protested Paul-Henri Spaak (1971, p. 375), 'a lack of consideration unexampled in the history of the EEC, showing utter contempt for his negotiating partners, allies and opponents alike'. He added insult to injury by making the announcement as an answer to a prearranged question posed by a journalist at a press conference in Paris. De Gaulle argued that integrating the British economy into the EEC would be too difficult, and allowing Britain in would mean having to allow other countries in, and would complicate the EEC's relations with other parts of the world. He dismissed Britain as 'insular' and 'maritime', and as a country with 'very marked and very original habits and traditions' (WEU, 1964, pp. 85–9). And since Britain's application was part of a four-state package, Denmark, Ireland and Norway were also denied entry.

Britain applied again in 1967 and was again unilaterally vetoed by de Gaulle, still trying to protect French interests in the CAP and still seeing Britain as a

European Free Trade Association (EFTA): A free trade grouping championed by Britain and founded in 1960, with more modest goals and looser organization than the EEC.

Trojan horse for the Americans; letting Britain and the other countries in at this point, he claimed, 'would lead to the destruction of the European Community' (quoted in Dinan, 2014, p. 115). Britain and the others had to bide their time until de Gaulle's resignation as president of France in 1969, when a third application was lodged and this time accepted. Following remarkably rapid membership negotiations in 1970–71, Britain, Denmark, Ireland and Norway were all cleared for EEC membership. When the Norwegians turned down the offer in a September 1972 national referendum, thanks mainly to the concerns of farmers and fishing communities, it was with Britain, Denmark and Ireland that the EEC saw its first enlargement on 1 January 1973. The Six had now become the Nine.

Interest in the Community was also emerging elsewhere. Greece had made its first overtures in the late 1950s but had an underdeveloped and mainly agricultural economy, so was given only associate membership in 1961. Full membership might have come much sooner had it not been for the Greek military coup of April 1967, following which even its association agreement was suspended. With its return to civilian government in 1974, Greece applied almost immediately for full Community membership. Portugal and Spain had also shown early interest in associate membership, but both were still dictatorships with underdeveloped and mainly agricultural economies; it was only with the overthrow of the Caetano regime in Portugal in 1974 and the death of Franco in Spain in 1975 that full EEC membership for the two states was taken seriously. The EEC felt that welcoming the three countries would strengthen their democracies and help link them more closely to NATO and western Europe, so negotiations were opened, leading to Greek membership in January 1981, and to Spain and Portugal joining the EEC in January 1986. The Nine had now become the Twelve.

Illustration **5.2**
Britain joins the Community
British Prime Minister Edward Heath signs the UK's Treaty of Accession on 22 January 1972, paving the way for his country to be part of the first enlargement of the EEC in January 1973.

Map **5.2** **The first two rounds of enlargement, 1973–86**

The doubling of the membership of the EEC between 1973 and 1986 had several consequences. It changed the economic balance among the member states, by bringing in first the poorer British economy and then the even poorer Mediterranean states, which in turn meant a redistribution of EEC spending. It also increased the international influence of the EEC, which was now the largest economic bloc in the world. At the same time, it complicated the Community's decision-making processes by requiring that a wider range of opinions and interests be considered. Although membership applications were also received from Turkey in 1987, Austria in 1989, and Cyprus and Malta in 1990, there was now to be a focus on deepening rather than widening. East Germany was to enter the Community through the back door with the reunification of Germany in October 1990, but there would be no further enlargement until 1995.

First steps to monetary union (1969–92)

In order to avoid a repeat of the economic problems of the mid-war years, exchange rate stability had been established as a lynchpin of the Bretton Woods system (see Hosli, 2005, pp. 17–19). The International Monetary Fund was charged with helping maintain that stability, based on the convertibility of the world's major currencies with gold and the US dollar. In 1950 the European Payments Union was set up to help encourage the convertibility of European currencies by setting realistic exchange rates (see Chang, 2009, p. 17). In 1958 it was replaced by the European Monetary Agreement, under which EEC members (along with Britain, Ireland and Sweden) worked to keep exchange rates within 0.75 per cent either way of the US dollar. In 1964, a committee of governors of the central banks began meeting to coordinate monetary policy, becoming the forerunner of today's European Central Bank.

While monetary cooperation was one challenge, monetary union was quite another, with its troubling implications for loss of national sovereignty; a state that gave up its national currency would lose much of its economic independence. But changes of leadership in France and West Germany in 1969 brought new ideas and fresh perspectives. At a summit of Community leaders in The Hague in December, the main items on the agenda were enlargement, agriculture and economic and monetary union (EMU) (Dinan, 2014, p. 135). A year later, a committee headed by Luxembourg Prime Minister Pierre Werner came down in favour of parallel efforts to coordinate national economic policies while also working to hold exchange rates steady (Commission of the European Communities, 1970).

Then came another political shock. The Bretton Woods system had been based on confidence in the US dollar, which in turn depended on the strength of the US economy and the convertibility of US dollars and gold (Spero and Hart, 2003, p. 17). But western European economies saw rapid growth in the 1960s, while the costs of fighting the war in Vietnam caused inflation in the US and reduced international confidence in the dollar. The Nixon administration tried to deflect some of the blame onto the EEC, charging it with protectionism and an unwillingness to take more responsibility for the costs of defence (Judt, 2005, p. 454). Then, in August 1971, it unilaterally decided to end the convertibility of the US dollar with gold, ending the Bretton Woods system and ushering in an era of international monetary turbulence. This was made worse by an international energy crisis set off by the October 1973 Yom Kippur War between Israel and the Arabs, which resulted in Arab oil producers quadrupling the price of oil.

In a frantic attempt to control the threat that floating exchange rates posed to the CAP, Community leaders agreed in February 1972 to a structure known as the 'snake in the tunnel', within which EEC member states would work to hold the value of their national currencies within 2.25 per cent either way of the US dollar, preparing the way for monetary union by 1980. The snake was launched in April 1972, with all six EEC member states participating, along with Britain, Denmark and Norway. But exchange rate volatility quickly forced Britain, Denmark and Italy out. France left in 1974, rejoined in 1975, then left again in 1976 (Eichengreen, 2007, pp. 248–9).

Economic and monetary union (EMU): A programme agreed by the EEC in 1969 to coordinate economic policy in preparation for the switch to a single currency.

Meanwhile, enlargement was creating new pressures. Economic disparities among the members of the EEC grew with the accession of Britain and Ireland, an official report concluding that the differences were big enough to be an obstacle to a 'balanced expansion' in economic activity and EMU (Commission of the European Communities, 1973). With France and West Germany supporting Community spending as a means of helping Britain integrate into the Community, and the government of Prime Minister Edward Heath seeing it as a way of making EEC membership more palatable to British voters (Dinan, 2014, p. 155), a decision was taken in 1973 to launch the European Regional Development Fund. This would match existing national development spending, with an emphasis on improving infrastructure and creating new jobs in industry and services.

In March 1979, the snake was replaced by a European Monetary System (EMS), using an Exchange Rate Mechanism (ERM) based on the European Currency Unit (ecu). This was a unit of account whose value was determined by a basket of the EEC's national currencies, each weighted according to their relative strengths. Participants undertook to work to keep their currencies within 2.25 per cent either way of the ecu (or 6 per cent in the case of Italy). In addition to creating a zone of monetary stability, the hope was that the ecu would become the normal means of settling debts between EEC members, and that it would psychologically prepare Europeans for the idea of a single currency. Since *ecu* also happened to be the name of an ancient French coin, there was speculation that it might become the name of the new single currency.

But while the Commission argued that EMU was helping encourage more economic efficiency and allowing the EEC to take a stronger role in the international economy, several member states found it difficult to control exchange rates. The problems worsened in the early 1990s with turbulence in world money markets, Germany had problems trying to adjust to its 1990 reunification (Gilbert, 2003, pp. 227ff.), and Britain found the demands of staying in the ERM too much to bear. It had delayed joining until 1990, by which time inflation and interest rates were high, and its efforts to keep the pound stable were undermined by speculation on international currency markets; the investor George Soros famously made an estimated $1 billion profit by short selling (profiting from a decline in the price of assets between their sale and repurchase) his holdings of sterling. After furiously trying to prop up the pound, mainly by raising interest rates in order to encourage investors to buy sterling, Britain withdrew from the ERM on 16 September 1992, a date that became known as 'Black Wednesday'.

European Monetary System (EMS): An arrangement introduced in 1979 by which EEC member states linked their currencies to one another through an Exchange Rate Mechanism designed to keep exchange rates stable.

Summary

- Attempts to clear the way to West German remilitarization, while tying it closely into western Europe, led to the signature in May 1952 of a treaty setting up a European Defence Community (EDC), and the creation in 1954 of a Western European Union.

- There were hopes, too, of creating a European Political Community (EPC), but political opposition within France to the EDC led to its collapse in August 1954, along with plans for the EPC.

- Economic cooperation was behind the signature in 1957 of the Treaties of Rome, creating the European Economic Community (EEC) and the European Atomic Energy Community.

- The goals of the EEC included a single market, a common external customs tariff, and common policies on agriculture, trade, transport and competition.

- Progress on the single market was mixed, with many barriers coming down but many non-tariff barriers remaining, and slow progress on the development of a common transport policy and addressing regional economic disparities.

- The 1960s were a time of Cold War nervousness, opening with the Berlin crisis and the Cuban missile crisis and closing with an escalation of the war in Vietnam. These events impacted the tripartite relationship among Europe, the US and the USSR.

- Enlargement of the EEC moved up the agenda, but British applications were twice vetoed by Charles de Gaulle.

- Britain, Denmark and Ireland joined the EEC in 1973, followed in 1981 by Greece and in 1986 by Spain and Portugal. The political and economic personality of the EEC changed as a result.

- Exchange rate stability had been central to western economic and monetary policy since Bretton Woods. The first attempt to pave the way to a single currency – the 1972 'snake in the tunnel' – failed mainly because of bad timing, and it was replaced by the 1979 European Monetary System.

Key terms and concepts

Economic and monetary union

Empty chair crisis

Enlargement

European Atomic Energy Community

European Defence Community

European Economic Community

European Free Trade Association

European Monetary System

European Political Community

Luxembourg Compromise

Single market

Suez crisis

Western European Union

Further reading

Gorst, Anthony, and Lewis Johnman (1997) *The Suez Crisis* (Abingdon: Routledge). Kyle, Keith (2003) *Suez: Britain's End of Empire in the Middle East* (London: I.B. Taurus). Two studies of the landmark events of 1956.

Griffiths, Richard T. (2000) *Europe's First Constitution: The European Political Community, 1952–1954* (London: Kogan Page). Study of the draft EPC Treaty, drawing parallels between the political situation in the 1950s and that in the early years of the EU.

Mangold, Peter (2006) *The Almost Impossible Ally: Harold Macmillan and Charles de Gaulle* (London: I.B. Taurus). Fenby, Jonathan (2010) *The General: Charles de Gaulle and the France he Saved* (London: Simon & Schuster). Two studies of Charles de Gaulle, the former focusing on his critical relationship with British Prime Minister Harold Macmillan.

6 From Single Market to European Union

Preview

Although the single market topped the agenda of European integration in the 1960s, progress had been slow. Prompted by worries about rising international competition and inflexible European labour markets, there was a renewed effort in the 1980s to complete the single market, resulting in agreement on the first major new treaty since Rome, the 1986 Single European Act (SEA). This gave the European Economic Community – now more often known as the European Community, or simply 'the Community' – a new sense of mission and identity.

Meanwhile, the collapse of the Berlin Wall in 1989 symbolized the end of the Cold War division of the continent, and emphasized the need for the Community to assert itself on the global stage. Serial embarrassments followed as the Community failed to agree on a response to the 1990–91 Gulf War or the crisis in the Balkans. But with new leadership came new ideas, leading to the agreement in 1992 of the Maastricht treaty. This confirmed plans for a single European currency, gave new emphasis to a common foreign policy, and brought a change of name: the Community would now be part of a broader based European Union.

There was also a new focus on enlargement, with EFTA members given access to the single market through a new European Economic Area in 1994, followed in 1995 by the accession of Austria, Finland and Sweden. But there was also a backlash against integration, and signs that many Europeans had new doubts about the decisions being taken in their name by their leaders. Even so, more new member states were lining up to join, and two more treaties – Amsterdam in 1997 and Nice in 2001 – were agreed in order to amend institutional rules and confirm new policy responsibilities.

Key issues

- How important was the Single European Act to the history of European integration?
- What did the end of the Cold War mean for European integration?
- What were the effects of the Community's failures in the Gulf and the Balkans?
- What were the relative roles of political leadership and international circumstances in pushing forward the process of European integration?
- Why was the Maastricht treaty more controversial than the Single European Act, and why was it so central to the backlash against integration?

The Single European Act (1983–93)

While there had been progress during the 1960s on building the single market, many non-tariff barriers persisted, including different technical standards, quality controls, health and safety standards, and levels of indirect taxation. Travellers still had to go through customs and immigration checks at borders, and anyone planning to move permanently to another Community state still came up against efforts to protect jobs and home industries (see Armstrong and Bulmer, 1998, Ch. 1; Gilbert, 2003, Ch. 6).

Meanwhile, European corporations were not taking full advantage of the single market, still looked outside Europe for merger and joint venture opportunities, and had lost market share to competition, first from the US and then Japan. By the early 1980s there was worried speculation about the effects of what came to be known as Eurosclerosis (Giersch, 1985): the role of excessive regulation and generous welfare systems in contributing to high unemployment and slow job creation in western Europe. The inflexibility of its labour market was contrasted – and continues to be contrasted even today – with the more dynamic and open market of the US.

For Jacques Delors, who took office as the new president of the Commission in January 1985, pulling the Community out of its lethargy and responding to the accelerating effects of globalization and technological change were priorities. A committee chaired by Irish politician Jim Dooge identified the need for a new focus on the single market, and an intergovernmental conference (IGC) was convened to discuss the necessary steps. A Commission White Paper – named for its primary author, internal market commissioner Lord Cockfield – was published within months, listing 282 pieces of legislation that would need to be agreed and implemented in order to remove all remaining non-tariff barriers and create a truly open market (Commission of the European Communities, 1985). The result was the signature in February 1986 of the Single European Act (SEA), the first substantial expansion of Community powers since the Treaty of Rome.

Compared to later treaty changes, the SEA was not particularly controversial; it had mainly economic goals, few Europeans had yet fully grasped the implications of integration, and the treaty was not so much a new project as the relaunching of an old one. (By contrast, the 1992 Maastricht treaty would move European integration in a different direction and faced stiffer resistance; see later in this chapter.) The biggest misgivings were in Denmark, whose parliament failed to approve the draft treaty for fear of its implications for national sovereignty. When other member states refused to make changes to meet its objections, in February 1986 Denmark became the first Community state to put a treaty to a national referendum, resulting in 56.2 per cent of votes in favour, with a healthy 74 per cent turnout. In Ireland, too, there were problems, this time of a constitutional nature (see Chapter 8 for details), but the issue was resolved by a May 1987 referendum that came down heavily in favour of the SEA, clearing the way for its entry into force two months later.

The passage of the SEA was made possible by a combination of economic and political factors: member states were increasingly dependent on intra-EC trade, they were experiencing reduced growth and worsening unemployment, the European Monetary System was off the ground, and European business strongly favoured the single market. The SEA also had political support: Jacques

Eurosclerosis: A term coined in 1985 to describe the inflexibility of the western European labour market, and its failure to create new jobs quickly enough to meet demand.

Single European Act (SEA): The first major change to the treaties, signed in 1986, with the goal of reviving plans to complete the single European market.

Profile *Jacques Delors*

Arguably the most influential and dynamic of all the European Commission presidents, Jacques Delors (1925–) made his mark on European integration during two terms in office (1985–95). He oversaw the negotiation and signature of the Single European Act and the Maastricht treaty, more enlargement, reforms to the Community budget, the creation of the European Economic Area, and the laying of groundwork for the later adoption of the euro, as well as witnessing the end of the Cold War and the outbreak of civil war in the Balkans. Born in Paris, he trained as an economist and worked in the banking industry before serving briefly as a Member of the European Parliament (1979–81), and as French economics and finance minister between 1981 and 1984. As president of the Commission, he was known for his ambitious plans and assertive style of management, and for capturing the headlines more than any of his predecessors. He stepped down in 1995, resisting suggestions that he run as the socialist candidate in that year's French presidential election.

Delors had built a strong case for the single market, and there was (for once) a congruence of opinion among the leaders of Britain, France and West Germany (Eichengreen, 2007, pp. 338–41). Even British Prime Minister Margaret Thatcher (1993, p. 556) was supportive: 'At last, I felt, we were going to get the Community back on course, concentrating on its role as a huge market, with all the opportunities that would bring to our industries.'

But for some, the goals of the SEA were not sufficiently ambitious, and several states had already gone ahead with a side agreement on a border-free Europe. In June 1985, representatives of France, West Germany and the Benelux countries met on a river boat moored near the village of Schengen in Luxembourg, which symbolically lay at the confluence of the borders of France, Luxembourg and West Germany. There they signed the Schengen Agreement providing for the fast-track removal of border controls. A second agreement was signed in June 1990, and 'Schengenland' finally came into being in March 1995. It was incorporated into the EU treaties by the 1997 Treaty of Amsterdam, and it has now been adopted by 26 countries: all EU member states except Britain, Croatia, Bulgaria, Cyprus, Ireland and Romania, along with Iceland, Liechtenstein, Norway and Switzerland. Britain has stayed out because of concerns about the need for its residents to carry ID cards in order to monitor movement in an area without internal border checks, while Ireland has stayed out mainly because it has a passport union with Britain. Conditions for the membership of Bulgaria, Croatia, Cyprus and Romania have not yet been met.

Meanwhile, ordinary Europeans were starting to feel the effects of integration for themselves. Cross-border travel was becoming easier, foreign corporations were becoming more visible as they merged with (or bought up) businesses in other EU states, and two important new symbols of European integration were adopted in 1985. The first of these was a passport with a standard design, first proposed in 1974 and issued for the first time in January 1985. Holders were still citizens of their home states, but all Community passports were now the same burgundy colour and bore the words 'European Community' alongside the state coat of arms. The second was the Community flag (12 gold stars on a blue back-

Schengen Agreement: A fast-track agreement to set up a border-free Europe, signed in 1985 among 5 Community states, which has since expanded to 26 states.

ground), adopted from the Council of Europe in June 1985 and soon to become a common sight throughout the Community.

The SEA entered into force amid great fanfare in July 1987, setting midnight on 31 December 1992 as the target date for completion of 'an area without internal frontiers in which the free movement of goods, persons, services and capital is ensured'. As well as relaunching 'Europe' as the biggest market and trading bloc in the world, the SEA brought other changes:

- Legal status was given to meetings of the heads of government within the European Council, and to Community foreign policy coordination.
- New powers were given to the European Court of Justice, and a new Court of First Instance (since renamed the General Court) was created to help deal with the growing legal caseload.
- The European Parliament (EP) was given more power relative to the Council of Ministers through the introduction of a new cooperation procedure and a new assent procedure (see Chapter 12 for details).
- Many internal passport and customs controls were eased or lifted.
- The Community was given more responsibility over environmental policy, research and development, and regional policy.
- Banks and companies could now do business and sell their products and services throughout the Community.

New prominence was also given on the Community agenda to 'cohesion' (balanced economic and social development), and the target was set of creating a European social area in which there were equal employment opportunities and working conditions. There was to be new spending under the so-called structural funds of the Community, including the European Regional Development Fund, the European Social Fund and the Cohesion Fund, and another boost for social policy came in 1989 with the Community Charter of Fundamental Social Rights of Workers (the Social Charter). This was designed to encourage free movement of workers, fair pay, better living and working conditions, freedom of association, and protection of children and adolescents (see Chapter 21).

International developments: the end of the Cold War (1989–99)

Changes in the Community were taking place against a background of dramatic political events that would redefine the meaning of Europe and fundamentally alter its place in the world. The first hint of an impending new order had come in March 1985 when Mikhail Gorbachev was appointed general secretary of the Soviet communist party, and quickly made clear that it would not be business as usual in the USSR. He set out to restructure the inefficiencies of the centrally planned Soviet economic system and the inadequacies of its one-party political system, and to encourage more public discussion about the problems the USSR faced and how they might be addressed. But he quickly lost control of his own agenda, which was hijacked by a struggle for power between conservatives opposed to change and progressives seeking its acceleration.

Timeline *From single market to European Union*

1975	**March**	First meeting of European Council
1979	**June**	First direct elections to European Parliament
1985	**January**	Jacques Delors takes over as president of the Commission; first burgundy European passports issued
	June	Signature of Schengen Agreement
1986	**February**	Signature of Single European Act (SEA); Danish referendum supports SEA
1987	**May**	Irish referendum supports SEA
	July	Single European Act enters into force
1989	**April**	Announcement of Delors three-stage plan to monetary union
	Sept-Dec	Collapse of communist governments in eastern Europe; fall of Berlin Wall
1990	**August**	Iraqi invasion of Kuwait
	October	German reunification
1991	**February**	Ground war in Kuwait/Iraq
	June	Slovenia and Croatia declare independence; outbreak of war in Yugoslavia
1992	**February**	Signature of Treaty on European Union
	June	Danish referendum rejects Maastricht
1993	**January**	Single European market enters into force; break-up of Czechoslovakia
	May	Second Danish referendum on Maastricht
	June	Agreement of Copenhagen conditions
	November	Treaty on European Union enters into force
1994	**January**	Creation of European Economic Area
1995	**January**	Austria, Finland and Sweden join the EU, taking membership to 15
	March	Schengen Agreement enters into force
	December	Dayton Peace Accords end war in Yugoslavia
1997	**October**	Signature of Treaty of Amsterdam
1999	**May**	Treaty of Amsterdam enters into force
2000	**March**	Agreement of the Lisbon Strategy
2001	**February**	Signature of Treaty of Nice
	June	Irish referendum rejects Nice
2002	**October**	Second Irish referendum accepts Nice
2003	**February**	Treaty of Nice enters into force

The new openness in the USSR was interpreted in eastern Europe as an opportunity to press for long-wished-for democratic and free-market changes, which soon followed:

- In Poland, the creation in 1980 of Solidarity as the first non-communist party controlled trade union posed deep challenges to the government, which reacted at first with efforts to close it down, but was eventually obliged to open negotiations. These changes paved the way for more democracy and the election of Solidarity leader Lech Walesa as president of Poland in 1990.
- In East Germany, rigged elections in May 1989 sparked anger, and when Hungary opened its borders with Austria in September, several thousand East Germans fled to the West via Hungary. Demonstrations broke out in

October in East Berlin, and in November access was made available to West Berlin through the Berlin Wall, which began to be dismantled. In place since 1961, one of the most potent symbols of Cold War division was removed on 3 October 1990 with the reunification of Germany. Segments of the wall still remain, but they serve only as a tourist attraction.

- In Czechoslovakia, the anti-communist Velvet Revolution broke out in November 1989, leading to the end of the one-party state and the holding of democratic elections in June 1990. Economic and nationalist tensions fed into demands for a looser political association between Czechs and Slovaks, who had lived together in an uneasy arrangement since the creation of Czechoslovakia in 1917. These demands led eventually to the 'velvet divorce', and in January 1993 the Czech Republic and Slovakia came into being as independent states.

- In Romania, the most authoritarian of eastern European states, Nicolae Ceauşescu (in power since 1965) was re-elected as leader of the Romanian communist party in November 1989 and indicated no change in direction. Years of resentment immediately boiled over, and when the military took the side of demonstrators, Ceauşescu and his wife were arrested, tried and executed.

- Democracy also came to Albania, Bulgaria and Hungary, and – with the dissolution of the Soviet Union on Christmas Day, 1991 – independence came to Belarus, Estonia, Latvia, Lithuania, Moldova and Ukraine.

Meanwhile, the Middle East entered the equation once again when Iraq invaded Kuwait in August 1990. The US quickly orchestrated the formation of a multinational coalition and the launching of an air war against Iraq, followed by a four-day ground war in February 1991. But the Community dithered in its response (see van Eekelen, 1990; Anderson, 1992). Britain fell in with the Americans and placed more than 40,000 troops under US operational command, while France committed 18,000 troops but emphasized a diplomatic resolution in

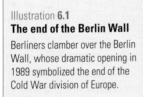

Illustration **6.1**
The end of the Berlin Wall
Berliners clamber over the Berlin Wall, whose dramatic opening in 1989 symbolized the end of the Cold War division of Europe.

Concept

European Political Cooperation

The arrangement by which Community foreign ministers met on a regular basis with the goal of agreeing common foreign policy positions. Foreign ministers learned the value of multilateral discussions, national diplomats set up networks of communication, and EPC became 'a working model of intergovernmental cooperation without formal integration' (Wallace, 2005, p. 435). But while it encouraged helpful new habits, it had little impact on public opinion, and did little to bring national policies in the EEC into closer convergence.

order to maintain good relations with Arab oil producers and protect its weapons markets. Germany could do little, constrained as it was by a postwar tradition of pacifism and constitutional limits on the deployment of German troops outside the NATO area. Fearing retribution, Belgium refused to sell ammunition to Britain and, along with Portugal and Spain, refused to allow its naval vessels to be involved in anything more than minesweeping or enforcing the blockade of Iraq. Meanwhile, Ireland remained neutral.

A frustrated Luxembourg Foreign Minister Jacques Poos bemoaned the 'political insignificance' of the Community, dismissed by Belgian Foreign Minister Mark Eyskens as 'an economic giant, a political dwarf, and a military worm' (Whitney, 1991). Jacques Delors (1991) summed up the implications of the problem when he mused that while the member states had taken a firm line against Iraq on sanctions, once force entered the equation, it was clear that the Community had neither the institutional machinery nor the military force to allow it to act in concert.

Worse was to follow in the Balkans, where nationalist tensions had been building since the death of Josip Broz Tito in 1980. Yugoslavia began to break up in June 1991 when Slovenia and Croatia declared independence, followed in September by Macedonia. There followed a bloody melange of war, sieges, massacres, genocide and ethnic cleansing, and once again the response of the Community was indecision. When it tried to broker a peace conference, a confident Jacques Poos was moved to declare: 'This is the hour of Europe, not of the United States' (*The Economist*, 1991). But when the Community recognized Croatia and Slovenia in January 1992, its credibility as a neutral arbiter collapsed. The EU monitors sent to Bosnia – garbed all in white and derided as 'ice-cream men' – were powerless to stop the slaughter, and it was left to the US to lead the way to the December 1995 Dayton Peace Accords. Later, when ethnic Albanians in Kosovo tried to break away from Yugoslavia in 1997–98, it was left to NATO – again under US leadership – to organize a bombing campaign against Serbia between March and June 1999. The Community was clearly failing to match its economic power with an international political presence.

The Community becomes a Union (1990–93)

In spite of concerns about the surrender of national sovereignty, the demands of economic integration had always meant pressure for wider political coordination in the Community. The occasional summits among EEC leaders in the 1960s led to new thinking about imposing order on the process, and a 1970 report authored by Belgian diplomat Etienne Davignon identified foreign policy coordination as a potentially useful first step. The report recommended quarterly meetings of the six foreign ministers, liaison among EC ambassadors in foreign capitals, and common EC instructions on certain matters for those ambassadors (Urwin, 1995, p. 148).

Thus had been born European Political Cooperation (EPC), a process of foreign policy coordination that encouraged new habits and focused political minds. Among its early results were a 1970 joint EC policy declaration on the Middle East, the signing of the 1975 Lomé Convention on aid to poorer countries, and joint Community responses during the 1980s to the Anglo-

Argentinean war in the Falklands, developments in Poland and Iran, and apartheid in South Africa (White, 2001, Ch. 4). But EPC was more reactive than proactive, and a more substantial step towards political coordination among Community leaders was taken in December 1974 with the creation of the European Council. Less an institution in the mould of the European Commission and more a forum, the Council formalized the holding of periodic summits among Community heads of government, allowing them to reach decisions on strategy without becoming bogged down in detailed administrative issues. It met for the first time in March 1975 and went on to launch some of the defining initiatives in the process of integration, as well as being the site of some of its most bitter political squabbles.

Another attempt was made to move forward in 1975 when the report of a committee headed by Belgian Prime Minister Leo Tindemans described European union as the next logical step in the journey from the EEC to an eventual European federation. It recommended institutional changes, including a stronger Commission and Parliament, and greater use of qualified majority voting in the Council of Ministers, and also recommended further movement on economic and monetary union (EMU), foreign and security policy, and social and regional policy. These suggestions were too radical for the 1970s (Dinan, 2004a, pp. 162–3), but their time would come.

EMU was given a boost in 1989–90 with a favourable alignment of circumstances. First, France, West Germany and Spain had new leaders (François Mitterrand, Helmut Kohl and Felipe González) who had won office in part on the strength of their support for integration, and the European Commission was still being run by the dynamic and ambitious Jacques Delors. Second, when the 1989 revolutions in eastern Europe helped pave the way to German reunification, France expected a reaffirmation of Germany's commitment to Europe so that German and European unification could move ahead in parallel (Dyson and Featherstone, 1999, p. 4). Finally, in spite of problems with the European Monetary System, there was widening political agreement to move ahead with the single currency. Delors now headed a committee that reviewed the necessary steps, and its April 1989 report (Commission of the European Communities, 1989) suggested a three-stage process:

- Stage I, to begin by July 1990, was to be based on free use of the European currency unit, increased cooperation between central banks, and free capital movement.
- Stage II would involve new independence for national central banks, increased coordination of monetary policies, and the establishment of a European Monetary Institute as a precursor to a European central bank.
- Stage III, to be achieved by January 1997, would involve a single monetary policy under the control of the European System of Central Banks, the introduction of the single currency, and the permanent fixing of exchange rates.

Most Community leaders were supportive, so the June 1990 European Council decided to open a new IGC on economic and monetary union, and later a second IGC to discuss political union. This latter notion was less than it sounded: it involved not so much the laying of foundations for a federal Europe as the transfer of more policy responsibilities to the European level, giving more powers to the Commission and Parliament, and extending the use of qualified majority voting in the Council of Ministers (Dinan, 2004a, p. 246).

Negotiations in 1990–91 resulted in the Treaty on European Union, signed in February 1992 in Maastricht in the Netherlands. The original draft had included mention of a 'federal goal' for Europe, but this was firmly opposed by Britain, so the wording reverted to that found in the preamble to the Treaty of Rome, which spoke of 'an ever closer union' among the peoples of Europe. A cumbersome agreement was also reached by which a new European Union would be created, resting on three organizational 'pillars': the renamed European Community, foreign and security policy, and justice and home affairs (see Chapter 8 for details). There was also agreement to begin work on a new Common Foreign and Security Policy (CFSP), confirmation of the three-stage plan to monetary union, and several other changes:

- New powers were given to the European Parliament relative to the Council of Ministers, and a new Committee of the Regions was created to represent local interests.
- The EU was given new responsibility in policy areas such as consumer protection, industrial policy, education, and social policy, and there was to be more cooperation on immigration and asylum, including the creation of a European police intelligence agency (Europol) to combat organized crime and drug trafficking.
- More regional funds would be set aside for poorer member states.
- There were new rights for European citizens and the creation of an ambiguous EU 'citizenship' allowing citizens of EU states to live wherever they liked in the EU and to stand and vote in local and European elections.

Treaty on European Union: A treaty signed in February 1992, which came into force in November 1993, creating the European Union and outlining a commitment to a single European currency and a common foreign policy.

Illustration **6.2 The Maastricht treaty**
The signing ceremony for the Treaty on European Union, held in Maastricht on 7 February 1992.

Document 6.1 *Opening articles of the Treaty on European Union, 7 February 1992*

Article A

By this Treaty, the HIGH CONTRACTING PARTIES establish among themselves a EUROPEAN UNION, hereinafter called 'the Union'.

This Treaty marks a new stage in the process of creating an ever closer union among the peoples of Europe, in which decisions are taken as closely as possible to the citizen.

... Its task shall be to organise, in a manner demonstrating consistency and solidarity, relations between the Member States and between their peoples.

Article B

The Union shall set itself the following objectives:

– to promote economic and social progress which is balanced and sustainable, in particular through the creation of an area without internal frontiers, through the strengthening of economic and social cohesion and through the establishment of economic and monetary union, ultimately including a single currency in accordance with the provisions of this Treaty;

– to assert its identity on the international scene, in particular through the implementation of a common foreign and security policy including the eventual framing of a common defence policy, which might in time lead to a common defence;

– to strengthen the protection of the rights and interests of the nationals of its Member States through the introduction of a citizenship of the Union;

– to develop close cooperation on justice and home affairs;

– to maintain in full the *acquis communautaire*.

Where the SEA had been approved without much debate, the Maastricht treaty represented a significant change of direction, was more political in its intent, and so was always going to be more controversial. Denmark once again opted for a national referendum, and in June 1992 sent shockwaves through the Community by becoming the first member state ever to reject a European treaty in a national referendum (albeit by the narrow margin of just 50,000 votes; 50.7% of voters were opposed, with 83% turnout). There was also a debate about the treaty in Ireland, where, after agreement of a protocol guaranteeing that the Irish ban on abortion would not be affected, it was passed with a majority of nearly 69% in favour in a June 1992 referendum. This was followed by a *petit oui* (literally, 'small yes') in France in September, when Maastricht was approved by just 51.04% of voters, with 70% turnout – an outcome explained, at least in part, by the declining popularity of French President François Mitterrand (Criddle, 1993).

Once the dust had settled, a compromise was arranged by which Denmark was given opt-outs from the clauses dealing with the single currency, defence, citizenship, and justice and home affairs. A second Danish referendum was then held in May 1993, in which the treaty was approved by 56.8% of voters. With all other member states also on board, the Maastricht treaty entered into force in November 1993, nearly a year late.

More enlargement (1990–95)

As noted in Chapter 5, the doubling of Community membership between 1973 and 1986 had brought key changes to the relationship among the member states, to the institutional character and policy agenda of the Community, and to its international role and standing. But enlargement had been a piecemeal affair, lacking either a grand plan or specific rules on the credentials that states should have in order to qualify for membership. There was an understanding that they should be European (so there was little question about rejecting an application from Morocco in 1987), but beyond that the rules were vague. By the early 1990s the question of clarity was pressing for attention, because applications for membership had been lodged by Austria, Cyprus, Finland, Malta, Norway, Sweden, Switzerland and Turkey, and the end of the Cold War had raised the prospect of enlargement to the east.

By way of preparation (or, in the view of Dinan (2004a, p. 268), to fob off the new aspirant members), negotiations began in 1990 on the creation of a European Economic Area (EEA), under which the terms of the SEA would be extended to the seven members of the European Free Trade Association (EFTA: Austria, Finland, Iceland, Liechtenstein, Norway, Sweden and Switzer-

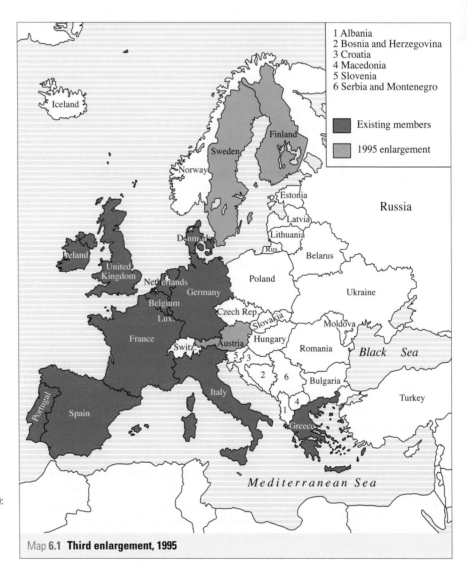

European Economic Area (EEA):
An agreement under which EFTA member states were given access to the single European market without full EU

Map **6.1 Third enlargement, 1995**

Concept

Acquis communautaire

The body of treaties, laws and regulations adopted by the EU. Derived from the French *acquis* (meaning *accepted* or *acquired*) and *communautaire* (of the community), the term is most often used in the context of the obligations of aspirant new members of the EU. Negotiations on membership split the *acquis* into multiple chapters that are used as the basis of discussions, and new members must agree to transpose the *acquis* into national law and implement it upon accession.

Concept

Permissive consensus

This refers to the idea that political elites could pursue their own plans for European integration, given the widespread lack of public interest in what they were doing. How far this has been a problem depends on whether we think of the EU as an international organization or as a proto-state, on how confident we are about the extent to which elected leaders take account of public opinion, and how much faith we have in the European public to make informed decisions about the process of integration (see discussion in Chapter 17 about the knowledge deficit).

land). They, in return, would accept the rules of the single market. Negotiations were completed in February 1992, but the Swiss turned down membership in a December 1992 referendum, so only six EFTA states joined when the EEA came into force in January 1994. Even as the EEA was being negotiated, however, agreement was reached to open talks on Community membership for Austria, Finland, Norway and Sweden, and in June 1993 the first set of formal requirements for EU membership was agreed at the Copenhagen European Council. Henceforth, the 'Copenhagen conditions' would require that applicant states should be democratic, should have functioning free markets, and should be able to take on the obligations of the *acquis communautaire* – the body of laws and regulations already adopted by the EU (see Chapter 9 for more details).

With membership terms agreed in March 1994, referendums were held in Austria, Finland, Norway and Sweden, and majorities came down in favour in all but Norway. Austria, Finland and Sweden joined the EU in January 1995, pushing membership to 15, increasing the land area of the EU by one-third, and for the first time giving it a shared border with Russia. Although there was to be a break of nine years before the next round of enlargement, the wheels had already been set in motion with the 1990 applications from Cyprus and Malta, followed in 1994 by those from Poland and Hungary, and in 1995–96 by those from Bulgaria, the Czech Republic, Estonia, Latvia, Lithuania and Slovenia. A taste of the implications of eastern enlargement had been offered by German reunification in October 1990; although this was the result of a domestic German decision (and not one that was entirely popular in other Community states), it gave some insight into the problems and promises involved in trying to integrate communist states into the capitalist EU.

The backlash against Europe

In its early years, the speed and content of integration was set by bureaucrats and government ministers meeting in closed session, emerging with agreements that were barely tested in the court of public opinion. These agreements were not reached easily, and often saw governments fighting to protect state interests, leaders imposing on their peers their personal views about the process of integration, and bitter struggles to move the debate in new directions. The issues at stake were primarily economic, the process was elitist and technocratic, and integration attracted little public attention. Integration was driven by a culture of permissive consensus, in which political leaders had been able to exploit the lack of public interest in European integration to move ahead at their own pace and to assume that national votes were not needed (see discussion in Carubba, 2001).

As the reach of the European Community expanded, however, and as its work began to have a greater impact on the lives of ordinary Europeans and to take on more of a political quality, so it drew new public attention. Most Europeans knew it as the 'Common Market', a relatively benign economic concept with which few could find serious fault. And when the SEA came along, it was not much more than an affirmation of the original core goals of the Treaty of Rome, and generated little controversy. At the same time, though, the '1992 programme' (a reference to the target date for completion of the single market) had the effect of making more Europeans familiar with integration. Inevitably, then, the debate over the Maastricht treaty in 1992–93 was going to be more animated. The new treaty was long and dense, its implications demanded more thought, it raised more troubling questions about national sovereignty, and two new terms now entered the debate over Europe.

The first of these was *euroscepticism*, suggesting hostility to the idea of integration. Although it came in many different shades (see Chapter 17 for more discussion), it reflected growing doubts about the direction being taken by Europe. One of the earliest hints of such doubts had come in 1972 with the Norwegian vote against membership of the EEC. More doubts surfaced in 1986 when Denmark became the first country to put a European treaty (the SEA) to a national referendum. Six years later, far greater public attention was generated by the June 1992 Danish rejection of the Maastricht treaty, the near miss in France three months later, and the rejection by the Swiss in December of membership of the EEA.

The second new term was *democratic deficit*, referring to the gap between the authority of EU institutions and the ability of EU citizens to impact their work (see Chapter 18 for more discussion). Ironically, the concerns over this deficit grew even as European public opinion played a greater role in the decisions over Europe. Meanwhile, EU voters had been given the opportunity since 1979 to take part in direct elections to the European Parliament, and Parliament's powers over the legislative process had grown. But most voters still understood little of

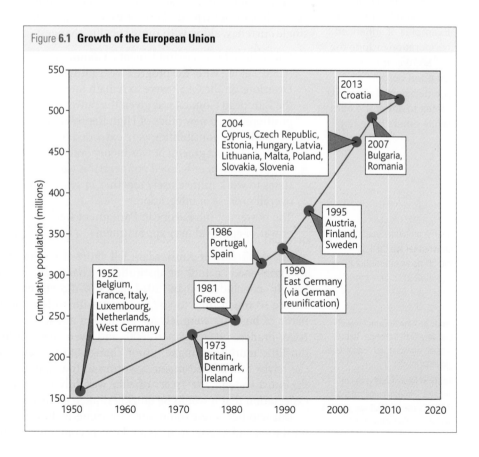

Figure **6.1 Growth of the European Union**

Concept

Enhanced cooperation

A procedure allowing those member states that wish to proceed more rapidly in a particular policy area to do so within the EU legal framework, but without extending the powers agreed under the treaties. Otherwise known as 'multi-speed integration', or 'Europe à la carte', enhanced cooperation represents the failure of the EU partners to agree, but also prevents foot-draggers from placing a brake on the process. Examples of enhanced cooperation include the Schengen Agreement on open borders and the decision of some EU states to adopt the euro while others have not.

the manner in which decisions were taken at the Community level, and they turned out at EP elections in declining numbers: from a high of 63 per cent at the first elections in 1979, turnout by 1999 was down to 49 per cent.

The three 1992 votes were symptomatic of an increasingly heated public debate about the merits of integration, which showed that even though many Europeans were still confused about its implications, and so were more easily swayed in their opinions by supporters and critics of integration, they cared much more than they had even a decade before. Where decisions about Europe in the 1950s and 60s could be taken by bureaucrats meeting in closed session, by the 1990s this was no longer possible, and the dynamics of the debate over Europe had taken on an entirely new character.

From Amsterdam to Nice (1997–2002)

Because the Maastricht treaty had left a number of items of business unfinished, another IGC was convened in 1996–97 that resulted in agreement of the Treaty of Amsterdam. Signed in October 1997, and entering into force in May 1999, it was less important than either the SEA or Maastricht, and focused on consolidation rather than innovation. It was designed mainly to make some of the institutional and political changes needed to deal with enlargement, and to help the EU better address issues such as globalization, terrorism and international crime. It also confirmed plans for eastern enlargement and for the launch of the single currency, along with more specific changes:

- It formalized plans to implement a Common Foreign and Security Policy (CFSP) along with 'the progressive framing of a common defence policy'. Decisions on the CFSP were to remain intergovernmental and unanimous, but the European Council was given the power to agree common strategies and positions, and a new office of High Representative for the CFSP was created.
- EU policy responsibilities were extended to health and consumer protection.
- The Schengen Agreement was incorporated into the treaties.
- The principle of enhanced cooperation was established, allowing member states to work more closely together in selected areas without harming the overall process of integration.
- The powers of the European Parliament were expanded, and it was given the power of approval over appointments to the College of Commissioners.

Treaty of Amsterdam: A set of relatively limited changes to the treaties, signed in 1997 and entered into force in 1999.

Treaty of Nice: Another set of relatively limited changes to the treaties, signed in 2001 and entered into force – after unexpected delays – in 2003.

But the Treaty of Amsterdam fell short of requirements, so yet another IGC was convened to look at institutional change in anticipation of enlargement. 'Rarely', concludes Dinan (2014, p. 290), 'did an intergovernmental conference devote so much time to so few issues with so few consequential results.' Many items of business were left for discussion at the European Council meeting in Nice, France, in December 2000, and even then the resulting Treaty of Nice did little more than make minor changes to the structure of the Commission, the terms of qualified majority voting in the Council of Ministers, the EP, and the court system. The Treaty of Nice was duly signed in February 2001 with the expectation that it would be quickly ratified by member states.

But another referendum surprise came in June, this time in Ireland, which until then had a reputation as a relatively contented member of the EU. A surfeit of confidence had led the Irish government to make little effort to educate voters on Nice, creating an information breach into which stepped an unlikely coalition of environmentalists, religious conservatives and those concerned with preserving Ireland's neutrality (Costello, 2005). On referendum day, barely one-third of voters turned out, and 54% of those rejected the treaty. EU leaders refused to renegotiate the terms of the treaty, but the European Council did confirm that Ireland would not have to be party to any mutual defence obligations. A second Irish referendum was held in October 2002, this time prefaced by a spirited information campaign and more active debate of the issues. The new vote resulted in nearly 63% approval with a 50% turnout, and the Treaty of Nice finally entered into force in February 2003.

While public attention was focused on Amsterdam and Nice, another initiative with important implications for the political lives of Europeans was completed with less fanfare in the form of the Charter of Fundamental Rights of the European Union. Sparked by a 1996 decision by the European Court of Justice that its treaties did not allow the EU to accede to the 1950 European Convention on Human Rights, the charter was discussed and approved during 2000, and 'proclaimed' at the Nice European Council in December. Reaffirming a selection of rights with which few Europeans could take much issue, the charter came into force with the Treaty of Lisbon in 2009 (see Chapter 7), since when it has been part of the legal structure of the EU.

Meanwhile, there were new initiatives on the economic front. In spite of progress on the single market and preparations for the single currency, many still worried that the EU was not fulfilling its potential as the largest marketplace in the world. Planners contemplated lagging productivity rates, high unemployment in parts of the EU, an inflexible labour market, and continued economic disparities among member states. In order to set new targets, the Lisbon European Council in March 2000 agreed the Lisbon Strategy, which set the ambitious goal of making the EU – within 10 years – 'the most dynamic and competitive knowledge-based economy in the world capable of sustainable economic growth with more and better jobs and greater social cohesion, and respect for the environment'. To do this, employment rates would be raised, more women would be brought into the workplace, telecommunications and energy markets would be liberalized, transport would be improved, and labour markets opened up (Wallace, 2004). Sceptics doubted that this was possible, and were to be proved correct.

Lisbon Strategy: An attempt made in 2000 to set economic modernization targets for the EU, with the goal of making it the world's most dynamic marketplace within 10 years.

Summary

- In the mid-1980s an attempt was made to refocus attention on completion of a European single market. The result was the signature in 1986 of the Single European Act, the first major amendment to the founding treaties of the European Community. Its key goal was a single market by the end of 1992.

- Concerned about the slowness with which borders were being opened within the EEC, several member states signed the Schengen Agreement in 1985, aimed at a fast-track lifting of customs and immigration checks.

- The political revolutions of 1989 brought an end to the Cold War and began lifting the divisions between western and eastern Europe.

- The signature of the 1992 Treaty on European Union confirmed the three stages to the achievement of a single currency, expanded the policy reach of integration (notably into foreign and security policy), and created a new three-pillar EU. The treaty proved controversial, and was delayed by a negative vote (later reversed) in a Danish national referendum.

- With more countries hoping for EU membership, the European Economic Area was created in 1994 to give EFTA members access to the single market, and 1995 saw the entry of Austria, Finland and Sweden.

- The process of integration had at first attracted little public attention. But the passage of the Single European Act made the headlines, paving the way for a heated debate over Maastricht that changed the nature of the debate. Supporters and opponents of integration became more vocal, and national governments had no choice but to pay more attention to public opinion.

- Unfinished organizational business from Maastricht was addressed in the treaties of Amsterdam (1999) and Nice (2003), but only limited changes were agreed. Shock was generated, however, by a negative vote on Nice in Ireland.

Key terms and concepts

Acquis communautaire

European Economic Area

European Political Cooperation

Eurosclerosis

Lisbon Strategy

Permissive consensus

Schengen Agreement

Single European Act

Treaty of Amsterdam

Treaty on European Union

Treaty of Nice

Further reading

Christiansen, Thomas, and Simon Duke (eds) (2015) *The Maastricht Treaty: Second Thoughts after 20 Years* (Abingdon: Routledge). Edited collection that looks at the changes brought by the Maastricht treaty and their long-term effects.

Drake, Helen (2000) *Jacques Delors: Perspectives on a European Leader* (Abingdon: Routledge). Profile of the most influential and controversial president of the European Commission to date, which sets out to pin down the 'Delors factor' in politics.

Padoa-Schioppa, Tommaso (2000) *The Road to Monetary Union in Europe: The Emperor, the Kings, and the Genies* (Oxford: Oxford University Press). Review of the background to the SEA and Maastricht, written by an Italian banker who later became Italy's minister of finance.

7 To the Euro Crisis and Beyond

With Maastricht having made the European Community part of the new European Union, the focus of integration shifted to the single currency; it was named the euro in 1995, exchange rates in participating states were locked in place in 1999, and euro banknotes and coins began circulating in 2002.

Barely had this happened when world events impinged again as several EU governments, led by Germany and France, fell out with the US over the 2003 invasion of Iraq. Events showed that while at least some European governments were willing to go public with their opposition to US policy, they still were unable to agree on critical foreign policy issues. But they were able to agree on enlargement, and 2005 saw the entry into the EU of its first eastern European members, giving new meaning to the idea of Europe.

Meanwhile, an attempt was made in 2002–03 to agree a draft constitutional treaty for the EU, but while it was approved by 17 member states, the treaty was turned down by French and Dutch voters in 2005. The failed constitution was reinvented as the Treaty of Lisbon, which entered into force in 2009, just as the most serious crisis in the history of the EU was breaking.

Already reeling from the effects of the global financial crisis that had begun in the US in 2007, the EU was struck a second economic blow when it became clear during 2009 that Greece had failed to respect the terms of euro membership, and other euro zone countries were facing severe economic difficulties. Meanwhile, criticism of the EU continued to grow as populist parties made gains at elections, while its contributions to peace were recognized by the award of the 2012 Nobel Peace Prize.

- Was the euro launched too soon, and to what extent were its later problems a reflection of design flaws, underlying economic problems in euro zone states, or the failure by some of those states to respect the rules of membership?
- Given the history of postwar transatlantic relations, what was the significance of the dispute over Iraq?
- How much did the negative votes against the treaties or the euro in Denmark, France, Ireland, the Netherlands and Sweden reflect on the direction being taken by European integration, and how much did they reflect domestic political dissatisfaction in these countries?
- How politically significant was the EU enlargement to eastern Europe?
- Was the Treaty of Lisbon a constitution by another name?

Arrival of the euro (1995–2002)

As we saw earlier, Maastricht had outlined a three-stage plan for the achievement of the single currency: Stage I (new levels of cooperation among banks) had been in place since 1990, and Stage II had been launched in January 1994. This led to the establishment of the European Monetary Institute, designed to oversee preparations for Stage III, the creation of a European single currency, which in 1995 was named the euro. Maastricht had set five convergence criteria that a state would have to meet in order to qualify to adopt the new currency (see Table 7.1).

Because several states had trouble achieving the criteria, the target date for Stage III was postponed from January 1997 to January 1999. When EU leaders met in 1998 to decide which states qualified to make the switch, they found varied levels of readiness; all had met the budget deficit goal, for example, but only seven had met the debt target. Since Maastricht allowed member states to qualify if their debt-to-GDP ratio was 'sufficiently diminishing and approaching the reference value at a satisfactory pace', strict adherence to the criteria was set aside, immediately raising questions about how seriously they were being taken. The decision to bring Greece into the euro zone, in particular, would later come home to roost with a vengeance.

In June 1998 the new European Central Bank (ECB) replaced the European Monetary Institute and became responsible for monetary policy in the euro zone. On 1 January 1999 the euro was launched, becoming available as an electronic currency (but not yet a physical currency) and participating countries permanently fixed the exchange rates of their national currencies against one another and against the euro. All dealings of the ECB with commercial banks and all its foreign exchange activities were now transacted in euros, which began to be quoted against the yen and the US dollar in international financial markets. The euro started out at a healthy $1.18, fell to a low of 82 cents in late 2000 (sparking claims of crisis), climbed back up to reach parity in mid-2002, and was to reach a high of nearly $1.60 in mid-2008 before falling again (see Chapter 20).

Discussion about the design of the new euro banknotes and coins had been resolved fairly easily. In the case of the banknotes, it was felt that the designs could not be tied to any one country but instead had to capture general European themes, so it was decided to use designs based on styles of European architecture. Sophisticated anti-counterfeiting measures were also built into the designs, including raised print, security threads and holograms. As for the coins, one side had a common design including a map of Europe (without Turkey, it is interesting to note), while the other had designs peculiar to the participating

Convergence criteria: Standards that EU member states must achieve before being allowed to adopt the euro, including low national budget deficits and inflation, and controls on public debt and interest rates.

Table **7.1 The convergence criteria**

Budget deficit	Less than 3% of GDP
Public debt	Less than 60% of GDP
Inflation	Within 1.5% of the average in the three countries with the lowest rates
Interest rates	Within 2% of the average in the three countries with the lowest rates
Exchange rates	Kept within Exchange Rate Mechanism fluctuation margins for two years

Illustration 7.1
Launch of the euro
Commission President Jacques Santer (*right*) and economics and financial affairs commissioner Yves-Thibault de Silguy (*left*) pose with a reproduction of the new 1 euro coin, May 1998.

states: Belgium, Luxembourg, the Netherlands and Spain chose images of their monarchs, Ireland opted for the Celtic harp, France included images of Marianne (a mythical icon of liberty), and Germany used oak twigs, the Brandenburg Gate and the German eagle.

But even as governments and bankers made their preparations, ordinary Europeans had doubts about the euro. Opinion polls found support between 1993 and 1996 running at about 51–54 per cent, with 36–37 per cent opposed (Eurobarometer 49, September 1998). Opposition in 1998 was greatest in Denmark, Sweden and Britain, but even among member states planning to adopt the euro there were mixed opinions; enthusiasm was highest in Ireland, Luxembourg, the Netherlands and Spain, and lowest in Finland, Germany and Portugal. The German figure was particularly worrying, given that Germany was critical to the exercise of monetary union: in the end, suggests Tsoukalis (2003, pp. 34–5), most Germans ultimately signed on only because they saw a need to reaffirm their commitment to Europe in the wake of German reunification.

In January 2002 euro coins and notes began circulating in all EU-15 member states except Britain, Denmark and Sweden. This final launch of the physical euro was a monumental task, involving the challenge of preparing consumers and businesses, making sure that enough coins and notes were available to meet demand (14 billion banknotes were printed and 56 billion coins minted), and converting ATMs, cash registers and vending machines throughout the euro zone. It had been assumed that the transition would be expensive and complicated, so national currencies were to be allowed to circulate alongside the euro for six months. But the problems proved unfounded; within a month euros were accounting for 95 per cent of cash payments in the euro zone, and the transition was over by the end of February. For the first time since the Roman era much of Europe had a single currency.

Shockwaves from Iraq (2003–05)

The US has always played a critical role in the process of European integration, intentionally and unintentionally. Intentionally, it provided the political and economic support needed to help get the process off the ground in the late 1940s and early 1950s, it provided security guarantees through NATO, and economic leadership and opportunity through the Bretton Woods system and the Marshall Plan. Unintentionally, it helped bring western Europeans together by pursuing policies during the Cold War that alarmed and repelled. Starting with Korea, and moving through Suez, the Cuban missile crisis, Vietnam, the Middle East, Central America and beyond, western Europeans regularly found themselves looking askance at US policy. But while public opinion was often openly hostile, governments rarely made their disquiet public. All now changed with the controversy over Iraq, which not only brought transatlantic political tensions into the open, but also showed that the EU member states had much work to do in developing common foreign policies.

The September 2001 terrorist attacks on New York and Washington DC at first generated an unprecedented degree of transatlantic solidarity, suggesting that international terrorism might be a new challenge around which a new Atlantic Alliance might be forged. More than 120 Europeans died in the twin towers, the EU

Timeline *To the euro crisis and beyond*

1995	December	Single currency named the euro
1998	June	Creation of European Central Bank
1999	January	Launch of the euro
2000	December	Proclamation of Charter of Fundamental Rights of the EU
2001	September	Terrorist attacks in the US
2002	January	Euro coins and banknotes begin circulating
	March	Opening meetings of Convention on the Future of Europe
2003	February	Large anti-war demonstrations in major European cities
2003	March	Launch of US-led invasion of Iraq
2004	March	Terrorist bombings in Madrid
	May	Ten mainly eastern European states join the EU, taking membership to 25
	October	Signature of Treaty on the European Constitution
2005	May–June	French and Dutch voters reject the constitutional treaty
	July	Terrorist bombings in London
2007	January	Bulgaria and Romania join the EU, taking membership to 27
	December	Signature of Treaty of Lisbon
2008	June	Irish referendum rejects Lisbon
2009	January	Slovakia becomes 13th EU member state to adopt the euro
	October	Second Irish referendum accepts Lisbon
	October	Greek admission of budget deficit marks beginning of crisis in euro zone
	November	Treaty of Lisbon enters into force
2012	March	All but two EU states adopt fiscal compact
	December	EU awarded Nobel Peace Prize
2013	July	Croatia becomes 28th member state of the EU
	October	Launch of European Stability Mechanism
2014	May	European Parliament elections result in gains for populist parties
2015	January	Lithuania becomes 19th EU member state to adopt the euro

was quick to express its moral outrage, its foreign ministers described the attack as an assault 'against humanity itself', and the French newspaper *Le Monde* famously declared '*Nous sommes tous Americains*' (We are all Americans). EU leaders were also generally in support of the US case for quick action to be taken against the Taliban in Afghanistan, a haven for terrorists. But when the administration of George W. Bush began preparing for a pre-emptive invasion of Iraq, claiming that its leader Saddam Hussein possessed weapons of mass destruction and thus posed a threat to neighbouring states and US interests, everything changed.

In notable contrast with earlier such international crises, where EU leaders would have chosen among open support, qualified support or diplomatic silence, several were now openly critical of US policy. Supporters included the governments of Britain, Denmark, Italy, the Netherlands, Spain and many of those in eastern Europe, while the opposition – which included Austria, Belgium and Greece – was led vocally and openly by President Jacques Chirac of France and Chancellor Gerhard Schroeder of Germany.

But largely overlooked in the mix was the deep and near uniform public hostility to the invasion across the EU. This was reflected in opinion polls that found majorities of between 70 and 90 per cent opposed in Britain, Denmark, France, Germany, and even in 'new' European countries such as the Czech Republic and Hungary (see Figure 7.1). It was also reflected in the massive and coordinated

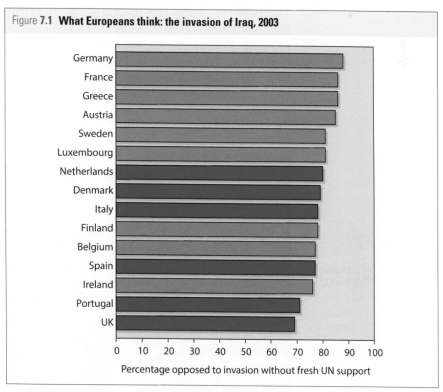

Figure **7.1** **What Europeans think: the invasion of Iraq, 2003**

Percentage opposed to invasion without fresh UN support

Note: Bold indicates governments that supported the invasion. Support also came from the governments of all eight prospective eastern European member states of the EU: the Czech Republic, Estonia, Hungary, Latvia, Lithuania, Poland, Slovakia and Slovenia.

Source: EOS Gallup poll, January 2003.

anti-war demonstrations held in EU capitals on 15 February 2003, and in the unpopularity of several pro-war European governments; these included Spain – where government support for the war was a factor in the unexpected loss of the April 2004 election by the ruling conservative government of José Maria Aznar – and Britain, where Tony Blair was never able to recover politically from the domestic unpopularity of his decision to support the invasion, struggling on in office until stepping down in June 2007.

This was more than just a dispute over Iraq, or even an EU response to George W. Bush, clearly among the most reviled (in Europe) of all US presidents. Instead, the breach over the invasion could be seen as symptomatic of the new willingness of the EU to assert itself in its relations with the US. The transatlantic relationship since 1945 had always been more nervous than many had realized, but while western European governments had occasionally resisted American leadership and criticized US policy, the split was now in the open. The end of the Cold War had removed much of the glue that had kept the Americans and the western Europeans on the same page, and the division over Iraq showed how much postwar Europe had grown, and how much it now sought to express its independence.

The EU looks east (1994–2013)

The 1995 enlargement of the EU to Austria, Finland and Sweden had gone relatively easily. Far more challenging – and also politically significant – was the prospect of enlargement to the east. While it would put the final cap on the end of the Cold War division of Europe, it also meant bringing in states that had long been guided by communism, and were far poorer than any western states had been when they had joined the EC/EU. By way of preparation, the Community had agreed to take responsibility for coordinating western European aid to the east following the end of the Cold War. To this end, the European Bank for

Illustration 7.2 Croatians celebrate joining the EU

Croatians gather in the main square in Zagreb to celebrate the accession of their country to the European Union on 1 July 2013.

Reconstruction and Development was founded in 1991 to provide loans, encourage capital investment and promote trade; Europe Agreements were signed with several eastern countries to allow for progress on free trade; and in 1997 the EU launched Agenda 2000, listing the changes needed to prepare 10 eastern European states for EU membership.

Negotiations opened between 1998 and 2000 with Bulgaria, Cyprus, the Czech Republic, Estonia, Hungary, Latvia, Lithuania, Malta, Poland, Romania, Slovakia and Slovenia. Following their completion in December 2002, all but Bulgaria and Romania were invited to join in an initial wave of enlargement. All accepted, all but Cyprus held referendums that confirmed support for membership, and in May 2004 the biggest round of enlargement to date was completed when 10 new states joined the EU. Membership of the EU was now up to 25, and for the first time former Soviet republics (Estonia, Latvia and Lithuania) were members of the club. But while the population of the EU grew by more than 23 per cent

Map **7.1** **Eastern enlargement, 2004–13**

(from nearly 380 million people to 467 million), its economic wealth grew by just 5 per cent (less than the GDP of the Netherlands). In a second phase of eastern enlargement, Bulgaria and Romania joined in January 2007 and Croatia in 2013, pushing the EU population up to just over half a billion.

The symbolism of eastern enlargement was unmistakable: as well as sealing the end of the Cold War division of Europe, it was a dramatic step in the transformation of former Soviet bloc states from communism to liberal democracy, and gave new meaning to the word *European*. Until 2004 the 'European' Union had ultimately been a western European league, and the absence of its eastern neighbours reflected the political, economic and social divisions of the continent. By 2013, 28 of the 40 sovereign states of Europe – containing 84 per cent of the population of Europe – had been brought together under the aegis of the European Union.

The process was by no means simple or trouble free, to be sure. Neither was it quick (see Figure 7.2). There were arguments over the terms of entry, questions about how much access workers from the new member states would have to free movement and residence, objections from Turkey to claims that the government of Cyprus represented the whole of the divided island and that Cyprus had

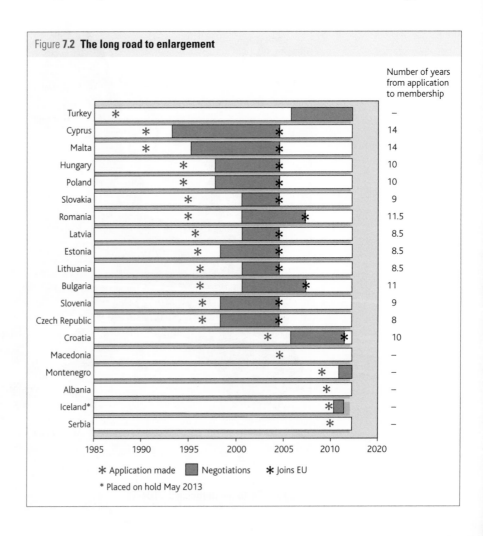

Figure **7.2 The long road to enlargement**

slipped past Turkey in the queue to join the EU, and much political resistance in Malta to joining. There was also a new sense of 'enlargement fatigue' in some of the existing member states, and new concerns about immigration, which contributed in turn to new levels of support for right-wing political parties in Austria, Belgium and the Netherlands. And yet the queue of prospective members has never stopped growing.

As of late 2014, Albania, Iceland, Macedonia, Montenegro, Serbia and Turkey had been accepted as 'candidate countries', meaning that membership has been agreed in principle for all six, and negotiations on terms have begun with most of them. Turkey poses the greatest challenges because of the combination of its size, poverty, religion and mixed political record, as well as concerns over its attitude towards Cyprus and questions about whether it is a European country (see Chapter 9 for more discussion). Two more countries – Bosnia and Kosovo – are considered potential candidate countries.

The failed constitutional treaty (2001–05)

Although the treaties of Amsterdam and Nice had taken care of most of the immediate institutional needs of the expanding EU, there was support for the idea of taking a new approach to organizing the EU. Nothing could be more emphatic in this regard than the idea of a constitution for Europe, and it was with this in mind that the Laeken European Council in December 2001 decided to set up a Convention on the Future of Europe, or the European Convention. This met for the first time in March 2002, with former French President Valéry Giscard d'Estaing in the chair, and former Italian Prime Minister Giuliano Amato and former Belgian Prime Minister Jean-Luc Dehaene as vice-chairs. It brought together 105 delegates drawn carefully from a variety of sources and designed to ensure that a wide range of opinions were heard; all 15 member states were represented, along with 13 potential member states, national legislatures, the European Parliament, and the European Commission.

Several guiding questions dominated the thinking of the convention:

- how the EU might play a more effective role in the world
- how ordinary Europeans could connect more fully and effectively with the EU
- how the division of responsibilities between the EU and the member states could be more clearly explained
- how the organizational rules of the EU could be simplified
- what arrangements needed to be made to pave the way for more enlargement of the EU
- how the EU could achieve greater democracy, transparency and efficiency.

European Convention: A series of meetings held during 2002–03 to draft a constitution for the EU.

Treaty Establishing a Constitution for Europe: A treaty signed in 2004, which was intended to replace the process of developing new treaties with a constitution for the EU. It failed when rejected by French voters in 2005.

Public plenary sessions were held monthly, the convention breaking out between sessions into working groups to discuss particular issues in more detail.

After months of debate, focusing often on the minutiae of how to reform EU institutions and structure the decision-making process, the convention agreed a draft Treaty Establishing a Constitution for Europe. This was intended to combine all the rules and principles established by past treaties and the growing body of European case law, and to bring an end to the process of changing the rules of the EU by drawing up new treaties. A final draft was published in July

2003, was further discussed at an IGC beginning in October and at the European Council in June 2004, and the treaty was signed in October (for details, see Dinan, 2014). Some of its provisions were new, bringing changes to the institutional structure of the EU, while others simply confirmed established habits.

As usual, ratification was needed by all EU member states. But in a departure from past practice, it was agreed that a negative vote by even one state would be enough to terminate the treaty; most assumed that Britain – where the Blair administration was in favour but public opinion was not – would be the spoiler. Lithuania became the first member state to ratify in November 2004 with a parliamentary vote, followed by Hungary, Slovenia and Italy. The treaty then passed its first national referendum in Spain in February 2005, when 77% voted in favour with a lethargic turnout of 42%. More parliamentary votes followed in Greece, Austria, Belgium, Estonia, Slovakia and Germany, at which point, with 11 positive votes in the bag, the spotlight shifted to France, where a referendum had been arranged for 29 May.

Both the governing conservatives and the opposition socialists campaigned in favour of the treaty, and opinion polls suggested that it would be approved by a healthy majority. But opposition began to build around concerns on the left that the treaty would force a neoliberal economic model on France, and on the right that it would entail too great a loss of national sovereignty. Matters were complicated by the unpopularity of President Jacques Chirac, a champion of the constitution (*The Economist*, 2005). Although there was high turnout (69%) on polling day, nearly 55% of voters rejected the constitution. For the first time in the history of the EU, one of its two major founding powers had dealt a blow to the process of European integration, and there was no possibility of the treaty being renegotiated. In spite of this, the Netherlands went ahead with a planned referendum three days later, and all doubts were laid to rest with its rejection there by 62% of voters, with turnout of more than 63%.

All major Dutch political parties had campaigned for the treaty, but polls showed a split in public opinion, with about half the voting population admitting to knowing almost nothing about its content. In the end, the result was explained by a combination of the unpopularity of the Dutch government, a perception that the European project was one generated by elites with too little reference to ordinary Europeans, public resentment that the Netherlands had never before been given the opportunity of a referendum (notably on adoption of the euro), concerns about immigration from Turkey and eastern Europe, concerns that the treaty would mean reduced influence for the Netherlands in Europe, and the negative vote in France. Luxembourg went ahead with a planned referendum in July, at which 56% voted in favour of the treaty, and there were successful legislative votes in Latvia, Cyprus, Malta, Bulgaria and Romania. But in spite of the fact that 17 member states eventually ratified the treaty, the French and Dutch results made the matter moot; the constitution was dead.

The Treaty of Lisbon

Writing in his memoirs in 1978, Jean Monnet (1978, p. 518) had warned that Europe would be 'established through crises and … the outcome will be the sum of the outcomes of those crises'. The tale of integration can indeed seem to be one of crisis following crisis, and the process has been declared dead or dying more times than can be counted. In this time-honoured tradition, the collapse of the constitutional treaty in 2005 was greeted as another blow to Europe, and one that clouded the entire direction being taken by European integration.

But just as with all earlier cries of 'wolf!', the EU continued to function, even if its institutions were becoming increasingly creaky; it was even able to absorb Bulgaria and Romania when they joined in January 2007 (albeit by sweeping many problems under the carpet). After a 'period of reflection', European leaders regrouped to pick up the pieces, and did so in what was widely criticized as a devious manner. The German presidency of the EU declared in January 2007 that a new treaty was needed in order to take care of outstanding organizational needs, and used the occasion of the 50th anniversary of the Treaty of Rome in March 2007 to issue the Berlin Declaration, which hinted at the hope that there would be a new agreement in place before the June 2009 European Parliament elections. A draft of what was initially known as the reform treaty was duly discussed at an IGC in Lisbon in July 2007, and signed there the following December.

It quickly became clear that the content of what eventually became the Treaty of Lisbon was much the same as that of the constitutional treaty; it was 'different in approach but not in content', noted Valéry Giscard d'Estaing. It was another amendment to the treaties rather than a reformulation of the treaties as a constitution, to be sure, but beyond that the differences were marginal, and most of the key changes intended by the stillborn constitution survived:

- A new president for the European Council, appointed by its members and approved by Parliament.

Illustration **7.3 The Treaty of Lisbon**

The ceremony for the signature of the Treaty of Lisbon in December 2007. It may be many years before another effort is made to agree a new European treaty.

Treaty of Lisbon: The most recent change to the EU treaties, signed in 2007 and entered into force in 2009. It makes most of the changes that had been intended by the stillborn constitutional treaty.

- A High Representative of the Union for Foreign Affairs and Security Policy, appointed by the European Council and backed up by a new European External Action Service.
- Abolition of the pillar system, introduced by Maastricht, and the European Community.
- Equal powers for the European Parliament and the Council of Ministers over proposals for almost all EU legislation.
- Recognition of the rights laid out in the Charter of Fundamental Rights, and accession to the European Convention on Human Rights.
- More responsibilities for the EU in the areas of energy policy, public health, climate change, crime and terrorism, commercial policy, humanitarian aid, sport, tourism, research and space.
- A new formula for qualified majority voting in the Council of Ministers to take effect in 2014.
- Expansion of the use of qualified majority voting, but the national veto to be retained for foreign and defence policy and taxation.
- A single legal personality for the EU, designed to strengthen its negotiating powers on the international stage.
- Formal recognition, for the first time, of the freedom of a member state to leave the EU.

With the exception of Ireland, all member states argued that the Lisbon treaty was an amendment to past treaties and so did not require national referendums, a position that was criticized by Lisbon's opponents as a ploy to push through the constitution by other means and with a different name. It was widely assumed that it would go through with few difficulties, but Ireland was once again required to organize a referendum to change its constitution, and, on 12 June 2008, 53 per cent of Irish voters rejected the treaty (with 53 per cent turnout). Few had taken the time to read the treaty or understand its critical components, creating a breach into which supporters and opponents stepped with alacrity. Opponents wrongly claimed that Lisbon would mean legalized abortion in Ireland, compromised Irish neutrality, and a change to tax policy.

A protocol for Ireland was negotiated and agreed in June 2009, including confirmation of neutrality and guarantees that Lisbon did not provide for the creation of a European army, the powers of member states on tax issues remained unchanged, the number of European commissioners would not be reduced, and Ireland's constitutional provisions for the right to life, family and education would not be impacted. Against this background, a second Irish referendum was held in October 2009, resulting in a 67 per cent majority in favour, with 59 per cent turnout. In spite of the unpopularity of the Irish government, the Yes campaign was helped by the perception that EU membership had helped Ireland weather some of the effects of the global financial crisis. Lisbon came into force in November.

Apart from putting an end to the clumsy three-pillar arrangement introduced by Maastricht, the most significant institutional change to come out of Lisbon was the creation of the two key new positions of president of the European Council, and high representative for foreign affairs. Their creation was seen as an opportunity to give the EU new direction and make it a more effective player in the international system, the hope among some being that the new president would be someone with a strong international profile and a proven leadership style. What the European Council needed, said British Foreign Secretary David Miliband, was someone who could 'do more than simply run through the agenda', who was guaranteed access to political leaders at the highest level, and who could bring traffic to a halt when they landed in Beijing or Washington or Moscow (quoted in *The Guardian*, 2009).

Early speculation focused on former British Prime Minister Tony Blair, who had the necessary credentials and reputation but whose candidacy was sullied by his support of the US-led invasion of Iraq in 2003, and Britain's refusal to adopt the euro. There was also a preference among the leaders of smaller countries for the job to go to one of their own, and in the end their views prevailed: the job was given to the little-known Belgian Prime Minister Herman van Rompuy, who had a reputation as a consensus-builder, and who – like most of those on the council – was a moderate conservative.

The council also reached into the ranks of the relatively unknown in their choice for the new EU foreign minister, appointing the incumbent trade commissioner from Britain, Catherine Ashton. Never elected to public office, and all but unknown outside her home state, she had no foreign policy experience, but was well regarded by Commission President José Manuel Barroso, and by coming from the ideological left gave political balance to the two positions. Given the staff and the resources that Ashton would have at her disposal, it was widely thought that her position might end up being the more significant of the two. But little traffic would have had to have been halted to allow for the foreign visits of either van Rompuy or Ashton.

Crisis in the euro zone

Barely had speculation begun about the implications of the death of the constitutional treaty and the passage of the Treaty of Lisbon when the EU faced two critical challenges that cast all its earlier problems into the shade: the breaking in 2007 of a global financial crisis that began in the US and quickly impacted economies all over the world, followed by the breaking in 2009 of a crisis in the euro zone so serious that it led to speculation not just of the end of the euro but also possibly of the EU itself.

The global financial crisis had its origins in the subprime mortgage industry in the US. Seeking new profits and encouraged by weak financial regulations, banks and financial companies had lent to low-income home-buyers, encouraged by growing home prices. These loans could be turned into securities and sold off, earning large profits while also passing on the risk. When the US housing bubble burst in 2007, the value of assets held by banks and financial institutions fell. With few reserves to back them up, many either went bankrupt or turned to the government for help, stock prices plummeted, many people lost their jobs and their homes, and shrinking consumer demand led to financial woes for business. Many of these so-called 'toxic assets' had been sold to European financial institutions, so the crisis quickly spread to the EU.

Although the crisis indicated that the EU had neither the institutions nor the processes to respond, EU leaders were commendably quick to cooperate, raising guarantees for individual bank deposits, and not allowing any bank whose failure

Focus on... *The EU as winner of the Nobel Peace Prize*

Amid all the worries and speculation about the euro zone crisis and its implications for European integration, there was one piece of good news (for supporters of the EU, at least) when it was awarded the 2012 Nobel Peace Prize. In presenting the award, Nobel committee chairman Thorbjørn Jagland (2012) described the reconciliation between France and Germany as 'probably the most dramatic example in history' of war and conflict being turned so rapidly into peace and cooperation. He went on: 'What this continent has achieved is truly fantastic, from being a continent of war to becoming a continent of peace. In this process the European Union has figured most prominently. It therefore deserves the Nobel Peace Prize.'

European Council President Herman van Rompuy shared his hope that future generations would say with pride 'Ich bin ein Europaer', 'Je suis fier d'etre Europeen', 'I'm proud to be European'. The German newspaper *Bild* carried a front page story with the headline 'This prize belongs to us all', while Spain's *El Mundo* recorded that in the chronicles of the EU, the date of the award ceremony would 'appear in bold and underlined'.

But just as with many earlier decisions about the award of the prize, the decision to recognize the EU was widely questioned. Some suggested that NATO was at least an equally worthy winner, to which others responded that NATO was a military alliance that kept peace mainly by threatening violence against anyone who might undermine that peace, while the EU was always focused on peace through opportunity, cooperation and the rule of law. Critics also questioned the timing of the award, presented as it was against a background of crisis, austerity and high unemployment in many EU countries. The award, said others, had come as euro zone governments were showing a distinct lack of goodwill towards one another, and bickering over how the debt crisis might best be resolved.

But there was no question that, since 1945, Europe had enjoyed the longest spell of general peace in its recorded history. And while it was impossible to say with any certainty how much the EU had contributed, it had unquestionably been a force for cooperation and peace, has not maintained a military or had aspirations so to do, and has not been involved in conflicts with other actors.

might pose systemic risks to the EU financial system to fail. The Commission issued guidelines on bank recapitalization, and announced a stimulus package to which EU leaders quickly agreed. Help was also offered to non-euro eastern European states and any euro zone state facing a balance of payments crisis. These responses showed how much the structure of European economies had been homogenized by the single market, increased intra-European trade and investment, corporate mergers and acquisitions, and common policies on competition.

But barely had the response begun when a home-grown crisis emerged in the euro zone. After being allowed to join the euro in spite of its failure to meet the budget deficit terms of entry, Greece went on a spending spree fuelled by cheaper borrowing, manipulated statistics to exaggerate its levels of economic growth, ran a budget deficit that – at nearly 13 per cent – was far above the 3 per cent limit set for euro zone membership, and accumulated a national debt that was ultimately bigger than its national economy. This was despite the existence of a Stability and Growth Pact among euro zone governments, designed to limit borrowing and budget deficits. To make matters worse, the Greek government was not attracting enough revenue, thanks in part to widespread tax evasion. The breaking of the global financial crisis found the Greek economy weak and exposed, and Greece's credit rating was downgraded, reducing the prospect of badly needed foreign investment.

But Greece was not alone in experiencing problems, and other euro zone countries also faced budgetary pressures, if not always for the same reasons. In Ireland, the root of the problem was the bursting of a housing bubble in 2008, when Ireland declared itself in a recession, government revenues fell, unemployment levels rose, bankruptcies grew, and bad debts brought problems for Irish banks. For Spain, the problem grew out of a combination of inflation, a large trade deficit, the bursting of a property bubble, and loss of competitiveness that had brought economic weakness even before the breaking of the euro zone crisis. For Italy, which sparked some of the greatest worries because it was the third largest economy in the euro zone, the economic downturn grew out of a large decline in industrial production, bankruptcies and failures in the corporate sector, and widespread corruption.

The euro crisis broke in October 2009 when the new Greek government admitted that the country had accumulated a massive deficit. Euro zone leaders at first avoided offering Greece a bailout, but when it became too expensive for the more troubled euro states to borrow on the open market (rates for lending went up and some speculators even bet on the possibility of a default), a package was offered by the European Commission, the International Monetary Fund and the European Central Bank (the so-called 'troika') on condition that Greece cut public spending and boosted tax revenue. This sparked riots in the streets of Athens and encouraged little improvement in investor confidence. Spain, Italy, Ireland and Portugal were also asking for help, and even non-euro states such as Britain were having problems. Speculation grew of a 'Grexit' – Greece leaving the euro – and the possible collapse of the euro, followed by the break-up of the EU.

In the end, a two-pronged approach was taken, based on safeguarding the financial stability of the euro zone and strengthening its institutional architecture. A legislative package known as the 'six-pack' was adopted at the end of 2011; it included a stronger Stability and Growth Pact, which moved beyond budget deficits to include public debts, and required that member states focus more on long-term economic sustainability. In an effort to improve economic policy coordination, in 2012 all EU countries, with the exception of Britain and the Czech Republic, adopted a new fiscal compact formally titled the Treaty on Stability, Coordination and Governance in the Economic and Monetary Union. Entering into force in January 2013, it formalized fiscal rules into national law, including provisions of balanced budgets.

In the meantime, agreement was reached on the creation of a new European System of Financial Supervision, which began work in 2011 with three institutions:

1 The European Banking Authority was designed to check on the efficiency and functioning of the banking sector.
2 The European Securities and Markets Authority was designed to do the same for securities markets and to protect investor interests.
3 The European Insurance and Occupational Pensions Authority was designed to protect the interests of insurance policyholders and the members and beneficiaries of pension schemes.

Meanwhile, a European Stability Mechanism was instituted in 2013 with the goal of providing financial assistance to euro zone states in difficulty (it allows capital to be raised by issuing bonds and other debt instruments, and can lend up to €500 billion), and under the European Semester scheme, the European

Commission regularly analyses the fiscal situation in every member state, providing recommendations for reforms and monitoring their implementation.

As if its economic woes were not enough, there were signs of declining faith in the EU. As we saw in Chapter 6, there had been a growing backlash underway since the passage of the Maastricht treaty, with concerns about the implications of integration for national sovereignty, and criticisms of an EU that seemed elitist and aloof. Anti-EU sentiment also overlapped with populist resistance to immigration, spawning new political parties that were both anti-EU and anti-immigration. Euroscepticism reached new political levels in Britain when the Cameron government – attempting to address another squabble over the EU within the Conservative Party – promised to hold a referendum on continued British membership of the EU. The results of the 2014 European Parliament elections seemed to confirm the trend, with anti-EU parties doing well in France and Britain (where they won more votes and seats than any other domestic party), and also doing well in Denmark, Greece, the Netherlands and Austria. Mainstream conservative, socialist and liberal parties still won by far the largest share of votes and seats, but the election results, combined with strong feelings in many EU countries about the effects of recession and austerity, raised troubling questions about the future of the EU.

Summary

- The European single currency was named the euro in 1995, was launched as an electronic currency in January 1999, and the final switch was made in 12 EU countries in early 2002 when national currencies were abolished.

- The 2001 terrorist attacks on the US were condemned by all EU governments, but when the US made plans to attack Iraq on what were widely regarded as spurious grounds, a split emerged among EU leaders; public opinion in the EU, however, was overwhelmingly opposed to the invasion.

- In May 2004, eight eastern European states, together with Cyprus and Malta, joined the EU. They were followed in January 2007 by Bulgaria and Romania, and in 2013 by Croatia. The new round of enlargement confirmed the end of the Cold War, and the EU was now truly European rather than a club of western states.

- The Convention on the Future of Europe in 2002–03 resulted in the drafting of a constitutional treaty for the EU. But its passage required ratification by all EU member states, and when French and Dutch voters rejected the treaty in 2005, plans for the constitution died.

- The constitution was reinvented as the Treaty of Lisbon, which – following a delay after a negative vote in Ireland, followed by a second positive vote – entered into force in 2009.

- Following hard on the heels of the global financial crisis that broke in 2007, the euro zone crisis broke in 2010, and the EU was given insight into the consequences of not respecting its own rules. Some spoke of exits from the euro zone, and the possible collapse of the euro, and even of the EU.

- In spite of the EU's economic and political problems, the line of states hoping to join remained long.

Key terms and concepts

Convergence criteria

European Convention

Treaty Establishing a Constitution for Europe

Treaty of Lisbon

Further reading

Hix, Simon (2008) *What's Wrong with the European Union and How to Fix It* (Cambridge: Polity Press). Argues that the EU needs more political competition in order to encourage policy innovation and address public apathy.

Meunier, Sophie, and Kathleen R. McNamara (eds) (2007) *Making History: European Integration and Institutional Change at Fifty* (Oxford: Oxford University Press). Most recent in a series of periodic reviews of the state of the EU.

Peterson, John, and Mark A. Pollack (eds) (2003) *Europe, America, Bush: Transatlantic Relations in the Twenty-First Century* (London: Routledge). Mowle, Thomas A. (2004) *Allies at Odds? The United States and the European Union* (Basingstoke: Palgrave Macmillan). Two studies of transatlantic relations written just before the Iraq War and still interesting for what they have to say.

8 The Treaties

Almost all democratic bodies, whether states, international organizations, corporations, or institutions with members and a governing structure, are based on constitutions. These outline the purposes and rules of the body, list its governing principles, and provide it with legal authority. The EU has no formal constitution as such, having instead agreed a series of treaties among its members that have played almost the same role: they include declarations about the purposes and powers of the EU, and rules on the functioning of its institutions and the obligations of its members.

These treaties have evolved in two phases: phase I lasted from 1951 to 1987 and involved minimal public input, while phase II began with Maastricht and has proved more controversial and involved greater public debate. It could be argued that the EU cannot establish real permanence until it agrees and governs itself on the basis of a constitution, but just as many Europeans shy away from the term *federalism* for what it implies about loss of state sovereignty, so they shy away from the term *constitution* out of concern that it will confirm and make permanent that loss.

The difficulties of agreeing new treaties over the years have sparked regular warnings of impending chaos. But the EU has managed regardless, and it has been argued that a kind of constitutional equilibrium has now been achieved. Although there has been talk since the euro zone crisis of more treaty reform, it is unlikely that public or political opinion could stomach more changes any time soon.

In addition to the seven major treaties, the EU has also reached a number of more focused agreements, including Acts of Accession for new members, two treaties designed to improve management of the euro, and two treaties dealing with human rights.

- What are the differences between treaties and constitutions?
- To what extent are the EU treaties the functional equivalent of a constitution?
- Have changes in the way the treaties have been negotiated and confirmed reflected well or badly on the nature of European democracy?
- Since it is not a fully fledged state, does the EU need a formal constitution, or can it continue to rely on the treaties?
- What are the likely long-term effects on human rights of the EU having its own legal personality?

Understanding the treaties

A **constitution** is a document (or set of documents) that sets out the general rules by which a state (or almost any formally constituted body) is governed. At its most basic, a constitution is 'the law that establishes and regulates the main organs of government ... [and] that establishes the general principles under which [a] country is governed' (Raz, 1998, p. 153). State constitutions usually include the following:

- A listing of the general goals, values and aspirations of the state, such as democracy, equal rights and the rule of law.
- An outline of the powers and responsibilities of its governing bodies.
- An outline of the procedures used in electing or appointing government leaders, and the limits on their powers.
- A listing of the rights of its citizens.
- The steps needed to change or amend the constitution.

Constitutions are typically codified, that is, arranged as an organized legal code in a single document (Britain is one of the few exceptions to this rule), and supported by a constitutional court. The job of the latter is to protect and interpret the constitution, and to issue judgments when questions are raised about whether or not the actions of government fit with the goals and principles of the constitution. The level of detail contained in a constitution varies; some lay out only the core rules and general aspirations of government, while others (particularly in younger and more politically divided states) go into greater detail. Some reflect the realities of the state they are intended to guide, while others will try to change political behaviour, in a process known as 'constitutional engineering'.

The US constitution is often taken as the benchmark for all others, because it was the first modern document of its kind. It was drawn up in 1787 when delegates from the states met at a Constitutional Convention in Philadelphia to replace the flawed Articles of Confederation adopted in 1781. In spite of much drama and disagreement, they spent just two months on the task, producing a document that remains the legal foundation of one of the world's most successful democratic societies (and a template for many others). There have since been numerous disputes over the meaning of the details contained in the US constitution, to be sure, and it has had to be clarified and expanded by amendments, new laws, the judgments of a federal judicial system topped by the US Supreme Court, and in the wake of the growing size and diversity of the US population. But it has, overall, proved stable and durable.

The EU experience has been rather different. To begin with, the EU is not a united state, but began life as an international organization whose qualities it has never fully shaken off. Its population has always been large and diverse, and the interests of its member states have become more complex as it has grown; a population of more than half a billion people living in a cluster of vibrant democracies is bound to generate a wide range of opinions that elected officials ignore at their peril. The relative tidiness of the American Constitutional Convention of 1787 (when the US population was less than 4 million) stands in contrast to the wide variety of opinions and interests represented at the European constitutional convention of 2002–03.

Constitution: A document, usually codified, that spells out the principles and powers of government, limits on the powers of government, and the rights of citizens.

Concept

Constitutionalization

The process by which rules and treaties have been agreed that have conferred a constitutional status on the EU without the agreement of a formal constitution. Although the treaties have outlined rules and responsibilities in much the same way as a constitution, they have been legal agreements among member states rather than a finished constitution. The EU has been moving along the road to agreeing a constitution without so far taking that last, critical step.

The most important difference between the US and EU cases, though, is that while the US began life with a constitution, European integration began with a treaty, and has since proceeded with the agreement of more treaties and side agreements that have added to and amended those that came before. Unlike constitutions, which are typically holistic, in the sense that they deal with entire and self-contained systems of government, treaties are agreements reached among the constituent parts of those systems, meaning – in the case of the EU – the member states. This reliance on treaties has, in turn, meant that Europeans have had to live with a process of constitutionalization by which a constitutional status has been conferred on the treaties that make up the basic legal framework of the EU (Snyder, 2003). This process is described by Haltern (2003) as having taken the EU from being an international organization based on a set of legal agreements binding together sovereign states to a polity with 'a vertically integrated legal regime conferring judicially enforceable rights and obligations on all legal persons and entities' within its sphere.

Put another way, where the typical experience with states has been to intentionally design and agree a (hopefully finished and final) constitution and then fine-tune it through amendments and judicial interpretation, the EU has been incrementally constitutionalizing its legal order through a process that is formal and informal, explicit and implicit, and that connects each of the steps in the process of constitutional change (Christiansen and Reh, 2009, pp. 4–5). As to whether the EU now has a de facto constitution, opinion is divided. EU leaders apparently felt that it did not, which is why they tried to win agreement in 2002–05 on a constitutional treaty. Brunkhorst (2004, p. 89) has 'no doubt' that the EU has a constitution, while Keleman (2006) argues that the treaties are a constitution

Treaty: An agreement under international law entered into between sovereign states and/ or international organizations, committing all parties to shared obligations, with any failure to meet them being considered a breach of the agreement.

Illustration **8.1 The constitutional treaty**

EU heads of government and their foreign ministers gather in Rome in November 2004 to sign the new constitutional treaty. Comparisons with the American Constitutional Convention nearly 220 years earlier ended abruptly when the treaty was rejected by French and Dutch voters.

in all but name. At the very least, the EU has what might be called a 'material constitution', in the sense that the treaties are legally binding, the EU institutions amount to a political community that is separate from the member states, and EU law amounts to a constitutional legal order (Eriksen et al., 2004, pp. 4–5). This order has several key elements, ranging from treaty articles to judgments of the European Court of Justice and the obligations of international law (see Figure 8.1).

Coming to grips with the treaties can be confusing, even for experts. It does not help that most have had formal and informal names: hence the Merger treaty of 1965 is formally the Treaty of Brussels, and the Maastricht treaty of 1992 is formally the Treaty on European Union. More troublesome by far is the curious use of the plural. Although there have been eight major treaties dating back to the 1951 Treaty of Paris, they do not continue to exist today as a working set of eight. The 1951 Treaty of Paris was an anomaly, because it was never amended, and it was the only one of the treaties to be agreed with a time limit: it had a life of 50 years, and duly expired in July 2002. The 1957 Euratom Treaty continues to exist today (guiding the Luxembourg-based Euratom Supply Agency, which ensures an equitable supply of materials to the European nuclear industry), and was amended significantly in 2007 following agreement of the Treaty of Lisbon. But the real focus of treaty building has been on the 1957 EEC Treaty, which has undergone several changes of identity:

- It came into force in 1958 as the Treaty Establishing the European Economic Community (TEEC), and was later amended by the Single European Act.
- In 1992, when the word 'Economic' was dropped from 'European Economic Community', the TEEC became the Treaty Establishing the European

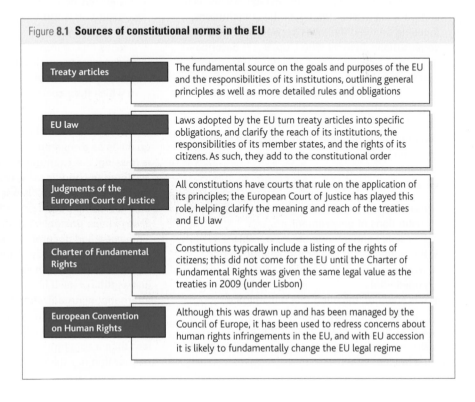

Figure **8.1 Sources of constitutional norms in the EU**

Treaty articles	The fundamental source on the goals and purposes of the EU and the responsibilities of its institutions, outlining general principles as well as more detailed rules and obligations
EU law	Laws adopted by the EU turn treaty articles into specific obligations, and clarify the reach of its institutions, the responsibilities of its member states, and the rights of its citizens. As such, they add to the constitutional order
Judgments of the European Court of Justice	All constitutions have courts that rule on the application of its principles; the European Court of Justice has played this role, helping clarify the meaning and reach of the treaties and EU law
Charter of Fundamental Rights	Constitutions typically include a listing of the rights of citizens; this did not come for the EU until the Charter of Fundamental Rights was given the same legal value as the treaties in 2009 (under Lisbon)
European Convention on Human Rights	Although this was drawn up and has been managed by the Council of Europe, it has been used to redress concerns about human rights infringements in the EU, and with EU accession it is likely to fundamentally change the EU legal regime

Community (TEC) and was subsumed under the Treaty on European Union (TEU, or the Maastricht treaty). Put another way, the European Community became part of the European Union.

- More amendments came as a result of the treaties of Amsterdam and Nice.
- The formal name of the Treaty of Lisbon was 'The Treaty of Lisbon amending the Treaty on European Union and the Treaty Establishing the European Community'. One of its effects was to abolish the European Community, so the TEC became the Treaty on the Functioning of the European Union (TFEU), and the current source of legal authority in the EU is the consolidated version of the TEU and the TFEU. (In reading the treaties, a careful distinction must be made between each individual treaty – indicated from the SEA onwards by tell-tale phrases such as 'Article I will be amended as follows' – and the single consolidated treaty, of which there is only ever one, incorporating all the amendments agreed to that point.)

As if all this is not confusing enough, more potential confusion is added by the distinction between the big seven major treaties – Paris, the Rome treaty on the EEC, the Single European Act, Maastricht, Amsterdam, Nice and Lisbon – and a cluster of mini-treaties and side agreements that have had constitutional implications, in the sense that they have changed the rules of the game (see Figure 8.2). There have, for example, been several housekeeping treaties focused

Understanding Integration... *Comparing constitutions*

One way of understanding the EU experience is to compare the treaties with national constitutions, focusing on the differences between **thin** and **thick** **constitutions**. Tushnet (2000, pp. 9–17) describes the former as aspirational, mainly philosophical, and focused more on rights than on rules, and the latter as functional and containing detailed provisions about how government should be organized. Raz (1998, pp. 153–4) describes a thin constitution as one that establishes and regulates the main bodies of government and the general principles under which a state is governed, while a thick constitution has seven key qualities:

1 It outlines the structure and powers of the main institutions of government.
2 It is stable and intended to be durable.
3 It is contained in one or a small number of written documents, hence references to *the* constitution.
4 It is superior, meaning that it invalidates conflicting ordinary laws.
5 It is justiciable, meaning that there are procedures in place by which its superiority can be implemented.
6 It is entrenched, meaning that amending the constitution is more difficult than passing ordinary laws.
7 It relies on common ideological principles such as democracy and individual rights, which reflect the beliefs of a population about the way in which their society should be governed.

Christiansen and Reh (2009, p. 42) argue that while the EU treaties have many of the same qualities as a constitution, there is also much that is missing. For example, their superiority is not accepted unconditionally, the EU institutions lack the power to make decisions on the definition of their tasks and authority, and the treaties have always been unstable: rather than there being a single codified document that can be amended, amendments are made to the structure and work of the EU with every new treaty. The result is that just as the EU itself is described as more than an international organization but less than a European superstate, or more than a regime but less than a federation, so the EU has more than a treaty but less than a constitution. In short, the treaties are neither thin nor thick, but somewhere in between.

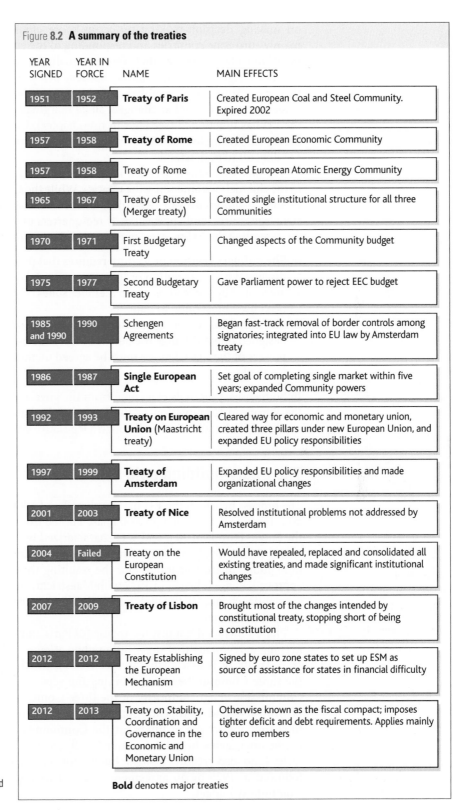

Figure **8.2 A summary of the treaties**

YEAR SIGNED	YEAR IN FORCE	NAME	MAIN EFFECTS
1951	1952	**Treaty of Paris**	Created European Coal and Steel Community. Expired 2002
1957	1958	**Treaty of Rome**	Created European Economic Community
1957	1958	Treaty of Rome	Created European Atomic Energy Community
1965	1967	Treaty of Brussels (Merger treaty)	Created single institutional structure for all three Communities
1970	1971	First Budgetary Treaty	Changed aspects of the Community budget
1975	1977	Second Budgetary Treaty	Gave Parliament power to reject EEC budget
1985 and 1990	1990	Schengen Agreements	Began fast-track removal of border controls among signatories; integrated into EU law by Amsterdam treaty
1986	1987	**Single European Act**	Set goal of completing single market within five years; expanded Community powers
1992	1993	**Treaty on European Union** (Maastricht treaty)	Cleared way for economic and monetary union, created three pillars under new European Union, and expanded EU policy responsibilities
1997	1999	**Treaty of Amsterdam**	Expanded EU policy responsibilities and made organizational changes
2001	2003	**Treaty of Nice**	Resolved institutional problems not addressed by Amsterdam
2004	Failed	Treaty on the European Constitution	Would have repealed, replaced and consolidated all existing treaties, and made significant institutional changes
2007	2009	**Treaty of Lisbon**	Brought most of the changes intended by constitutional treaty, stopping short of being a constitution
2012	2012	Treaty Establishing the European Mechanism	Signed by euro zone states to set up ESM as source of assistance for states in financial difficulty
2012	2013	Treaty on Stability, Coordination and Governance in the Economic and Monetary Union	Otherwise known as the fiscal compact; imposes tighter deficit and debt requirements. Applies mainly to euro members

Bold denotes major treaties

Thin and thick constitutions: Constitutions that differ in their intent and character, the latter being more detailed, consistent and permanent than the former.

on making decision-making processes more efficient, two treaties involving mainly euro zone countries and responding to the euro crisis, and several agreements outside the treaties that were eventually integrated into the treaties – the Schengen Agreement on internal borders being a prime example. Added to this, every time a new member state has joined the EU, there has been a new agreement signed that has changed, albeit marginally, some of the details of how the EU has functioned (see later in this chapter). Under the circumstances, it is hardly surprising that so many Europeans find the structure and powers of the EU difficult to understand.

The final distinction between the EU treaties and a constitution can be found in the channels for amending the treaties. While the US constitution, for example, requires a proposal from two-thirds of members of Congress or two-thirds of state legislatures, and approval by three-quarters of states, there are two options for amending the EU treaties, one broad and one quite focused:

- The ordinary revision procedure requires that proposals for amendments be discussed by a convention or intergovernmental conference, after which they are signed by the leaders of the member states. This is the method that has been used most often to date.
- The simplified revision procedure was established by the Treaty of Lisbon, designed only to change the details of EU policies, and cannot increase the powers of the EU. Changes must be agreed unanimously by the European Council.

In both cases, proposals can come from the governments of the member states, the European Commission or the European Parliament, and changes must be approved by the states, either through a legislative vote or a national referendum.

The treaty-building epic

The process by which the EU has developed and adopted its guiding treaties has gone through two distinct phases. Phase I lasted from 1951 to 1987, from Paris to the Single European Act, and was characterized by debates held mainly behind closed doors, involving technocrats and government representatives, attracting little public interest or input, and the resulting treaties being relatively quickly approved. Phase II began in 1992 with Maastricht, and has been characterized by substantial changes to the direction of European integration, and far more public and political interest.

Phase I included not just the treaties of Paris and Rome but also three housekeeping agreements that drew little public attention. The first of these was the 1965 Treaty of Brussels (the Merger treaty), which tidied up the structure of the three Communities by combining the separate Councils of Ministers and Commissions/High Authority of the three Communities into a single Council of Ministers and European Commission. Then in 1970 came an agreement to change the source of funds for the Community budget from contributions by member states to 'own resources' such as customs duties and agricultural levies (and also creating a single budget for the three Communities). This was followed in 1975 by an agreement to give Parliament the power to reject the Community budget.

The lack of more ambitious goals and the absence of greater political rancour during phase I can be ascribed to five main causes:

1 The member states were too focused on implementing the terms of the first three treaties to consider a major expansion of objectives, and had learned the dangers of overreaching from the failures of the European defence and political communities.
2 There were only six member states at first, with similar political and economic personalities, and governments that were mainly agreed on the goals and purposes of integration. Enlargement during this phase brought in only six more members with mainly similar views about integration.
3 There was an absence of the kind of political leadership and initiative that would spark more ambitious amendments to the treaties in the 1980s and 90s.
4 The early years of the EC were ones of economic growth and relative political harmony (Dinan 2010, pp. 47–8), and it would not be until later that concerns about Europe's declining place in the world would become clearer, helping prompt new treaty initiatives.
5 Several later treaties were drawn up to account for enlargement, a process that would not begin to significantly alter the character of the EU until the 1990s.

Compared to what would follow, even the Single European Act (SEA) went through a relatively easy approval process, the only serious misgivings being (as we saw) in Denmark and Ireland. The Danish situation was resolved by the February 1986 referendum, but in Ireland there was a more complex problem. An anti-EEC campaigner and economist named Raymond Crotty, who was concerned about the implications of the foreign policy provisions of the SEA for Irish neutrality, took legal action against the Irish government, which led to an Irish Supreme Court decision that the state did not have the authority to ratify the SEA because it would mean a reduction of government control over foreign policy. As a result, a public referendum had to be held in May 1987 on an amendment to the constitution allowing the government of Ireland to ratify the SEA. Nearly 70 per cent voted in favour, clearing the way for the SEA to come into force in July 1987.

Phase II has been an animal of a very different stripe. It began with the controversies over the 1992 Treaty on European Union, which marked the beginning of nearly two decades of intensive treaty drafting, accompanied by often strident political and public debate. This was a result partly of the growing stakes in each new treaty, and partly of the better organization of movements of supporters and opponents of integration. The meetings organized to draft and amend the treaties in this phase were often long and contentious, and often ended only with bad-tempered eleventh-hour compromises. The resulting draft treaties were occasionally voted down or only narrowly approved in national referendums, and each successive failure was greeted as a crisis, calling into question the very nature and future of European integration.

Three pillars: A compromise reached in the Maastricht treaty by which intergovernmental decision-making for foreign and security policy and justice and home affairs was preserved by making them legally separate from the European Community.

The content of Maastricht was impacted by concerns (mainly from Britain) about the growth of Community powers, resulting in a peculiar compromise in which **three pillars** were created (see Figure 8.3). This allowed the supranational qualities of the European Community to be preserved while making provision for intergovernmental decision-making on matters related to foreign and security policy, and justice and home affairs. The whole edifice was to support a new

Figure **8.3 The three pillars**

THE EUROPEAN UNION		
Supranational Existing procedures and powers of the European Communities. Covered economic, agricultural, environmental, social and immigration policy	Intergovernmental Cooperation on foreign and security policy	Intergovernmental Cooperation in the field of justice and home affairs, including issues such as customs, immigration, asylum and cross-border crime

European Union; although the European Community still existed in law, and all European law was technically Community law rather than EU law, it now became more usual to use the label European Union. (The pillars were thankfully abolished under the terms of Lisbon.)

As we saw earlier, adoption of the Maastricht treaty was slowed down by the negative vote in June 1992 in Denmark, a barely affirmative vote in France, doubts in Ireland, and negotiations leading to the second (and affirmative) vote in Denmark in May 1993. There were two major reasons for Maastricht's problems. First, it was launched against a background of major problems, including a slowdown in economic growth, rising unemployment, and emerging security problems in the Balkans. Second, the treaty itself was dense and

---

Focus on... *Intergovernmental conferences*

The meetings at which leaders of the member states sign new treaties attract considerable media attention, but they are only the final and usually brief step in a process that may have taken several years and involved intensive negotiations among national government ministers and permanent representatives of the member states. These representatives meet at **intergovernmental conferences** (IGCs), which take place outside the decision-making framework of the EU, and may last days, weeks or even months. (For a detailed analysis of the dynamics of IGCs, see Christiansen and Reh, 2009, Chs 6–8). Their use emphasizes the extent to which decision-making on the major initiatives of the EU still rests with the member states.

Depending on how they are defined, there have been as many as a dozen IGCs since 1950:

- The first (1950–51), chaired by Jean Monnet, discussed plans for the European Coal and Steel Community and resulted in the Treaty of Paris.

- The second (1955–56) resulted in the two Treaties of Rome.
- Several more in the 1960s and 70s dealt with more limited issues: a one-day IGC in April 1965 led to the Merger treaty, another in 1970 discussed budgetary issues, and another in 1975 discussed the terms of the European Investment Bank (Pijpers, 1998, p. 294).
- The third major IGC (1985–86) developed the framework for the Single European Act.
- Two more IGCs (1991) separately discussed political and monetary union, resulting in the signature in 1992 of the Treaty on European Union.
- IGCs in 1996, 1997 and 2000 focused on institutional reform and preparations for eastward enlargement, drafting the treaties of Amsterdam and Nice.
- Undoubtedly the grandest of all IGCs was the Convention on the Future of Europe, which met in 2002–03 to draft the constitutional treaty.
- A 2007 IGC drafted the Treaty of Lisbon, which was signed in December 2007.

complex, meaning that few Europeans read or understood it, giving opponents more leeway to manipulate public opinion by making the case that it involved the surrender of too much national sovereignty. It was eventually adopted, but nothing would ever be quite the same: all new treaties have since been subjected to closer public scrutiny and generated more intense political debates, more national governments have felt obliged to hold referendums (see Chapter 16), the arguments of pro- and anti-Europeans have been louder, and a renegotiation of the terms of the treaties – or, at least, the provision of opt-outs or assurances for states where votes went against a treaty – has been more usual.

The treaties of Amsterdam and Nice dealt with relatively uncontroversial issues, and – except for the surprise rejection of Nice in a June 2001 Irish referendum (accepted in a later referendum) – were relatively problem free. The next step was the ambitious but ultimately failed attempt by European leaders in 2002–03 to agree a constitution (actually, a constitutional treaty) for the EU. In the public debates over the draft, it became clear that bigger states were more comfortable than smaller states, which were concerned that their voices would not be heard. But for Moravcsik (2007, pp. 23, 24) the treaty was less than it was made out to be by critics. It was, in his view, 'a conservative document that consolidated rather than transcended the constitutional status quo' and that 'reaffirmed rather than fundamentally reformed the existing scope of European integration'. Some states opted to put the issue to a national referendum (in some cases because they were required to by national law), while others opted – often controversially – for ratification in a legislative vote. In the event, the treaty was terminated by negative votes in the summer of 2005 in France and the Netherlands.

After taking a break of about 18 months, EU leaders revisited the questions and problems left unanswered by the failure of the constitutional treaty, and 2007 saw the drafting of what was to become the Treaty of Lisbon. Following another

Intergovernmental conferences (IGCs): Conferences convened among representatives of the governments of the EU member states to discuss and agree amendments to the treaties.

Illustration **8.2 The Treaty of Amsterdam**

The signature of the Treaty of Amsterdam in October 1997 represents – in hindsight – the calm before the storms that were to confirm the end of the permissive consensus in European treaty making.

No vote in Ireland, followed by a Yes vote, Lisbon came into force in December 2009. After nearly 20 years of often heated constitutional activity (from the start of the 1991 IGC that led to the Maastricht treaty to the second Irish vote on Lisbon in 2009), it seemed unlikely that European leaders or publics would any time soon want to consider another new treaty, for three main reasons:

1 Almost all the changes planned by the stillborn constitution were effected by Lisbon, so there was no longer a pressing need to change the treaties to keep up with the needs of the growing membership of the EU.
2 The political challenges of drafting and agreeing new treaties had become increasingly difficult to address, the criticism directed at the ways in which national leaders work their way around the democratic process has done the EU no good, and each new controversy has served to undermine the credibility of the European project.
3 Few Europeans could stomach the idea of more national referendums and the risk of more division and rejection. In short, they needed time to recover from 'reform fatigue'.

It has also been argued that a political and constitutional plateau has been reached. For Moravcsik (2007, pp. 23, 24, 47), the process of integration has achieved 'a stable constitutional equilibrium' that is 'likely to endure, with incremental changes, for the foreseeable future', and while the EU may enlarge, may continue to reform, and may deepen its reach, the time has come to acknowledge a 'European constitutional settlement'. It is no longer necessary, Moravcsik argues, for the EU to move forward to consolidate its achievements: 'When a constitutional system no longer needs to expand and deepen in order to assure its own continued existence, it is truly stable. It is a mark of constitutional maturity.' Duff (2008, p. 13) makes similar arguments, suggesting that while some additional rationalization and simplification may be needed, the system achieved by Lisbon should be 'strong and durable'.

Illustration **8.3**
Ireland rejects Lisbon
Members of an Irish anti-Lisbon treaty group celebrate the result of the June 2008 national referendum in which a majority of voters rejected the new treaty. The result was reversed in a second vote 16 months later.

Debating... *Does the EU need a constitution?*

YES

Understanding how the EU works is difficult enough without additional complications being created by the absence of a succinct (ideally) set of rules and guiding principles to which Europeans can refer for clarification, and by the political stresses and confusion surrounding the writing and adopting of new treaties.

The lack of a constitution undermines the legitimacy of the EU by raising questions about the significance and openness of the process by which decisions are taken at the EU level.

The lack of a constitution makes it harder for governments and courts to settle questions over the jurisdiction and authority of the EU, particularly if its reach is constantly changing.

Developing new treaties to keep up with the changing needs and personality of the EU is a more complex and time-consuming process than amending a constitution.

The individual EU member states can no longer be relied on to deal with the pressures of globalization, and a constitution offers the best means of protecting Europe's distinctive features in the face of globalization (Habermas, 2004).

NO

It already has one in the form of the treaties, and the passage of the Treaty of Lisbon provided all the remaining changes needed to allow the EU to work efficiently. As Moravcsik (2007) puts it, the EU now has a stable constitutional settlement.

The British case, where there is no single, codified constitution, but a large body of laws, commentaries and traditions, shows that it is possible for a political entity to function well without a finished constitution.

The debates over the writing and adoption of new treaties have been increasingly harmful to the process of integration, because they have been dominated by supporters and detractors who manipulate the argument to their own ends, and because experience has shown that votes in national referendums are often driven less by opinions about the new treaties than about the standing of the national governments in referendum states. This problem will only be exacerbated by another debate over a constitution.

The efforts of the member states and national leaders should be focused on making the existing system work more efficiently, and EU citizens need time to learn more about how that system works.

Yet calls were already being made in late 2010 by Angela Merkel of Germany and Nicolas Sarkozy of France for an amendment to Lisbon designed to tighten the rules on national debt. Arguing that unsustainable debts posed a major threat to the stability of the euro, they proposed changes that would allow sanctions to be brought against EU member states exceeding the debt ceiling of 60 per cent of GDP set under the Stability and Growth Pact designed to sustain the euro (see Chapter 20). The sanctions would be tightened progressively in the light of failure to act, with the possibility of a recalcitrant euro zone state even losing its voting rights on monetary matters. The proposal met with a mixed response, but what it also helped emphasize was the absence in the treaties of a key mechanism associated with constitutions: the ability to propose and vote on amendments without having to make wholesale changes.

Other elements of the EU legal order

Discussions about the EU treaties usually focus on the big seven (from Paris to Lisbon), and all the similar major agreements reached by the EU member states that might be seen as part of the process of building an EU constitution. Often overlooked have been other treaties and agreements that have had more limited effects, but that have nonetheless resulted in changes to the EU legal order. Among these are the accession agreements that are signed each time a new member state joins the EU.

The first nine of these were Acts of Accession, signed between the Community and each of the nine states that joined between 1972 and 1994. With eastern enlargement, the EU opted for joint treaties of accession; the first was signed in 2003 with the 10 states that joined in 2004, and the second was signed in 2005 with Bulgaria and Romania. As well as outlining the obligations of membership, these joint treaties – unlike the Acts of Accession – had the effect of modifying the EU treaties, for example changing the number of votes involved in qualified majority voting, and the number of seats in the European Parliament, and had to be ratified in legislative votes by all existing member states before they came into force.

Other European agreements have been more substantial, in that they have impacted policy developments in multiple states. Three in particular are noteworthy:

1 The Schengen Agreements, signed in 1985 and 1990, allowed a subgroup of Community states to work independently to accelerate the process of bringing down barriers among the member states. Originally signed by France, West Germany and the Benelux countries, Schengen has since expanded to include all EU member states except Britain and Ireland, along with non-EU members Iceland, Norway and Switzerland. The agreements were made part of the EU legal structure by the Treaty of Amsterdam, although there is no obligation on EU member states to join. A lesser known treaty, the Prüm Convention (sometimes known as Schengen III), was signed in Germany in May 2005 with the goal of improving cross-border cooperation in the fight against terrorism, cross-border crime and illegal migration.

2 The Social Charter, signed in 1989 with the goal of creating uniform rights for workers throughout the Community. It was incorporated into the legal framework of the EU by the Treaty of Amsterdam (see Chapter 22).

3 Two treaties were agreed in response to the euro crisis, one establishing the European Stability Mechanism and one (the fiscal compact) imposing tight deficit and debt requirements on euro zone states.

Opt-outs are also part of the EU legal order, even if they apply only to a limited number of countries. They allow the majority of member states to go ahead with an agreement, avoiding the prospect of a minority of states blocking the entire agreement. So, for example, the UK and Ireland have opted out of the Schengen Agreement, Denmark and the UK have opted out of the euro, and Denmark has opted out of an EU defence policy. Meanwhile, opt-ins allow non-EU states to sign on to EU agreements; hence, Iceland, Norway and Switzerland are all part of the Schengen area.

In terms of their legal and constitutional implications, arguably the most important of all the agreements outside the major treaties are those dealing with human rights. As the reach of integration expanded, so the need for an elaboration of these rights became more acute, producing two documents that are regularly confused with the other. The first is the Charter of Fundamental Rights of the European Union, which was drawn up at the suggestion of the

Accession agreement: A membership agreement signed between a new member state and the Community or the EU.

Opt-outs: Agreements reached by which one or more EU member states are not subject to the terms of agreements reached by the others.

Charter of Fundamental Rights: A document adopted in 2000 that collected together statements on human rights outlined in other EU agreements.

European Council, adopted in 2000, integrated into the treaties by the Treaty of Nice, and came into force with the Treaty of Lisbon. But in spite of concerns about what the charter might mean in legal terms (concerns that encouraged Britain, Poland and the Czech Republic to negotiate opt-outs), it was no more than a gathering of existing rights already recognized by EU member states into a single document. These include:

- the right to life (confirming the abolition of the death penalty throughout the EU)
- the right to physical and mental integrity
- protection against torture and slavery
- respect for private and family life
- protection of personal data
- freedom of thought and religion
- freedom of expression and association
- respect for cultural diversity
- the right to a fair trial
- rights for children, the elderly, the disabled and workers
- expectations about environmental and consumer protection.

The second document with legal implications for the EU is the European Convention on Human Rights (ECHR), drawn up in 1950 by the Council of Europe, and entered into force in September 1953. It applies to members of the Council of Europe, which includes all EU member states, and any citizen of the EU who feels that their rights have been limited by EU law can use the Strasbourg-based European Court of Human Rights (see Chapter 13) for redress. Signature of the ECHR is a requirement of membership of the Council of Europe, which has 47 members: every European state except Belarus and Kosovo, along with Andorra, Lichtenstein, Monaco, San Marino and Russia. The ECHR covers

European Convention on Human Rights (ECHR): An agreement drawn up by the Council of Europe in 1950 that provides the right of petition for citizens, which has taken on a new life and legal significance since the late 1990s.

| Document 8.1 | *Charter of Fundamental Rights of the European Union, Preamble* |

The peoples of Europe, in creating an ever closer union among them, are resolved to share a peaceful future based on common values.

Conscious of its spiritual and moral heritage, the Union is founded on the indivisible, universal values of human dignity, freedom, equality and solidarity; it is based on the principles of democracy and the rule of law. It places the individual at the heart of its activities, by establishing the citizenship of the Union and by creating an area of freedom, security and justice.

The Union contributes to the preservation and to the development of these common values while respecting the diversity of the cultures and traditions of the peoples of Europe as well as the national identities of the Member States and the organisation of their public authorities at national, regional and local levels; it seeks to promote balanced and sustainable development and ensures free movement of persons, services, goods and capital, and the freedom of establishment.

To this end, it is necessary to strengthen the protection of fundamental rights in the light of changes in society, social progress and scientific and technological developments by making those rights more visible in a Charter. ...

Enjoyment of these rights entails responsibilities and duties with regard to other persons, to the human community and to future generations.

Source: EUR-Lex website, http://eur-lex.europa.eu/legal-content/ EN/TXT/?uri=CELEX:12012P/TXT (retrieved July 2014).

much of the same ground as the Charter of Fundamental Rights, but the former focuses on civil and political rights, while the the latter ranges across social, economic, cultural and citizenship rights (Greer, 2006, p. 50).

The ECHR had little effect on the early stages of European integration, the prevailing view in the EEC being that while human rights were important, they were not integral to the project of integration, and were covered anyway by the ECHR. But then the EEC/EU began to require respect for human rights as a condition for the entry of new members, issues relating to justice and home affairs moved up the agenda, and more effective monitoring of human rights matters were seen as part of the solution to the post-Maastricht backlash against integration (Greer, 2006, pp. 48–9). When the European Court of Human Rights became a permanent institution in 1998, the right of petition to the court became more widely known, changing the nature of the European legal regime.

Interestingly, because the Treaty of Lisbon created a legal personality for the EU, as distinct from each of the member states, it is now in a position to be able to ratify agreements such as the ECHR, with profound potential legal implications for the character of the EU. Lisbon also made the accession of the EU to the ECHR a legal obligation, so negotiations began in 2010 and a draft agreement was finalized in 2013. Greer (2006) argues that while the ECHR was originally an expression of the identity of western European liberal democracy, emphasizing its contrasts with eastern European communism, the end of the Cold War division of Europe meant that the ECHR evolved into something more like an 'abstract constitutional model' for the whole of Europe, possibly leading to convergence in the operation of public institutions at every level.

Summary

- The EU does not have a constitution as such, but it has a body of treaties that have almost the same role, in the sense that they outline the principles and rules by which the EU functions.

- The process of integration was guided initially by treaties agreed between sovereign states, but through a process of constitutionalization those treaties have since taken on most of the features of a constitution.

- There have been two phases in the development of the treaties: phase I lasted until 1986 and was mainly intergovernmental with little public input or interest (influenced by an atmosphere of permissive consensus), while phase II has been more open and affected by public debate.

- The process of treaty drafting has mainly taken place in intergovernmental conferences, the meetings of which have been subject to more public and political pressure since the early 1990s.

- The Treaty of Lisbon may be the last major amendment to the rules of the EU for some time to come, given that most of the rules needed to allow it to function efficiently are now in place, and that 'reform fatigue' has settled in. It has also been argued that a plateau has been reached and there is a 'constitutional settlement' that obviates the need for additional treaties.

- The major treaties are the foundations of the European legal order, but there have also been other agreements that have contributed to that order: these include accession agreements, agreements among subgroups of member states (such as Schengen and the Social Charter), the Charter of Fundamental Rights of the European Union, and the European Convention on Human Rights.

Key terms and concepts

Accession agreement

Charter of Fundamental Rights

Constitution

Constitutionalization

European Convention on Human Rights

Intergovernmental conferences

Opt-outs

Thin and thick constitutions

Three pillars

Treaty

Further reading

Christiansen, Thomas, and Christine Reh (2009) *Constitutionalizing the European Union* (Basingstoke: Palgrave Macmillan). Assessment of the story of constitution building in the EU, looking at the mechanics of IGCs, the actors involved and the issues at stake.

Greer, Steven (2006) *The European Convention on Human Rights: Achievements, Problems and Prospects* (Cambridge: Cambridge University Press). Compelling review of the achievements and possible long-term effects on European integration of the European Convention on Human Rights.

Piris, Jean-Claude (2006) *The Constitution for Europe: A Legal Analysis* (Cambridge: Cambridge University Press). Assessment of the background to, and potential legal, institutional and practical consequences of, the proposed European constitution.

9 The Member States

Debates about the nature of the relationship between the EU institutions and the member states have heated up as the reach and the membership of the EU have expanded, and as more Europeans have come to feel its influence. Within their home states, they know approximately what to expect from their home governments, that is, if they follow public affairs. But there is much less understanding about the political status of the member states within the EU. As we saw in Chapter 2, the EU has some qualities that are federal, others that are confederal, and yet others that fit none of the mainstream explanations of how power is shared, divided, or expressed. And even if we could agree on how to characterize the EU, it is, like all systems of government or governance, in a constant state of evolution.

This chapter looks at the relationship between the EU and its member states and their changing levels of authority over law and public policy. It examines clues regarding the division of policy authority, noting that there has been almost no field of policy on which European integration has not had some impact, whether direct or indirect, obvious or subtle, deliberate or accidental. But it also notes that the jury is still out on the relative balance of powers and authority in most fields of policy; the EU dominates the making of economic, agricultural and environmental policy, and the member states still have a high degree of control over tax policy, policing, education, and criminal justice, but in most areas of policy there is a wide overlap of powers. It ends with a review of the prospects for future enlargement of the EU, and how this will continue to change the relative roles of the EU and the member states.

- How can we measure the relative levels of policy independence of the member states?
- In which areas of policy does it most clearly make the most sense for EU member states to act together, and in which is it better to leave responsibility with individual states?
- Is Europeanization a useful conceptual term?
- What do the four measures used in this chapter – length of EU membership, economic size, population size, and attitudes towards integration – tell us about the relative powers and influence of different member states?
- Should the EU focus on widening or deepening?

Competence

A term used to indicate responsibility or authority in an area of public policy. Article 2 of the Treaty of Lisbon points out that exclusive competence in a policy area means that only the EU can legislate or adopt legally binding acts related to that area, and that the member states can only do this themselves if specifically empowered by the EU or in the interests of implementing an act of the EU. The EU has exclusive competence in only five policy areas – competition, customs, fisheries conservation, trade and – within the euro zone – monetary policy. Levels of competence in all other policy areas (except those where the member states have clearly retained their authority) are debatable.

The place of the member states

The member states of the EU have a peculiar position in international law. On the one hand, they are sovereign actors in the international system, with territory, sovereignty, independence and legitimacy. On the other hand, they have pooled or transferred authority to the extent that it is no longer accurate or practical to think of them as independent actors. They are still free to take unilateral action on many issues, and they still have separate votes in the European Council and the Council of the EU, but in multiple areas of law and policy they are subject to the common rules of the EU. At the same time, though (as we saw in Chapter 2), they have not yet built the kind of legal and political ties that make them members of a European superstate.

In many ways, the EU still reflects its modest origins in the European Coal and Steel Community: it consists of member states that were each accepted as partners in the club, and they are expected to adhere to its rules as long as they stay. Yet they are free to leave the club any time they wish. If citizens of a region within a state decided to leave and form their own state, their action would be regarded as secession and would likely spark legal battles, political resistance, and perhaps even violence of the kind that accompanied the break-up of Yugoslavia in the 1990s. (For a discussion of the implications of secession, see Buchanan, 1991.) But while a decision by a member state to leave the EU would be disappointing to some and welcomed by others, there would be no need for a legal declaration of independence (see Focus on prospects of the EU losing members below).

It is important to be clear about the meaning of the term 'member state'. Bulmer and Lequesne (2005, p. 2) argue that it should not just be thought of as a synonym for the national governments of the member states, but instead as shorthand for all the political actors and institutions within a member state. But the nature of the relationship between the member states and the EU institutions is complex and constantly evolving, varying from one policy area to another. A good starting point for understanding that relationship is to look at four principles contained in the treaties (specifically Article 5 of the Treaty of Lisbon):

1 Competence: This is another term for *authority*, and is used to describe the areas of policy for which the EU is responsible. Hence, it has a high level of competence in the fields of competition and trade, for example, but much less over education and taxation.

2 Conferral: This principle holds that the EU can act only where it has been given authority by the member states to achieve objectives set out in the treaties, and that any areas of competence not specifically listed in the treaties default to the member states. (It mirrors the 10th amendment to the US constitution, which declares that powers not delegated to the federal government by the constitution, nor prohibited by it to the states, are reserved to the states or to the people.)

3 Subsidiarity: By this principle, the EU can only act in areas outside its exclusive competence if the action needed cannot be better taken by the member states. In other words, the EU should only do what it does best.

4 Proportionality: This principle establishes that the EU should not go beyond taking the action needed to achieve the objectives of the treaties. But just where that line is drawn is, of course, a matter for debate.

Secession: The act of withdrawing from membership of an association, usually taken to mean some kind of political organization or union.

Subsidiarity: The principle that the EU should limit itself in policy terms to undertaking tasks better dealt with jointly than at the level of the member state.

Focus on... *Prospects of the EU losing members*

Rarely seriously discussed (but always a theoretical possibility) is the prospect of an EU member state leaving the EU. This has already happened in the case of a territory, when, in February 1985, Greenland became the first and so far only community to leave the EEC. As a colony of Denmark, it had become part of the EEC in January 1973, despite its 32,000 residents voting against membership out of concern over loss of control of fishing rights. It was granted self-government by Denmark in May 1979, clearing the way for a 1982 vote to leave the Community. But no member state of the EU has yet followed the same path. (There was more than passing discussion in 2010 about the possibility of states being expelled from the euro zone, but this is not allowed under the treaties.)

Article 50 of the Lisbon treaty says that 'any Member State may decide to withdraw from the Union in accordance with its own constitutional requirements', and that all it must do is notify the European Council, which would then direct the negotiations leading to an agreement 'setting out the arrangements for its withdrawal, taking account of the framework for its future relationship with the Union'. If the state later changed its mind and decided to apply for re-entry, it would have to go through the same steps as a new applicant (see later in this chapter). An interesting twist was added to the debate when questions were asked about whether Scotland would have been allowed to stay in the EU or would have had to reapply for membership, had it voted for independence in a September 2014 referendum.

Since the EU is not a state, withdrawal of a member would not have the same legal significance or implications as when, for example, Montenegro and Kosovo declared their independence from Serbia in 2006 and 2008. Nor would there be the same violent response as accompanied the secession of Katanga from the Congo in 1960, Biafra from Nigeria in 1967, or the formation of Eritrea and Timor Leste in 1993 and 2002. Nor would it have the same effect as secessionist movements in Canada, India, Russia, Spain and Sri Lanka, all of which have been vigorously resisted, sometimes with violence.

Several EU member states have political parties and movements that campaign for an exit from the EU. In few has the issue been more widely discussed than in Britain, which in 1975 became the first and so far only EEC/EU member state to put membership to a national referendum (see Chapter 16). But while polls reveal that enthusiasm for the EU is lower in Britain than in almost any other member state, they also reveal that the British know less about the EU than the citizens of almost any other EU member state (see Chapter 17). This raises questions about the quality of British public opinion, and makes it difficult to be sure how much the hostility held by many Britons towards the EU is based on a real understanding of the issues. The UK Independence Party was formed in 1993 to campaign for British withdrawal from the EU, but while it has done well in local and European elections, it has not fared well in British general elections.

The challenge of deciding how powers are divided in practice in the EU is heightened by the changing rules of the game: the role of the member states has declined as the competence of the EU institutions has grown, but their powers vary from one set of policies to another. At first, member states gave up only the powers agreed under the terms of the Treaty of Paris, but even in this limited area, there was the promise of change to come: the ECSC was allowed to ensure the rational use of coal resources (a precursor to environmental policy), to promote improved working conditions (a precursor to social policy), and to promote international trade in coal and steel (a precursor to trade and foreign policy). The EU institutions have since won competence over a broadening set of policy issues, or have accumulated more powers through the pressures of spill-

Illustration **9.1 Conserving North Sea fisheries**

Fisheries conservation is one of the few policy areas in which the EU has exclusive competence. Here, coastguards and fisheries inspectors prepare to control fishing vessels in the North Sea.

over, the authority of the member states declining along the way. But there has always been much ambiguity built into the system, the result being that authority in most areas is divided. Three sets of clues offer us some guidance.

First, we can look at the Treaty of Lisbon, but while Articles 3–6 of the Treaty on the Functioning of the EU provide what looks like a comprehensive listing of EU areas of competence (see Figure 9.1), the list is not always as clear as it seems. Missing, for example, are external relations and immigration, both areas in which the EU is active. Environmental policy may be listed as a shared responsibility, but in practice it is now almost entirely made at the EU level. And while human health is listed as a shared responsibility, healthcare is almost entirely a responsibility of the member states. Even in policy areas where competence is shared, it is not always clear how far it is shared; in some areas the EU has authority only to support or supplement the work of the member states.

A second set of clues is offered by policies that are prefaced with the word 'Common', such as the Common Agricultural Policy (CAP), the Common Commercial Policy (CCP), the Common Fisheries Policy, the Common Foreign and Security Policy and the Common Transport Policy. But this is not an entirely accurate indicator; while it would be hard to find a European farmer or national agricultural department whose work has not been affected by the CAP, and the CCP has allowed the European Commission to negotiate trade agreements on behalf of all the member states, the division of authority for the 'Common' Foreign and Security Policy is not quite so clear. The interests of former colonial powers such as Britain and France are still quite different from those of smaller states with few political or cultural interests outside Europe, or officially neutral states such as Austria and Ireland. Meanwhile, progress on the security front has been compromised by a difference of opinion about priorities and the lack of a combined European military that would allow words to be backed up by deeds (see Chapter 24).

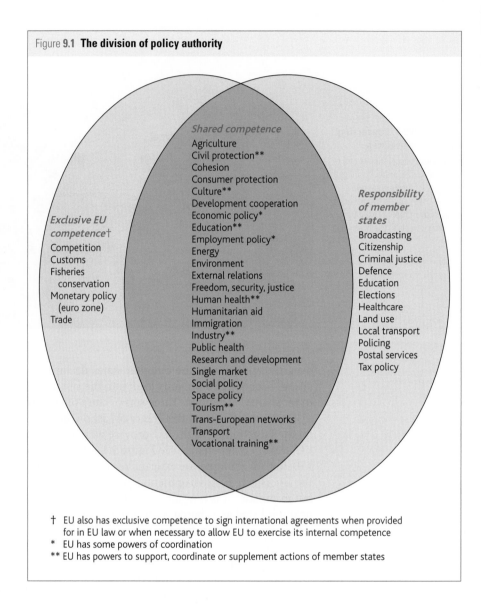

Figure **9.1 The division of policy authority**

Shared competence
Agriculture
Civil protection**
Cohesion
Consumer protection
Culture**
Development cooperation
Economic policy*
Education**
Employment policy*
Energy
Environment
External relations
Freedom, security, justice
Human health**
Humanitarian aid
Immigration
Industry**
Public health
Research and development
Single market
Social policy
Space policy
Tourism**
Trans-European networks
Transport
Vocational training**

Exclusive EU competence†
Competition
Customs
Fisheries
  conservation
Monetary policy
  (euro zone)
Trade

Responsibility of member states
Broadcasting
Citizenship
Criminal justice
Defence
Education
Elections
Healthcare
Land use
Local transport
Policing
Postal services
Tax policy

† EU also has exclusive competence to sign international agreements when provided
  for in EU law or when necessary to allow EU to exercise its internal competence
* EU has some powers of coordination
** EU has powers to support, coordinate or supplement actions of member states

A final set of clues to the division of policy authority can be found in the body of EU laws, the subjects of which provide insight into areas where the EU is most active and where the member states, by implication, have most thoroughly pooled authority. The data shown in Figure 9.2 reveal the dominance of economic law, and more specifically agriculture and fisheries, and external relations and foreign policy, which each accounted for 21 per cent of the nearly 22,000 pieces of legislation then in force. But again, this source cannot be taken too literally because the reach and significance of laws vary: some cover a large area of ground and have major policy effects, while others are more focused in policy and territorial terms. Some areas of policy also demand more technical and finely tuned pieces of law, hence the volume of laws adopted in a given area may be more an indication of the depth rather than the breadth of EU activity.

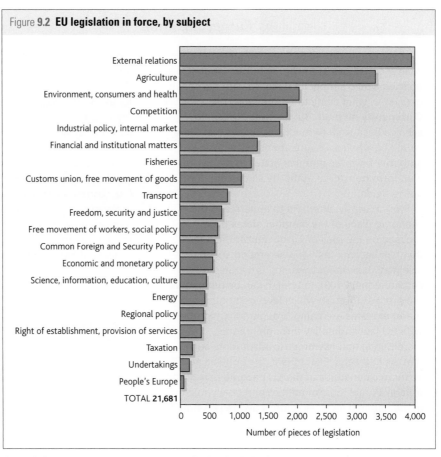

Figure **9.2** **EU legislation in force, by subject**

Number of pieces of legislation

Source: EUR-Lex website, http://eur-lex.europa.eu (retrieved July 2014).

Understanding the place of the member states in the EU is only partly a question of pinning down their powers relative to the EU institutions. It also demands an appreciation of the relative powers and influence of different member states, whose role within the EU is impacted by at least four key factors, as Laffan and Stubb (2003) suggested. First, there is the question of how long each state has been a member, although date of entry can only be taken so far as an analytical tool. While France and Germany played a critical role in the foundation and early formation of the EEC, their influence has been diminished by enlargement; where they once had 47 per cent of the votes on the Council of the EU, today they have only 17 per cent. Meanwhile, Italy, the other large founding member state of the EEC, has rarely lived up to its potential, handicapped by political and economic dysfunction, and now by declining population numbers. This said, though, the founding members of the ECSC/EEC were able to set many of the rules and principles of integration to their own liking, while newer members had to adapt to pre-existing arrangements on whose formation they had little influence.

The second telling factor in the determination of influence and power is economic wealth, in the sense not just that the biggest or wealthiest economies have had the most political influence, but also in the sense that the poorest econ-

Understanding Integration... *Europeanization*

In contemplating the EEC/member state dynamic, Jean Monnet was of the opinion that national policies would simply be replaced with European policies in what came to be known as the **Community method**. But this was difficult to achieve because it (wrongly) assumed that there would be wholesale agreement on switching authority from the member states to the EU, and a uniform transfer of authority across different policy fields.

More recently, attempts to understand the changing place of the member states have focused on the idea of **Europeanization**, a term that has become fashionable among social scientists but whose meaning is contested (see Featherstone, 2003). In brief, it can be defined as the process through which laws and policies in the member states are being brought into alignment with EU law and policy through gradual, incremental and asymmetric adaptation, such that, as Ladrech (1994) puts it, the political and economic dynamics of the EU become part of the organizational logic of politics and policy-making at the national level. Opinion is divided on how far

the process has gone, or even how useful it is as a means of understanding the EU policy process (Page, 2003; Graziano and Vink, 2007). Much of the focus in the debate in recent years has been on the effect of Europeanization on the new member states of eastern Europe (Schimmelfennig and Sedelmeier, 2005).

Bulmer and Lequesne (2005, p. 12) make a distinction between European integration (concerned with political and policy developments at the supranational level) and Europeanization (concerned with the consequences of integration for the member states). Olsen (2002) lists five aspects of Europeanization:

1 changes in the external boundaries of Europe
2 the development of European-level institutions
3 the adaptation of national and subnational systems of governance to European-wide norms
4 the export of distinctively European forms of political organization beyond the borders of Europe
5 the extent to which Europe is becoming a more unified and stronger political entity.

omies have been the target of so much political attention, and have occasionally acted as a drag on European growth. By economic size, the member states can be clustered fairly naturally into three groups: large, medium and small (see Table 9.1). The six founding EEC states were similarly placed in terms of per capita wealth, but enlargement to many often poorer countries has broadened the economic spread. Structural funds that were created to invest in the EU's poorer regions have taken up a growing share of the EU budget, with wealthier states taking on the burden of helping poorer states. The fallout from the 2007–10 global financial crisis and the euro zone crisis further illustrated which countries had economic power (Germany was prime among them) and which did not, such as Greece, Portugal and Ireland.

The third power factor has been population size: the bigger states have more votes in the Council of the EU, more members in the European Parliament, louder voices in the European Council, and more prospects of taking policy initiatives and providing leadership on EU issues. By size, the member states can be clustered fairly naturally into four groups: large, medium, small and micro (see Table 9.2). Population numbers have repeatedly been a factor in debates over voting systems and appointments to key EU offices, with smaller member states worried that they will be outvoted or outsmarted by larger ones. As a result, the large states have not always been able to have their way on policy, and the voting system in the EU has been set up such that – per capita – the smaller states have

Community method: The process by which it was thought that public policies in the member states would gradually be replaced with European policies.

Europeanization: The process by which public policies in the member states are brought into alignment with one other.

more influence: while Germany, for example, has one vote in the Council of the EU per 2.8 million people, Malta has one vote per 140,000 people. Similarly, while each German Member of the European Parliament (MEP) represents 840,000 people, each Maltese MEP represents 70,000 people.

The final determinant of the influence of member states on the EU has been their contrasting attitudes towards the process of integration, much less easy to quantify than economic or population size. The drivers of integration have been those states whose governments and/or publics have been most enthused about integration; although, given its small size, there is only so far that Luxembourg, among the most enthusiastic of EU states, can lead the way. The initial impetus for integration came mainly from Germany and France; even if, in the case of

Table **9.1 EU member states by economy**

Large ($1–4 trillion)	
Germany	$3.6
France	$2.7
UK	$2.5
Italy	$2.0
Spain	$1.4

Medium ($100–900 billion)	
Netherlands	$800
Sweden	$558
Poland	$517
Belgium	$508
Austria	$416
Denmark	$331
Finland	$257
Greece	$242
Portugal	$220
Ireland	$218
Czech Republic	$198
Romania	$190
Hungary	$125

Small (less than $100 billion)	
Slovakia	$91
Luxembourg	$60
Croatia	$58
Bulgaria	$53
Slovenia	$45
Lithuania	$42
Latvia	$28
Estonia	$24
Cyprus	$23
Malta	$9

Note: Figures refer to gross domestic product.

Source: World Bank data for 2013, http://web.worldbank.org (retrieved July 2014).

Table **9.2 EU member states by population**

Large (35–85 million)	
Germany	80.6
France	66.0
UK	64.1
Italy	59.8
Spain	46.6
Poland	38.5

Medium (7–20 million)	
Romania	20.0
Netherlands	16.8
Belgium	11.2
Greece	11.0
Portugal	10.5
Czech Republic	10.5
Hungary	9.9
Sweden	9.6
Austria	8.5
Bulgaria	7.3

Small (1–6 million)	
Denmark	5.6
Slovakia	5.4
Finland	5.4
Ireland	4.6
Croatia	4.3
Lithuania	3.0
Latvia	2.0
Slovenia	2.0
Estonia	1.3

Micro (less than 1 million)	
Cyprus	1.1
Luxembourg	0.5
Malta	0.4

Source: World Bank data for 2013, http://web.worldbank.org (retrieved July 2014).

de Gaulle, that impetus was based on suspicion rather than support. Britain has since earned a reputation as something of a brake on integration, changing its direction and its priorities in several key ways, and yet it has also been a champion of the single market, trade liberalization and a common security policy. The possibility even of small states occasionally being the tails that wag the dog was shown by the negative votes in Denmark and Ireland on the Maastricht treaty, the Treaty of Nice, and the Treaty of Lisbon, and the negative vote on the constitutional treaty in the Netherlands in 2005.

But to characterize some states as consistently pro-European and others as consistently anti-European is to ignore many of the nuances in the debate about Europe. A pro-European state is not necessarily one that agrees to every initiative, but rather one that works to promote the initiatives it defines as being in the best interests of effective and efficient integration. Equally, resistance is not an indication of being anti-European, but rather, perhaps, of caution and care. Also, opinions on Europe vary within member states by social class, age, education, wealth, strength of national identity, time and even the policy under consideration. France, for example, has always been more interested in agricultural policy than Germany, poorer EU states are more interested in regional policy than richer states, wealthier states have been more willing to tighten environmental regulations than poorer states, and states with global interests have a clearer stake in how EU foreign policy evolves. Finally, we have to make a distinction between public and political opinion; governments and voters will not always agree on policy towards Europe.

Prospects for future enlargement

Enlargement has been one of the most telling influences on how the EU has evolved and how the role of its member states has changed. If we agree that there are 44 sovereign states in Europe today (see discussion in Chapter 3), and given that 28 are currently members of the EU, then there are 16 potential future additional members, containing a total population of just over 182 million. (Table 9.3 below provides a summary.) Their membership prospects vary not just in terms of meeting the formal negotiated terms of entry but also in terms of passing an array of political and economic tests. Not least among these are the levels of political support for membership in aspirant states and within existing states.

In the early years of integration, there were few formal rules on membership; the Treaty of Rome noted that 'any European state' could apply for membership (the term 'European' was never defined), the only conditions being agreement on the terms of membership and the approval of all existing members. But as the EC grew and its rules became more detailed, so the process of applying for membership became more formalized and complex. Articles 2 and 49 of the Maastricht treaty noted that any European state that respected the values of 'human dignity, freedom, democracy, equality, the rule of law ... [and] human rights' could apply to join. More detailed guidance was provided by the Copenhagen conditions, agreed at the Copenhagen European Council in 1993 and expanded at the Madrid European Council in 1995:

Copenhagen conditions: The requirements for membership of the EU, including democracy, capitalism and a willingness and ability to adopt all existing EU laws.

- ◼ Democracy: States must meet the Maastricht terms on freedom, democracy, human rights and the rule of law.

- Capitalism: States must have viable free-market economies and the ability to respond to market forces within the EU.
- The *acquis*: States must be willing and able to assume the obligations of the existing body of EU laws and policies (the *acquis communautaire*).
- Administration: States must have adapted their administrative structures in order to create the necessary conditions for integration.

But nothing is that simple, and the various formulae provide no hints of the troubling political, economic and social questions that have arisen with every round of enlargement to date, and are likely to continue so to do in future. At the core of the problem is the debate about widening vs. deepening, or the respective views of those who argue that continued enlargement is in the best interests of everyone, and those who argue that deeper and better integration among existing members should be the priority.

Membership applications are submitted to the European Council, which then consults with the Commission and must have the consent of Parliament before making a decision, which must be unanimous. A country can be declared a potential candidate by being promised the possibility of join the EU when it is ready. If an application is approved, the state is considered a candidate country, and negotiations open (not necessarily immediately) on the terms of membership and the changes needed in the applicant state to clear the way. Each set of negotiations is tailored to the needs and qualities of the applicant state, and is designed to pin down the adjustments needed by that state to qualify for membership. Discussions are divided into chapters dealing with different aspects of EU policy, within which benchmarks (or targets) are set by the Council. The process begins with an assessment by the Commission on where the applicant stands in relation to each chapter, and negotiations end on a given chapter when the Council and Parliament (on the recommendation of the Commission) agree that the applicant has met the benchmarks. In the case of serious and persistent disagreements, negotiations on individual chapters can be suspended and conditions set for their reopening.

A series of options and steps are made available to help with the transition to membership, including pre-accession strategies to identify the changes needed to smooth the transition, bilateral agreements between the EU and the applicant states, participation in EU programmes that allows applicant states to learn more at first hand about how the EU works, and Commission monitoring aimed at outlining the progress (or lack thereof) made by applicants in meeting the terms of membership. Pre-accession aid is also usually made available to help applicants strengthen institutions, improve infrastructure, and improve cross-border cooperation.

Once all the benchmarks have been met – a process that can take several years – an Act of Accession is drawn up and signed, which includes the date of entry of the new state into the EU, the changes needed to the EU institutions to accommodate the new member, and a summary of the agreements reached and the conditions set. Assuming that the Act of Accession is ratified by the applicant state (which may or may not decide to hold a national referendum) and all existing member states, the new member joins the EU on the agreed date. But behind this rather bland formula lies a cornucopia of political, economic and social considerations that leave the non-EU states at varying levels of readiness for membership:

Widening vs. deepening: The competing arguments about whether the EU should continue to expand its membership, or focus on improving the efficiency of the existing club.

Candidate country: A non-member state of the EU whose application to join has been accepted and with which negotiations on the terms of entry are either planned, under way, or have been completed.

Benchmarks: Measurable targets set by the Commission in order to provide a focus for applicant states as they work to meet the terms of entry into the EU.

- **Albania** became a candidate country in 2014. It has been receiving EU development funding since the early 1990s, but is handicapped by corruption and the influence of organized crime. It was part of the Stabilization and Association Process (SAP) adopted by the EU in 2003 and aimed at building a free trade area and preparing several states for the adoption of EU standards, and it signed a Stabilization and Accession Agreement (SAA) with the EU, which entered into force in April 2009, the same month Albania applied for EU membership.
- **Armenia** is economically troubled (more than a quarter of its population has left the country since independence in 1991), and is heavily reliant on Russia from which it imports almost all its natural gas. Armenia also has an unresolved dispute with Turkey over the killing by Ottoman Turks of hundreds of thousands of Armenians during the First World War; Armenia defines this as genocide but Turkey defines it as a result of war.
- **Azerbaijan** has the benefit of large oil and natural gas reserves, but has a poor political record, with accusations of vote rigging and voter intimidation during the 2003 elections that saw Ilham Aliyev succeed his father Heydar as president. Doubts about the country's commitment to democracy undermine its prospects for closer ties with the EU.
- **Belarus** has major political difficulties. Belarusians are regarded ethnically as Europeans, and make up more than 80 per cent of the population of the country, but the dictatorship of Alexander Lukashenko has controlled Belarus since 1994 (it remains the only European state that has been denied entry to the Council of Europe), and a confederal union between Russia and Belarus has been under discussion since the late 1990s. Bilateral relations have not always been smooth, however, with particular tensions over Russian energy imports.
- **Bosnia and Herzegovina** is a potential candidate, and has had an SAA with the EU since 2007. It has also been influenced by the EU Police Mission set up in 2003 and by the replacement in 2004 of the NATO peacekeeping mission 'Stabilisation Force' with the EU's mission 'European Union Force'. There has been work on visa liberalization with the EU, and the EU accounts for about two-thirds of Bosnia's trade and about half its foreign direct investment. But corruption, organized crime and internal ethnic tensions remain barriers to EU membership, as does a division of public opinion about joining the EU.
- **Georgia** aspires to join the EU but faces many difficulties. After 11 years of corruption and poverty, the Rose Revolution of 2004 saw the replacement of President Eduard Shevardnadze by Mikheil Saakashvili, but relations with Russia, on which Georgia relies for natural gas, have been tense, reaching a new low in 2008 with fighting sparked by the separatist aspirations of Abkhazia and South Ossetia, which led to a military intervention by Russia.
- **Iceland** became a candidate country in June 2010. It became part of EFTA in 1970, joined the European Economic Area (EEA) in 1994, and signed the Schengen Agreement in 2000, but kept EU membership at arm's length out of concerns for Icelandic fisheries. Then came the 2007–10 global financial crisis, the near collapse of the Icelandic banking system, and the devaluation of its currency, helping spark an application for EU membership in July 2009. It was given candidate status, but brewing disputes over fishing rights and financial reform led the new centre-right government to place a hold on accession negotiations in May 2013. Iceland is a democratic free-market

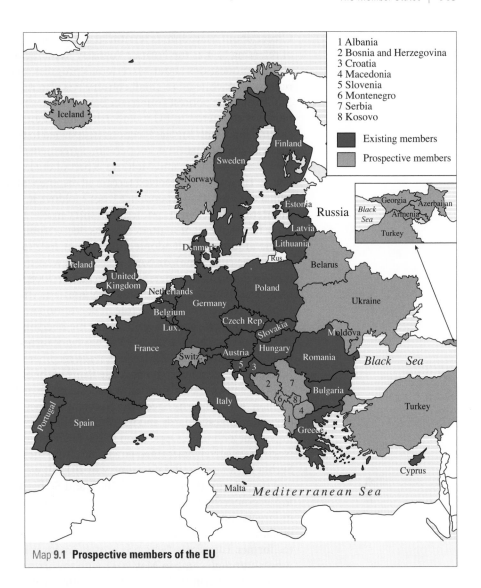

Map **9.1 Prospective members of the EU**

system, has already adopted many EU laws and policies as a result of being in the EEA, and has a small and wealthy population.

■ **Kosovo** is a potential candidate, but its prospects are complicated by its contested legal status. Once part of Serbia, it declared independence in February 2008 and has unofficially adopted the euro, but while nearly 65 UN members have recognized its independence, several EU states (Cyprus, Greece, Romania, Slovakia and Spain) have not. EULEX, the EU police and legal mission to Kosovo, has pointed out problems with corruption, organized crime and the smuggling of drugs, humans and weapons.

■ **Macedonia** became a candidate country in 2005. It was the first Balkan country to sign an SAA with the EU (in April 2001), applied for EU membership in March 2004, and quickly became a candidate, but as of late 2014 negotiations had not yet begun. There is an unresolved dispute over its name, which it shares with a northern Greek province (raising concerns in

Greece about Macedonia's territorial aspirations), leading to the compromise of referring to it as the Former Yugoslav Republic of Macedonia. There have also been questions about Macedonia's progress on democratic and economic reform, and while it is a small country it is also relatively poor.

- **Moldova** is the poorest country in Europe, and while its political leaders have hinted at an interest in EU membership, the country has strong historical and cultural links with Russia. Elections in 2009 led to the communists losing their majority for the first time, cooperation agreements have been signed between the EU and Moldova, and Moldova is part of the European Neighbourhood Policy. There is an unresolved territorial dispute with the region of Transnistria, which declared its independence from Moldova in 1990.

- **Montenegro** became a candidate country in 2010. It has only been a distinct actor in enlargement matters since its declaration of independence from Serbia in June 2006. It adopted the euro in 2002 (although it is not formally part of the euro zone), an SAA was signed with the EU in October 2007, and it applied for EU membership in December 2008. But unresolved questions hang over its transition to democracy, and – as with other Balkan countries – there are concerns about the role of corruption and organized crime.

- **Norway** has twice applied for EEC/EU membership (in 1970 and again in 1992), has twice been accepted, and has twice turned down membership in national referendums. Like Iceland, it is a member of EFTA, the EEA and the Schengen Agreement, so it has made many of the adjustments needed to be an EU member, the only remaining substantial barrier being domestic public opinion. Past concerns have focused on the impact of membership on Norway's environmental standards and its fishing industry, but these have become less important with time. Opposition to EU membership was strengthened by Norway's relatively unscathed emergence from the global financial crisis.

- **Serbia** became a candidate country in 2012. It was part of the SAP, an SAA was signed with the EU in April 2008, and Serbia applied for EU membership in December 2009. The EU has become its major trading partner and its largest source of foreign direct investment, but unresolved questions remain over Serbia's position on the International Criminal Tribunal for the former Yugoslavia (which is prosecuting war crimes from the 1990s). A breakthrough came in May 2011 with the arrest of Europe's most wanted suspected war criminal, Ratko Mladic, after 16 years on the run. But concerns remain about corruption, organized crime, bureaucratic reform, media freedom, and the rights of minorities such as the Roma.

- **Switzerland** signed an EEA membership agreement in May 1992 and also applied to join the EEC, but when EEA membership was turned down in a national referendum in December 1992, the EEC membership application was placed on hold. EU membership was finally turned down in another referendum in 2001, but in 2008 Switzerland became part of the Schengen area. This 'on-again, off-again' approach to the EU reflects Switzerland's concerns about protecting its neutrality and sovereignty. A February 2014 Swiss referendum that supported restrictions on immigration raised difficult questions about the future of the country's relations with the EU.

- **Turkey** is the troubled outlier on the future enlargement agenda, being both the non-member with the longest history of aspirations to join the EU, and also the one that has faced the strongest political resistance. Turkey applied for associate membership of the EEC in 1959, and then for full EEC membership in April 1987. It was given candidate status in December 1999, but negotiations (which opened only in 2005) have been rocky; the EU has refused to open several chapters until there is a resolution of the dispute over Cyprus, which is split between a Turkish north and a Greek south. Trade between Turkey and the EU has grown, Turkey has made numerous changes to domestic law and policy to meet EU requirements (including the abolition in 2004 of the death penalty), but still has only a mixed record on democracy and human rights. Turkish membership would mean critical new EU influence in the Middle East, but Turkey is large (nearly 75 million people), poor (economic integration would pose considerable challenges) and Islamic (raising numerous troubling religious and cultural issues). Public support in Turkey for EU membership has been declining.

- **Ukraine** was initially faced with the challenge of building on the democratic changes that came in the wake of its 2004 Orange Revolution (sparked by an outcry over rigged elections), while maintaining a balancing act in keeping on good terms with Russia and the EU. There was talk of instituting pre-accession arrangements and setting up a free trade agreement, and major Ukrainian political parties made public their support for EU membership, but public opinion in Ukraine was mixed. Then came developments in 2013–14. When President Viktor Yanukovych decided to pull out of an agreement for closer trade ties with the EU, street protests broke out that resulted in his downfall in February 2014. The appointment of an interim government sparked a takeover of Crimea by Russia, and economic sanctions against the Putin administration. Ukraine continues to find itself split between those wanting closer ties with the EU, and those wanting closer ties with Russia.

Table **9.3 Prospective members of the EU, 2014**

Country	Population (millions)	Per capita gross national income	Status
Turkey	74.9	10,950	Candidate (Dec 1999)
Macedonia	2.1	4,800	Candidate (Dec 2005)
Iceland	0.3	43,930	Candidate (June 2010)
Montenegro	0.6	7,260	Candidate (Dec 2010)
Serbia	7.2	5,730	Candidate (March 2012)
Albania	2.8	4,700	Candidate (June 2014)
Bosnia & Herzegovina	3.8	4,740	Potential candidate
Kosovo	1.8	3,890	Potential candidate
Armenia	3.0	3,790	Long shot
Azerbaijan	9.4	7,350	Long shot
Belarus	9.5	6,720	Poor prospects
Georgia	4.5	3,570	Mixed prospects
Moldova	3.6	2,460	Mixed prospects
Norway	5.0	102,610	Improving potential
Switzerland	8.1	80,950	Mixed prospects
Ukraine	45.5	3,960	Mixed prospects

Source: Population and economic data: World Bank data for 2013, http://web.worldbank.org (retrieved July 2014).

Illustration **9.3**
Turkey and the EU
Few membership applications have been more troubling than the one involving Turkey. The difficulties are reflected in the expressions on the faces of (*left to right*) enlargement commissioner Olli Rehn, Commission President José Manuel Barroso and Marc Pierini, head of the Commission delegation to Turkey, during an April 2008 press conference in Ankara.

Just as past rounds of enlargement have changed the personality and reach of integration, and even the meaning of 'Europe', so will future rounds. Enlargement has long been one of the most effective means for the spread of democratic and capitalist ideas (see Chapter 24), and if history is any indication, then the promise of enlargement will likely continue to encourage change in the former Soviet republics, and ultimately change the personality of the EU and its relations with Russia. But the question of the EU's absorption capacity remains unanswered: How far can the EU expand while also remaining manageable, efficient and true to its core goals?

Summary

- The place of the member states of the EU in international law is unusual, because while they are sovereign states, they have also pooled unprecedented amounts of authority within the EU.

- Guidance on the relative powers of the member states and the EU institutions can be found in the treaties, common policies and the body of EU law, but in all three cases there are ambiguities.

- The dynamic of member state/EU relations was once explained by the Community method, but Europeanization has become more popular as an analytical tool, even if there is no agreement on what it means or its lasting value.

- Understanding the relative powers and influence of the EU member states is partly a function of how long they have been members, the size and wealth of their national economies, their population size, and their attitudes towards the process of integration.

- Where once the process of applying to join the EU was relatively simple, it has become more demanding and complex as the reach and effect of integration has expanded.

- The Copenhagen conditions require that an aspirant member state should be democratic, a free-market economy, and willing to adopt the existing body of EU laws and policies and adapt its administrative structures to fit with the needs of integration.

- Applicant countries in late 2014 included Albania, Iceland, Macedonia, Montenegro, Serbia and Turkey. Countries that face the most challenging barriers to EU membership include Armenia, Azerbaijan, Belarus, Georgia, Moldova and Ukraine.

Key terms and concepts

Benchmarks

Candidate country

Community method

Competence

Copenhagen conditions

Europeanization

Secession

Subsidiarity

Widening vs. deepening

Further reading

Bulmer, Simon, and Christian Lequesne (eds) (2005) *The Member States of the European Union* (Oxford: Oxford University Press). Zeff, Eleanor, and Ellen Pirro (eds) (2015) *The European Union and the Member States*, 3rd edn (Boulder, CO: Lynne Rienner). Two edited collections looking at relations between the EU and the member states, with a survey of analytical approaches, chapters on key states, and a discussion of the effects of Europeanization.

Featherstone, Kevin, and Claudio M. Radaelli (eds) (2003) *The Politics of Europeanization* (Oxford: Oxford University Press). Edited collection dealing with the many facets of the debate over Europeanization.

Nugent, Neill (2004) *European Union Enlargement* (Basingstoke: Palgrave Macmillan). Edited collection of studies of the mechanics and implications of enlargement.

2 POLITICS AND GOVERNANCE

Part 2 focuses on the major institutions of the European Union, and the manner in which Europeans relate to them and make their views known about the directions being taken by integration. Chapters 10–13 deal with the key institutions: the European Commission, the Council of Ministers, the European Council, the European Parliament, and the European Court of Justice. Chapter 14 looks at the more specialized agencies (some of them part of the EU, some of them not) that participate in decision-making at the EU level. Following a brief review of the evolution of these institutions, each of the chapters explains how they are structured, then looks at what the work of the institutions.

Chapters 15–17 look at the different ways in which the views of Europeans impact the process of integration. Political parties and interest groups play an important role, even if many still function at a national rather than a European level. Elections to the European Parliament are held every five years, although turnout has been declining. Meanwhile, national referendums on EU issues have occasionally changed the debate about the EU in a dramatic fashion. Finally, public opinion on the EU has been the subject of renewed interest, the results of polls finding that there has been reduced support for the EU, but also finding that there has been reduced support for government in general, and that many Europeans do not understand how the EU works.

10 The European Commission

Preview

The European Commission is the most prominent of the major EU institutions: it is the one most often in the news and most often blamed by critics for the excesses of 'Brussels'. Yet, despite its visibility, the Commission is both less and more than it seems. It is often portrayed as powerful, secretive, expensive and undemocratic, but in fact it has few independent decision-making powers, is one of the most open of all large bureaucracies found anywhere in the world, and has an institutional budget smaller than that of an average mid-sized European city. As for charges that it is undemocratic, it is not much different from national bureaucracies, few of whose staff members are held directly accountable to voters.

Headquartered in Brussels, the Commission is both the bureaucratic arm of the EU, responsible for proposing new laws and policies, and its executive, responsible for overseeing their implementation through the member states. It is headed by a president and a 28-member College of Commissioners that functions something like a European cabinet; beneath them work several thousand career European bureaucrats responsible for the day-to-day work of the Commission, divided up among directorates-general (DGs) that are the functional equivalent of national government departments.

The Commission is one of the most supranational of the major EU institutions, and has long been at the heart of European integration, charged with making sure that EU policies are given substance according to the goals and principles outlined in the treaties. Commissioners and staff members may be citizens of individual states, but they are discouraged from pursuing the interests of those states, and work to promote a policy agenda that focuses on the interests of the EU as a whole.

Key issues

- What are the similarities and differences between the European Commission and a typical national bureaucracy?
- Should Parliament have the right to confirm individual nominees to the College of Commissioners, rather than the College as a whole?
- Should the president of the Commission be directly elected by EU voters?
- The Commission has been described as the barometer of integration. What is the evidence for this?
- Should the Commission's legislative powers be transferred to Parliament?

How the Commission evolved

The origins of today's European Commission lie in the nine-member High Authority of the ECSC, which was based in Luxembourg, began work in August 1952, and was charged with encouraging the opening of the western European market in coal and steel. Jean Monnet's original hope was that the High Authority would be powerful and independent, but concerns among the Benelux governments that it would be dominated by West Germany and France led to the decision to create a Special Council of Ministers through which member state governments could offset and balance the work of the High Authority (Nugent, 2001, p. 20).

The ECSC High Authority was joined in 1958 by separate commissions for the EEC and Euratom, each headquartered in Brussels and led by nine-member Colleges of Commissioners appointed by national governments for four-year terms. Under the changes made by the 1965 Merger treaty, the three commissions were combined in 1967 into a new Commission of the European Communities, which soon became more commonly known as the 'European Commission'. As membership of the Community expanded in the 1970s and 80s, the number of commissioners grew, with two more added for each of the bigger member states and one each for the smaller states. Under the terms of the Treaty of Nice, each member state was given just one commissioner, leaving today's College with 28 members.

The Commission has always been a champion of the supranational qualities of the EEC/EU, its powers waxing and waning with changes in the political environment. As we saw in Chapter 5, early attempts to build its powers sparked the 1965 empty chair crisis, from which it emerged bloodied and weakened. It continued to lose powers with the creation in 1974 of the European Council, and with the introduction in 1979 of direct elections to the European Parliament (EP). After enjoying a newly assertive phase under President Jacques Delors during the late 1980s and early 1990s, the Commission saw its powers declining once again relative to those of the Council of Ministers and the EP. At the same time, though, it also saw its visibility increasing.

Under the failed constitutional treaty, there was a plan to stop the growth in the number of commissioners, which was becoming unsustainable: with a 28-member College it was becoming harder to give everyone meaningful tasks. Under Lisbon, the number of commissioners from November 2014 would have been capped at two-thirds of the number of member states (or 18 commissioners in a 28-member EU), but this was not a popular idea with smaller EU states, and one of the concessions made to Ireland as it sought guarantees in the lead-up to its second referendum on Lisbon in October 2009 was a reinstatement of the rule of one commissioner per member state.

How the Commission is structured

The European Commission is headquartered in Brussels, in the European Quarter that lies east of the city centre. It was not given a permanent home until the building in 1963–67 – on the site of a vacated 300-year old convent run by the Dames de Berlaymont – of a new shared seat for the Commission,

Illustration **10.1**
The European Commission
The Berlaymont building in Brussels, seat of the European Commission and the heart of the European Quarter in Brussels.

the Council of Ministers and the EP. The star-shaped floor plan of the new Berlaymont building provided an architecturally distinctive personality, passed on to the Commission when it eventually took over the entire building. In 1990 asbestos was found in the Berlaymont, so it was emptied and renovated at an estimated cost of more than €800 million. Following the overhaul, senior staff and some of the directorates-general moved back into the building in 2004, but the size of today's Commission makes it impossible to house them all there, so most of its staff have been dispersed to more than 60 buildings scattered around Brussels. In 2009 a master plan was announced aimed at addressing this problem and giving the European Quarter a facelift.

The Commission has five main components: the College of Commissioners, the president of the Commission, the directorates-general and services, a network of advisory and executive committees, and the Secretariat-General (see Figure 10.1).

The College of Commissioners

Confusingly, the term 'the Commission' refers to the entire European Commission with its 24,000 staff, and the College of 28 commissioners who head the institution. The College of Commissioners is the public face of the Commission, its more influential or active members (particularly the commissioners for trade or competition) being among the few leaders of the EU institutions likely to make much of an impression on the European public. Functioning much like a cabinet of ministers in national government, the College consists of commissioners responsible for each of the policy areas in which the EU is active, appointed for renewable five-year terms beginning six months after elections to the EP. Commissioners are chosen by the president from lists submitted by the governments of the member states, and a final draft list is submitted to the European Council, which must approve it by a qualified majority vote.

College of Commissioners: The group of 28 commissioners who head the European Commission. They are appointed for five-year renewable terms, one from each of the member states, and each is given responsibility over a particular area of policy.

Figure **10.1** **Structure of the European Commission**

- The bureaucratic-executive arm of the EU

- Headquartered in Brussels

- Headed by a president nominated by the European Council and approved by the European Parliament for renewable five-year terms

- Managed by a 28-member College of Commissioners, with one commissioner nominated by each member state, approved by the European Council and the European Parliament, and each given responsibility over a particular policy area

- Divided into directorates-general and services responsible for a combination of internal and external policy areas or administrative functions

- Work supported by a Secretariat-General

- Supranational and confederal in character

All nominees must attend confirmation hearings before the relevant committees of the EP, which cannot accept or reject them individually, but can only accept or reject the College as a whole. Reservations about an individual nominee can be enough to force a withdrawal (see Nugent, 2001, pp. 82–7; Spence, 2006a, pp. 34–8), as happened in 2004 when the Italian government nominated Rocco Buttiglione for consideration as justice commissioner. In hearings before the EP, Buttiglione defended comments he had made about homosexuality being a 'sin' and the family existing 'in order to allow women to have children and to have the protection of a male who takes care of them'. When it became clear that Parliament would not approve the College with Buttiglione as a member, he was replaced by Franco Frattini. Another rejection came in 2010 when nominee Rumiana Jeleva (the incumbent Bulgarian foreign minister) withdrew her nomination after facing tough questioning about her financial declaration and her ability to be the new commissioner for humanitarian aid. She was replaced by Kristalina Georgieva.

Parliament can also remove the College through a motion of censure, although this has never happened. It came closest in January 1999, when – after charges of fraud, nepotism and cronyism in the Commission – Parliament tried to dismiss the College. It could not muster the necessary two-thirds majority, but the College dramatically resigned within hours of the publication on 16 March of a report by a committee appointed to investigate the allegations (see Georgakakis, 2004). Individual commissioners can also be asked to resign from office by the president, or can be compulsorily retired by the European Court of Justice in cases of failure to do their job or engaging in serious misconduct. Commissioners can also retire from office, as several have, often to re-enter national politics or run for the European Parliament.

Despite being nominated by the governments of the member states, commissioners are expected to promote the interests of the EU and must swear an oath of office before the European Court of Justice agreeing 'neither to seek nor to take instructions from any Government or body'. Their independence is helped by the fact that they cannot be removed in mid-term by their home governments,

Illustration **10.2** **The College of Commissioners**

The incoming College of Commissioners poses for a family photo in October 2014. Much was expected of this group as they were presented with an agenda topped by numerous economic and social problems.

although they can be recalled at the end of their terms if there is a change of political leadership at home or a disagreement with their national leaders; hence commissioners hoping to stay in the job will always be keeping a close eye on political opinion at home.

Most commissioners have political reputations in their home states (see MacMullen, 2000), and the pool of potential candidates has grown in quality as the visibility and reach of the EU has grown, as the Commission has become a more significant force in European politics, and as nominations to the College have become more desirable (Nugent, 2001, pp. 88–91). Top-level national government experience is now all but required, and the College usually counts among its number former prime ministers, foreign ministers, finance ministers, labour and trade ministers, and former Members of the European Parliament (MEPs). Although national party affiliation is often a factor in deciding nominations, and party balance has become more of a factor in speculation about the work of the College, most of that work tends to be non-political; the College's policy debates are more technical and administrative in nature than ideological.

At the beginning of each term, all commissioners are assigned policy portfolios, which are distributed at the prerogative of the president (see Table 10.1). Assignments will be influenced by the abilities, political skills and experience of individual commissioners, as well as lobbying by national leaders keen to see 'their' commissioner win a strong portfolio or one of particular interest to their country. Turnover is high and reassignments common at the end of a term; it is rare that a commissioner will return for a second term, let alone to the same portfolio. In 2014 there were only five returning commissioners and all were assigned to new portfolios.

Table **10.1** **Portfolios in the College of Commissioners**

Agriculture and Rural Development
Budget
Climate Action
Competition
Development
Digital Agenda
Economic and Monetary Affairs
Education, Culture, Multilingualism and Youth
Employment, Social Affairs and Inclusion
Energy
Enlargement
Environment
Health and Consumer Policy
High Representative of the Union for Foreign Affairs and Security Policy
Home Affairs
Industry and Entrepreneurship
Inter-Institutional Relations and Administration
Internal Market and Services
International Cooperation, Humanitarian Aid and Crisis Response
Justice, Fundamental Rights and Citizenship
Maritime Affairs and Fisheries
President
Regional Policy
Research and Innovation
Taxation and Customs Union
Trade
Transport

Details on current holders of these portfolios can be found at http://ec.europa.eu/index_en.htm.

Just as in national cabinets, there is an internal hierarchy of portfolios, the most powerful including those dealing with the budget, agriculture, trade and the single market. A new twist was added by Lisbon, which replaced the external relations commissioner with a redesigned High Representative of the Union for Foreign Affairs and Security Policy. The post was created as the latest of a series of steps taken to place responsibility for external relations in one office (there had once been four commissioners dealing with separate parts of the world). The High Representative is appointed by the European Council, with the agreement of the president of the Commission, and not only chairs the Foreign Affairs Council of the Council of Ministers, but is also a vice-president in the Commission, so straddling both institutions (see Chapter 24).

Although there are similarities between the College of Commissioners and national cabinets when it comes to the management of portfolios, the comparison can only be taken so far; commissioners do not have the same kind of political responsibilities as national ministers, nor the same control over administrative departments, nor the same responsibility to the public. (In terms of running the departments and services of the Commission, directors-general are actually more like national government ministers than are commissioners.) And while

Understanding Integration... *New institutionalism*

One of the effects of the new emphasis on studying the EU as a political system in its own right has been to revive and elevate the importance of the study of institutions such as the European Commission. Political science was once focused almost entirely on the study of institutions, so much so that it came to be criticized for looking at the formal rules of government at the expense of politics in its many different forms. Conversely, most early theories of integration were too focused on relations among states to pay much attention to systems, and it was only with efforts in the 1990s to look at the EU as a political system that there was a renewed focus on institutions. New institutionalism looks not just at the formal rules but also how institutions shape political decisions, and the informal patterns of behaviour that have arisen with the formal institutions.

New institutionalism is a middle-range theory that does not attempt to explain everything that happens in the EU, instead making the argument that institutions are critical, deserve particularly

focused study, and have much greater impact on the day-to-day story of integration than the broader bargains negotiated by states. It is not so much a single theory as a group of three theoretical approaches:

1 *Historical institutionalism* looks at the long-term implications of past decisions and how member states created institutions that resulted in a pattern of path dependency (new decisions being driven and limited by past decisions) and unintended consequences (outcomes that were not anticipated).

2 *Rational choice institutionalism* focuses on trying to understand how and why states as self-interested actors delegate responsibilities to institutions, the assumption being that they work rationally and strategically to reduce transaction costs and maximize benefits.

3 *Sociological institutionalism* focuses on the norms, values and culture of institutions and the ways in which these help shape policy.

national cabinet ministers usually owe their positions to the national leader of the day, commissioners do not owe their chairs in the College to the president of the Commission.

Each commissioner is supported by a staff of assistants and advisers known as a *cabinet* (pronounced *cabiney*), headed by a *chef de cabinet*. Most members of *cabinets* once came from the same member state and the same national political party as their commissioners, but changes to the rules in 1999 required that *cabinets* should be more nationally diverse. The quality of the *cabinet* staff can have a close bearing on the performance of a commissioner, and the *cabinets* collectively have become a key influence on the operations of the Commission (Spence, 2006a, pp. 60–72). Members keep their commissioners informed, provide policy advice, act as a point of contact for lobbyists, keep in touch with other *cabinets* on Commission business, and provide an essential link between commissioners and the DGs and services (Nugent, 2001, pp. 123–32).

The president

The **president of the Commission** is the most dominating figure and usually the most public face of the EU. As well as running the Commission, the president appears alongside meetings of world leaders, plays an often critical role in negotiations at European Council summits, is expected to make public statements on critical issues, and has bilateral meetings with national leaders ranging from the president of the US to the leaders of countries receiving EU development aid.

Cabinet: The small group of assistants and advisers that works for each of the commissioners. Headed by a *chef de cabinet,* members provide advice, information and other services to the commissioners.

President of the Commission: The head of the Commission and one of the most visible of all the staff of the EU institutions. Appointed by the European Council for renewable five-year terms, and charged with giving the Commission direction.

Where candidates for the job were once expected to have only modest political experience, and their terms in office were relatively quiet and non-controversial, appointments have become more significant and more hotly contested, and opinions about the performance of presidents in office have become stronger.

Presidents are appointed for renewable five-year terms, taking office – like the commissioners – six months after elections to the EP. The president is expected to give political guidance and direction to the Commission, which also means playing a central role in giving impetus to the direction taken by the EU. Specifically, presidents have the following powers:

- To convene and chair meetings of the College, and approve agendas for College meetings.
- To lay down the guidelines for the work of the Commission, and decide its internal organization.
- To distribute policy portfolios in the College at the beginning of each term, reshuffle portfolios mid-term, and ask members of the College to resign if necessary.
- To assign themselves whatever duties and policy responsibilities interest them.
- To regularly take questions before the European Parliament, on the model of Prime Minister's Question Time in the British House of Commons.
- To represent the Commission in dealings with other EU institutions and at key meetings of national governments and their leaders.

These are the formal aspects of the job, some of which are outlined in the treaties and the operating rules of the Commission. But as with all major leadership positions, the character of the office changes according to the personality and management style of the office-holder, the agenda each brings to the task, the prevailing political climate, and the ability of a president to work with and command the respect of EU leaders (Spence, 2006a, pp. 27–8). Some presidents, notably Hallstein, Jenkins and Delors, have been more ambitious and effective, while others, notably Malfatti, Santer and Prodi, have been more low key in their approach (see Figure 10.2).

Profile Jean-Claude Juncker

Jean-Claude Juncker (1954–) took office in December 2014 as the twelfth president of the European Commission, and the third from Luxembourg. He had a background in national government, serving as minister of finance (in which role he chaired the EC Council of Ministers and was at the heart of discussions over the Maastricht treaty) and as prime minister between 1995 and 2013. In 2005 he became the first president of the Eurogroup of euro zone finance ministers, in which role he was deeply involved in efforts to resolve the euro crisis. He was nominated as the candidate of the European People's Party (EPP) for president of the Commission in 2013, winning confirmation on the back of the EPP winning the largest share of seats in the 2014 European Parliament elections, and in spite of efforts by British Prime Minister David Cameron to block his appointment on the grounds that Juncker was too much of a European federalist.

Figure 10.2 Past presidents of the European Commission

1958–67

Walter Hallstein
West Germany
Christian democrat
Foreign minister

Helped establish role of Commission in Community affairs, laid groundwork for common market and CAP, and was involved in 1965 empty chair crisis.

1967–70

Jean Rey
Belgium
Centrist
Economics minister

Won new powers for European Parliament, and was in office for launch of economic and monetary union and European Political Cooperation.

1970–72

Franco Maria Malfatti
Italy
Christian democrat
Minister for state industries

Voluntarily resigned from office, a reflection of how weak the position then was and the trough into which Community had sunk.

1972–73

Sicco Mansholt
Netherlands
Social democrat
Agriculture minister

Interim president.

1973–77

François-Xavier Ortoli
France
Conservative
Economic affairs and
finance minister

President during first enlargement of EEC and global energy crisis, but more influential as economics and finance commissioner (1977–81) when he oversaw launch of European Monetary System.

1977–81

Roy Jenkins
UK
Social democrat
Home secretary and
finance minister

Oversaw creation of EMS and established right of Commission president to represent Community at world economic summits.

1981–85

Gaston Thorn
Luxembourg
Socialist
Prime minister 1974–79

Oversaw British budget rebate talks and growth of Commission power, laying groundwork for his successor, Jacques Delors.

1985–94

Jacques Delors
France
Socialist
Economics and finance minister

The towering figure in history of the office. His two terms remembered for completion of single market, plan for economic and monetary union, and negotiations leading to Maastricht.

1995–99

Jacques Santer
Luxembourg
Christian democrat
Prime minister 1985–95

Guided EU towards economic and monetary union, enlargement, and Common Foreign and Security Policy, but allowed culture of complacency and inefficiency, leading to resignation of College in March.

1999–2004

Romano Prodi
Italy
Centrist
Prime minister 1996–98

Oversaw the launch of euro, enlargement negotiations, and draft European constitution, but widely regarded as disorganized and as a poor communicator.

2004–14

José Manuel Barroso
Portugal
Centrist
Prime minister 2002–04

His two terms saw much change and uncertainty: eastern enlargement still new, EU–US relations in trouble, European constitution collapsed, global financial crisis, euro crisis, and declining confidence in EU.

The process by which presidents are appointed is technically simple but in reality complex. First, the credentials for aspirant presidents have become more demanding: where experience as a national government minister was once enough, experience as a prime minister is now all but required. Second, presidents long had to be acceptable to all the leaders of the EU member states, with the consequence that candidates with well-formed opinions and substantial track records were often dismissed in the search for consensus. The result, argues Spence (2006a, p. 32), was that the strongest candidate was rarely chosen. This was clear in the 2004 appointment season, when several leading candidates emerged, including Belgian Prime Minister Guy Verhofstadt, Austrian Chancellor Wolfgang Schüssel and former NATO chief Javier Solana. In the end, the compromise candidate was Portuguese Prime Minister José Manuel Barroso, who was confirmed to a second term in 2009 despite concerns that his lack of strong positions made him easier for EU leaders to control (Peter, 2009).

The appointment of Jean-Claude Juncker in 2014 saw the new rules introduced by Lisbon being used for the first time. These said that candidates would be proposed by the European Council using a qualified majority vote (QMV; see Chapter 11 for explanation), and had to be confirmed by a majority vote in the European Parliament. But Parliament interpreted this to mean that the political group that won the most seats in the EP elections should automatically have its preferred candidate confirmed. The major political groups nominated *spitzencandidaten*, or 'top candidates', who engaged in campaigning as well as TV debates prior to the EP elections. When the conservative European People's Party won a plurality of the seats, their candidate Jean-Claude Juncker became the frontrunner, and eventually won appointment. The switch to QMV means that no one national leader can any longer veto the choice of president, thus significantly changing the dynamics of the process.

Directorates-general and services

If the College is the 'cabinet of ministers' of the EU, then the body of the EU civil service is found in its directorates-general (DGs) and services (see Table 10.2). The DGs are the equivalent of national government departments in the sense that each is responsible for overseeing the development and implementation of laws and policies in specific areas. They are not, however – like most national government departments – executive bodies with direct links to the public (Spence, 2006b). The services, meanwhile, are much as the name implies. Some work externally; for example, the Anti-Fraud Office investigates charges of fraud in relation to the EU budget, and cases of corruption and serious misconduct in the EU institutions. Others are focused internally; for example, the Legal Service provides in-house legal counsel to the Commission and represents it in cases brought before the European Court of Justice.

The DGs and services are staffed mainly by a mix of full-time European bureaucrats, known as *fonctionnaires*, and national experts seconded from the member states on short-term appointments. Permanent jobs in the Commission are highly sought after and demanding, with thousands of applicants chasing the positions that become available each year, keeping the Personnel Selection Office busy. Citizenship of an EU member state is usually needed, and the Commission

Directorate-general (DG):
A department within the Commission, headed by a director-general and given responsibility for generating and overseeing the implementation of laws and policies in particular areas.

Table **10.2** **Commission directorates-general and services**

Directorates-general

Agriculture and Rural Development	Home Affairs
Budget	Humanitarian Aid and Civil Protection
Climate Action	Human Resources and Security
Communication	Informatics
Communication Networks, Content and Technology	Internal Market and Services
Competition	Interpretation
Economic and Financial Affairs	Joint Research Centre
Education and Culture	Justice
Employment, Social Affairs and Inclusion	Maritime Affairs and Fisheries
Energy	Mobility and Transport
Enlargement	Regional Policy
Enterprise and Industry	Research and Innovation
Environment	Services for Foreign Policy Instruments
EuropeAid Development and Cooperation	Taxation and Customs Union
Eurostat	Trade
Health and Consumers	Translation

Services

Bureau of European Policy Advisers	Internal Audit Service
Central Library	Legal Service
European Anti-Fraud Office	Office for Administration and Payment
European Commission Data Protection Officer	of Individual Entitlements
Historical Archives	Publications Office
Infrastructure and Logistics	

For more details, see European Commission website, http://ec.europa.eu/about/ds_en.htm.

is required to ensure balanced representation by nationality at every level. While it expects all non-support staff applicants to speak at least two languages, multilingualism is increasingly the norm, along with a university degree and professional training in law, business, finance, science, or a related area. Applicants sit entrance exams (the *concours*) and may have to wait as long as three years to find out whether or not they have been accepted. Once appointed, though, they are well paid and redundancies are rare.

Each DG is headed by a director-general, usually someone who has worked their way up through the bureaucracy of their home state and then through the ranks of the Commission, although the higher the level of appointment, the stronger the role that nationality and political affiliation will play in appointments. Directors-general are the main link between the DG and the relevant commissioner, and oversee DGs that vary in size, but not always in relation to the importance of the job they do: the biggest is the DG for Translation with nearly 2,300 staff, while the Joint Research Centre has 1,800, and DGs for Research and for Development Cooperation have just over 1,000 each. The DG for Trade is surprisingly small with 550 staff, Budget has 400, and Enlargement employs just 260 (see European Commission website). Most Commission staff work in Brussels, while several thousand work in Luxembourg and other parts of the EU.

Concept

Comitology

The process by which executive decisions within the Commission are monitored and influenced by a network of advisory, management and regulatory committees. It traces its roots back to concerns among member states that the Commission might try to change policy in the course of implementing it. Committees were once powerful, feeding charges of the secretive and undemocratic character of the Commission. After years of complaints from the EP, a 2006 decision gave the EP the power to block decisions coming out of the Commission where they were quasi-legislative and adopted using the co-decision procedure (see Chapter 12).

Committees

The process of implementation is monitored by a network of several hundred committees and subcommittees participating in a phenomenon known as comitology (Bergström, 2005). The committees take four different forms:

1 Advisory committees look at less politically sensitive issues and provide opinions to the Commission, which must make an effort to take them into account. They have no power to block Commission action.
2 Management committees focus on areas such as agricultural and fisheries policy, and have the power to refer Commission measures to the Council of Ministers, which then has the option of overruling the Commission.
3 Regulatory committees have the power to refer Commission measures to the Council of Ministers and the European Parliament.
4 Regulatory committees with scrutiny must allow the Council and Parliament to check proposed measures taken by the Commission before they are adopted, and if either institution objects the Commission cannot proceed.

The Secretariat-General

The Commission has its own internal bureaucracy in the form of the Secretariat-General, which employs about 460 staff who provide technical services and advice to the Commission, prepare the annual work programme of the Commission, and organize and coordinate the work of the DGs and services (Kassim, 2006). Answering to the president of the Commission, it is headed by a secretary-general who chairs the weekly meetings of the *chefs de cabinet*, sits in on meetings of the College of Commissioners, directs Commission relations with other EU institutions, and generally works to ensure that the Commission runs smoothly. The position was held for nearly 30 years (1958–87) by Emile Noël of France, whose belief in an activist Commission and a leadership role for the Secretariat-General influenced its development. In 2005, Catherine Day of Ireland, former director-general for the environment, became the first woman to hold the job.

What the Commission does

Article 9 of the Treaty of Lisbon says that the task of the European Commission is to 'promote the general interest of the Union', to 'ensure the application of the Treaties', and to 'oversee the application of Union law'. It does this mainly through its powers of initiation and implementation, its responsibilities for managing the EU budget, and its responsibilities for the external relations of the EU (Figure 10.3). Thanks to all this work, it has been described as the 'barometer of integration' and the key organization whose activities reflect the patterns of European integration (Dimitrakopoulos, 2004, p. 2).

Most of its work revolves around the development and implementation of EU law, which comes in several different forms (see Figure 10.4).

Powers of initiation

The Commission has a monopoly over the generation of most new European laws, and can also draw up proposals for new policy areas, as it did with the

Figure **10.3 Powers of the European Commission**

- Develops and makes proposals for new EU laws and policies
- Oversees implementation of laws and policies through the member states
- Develops and manages the EU budget
- Represents the EU in international trade negotiations
- Oversees process by which applications for membership of the EU are considered
- Coordinates the EU's official development assistance and humanitarian aid

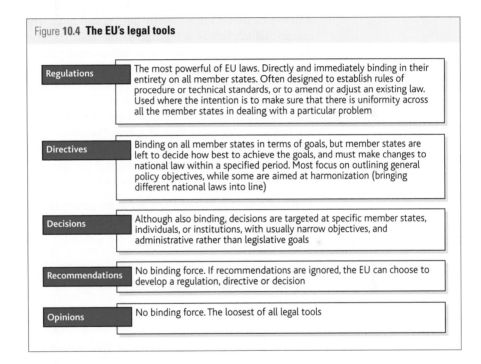

Figure **10.4 The EU's legal tools**

Regulations
The most powerful of EU laws. Directly and immediately binding in their entirety on all member states. Often designed to establish rules of procedure or technical standards, or to amend or adjust an existing law. Used where the intention is to make sure that there is uniformity across all the member states in dealing with a particular problem

Directives
Binding on all member states in terms of goals, but member states are left to decide how best to achieve the goals, and must make changes to national law within a specified period. Most focus on outlining general policy objectives, while some are aimed at harmonization (bringing different national laws into line)

Decisions
Although also binding, decisions are targeted at specific member states, individuals, or institutions, with usually narrow objectives, and administrative rather than legislative goals

Recommendations
No binding force. If recommendations are ignored, the EU can choose to develop a regulation, directive or decision

Opinions
No binding force. The loosest of all legal tools

Single European Act and the Delors package for economic and monetary union. Its main guidance comes from the treaties, whose general principles it works to turn into practical laws and policies, but it can also be nudged into action by the European Council, the Council of Ministers, Parliament, a ruling by the Court of Justice, by emergencies and political need, or by pressure from member states, interest groups and corporations. Proposals for new laws can also come from a commissioner or a staff member of one of the DGs.

A proposal for a new law (or an amendment to an existing law) usually begins as a draft written by middle-ranking Eurocrats in the relevant DG. If several DGs have an interest in the topic, then one will be selected as *chef de file*, or lead DG. The proposal then works its way through interested DGs, the Commission's Legal Service, *cabinets* and advisory committees, meetings of interested external policy actors, and the office of the relevant commissioner. This process can take months or even years to complete. Finished proposals will then be reviewed by the *chefs de cabinet*, meeting together weekly on Mondays, who will decide which proposals need discussion by the College and which do not. The proposals are then reviewed by the College, gathering on Wednesdays in Brussels, or in Strasbourg if Parliament is in plenary session. Using a majority vote, the College can accept or reject the proposal, send it back for redrafting, or defer making a decision. If accepted, it is sent to the Council of Ministers and the EP for a decision (see Figure 10.5).

Powers of implementation

Once a law has been adopted by the Council of Ministers and Parliament, the Commission is responsible for making sure that it is implemented by the member states. It cannot do this directly but instead must work through national bureaucracies, which leaves it hostage to the abilities, energies and cultures of those bureaucracies, which vary from one member state to another. Every member state is required to report to the Commission on the progress it is making, but this is sometimes easier said than done: the Commission only has a limited number of staff, and while member states may not openly refuse to implement a law, they may drag their feet, or there may be genuine problems with interpreting the meaning and effect of a law. For these reasons, the Commission often relies on less formal means of gathering information, including whistle-blowing by individuals, corporations and interest groups.

If a member state is slow, the Commission has three options available:

1 It can issue a Letter of Formal Notice giving the member state time to comply (usually about two months). Most problems are resolved at this stage.

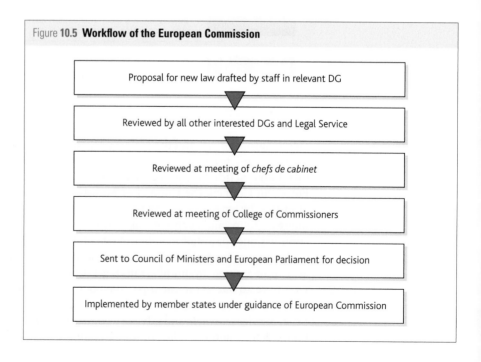

Figure **10.5 Workflow of the European Commission**

Proposal for new law drafted by staff in relevant DG

Reviewed by all other interested DGs and Legal Service

Reviewed at meeting of *chefs de cabinet*

Reviewed at meeting of College of Commissioners

Sent to Council of Ministers and European Parliament for decision

Implemented by member states under guidance of European Commission

2 If there is still no progress, the Commission can issue a Reasoned Opinion explaining why it feels there may be a violation.

3 If there is still no compliance, the Commission can take the member state (or an individual, corporation, or other institution) to the European Court of Justice for failure to fulfil its obligations. The Commission can recommend a fine or a penalty for the member state, but the final decision is left with the court.

At the same time, the Commission adds pressure by publicizing progress on implementation. Over time, Greece and Italy have been among the worst offenders (see Figure 10.6), mainly because their bureaucracies are relatively slow and inefficient. The lead-up to the 2004 eastern enlargement of the EU was a particularly busy time for the Commission, checking that the new incoming members were keeping up with their obligations to implement existing EU law. Just months before the new states joined, the Commission published a report warning of problems in all 10 countries, opening them to the risk of fines, export bans and the loss of EU subsidies. Lithuania and Slovenia had made the

Focus on... *The number of EU laws*

One of the most controversial issues in the debate about the EU is the question of how many laws the EU has adopted, and how far national laws in the member states are affected by those laws. The extent of the uncertainty is reflected in the range of estimates, which suggest that anything from 6 per cent to 84 per cent of national laws in the member states trace their origins to EU law.

It is hard to be sure of the exact size of the EU body of law – or even national bodies of law – because it is difficult to be sure how many laws are active at any given time. It must also be understood that not all laws are equal in terms of their reach; some are short, technical and narrow in their goals, while others are more widely applicable and bring about wider change. And it must also be remembered that many EU laws have had the effect of harmonizing (and thus often replacing) different and contradictory national laws, leading to a net decrease in regulation.

In 2010, the European Commission claimed that there were about 8,400 regulations and nearly 2,000 directives in force in the EU (European Commission, 2011, p. 3). Adding in EU decisions (which have narrow and specific targets, and administrative rather than legislative goals) and miscellaneous other acts takes the total to just short of 26,000 (Persson, 2012).

As to the question of how far national law in the member states is impacted by EU law, one of the few authoritative studies so far undertaken of this issue was a 2010 paper published by the British House of Commons Library. After pointing out that

- EU and national databases were not always reliable
- differentiating between EU-generated and nationally generated changes to the law was not easy
- there was little data on the relative material impact of EU and national laws
- EU law had different levels of impact from one member state to another
- in the British case, 'there is no totally accurate, rational or useful way of calculating the percentage of national laws based on or influenced by the EU'

the report concluded that between 1997 and 2009, just under 7 per cent of primary legislation in the UK and just over 14 per cent of secondary legislation could be tied to the obligations of implementing EU rules (House of Commons Library, 2010, pp. 13–14). Assuming that all the member states have had approximately similar experiences (with the exception of newer eastern European states that had to make more adjustments), it seems clear that many of the estimates broadcast by the EU's critics are far off the mark.

For a full listing of EU laws, see EUR-Lex and SCAD+ websites, http://ec.europa.eu/legislation/index_en.htm.

most progress, while Poland was singled out for its poor performance in areas as diverse as farm subsidies, inadequate standards at meat and dairy plants, dealing with corruption, and making changes to its fishing industry. Its problems continue today.

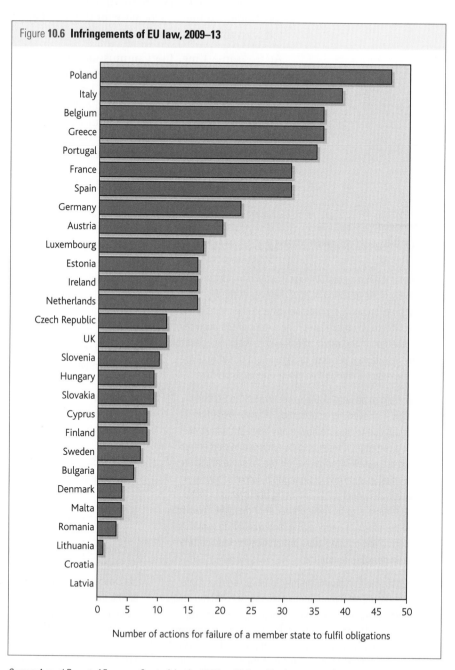

Figure **10.6** **Infringements of EU law, 2009–13**

Number of actions for failure of a member state to fulfil obligations

Source: Annual Report of European Court of Justice 2013, p. 87, http://curia.europa.eu (retrieved July 2014).

Managing EU finances

Control over the purse strings is one of the most potent of all political powers, and while the EU budget is relatively small (see Chapter 18), the reach of the Commission is extended by its role in drafting the budget, monitoring its progress through the Council of Ministers and Parliament, and making sure that all revenues are collected and funds are spent correctly. This means working with national agencies, monitoring the collection of funds, and ensuring that the member states make their required contributions (Nugent, 2001, pp. 287–8).

External relations

Although the process of European integration was inwardly focused in its early years, as the reach of the EEC expanded so its effects were felt outside its member states, and the role of representing the EEC/EU externally largely defaulted to the Commission. The basis of its role lies in the Treaty of Rome, which gave the Commission the authority in areas of exclusive Community competence to negotiate international agreements on behalf of the member states. The EU is now one of the world's dominating political and economic actors (see Chapter 24), and as such the activities and visibility of the Commission in external relations have grown exponentially (Smith, 2006). Those activities fall into three main categories.

1 It represents the EU in international trade negotiations. The member states agree common positions and it is left to the Commission to negotiate, whether on bilateral deals or in multilateral negotiations or dispute resolution through the World Trade Organization (WTO). Backed by a market of more than 500 million people, and with the EU's share of world trade standing at one-sixth of merchandise and about a quarter of commercial services (see Chapter 24), the EU's trade commissioner is the representative of an economic and trading behemoth.
2 It processes applications for full or associate membership of the EU. This was not the case in the early years of the EEC, but as the number of interested potential members grew, so the Commission helped develop a more strategic approach to the process, evaluating the quality and implications of new applications. If the European Council decides to open negotiations with an applicant country, the Commission manages the process.
3 It is the EU's coordinator for official development assistance (ODA) and humanitarian aid, a role whose significance has grown as the volume of aid has grown: the EU is now the source of 51 per cent of the ODA provided by the world's wealthiest countries (see Chapter 25).

The precise status of the EU in international forums is not always easy to understand; there is no single EU seat in the UN or NATO, for example, but the EU is a member of the WTO along with all the individual EU member states, even though the Commission speaks on behalf of all 28 states at most WTO meetings.

Summary

- The European Commission (headquartered in Brussels) is the bureaucratic-executive arm of the EU, responsible mainly for developing proposals for new laws and policies, and then for overseeing implementation in the member states.

- It also manages the EU budget, has responsibilities in external relations, represents the EU in international trade negotiations, and processes applications for membership of the EU.

- It is headed by a College of Commissioners, whose members are nominated by the governments of each of the member states to five-year renewable terms and must be confirmed by the European Council and the European Parliament.

- The College is headed by a president, formally nominated by the European Council to a five-year renewable term and confirmed by a majority vote in the European Parliament. Commission presidents have become the most public face of the EU institutions.

- Most Commission staff work in Brussels-based directorates-general and services, but some work in Commission offices in EU member states and abroad.

- The detailed work of the Commission is undertaken by a network of advisory, management and regulatory committees, supported by a Secretariat-General.

- The work of the Commission is widely misunderstood, critics claiming that it is too powerful, secretive and expensive. In fact, it can only do what the member states allow it to do, it is no more secretive than national bureaucracies, and its operating budget is modest compared to those of national bureaucracies.

Key terms and concepts

Cabinet

College of Commissioners

Comitology

Directorate-general

President of the Commission

Further reading

Cini, Michelle (2007) *From Integration to Integrity: Administrative Ethics and Reform in the European Commission* (Manchester: Manchester University Press). Bauer, Michael W. (ed.) (2008) *Reforming the European Commission* (London: Routledge). Look at recent reforms to the European Commission and the implications for the EU policy process.

Nugent, Neill (2001) *The European Commission* (Basingstoke: Palgrave Macmillan). Spence, David (ed.) (2006) *The European Commission*, 3rd edn (London: John Harper Publishing). Two standard texts on the Commission, covering its structure, powers and responsibilities, the second written by someone with many years of experience working in the Commission.

Smith, Andy (ed.) (2004) *Politics and the European Commission: Actors, Interdependence, Legitimacy* (London: Routledge). Study of the political forces that come to bear on the Commission, arguing that studying the links between politics and technical expertise helps us better understand how it works.

11 The Councils

The Council of the European Union and the European Council are often confused with each other, but are quite different. The Council of the EU (more often known as the Council of Ministers) consists of national government ministers and shares responsibility with the European Parliament for making EU law and approving the EU budget. The European Council, meanwhile, is the meeting place for the heads of government of the member states, in which they make broad strategic decisions and key appointments to other EU institutions.

Both institutions are primarily intergovernmental and confederal, even if they are expected to work in the general interest of the EU. Their members are government leaders from the member states, they provide indirect representation of the interests of citizens, and they defend national interests while trying to balance them with the goals of European integration. The Council of Ministers makes decisions on the basis of consensus or using a system of qualified majority voting, while the European Council relies on consensus, informality and flexibility. The presidency of the Council of Ministers is held by each member state in six-month rotations, while its detailed work is undertaken by the permanent representatives of the member states based in Brussels. Meanwhile, the European Council is headed by a president appointed to limited terms by members of the Council.

This chapter looks first at the changing role of the Council of Ministers in the EU decision-making process and the implications of qualified majority voting. It then looks at the work of the European Council, with an emphasis on the political dynamics of summitry and the role of the president of the European Council. It argues that the work of the Council of Ministers has been too often overlooked, thanks mainly to the attention paid to the Commission.

- Is the Council of Ministers primarily intergovernmental or supranational in character?
- Is the work of the Council more legislative or executive in nature?
- Which is more important to the EU decision-making process: the ministers themselves or the Committee of Permanent Representatives (Coreper)?
- Is summitry an effective and efficient way of reaching decisions, and how does it compare to the often lengthy discussions that take place in committees of the Council of Ministers?
- Should the president of the European Council be a leader or a conductor?

How the Councils evolved

The Council of the European Union, also known as the Council of Ministers or just 'the Council', traces its roots back to the Special Council of Ministers that was part of the ECSC. While the High Authority dealt exclusively with matters relating to coal and steel, all other initiatives needed the approval of the Council of Ministers. The Council was designed to be a link between the High Authority and national governments, balance the supranational character of the High Authority, and assuage the concerns of the Benelux countries about the political dominance of France, West Germany and Italy (Westlake and Galloway, 2004, p. 6).

Separate Councils of Ministers were created for the EEC and Euratom in 1958, and national interests moved to the fore as the balance of power shifted from the three Commissions to the three Councils. A qualified majority voting system was created that was designed to protect smaller member states from being overwhelmed by larger states: each Council had only six members, but they shared 17 votes that were shared out in rough proportion to the size of each country. On some issues a simple majority was enough, but on others a minimum of 12 votes (70 per cent of the total) was needed. Under the Merger treaty, the three councils were combined in 1967 into a single Council of Ministers.

Meanwhile, the broader strategic interests of the Community were discussed at several ad hoc summits of leaders of the member states during the 1960s, all held to address various crises (Werts, 2008, pp. 3–11). As the goals and obligations of the Treaty of Rome became more clear, so it also became clear that the Community lacked a sense of overall direction, and was becoming bogged down by intergovernmental struggles within the Council of Ministers. The inability of the Community to respond effectively to major international crises was illustrated by the confusion that came in the wake of the end of the Bretton Woods system in 1971 and the energy crisis of 1973, which prompted French Foreign Minister Michel Jobert to dismiss Europe as a 'nonentity' (Defarges, 1988, pp. 38–9).

At a summit in Paris in 1974 it was agreed to create a new forum that would take 'an overall approach' to internal and external problems and provide policy progress and consistency (see Document 11.1). The new forum was given neither formal rules nor legal standing nor a separate bureaucracy, and lacked even a name until French President Giscard d'Estaing's announcement at a press conference at the close of the meeting that 'the European summit is dead, long live the European Council' (Morgan, 1976, p. 5). Given the surfeit of councils in the European system (including the European Council, the Council of Ministers and the Council of Europe), this was an unfortunate choice.

The new body met for the first time as the European Council in Dublin in March 1975, then triannually until 1985, then biannually (with additional special meetings as needed) until the Treaty of Lisbon, since when it has been committed to four annual meetings. The Council usually used to convene in the country holding the presidency of the Council of Ministers, but the organization and security needed to set up summits became too onerous, so since 2003 all routine European Council meetings have been held in Brussels. The European Council was finally given formal recognition as an EU institution with the passage of the Treaty of Lisbon in 2009.

Document 11.1	*Final communiqué of the meeting of heads of government of the Community, 9 and 10 December 1974 (excerpts)*

1 The Heads of Government of the nine States of the Community, the Ministers of Foreign Affairs and the President of the Commission, meeting in Paris at the invitation of the French President, examined the various problems confronting Europe. …

2 Recognizing the need for an overall approach to the internal problems involved in achieving European unity and the external problems facing Europe, the Heads of Government consider it essential to ensure progress and overall consistency in the activities of the Communities and in the work on political co-operation.

3 The Heads of Government have therefore decided to meet, accompanied by the Ministers of Foreign Affairs, three times a year and, whenever necessary, in the Council of the Communities and in the context of political co-operation. …

In order to ensure consistency in Community activities and continuity of work, the Ministers of Foreign Affairs, meeting in the Council of the Community, will act as initiators and co-ordinators. They may hold political cooperation meetings at the same time. …

4 With a view to progress towards European unity, the Heads of Government reaffirm their determination gradually to adopt common positions and co-ordinate their diplomatic action in all areas of international affairs which affect the interests of the European Community. …

5 The Heads of Government consider it necessary to increase the solidarity of the Nine both by improving Community procedures and by developing new common policies in areas to be decided on and granting the necessary powers to the Institutions.

6 In order to improve the functioning of the Council of the Community, they consider that it is necessary to renounce the practice which consists of making agreement on all questions conditional on the unanimous consent of the Member States, whatever their respective positions may be regarding the conclusions reached in Luxembourg on 28 January 1966.

Source: www.cvce.eu/content/publication/1999/1/1/…/ publishable_en.pdf (retrieved October 2014).

How the Council of Ministers is structured

The Council of Ministers is headquartered in the Justus Lipsius building (also known as the Consilium) in the European Quarter of Brussels, across from the Berlaymont, seat of the European Commission. Named for a little-known sixteenth-century Flemish humanist, the Justus Lipsius is a large, marble-clad building that was opened in 1995 at a cost of €450 million, allowing the Council to move from the nearby Charlemagne building and a network of rented offices into a single home. But the new building was already too small to account for enlargement of the EU or the decision to hold all European Council summits from 2003 in Brussels. As the Council spilled over into neighbouring buildings, renovations were made to the Lipsius building to absorb the growth, and the European Council moved next door to the Europa building, renovated at an estimated cost of €315 million.

The Council of Ministers has five main components: the councils themselves, the presidency of the Council, Coreper, committees and working groups, and the General Secretariat (see Figure 11.1).

Figure **11.1** **Structure of the Council of Ministers**

- The quasi-legislative arm of the EU, sharing powers with the European Parliament
- Headquartered in Brussels
- Presidency held by member states taking turns in a pre-agreed rotation. Foreign Affairs Council chaired by the High Representative for Foreign Affairs
- Consists of the relevant national government ministers of the member states, membership changing according to the policy area under consideration
- Most negotiations within the Council take place in the Committee of Permanent Representatives, made up of representatives from the member states
- Work supported by a General Secretariat
- Intergovernmental and confederal in character, but with supranational aspects

The Councils

The different groups of ministers that make up the Council are known either as technical councils, formations or configurations. Where once there were nearly 24, there are now just 10 (see Table 11.1). Whichever of these groups is meeting, they always act as 'the Council', and in legal terms their decisions are always taken as 'the Council'. The major councils are:

- General Affairs, which prepares and ensures follow-up to meetings of the European Council
- Foreign Affairs, which deals with external relations, trade issues and development cooperation
- Economic and Financial Affairs (Ecofin), which deals with economic policy coordination
- Agriculture and Fisheries.

Illustration **11.1** **The Council**
The Justus Lipsius building in Brussels, seat of the Council of Ministers.

Table **11.1** **Council of Ministers configurations**

Agriculture and Fisheries
Competitiveness
Economic and Financial Affairs
Education, Youth, Culture and Sport
Employment, Social Policy, Health and Consumer Affairs
Environment
Foreign Affairs
General Affairs
Justice and Home Affairs
Transport, Telecommunications and Energy

For more details, see Council of Ministers website, www.consilium.europa.eu/council/council-configurations?lang=en.

These four councils meet monthly, while the rest meet between two and four times a year, for a grand total of about 50–60 Council meetings per year. Almost all are held in Brussels, except in April, June and October when they are held in Luxembourg. Sessions usually last no more than one or two days, depending on how much business they have. Since 1998, finance ministers from the euro zone have also met as the Eurogroup, which is not formally part of the Council of Ministers but works in much the same way, and meets the day before meetings of Ecofin.

The Treaty of Lisbon says that representatives of the member states must be 'at ministerial level', but meetings of the Council do not always attract a matching set of ministers. Some may opt out and send a deputy because they want to avoid political embarrassment on a sensitive issue, or because they may have more pressing matters to attend to at home, and not all member states divide policy portfolios up the same way; prime ministers, for example, sometimes give themselves key policy portfolios such as foreign or economic affairs, while some of the less important portfolios may be combined with the responsibilities of senior ministers.

The Presidency

Until the Treaty of Lisbon, the presidency of the Council of Ministers and the European Council was held not by a person but by the government of a member state, with each taking turns in a pre-agreed rotation for six months, beginning in January and July each year. All meetings of the Council were organized and chaired by the relevant ministers from the country holding the presidency, giving its government a key role in setting the EU agenda for six months. Lisbon gave the European Council its own president, while arranging for the Foreign Affairs Council to be chaired by the High Representative (HR) of the Union for Foreign Affairs and Security Policy. All other meetings of the Council are still chaired by representatives of the member states in a pre-agreed rotation (see Table 11.2).

Presidency of the Council of Ministers: The leadership of all meetings of the Council of Ministers except the Foreign Affairs Council. Held by the governments of EU member states in a rotation of six months each.

This arrangement has the advantage of giving each member state the opportunity to guide the direction of the EU. This, in turn, helps make the EU more real to the citizens of the member state in control, allows member states to bring issues of national interest to the top of the agenda, and gives smaller member states an opportunity to counter the influence of bigger states. But while the

Table **11.2 Rotation of the Council presidency**

	First half	*Second half*
2010	Spain	Belgium
2011	Hungary	Poland
2012	Denmark	Cyprus
2013	Ireland	Lithuania
2014	Greece	Italy
2015	Latvia	Luxembourg
2016	Netherlands	Slovakia
2017	Malta	UK
2018	Estonia	Bulgaria
2019	Austria	Romania

rotation was viable when there were only 6 or even 12 member states, it has lengthened as membership has grown, so that with 28 members they must each wait fourteen years for their turn at the helm.

The workload that comes with the job has also grown, creating a burden that is especially onerous on smaller member states with limited resources and small bureaucracies. The rotation also has the effect of holding the rest of the EU hostage to the different styles, interests and political abilities of the countries in the presidency, and means a constant change of personnel at the top. This is offset to some extent by the use of a trio system, under which each presidency cooperates with its predecessor and successor. With Lisbon, this has evolved into a virtual 18-month, three-state team presidency, which has the advantage of encouraging EU governments to work together and to better know each other.

The duties of the presidency are as follows (Elgström, 2003, pp. 4–7):

- It prepares and coordinates the work of the Council of Ministers, setting the agendas for several hundred annual meetings of ministers, working parties and committees.
- It arranges and chairs most meetings of the Council of Ministers and Coreper, and represents the Council in dealings with other EU institutions.
- It mediates, bargains, promotes cooperation among member states, and tries to ensure that policy development has consistency and continuity.

Over the years, the Council of Ministers has increasingly followed the lead of the European Council, opening up the prospect of the still evolving office of the president of the European Council making arrangements that will influence the entire structure of the Council.

Permanent representatives

Although ministers are the most visible and senior members of the Council hierarchy, much of the work of the Council has already been settled before the ministers meet. This is made possible by the Committee of Permanent Representatives, or Coreper (*Comité des représentants permanents*). Each member state maintains a permanent representation in Brussels, in effect an embassy to the EU that works alongside member state embassies to Belgium. The staffs

Trio system: The arrangement under which the member state holding the presidency works closely with its predecessor and successor in order to help encourage policy consistency.

Coreper: The Committee of Permanent Representatives, in which delegates from each of the member states meet to discuss proposals for new laws before they are sent to the Council of Ministers for a final decision.

Understanding Integration... *Intergovernmentalism*

Intergovernmentalism is an approach to understanding international relations that focuses on how governments interact with each other in the meeting rooms of intergovernmental organizations. In relation to the EU, it is:

- a theory based on the argument that states are the key actors in the process of integration, and that they behave as rational actors
- a model describing how representatives of the member states negotiate and make decisions.

In theoretical terms, it looks at the costs and benefits to states of their participation in the EU; they want to protect national interests, but they will also look at the extent to which integration results in more efficient decision-making. It also assumes that states work hard to remain in control of decision-making at the EU level, and that rather than transferring sovereignty to the EU institutions, the most they are prepared to do is to pool or share that sovereignty (Keohane and Hoffmann, 1991, p. 227). Using this logic, the most important of the EU institutions are the Council of Ministers and the European Council, both of which are made up of representatives from the member states, and where the interests of the member states are most obviously defended. By comparison, the other EU institutions are considered to be agents of the member states, whose core tasks are to follow the lead of the councils.

Opinion is divided on the extent to which the councils are intergovernmental or supranational, and whether they are becoming stronger or weaker with time. Westlake and Galloway (2004, p. 8) argue that to portray the Council of Ministers as intergovernmental is misleading, and that it is 'first and foremost a supranational institution' because it acts as a collective body when defending the Council's interests relative to other EU institutions, or the EU's interests to the outside world. The ministers are domestic politicians, so they are driven by national political interests, ideology, the popularity and stability of their home governments, and the attitude of those governments towards European integration. At the same time, they are pulled in several directions, it is difficult always to be sure to whom they are responsible, and the character of the Council remains ambiguous at best (Hayes-Renshaw and Wallace, 2006, pp. 4–5, 27–8).

Routinely overlooked in discussions about the councils is the extent to which they are not just intergovernmental in nature, but also confederal. A confederation, as we saw earlier, is a group of sovereign states with a central authority deriving its authority from those states, and where the interests of citizens are represented indirectly through the governments of the states meeting in common institutions. This precisely describes the dynamic of the Council of Ministers and the European Council, the membership of which is not determined directly by elections, but indirectly through an ex officio arrangement; the members of both bodies are there by virtue of being senior members of their national governments.

of the permanent representations include experts in each of the policy areas addressed by the EU, and these experts will meet regularly as Coreper (often multiple times each week, and altogether about 2,000 times a year) to go through the proposals for new laws, argue national positions, and work out agreements and compromises. All but unknown outside the corridors of Brussels, and the subject of surprisingly little academic study, Coreper is one of the most powerful parts of the EU decision-making structure.

Thanks to Coreper, most of the detailed work of the Council is finished before the ministers even meet (Hayes-Renshaw and Wallace, 2006, p. 77), with only the most politically sensitive and controversial proposals left for the ministers to discuss. This arrangement was described colourfully by Alan Clark (1993, p. 139), a former British government minister, when he noted in his diaries that:

it makes not the slightest difference to the conclusions of a meeting what Ministers say at it. Everything is decided, and horse-traded off by officials at Coreper … The ministers arrive on the scene at the last minute, hot, tired, ill, or drunk (sometimes all of these together), read out their piece and depart.

Working parties and committees

In addition to Coreper, the Council of Ministers has a complex network of working parties and committees (about 250 in all, together meeting more than 4,000 times each year) that support the work of Coreper, and in this sense function as the foundations of the Council edifice. The first port of call for a proposal from the Commission is usually a working party, which reviews the technical details and makes a recommendation to Coreper. The working parties are organized along policy lines, with a variety of charges: some are permanent, some are temporary, some meet weekly, some biannually, and some only once before being disbanded. They bring together policy specialists, national experts, members of the permanent representations, and staff from the Commission. The Council also has several standing committees, dealing with economic and financial matters, employment, social protection, security matters, financial services, and other key issues.

The General Secretariat

The General Secretariat is the bureaucracy of the Council, staffed by about 3,000 employees based in Brussels, most of them translators and service staff. It helps prepare Council meetings, provides advice to the presidency, provides legal support to the Council and Coreper, briefs Council meetings on the status of agenda items, keeps records, manages the Council budget, and generally gives the work of the Council some continuity. It was originally focused mainly on secretarial work, but has since become more political, helping manage negotiations, offering counsel to the presidency, and helping with the executive duties of the secretary-general (Westlake and Galloway, 2004, pp. 347–9).

The secretary-general is appointed by the Council of Ministers to five-year renewable terms. The job was briefly given a new personality and a higher public profile in 1999 when it was combined with the (then) new office of the High Representative for the Common Foreign and Security Policy, a move which had the effect of making the General Secretariat a hub for the development of the EU's foreign and security policies (Christiansen, 2006, pp. 164–7). The first holder of this combined position was Javier Solana, a former minister in the Spanish government and a former secretary general of NATO. With the passage of the Treaty of Lisbon, the job of High Representative was redefined so that the office-holder is now both chair of the Foreign Affairs Council within the Council of Ministers, and also a vice-president of the European Commission. Meanwhile, the job of secretary-general reverted back to something more like its pre-1999 character when Solana was succeeded in December 2009 by Pierre de Boissieu, a French diplomat and grand-nephew of Charles de Gaulle. He was succeeded in 2011 by Uwe Corsepius, a German economist.

What the Council of Ministers does

The main job of the Council is to decide – in conjunction with Parliament – which proposals for new European laws and policies will be adopted and which will not (see Figure 11.2). When the College of Commissioners has approved a proposal for a new law, it is sent to the Council, the more complex proposals usually going first to one or more of the Council working parties or committees, which identify points of agreement and disagreement (for more details, see Hayes-Renshaw et al., 1989). Proposals are then sent to Coreper, listed as a Part I item if there is agreement and as a Part II item if further discussion is needed. Coreper reviews the political implications and tries to clear up as many of the remaining problems as possible. If agreement is reached, the proposal is sent as an A item to the relevant council, which will usually approve it without debate – this is the case with about two-thirds of council decisions (Westlake and Galloway, 2004, p. 38). If agreement has not been reached, or if the item was left over from a previous meeting, it is listed as a B item, meaning that it needs further discussion (see Figure 11.3).

The voting system within the Council has changed over the years, the options reflecting changing attitudes towards integration. Where once unanimity was required for almost every major vote, it is now all but unknown and ministers mainly have three options:

1   If they are dealing with a procedural issue, or one of a small number of specific policy issues, they can use a simple majority.
2   The second option is consensus, where outcomes may be determined by silence or the absence of opposition.
3   For all other business where a vote is needed, the ministers use a qualified majority vote (QMV), by which each is given several votes roughly in proportion to the population of their member state, for a total of 345 (see Table 11.3).

For a proposal to succeed, it must win a triple majority: 55% of the votes in the Council, from at least 15 member states that must together be home to 65% of the population of the EU. A blocking minority is also available, requiring at least four states representing 35% of the population of the EU. And that is not

Qualified majority vote: A system of voting used in the Council of Ministers, by which proposals must win substantially more than a simple majority.

Figure **11.2 Powers of the Council of Ministers**

- Shares powers with the European Parliament for discussing and passing laws
- Shares powers with Parliament for approving and adopting the EU budget
- Coordinates the economic policies of the member states
- Coordinates justice and home affairs policies of the member states
- Defines and implements the Common Foreign and Security Policy
- Concludes international agreements on behalf of the EU

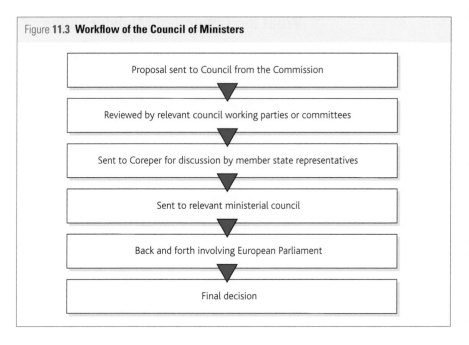

Figure **11.3 Workflow of the Council of Ministers**

> Proposal sent to Council from the Commission
>
> ▼
>
> Reviewed by relevant council working parties or committees
>
> ▼
>
> Sent to Coreper for discussion by member state representatives
>
> ▼
>
> Sent to relevant ministerial council
>
> ▼
>
> Back and forth involving European Parliament
>
> ▼
>
> Final decision

all: if the Council acts without a proposal from the Commission, a reinforced qualified majority comes into play by which a proposal must win at least 72% of the votes from countries representing at least 65% of the population of the EU. This convoluted arrangement reduces the power of big states and encourages states to form coalitions, but it also emphasizes the extent to which the ministers seek to protect national interests.

The allocation of votes has long been a bone of contention. Consternation was generated during the debate over the constitutional treaty when Poland, which had been given 27 votes under the Treaty of Nice, refused to have its quota

Illustration **11.2**
Council of Ministers

A meeting of the Council of Ministers in Brussels. Many of the key decisions on new EU law are taken by such gatherings of the national ministers from the member states.

Table **11.3 Qualified majority voting in the Council of Ministers**

Germany	29	Belgium	12	Lithuania	7
UK	29	Hungary	12	Slovakia	7
France	29	Portugal	12	Cyprus	4
Italy	29	Austria	10	Estonia	4
Spain	27	Bulgaria	10	Latvia	4
Poland	27	Sweden	10	Luxembourg	4
Romania	14	Croatia	7	Slovenia	4
Netherlands	13	Denmark	7	Malta	3
Greece	12	Finland	7		
Czech Republic	12	Ireland	7	TOTAL	**345**

To pass, a proposal must win at least 55 per cent of the votes from 15 member states that together are home to 65 per cent of the EU population.

reduced, even when it was pointed out that Germany – with twice the population and an economy ten times larger – had just 29 votes. Poland also baulked during the debate over the Treaty of Lisbon at the suggestion to change QMV from a triple to a double majority. The then Polish President Lech Kaczynski claimed that such a change would hurt Poland to the benefit of large states such as Germany, and shocked his peers by arguing that Poland would have had a much bigger population had it not been for the ravages of the Second World War; 'Poles like Germans,' he mused, 'while Germans do not like Poles' (Mulvey, 2007). He was eventually placated by an agreement to delay switching to the new voting system until 2014.

Once the Council has reached a decision, proposals are subject to a complex process of review involving the European Parliament in which – depending on the nature of the topic – they can be discussed and voted upon in each body up to three times. If there is still a failure to agree, proposals are sent to a Conciliation Committee made up of 28 representatives each from Parliament and the Council of Ministers, with representatives of the Commission also in attendance (see Chapter 12 for more details).

The European Council

The European Council is the meeting place for the heads of government (or the heads of state in the cases of Cyprus and France) of the EU member states. Until the Treaty of Lisbon, the Council would usually meet every June and December, with additional meetings as needed, but the Council is now committed to meeting four times per year, with additional special meetings as needed. (Since 2010, several euro summits have also been held, involving only the heads of government of the euro member countries.) It usually meets (in closed session) for no more than two days, the heads of government being accompanied by a minister (usually the foreign minister). Also present will be the president of the European Council, the president of the Commission (with a deputy commissioner as needed), the HR of the Union for Foreign Affairs and Security Policy, and small retinues of staff and advisers, including permanent representatives. The president of the Council chairs the meetings, and decisions are taken on the

European Council: The forum in which the heads of government of the member states meet regularly to make strategic decisions on the progress of integration.

basis of a consensus (except where the treaties provide otherwise). Meetings have taken place in the Justus Lipsius building pending completion of renovations to the Europa building next door.

The European Council and the Council of Ministers are often confused, and sometimes interchangeably referred to as 'The Council', but their membership, rules, structure and legal personalities are quite distinct. Among the critical differences:

- Its members are the heads of government of the EU member states, not the ministers.
- It has its own appointed president, and is no longer chaired by a presidency from a member state, as it once was.
- It discusses broad strategic issues, not proposals for new laws.
- It mainly uses only one means of decision-making (consensus).
- It has no legislative functions and no direct relationship with the European Parliament.

In spite of its clearly dominating role, the duties of the European Council were long kept deliberately vague and ambiguous, its membership first confirmed by the Single European Act, its role only given a basis in the treaties by Maastricht (Westlake and Galloway, 2004, p. 179), and final confirmation that it was an institution of the EU coming only with the Treaty of Lisbon, which describes its job as follows (Article 15):

> The European Council shall provide the Union with the necessary impetus for its development and shall define the general political directions and priorities thereof. It shall not exercise legislative functions.

Put another way, the Council rises above the details and focuses on key decisions about the strategic direction of political integration. This includes launching policy cooperation in new areas, helping drive the EU policy agenda, ensuring policy consistency, and promoting the development of a common EU foreign policy.

Beyond policy-making, the Council also makes appointments to several of the key positions in the EU hierarchy (see Figure 11.4). Aside from the Council's own president, the most important of these is the president of the Commission. The decision to appoint formally begins with a review of potential candidates in the Council, which makes a decision using QMV, and sends the name of its

---

Figure **11.4 Structure and powers of the European Council**

- The 'board of directors' of the EU, consisting of the heads of government of the member states
- Based in Brussels, where it meets at least four times annually
- Chaired by a president appointed by the European Council for a term of two and a half years, renewable once
- Responsible for taking strategic decisions
- Responsible for making nominations to senior positions, including president of the European Commission, the High Representative of the Union for Foreign Affairs and Security Policy, and president of the European Central Bank

nominee to the European Parliament, which then votes using a simple majority. If the nominee fails to win a parliamentary majority, the European Council has one month to propose a new nominee. But as we saw in Chapter 10, Parliament has won a new role for itself with the nomination of candidates by the major political groups. The Council also has a role in confirming the list of new commissioners, based on suggestions made by the governments of the member states, and is responsible for appointing – again by QMV – the HR of the Union for Foreign Affairs and Security Policy.

Its interest in the big picture does not mean that the Council always avoids service in the trenches of political warfare, and in fact many of the most bruising and tiring of all the debates surrounding the process of European integration have taken place in the meeting chambers of the Council. But where the job of the other institutions is to work out the details, the European Council tries to focus on the longer term needs of the EU, using summitry rather than meetings designed to pore over the details of policy.

Because summitry is only loosely institutionalized, if at all, the rules are informal and meetings of the Council take place using a combination of brainstorming, intensive bilateral and multilateral discussions and bargaining. The outcome is a formal set of conclusions, whose content depends on a combination of the management skills of the president, the quality of organization and preparation, the negotiating skills of the individual leaders, the personal relationships among those leaders, how they choose to balance their defence of national and European interests, and the prevailing international environment. Because summits must often deal with crises, decisions are often made in a pressure-cooker environment, with meetings lasting longer than planned, running on into the small hours, and dominated by the expectation of agreements being reached at almost any cost for fear that summits will be declared to be failures.

Much like meetings of the Council of Ministers, national delegations are ranged around a room, their numbers limited in order to keep meetings

Illustration **11.3**
The European Council
EU leaders gathering for their traditional family photo at the European Council summit in Brussels in October 2014.

manageable; typically, only the heads of government and their foreign ministers are allowed to be present, along with representatives of the Commission and the Council of Ministers, and no more than one adviser per member state, making a total of about 90–100 people. Additional members of national delegations are restricted to nearby suites that they use as a base. Summits combine plenary sessions with breakouts involving different combinations of leaders, officials from the Council of Ministers working hard to draft a set of conclusions whose content is usually announced at a closing press conference.

Some agenda issues (particularly economic problems) have been perennial, while others have come and gone in response to emergencies, crises and changes in the international environment (Table 11.4 lists some key summits). Between 1957 and 2014 there were more than 160 meetings of European leaders, dealing with a wide variety of needs and problems:

- Launching major new initiatives, including the single market programme during the 1980s, and every new EU treaty.
- Addressing key economic matters, including the steps leading to the launch of the euro, and the EU responses to the 2007–10 global financial crisis and the euro zone crisis.
- Dealing with emergencies and rapidly unfolding events, such as developments in eastern Europe in 1989, the crisis in the Exchange Rate Mechanism in 1992, rifts over the impending invasion of Iraq in 2003, and responding to the crisis in Ukraine in 2014.
- Giving momentum to the development of an EU foreign policy.
- Resolving budget disputes.
- Making decisions on new member applications.
- Agreeing critical institutional reforms.

Table **11.4** **Key summits of the European Council**

Date	Venue	Highlights
1975 March	Dublin	First meeting of the Council
1978 July	Bremen	Creation of European Monetary System
1985 December	Luxembourg	Signature of Single European Act
1991 December	Maastricht	Signature of Treaty on European Union
1995 December	Madrid	Naming of the euro
1997 June	Amsterdam	Signature of Treaty of Amsterdam
2000 March	Lisbon	Agreement of Lisbon Strategy
2000 December	Nice	Signature of Treaty of Nice
2003 February	Brussels	Discussed growing crisis over Iraq
2003 October	Rome	Initiated IGC leading to EU constitutional treaty
2007 December	Lisbon	Signature of Treaty of Lisbon
2008 March	Brussels	Climate change
2008 September	Brussels	Crisis in Georgia
2010–11	Brussels	Several summits to address the euro crisis
2014 March	Brussels	Crisis in Ukraine

For a full list of meetings, see European Council website, www.european-council.europa.eu/council-meetings?lang=en.

Along the way it has had successes, but it has also had its failures, including a slow response to pressures for agricultural and budgetary reform, and a failure to clear the way to agreements on a common EU response to the two Gulf Wars, the Bosnian conflict, and the crisis in Kosovo in 1998–99. Some of its problems could be traced to the way it was once chaired and managed: with its presidency in the hands of the government of member states, and leadership changing every six months, providing leadership and continuity was always a problem. The dynamics of Council decision-making have also been left hostage to at least five sets of internal pressures:

1   The Franco-German axis has often been at the heart of the work of the Council, the state of personal relations between the leaders of the two states being a key determinant of the agreements reached. Their role was diminished as eastern enlargement helped change the balance of Council membership, but still crops up occasionally.
2   The ideological and personal agendas of individual leaders.
3   The levels of experience of individual leaders; membership changes often as elections and political crises bring political change in the member states.
4   The levels of support enjoyed at home by individual leaders. Those with a solid base of support are in different negotiating positions from those who are unpopular, or who lead weak or unstable coalition governments, or who are facing a new election that they may lose.
5   The different levels of respect and credibility earned by different leaders. Some become (or have tried to become) major players in EU debates, but with enlargement there has been less opportunity for individual leaders to exert themselves in anything more than a passing fashion.

A key change made by the Treaty of Lisbon was to take the position of chair out of the hands of the head of government of the member state holding the presidency of the Council of Ministers, and to give it instead to a president appointed for two and a half years (renewable once) by the European Council. The president of the European Council is elected using QMV, the incumbent cannot hold national office while serving as president, and they can be removed by QMV 'in the event of an impediment or serious misconduct' (Article 15(5)). With the new office having been created only in 2009, and with only two holders to date, it is still too early to be sure how the post will impact the Council's leadership dynamic, particularly as the terms of the job, as outlined in Article 15(6) of the Treaty of Lisbon, are remarkably vague:

■   The president shall chair, 'drive forward' and 'ensure the preparation and continuity' of the work of the Council.
■   The president shall 'endeavour to facilitate cohesion and consensus' in the Council.
■   The president shall 'ensure the external representation of the Union on issues concerning its common foreign and security policy, without prejudice to the powers of the High Representative of the Union for Foreign Affairs and Security Policy'.
■   The president must report to Parliament after each meeting.

President of the European Council: The head of the European Council, appointed by the Council for a term of two and a half years, renewable once, and charged with giving it direction.

Profile *Donald Tusk*

Donald Tusk (1957–) (*left*), the Polish prime minister, was chosen in August 2014 by the leaders of the EU member states to be the second president of the European Council. He took office in December that year, replacing former Belgian Prime Minister Herman van Rompuy (*right*), who had served the maximum possible two terms of two and a half years each. Van Rompuy's skills as a negotiator and consensus builder had helped give more shape to the nature of the position, and Tusk was expected to follow in a similar vein. Tusk was elected to the Polish parliament in 1991, was appointed deputy speaker of the Senate in 1997, became leader of the opposition in 2003, and became prime minister of Poland at the head of a centre-right Civic Platform government in 2007. With his appointment to the presidency of the European Council, he became the first East European to hold one of the EU's top jobs.

History has repeatedly shown that the first holder of a new office can often have a major impact on how the office evolves. As we saw in Chapter 7, the choice of Herman van Rompuy as the first president of the Council was controversial, with some arguing that he was the perfect deal-maker, in the sense that he would not rattle the egos of more than two dozen national leaders meeting in committee, while others argued that the appointment of the so-called 'grey mouse' was a missed opportunity to provide the EU with a new sense of leadership. For now, opinion remains split on whether the Council best works as a collective, or whether it still needs the kind of president who can lead from the front.

Summary

- The Council of Ministers is where national government ministers make decisions on proposals for new laws, and the European Council is where heads of government discuss broad strategic issues.

- The Council of Ministers is headquartered in Brussels, its membership changing according to the policy area under discussion.

- Meetings of the Council of Ministers are chaired by representatives from the presidency of the Council, which rotates among member states every six months.

- Most of the work of the Council is undertaken by the Committee of Permanent Representatives (Coreper), one of the most influential and most often overlooked institutions in the EU system of governance.

- The main job of the Council is to decide – in conjunction with Parliament – which proposals for new EU laws and policies will be adopted and which will not. It also shares powers with Parliament for approving the EU budget.

- Most Council decisions are either unanimous or use a qualified majority, with each member state given a number of votes roughly in proportion to the size of its population.

- The European Council is much like a board of directors for the EU, meeting at least four times annually in Brussels to address broader issues.

- The European Council uses summitry and bargaining, works on the basis of achieving a consensus, appoints its own president and the High Representative of the Union for Foreign Affairs and Security Policy, and plays a key role in the appointment of members of the College of Commissioners.

- The European Council is headed by an appointed president whose job is to provide it with direction and consistency.

- The Council of Ministers and the European Council have a mix of intergovernmental, supranational and confederal qualities.

Key terms and concepts

Coreper

European Council

Presidency of the Council of Ministers

President of the European Council

Qualified majority vote

Summitry

Trio system

Further reading

Foret, François, and Yann-Sven Rittelmeyer (eds) (2014) *The European Council and European Governance: The Commanding Heights of the EU* (Abingdon: Routledge). Edited collection of studies of the European Council as an institution and a policy-maker.

Hayes-Renshaw, Fiona, and Helen Wallace (2006) *The Council of Ministers*, 2nd edn (Basingstoke: Palgrave Macmillan). A more analytical text than Westlake and Galloway (below), with more emphasis on the functions of the Council and its relations with other EU bodies.

Westlake, Martin, and David Galloway (eds) (2004) *The Council of Ministers of the European Union*, 3rd edn (London: John Harper). Detailed survey of the workings of the Council, with chapters on key councils, supporting bodies and procedures.

12 The European Parliament

Preview

The European Parliament (EP) is the only directly elected European institution, and has won new powers for itself that have made it an increasingly important actor in European affairs. Logically, then, the EP should be the one EU institution that has developed the closest political and psychological ties to Europeans, particularly those who worry about the EU's democratic deficit. And yet most European voters remain disengaged from its work, turning out in low numbers at EP elections, and taking less interest in its work than in the work of national legislatures.

Dividing its time between Brussels in Belgium and Strasbourg in France (with an administrative Secretariat in Luxembourg), the EP is the legislative arm of the EU, sharing responsibility with the Council of Ministers for debating, amending and taking the final vote on proposals for new EU laws and the EU budget, and having the power to confirm or reject senior institutional appointments (such as the president of the Commission). However, it lacks two of the typical powers of national legislatures: it can neither introduce new laws nor raise revenues. It consists of 751 members elected from the 28 EU member states for fixed and renewable five-year terms, who sit together not in national blocs but in cross-national party groups.

The EP's structural problems are manifold: it is not part of a European 'government', there is no change of 'government' at stake in EP elections, there are few prominent personalities in the EP who can fire public imaginations, and the links between national political parties and political groups in the EP are still not clear (see Chapter 15). Until European voters can see how the EP impacts their lives, and until they make choices at European elections on European rather than national issues, it is unlikely that the EP's situation will improve.

Key issues

- Is the European Parliament more or less than it seems?
- Should the EP have more powers over the legislative process?
- How far has the EP gone to help close the EU's democratic deficit, and what is still missing from the equation?
- Do critics of the procedure by which the EP president is chosen have a point?
- What powers over the other institutions does the EP most obviously lack?

How Parliament evolved

The European Parliament traces its roots back to the first meeting in Strasbourg on 10 September 1952 of the Common Assembly of the ECSC. Its 78 members had no power to propose or amend ECSC laws, and although the High Authority was required to answer questions put to it by the Assembly, and could be forced to resign by an Assembly vote of censure, the Assembly was little more than a forum for the discussion of proposals from the High Authority (Gillingham, 1991, p. 282). It could develop its own rules of procedure, however, and used this to good effect by allowing for the formation of cross-national party groups and creating standing committees.

The Treaties of Rome created a 142-member European Parliamentary Assembly shared by the ECSC, the EEC and Euratom, which met for the first time in Strasbourg in March 1958 with Robert Schuman as its president. It was given joint powers with the Council of Ministers for approving the Community budget, and in 1962 was renamed the European Parliament. Many members had a dual mandate, meaning that they served in the European Parliament and their national legislatures, but the workload of the EP grew, so the dual mandate became more impractical and was eventually abolished.

The EP crossed a political watershed in 1976 when the European Council agreed to an EP proposal that it should be directly elected. The first elections were held in June 1979, and with Members of the European Parliament (MEPs) now given a democratic mandate and meeting in public session, they argued that they should be given new powers to represent voter interests and offset and balance the powers of the other EU institutions. Unfortunately, voters were slow to back up the EP; even today, few know what it does and turnout at elections has fallen steadily from 63 per cent in 1979 to just over 43 per cent in 2014 (see Chapter 16).

The membership of the EP more than tripled between 1973 and 1995 from 198 to 626 as the membership of the EEC/EU grew, and it was given shared responsibility with the Council of Ministers over the Community budget; within limits, it could now raise, lower or reallocate spending, and even – if necessary – reject the annual budget altogether (Corbett et al., 2011, p. 225). It was given an additional boost in 1980 by a decision from the European Court of Justice (ECJ) – *SA Roquette Frères* v. *Council* (Case 138/79). This sided with a French company that challenged a Council regulation placing production limits on isoglucose (a starch-based food sweetener), partly on the basis that it had been adopted without an opinion from Parliament. The ECJ thus established the right of the EP to be consulted on draft legislation, giving it standing to bring cases to the ECJ (Dehousse, 1998, p. 98).

The EP also used parliamentary questions to hold the other Community institutions more accountable, and steadily won more powers over new policy areas and greater input into the law-making process (see Rittberger, 2005, Chs 5 and 6). The Single European Act brought a key change: where the EP's opinions on proposals for new laws had been non-binding (the so-called 'consultation procedure'), the SEA introduced a cooperation procedure under which all laws relating to the single market could be subject to two readings by the EP. Maastricht and Amsterdam introduced the co-decision procedure (since renamed the 'ordinary procedure'), under which a third reading was possible, giving the EP the effective right of veto over most new legislation.

How Parliament is structured

The European Parliament is the only directly elected transnational legislature in the world, and the only directly elected EU institution. It consists of a single chamber with 751 MEPs elected by universal suffrage for fixed and renewable five-year terms (see Figure 12.1). Controversially, it is divided among three different locations: plenary sessions (meetings of the whole, or part-sessions) take place in Strasbourg, while parliamentary committees meet in Brussels for two weeks every month (except August), and the administrative Secretariat is based in Luxembourg.

The problem dates back to the era of the European Parliamentary Assembly, which held committee meetings in Brussels and plenaries in Luxembourg and Strasbourg. The latter was chosen in part because the Council of Europe building was the only one available at the time that was big enough, and in part because many members of the Assembly were also members of the Parliamentary Assembly of the Council of Europe. Since 1981, plenaries have been held in Strasbourg alone, and the split between Strasbourg, Brussels and Luxembourg was confirmed in 1992. The French government went further in 1999 by opening a new €470 million home for the EP in Strasbourg. Named for Louise Weiss, a French journalist and MEP, the building was immediately branded a white elephant; because plenary sessions last only three to four days each month (again, except August), the building is almost empty for most of the year. Meanwhile, the Espace Léopold complex in Brussels, built for the EP in stages between 1989 and 2009, was big enough to meet all the EP's needs.

The division (long opposed by the EP itself) not only forces a tiring and time-consuming travel schedule on MEPs (who must also regularly travel home to meet with their constituents and parties), but inflates the EP's annual budget by an estimated €200 million. Meanwhile, Strasbourg continues to press its demands, laying claim to being symbolic of European unity because it is sited in the French province of Alsace, which was long at the heart of Franco-German hostilities (see discussion in Judge and Earnshaw, 2008, pp. 148ff.). But this is

Illustration **12.1**
The European Parliament
The buildings housing the European Parliament: the Louise Weiss plenary chamber in Strasbourg on the left and the Espace Léopold in Brussels on the right.

Figure **12.1** **Structure of the European Parliament**

- Legislative arm of the EU (but shares powers with Council of Ministers)
- Plenary sessions meet in Strasbourg, committees meet in Brussels, administrative offices in Luxembourg
- Headed by a president elected from among the party groups in Parliament for renewable five-year terms
- Consists of 751 MEPs directly elected by voters in the member states for fixed and renewable five-year terms, the number of MEPs being divided among member states approximately on the basis of population
- MEPs are organized into cross-national political groups, or may sit as independents
- Detailed work undertaken by 20 standing committees, and temporary committees and committees of inquiry
- Work supported by a Secretariat
- Federal in character, and driven by a combination of supranationalism, nationalism and ideology

an increasingly weak argument, and the French government is almost alone in insisting that the EP continues to meet in Strasbourg.

The EP has five main components: Members of the European Parliament, the president of the EP, parliamentary committees, rapporteurs, and the Secretariat.

Members of the European Parliament

Seats in the EP are divided up among the member states roughly on the basis of population, with a cap of 751 and no state allowed more than 96 or less than 6. While Germany today has the full allotment of 96, Malta, Luxembourg, Cyprus and Estonia have 6 each (see Table 12.1). If seats were divided strictly by population, with each Member of the European Parliament (MEP) representing the same number of people (673,000), then Germany would have 120 MEPs, while Cyprus would have 1 and Malta and Luxembourg would have 0. Under the current formula, the French and the British have fewer MEPs per capita (about

Member of the European Parliament (MEP):
A representative elected from any of the EU member states to serve in the European Parliament.
Elected for fixed and renewable five-year terms.

Table **12.1** **Seats in the European Parliament**

Germany	96	Portugal	21	Ireland	11
France	74	Czech Republic	21	Lithuania	11
UK	73	Hungary	21	Latvia	8
Italy	73	Sweden	20	Slovenia	8
Spain	54	Austria	18	Cyprus	6
Poland	51	Bulgaria	17	Estonia	6
Romania	32	Denmark	13	Luxembourg	6
Netherlands	26	Finland	13	Malta	6
Greece	21	Slovakia	13		
Belgium	21	Croatia	11	TOTAL	**751**

Illustration **12.2**
A parliamentary plenary
Members of the European Parliament meeting in a plenary session in Strasbourg.

one per 885,000 people), while the Maltese and Luxembourgers have many more (about one MEP per 75,000 people).

Candidates for European elections are chosen according to the rules of their national parties, but once in office they have an independent mandate and cannot always be bound by those parties (Hix and Lord, 1997, pp. 85–90). What this means for the personality of the EP is debatable. It is often assumed that anyone working within an EU institution will undergo a process of socialization that encourages them to become more pro-European. But the ranks of MEPs include representatives of political parties that are lukewarm and even hostile towards integration, and Scully (2005) has argued that MEPs do not necessarily become more pro-integration and often think and act like national politicians, and that to think of the EP as supranational in character is misleading.

MEPs are paid by their home governments, and long received the same as members of their respective national parliaments. This created large income disparities with the arrival in 2004–07 of new and relatively poorly paid eastern European MEPs. Since 2009, all MEPs have been paid the same; in the 2013–14 term, this was €95,483 per year (plus office and travel expenses), and they pay their taxes into the EU budget. MEPs are not allowed to hold other significant political offices, such as a member of a national government or a legislature of a member state, a European commissioner, a judge on the ECJ, or a member of the board of directors of the European Central Bank.

The political experience of MEPs has improved over the years. Where once the EP was seen as something of a haven for politicians who had failed to win office at home or had been temporarily sidelined, its new powers have attracted more seasoned legislators. Its ranks have included former chancellors of Germany, former presidents of France and Lithuania, and former prime ministers of Italy and Belgium. Many MEPs have served as elected representatives in their national legislatures, and others have had experience as national government ministers. Meanwhile, experience as an MEP has counted for more, and has appeared on the résumés of several members of the European Commission and several high-ranking members of national governments.

In economic, gender and social terms, the EP looks much like most national legislatures, with a preponderance of white, middle-aged, middle-class professional men from urban backgrounds. But the proportion of women in the EP has grown from a low of 16% in 1979 to just under 37% in 2014. This is still far short of the EP's own goal of 50% by 2050, and below the average for the national legislatures of several Scandinavian countries (42–45%), but well above that for Britain (23%), the US (18%), or Russia (14%) (Inter-Parliamentary Union figures for 2010–13, for lower or single chambers of national legislatures, see www.ipu.org/english/home.htm). Turnover for MEPs at elections is higher than is the case in most national legislatures; typically about half the members arriving after an election are newcomers (Corbett et al., 2011, p. 45).

The president

The European Parliament is chaired by a president elected by MEPs from among their number for renewable terms of five years, or the span of a parliamentary term. The functional equivalent of the presidents or speakers found in most national European legislatures, the president of the EP works with vice-presidents representing the EP's political groups, and has several responsibilities:

- To open, chair and close EP debates during plenary sessions.
- To apply the rules of parliamentary procedure.
- To sign the EU budget and all legislative proposals decided by co-decision.
- To pass proposals to committees.
- To represent Parliament in legal matters and in its relations with other institutions (including national legislatures), and to address meetings of the European Council.
- To preside over meetings of the Conference of Presidents and the Bureau of the EP (see later in this chapter).

In theory, the president is elected in a vote by MEPs choosing from a slate of competing candidates, with the preferred candidate of the biggest political group in the EP having a clear advantage. Also in theory, the president is elected for five-year terms and can remain in office for as long as they want the job and have the support of a majority of MEPs. But because no one political group has yet won a majority of seats in the EP, since 1989 the president has been chosen as a result of bargaining among the leaders of the major groups, particularly the two biggest: the centre-right European People's Party (EPP) and the centre-left Progressive Alliance of Socialists and Democrats (S&D). These groups have taken turns controlling the office for half terms of two and a half years, with the smaller liberal democrats occasionally being given a turn (see Table 12.2) (Judge and Earnshaw, 2008, pp. 160–1). The first break in this pattern came in 2014 when the S&D dropped its support for its favoured candidate for president of the Commission, Martin Schulz, and backed Jean-Claude Juncker in return for an agreement that Schulz be returned to a second half term.

President of the EP: The leader of the European Parliament, elected by MEPs from among their number, the selection being predetermined as a result of negotiations among the major party groups.

Profile *Martin Schulz*

Martin Schulz (1955–) was elected president of the European Parliament in January 2012, and in July 2014 became the first ever president confirmed to a full five-year term. A German socialist, he began his working career as a bookseller after his hopes of being a professional footballer were dashed by injury, and at age 31 was elected mayor of Würselen in North Rhine-Westphalia. In 1994 he was elected to the European Parliament, becoming leader of the SPD political group in 2000, then the Socialist Group, and then the S&D. In late 2013 he was nominated to be the socialist candidate for the presidency of the European Commission, his plans ending when the S&D switched its support to Jean-Claude Juncker in return for an agreement that Schulz be elected to a second half term as president of the EP.

The arrangements made for the election of Jerzy Buzek in 2009 illustrate how the system works. With EPP president Hans-Gert Pöttering stepping down, British MEP Graham Watson – leader of the liberal democratic group in the EP – launched a campaign in January 2009 for the presidency, saying that he wanted to end the cycle of back-room deals. He hoped to win the support of Joseph Daul, leader of the EPP, but Daul had no incentive to offer Watson his support, given that the EPP and the S&D had enough votes in the EP to continue with the tradition of the rotating presidency. Italian MEP Mario Mauro announced that he would run against Buzek in an internal EPP contest, but was encouraged by Daul to withdraw his candidacy. Watson then withdrew after a deal was struck by which the liberal democratic group was given its wish for the setting up of a special parliamentary committee to investigate the causes of the 2007–10 global financial crisis. This cleared the way for Buzek – after facing the token opposition of Eva-Britt Svensson, leader of the left-wing European United Left/Nordic Green Left group in the EP – to be elected president in July 2009, becoming the first East European to hold the job (Taylor, 2009).

This system encourages critics to scoff at the EP's claims to be the democratic conscience of the EU. Furthermore, the fact that only one president has ever served a full term makes it difficult for incumbents to come to grips with the job or become well-known public figures, making it more difficult to draw public attention to the work of the EP. Few presidents were less prepared for the job than the Spanish socialist Josep Borrell Fontelles, who became president in 2004 within weeks of the start of his first term as an MEP. And the fact that the deal on the presidency is worked out between two political groups with dissimilar ideological identities makes it seem all the more artificial and opportunistic. Opposition to the deal-making has been growing within the EP, to be sure, but until one group wins a majority of seats in the EP, or is willing and able to form a coalition with smaller groups, lasting change is unlikely.

The EP is managed by three different committees:

Conference of Presidents:
The major administrative body of the EP, consisting of the president and the heads of the party groups, and responsible for managing plenary sessions and the EP committee system.

1 The most politically powerful is the Conference of Presidents, consisting of the president and the heads of the EP political groups, and responsible for deciding the timetable and agenda for plenary sessions and managing EP committees.

Table **12.2** **Presidents of the European Parliament**

Beginning of term		Name	Member state	Party group
Sept	1952	Paul-Henri Spaak	Belgium	Socialist
May	1954	Alcide de Gasperi	Italy	Christian Democrat
Nov	1954	Giuseppe Pella	Italy	Christian Democrat
Nov	1956	Hans Furler	Germany	Christian Democrat
Mar	1958	Robert Schuman	France	Christian Democrat
Mar	1960	Hans Furler	Germany	Christian Democrat
Mar	1962	Gaetano Martino	Italy	Liberal Democrat
Mar	1964	Jean Duvieusart	Belgium	Christian Democrat
Sept	1965	Victor Leemans	Belgium	Christian Democrat
Mar	1966	Alain Poher	France	Christian Democrat
Mar	1969	Mario Scelba	Italy	Christian Democrat
Mar	1971	Walter Behrendt	Germany	Socialist
Mar	1973	Cornelis Berkhouwer	Netherlands	Liberal Democrat
Mar	1975	Georges Spénale	France	Socialist
Mar	1977	Emilio Colombo	Italy	European People's Party (EPP)
July	1979	Simone Veil	France	Liberal Democrat
Jan	1982	Pieter Dankert	Netherlands	Socialist
July	1984	Pierre Pflimlin	France	EPP
Jan	1987	Sir Henry Plumb	UK	Conservative
July	1989	Enrique Barón Crespo	Spain	Socialist
Jan	1992	Egon Klepsch	Germany	EPP
July	1994	Klaus Hänsch	Germany	Socialist
Jan	1997	José Maria Gil-Robles	Spain	EPP
July	1999	Nicole Fontaine	France	EPP
Jan	2002	Pat Cox	Ireland	Liberal Democrat
July	2004	Josep Borrell Fontelles	Spain	Socialist
Jan	2007	Hans-Gert Pöttering	Germany	EPP-European Democrats
July	2009	Jerzy Buzek	Poland	EPP
Jan	2012	Martin Schulz	Germany	S&D
July	2014	Martin Schulz	Germany	S&D

2 The Bureau functions much like the EP's governing council, and is responsible for administrative, organizational and staff issues, monitoring the rules on party groups, appointing the EP secretary-general, and administering the EP budget. It consists of the president and the 14 vice-presidents, joined in a non-voting capacity by the five quaestors of the EP, who are responsible for the administrative and financial rules relating to MEPs.

3 Finally, the Conference of Committee Chairs discusses organizational issues, watches the progress of legislative proposals, and brokers deals between the political groups over the drafting of the parliamentary agenda (Corbett et al., 2011, p. 101).

Rapporteurs

One of the most important and influential roles in the EP is that of the rapporteur, an MEP who is appointed to a committee to draft a report on a legislative proposal and recommend a position or political line to be followed. Appointments are based on a points system, with the different political groups in the EP being given points in relation to their size and essentially bidding against each other for the appointment of rapporteurs to proposals. On recurring proposals such as the annual EU budget, assignment takes place on a rotation. With the help of policy specialists, members of EP committees, and even interest groups, rapporteurs will solicit information on the subject of the proposal and prepare a report to be put before a plenary session of the EP.

Secretariat

Parliament has its own internal bureaucracy, to match those of the Commission and the Council of Ministers. Based in Luxembourg, the job of the EP Secretariat is to coordinate legislative work, organize plenary sittings and meetings, and provide MEPs with technical and expert assistance. It employs about 6,000 staff, about 2,000 of whom work on translation and interpretation, and about 1,000 of whom are employed temporarily by the EP political groups. The balance are permanent EU civil servants, recruited with an eye to ensuring a spread of nationalities; at the higher levels political affiliation is a factor in determining appointments. As with the Secretariat-General of the Commission, there has been little turnover in the office of EP secretary-general, so that when Klause Welle of Germany replaced Harald Rømer of Denmark in 2009, he became only the seventh person to hold the job in just over 50 years.

Parliamentary committees

As with conventional national legislatures, most of the detailed work of the EP is addressed by a network of committees in which MEPs meet to discuss and amend legislative proposals (Neuhold and Sttembri, 2007). Convening monthly or bimonthly in Brussels, there are now 20 standing (permanent) committees (see Table 12.3), ranging in size between 24 and 76 members, their responsibilities reflecting the priorities of European integration. EP committees are in some ways more important than their national equivalents: Ringe (2009) argues that since MEPs lack the resources to make equally informed decisions across all areas of policy, they often adopt the positions of their expert colleagues in EP committees that most closely match their own.

Table **12.3 Committees of the European Parliament**

Agriculture and Rural Development	Fisheries
Budgetary Control	Foreign Affairs
Budgets	Industry, Research and Energy
Civil Liberties, Justice and Home Affairs	Internal Market and Consumer Protection
Constitutional Affairs	International Trade
Culture and Education	Legal Affairs
Development	Petitions
Economic and Monetary Affairs	Regional Development
Employment and Social Affairs	Transport and Tourism
Environment, Public Health and Food Safety	Women's Rights and Gender Equality

Winning appointment to a committee is desirable and competitive, because this is where most of the work of shaping legislation is done. Some committees (particularly Budgets, Environment, and Foreign Affairs) are more influential than others, and national interests also drive MEP choices; so, for example, Polish and Irish MEPs have more interest in agriculture than in foreign and security issues. Membership of committees is determined in part by the seniority of MEPs and in part by the size of political groups in the EP. In most national legislatures, committee chairs are appointed out of the majority party or coalition. But because there is no majority party in the EP, committee positions and chairmanships are divided up among political groups using the d'Hondt method of apportionment (named for a nineteenth-century Belgian mathematician), which uses a formula based on the number of votes each party receives and the number of seats it is allocated. Controversially, the three major pro-EU political groups worked together in 2014 to block the appointment of a eurosceptic MEP from Italy as chair of the Petitions committee.

In addition to standing committees, the EP also has temporary committees set up to examine a variety of politically pressing issues, including (in recent years) human genetics and other medical technologies (2001), the foot-and-mouth crisis (2002), allegations of illegal CIA activities in Europe (2006–07), climate change (2007–08), and the global financial crisis (set up in 2009). The EP can also set up committees of inquiry to investigate breaches or poor application of EU law, their work designed to assert the EP's rights of scrutiny over other institutions. Finally, there is a Conciliation Committee that meets when the EP and the Council of Ministers have disagreed on the wording of a legislative proposal. There are 28 members from each side, with representatives of the Commission also attending.

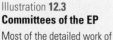
Illustration **12.3**
Committees of the EP

Most of the detailed work of the European Parliament is undertaken in committees such as this, which meet mainly in Brussels.

Comparing the European Parliament with national legislatures gives us more insight into how it works, and also helps us identify its more unusual qualities. It is most clearly distinctive in being the only international legislature in the world, but it is also unusual in the array of its powers and the manner in which it relates to the other EU institutions and the national parliaments of the member states. It has no significant intergovernmental qualities, because it is not a meeting place for the governments of the member states. It is, however, supranational because it works above the level of the member states on matters of broad EU interest, and it is also the most federal of the EU institutions.

The EP has five of the powers of a conventional national legislature:

1 It represents the interests of voters.
2 It deliberates on matters of public importance.
3 It has powers to make laws.
4 It has authority over the EU budget.
5 It has the power of scrutiny over the other institutions, keeping a particularly close eye on the work of the Commission.

But, in almost every regard, its powers are conditional:

■ It lacks the critical ability to draw up and propose legislation, which belongs to the Commission.
■ It shares the power to amend and adopt legislation with the Council of Ministers.
■ It shares power to approve the EU budget with the Council of Ministers.

■ Its ability to hold the other EU institutions accountable is limited.

The most important power that the EP lacks is that of making and bringing down governments. In most member states, the government (or the executive) is decided on the basis of the balance of political parties in the legislature and in order to stay in power, it must keep the support and confidence of the legislature. In the case of the EU, the political make-up of the EP has little bearing on the membership or stability of the other EU institutions. There is a distant relationship between the balance of political opinion in the EP and that in the member states, and a growing ideological relationship between the EP and the Commission, but the dynamic is quite different from that found in national governments.

At the same time, the EP is in the position of having a power relationship with the legislatures of the member states, who have been losing authority as the list of policies on which the EP can legislate has grown. National legislatures also find themselves regularly developing new laws on the basis of the requirements of EU law. This is what helps make the EP the most federal of the EU institutions, and the most obvious exception to, or variation on, the idea of the EU as a confederation.

Finally, where there is speculation about the declining powers of national legislatures and the growing powers of executives, the opposite is true of the EP. It is one legislature whose powers are growing, in part as a result of changes to the terms of the treaties, and in part due to some astute exploitation of its advantages by the EP itself.

What Parliament does

The European Parliament does not yet have all the conventional powers of a legislature (see Understanding Integration), but as time has gone on, it has become more like a conventional legislature, winning new authority mainly at the cost of the Council of Ministers. It is still a work in progress, however, and more changes are sure to come. For now, though, the jockeying for power and influence among the EU institutions has left it with powers ranging from the formal to the informal, the modest to the significant (see Figure 12.2). These powers fall broadly into three main groups: those over legislation, those over the budget, and those over other EU institutions.

Powers over legislation

Although Parliament cannot draft proposals for new laws (a job that belongs to the European Commission), there are several ways in which it can play a role in this part of the legislative process:

1 It can send representatives to the initial meetings held by the Commission to start the drafting process, helping shape legislation and encouraging the Commission to address issues it thinks are important.
2 It can publish 'own initiative' reports that draw attention to a problem, encouraging the Commission to respond.
3 It can send a request to the Commission that it submit a proposal on a problem related to the implementation of treaty obligations.

Most of the EP's legislative work, though, is focused on reviewing proposals received from the Commission, at which point it enters a complex process of bargaining with the Council of Ministers. When proposals are received by the EP, a report is drawn up by a rapporteur and discussed in committee, then sent for a vote in plenary session, the result being the 'position' of the EP. In its early years, the EP was mainly limited to the consultation procedure, by which it could accept, reject, or propose amendments to a proposal. Amended proposals would be sent back to the Council of Ministers, which then decided whether to accept, reject, or further amend the proposal. There was no time limit on how long the EP could take to give its opinion, so it had the power of delay, but consultation ultimately meant little more than the term implied, and it was the Council that had the final say over adoption.

The Single European Act changed the balance of power by introducing a new cooperation procedure, giving the EP a second reading for laws in areas relating to the single market, regional policy, the environment, and the European Social Fund. Maastricht changed the balance still further by extending cooperation to cover new policy areas, and introducing a new co-decision procedure that allowed for a third reading (see Figure 12.3). Renamed the ordinary legislative procedure

Consultation procedure: The original legislative procedure used in the EP, by which it could comment on proposals from the Commission but had little more than the power of delay.

Cooperation procedure: A legislative procedure introduced by the Single European Act, giving the EP the right to a second reading on selected proposals. All but eliminated by the Treaty of Amsterdam.

Ordinary legislative procedure: The most common legislative procedure now used in the EP, under which it has the right to as many as three readings on a legislative proposal, giving it equal powers with the Council of Ministers.

Figure **12.2 Powers of the European Parliament**

- Under the ordinary procedure, shares powers with the Council of Ministers over discussion and approval of new legislative proposals, and of the EU budget

- May encourage or pressure the Commission to develop new proposals

- Commission, Council of Ministers, and presidency of Council of Ministers must regularly report to the EP on their activities

- Right to confirm or reject the European Council's nominees for president of the European Commission and High Representative for Foreign Affairs and Security Policy

- Right of approval over appointments to the College of Commissioners, the management team of the European Central Bank, and the Court of Auditors

- May compel removal of the College of Commissioners

- Manages the office of the European ombudsman

by Lisbon, this is now the standard approach to law-making, giving the EP virtually equal powers with the Council of Ministers over the adoption of new laws, and making the two bodies 'co-legislatures'.

The last of the EP's legislative powers is the **consent procedure**, by which the support of the EP is needed in four kinds of decisions:

1 The accession of new member states to the EU and the granting of associate status to others.
2 The withdrawal of a member state from the EU, although what would happen if the EP did not give its consent is unclear.
3 The conclusion of international agreements, such as those reached by the EU after negotiations under the auspices of the WTO.
4 The imposition of penalties by the Council of Ministers on a member state for serious and persistent violations of fundamental rights.

One area in which the EP has won only limited powers is foreign policy, but the EP has creatively used the consent procedure to extend its authority. Maastricht obliged the presidency of the Council of Ministers to consult with the EP on the development of the Common Foreign and Security Policy, for example, and during the 1990s the EP used the consent procedure several times to delay agreements between the EU and third countries. These included an agreement with Russia in protest over Russian policy in Chechnya, with Kazakhstan in

Consent procedure: A legislative procedure under which the EP has veto rights in selected areas, including the admission of new member states to the EU, and the conclusion by the EU of new international agreements.

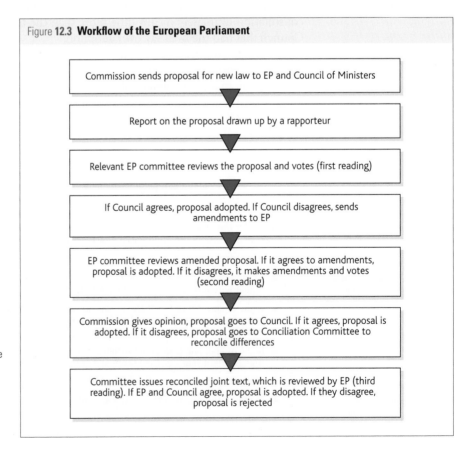

Figure **12.3 Workflow of the European Parliament**

Commission sends proposal for new law to EP and Council of Ministers

Report on the proposal drawn up by a rapporteur

Relevant EP committee reviews the proposal and votes (first reading)

If Council agrees, proposal adopted. If Council disagrees, sends amendments to EP

EP committee reviews amended proposal. If it agrees to amendments, proposal is adopted. If it disagrees, it makes amendments and votes (second reading)

Commission gives opinion, proposal goes to Council. If it agrees, proposal is adopted. If it disagrees, proposal goes to Conciliation Committee to reconcile differences

Committee issues reconciled joint text, which is reviewed by EP (third reading). If EP and Council agree, proposal is adopted. If they disagree, proposal is rejected

protest over that country's poor democratic record, and with Turkey in protest over human rights violations (Pienning, 2001).

Although it is not a legislative power, the EP has also taken a leading role in drawing attention to human rights issues inside and outside the EU. Debates on human rights problems are held during plenary sessions, the EP participates with the Council of Ministers in agreements to pressure states to release political prisoners, and since 1988 it has awarded the annual Sakharov Prize for Freedom of Thought to individuals or organizations active in the promotion of human rights. Past winners include Nelson Mandela, Burmese democracy leader Aung San Suu Kyi, UN Secretary-General Kofi Annan, and Malala Yousafzai, the (then) 16-year-old campaigner for education rights for girls in Pakistan.

Powers over the budget

Parliament and the Council of Ministers share powers over agreeing the EU budget, making them jointly the budgetary authority of the EU. As with new laws, it is the Commission that drafts the budget, which is then sent to the Council of Ministers (usually in April each year), and then to the EP where it is reviewed by the Committee on Budgetary Control and sent to a plenary session for a first reading. The EP can accept the draft or propose changes, which are forwarded to the Council of Ministers, which can either accept the changes or add its own, returning the new draft to the EP for a second reading. If there is strong opposition to the budget, then the EP – with a two-thirds majority – can reject it, but it has only done this three times so far (in 1979, 1982 and 1984). For the budget to come into force, it must be adopted by the EP and signed by the president of the EP.

Powers over other institutions

Parliament has several direct powers over other EU institutions that have helped it develop a modest system of checks and balances, and have given EU citizens more of a role (via the EP) in influencing those institutions. The most compelling relate to the Commission, which must submit regular reports to the EP, including its annual legislative programme and its report on the implementation of the EU budget. The presidency of the Council of Ministers must also report to the EP on its plans and its achievements. The EP can submit questions to the Commission and the Council, and can even take the Commission or the Council to the ECJ over alleged infringements of the treaties.

The EP's most substantial power over the Commission, often described as the 'nuclear option' because of its deterrent qualities, is to force the resignation of the College of Commissioners through a motion of censure. Several censure motions have been proposed over the years, but all have been defeated or withdrawn because they failed to win the two-thirds majority needed to succeed. As noted in Chapter 10, the closest the EP came to removing the College was during a vote in January 1999 over charges of fraud and corruption. While only 232 MEPs voted in favour, falling far short of the two-thirds majority of 416, the size of the negative vote sparked the creation of a committee of inquiry, whose report ultimately brought down the College.

Parliament also confirms the nominee of the European Council for president of the European Commission. If the nominee fails to win an EP majority, the

Council must submit a second nominee within a month. The Council's nominee for High Representative of the Union for Foreign Affairs and Security Policy must also be confirmed by the EP, along with the College of Commissioners as a whole. All nominees to the College must appear before the EP, and while it cannot block individual nominations, its reservations can be enough to lead to the withdrawal of nominations (see Chapter 10). Parliament also has the right to review and confirm the appointment of the president, the vice-president and the executive board of the European Central Bank; and must be consulted on appointments to the Court of Auditors.

The EP's relationship with the Council of Ministers is one of the most important in the EU institutional system. Apart from sharing powers with the Council over the adoption of most new laws, the EP also closely monitors the work of the Council, regularly submitting oral and written questions on matters of policy. The two institutions work particularly closely together on the Common Foreign and Security Policy, judicial cooperation, asylum and immigration issues, and international crime. The president of the EP also makes an address at the opening of every meeting of the European Council, providing an opportunity for the EP to comment on the Council agenda.

Parliament has also taken the initiative through the years to win new powers for itself over the work of EU institutions. As well as its early campaign to introduce direct elections, it introduced its own Question Time in 1973 – allowing it to demand oral or written replies to questions from commissioners – and initiated the 1992 reconfiguration of the number of seats in the EP. It has also worked to increase its role in the appointment of the directors and boards of the EU's specialized agencies; an EP campaign led to the creation of the Court of Auditors in 1993, since when it has exerted its moral and legal right to monitor the work of these agencies.

No coverage of the EP's relationship to other institutions would be complete without an assessment of the work of the European ombudsman. Created as a result of changes made by Maastricht, the ombudsman is charged with investigating complaints of maladministration by any of the EU institutions except the ECJ. The office is something of a branch of the EP, since the ombudsman is appointed by the EP with no input from the member states, has a term of office that coincides with that of the EP, has an office physically located in the EP buildings in Strasbourg, has a budget that comes out of that of the EP, and can be dismissed by the ECJ on a request from the EP. In 2013, Emily O'Reilly, the former national ombudsman of Ireland, became the first woman to be appointed to the position. (For more on the ombudsman, see Giddings et al., 2002.)

Complaints can be lodged by anyone who is a citizen or a legal resident of the EU, and the ombudsman's office can launch its own investigations if necessary. Complaints can be directed at discrimination, abuse of power, failure to reply, delays in taking action, and administrative irregularities. The ombudsman then informs the institution concerned, tries to find a solution to the problem, and can send a report to the EP if no resolution is achieved. Recent cases have included an attempt by the Commission to blacklist a German nongovernmental organization that had raised allegations of maladministration by the Commission, allegations of age discrimination against an Irish language translator employed by the Council of Ministers, and several complaints regarding late payment or non-payment of fees related to contracted work.

European ombudsman: An official appointed and monitored by the European Parliament and charged with investigating complaints of maladministration by any of the EU institutions except the ECJ.

Summary

- The European Parliament is the legislative arm of the EU, sharing powers with the Council of Ministers over the discussion and approval of legislative proposals developed by the European Commission, and over approving the EU budget.

- Plenary meetings of Parliament are held in Strasbourg, its committees meet in Brussels, and its Secretariat is based in Luxembourg. Pressure to move Parliament to Brussels has been resisted by France.

- The EP has 751 members elected to renewable five-year terms, the number of seats being divided up among the member states on the basis of population.

- The EP is headed by a president elected by its members. Since no one party group has yet won a majority in the EP, the presidency is decided by a bargain between the two largest political groups.

- Detailed parliamentary work is undertaken in a network of 20 standing committees.

- Most decisions are made under the ordinary legislative procedure, by which the EP and the Council can discuss and amend a proposal up to three times.

- The EP has the right to confirm nominees to the presidency of the European Commission, the High Representative for Foreign Affairs, the College of Commissioners, and the office of European ombudsman, and also has powers of scrutiny over the Commission.

- The powers of the EP have grown, thanks in part to changes in the treaties and in part to its own initiatives, and yet most EU citizens know little about what it does, and turnout at EP elections has been declining.

Key terms and concepts

Conference of Presidents

Consent procedure

Consultation procedure

Cooperation procedure

European ombudsman

Member of the European Parliament

Ordinary legislative procedure

President of the EP

Further reading

Corbett, Richard, Francis Jacobs and Michael Shackleton (2011) *The European Parliament*, 8th edn (London: John Harper). Judge, David, and David Earnshaw (2008) *The European Parliament*, 2nd edn (Basingstoke: Palgrave Macmillan). Two standard texts on the EP, the former written by insiders with an intimate knowledge of the workings of the EP.

Ringe, Nils (2009) *Who Decides, and How? Preferences, Uncertainty, and Policy Choice in the European Parliament* (Oxford: Oxford University Press). Study of how MEPs make decisions and choices, and the role of parties and committees in the process.

Whitaker, Richard (2010) *The European Parliament's Committees* (Abingdon: Routledge). First full-length study of the EP's committees, assessing their relationship with political parties.

13 The European Court of Justice

Preview

The European Court of Justice (ECJ) does not often make the news, and yet its role in European governance is critical: its task of ensuring that the terms of the treaties are respected, understood and applied as accurately as possible has made it essential to the process of integration. As the judicial arm of the EU, it has made decisions that have expanded and clarified the reach and meaning of integration, established key principles (such as direct effect and the supremacy of EU law), and helped transform the treaties into something like a constitution for Europe. It is one of the most clearly supranational of EU institutions.

Headquartered in Luxembourg, the ECJ has three parts. The Court of Justice works as the final court of appeal on matters of EU law, and is helped by the General Court, created in 1989 to deal with less complex cases, and by the EU Civil Service Tribunal, created in 2004 to deal with EU staff matters. The two upper courts each have 28 judges while the Tribunal has 7. And, although it is an entirely separate institution, the work of the European Court of Human Rights cannot be ignored, because its rulings have had important implications for the process of European integration.

The treaties may not be a constitution in the formal sense, and the Court of Justice may not strictly fit the definition of a typical constitutional court (if only because there is no EU constitution), but the progress of integration and the efficiency of the European institutions have depended heavily on the Court clarifying the meaning of the treaties and EU law. Its decisions have had an influence on matters as varied as the single market, competition policy, human rights, gender equality, and external trade.

Key issues

- Can the Court of Justice be a constitutional court without there being an EU constitution?
- Whose interests are represented by the Court of Justice?
- What (if any) is the political role of the Court of Justice?
- Is it possible, as Vassilios Skouris argues, for the Court of Justice to do 'nothing more' than rule on cases? In other words, can judges be objective and neutral?
- Should members of the Court of Justice be elected, or at least subject to approval by the European Parliament?

How the Court evolved

The European Court of Justice traces its roots back to the founding in 1952 of the Court of Justice of the ECSC. Consisting of seven members (six judges and a representative of the trade unions in the coal and steel industry), its job was to guard the Treaty of Paris by ruling on the legality of decisions made by the ECSC High Authority in the event of complaints lodged by member states or their national coal and steel industries. During its brief existence, it reviewed just over 50 cases and issued 16 judgments.

The treaties of Rome created separate courts for the EEC and Euratom, but a subsidiary agreement gave jurisdiction over all three founding treaties to a single seven-member Court of Justice of the European Communities. The new Court had a modest workload at first, but as the reach of integration expanded, it became busier, and by the early 1980s was taking on hundreds of new cases and issuing between 130 and 200 judgments per year (a figure that had risen to about 600 per year by 2008–12).

The number of judges grew with enlargement, but so did the workload of the Court, the backlog of cases meaning that it was taking up to two years to issue its more important judgments (Millett, 1990, p. 2). As a result, a new subsidiary Court of First Instance was created in 1989 to review less complicated cases, issuing its first judgment in February 1990. In 2004 the EU Civil Service Tribunal took over responsibility for cases involving disputes between the EU institutions and their staff. A final change came with the Lisbon treaty: the Court of First Instance was renamed the General Court, and the two courts together are now formally known as the Court of Justice of the European Union, although informally they are known as the European Court of Justice (ECJ).

Over the years, the ECJ has made numerous judgments that have clarified the meaning of the treaties, expanded the reach of the EU, and expanded the authority of the Court itself. Three in particular stand out for their importance. First, the principle of **direct effect** holds that EU law is directly and uniformly applicable in all member states, and that individuals can invoke EU law regardless of whether or not a relevant national law exists. It was established by the 1963 Court decision *Van Gend en Loos* v. *Nederlandse Administratie der Belastingen* (Case 26/62).

The Dutch transport company Van Gend en Loos complained that the Dutch government had increased the duty it charged on a chemical imported from Germany. Its lawyers argued that this was a violation of Article 12 of the EEC Treaty, which prohibited new duties on imports and exports or increases in existing duties. The Dutch government claimed that the Court had no jurisdiction, but the Court responded that the treaties were more than international agreements and that EC law was 'legally complete … and produces direct effects and creates individual rights which national courts must protect'.

Second, the principle of the **supremacy of EU law** holds that EU law trumps national law in policy areas where the EU has responsibility. This was established by the 1964 Court decision *Flaminio Costa* v. *ENEL* (Case 6/64). Costa was an Italian who had owned shares in Edison Volta, an electricity supply company that was nationalized in 1962 and made part of the new National Electricity Board (ENEL). Costa refused to pay his electricity bill, arguing that he had been hurt by nationalization, which was contrary to the spirit of the Treaty of Rome. When

Direct effect: The principle that EU law is directly and uniformly applicable in all EU member states, and that challenges can be made to the compatibility of national law with EU law.

Supremacy of EU law: The principle that in areas where the EU has competence (authority), EU law supersedes national law in cases of incompatibility.

Judicial authority

The power given to judges to interpret and apply law, and adjudicate disputes. Judges are expected to consider all aspects of a case and deliver their opinions impartially, typically being guided by the principles contained in a constitution. But they are only human, and are subject to biases, ideological leanings and subjective ideas about the meaning of law and constitutions. This raises the fundamental question of whether or not their appointments should be subject to public confirmation.

the local court in Milan asked the Court of Justice for a preliminary ruling, the Italian government argued that the ECJ had no jurisdiction. The Court disagreed, arguing that by creating 'a Community of unlimited duration … [with] its own legal capacity', the member states had 'limited their sovereign rights, albeit within limited fields, and have thus created a body of law which binds both their nationals and themselves'.

Third, the principle of mutual recognition holds that a product or service provided and sold legally in one member state cannot be barred from another. When West Germany refused to allow imports of Cassis de Dijon (a French blackcurrant liquor) because its wine-spirit content (15–20 per cent) was below the German minimum for fruit liqueurs (25 per cent), the importer charged that this amounted to a restriction on imports, prohibited under the Treaty of Rome. In its 1979 decision *Rewe-Zentral AG* v. *Bundesmonopolverwaltung für Branntwein* (Case 120/78), the ECJ agreed.

The issue came up again in the 1984 case *Commission* v. *Federal Republic of Germany* (Case 178/84) over a 1952 West German law that prevented beer being imported or sold in Germany that did not meet the *Reinheitsgebot*, a purity law passed in 1516 by the Duke of Bavaria that allows beer to contain only malted barley, hops, yeast and water. The West German government argued that because German men relied on beer for a quarter of their daily nutritional intake, allowing imports of 'impure' foreign beer would pose a risk to public health. The Court disagreed and ruled in 1987 that Germany had to accept foreign beer imports as long as brewers printed a list of ingredients on their labels.

With the abolition by Lisbon of the three-pillar arrangement, the Court's authority over matters of criminal law has expanded, with criminal sentences for environmental crimes being a valuable test. An attempt to prevent the Commission winning new powers worked its way up to the ECJ, which ruled in 2005 (*Commission of the European Communities* v. *Council* (Case 176/03)) that while criminal law as a general rule did not fall within the scope of the treaties, this did not prevent the Commission from proposing criminal sanctions when they were needed for the effective implementation of EU law (see discussion in Jacobs, 2006). New attention was drawn to the problem in 2006 when toxic waste carried by a European ship was dumped in Côte d'Ivoire, resulting in the deaths of ten people, numerous hospitalizations, and the dismissal of government ministers. The first EU law aimed at harmonizing national criminal law (a directive requiring all member states to consider intentional infringements of intellectual property rights carried out on a commercial scale a criminal offence) was soon working its way through the legislative process.

Mutual recognition: The principle that a product or service provided legally in one member state cannot be barred from provision in another member state.

Constitutional court: A court created to deal with matters of constitutional law, and to decide whether or not laws or the actions of elected officials respect the terms of a constitution.

How the Court is structured

By definition, a constitutional court is one created to issue judgments on questions of whether or not the laws or actions of governments and government officials conflict with the spirit or the letter of constitutionally established powers, rights and freedoms. Not all states have constitutional courts, some choosing to delegate judicial authority to supreme courts that also deal with issues of civil law (laws created by legislatures) and common law (laws created and developed through court decisions). Among the EU member states with constitutional courts are Austria, France, Germany, Italy and Spain, and all the eastern European states; those without constitutional courts include Denmark, Ireland, Malta, the Netherlands and Sweden. The ECJ clarifies the meaning and application of the treaties (the functional equivalent of a European constitution), but the idea of a constitutional court is one that some Europeans still find alien.

The ECJ is headquartered in Luxembourg, in the Centre Européen on the Kirchberg Plateau above the city of Luxembourg. When the ECSC was created, there was some debate about where its institutions would be based, Luxembourg eventually being chosen as a provisional home. Temporary buildings were used until the opening in 1973 of the Court's new black steel and glass Palais de Justice. But with the Court still growing, the Erasmus building was opened in 1988 to house the Court of First Instance, and two more extensions were opened in the early 1990s. It was only in 1992 that Luxembourg was formally confirmed as the home of the ECJ, which now shares the Centre Européen with a cluster of other European institutions that includes the Secretariat of the European Parliament, buildings for the Commission and the Council of Ministers, the seat of the Court of Auditors, and the headquarters of the European Investment Bank.

The Court of Justice has five main components: the judges, the president, the advocates-general, the General Court and the EU Civil Service Tribunal (see Figure 13.1).

The judges

The Court of Justice is headed by 28 judges, each appointed for a six-year renewable term of office, the beginnings of their terms staggered so that about half come up for renewal every three years. According to treaty rules, nominees must be 'persons whose independence is beyond doubt and who possess the qualifications required for appointment to the highest judicial offices in their respective countries or who are jurisconsults of recognized competence'. Most judges come to the Court having worked their way up through their national court systems, while some also have experience as government ministers, in elective office, with

---

Figure **13.1** **Structure of the European Court of Justice**

- Judicial arm of the EU
- Headquartered in Luxembourg
- Headed by a president elected from among its judges for renewable three-year terms
- Consists of 28 judges, each appointed for renewable six-year terms of office, with each member state having control over one appointment
- Judges rarely meet as a full court, more often meeting as chambers of 3 or 5 judges, or as a Grand Chamber of 13 judges
- Assisted by 11 advocates-general appointed for renewable six-year terms and charged with reviewing cases, studying arguments and delivering opinions
- Further assisted by the lower 28-member General Court, which hears less complicated cases in selected areas, and by the 7-member EU Civil Service Tribunal, which hears disputes between the EU institutions and their staff
- Supranational in character

Illustration 13.1 The European Court of Justice

Part of the headquarters complex of the European Court of Justice in Luxembourg.

international organizations, or as lawyers or academics. The European Parliament has almost no say in the appointment process, although it has argued that there should be confirmation hearings on the model of those used in the US for appointments to the US Supreme Court. The Court of Justice has opposed this idea on the grounds that its deliberations are secret, and confirmation hearings would force nominees to make public their views on judicial issues (Arnull, 2008, p. 21).

Although the judges are appointed by 'common accord' of the governments of the member states, and each member state controls one of the nominations, there is no requirement that the judges come from different member states, nor even from *any* member state. Theoretically, at least, they could all be Estonian or Polish or Spanish, and the Court could even – in the words of former President Lord McKenzie Stuart – be made up 'entirely of Russians' (Brown and Kennedy, 2000, p. 45). But the desire of member states to control as many appointments as possible to the EU institutions has meant that so far there has never been more than one judge from any member state (see Table 13.1).

Nominees to the Court must first be vetted by a seven-member panel made up of former members of the ECJ, members of national constitutional courts and lawyers, of whom one is nominated by the European Parliament. Once confirmed to the Court, judges – like members of the College of Commissioners – must maintain their independence and avoid promoting the national interests of their home states. Upon appointment, each takes a short oath: 'I swear that I will perform my duties impartially and conscientiously; I swear that I will preserve the secrecy of the deliberations of the Court.' In order to protect their independence, they are immune from having lawsuits brought against them while they are on the Court and even once they have retired. And while they can resign from the Court, they can only be removed against their will by the other judges and the advocates-general (not by the governments of member states or

Understanding Integration... *Supranationalism*

Supranationalism is a concept very much associated with the EU, but, unlike intergovernmentalism, is more a model than a theory (although efforts have been made to explore its theoretical possibilities). Sometimes portrayed as the opposite end of a continuum that begins with intergovernmentalism, it was used for the first time in an international agreement in the Treaty of Paris, and broadly refers to a political activity involving two or more states and taking place above the level of those states. As we saw in Chapter 11, intergovernmentalism refers to an arrangement within which governments work together to make decisions on matters of shared interest, retaining the right of veto to protect national interests, and giving up none of their sovereignty. In contrast, supranationalism refers to an arrangement within which decision-making is delegated to an institution working above the level of the states involved, and involving some degree of loss of control or sovereignty by the states involved.

Although none of the five major EU institutions are either entirely intergovernmental or supranational, the ECJ is arguably the most supranational of them all. The judges are not the representatives of national governments, are not expected to pursue national interests, are protected from coming under the influence of the member states, are not required to come from the member states, participate in governance above the level of individual states, and are expected to focus on making decisions that are in the broad interest of the EU, using the treaties as their guide.

One of the arguments made by neofunctionalists is that because supranational institutions have their own political agenda, they are likely to see national interests being replaced over time with a focus on supranational interests. In the case of the European Parliament, for example, MEPs may be elected by national voters to represent local or national interests, but once in the EP they work with like-minded colleagues from other countries and are thus more likely to become European in their thinking. These arguments apply to a lesser degree to the European Council and the Council of Ministers, but not to the Court of Justice or the European Commission, where national interests were rarely, if ever, a factor. In other words, while all five major EU institutions are supranational in the sense that they work above the level of the member states, not all are supranational in they way they think and make decisions.

the other EU institutions), and then only as a result of a unanimous agreement that they are no longer doing their job adequately (Lasok, 2007, pp. 7–8).

Although most judges are renewed at least once, the Court has more turnover than the national courts of the US, the Netherlands and Belgium, where appointments are for life. Life appointments have the benefit of exploiting the experience of judges and encouraging their independence, but they also restrict the flow of new thinking into the deliberations of a court, and make new appointments more highly contested. But limited appointments means new ideas and higher turnover; in 2014 almost half of the 28 judges were still in their first term. And yet the Court has not yet matched other EU institutions on diversity: the first female advocate-general was appointed in 1981, the first female judge on the General Court was appointed in 1995, and the first female judge on the Court of Justice was appointed in 1999. In 2014 the Court had only five women judges: Rosario Silva de Lapuerta of Spain, Camelia Toader of Romania, Maria Berger of Austria, Alexandra Prechal of the Netherlands, and Küllike Jürimäe of Estonia.

For all 28 judges to hear cases together and to meet as a full court would be an inefficient use of time and resources, so meetings of the full court are reserved only for proceedings to dismiss a European commissioner, a member of the

Table **13.1** **Judges of the European Court of Justice, August 2014**

Name	Member state	Year of birth	Year of appointment
Vassilios Skouris	Greece	1948	1999
Allan Rosas	Finland	1948	2002
Rosario Silva de Lapuerta	Spain	1954	2003
Koen Lenaerts	Belgium	1954	2003
Endre Juhász	Hungary	1944	2004
George Arestis	Cyprus	1945	2004
Anthony Barthet	Malta	1947	2004
Marko Ilešič	Slovenia	1947	2004
Jiří Malenovský	Czech Republic	1950	2004
Egils Levits	Latvia	1955	2004
Aindrias Ó Caoimh	Ireland	1950	2004
Lars Bay Larsen	Denmark	1953	2006
Antonio Tizzano	Italy	1940	2006
Jean-Claude Bonichot	France	1955	2006
Thomas von Danwitz	Germany	1962	2006
Alexander Arabadjiev	Bulgaria	1949	2007
Camelia Toader	Romania	1963	2007
Marek Safjan	Poland	1949	2009
Daniel Šváby	Slovakia	1951	2009
Maria Berger	Austria	1956	2009
Alexandra Prechal	Netherlands	1959	2010
Egidijus Jarašiūnas	Lithuania	1952	2010
Carl Gustav Fernlund	Sweden	1950	2011
José Luís da Cruz Vilaça	Portugal	1944	2012
Christopher Vajda	United Kingdom	1955	2012
Sinisa Rodin	Croatia	1963	2013
François Biltgen	Luxembourg	1958	2013
Küllike Jürimäe	Estonia	1962	2013

For a current listing of judges, see Court website, http://curia.europa.eu.

Court of Auditors, or the European ombudsman. All other cases are heard by chambers of 3 or 5 judges, or by a Grand Chamber of 13 judges when a member state or another EU institution makes a specific request. To further help manage the workload, each judge has their own cabinet of assistants and legal secretaries, equivalent to the *cabinets* of European commissioners, and responsible for helping with research and keeping records. The Court also has about 1,500 staff members, most of whom are bureaucrats or translators.

The president

Judge-rapporteur: A judge on the Court of Justice who is appointed to oversee the different stages through which a case is reviewed. Equivalent to rapporteurs in the European Parliament.

The Court of Justice is headed by a president elected by the judges from among their own number in a secret ballot by majority vote to serve a three-year renewable term (see Table 13.2). As well as presiding over meetings of the Court, the president is responsible for organizational matters such as assigning cases to chambers, appointing judge-rapporteurs (the judges responsible for shepherding a case through the review process), and deciding the dates for hearings.

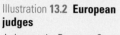

Illustration **13.2** **European judges**

Judges at the European Court of Justice take part in the swearing-in of the new European Commission in 2010.

Despite the growing powers of the Court, presidents are the least known of the senior figures in the EU institutional hierarchy and their work is subject to little public and political scrutiny. When President Skouris was first elected to his position in 2003, it was barely reported by the European media, and his election to a unprecedented fourth term in 2012 also passed almost unnoticed.

Just how political the role of president (or even judges) has become is open to debate. President Skouris (2004) was clear when he argued that the Court was not 'a political body with the right of initiative', and that its job was to 'rule on the cases, and nothing more'. But is there really 'nothing more'? Even with the best will in the world, judges will bring personal biases (including political views) into their assessments; they are, after all, only human. And the role of politics in court decisions has long been very much part of the debate in the US about the work of its Supreme Court, with an ongoing discussion about the merits of constructionists (judges who interpret the US constitution literally, to the extent that this is possible) and activists (those who bring their own views into their judgments).

Profile *Vassilios Skouris*

Vassilios Skouris (1948–) is the president of the European Court of Justice. A lawyer and professor of public law from Greece, he was educated in Germany, earning degrees in constitutional and administrative law from the Free University of Berlin and Hamburg University. He was then a professor of law for several years in German and Greek universities, and served twice in the Greek government as minister of internal affairs. He was first appointed as a Court judge in 1999, was elected as the ninth president of the Court in 2003, and to a fourth term in October 2012.

Table **13.2** **Presidents of the European Court of Justice**

Term	Name	Member state
1958–61	A.M. Donner	Netherlands
1961–64	A.M. Donner	Netherlands
1964–67	Charles Hammes	Luxembourg
1967–70	Robert Lecourt	France
1970–73	Robert Lecourt	France
1973–76	Robert Lecourt	France
1976–79	Hans Kutscher	West Germany
1979–80	Hans Kutscher	West Germany
1980–84	Josse Mertens de Wilmars	Belgium
1984–88	Lord McKenzie Stuart	United Kingdom
1988–91	Ole Due	Denmark
1991–94	Ole Due	Denmark
1994–97	Gil Carlos Rodríguez Iglesias	Spain
1997–2000	Gil Carlos Rodríguez Iglesias	Spain
2000–03	Gil Carlos Rodríguez Iglesias	Spain
2003–06	Vassilios Skouris	Greece
2006–09	Vassilios Skouris	Greece
2009–12	Vassilios Skouris	Greece
2012–15	Vassilios Skouris	Greece

The advocates-general

Advocates-general are court officers whose job is to review cases as they come to the Court of Justice, study the arguments involved, and deliver independent opinions in Court before the judges decide which laws apply and what action to take. The opinions of the advocates-general are not binding on the judges, but they provide a valuable point of reference (Burrows and Greaves, 2007). The Court has nine advocates-general appointed to renewable six-year terms. Like the judges, they are theoretically appointed by the 'common accord' of the governments of the member states, but in practice an informal system has developed by which one post is held by nationals of each of the big five member states (Germany, Britain, France, Italy and Spain), and the rest are held on a rotating basis by nationals of the smaller states. If needed, the number of positions can be increased by a simple decision of the Council of Ministers. One is appointed first advocate-general on a one-year rotation.

The General Court

With the workload of the Court of Justice growing in the 1980s, a decision was taken under the Single European Act to create a new Court of First Instance that could rule on less complicated cases. These included actions against EU institutions, actions brought by member states against the Commission, selected actions brought by member states against the Council of Ministers, actions for damage against EU institutions or their staff, actions on trademarks, and appeals from the Civil Service Tribunal. If a case is lost at this level, the parties involved have the right to appeal to the Court of Justice, but only on points of law.

Advocates-general: Officers of the Court of Justice who review cases as they arrive and deliver preliminary opinions to the Court about which laws apply and what action to take.

Renamed the General Court by the Treaty of Lisbon, it has roughly the same institutional structure as the Court of Justice: it has the same number of judges as there are member states of the EU, they are appointed for six-year renewable terms, and its rules of procedure are similar to those of the Court of Justice (although it has no advocates-general). The number of judges can be changed by a decision of the Council of Ministers without an amendment to the treaties. The Court usually sits as a chamber of 3 judges, but a single judge can hear and decide a case, while there can also be chambers of 5 judges, a Grand Chamber of 13 judges, and for the most important cases the entire court can sit together. It is overseen by a president elected by the judges for three-year renewable terms. In 2007, Marc Jaeger – a lawyer from Luxembourg and a member of the General Court since 1996 – was elected president. He was confirmed to a third term in 2013.

The General Court has been particularly active in cases dealing with competition, state aid and intellectual property. In the 2005 case *Laurent Piau* v. *Commission of the European Communities* (Case 193/02), for example, a player's agent named Laurent Piau complained to the European Commission that new rules adopted by FIFA, the international governing body of football, discriminated against agents for football players, amounted to abuse of dominant position and contravened EU competition law. The Commission dropped the case after FIFA changed its rules, but Piau challenged the decision to drop the case, which went to the General Court. In a 2005 judgment, the Court argued that the activities of football clubs and their national associations – as well as FIFA – were economic activities and so were subject to EU competition law, and that while the FIFA rules did not break EU competition rules, those rules could occasionally apply to sport.

The EU Civil Service Tribunal

The EU Civil Service Tribunal is one of the EU's newer institutions, created in 2004 to take over from the General Court any cases involving disputes between the EU institutions and their staff. It began work in 2005 under the jurisdiction of seven judges appointed for six-year renewable terms, with as broad a geographical range as possible, and overseen by a president. Its decisions can be appealed on questions of law to the General Court, and in exceptional situations to the Court of Justice. The Commission has been the target of more than half the cases brought to the Tribunal (a reflection as much as anything of its relative size), and the subjects range from contracts to pensions, job appraisals, promotions, discrimination, salaries and workplace facilities.

What the Court does

General Court: A subsidiary court created in 1989 (as the Court of First Instance) to review less complicated cases coming before the Court of Justice.

EU Civil Service Tribunal: A subsidiary court created in 2004 to take over from the Court of Justice cases involving complaints by EU employees.

The Court of Justice is responsible for making sure that the treaties are correctly interpreted, and that EU law is equally, fairly and uniformly applied throughout the member states. In other words, the Court is the supreme legal body of the EU and the final court of appeal on all matters relating to EU law (see Figure 13.2). In meeting its obligations, it has been at the heart of the process of European integration, playing a particularly important role in the late 1970s and 80s when the Community slipped into a hiatus and the Court kept alive the idea of integration as being something more than the building of a customs union (Shapiro, 1992). It is

---

Figure **13.2 Powers of the European Court of Justice**

- Supreme legal body of the EU and the final court of appeal on all matters relating to EU law
- Issues preliminary rulings when national courts ask for a ruling on the interpretation or validity of an EU law that arises in a national court case
- Makes decisions on direct actions when an individual, corporation, member state or EU institution brings proceedings directly before the Court, usually with an EU institution or a member state as defendant

---

the most powerful international court in the world, and yet it has no direct powers to enforce its decisions, instead exerting its influence through the work of other actors – institutions, states and individuals – who support its work (Conant, 2002).

Work on a case begins with a written application made by a lawyer or agent for the party bringing the case, which is filed with the registrar of the Court and published in its *Official Journal*. This describes the dispute and explains the grounds on which the application is based. The defendant is also notified and given a month to respond. A judge-rapporteur is assigned to the case by the president, and an advocate-general by the first advocate-general. These two officials present their preliminary reports to the Court, at which point the case is assigned to a chamber. The Court then decides whether documents need to be provided, witnesses interviewed, or an expert's report commissioned, after which the case is argued before the Court by the parties involved at a hearing. At the end of the oral phase, the advocate-general delivers an opinion, and once the chamber has reached a decision, it delivers judgment in open court (see Figure 13.3). Once a judgment has been made, details of the case are published in the *Report of Cases before the Court* (also known as the *European Court Reports*).

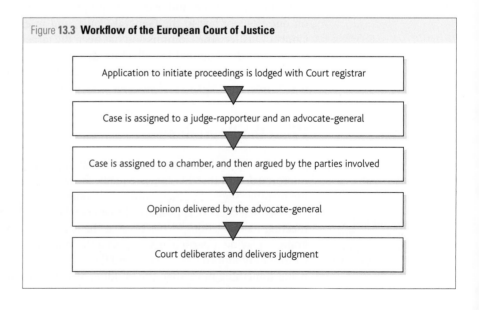

Figure **13.3 Workflow of the European Court of Justice**

Application to initiate proceedings is lodged with Court registrar

Case is assigned to a judge-rapporteur and an advocate-general

Case is assigned to a chamber, and then argued by the parties involved

Opinion delivered by the advocate-general

Court deliberates and delivers judgment

The whole process may take months, or years in more complex disputes; the average time has fallen, though, since the creation of smaller chambers, the General Court and the Civil Service Tribunal. Cases can also be heard on an expedited basis if an urgent decision is needed. Court decisions are technically supposed to be unanimous, but votes are usually taken on a simple majority; all votes are secret, so it is never publicly known who – if anyone – dissented. Judges were not given the right to publicly issue dissenting or concurring opinions, argues Arnull (2008, p. 11), for two main reasons. First, given that they serve short and renewable terms, they might have been tempted to go public in order to curry favour with their home governments in an attempt to be reappointed. Second, there were concerns in the early years of the Court that dissenting opinions might have undermined the Court's authority.

The work of the Court falls into two main parts, preliminary rulings and direct actions (see Figure 13.4).

Preliminary rulings

In order to ensure consistency in the application of EU laws, national courts can (and sometimes must) ask the Court of Justice for a preliminary ruling on the interpretation or validity of an EU law that arises in a national court case. EU institutions can also ask for preliminary rulings, but most are made on behalf of a national court, which is then bound to respect and apply the Court's response. The word *preliminary* is misleading, because the rulings are usually requested and given *during* a case, not before it opens; hence the rulings are actually concurrent rather than preliminary.

Both *Van Gend en Loos* and *Flaminio Costa* are classic examples of preliminary rulings. Another, with important implications for questions of citizenship, came in 2004. The Chens, a Chinese couple living in Britain, moved temporarily

Preliminary ruling: A ruling by the Court of Justice on the interpretation or validity of an EU law that arises in a national court case.

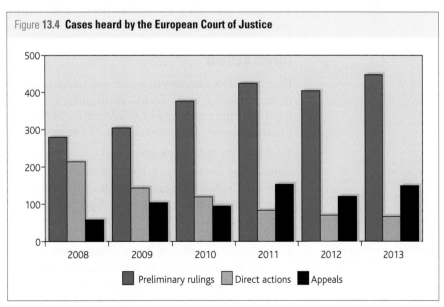

Figure **13.4 Cases heard by the European Court of Justice**

Legend: ■ Preliminary rulings □ Direct actions ■ Appeals

Source: Annual Report of the European Court of Justice, 2013, http://curia.europa.eu (retrieved August 2014).

Illustration **13.3**
The Court in session
A chamber of the European Court of Justice in session.

to Northern Ireland to have their second child, Catherine, who, by virtue of being born there, could claim Irish citizenship (she could not have claimed British citizenship because her parents were only temporary residents). Using the child's status as a citizen of an EU member state, the Chens hoped to move permanently back to Britain, but were barred by the British authorities. The case went to the Court of Justice, which ruled in *Zhu and Chen* v. *Secretary of State for the Home Department* (Case 200/02) that Catherine Chen could live anywhere in the EU, that denying her parents a similar right would interfere with Catherine's rights, and that it was not an abuse of EU rights to take advantage of Irish citizenship laws. Ireland was quick to change its constitution in order to deny automatic citizenship to children born on the island of Ireland unless one of the parents was an Irish citizen.

Direct actions

Direct actions are cases in which one party, which may be an individual, corporation, member state, or EU institution, brings proceedings against another, often a member state or an EU institution, before the Court of Justice rather than a national court. They can take one of five main forms:

1 *Actions for failure to fulfil an obligation:* These are cases where a member state has failed to meet its obligations under EU law, and can be brought either by the Commission or another member state, sometimes at the prodding of an interest group or a private company. They are by far the most common of direct actions, and most often deal with environmental and consumer law, freedom of movement, and freedom of establishment.

Direct action: A case in which there is a complainant, usually an individual, corporation, member state, or EU institution, and a defendant, usually an EU institution or a member state.

2 *Actions for annulment:* These (relatively rare) cases are aimed at making sure that EU laws conform to the treaties, and are brought in an attempt to cancel those that do not. The defendant is almost always the Commission or the Council, because proceedings are usually brought against an act that one of them has adopted (Lasok, 2007, p. 323).

3 *Actions for failure to act:* These are cases where an EU institution has failed to act in accordance with the terms of the treaties, and can be brought by other institutions, member states, or individuals. The first such action was brought in 1983 (*European Parliament* v. *Council* (Case 13/83)), when the European Parliament charged the Council of Ministers with failing to agree a Common Transport Policy as required under the Treaty of Rome. The Court ruled that while there was an obligation, because no timetable had been agreed, it was up to the member states to decide how to proceed.

4 *Actions for damages:* These are cases in which damages are claimed by third parties against EU institutions and their employees. A claim could be made that the institution was acting illegally, or an individual could claim that their business was being hurt by a piece of EU law. Most of these cases are heard by the General Court.

5 *Actions by staff:* These are cases involving litigation brought by staff members against EU institutions as their employers, and are dealt with by the Civil Service Tribunal.

Appeals and other cases

In cases where the General Court has issued a judgment, and one of the parties in the case is unhappy with the outcome, an appeal can be lodged with the Court of Justice. The Court can also be asked by the Commission, the Council of Ministers or a member state to rule on the compatibility of draft international agreements with the treaties; if the Court gives an unfavourable ruling, the draft agreement must be changed before the EU can sign it. Finally, the Court can be called in to arbitrate on contracts concluded by or on behalf of the EU (conditional proceedings) and in disputes between member states over issues relating to the treaties.

The European Court of Human Rights

Although it is not part of the EU's network of institutions, no analysis of judicial life in the EU can be complete without addressing the work of the European Court of Human Rights (ECHR). All member states of the EU – and the EU itself – are signatories of the European Convention on Human Rights and members of the ECHR, which means that in decisions dealing with human rights, the Court of Justice must refer to precedent created by the decisions of the ECHR. There is another, more minor, link between the two institutions: it is not uncommon to find judges from the ECHR being appointed as judges on the ECJ (but not vice versa).

Headquartered in Strasbourg, the ECHR was founded in 1959 under the terms of the 1950 European Convention on Human Rights, which was in turn adopted under the auspices of the Council of Europe in order to promote the protection of human rights and fundamental freedoms. The Court remained a temporary body until 1998 when it became a permanent institution to which direct access was available to citizens of the member states of the Council of Europe, which are also parties to the European Convention. This new permanence, combined with expanded membership of the Council of Europe, greater media interest in

European Court of Human Rights (ECHR): A Strasbourg-based court that hears cases and issues judgments related to the 1950 European Convention on Human Rights.

the work of the Court and simplified procedures, led to a new burst of activity: in its first 30 years the Court issued less than 70 judgments, but in the 10 years after becoming permanent, it received an annual average of 45,000 applications and issued about 800–1,000 judgments per year (Greer, 2006, pp. 34–40). Turkey and Italy have topped the list of violators of human rights (see Figure 13.5); more than half the judgments for the former related to the right to a fair trial and the protection of property, and more than half for the latter related to the excessive length of proceedings.

The ECHR consists of 47 judges, one for each of the member states of the Council of Europe (but not necessarily one from each member state). Judges are appointed by the Parliamentary Assembly of the Council of Europe for six-year renewable terms of office (with an age limit of 70), and they in turn elect a president and two vice-presidents. The Court is divided into five Sections, each balanced by geography, gender and the different legal systems of the member states, the membership of which is changed every three years. Each Section selects a Chamber consisting of a Section president and a rotating group of six other judges, which deals with the more routine cases brought to the Court. The more important cases are dealt with by a 17-member Grand Chamber consisting of the president and the two vice-presidents (all three of whom are also Section presidents), the two other Section presidents, and 12 other judges appointed on a rotating basis.

Any contracting state or any individual who claims to have been harmed by the actions of a contracting state can bring a case to the Court. Most cases are dealt with in writing, a small minority going before a formal hearing. Each case

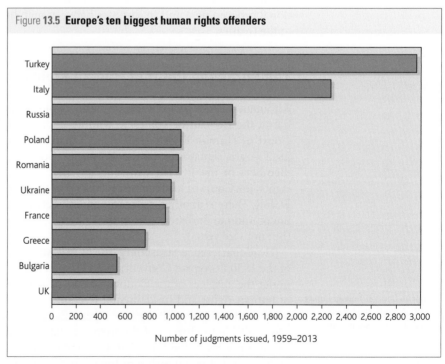

Figure **13.5 Europe's ten biggest human rights offenders**

Number of judgments issued, 1959–2013

Source: European Court of Human Rights website, http://www.echr.coe.int (retrieved August 2014).

Illustration **13.4 The European Court of Human Rights**

The headquarters of the European Court of Human Rights in Strasbourg.

is assigned to a Section, which can either declare it inadmissible or else decide to review it, in which case a decision is made by a simple majority vote. There is a right of appeal to a Grand Chamber, but otherwise a judgment becomes final within three months, and the Committee of Ministers of the Council of Europe is responsible for making sure that the state involved in the case has taken the necessary action to correct the problem.

This chapter would be incomplete without briefly mentioning two other courts with which the ECJ is sometimes confused, but with which there is a much looser judicial relationship. The first of these is the International Court of Justice, the major judicial arm of the UN. Founded in 1945, it is based in The Hague, and its job is to settle disputes between UN member states, and give opinions on legal questions submitted by international organizations and other UN bodies. The second is the International Criminal Court, also headquartered in The Hague, and founded in 2002 to prosecute individuals for crimes against humanity, war crimes and genocide. All EU member states are members of both courts, and while their rulings can have an impact on judicial matters in the EU, their relationship with the Court of Justice is not as close as that between the Court of Justice and the ECHR.

Summary

- The European Court of Justice (headquartered in Luxembourg) is the judicial arm of the EU, responsible for clarifying the meaning of the treaties and issuing judgments in disputes involving EU institutions, member states, and individuals affected by EU law.

- The Court is the least well known (and least controversial) of the EU institutions, yet it has made numerous decisions that have clarified the meaning of integration and established critical legal principles, such as direct effect, the supremacy of EU law and mutual recognition.

- The Court consists of 28 judges appointed for six-year renewable terms by 'common accord' of the member states. There is no approval process involving the European Council or the European Parliament.

- The Court is headed by a president elected to three-year renewable terms by the judges from among their number.

- The judges are assisted by nine advocates-general charged with reviewing cases as they come to the Court and with delivering independent opinions.

- Below the Court of Justice there is a General Court that is the first point of decision on less complicated cases, and an EU Civil Service Tribunal that takes cases involving disputes between EU institutions and their staff.

- Court actions are either preliminary rulings, where national courts ask for a ruling on a matter of EU law arising in a national court case, or direct actions, when a dispute between two parties is brought directly before the Court.

- Although it is an independent institution, the work of the Strasbourg-based European Court of Human Rights has an important bearing on EU law.

Key terms and concepts

Advocates-general

Constitutional court

Direct action

Direct effect

EU Civil Service Tribunal

European Court of Human Rights

General Court

Judge-rapporteur

Judicial authority

Mutual recognition

Preliminary ruling

Supremacy of EU law

Further reading

Alter, Karen J. (2009) *The European Court's Political Power: Selected Essays* (Oxford: Oxford University Press). Collection of articles on the ECJ written by one of its most active scholars.

Goldhaber, Michael D. (2007) *A People's History of the European Court of Human Rights* (Piscataway, NJ: Rutgers University Press). Compelling and readable survey of the work and effect of the ECHR.

Hartley, T.C. (2010) *The Foundations of European Union Law*, 7th edn (Oxford: Oxford University Press). One of the best of the many guides to EU law, with chapters on institutions, the legal system, legal principles, and the effects on the member states.

14 Specialized Agencies

European states have long cooperated on issues as varied as scientific research, patents, telecommunications, sports, higher education, postal services, and standardization, and have set up relevant international organizations. To these have been added more recently a network of specialized EU agencies: financial bodies such as the European Central Bank, decentralized agencies such as Europol and the European Food Safety Authority, executive agencies that manage specific EU programmes, and advisory bodies such as the Committee of the Regions.

There is no universal template for these agencies: some are part of the EU structure but others are independent, and most have been created since the 1990s as the policy reach of integration has widened and the need for better policy coordination has grown. Their size, reach and political role vary enormously: while the European Central Bank (ECB) is responsible for helping manage the euro, has a staff of 1,500, and makes decisions that impact business and consumers throughout the euro zone and much of the rest of the world, the European Training Foundation promotes vocational training in neighbouring states of the EU and employs just 130 people.

The creation of these agencies has happened mainly below the public radar, yet their growth has been significant because they have given the EU more of the trappings of a conventional system of government. Their creation has meant adjustments for national government agencies in the member states, better coordination of policy across the EU, and a pooling of policy authority between national governments and the EU institutions. But questions have been asked recently about the lack of a grand plan for agency development, how they should relate to equivalent national agencies, how they should be managed and held accountable, and how they will evolve in future.

- To what extent does the work of specialized agencies federalize the work of the EU?
- Does the European Central Bank have enough power to effectively do its job?
- Should selected decentralized agencies be converted into full-scale regulatory bodies with greater powers to implement laws and policies?
- Should the EU develop its own European criminal investigation force along the lines of the FBI in the US?
- Do the EESC and the Committee of the Regions (CoR) provide added value, or would the interests of their members be better represented by the European Parliament?

Financial bodies

The economy has long been at the heart of European integration; little surprise, then, that banks should be among the more influential of the specialized European agencies. By far the most powerful and important is the European Central Bank, which manages monetary policy in the euro zone. The oldest is the European Investment Bank, set up under the Treaty of Rome to encourage balanced economic development in the EEC. Meanwhile, the European Bank for Reconstruction and Development is not part of the EU but has played a critical role in integration by helping eastern European states make the transition to free-market economic policies. Most recently, one of the effects of the 2007–10 global financial crisis was to oblige member states to think long and hard about trans-European financial regulation, which led to the decision to set up several new institutions, including the European Systemic Risk Board and the European System of Financial Supervisors.

European Central Bank

Although it was created only in 1998, the European Central Bank (ECB) has quickly become one of the most influential and powerful of all pan-European institutions. Its core task was, at first, to help manage the euro by ensuring price stability, setting interest rates, controlling money supply, and managing the foreign reserves of the euro zone states. But this took on new meaning in the wake of the crisis in the euro zone, when it became clear that tighter management was needed in order to ensure that euro states met the terms of membership. The adoption of the euro was itself the biggest shift of monetary powers from individual states to a central authority in history. As the euro has now become more fully integrated into the global financial system, and faced substantial problems,

European Central Bank (ECB): The central bank of the euro zone, responsible for managing the euro by setting interest rates, encouraging price stability, and managing foreign reserves.

Illustration **14.1 European Central Bank**
The euro sculpture outside the former headquarters of the European Central Bank in Frankfurt.

so the stature and political significance of the ECB has grown, raising questions about whether it has overstepped its powers. The ECB has accumulated new powers to keep an eye on national budgets and supervise the euro zone's largest banks, and today it ranks today alongside the US Federal Reserve as the most powerful central bank in the world.

First proposed in 1988, the framework of the ECB was described in the Maastricht treaty, and the first step in its eventual creation was taken in January 1994 with the foundation of the European Monetary Institute, whose job was to promote cooperation and coordination among national central banks in order to clear the way for the launch of the euro. The ECB was formally established on 1 June 1998, replacing the European Monetary Institute and becoming part of two new bank networks:

1 the European System of Central Banks, comprising the ECB and the central banks of all the EU states
2 the Eurosystem, comprising the ECB and the national banks of member states that have adopted the euro.

Self-described as 'the monetary authority of the euro area', the Eurosystem works to promote price and financial stability, encourage financial integration, and hold and manage the foreign reserves of the euro zone states.

The ECB probably has more independence than any existing national central bank; where their powers can be changed by national law, the powers of the ECB are based on a treaty whose terms can only be changed by agreement of all the EU member states (Hodson, 2010, p. 166). Organizationally, it has a Governing Council charged with making policy and made up of the central bank governors from each state in the euro zone and the Bank's Executive Board. The latter manages the day-to-day business of the Bank, and consists of the president, the vice-president and four other members, all appointed by the governments of the member states to eight-year non-renewable terms. Finally, a General Council composed of the central bank governors of the 28 member states maintains links to non-euro zone countries. In May 2010, as the maelstrom of the Greek debt crisis swirled, the foundation stone was laid for a new dedicated headquarters for the ECB in Frankfurt, which opened in 2014.

The euro zone crisis not only emphasized the need for closer control of national budgets in the euro area, but also showed that the ECB was the only institution capable of intervening quickly and effectively in the event of problems in the euro zone; national leaders are too divided to take the kinds of decisions needed. The Bank's response to the crisis also raised questions among policy-makers as to whether or not the ECB should become the lender of last resort, along the lines of the Federal Reserve, and how far it should be allowed to intervene in euro zone fiscal policy. Particularly controversial has been the question of whether or not the ECB should be allowed to purchase government bonds, a power that would allow it to directly finance governments and might lead to the mutualization of debt, that is, pooling the debts of euro zone countries (Alessi, 2012).

A key development in the wake of the euro crisis has been the effort to build a European banking union, consisting of a single rulebook for the financial market, a single supervisory and resolution mechanism, and an emergency fund. Under this arrangement, the ECB would sit at the centre of a programme

Eurosystem: The monetary authority of the euro zone, made up of the ECB and national central banks, and charged with encouraging financial stability in the euro zone.

Profile *Mario Draghi*

Mario Draghi (1947–) was appointed as the third president of the European Central Bank – and thus head of the world's largest currency area – in 2011, taking over in the midst of the crisis in the euro zone. Born in Rome, he earned a PhD in economics from the Massachusetts Institute of Technology, and then joined the faculty of political science at the University of Florence. He served on the boards of several banks and corporations, including Goldman Sachs International, then became governor of the Bank of Italy, and a member of the Governing and General Councils of the ECB, in 2006. Such was his reputation for working through the complexities of the Italian political system that he earned the nickname 'Super Mario'. Within months of taking over as president of the ECB, he famously declared that the bank was ready to do 'whatever it takes' to preserve the euro, and he found himself with the challenge of trying to maintain financial unity among 18 countries, including several in a dire financial state. His term as president of the ECB runs until 2019.

to supervise banks in the EU, making sure that they complied with EU banking rules and watching out for potential problems. If approved, the banking union will not only substantially increase the powers of the ECB, but will also mean that all major banks in participating countries will, for the first time, report to a single supervisory body. Associated with the work of the ECB is that of the European Banking Authority, created in 2010, which is responsible for undertaking stress tests on banks to ensure that they have enough assets to withstand sudden economic shocks.

European Investment Bank

Headquartered in Luxembourg, the European Investment Bank (EIB) is the world's largest multilateral development bank. Set up in 1958 under the terms of the Treaty of Rome to encourage 'balanced and steady development' within the EEC, it describes itself as the long-term lending bank of the EU. Its funds come from subscriptions from EU member states and from borrowing on international capital markets, and it lends mainly to capital projects – long-term projects involving capital assets such as land, buildings and other structures – that support the policy goals of the EU. It gives priority to investments in poorer parts of the EU, with a focus on small and medium-sized companies (those with less than 250 employees), transport and communications networks, industry and infrastructure, the security of energy supply, and projects that promote environmental sustainability. It also manages a European Investment Fund that provides venture capital, equity and guarantees to small and medium-sized businesses.

Most of the EIB's investments have been within the EU, but about 10 per cent go to neighbouring states and developing countries. The EIB does not make a profit and rarely lends more than half the total investment cost of a project, often co-financing projects with other banks. In the wake of the global financial crisis, it almost doubled its annual levels of lending, providing just over €70 billion in 2013. Among its recent projects have been the conversion of athletes'

European Investment Bank (EIB): The investment bank of the EU, which supports economic development projects inside and outside Europe.

apartments in London's Olympic Village into affordable housing, the renovation of large parts of the ageing sewer system of Brussels, and helping develop a microinsurance scheme for small business owners in developing countries. Its single biggest project was the Eurotunnel that runs under the English Channel between England and France. Opened in 1994 after centuries of speculation and failed plans, the tunnel cost about $15 billion to build (nearly twice the original estimate) and had to wait until 2007 before turning in its first annual profits.

The EIB is managed by a board of governors consisting of representatives of the member states (usually their finance ministers), who decide policy and appoint a decision-making board of directors (28 members along with a representative from the European Commission) to five-year renewable terms, and a nine-member management committee to six-year renewable terms. The latter – consisting of the president (Werner Hoyer of Germany since 2012) and the eight vice-presidents of the Bank – is its main executive body, overseeing day-to-day operations and drafting decisions on spending for the consideration of the board of directors.

European Bank for Reconstruction and Development

The European Bank for Reconstruction and Development (EBRD) is not an EU institution, but its work has had an important impact on the economic development policies of the EU. Much like the World Bank, it was founded to provide loans, encourage capital investment and promote trade, but its specific focus has been on helping eastern European and former Soviet states make the transition to free-market economies. It began work in 1991 and is now the single largest investor in eastern Europe and central Asia. While the World Bank lends mainly to governments, the EBRD makes 60 per cent of its loans to the private sector, and also works with public sector companies to encourage privatization.

Headquartered in London, it is owned and operated by its 61 shareholder countries and the EU and the EIB; the biggest share (€2 billion) is held by the US, followed by Britain, France, Germany, Italy and Japan (€1.7 billion each). Like the EIB, it has a board of governors consisting of a representative from each shareholder country, typically the minister of finance. The board appoints a president who works with a 23-member board of directors to oversee the operations of the Bank; Thomas Mirow of Germany was appointed the Bank's fifth president in 2008. The EBRD ended its central European operations in 2010, shifting its focus to Russia, the Ukraine and the Balkans.

The new financial institutions

The 2007–10 global financial crisis emphasized the many problems in the way that EU financial markets had been regulated (or, at least, underregulated), the shortcomings in cross-border supervision made only too clear by how quickly problems in one country spread to others. As a result of what they learned, EU finance ministers held discussions in 2009 aimed at developing a new framework for financial supervision in the EU. While care was taken to ensure that EU powers did not stray into national tax policy, it was decided to set up a European System of Financial Supervision, consisting of several new institutions that began work in January 2011:

- The European Banking Authority (headquartered in London) replaced the advisory Committee of European Banking Supervisors, and has the task of encouraging consistent regulation and supervision in the banking sector, with a view to better protecting depositors and investors.
- The European Insurance and Occupational Pensions Authority (Frankfurt) encourages closer supervision of the EU insurance and pensions market.
- The European Securities and Markets Authority (Paris) oversees the EU market for financial services, and has the power to investigate selected financial products, such as credit default swaps, and ban them if needed.
- The European Systemic Risk Board (Frankfurt) is in charge of the macroeconomic supervision of the EU's financial sectors, and responsible for identifying emerging risks in the hope of avoiding more financial crises.

Decentralized and executive agencies

The EU has an expanding body of specialized agencies, including decentralized agencies with mainly technical and managerial responsibilities, executive agencies with powers of implementation (mainly in areas dealing with research funding support), and agencies dealing with specific aspects of the Common Security and Defence Policy. There are now more than 30 decentralized agencies and a changing number of executive agencies, and the ad hoc nature of the way they have been created has recently sparked a debate over the need for a more structured approach to their management and responsibilities.

Decentralized agencies

Set up under EU law, the decentralized agencies have their own legal personalities, are mainly funded out of the EU budget, and are given technical, management or informational responsibilities. Once more generally known as 'regulatory agencies', but now working under the less politically threatening and more accurate title of 'decentralized agencies', they lack the executive functions of most of their national equivalents. But they can take decisions on the application of EU standards, they influence policy-making through the expertise they provide to the Commission, and through their coordination work they are bringing the activities of national agencies more into line with one another. The Commission itself considers their main value to lie in helping it focus on its core tasks, helping pool technical and scientific expertise in the interests of better decision-making, and helping add to the visibility of the EU (European Commission, 2008; see also Géradin et al., 2005).

The first two decentralized agencies – dealing with vocational training and living and working conditions – were founded in 1975, since when many more have been set up, most of them since 1995 (see Table 14.1). (The Euratom Supply Agency is older, but its work relates only to Euratom.) Among them they employ nearly 4,000 staff and have a budget of €1.1 billion. The Commission (2008) divides them into four types:

Decentralized agencies:
Standing bodies set up under EU law with technical, management and/or informational responsibilities.

1 Those with the power to adopt decisions legally binding on third parties, such as the European Aviation Safety Agency and the European Chemicals Agency.

2 Those that provide scientific and technical advice to the Commission, and the member states where needed, such as the European Food Safety Authority.
3 Those with operational responsibilities, such as the European Global Navigation Satellite Systems Agency, which manages Europe's global navigation satellite systems programme.
4 Those acting as clearing houses for information.

One example of a clearing house is the European Environment Agency, set up in 1990 and headquartered in Copenhagen. It is small, with a staff of just 130, and its main job is to gather and process information from the EU member states, along with Iceland, Norway, Switzerland and Turkey. The idea of creating an inspectorate with powers to monitor national environmental conditions and the application of EU law was opposed by the governments of member states (Collins and Earnshaw, 1993, pp. 238–9), resulting in the much more modest responsibilities of the European Environment Agency. It partners with national environmental agencies through the European Information and Observation Network to collect information, which is then used to help improve the quality and effectiveness of EU and national environmental policies and measure the results of those policies.

Majone (1997) argues that, in their early years, the agencies were denied the powers normally granted to regulatory bodies and 'seemed to be doomed to play an auxiliary role'. But he also argues that they had the chance to turn their limitations into opportunities, given that 'regulation by information' could often be more effective than direct regulation. This would only work, though, if the information was credible, which in turn depended on the reputation of the agencies for independence and accuracy. Their role has been complicated by concerns in the member states about loss of control by national agencies, and the EU agencies have found themselves having to manoeuvre carefully between the member states, the Commission and related international organizations.

To ensure that they do not become too independent, their management boards consist of national representatives, controls are imposed on their decision-making, and their tasks are narrowly defined. Their role is also impacted by the 1958 ECJ ruling *Meroni* v. *High Authority* (Case 9/56), in which the Court said that while authority could be delegated to new bodies not mentioned in the Treaty of Rome, such delegation could only happen if that authority was compatible with the regulatory powers of EEC institutions and involved 'clearly defined executive powers' subject to strict review, and no discretionary powers (see Dehousse, 2002).

With the growth in their numbers and reach, questions have been asked about the accountability, cost and transparency of the decentralized agencies. Much like the Commission, they are often accused of being too big and having too many discretionary powers, yet they are small when compared to many national agencies and it is questionable how much real power they have. Borrás et al. (2007) point out that while there have been studies of the driving forces behind the delegation of policy-making powers and their influence on the design of specialized agencies, there is less understanding of what happens later. They argue the need for increased interaction between agencies and the communities in which they work in order to promote the credibility and legitimacy of the agencies.

Table **14.1** **EU decentralized agencies**

Name	Founded	Headquarters	Main interest
Euratom Supply Agency	1960	Luxembourg	Regular and equitable supply of nuclear fuels for EU users
European Centre for the Development of Vocational Training	1975	Thessaloniki, Greece	As title
European Foundation for the Improvement of Living and Working Conditions	1975	Dublin, Ireland	As title
European Environment Agency	1990	Copenhagen, Denmark	Information clearing house
EU Satellite Centre	1992	Madrid, Spain	Analyses satellite information in support of Common Foreign and Security Policy
European Monitoring Centre for Drugs and Drug Addiction	1993	Lisbon, Portugal	Information clearing house
European Training Foundation	1994	Turin, France	Promotes vocational education and training in states neighbouring EU
European Agency for Safety and Health at Work	1994	Bilbao, Spain	Information clearing house
Translation Centre for the Bodies of the EU	1994	Luxembourg	Provides translation services for agencies
Community Plant Variety Office	1995	Angers, France	Granting of intellectual property rights for new plant varieties
European Medicines Agency	1995	London, England	Evaluates applications for new medicinal products
Office for Harmonisation in the Internal Market	1996	Alicante, Spain	Oversees registration of trade marks and new designs
European Aviation Safety Agency	2002	Cologne, Germany	Helps Commission draft new rules
European Maritime Safety Agency	2002	Lisbon, Portugal	Helps Commission and national authorities
European Food Safety Authority	2002	Parma, Italy	Provides scientific advice
EU Institute for Security Studies	2002	Paris, France	Think tank
European Railway Agency	2004	Valenciennes, France	Safety and interoperability of railways as part of EU transport policy

The Commission has recently raised its own questions about the place and future of the decentralized agencies. In 2002 it proposed setting up an operating framework for the agencies, including details on how they would be set up, their legal basis, and even how decisions would be made on the location of their offices. This idea failed to win support in the Council of Ministers, so in 2008 the Commission issued a White Paper (European Commission, 2008), in which it argued that while agencies have a valuable role, they had been set up on an ad hoc basis without a clear idea of their place in the EU system, making it more difficult for them to work effectively. The time was ripe, argued the report, for an assessment of their purpose and role, and to 'develop a clear and coherent vision on the place of agencies in European governance'. It concluded that the Commission, the Council and Parliament needed to work together to develop more clarity on their different types of functions, along with the development of

Name	Founded	Headquarters	Main interest
European Agency for the Management of Operational Cooperation at the External Borders	2004	Wroclaw, Poland	Cooperation on management of EU's external borders
European Network and Information Security Agency	2004	Heraklion, Greece	Information clearing house
European Defence Agency	2004	Brussels, Belgium	Encourages systematic approach to European Security and Defence Policy and development of coordinated European defence industry
European Centre for Disease Prevention and Control	2005	Stockholm, Sweden	Defences against infectious disease
European Fisheries Control Agency	2005	Vigo, Spain	Uniformity of Common Fisheries control systems
European Police College	2005	Bramshill, England	Training courses for police officers
European Global Navigation Satellite Systems Agency	2007	Brussels, Belgium	Manages Europe's programme to build global navigation satellite systems, including Galileo
European Chemicals Agency	2007	Helsinki, Finland	Coordinates REACH, the programme to manage chemicals
EU Agency for Fundamental Rights	2007	Vienna, Austria	Information clearing house
European Institute for Gender Equality	2010	Vilnius, Lithuania	Information clearing house
Body of European Regulators for Electronic Communications	2010	Riga, Latvia	Single market for electronic communications networks and services
Agency for the Cooperation of Energy Regulators	2011	Ljubljana, Slovenia	Completion of single market for electricity and natural gas
European Asylum Support Office	2011	Valletta, Malta	Cooperation on asylum policy
European Agency for the Operational Management of Large-scale IT Systems in the Area of Freedom, Security and Justice	2012	Tallinn, Estonia	Manages EU asylum, migration and border management computer systems

a standard approach to their management, better regulation, and clearer rules on how agencies were set up and closed.

Executive agencies

In contrast to the decentralized agencies, which are permanent, executive agencies are set up for a fixed period with a specific task in mind. They are created and controlled by the Commission, their staff is appointed by the Commission, and they are almost always based in Brussels. Among those that have come and gone is the European Agency for Reconstruction, set up in 2000 to manage EU aid to Serbia, Kosovo, Montenegro and Macedonia, but whose mandate ended in 2008. In 2014 there were six executive agencies, dealing with issues ranging from competitiveness to transport and the management of EU research funding.

Executive agencies: Temporary bodies set up by the Commission to help carry out narrow and specific executive tasks.

The agencies each answer to a directorate-general in the Commission, and much of their work involves dispersing and managing EU research and development funds. One of the projects managed by the Executive Agency for Competitiveness and Innovation is the Marco Polo project, which aims to encourage the shift of freight transport from roads to sea, rail and inland waterways, helping reduce some of the congestion on Europe's increasingly busy highways. The Research Executive Agency is central to the EU's research funding programme, providing support for projects under the European Space Policy (see later in this chapter) and the Marie Curie grants that (among other things) encourage Europeans to begin a career in research, and encourage European researchers living overseas to return to Europe.

European Police Office (Europol)

With the opening up of the single market in the 1990s, it was felt that more direction needed to be given to police cooperation. With this in mind, the Europol Convention was signed in 1996, creating a European Police Office that became fully operational in July 1999. Based in The Hague, Europol is a criminal intelligence organization much like Interpol (the French-based international police organization founded in 1923). It has no powers of arrest and no autonomous powers of investigation, but instead oversees an EU-wide system of information exchange targeted at helping national police forces combat serious forms of international crime – including terrorism, organized crime, cybercrime, clandestine immigration networks, money forging and laundering, and the trafficking of drugs, vehicles, people, child pornography and radioactive materials. It coordinates operations among the national police forces of the EU, and can ask these forces to launch investigations. While some see it as the forerunner of a European police force, there is no common EU penal code or police law, making the development of such a force any time soon unlikely. (For a detailed study of Europol, see Occhipinti, 2003.)

Europol is overseen by a management board with one representative from each of the member states, run by a director and three deputies. The appointments are made by the Council of Ministers, and Europol answers to the Justice and Home Affairs Council. As well as its full-time staff, the Europol headquarters are also home to European liaison officers seconded from the member states as representatives of national police forces, and whose presence helps build networks and encourage police cooperation. Related to Europol is the European Police College, headquartered at Bramshill, England, which runs training courses for police officers from across Europe.

International terrorism may have moved up the policy agenda since the attacks in the US in 2001, Madrid in 2004 and London in 2005, but terrorism is nothing new to Europe (see Chapter 23). The threats it posed were part of the motivation behind the formation in 1975 of the TREVI group (Terrorism, Radicalism, Extremism and International Violence), which brought together police officials from EEC states, and paved the way for later EU cooperation.

Examples of recent Europol operations give a sense of where its services are most needed and effective. During 2008–09, there were ram raids in several

Europol: The criminal intelligence agency of the EU, which works to share information in order to address the most serious forms of international crime.

Illustration **14.2** **Eurojust**
The headquarters of Eurojust and the International Criminal Court in The Hague. Due to its increased workload, the construction of a new headquarters for Eurojust began in 2014.

continental EU states, where gangs drove stolen vehicles through the main entrances of electrical retailers, bagging as many high-value products as they could before dispersing, each raid usually taking less than 90 seconds. Austrian police discovered that the raiders were from Lithuania, and worked through Europol with the police in Belgium, France, Italy, Lithuania and Sweden to identify several separate criminal groups, and arrest the 18 leaders in early 2010. In 2012, arrests were made of 48 members of an Albanian-speaking organized crime ring operating between France, Germany and Switzerland, involved in facilitating illegal immigration, trafficking of heroin and cocaine, and forgery of documents. Europol also provided the Dutch government with help in identifying victims of the Malaysian Airlines jet shot down over Ukraine in July 2014, and with securing the site of the crash. Other cases involving Europol have included breaking up a Polish-based counterfeit euro operation, the arrest of child traffickers in Romania, and a six-nation operation to stop credit card fraud.

Another specialized agency related to Europol is Eurojust (the Judicial Cooperation Unit), set up in 2002 with headquarters in The Hague to improve investigations and prosecutions involving two or more member states. It has the authority to ask national authorities to launch an investigation or start a prosecution, coordinate the work of multiple national authorities, set up joint investigation teams, and provide supporting information. It is run by a College of 28 national members (most with backgrounds as judges, prosecutors or police officers), who elect one of their number as president and two as vice-presidents. Meanwhile, the work of Europol and Eurojust is complemented by the European Judicial Network, set up in 1998 in order to encourage judicial cooperation in criminal matters (see Chapter 23 for more details).

Eurojust: A judicial cooperation unit that works to improve the effectiveness of investigations and prosecutions across EU member states.

Advisory bodies

At the heart of the supporting framework of specialized European organizations are two Brussels-based advisory bodies designed to offer key groups input into the making of EU policy. The European Economic and Social Committee (EESC) was set up under the Treaty of Rome as a forum for representatives of employers and workers. It was joined in 1985 by an ad hoc assembly created to channel the opinions of local government into European decision-making, and formalized under Maastricht as the Committee of the Regions (CoR). The value of the two committees is debatable, given that the EESC was created out of unfounded fears that the European Parliament would not represent sectional interests and neither body has much power. Some would argue that they are more than advisory bodies and have developed modest political influence, but others would argue that they have not fulfilled the hopes of their founders for a corporatist Europe and a Europe of the regions.

Based in Brussels, the EESC was modelled on parallel bodies that existed in all the founder members of the EEC except West Germany. It has 353 members, divided up among the member states roughly in proportion to population size, nominated by national governments, and confirmed for renewable five-year terms by the Council of Ministers (see Table 14.2). It elects a president and a bureau from among its members for terms of two and a half years, and convenes two-day meetings in Brussels nine times each year.

The EESC is divided into three groups that represent, respectively, employers, employees and 'various interests', such as agriculture, small businesses, consumer and environmental groups, the academic community, nongovernmental organizations, and the professions. The three groups meet separately to discuss matters of common interest, breaking into smaller sections to deal with specific issues, such as agriculture, social policy, transport, energy, regional development and the environment. Consultation of the EESC by the Commission is mandatory in several policy areas, including agriculture, the movement of workers, social policy, regional policy, and the environment.

As for the Committee of the Regions (CoR), its role is to give a voice to the interests of local government, and help deal with the problem of regional economic disparities (see Chapter 22). As EU spending on regional development has grown, so the political role of the CoR has become more significant, and

Table **14.2 Membership of the EESC and the CoR**

Germany	24	Greece	12	Lithuania	9
UK	24	Hungary	12	Slovakia	9
France	24	Netherlands	12	Estonia	7
Italy	24	Portugal	12	Latvia	7
Spain	21	Sweden	12	Slovenia	7
Poland	21	Bulgaria	12	Cyprus	6
Romania	15	Croatia	9	Luxembourg	6
Austria	12	Denmark	9	Malta	5
Belgium	12	Finland	9		
Czech Republic	12	Ireland	9	TOTAL	**353**

given that so many EU laws are implemented at the local level, the CoR has a more overtly political role than the EESC. Based in Brussels, the CoR met for the first time in January 1994 and has the same membership structure as the EESC – 353 members chosen by the member states and appointed by the Council of Ministers for five-year renewable terms (see Table 14.2). They are mainly elected local government officials, including mayors and members of state, regional, district, provincial and county councils. The committee meets in plenary session five times per year and must be consulted by the Commission, the Council of Ministers and the European Parliament on issues relating to economic and social cohesion, trans-European networks, public health, education and culture. Being more political than the EESC, its members have formed themselves into political groups along the lines of those found in the European Parliament.

The core weakness of both bodies is that they can only issue opinions. Their role has been further undermined by their being brought into the legislative process only after proposals for new EU laws have reached an advanced stage of agreement by the Council of Ministers and Parliament; Lisbon changed the status of the CoR, however, by obliging the Commission to consult it as early as the pre-legislative stage, and giving it the authority to have EU laws reviewed by the Court of Justice if the CoR believes that those laws deal with areas outside the competence of the EU institutions. The two committees provide expert input into EU decision-making and can make the case that they encourage democracy by providing a link between EU institutions and key economic and social sectors.

Other institutions

Alongside the decentralized, executive and advisory bodies, there are several other EU or European institutions whose work either strengthens that of the major EU institutions or reflects the new opportunities for Europe-wide cooperation that have grown in recent decades. This section offers three examples, each quite different in terms of goals and structure: the Court of Auditors, Eurocorps and the European Space Agency.

European Court of Auditors

The Court of Auditors is the EU's financial watchdog, founded in 1975 to replace the separate auditing bodies for the ECSC and the EEC/Euratom. It is difficult to classify because it has been recognized since Maastricht as one of the formal institutions of the EU (along with the Commission, the Council of Ministers, Parliament, the Court of Justice and the European Council), but it has a more focused remit than any of those bodies. Headquartered in Luxembourg, the Court likes to describe itself as the 'financial conscience' of the EU. It carries out annual audits of the accounts of all EU institutions to ensure that revenue has been raised and expenditure incurred as planned and intended, and to monitor the EU's financial management. The Court reports back to the Commission, the Council of Ministers and Parliament by the end of November each year. Parliament is supposed to approve the Court's report by the following April, but can use the report to force changes in the Commission's spending and accounting habits.

The Court is headed by 28 auditors, one appointed from each member state for a six-year renewable term. Nominations come from the national governments and must be approved by the Council of Ministers on the advice of the European Parliament. The auditors then elect one of their number to serve as president for three-year renewable terms. Much like the Court of Justice, the members can sit in chambers of between three and six members each. The auditors must be members of an external audit body in their own country or have other appropriate qualifications, but they are expected to act in the interests of the EU and to be completely independent. A regular peer review by a team of international auditors carried out in 2008 confirmed that its record for independence and objectivity was strong.

The Court routinely finds errors in the management of funds, a problem that has encouraged critics of the EU to speak of waste and fraud in the use of EU funds. In recent years, the Court has approved the accounts as being complete and accurate, but has also argued that payments have not always been made in accordance with EU law; that is, it has not all been spent on the purpose intended or properly accounted for. There has certainly been waste and inefficiency, and over the years the Court has issued often scathing criticisms of waste and mismanagement. But the misuse of funds is a problem in national and local systems of spending and accounting too.

Eurocorps

Offering an example of how sub-clusters of EU member states have occasionally taken the initiative to move forward on policy cooperation without their partners, Eurocorps is seen by some as a potential foundation for a future EU military. Tracing its roots back to an experimental Franco-German brigade created in 1991, Eurocorps was formally launched in May 1992 and has been fully operational since November 1995. Today, it consists of 60,000 troops from its five participating states (Belgium, France, Germany, Luxembourg and Spain), along with staff from several other countries, including Austria, Greece, Poland and Turkey. It made its first significant military commitment in 1998 when nearly 500 Eurocorps personnel joined the NATO Stabilization Force in Bosnia. In 2000, it sent a mission to Kosovo, and in 2004–05 it briefly took over leadership of the NATO-run peacekeeping mission in the Afghan capital of Kabul.

Eurocorps is headquartered in Strasbourg. It is overseen by a Common Committee made up of the chiefs of defence staff and political representatives from the five member states, who meet annually. Day-to-day operations are overseen by the Eurocorps Committee, made up of representatives from the national ministries of defence and a commander appointed from one of the member states: Lt General Guy Buchsenschmidt of Belgium took over in 2013. Although participation in Eurocorps is open to all EU member states, the response to date has been disappointing to those who favour the building of an EU military capacity. Supporters of Eurocorps point to its role in bringing France and Germany into European defence matters, but critics note that it relies almost entirely on non-Eurocorps assets such as intelligence, advanced weapons and transportation.

Eurocorps: A multinational military force set up among several EU states, outside EU structures, that some see as the seed of a common European military.

European Space Agency

The European Space Agency (ESA) is not part of the network of EU agencies, but its creation and its work impact policy in the EU, and it provides an example of the expanding variety of cooperative ventures in which Europeans have become engaged. Headquartered in Paris, ESA has 20 member states: all 15 pre-2003 western European EU member states, along with the Czech Republic, Norway, Poland, Romania and Switzerland. It has a staff of nearly 2,000, and in 2013 had a budget of nearly €4.2 billion. It also operates a launch facility at Korou in French Guiana, and an astronaut training facility in Cologne, Germany. ESA focuses on space exploration and research, working mainly with the French commercial satellite company Arianespace (founded in 1980), and on human space flight through its participation in the International Space Station, in which 11 ESA member states cooperate with the US, Russia, Japan and Canada.

The ESA traces its roots back to the 1950s, when a combination of the 'brain drain' of European scientists to the US and the early ventures in space exploration prompted a group of western European scientists to talk of the need for coordination and cooperation among their peers. Two new bodies – the European Launch Development Organization and the European Space Research Organization – were founded in 1964, and made their first modest contributions with research satellites launched on American rockets. In 1975 the two organizations were merged to form the European Space Agency, and that same year ESA launched its first major mission, gathering information on gamma-ray emissions in the universe. In 1983, Ulf Merbold of West Germany became the first ESA astronaut to go into space, as a member of the NASA space shuttle *Columbia* mission. By 2014 the European Astronaut Corps had sent more than 50 astronauts into space, aboard either US space shuttles or Russian *Soyuz* missions to the International Space Station.

The ESA cooperates closely with the EU on policy (particularly on projects such as the Galileo satellite navigation system) and there has been talk of integrating the ESA more fully into EU institutional structures. In 2007 the EU adopted a European Space Policy emphasizing the importance of maintaining an independent launch capacity, the ongoing European commitment to the International Space Station, and the development of technologies that would allow Europe to be competitive in space policy. Ten mainly eastern European countries have applied to join ESA, so an expansion in its size and activities is on the cards.

Summary

- As the policy reach and responsibilities of the EU have grown, so a network of specialized agencies has grown, including financial bodies, advisory bodies, executive agencies, and a mix of EU and independent bodies whose work relates to that of the main EU institutions.

- Financial institutions include the European Investment Bank, the European Central Bank, and the independent European Bank for Reconstruction and Development. New regulatory institutions have been set up in the wake of the global financial crisis and the euro zone crisis.

- Other agencies have varying technical, managerial and executive responsibilities, dealing with such issues as vocational training, gathering environmental information, monitoring drug use, evaluating new medicinal products, and improving aviation, maritime and food safety.

- Executive agencies are set up for a fixed period of time with a specific task in mind, such as trans-European transport networks, education and training, and research.

- Police and judicial cooperation have been encouraged and promoted by Europol and Eurojust, which are active in helping deal with serious forms of cross-border crime.

- The two major advisory bodies are the European Economic and Social Committee, a policy forum for key economic and social groups, and the Committee of the Regions, which gives voice to the interests of local government.

- The European Court of Auditors is the EU's financial watchdog, charged with ensuring that the EU accounts are correct. It usually finds that they are not.

- Eurocorps maintains a multinational European military force for use mainly in humanitarian and peacekeeping operations, and the European Space Agency undertakes space research and manages Europe's astronaut programme.

Key terms and concepts

Decentralized agencies

Eurocorps

Eurojust

European Central Bank

European Investment Bank

Europol

Eurosystem

Executive agencies

Further reading

De Haan, Jakob, and Helge Berger (eds) (2010) *The European Central Bank at Ten* (Heidelberg: Springer). The turmoil in the euro zone has made it hard to publish studies of the euro and the ECB that do not quickly show their age. This collection of essays provides a snapshot of the ECB 10 years after its foundation.

Géradin, Damien, Rodolphe Muñoz and Nicolas Petit (eds) (2005) *Regulation Through Agencies in the EU: A New Paradigm of European Governance* (London: Edward Elgar). Edited collection of studies of the motives behind setting up specialized agencies and the potential effects.

Kaunert, Christian, Sarah Leonard and John Occhipinti (eds) (2014) *Justice and Home Affairs Agencies in the European Union* (Abingdon: Routledge). Study of the EU's police, justice and border control agencies, including Europol, Eurojust and Frontex.

15 Parties and Interest Groups

The EEC was designed and long run by bureaucrats and politicians, who referred little – if at all – to public opinion. But as the reach of integration expanded, so more Europeans became interested in expressing their views. For some, this was a positive interest, driven by a belief that European institutions deserved, even demanded, their attention. For others, it was a negative interest, driven by concerns that these institutions were undemocratic, too powerful and a threat to national sovereignty. For all political parties and interest groups have become key channels of engagement.

While political parties are at the heart of political life in the member states, we have yet to see transnational political parties fighting European election campaigns on European issues. Instead, elections to the European Parliament (EP) are contested by national political parties running in separate national contests. MEPs organize themselves into European political groups, or clusters of national parties based on alliances among like-minded legislators. But change is in the air, thanks to a network of European party organizations working to coordinate policy.

If political parties have not yet fully exploited what the EU might have to offer, interest groups have made more progress. National groups have paid more attention to Brussels, opening European offices and building transnational networks designed to capitalize on the strength of their numbers. They have been encouraged by the Commission, which uses groups as a source of expertise and to report on the implementation of EU law by the member states. The input of groups, even if they promote the interests of their members rather than working for the broader European interest, has helped strengthen the legitimacy and responsiveness of the EU decision-making system.

- Should national political parties work harder through Europarties to replace political groups in the EP, or is the current system sufficient?
- What would be the effect on the EP if a single political group won a majority of seats?
- Given the numerous parties represented in the EP, is there a problem of too much democracy in the EU system?
- What does the relative weakness of party activity at EU level mean for the character and quality of interest group activity?
- How are interest groups and their lobbying activities likely to affect levels of support for European integration?

European political groups

Political parties lie at the heart of democratic government, playing several critical roles in the way national political systems are ordered:

- They represent the views and interests of voters and party members.
- They recruit and provide a training ground for political leaders, who in turn become the personalities that drive politics and put a human face on government.
- They offer voters competing sets of public policy options.
- They help articulate and aggregate the collective goals of different interests in society.
- They help mobilize and engage voters in the political process.
- They provide the labels by which the philosophies of candidates for office can be better understood.
- They form governments and oppositions.

Although EU member states are replete with domestic political parties, catering for every ideological taste from the far left to the far right, party activity at the European level has had a rather different dynamic. When the Common Assembly of the European Coal and Steel Community first met in Strasbourg in 1953, its members were arranged in alphabetical order by name, but they were also members of national parliaments and political parties, and they naturally gravitated towards like-minded peers from other countries. Within months the Assembly had changed its own rules of procedure to allow for the formation of cross-national political groups, for each of which at least nine members were needed. The tradition of Members of the European Parliament (MEPs) sitting

Political groups: Groups formed within the European Parliament that bring together MEPs from like-minded political parties from the different member states.

Illustration **15.1 European political groups**

A meeting of the Progressive Alliance of Socialists and Democrats, one of the major party groups in the European Parliament.

in ideological groups – and not in national blocs, as some might expect – has continued since.

Although these groups are not formally political parties, they are not much different in terms of goals and structures: they consist of MEPs with common ideologies and policy preferences, their members tend to vote together on issues before Parliament, and they have their own budgets, leadership structures, operating rules and committees. One key difference between EP political groups and national political parties is that the groups do not campaign together across member states; EP elections are fought in 28 separate national contests by national parties that then form groups during the term of the EP. Another difference is that while parties in the member states form governments, and are intimately linked to executives, groups in the EP do not. Except for the EP's role in confirming and monitoring the Commission, there are few formal political links between the two institutions. For it to function more like its national equivalents, the membership of the College of Commissioners would have to come out of Parliament and be determined by the balance of parliamentary political groups.

In order for parties to form a group, they must have at least 25 members from at least one-quarter of member states, and no MEP is allowed to belong to more than one group. Participating MEPs must have a common 'political affinity', must inform the president of the EP of their plans, and must publish a statement in the *Official Journal of the European Union* (Rule 29, European Parliament Rules of Procedure, 16th edn, 2008). Groups then elect their own chairs (or co-chairs where the groups are confederal) and appoint governing bureaux and supporting secretariats.

The number and membership of EP political groups has changed as the balance of their constituent parties has changed, new parties have come and gone, and political philosophies, circumstances and opportunities have evolved. Some have been little more than marriages of convenience, bringing together MEPs with sometimes quite different philosophies, but others have built more focus and consistency over time and have become part of the permanent structure of Parliament. (For a history of EU party groups, see Bardi, 2002. For an overview of the groups, see Corbett et al., 2011, Ch. 5. For the dynamics behind transnational party cooperation, see Hanley, 2007.)

The greatest consistency has been on the mainstream left, centre-right and right of the political spectrum, where three groups – the socialists, the liberals and the European People's Party (EPP) – have a history dating back to the beginnings of the EP and have consistently won the largest share of seats in EP elections. They have been joined since the mid-1980s by green parties whose numbers in the EP have grown but have not yet achieved as much influence. Meanwhile, conservative, nationalist and eurosceptic groups have had a more chequered history, their memberships and labels changing more frequently according to the fluctuating interests and fortunes of their members (see Figure 15.1). No one political group has yet won enough seats to form a majority, and while it might be logical for like-minded groups to try and form a majority coalition, multi-partisanship has been the normal order of business.

Although there is no formal obligation for MEPs to vote with their political group, greater discipline gives groups greater impact, and research has revealed greater voting cohesion within parties: as the main groups have grown and the

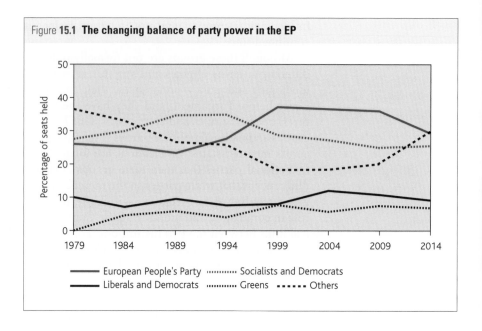

Figure **15.1** **The changing balance of party power in the EP**

powers of the EP have expanded, their policy distinctions have become clearer and cohesion among the major groups has grown (Hix et al., 2007). (For details on the positions on Europe of the major party families, see Marks et al., 2002.) Ringe (2009) argues that because MEPs lack the resources to be able to make informed decisions in every policy area, they often fall back on the positions taken by their political groups and the EP committees of which they are members. In spite of the structural weakness of political groups, the result of this reliance is more group cohesion and consistency.

Although the most visible arena of party activity in the EU is the European Parliament, party affiliations also factor into the work of the Councils and the European Commission. In the former, every minister and head of government is a member of a domestic political party and ideology and party platforms influence their decisions. While Parliament has seen a rise of centre-right parties at the expense of centre-left parties, there has been more volatility in the Councils, reflecting the ebb and flow of party fortunes in national elections. The right dominated in the 1980s, lost ground to the left in the 1990s, and was back in the early 2000s; in mid-2014, 14 of the 28 heads of government were on the right and just 8 on the left. As for the Commission, party politics are less openly on display, reflecting the bureaucratic qualities of the institution, but nominations are made by the national governments of the day, commissioners are typically members of national parties, and more attention is now paid to their affiliations. In spite of trends in national politics, however, there has been a shift to the left in the Commission in recent years.

After the 2014 EP elections, there were seven political groups in place (Figure 15.2). (Table 15.1 below shows the representation of the parties in the European Parliament in 2014, including non-attached members – NI.) Running from left to right on the ideological spectrum, they were as follows.

European United Left–Nordic Green Left (GUE/NGL)

This is the main left-wing group in the EP, and the product of complex changes that have taken place at this end of the spectrum since the mid-1980s. Less a fully fledged group than a confederation of two others, it traces its origins to a Communist Group formed in 1973. This broke up after the collapse of the Soviet Union in 1989, with Italian and Spanish communists forming the European United Left (GUE), while French, Greek and Portuguese communists formed Left Unity. GUE fell apart in 1993, was resurrected in 1994, and in 1995 teamed up with the Nordic Green Left, consisting of newly arrived leftist MEPs from Finland and Sweden. The 2014 elections saw the GUE/NGL's numbers in the EP rise from 35 to 52, its members coming from 15 EU states, with the biggest national delegations from Spain, Germany and Greece. The group is critical of the elitist qualities of the EU, opposes austerity measures introduced in the wake of the global financial and euro zone crises, campaigns for more direct democracy and enforcement of human rights, and, according to its website, supports 'a social union that places needs before profit and ends the destructive speculation that has provoked so much hardship and social discontent'.

Progressive Alliance of Socialists and Democrats (S&D)

The S&D is the main left-wing group in the EP, tracing its origins back to the creation in the ECSC Common Assembly of the Socialist Group. This went on to become the largest group in Parliament, its size adding to the concerns

Figure **15.2 Political groups in the European Parliament**

	NAME	ACRONYM	PHILOSOPHY	ASSOCIATED EUROPARTY
GUE/NGL	European United Left-Nordic Green Left	GUE/NGL	Left	Party of the European Left
S&D	Progressive Alliance of Socialists and Democrats	S&D	Social democrat	Party of European Socialists
The Greens : EFA	The Greens–European Free Alliance	Greens-EFA	Green/regionalist	European Green Party
	Alliance of Liberals and Democrats for Europe	ALDE	Centre-left	European Democratic Party
	European People's Party	EPP	Centre-right	European People's Party
ECR	European Conservatives and Reformists	ECR	Conservative	Movement for European Reform
EFDD	Europe of Freedom and Direct Democracy	EFDD	Eurosceptic	None

Focus on... *The rise of Europarties*

Party activity at the European level has been encouraged in recent years by a growth in the number and variety of Europarties, or pan-European party organizations and confederations. The most important of these parties are regulated and funded by the EU, and to be formally recognized by the EU must either have won at least 3 per cent of the vote in at least a quarter of EU member states in the most recent EP elections, or must have members elected to the EP or national or regional legislatures. While Europarties are not yet well known to the EU electorate and do not make much of a mark on national politics in the EU member states, their work helps improve coordination among like-minded national parties and helps give party groups in the EP greater stability and cohesion.

The first Europarties were founded in the 1970s in the lead-up to the first EP elections: the Confederation of Socialist Parties of the European Community was founded in 1973 (renamed the Party of European Socialists in 1992). It was followed by the moderately conservative European People's Party and the centre-left European Liberal Democratic and Reform Party in 1976, and a group of regional parties that created the European Free Alliance in 1981. But it has only been since 2002 that the real growth in Europarty activity has taken place, particularly at the conservative and eurosceptic end of the political spectrum (see Figure 15.3).

Europarties are still evolving, and have yet to run EU-wide campaigns for EP elections, which has led to questions about their significance and political role (Mair, 2006). They also face the challenge of attracting support in the face of declining support for political parties more generally. At the same time, they have become more adept at coordinating policy and building links between party leaders at the national and European levels (Hix and Hoyland, 2011, p. 201), and there have been growing efforts to give them more permanence and a more clearly defined role (Bartolini, 2012). One attempt to run a truly European campaign in 2009 was organized by an Irish businessman named Declan Ganley. In 2006 he formed a party named Libertas to campaign against the Treaty of Lisbon in the Irish referendum; this ran in the 2009 EP elections on a platform of greater democracy and transparency within the EU, but while it fielded several hundred candidates, only one (in France) was elected.

of conservative eurosceptics about the interventionist tendencies of European economic policies. At the first direct elections in 1979, it won a plurality of seats (113 to the 107 won by the EPP), picking up even bigger shares in the next three elections. A Confederation of Socialist Parties of the European Community had been created in 1973, and when it renamed itself the Party of European Socialists in 1992, the EP political group followed suit by renaming itself the Group of the Party of European Socialists (PES) (see Lightfoot, 2005).

During the late 1990s, PES felt the effects of a rightward shift within the European electorate, including a reaction in Britain against the governing Labour Party. In the 1999 elections, for the first time the EPP beat it into second place in the EP, where it has since remained. It became the Socialist Group in 2004, and in 2009 became the Progressive Alliance of Socialists and Democrats (S&D). Its numbers went up slightly at the 2014 elections, from 184 to 191, and it was the only political group with members from every EU member state, the biggest national blocs coming from Italy, Germany, the UK and Romania. It contains many shades of opinion, ranging from former communists on the left to more moderate social democrats towards the centre, but along with the EPP it is the most firmly pro-European of the political groups in the EP.

Europarties: Pan-European party organizations or confederations that coordinate policy and build links among national political parties in Europe.

Figure **15.3 Major Europarties**

NAME	YEAR FORMED	PHILOSOPHY
Party of European Socialists	1973	Social democratic
Alliance of Liberals and Democrats for Europe	1976	Liberal
European People's Party	1976	Christian democratic
European Free Alliance	1981	Regionalist
Party of the European Left	2004	Socialist/communist
European Green Party	2004	Green
European Democratic Party	2004	Centrist
Europeans United for Democracy	2005	Eurosceptic
Alliance of European Conservatives and Reformists	2010	Eurosceptic, conservative

The Greens–European Free Alliance (Greens-EFA)

This is another of the confederal marriages of convenience in the EP, bringing together national parties with approximately similar aims, but allowing each a high degree of independence. The Greens trace their roots back to the Rainbow Group formed in 1984 as a coalition of green parties (then making their first early mark on national politics in western Europe), regional parties and left-wing parties unaffiliated with other political groups. Green politics is popularly associated with environmental issues, but in fact greens pursue a wider variety of interests related to social justice, and refuse to be placed on the traditional ideological spectrum. In 1989 the greens formed their own Green Group, which entered into its current alliance with the European Free Alliance in 1999. The latter describes itself as the representative of stateless peoples and national minorities, and argues that regions should have more power. It lost ground slightly at the 2014 elections, its numbers falling from 55 to 50, with 17 states represented and the biggest national bloc coming from Germany.

Alliance of Liberals and Democrats for Europe (ALDE)

ALDE is the main centrist political group in the EP, although it long came a distant third in elections behind the socialists and the EPP, falling to fourth place in 2014. Most of its MEPs fall in or around the centre, with a wide range of opinions on the EU, and the group has suffered over the years from defections to the EPP. Its current name was agreed after the 2004 EP elections, and reflects its association with two Europarties: the European Liberal Democratic and Reform Party and the European Democratic Party. It is the only political group except the socialists and the EPP to have garnered enough support in the EP to have one of its members elected as president; this has happened four times so far, the last time being in 2002 when the conservatives and the socialists were unable to agree on whom to appoint as president, and chose Irish liberal democrat Pat Cox as a compromise. Its numbers fell substantially at the 2014 elections, from 84 to 67, leaving it with members from 21 EU member states, the biggest national blocs coming from Spain, France, the Netherlands and Germany.

Green politics: A political philosophy based on ecological wisdom, sustainability, social justice, grassroots democracy and non-violence.

European People's Party (EPP)

The EPP is the major political group on the centre-right and has been the biggest of the groups in the EP since 1999. It traces its origins to the formation of the Christian Democrat Group in the ECSC Common Assembly in 1953, which identified with the moderately conservative principles of Christian democracy, including social conservatism, liberal democracy, a mixed economy, European federalism, and a rejection of secularism. But the group's policies began to change as it incorporated centre-right parties from other member states that subscribed to neither Christian democracy nor European federalism (Judge and Earnshaw, 2008, p. 137). In 1976, in line with the creation that year of the European People's Party as a Europarty, it changed its name to the European People's Party Group.

The EPP might have been a natural fit for British and Danish conservatives, but their euroscepticism kept them functioning separately as the European Democrats (ED) until 1992, when they joined forces with the EPP. The new coalition contested the 1999 EP elections as the EPP–ED, and benefited from growing anti-European and anti-immigrant sentiment in several EU states to

Christian democracy: A political philosophy associated mainly with continental western Europe that applies Christian principles to public policy; moderately conservative on social and moral issues, and progressive on economic issues.

Table **15.1** **Party representation in the European Parliament, 2014**

	EPP	S&D	ECR	ALDE	GUE/NGL	Greens-EFA	EFDD	NI	Total
Germany	34	27	8	4	8	13	–	2	96
France	20	13	–	7	4	6	1	23	74
Italy	17	31	–	–	3	–	17	5	73
UK	–	20	20	1	1	6	24	1	73
Spain	17	14	–	8	11	4	–	–	54
Poland	23	5	19	–	–	–	–	4	51
Romania	15	16	–	1	1	–	–	1	32
Netherlands	5	3	2	7	3	2	–	4	26
Belgium	4	4	4	6	–	2	–	1	21
Czech Rep.	7	4	2	4	3	–	1	–	21
Greece	5	4	1	–	6	–	–	5	21
Hungary	12	4	–	–	–	2	–	3	21
Portugal	7	8	–	2	4	–	–	–	21
Sweden	4	6	–	3	1	4	2	–	20
Austria	5	5	–	1	–	3	–	4	18
Bulgaria	7	4	2	4	–	–	–	–	17
Denmark	1	3	4	3	1	1	–	–	13
Finland	3	2	2	4	1	1	–	–	13
Slovakia	6	4	2	1	–	–	–	–	13
Ireland	4	1	1	1	4	–	–	–	11
Croatia	5	2	1	2	–	1	–	–	11
Lithuania	2	2	1	3	–	1	2	–	11
Latvia	4	1	1	–	–	1	1	–	8
Slovenia	5	1	–	1	–	1	–	–	8
Cyprus	2	2	–	–	2	–	–	–	6
Estonia	1	1	–	3	–	1	–	–	6
Luxembourg	3	1	–	1	–	1	–	–	6
Malta	3	3	–	–	–	–	–	–	6
	221	191	70	67	52	50	48	52	**751**

overtake the socialists and win a plurality of seats in the EP for the first time. The political shift to the right continued in 2004, giving the group nearly 37 per cent of the seats in the EP despite a defection of British Conservatives to the ECR group. Its numbers fell substantially at the 2014 elections, from 265 to 221, but it still held the largest share of seats in the EP, with members from 27 member states, the biggest national blocs coming from Germany, Poland, France, Italy and Spain. The priorities of the EPP include a 'pragmatic' response to the global financial crisis (including better coordination of economic policies), reform of financing for the EU, the development of a joint EU immigration policy, and 'effective transatlantic solidarity'.

European conservatives

European conservatives – further to the right than the EPP, and more eurosceptic – have not had a stable history in the EP, but have been part of its group network since the early 1970s. In recent years its lynchpin has been the British Conservative Party, which was at the core of the European Democrats, which suffered from defections to the EPP during the 1980s, and in 1992 – on the brink of collapse – formed a coalition with the EPP, in spite of differences over the direction of European integration. After the 2009 elections, British Conservatives joined with Polish conservatives to form the new European Conservatives and Reformists (ECR) group. The 2014 elections saw its numbers grow from 54 to 70, making it the third largest group in the EP. It had members from 15 member states, but more than half were from the UK and Poland. It notes on its website that it opposes 'the ideological march towards a European federal super state' and supports 'a more flexible organization that listens to and respects people in all of its member countries'.

Eurosceptics

Political groups on this side of the EP have been the most unstable of all, repeatedly changing their name and structure, and united mainly by their hostility to the EU. The Europe of Nations group was founded in 1994, evolving in 1999 into Europe of Democracies and Diversities, becoming Independence/Democracy in 2004, and being reformed in 2009 as Europe of Freedom and Democracy, with 32 members from nine member states. It was renamed Europe of Freedom and Direct Democracy (EFDD) in 2014, and while its numbers increased from 32 to 48, they came from only seven member states, and all but seven came from the United Kingdom Independence Party (UKIP, which supports Britain's withdrawal from the EU) and Italy's populist Five Star Movement. EFDD is more conservative than its predecessors, noting on its website that it opposes further European integration 'that would exacerbate the present democratic deficit and the centralist political structure of the EU', and believing that member states 'have the right to protect their borders and strengthen their own historical, traditional and cultural values'.

Nationalists

Suffering similar levels of instability to the eurosceptics, the nationalists in the EP trace their origins back to the formation in 1984 of the European Right, consisting mainly of French and Italian right-wingers, notably the far-right French National Front led by Jean-Marie Le Pen. It was disbanded in 1994, and was briefly reformed in January 2007 as Identity, Tradition and Sovereignty, when the accession of Bulgaria and Romania gave it enough MEPs to apply for group status. Its members spoke of the need to defend 'Christian values, the family and European civilization', and included Le Pen and Alessandra Mussolini, granddaughter of the former Italian dictator. The group lasted less than a year before infighting tore it apart. The National Front did well in 2014, placing first in the EP elections in France under the leadership of Le Pen's daughter Marine, and winning 24 of France's 74 seats. But it was unable to attract enough MEPs from other countries to form a far-right EP group, and its members remained unattached.

Non-attached members

The EP has always had a small cluster of non-attached members (NI in Table 15.1), who have either been elected as members of parties that have not been able to reach agreement to join a political group, or who have deliberately chosen to remain outside the group structure. Their numbers have waxed and waned as the membership of groups has changed, but they have rarely numbered more than two or three dozen at a time. There were 52 following the 2014 elections.

Interest groups

Every EU member state has a diverse and active community of interest groups that works to influence government on a wide variety of issues. They use multiple methods, including political lobbying, support for election campaigns, and the provision of expertise and information. When public policy in Europe was made primarily at the national or local level, these groups naturally focused most of their efforts on national and local government. But as more decisions were made at the level of the EEC/EU, more groups began to pay more attention to European-level policy-making, with a particular interest in trying to influence the European Commission and the European Parliament (Mazey and Richardson, 2003, 2006).

Many either opened offices in Brussels or became part of Brussels-based umbrella organizations, contributing to the steady rise of a European lobbying industry. Counting only Eurogroups (those organized to work at the European level), there were estimated to be about 500 in 1985, rising to 700 in 1996, and 851 in 2006 (Philip, 1985; Aspinwall and Greenwood, 1998; Balme and Chabanet, 2008). Overall, the number of groups with offices in Brussels now runs well into the thousands, the majority representing business interests, while the balance represent mainly public interests and the professions.

Interest groups have benefited from two structural problems within the EU decision-making system. First, there has been the relative weakness of party activity in the EP, which has left Europe without the same degree of voter mobilization and engagement witnessed at the level of the member states, and has in turn helped lift the political profile of interest groups. Second, the small size of the European Commission has worked to the benefit of interest groups by allowing them to fill a structural need. With too few staff to manage the drafting

Interest group: An organization that represents and promotes the political, economic or social interests of its members, which may be individuals, cultural or social groups, professions or industries.

of new laws and the monitoring of implementation by the member states, the Commission has come to rely on interest groups for the provision of expertise at the drafting phase and to act as watchdogs at the implementation phase. Interest groups also benefit from the different points of contact and influence made available by the multilevel character of the EU.

The Commission has occasionally gone further than simply engaging groups for the support they might be able to offer, and has also funded the work of groups and set up formal channels through which groups can work directly with the Commission. This immediately raises the question, of course, of how far such groups can remain objective in their dealings with the Commission. On the environmental front, for example, the Commission has, since its creation in 1974, funded the European Environmental Bureau, a Brussels-based umbrella organization for local, national and regional environmental groups. In 2012 it received nearly 40 per cent of its funding from the Commission.

The Commission is not alone in attracting the attention of interest groups, which will also make sure to work with the national delegations of the member states in Brussels (because of their participation in the Committee of Permanent Representatives), the working parties and committees of the Council of Ministers, and the committees of the European Parliament. As we saw in Chapter 14, they also have direct representation in the European Economic and Social Committee (EESC), which despite its limited influence is another platform for the open discussion of the kinds of issues with which interest groups deal. The EESC has been instrumental in changes to laws dealing with a variety of issues, and also has a number of technical experts among its members and sets up its own working groups to which additional experts are invited to give evidence, so it can provide useful specialist comments on a proposal.

Reflecting the long emphasis of European integration on economic matters, business and labour groups have long been the most active and visible at the EU level. Individual corporations are represented either directly or through lobbying firms in Brussels, and several cross-sectoral and multi-state federations have been created to represent wider economic interests (see Figure 15.4). More numerous, but smaller, are the many groups representing special interests, such

Illustration **15.2**
Interest groups
Periodic European Business Summits bring together representatives of business and consumer interest groups, European corporations and the EU institutions.

as the European Platform for Social NGOs, Amnesty International, the European Youth Forum and the European Women's Lobby. They often lack the resources or expertise to compete with industry or business federations, and the compartmentalized nature of EU decision-making works to their disadvantage because it demands that groups be able to monitor and respond to policy developments in multiple different institutions. They will occasionally work to address these handicaps by building pan-European coalitions of national groups that are adept at mobilizing the interest and resources of millions of individual members.

One of the subspecies of interest groups that typically plays a critical role in the national capitals of liberal democracies is the think tank (or policy institute). These are private organizations set up to undertake research, organize conferences and seminars, sustain a public and political debate over the issues in which it is interested, and influence decision-makers either directly or indirectly. Most are privately funded, but some are supported by governments,

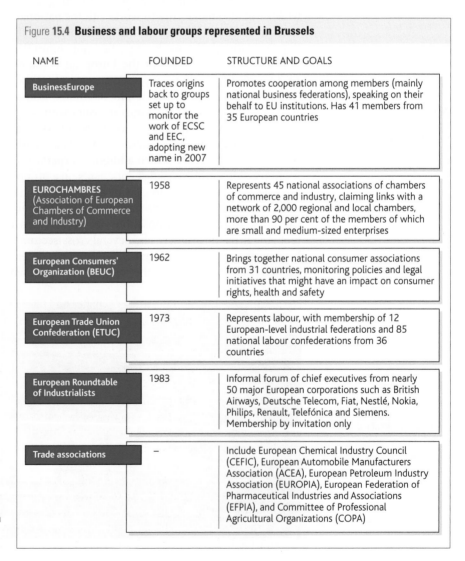

Figure **15.4 Business and labour groups represented in Brussels**

NAME	FOUNDED	STRUCTURE AND GOALS
BusinessEurope	Traces origins back to groups set up to monitor the work of ECSC and EEC, adopting new name in 2007	Promotes cooperation among members (mainly national business federations), speaking on their behalf to EU institutions. Has 41 members from 35 European countries
EUROCHAMBRES (Association of European Chambers of Commerce and Industry)	1958	Represents 45 national associations of chambers of commerce and industry, claiming links with a network of 2,000 regional and local chambers, more than 90 per cent of the members of which are small and medium-sized enterprises
European Consumers' Organization (BEUC)	1962	Brings together national consumer associations from 31 countries, monitoring policies and legal initiatives that might have an impact on consumer rights, health and safety
European Trade Union Confederation (ETUC)	1973	Represents labour, with membership of 12 European-level industrial federations and 85 national labour confederations from 36 countries
European Roundtable of Industrialists	1983	Informal forum of chief executives from nearly 50 major European corporations such as British Airways, Deutsche Telecom, Fiat, Nestlé, Nokia, Philips, Renault, Telefónica and Siemens. Membership by invitation only
Trade associations	–	Include European Chemical Industry Council (CEFIC), European Automobile Manufacturers Association (ACEA), European Petroleum Industry Association (EUROPIA), European Federation of Pharmaceutical Industries and Associations (EFPIA), and Committee of Professional Agricultural Organizations (COPA)

Think tank: An organization that conducts research into a given area of policy with the goal of fostering public debate and political change.

Concept

Civil society

A key indicator of a healthy political society is the willingness and ability of its individual members to organize themselves in order to address problems and provide services without the nudging or the support of government or the marketplace. This is the essence of a civil society, whose existence and functioning are also indicative of the willingness of government to entertain competing views about the sources and effects of societal problems. But citizen action can also be a sign that government is not responding adequately to the needs of society, thereby encouraging citizens to take matters into their own hands.

political parties or corporations, and have a clear national or ideological agenda. In the US, Washington DC is well known as the home of several hundred think tanks of many different persuasions, but Brussels is beginning to develop a similar reputation in Europe. Among the organizations based in Brussels with an EU focus are the following:

- The Centre for European Policy Studies: focuses on generating research and debate on pressing EU issues and managing a network of corporate and institutional partners.
- The European Policy Centre: dedicated to 'making European integration work' by developing recommendations to improve the way the EU operates and relates to ordinary Europeans.
- The European Enterprise Institute: encourages debate on issues relating to entrepreneurship and competitiveness.
- The European Trade Union Institute: promotes research and education on issues relating to labour in Europe.
- Friends of Europe: set up in 1999 to debate EU issues through the hosting of conferences and roundtables, and the publication of reports and a journal called *Global Europe*.

The work of interest groups has helped offset the national and intergovernmental influences in EU policy-making by reaching across state borders to promote the common sectional interests of groups of people in multiple member states. More of those interests are now part of European policy calculations, Eurogroups have helped promote a European consciousness in policy-making, and along the way they have become protagonists; where once they focused mainly on monitoring policy, they now try to change it using increasingly sophisticated means (Aspinwall and Greenwood, 1998). The work of interest groups has also helped offset concerns about the European democratic deficit, by offering a channel through which Europeans can lobby and influence the content of EU law and policy. This has in turn helped focus the attention of ordinary Europeans on how the EU influences the policies that affect their lives, helping draw them more actively into the process by which the EU makes its decisions, and encouraging them to bypass their national governments and focus their attention on European responses to shared and common problems.

To be sure, interest groups represent only the particular views of their members, and their leaderships are not elected and are therefore rarely accountable to any group bigger than the board of trustees. But most rely on the active support and input of their members, claim to speak on behalf of those members, and the competition among hundreds of interest groups can help provide some balance to policy debates. In this sense, interest groups are a critical part of a healthy civil society, or the arena that exists outside the state or the marketplace and within which individuals take collective action on shared interests. They will usually organize themselves into nongovernmental organizations (NGOs) in the form of charities, community groups, professional associations, cultural groups and trade unions, and take action outside government to deal with problems or provide services that have not been addressed by government.

If enough such organizations are working and cooperating on the same issues, the creation of these groups can coalesce into social movements. The existence of a diverse civil society is confirmation that individuals are engaging with their communities and government is willing to tolerate public discourse; civil societies barely exist in totalitarian regimes. Where each of the member states of the EU has a well-developed civil society of its own, however, the broader EU is only just catching up. Balme and Chabanet (2008) note the irony in the fact that as support for integration has declined, or has at least run into greater resistance, so social movements have flourished in the EU, addressing everything from unemployment and poverty to women's rights, migration policy and environmental protection.

One of the core functions of most interest groups is lobbying, or attempts to influence the decision-making process. This has long been part of political life at the national level in liberal democracies, although it is less developed in Europe than in the US, and its political role is quite different (see McGrath, 2005). Lobbying in the US is a major industry, with estimates of the number of lobbyists in Washington DC alone in the range of 20,000 or more, compared to Commission estimates of about 15,000 in Brussels (*EU Insight*, 2008). Washington lobbyists are professional and aggressive, are often generously funded, and long ago became part of the national political scene in the US. Americans, also, are more than familiar with the phenomenon of the revolving door, where former members of Congress, the White House staff, or government departments are

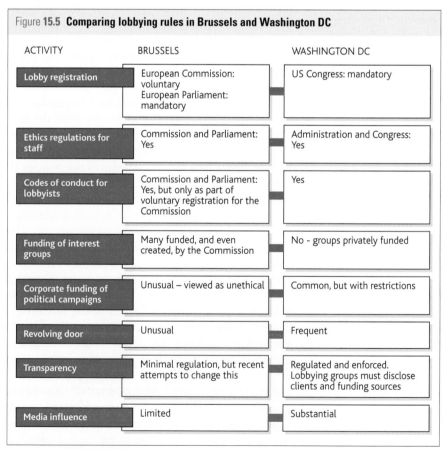

Figure **15.5** **Comparing lobbying rules in Brussels and Washington DC**

ACTIVITY	BRUSSELS	WASHINGTON DC
Lobby registration	European Commission: voluntary European Parliament: mandatory	US Congress: mandatory
Ethics regulations for staff	Commission and Parliament: Yes	Administration and Congress: Yes
Codes of conduct for lobbyists	Commission and Parliament: Yes, but only as part of voluntary registration for the Commission	Yes
Funding of interest groups	Many funded, and even created, by the Commission	No - groups privately funded
Corporate funding of political campaigns	Unusual – viewed as unethical	Common, but with restrictions
Revolving door	Unusual	Frequent
Transparency	Minimal regulation, but recent attempts to change this	Regulated and enforced. Lobbying groups must disclose clients and funding sources
Media influence	Limited	Substantial

Source: Based on *EU Insight*, 2008.

Lobbying: Efforts made to influence the decisions made by elected officials or bureaucrats on behalf of individuals, groups or organizations.

employed by lobbying organizations and paid large fees to exploit their insider knowledge and contacts in order to wield influence.

The lobbying world in Brussels is quite different, in part because of political realities and in part because of political culture. The political reality is that EU institutions have far less power than their American equivalents, so lobbyists have been less drawn to Brussels and still focus much of their attention on national government. Money also plays a smaller role in European politics, whereas campaigning in the US can be enormously expensive, and candidates rely heavily on corporate and interest group donations to support their efforts. As for political culture, Europeans are less used to lobbying than Americans and more sceptical about its role in the democratic process.

The differences are reflected in the extent to which lobbying is regulated in the two cities (see Figure 15.5). In Washington DC, lobbyists are required to register, and the Lobbying Disclosure Act obliges lobbying groups to list their clients and sources of funding. In Brussels, registration is voluntary for dealings with the Commission (although mandatory for Parliament), and it was only in 2005 that the Commission launched the European Transparency Initiative in an attempt to make the lobbying process more open. This led to the creation in 2008 of a voluntary Register of Interest Representatives, in which nearly 5,600 organizations were listed in 2013 (Zibold, 2013), and the development of a system for accrediting groups and individuals that want access to the European Parliament.

Summary

- MEPs organize themselves into like-minded political groups, which must have at least 25 members from at least one-quarter of member states.
- Groups have developed more consistency and cohesion with time, the most stability being found among the socialists, the liberals and the centre-right European People's Party (EPP). The socialists had the biggest bloc of seats in the EP until 1999, since when the EPP has had the biggest bloc. But no one political group has yet won a majority.
- Political groups have common ideologies and policy preferences, and their own leadership structures and operating rules, but do not campaign across member states during EP elections. There are no formal links between the political make-up of Parliament and the European Commission.
- The consistency of political groups has been encouraged by the creation of several Europarties
that bring together like-minded parties in different EU member states.
- National interest groups have increasingly turned their attention to the EU, with a particular focus on influencing the Commission, the Council of Ministers and the European Parliament.
- Group activity has helped offset the relative weakness of party activity at the European level, and groups have exploited the shortage of staff in the Commission to play a key role in the drafting and implementation of law and policy.
- Business and labour groups have long been the most active at the EU level, but the number of special interest groups and Brussels-based think tanks has grown.
- Lobbying is a growth industry in Brussels, although the opportunities have so far been fewer than those available at the national level and the rules looser.

Key terms and concepts

Christian democracy

Civil society

Europarties

Green politics

Interest group

Lobbying

Political groups

Think tank

Further reading

Arvanitopoulos, Constantine (ed.) (2010) *Reforming Europe: The Role of the Centre-Right* (New York: Springer). Lightfoot, Simon (2005) *Europeanizing Social Democracy? The Rise of the Party of European Socialists* (London: Routledge). Studies of the two major political groups in the European Parliament.

Coen, David, and Jeremy Richardson (eds) (2009) *Lobbying the European Union: Institutions, Actors, and Issues* (Oxford: Oxford University Press). Pedler, Robin (2002) *European Union Lobbying: Changes in the Arena* (Basingstoke: Palgrave Macmillan). Two studies of lobbying in the EU, including chapters on different EU institutions, key lobbies and major campaigns.

Lindberg, Bjorn, Anne Rasmussen and Andreas Warntjen (eds) (2010) *The Role of Political Parties in the European Union* (London: Routledge). Edited collection of studies of the mechanics and role of political parties in the European and national arenas.

16 Elections and Referendums

Preview

European integration has long been criticized for its weak democratic qualities. The treaties have too often been negotiated behind closed doors, argue the critics, and member states have had to surrender sovereignty with too little reference to the views of European voters. This has undermined enthusiasm for the European project, which has often seemed elitist and too far distant from the needs and interests of ordinary Europeans. Yet there are two key channels through which they can directly influence EU policy.

First, elections to the European Parliament are held every five years, and give voters the opportunity to elect representatives to the EP, which has become more powerful in recent years. But European voters have not taken full advantage of EP elections: turnout has fallen from a high of 63 per cent in 1979 to a low of 43 per cent in 2014, and many of those who cast their votes make their choices more on the basis of national issues than European issues; elections are often polls on the standing of incumbent governments, with the result that the bigger mainstream parties often do less well than smaller parties.

Second, national referendums on European issues have been held with growing frequency. There is no consistency as to when and where they will be held: thus, Ireland must hold referendums on amendments to its national constitution, and political pressures have led to several votes on European issues in Denmark and France, but most EU member states have avoided them. Nonetheless, the pressures to hold referendums on the adoption of new treaties have grown, and even a single national vote has occasionally been enough to spark a Europe-wide debate about the progress of integration. But whether referendums help or hinder the cause of democracy is a matter of debate.

Key issues

- How far does the arithmetic of proportional representation account for the difficulties of the EP?
- Which explanation for low voter turnout at EP elections is most compelling?
- What could or should be done to improve turnout at EP elections?
- Have referendums improved the quality of the democratic debate over Europe?
- Should national referendums become a more structured and regular part of the European political calendar?

European elections

Direct elections to the European Parliament (EP) have been held every five years since 1979 (in years ending with a four or a nine), but they have yet to earn a firm place in the European political consciousness. Theoretically, they should have been widely welcomed, because they give European voters a direct link with the work of the EU and help address concerns about the EU's democratic deficit: the EP is the only EU institution directly elected by voters, has won growing powers over the EU legislative and policy process, and should logically have attracted the interest and input of EU voters. But turnout at EP elections has been falling, and neither the EP nor the parties that contest its elections have been able to make the necessary psychological connection with voters on European issues.

The logistics of the elections are impressive: there were about 380 million eligible voters in 2014, making the EP elections the second largest democratic elections in the world after those held in India. Voters must be 18 years of age (16 in Austria), must be citizens of one of the EU member states, and can vote in whichever EU member state they are legally resident; all they need to do is make a declaration to the electoral authority of the member state in which they are living, meet local registration qualifications, and meet the terms of rules set by their home state. Member states once had different rules on the minimum age for candidates, but it has been established as 18 in all countries except Cyprus and Italy, where it is 25. They have different rules on how candidates qualify: some states do not allow independent candidates, some require candidates to pay deposits, others require them to collect signatures and so on.

For EP elections – and, in most cases, for national elections – every EU member state uses variations on the theme of proportional representation (PR). This contrasts with the single-member plurality (SMP) system used in national elections in Britain, Canada and the US, where each legislative district is contested by multiple candidates and the winner is the candidate who wins the most votes (a plurality). PR typically involves bigger and multi-member districts, with competing parties publishing lists of candidates for each district, and seats being distributed among parties according to the share of the vote each receives. While most EU member states structure their entire territory as a single electoral district and parties run with national lists of candidates, five states (Belgium, France, Ireland, Italy and the UK) are divided into between three and twelve Euro-constituencies, and their parties publish constituency lists of candidates.

All liberal democracies are representative democracies, which are, by definition, systems in which the votes of the public determine the make-up of legislatures, whose members are expected to represent the interests of voters. But no electoral system has yet been invented that is truly reflective of the balance of voter support for different political parties, and PR and SMP have their advantages and disadvantages (see Figure 16.1). For better or worse, PR has become the normal order of political business throughout Europe. The result is that politics in national legislatures and the European Parliament has come to be coloured by two main characteristics: coalition governments made up of two or more political parties, and the representation of a wide range of political opinion. This contrasts with the US, for example, which has only two parties that have any real chance of winning control – the Democrats and the Republicans – thereby almost always guaranteeing legislative majorities for one or the other.

Coalition government:
A government made up of representatives from more than one political party, demanding compromises among the participating parties.

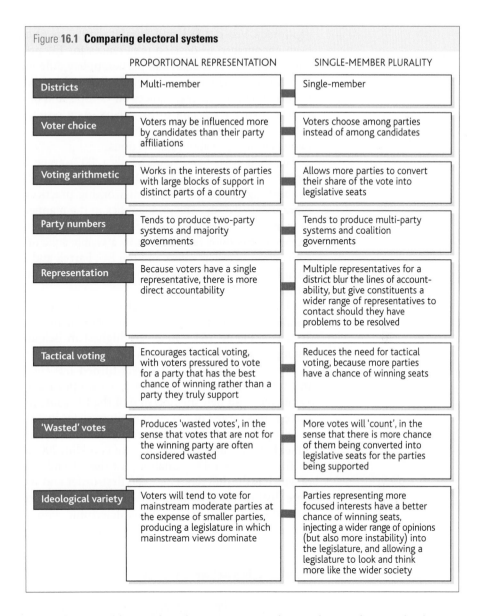

Figure **16.1 Comparing electoral systems**

	PROPORTIONAL REPRESENTATION	SINGLE-MEMBER PLURALITY
Districts	Multi-member	Single-member
Voter choice	Voters may be influenced more by candidates than their party affiliations	Voters choose among parties instead of among candidates
Voting arithmetic	Works in the interests of parties with large blocks of support in distinct parts of a country	Allows more parties to convert their share of the vote into legislative seats
Party numbers	Tends to produce two-party systems and majority governments	Tends to produce multi-party systems and coalition governments
Representation	Because voters have a single representative, there is more direct accountability	Multiple representatives for a district blur the lines of accountability, but give constituents a wider range of representatives to contact should they have problems to be resolved
Tactical voting	Encourages tactical voting, with voters pressured to vote for a party that has the best chance of winning rather than a party they truly support	Reduces the need for tactical voting, because more parties have a chance of winning seats
'Wasted' votes	Produces 'wasted votes', in the sense that votes that are not for the winning party are often considered wasted	More votes will 'count', in the sense that there is more chance of them being converted into legislative seats for the parties being supported
Ideological variety	Voters will tend to vote for mainstream moderate parties at the expense of smaller parties, producing a legislature in which mainstream views dominate	Parties representing more focused interests have a better chance of winning seats, injecting a wider range of opinions (but also more instability) into the legislature, and allowing a legislature to look and think more like the wider society

Coalitions oblige political parties to work together and party leaders to consider the views and interests of more than those who elected them. The result is a moderation of policies, except in those cases where the balance of power in a coalition is held by small parties, whose influence can be out of proportion to their size, and which end up becoming the tails that wag the dog. But moderation and consensus may not always be what is needed, and the energy generated by trying to reach agreement among the parties in a coalition can result in hamstrung leadership and an inability to take the sometimes unpopular steps needed to address pressing problems. (For a study of coalition governments in western Europe, see Müller and Strøm, 2003.)

There has long been a debate about the efficiency and efficacy of European elections in providing voters with real choices and the EU institutions with legitimacy. Van der Eijk and Franklin (1996, p. 6) argue that voters have never been encouraged to develop preferences for EU policies that would help them choose among candidates and parties, policy differences on Europe rarely figure in media coverage of news about the EU, and candidates and parties rarely offer policies that provide real choices on Europe, and often do not even put forward policies that are relevant to EU affairs. As a result, the opportunity to educate voters on European issues has been missed, as has the opportunity to generate public enthusiasm about EP elections.

For their part, Farrell and Scully (2007) argue that while the EP has been highly successful as an institution in terms of winning greater powers and establishing increasingly efficient working practices, it has been 'a failure as a representative body'. The problem lies in the manner in which MEPs are elected in many of the member states: most want to work in a powerful EP but find that European elections fail to result in a visible style of representation that offers a connection between voters and the EU. Farrell and Scully conclude that a more open list system is needed, along with a regionalization of electoral procedures for large member states.

One issue of concern in EP elections has been declining voter turnout, the number falling from a respectable 61.99% in 1979 to a disappointing 42.54% in 2014 (see Figure 16.2). Rates are highest in Belgium and Luxembourg, where voting is compulsory (although the laws are not enforced), but in most states in 2014 fewer than half of voters turned out (see Figure 16.3). Expectations that turnout might be high in eastern European states still in the flush of young democracy and new membership of the EU came to nothing; fewer than one in three voters turned out in eight of those states in 2014. Even in the two stalwarts of European integration – France and Germany – turnout has fallen to less than 50%. (For an analysis of turnout, see Franklin, 2006, pp. 233–7.)

There are several explanations for these trends, perhaps the most compelling of which is the difference between first-order and second-order elections. These were distinguished by Reiff and Schmitt (1980) according to how much was at stake: because national elections determine who controls national executives and legislatures, which in turn make the decisions that have the most immedi-

First-order and second-order elections: Elections with different stakes, the former for government institutions, such as national executives and legislatures, with significant powers, and the latter for institutions, such as local government and the European Parliament, with fewer powers.

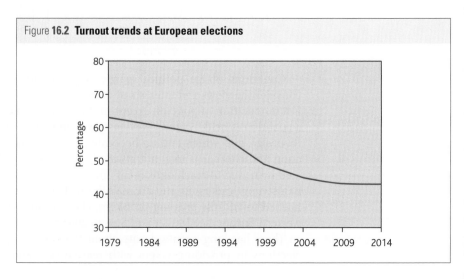

Figure **16.2 Turnout trends at European elections**

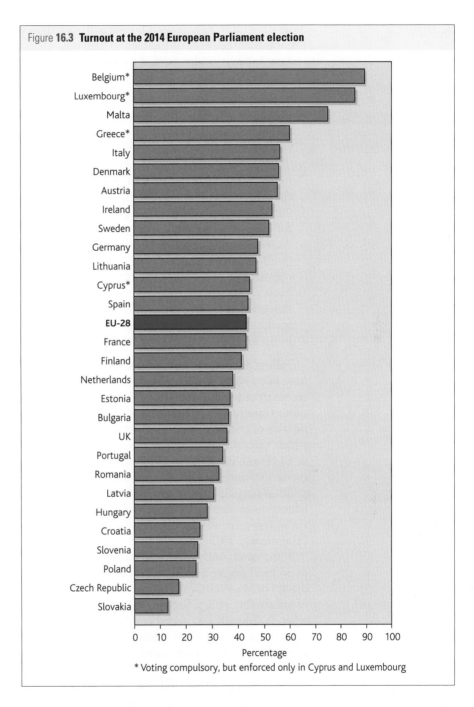

Figure **16.3 Turnout at the 2014 European Parliament election**

* Voting compulsory, but enforced only in Cyprus and Luxembourg

ate impact on the lives of voters, they also attract the most media attention, are more hard fought, and voters find it easier to engage with the issues (because they are more immediate), and hence are more likely to turn out on election day. By contrast, second-order elections, such as by-elections and local government elections, have lower stakes and attract less voter interest. EP elections are more clearly second-order: there is no change of government at stake, voters find it more difficult to engage with European issues than with national issues, and the result is that they are less inclined to turn out.

Low turnout is also related to several other factors (see discussion in Judge and Earnshaw, 2008, pp. 77–80):

- There is the simple problem of the fuzzy shape of the EP on the European political radar: few Europeans much know or care what it does, which is in turn a function of generally low voter knowledge on European integration (see Chapter 17). This makes them less inclined to make the effort to vote.
- There are few well-known figures in the EP who might act as a catalyst for higher turnout. Turnover among MEPs is relatively high, as are changes in the leadership of political groups, and no EP president until Martin Schulz in 2014 has served more than one term, all of which reduces the opportunities for individual MEPs to rise above the pack and energize voters.
- As we saw in Chapter 15, there is (as yet) no tradition of Europe-wide political parties running in EP elections, which means that there is less opportunity to mobilize voters and inject energy into election campaigns.
- Most voters still see EP elections very much in national terms, a problem exacerbated by the limited effect of Europarties and the focus in national media on the horse race between national parties and what the elections mean for the country rather than what they mean for the EU.

Falling turnout is also related to trends in national elections, where there have been signs of declining overall turnout in several EU member states over recent decades, although rates vary from one country to another and one election to another. Explaining voter turnout has been described as one of the great puzzles of political science, whether trying to understand trends in turnout, or which variables best explain voter turnout, or even why anyone bothers to vote at all (Franklin, 2005, p. xi). One explanation for falling turnout comes out of modernization theory, which argues that while it might be logical to think that political participation in general is a function of the amount of information and education available to voters, and the amounts of both have increased dramatically, there are at least two reasons why this has actually led to falling turnout (Thomassen, 2005, pp. 6–7).

First, voters with more resources are more likely to become directly involved in political decision-making, will be less likely to see political parties as intermediaries between citizens and the state, and may opt for less conventional means of influencing policy. Second, voters are more likely to turn out in elections only when faced with real choices and it is clear that real change will follow according to which party or coalition is in power. With party identification declining, voters will be motivated more by the changing stakes in each election, which means that they will decide from one election to another whether or not to vote.

The concept of second-order elections not only helps explain low voter turnout, but also helps explain the choices made by those who *do* vote:

- Voters will often treat EP elections less as an opportunity to determine the make-up and work of the EP than to comment on the national government of the day and its performance in dealing with domestic issues (Heath et al., 1999). In that sense, then, they are less European elections than subsidiary national elections. This has also been true of some of the referendums held on new EU treaties, where the result has been, at least in part, a reflection of the popularity or unpopularity of the national government and its position on the treaty under review (see later in this chapter).

■ Given that the political stakes in EP elections are seen as relatively low, there is an inclination for participating voters to make their choices with their hearts rather than their heads. In other words, they are more likely to express their feelings than to make hard-headed political choices. The result is that smaller parties which normally do not win much support in national elections will often do well in EP elections. This in turn means that true voter preferences are not reflected in the party make-up of the EP.

The effects of these two phenomena have been particularly clear in the UK, where the governing party has typically done poorly at EP elections and small parties have done well. For example, it took until 2010 for the Greens to win their first seat in the British Parliament, but they surprised even themselves by winning nearly 15% of the national vote in the 1989 EP elections, which converted into 12 seats in the EP (all but 3 of which were lost in 2014). Meanwhile, the often

---

Debating... *Does low voter turnout hurt democracy?*

YES

Levels of political accountability and representation are a function of levels of public engagement in politics.

Low voter turnout may reflect declining faith in the political process, a sense of disconnection with, and disengagement from, politics, and a belief among voters that the stakes are not high enough or important enough to merit investing time to go to the polls.

Voting is at the heart of the democratic process. Regardless of their wealth, position, race, gender or educational background, all members of society are politically equalized by the right to vote. A failure to vote is a form of voluntary disenfranchisement that gives more influence to those who do vote.

Government often looks like, and pays more attention to, the people who vote: turnout is highest among older, better educated and wealthier Europeans, while it is lowest among the young, the poor and racial minorities, whose interests are often lower down the list of national political priorities.

NO

Low voter turnout is not necessarily a sign of declining faith in politics: research has found that Europeans are shifting away from indirect participation in politics through their elected representatives in favour of direct participation by joining interest groups, voting in referendums, signing petitions, or taking direct political action. There has, in other words, been a shift away from representative democracy to participatory democracy (Almond et al., 2002, pp. 42ff.).

While many people do not vote because they feel disconnected from politics, there is another group of voters who are content as they are and feel that whoever is in office, it will not make much difference to their lives.

Lower turnout may be less an indication of declining faith in the political process than of declining faith in political parties.

Low voter turnout might suggest that politics has become marginal to the lives of many, which may be no bad thing. Politics sometimes comes to matter too much, and if disengagement with elections means devoting more time and attention to family, education, recreation and community service, society may benefit.

very different results of European and national elections in Britain were clearly illustrated by the outcomes of the May 2010 general election and the May 2014 EP election (see Figure 16.4). The unpopular governing Conservative Party was beaten into third place in the EP election by the UK Independence Party (UKIP), which won nearly 27% of the vote (and 24 seats in the EP). The junior partner in the governing alliance, the Liberal Democrats, fared even worse, losing all but 1 of its 10 seats in the EP. But while the UKIP vote was greeted by the party as a sound mandate for its anti-EU position, it had won only 3.1% of the vote in the 2010 general election, and turnout numbers were significantly different: 65% in 2010 and 35% in 2014.

As noted earlier, there has been much conjecture that declining voter turnout in Europe may be a function of a switch to alternative or less 'conventional' forms of political participation. The most telling of these has been support for the work of interest groups, which, as we saw in Chapter 15, are becoming more active at the European level. Europeans, like the residents of all democratic societies, also have the following options:

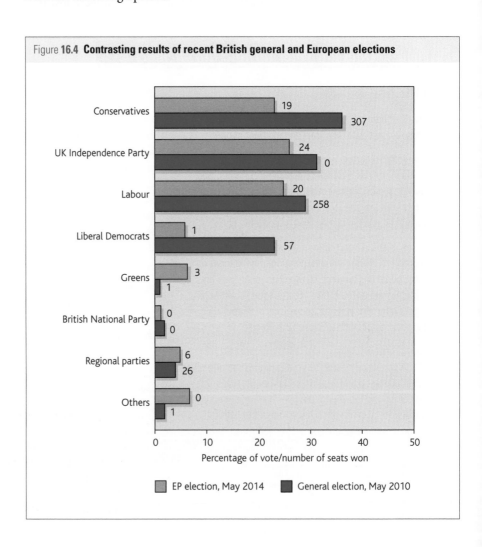

Figure **16.4 Contrasting results of recent British general and European elections**

Percentage of vote/number of seats won

■ EP election, May 2014   ■ General election, May 2010

- running for public office
- organizing or taking part in public demonstrations
- using social media to express their views or connect with others
- contacting elected officials
- volunteering for a local community organization
- signing a petition
- attending political rallies and speeches
- civil disobedience or passive resistance.

One new channel for the expression of citizen interests in the EU, introduced by the Treaty of Lisbon, is the petition or the citizen initiative. Article 11 of the treaty states:

> Not less than one million citizens who are nationals of a significant number of Member States may take the initiative of inviting the European Commission, within the framework of its powers, to submit any appropriate proposal on matters where citizens consider that a legal act of the Union is required for the purpose of implementing the Treaties.

Lisbon did not define what would constitute a 'significant' number of member states, nor is it clear how the details of the one million citizens would be recorded and confirmed as genuine, but this has not discouraged the generation of several initiatives: subjects have included allowing EU citizens be allowed to vote in all elections wherever they legally reside, setting a default speed limit of 30 kph (20 mph) in all urban areas in the EU, and improving EU legislation on access to drinking water.

Citizen initiative: An option introduced by Lisbon that allows a petition, signed by at least a million people, to be submitted to the Commission.

Illustration **16.1 European elections**
Incoming European Commission President Jean-Claude Juncker holds a press conference after the 2014 European Parliament elections, in which the European People's Party won the most seats.

National referendums

Less scholarly attention has been paid to the study of national referendums in the EU than the study of elections, yet they have been held with increased frequency, and they are the subject of often intense short-term public and political attention; at few times is voter attention drawn more actively to European issues than when one of the member states organizes (or even talks of the possibility of holding) a referendum. They have occasionally resulted in dramatic changes of political direction, and the EU's democratic deficit is rarely more apparent than when national governments refuse to put major European questions to a public test, usually out of fear of negative outcomes.

The use of national referendums varies from one country to another. At one end of the spectrum is Ireland, which has a constitutional requirement that all international treaties (including EU treaties) likely to impact national sovereignty need constitutional amendments, which in turn require a national referendum; hence Ireland has been active in holding referendums on EU treaties. In the middle of the spectrum lies Italy, whose voters since 1974 have often gone to the polls to express opinions on domestic issues as diverse as nuclear power, hunting, electoral reform, divorce and abortion. (They also voted in 1989 on whether the European Parliament should be given the power to adopt a treaty on European union developed at the prompting of Italian politician Altiero Spinelli.) Meanwhile, Denmark has had referendums on the rules of royal succession and changes to the minimum voting age, France has had several votes on changes to the constitution, and the UK has had several regional referendums on questions related to devolution (most recently, the 2014 referendum on Scottish independence). For most EU states, though, their experience with national votes on European matters has been something of a political novelty.

So far, a total of 43 referendums have been held dealing with European issues (see Table 16.1 below), making Europe – in the view of de Vreese and Semetko (2004, p. 4) – the single most voted-on issue in the world. More than half of the referendums have been held since 1998, and more than one-third of them in just two countries: Denmark and Ireland. In only seven EU member states (Belgium, Bulgaria, Cyprus, Germany, Greece, Portugal and Romania) has there never been a referendum on a European issue. Where there have been such votes, most have fallen into one of two major categories.

Membership of the EEC/EU or the euro

In none of the six founding states of the three European Communities was it considered politically or constitutionally necessary to put membership to a national vote. This was a reflection in part of the way the creation of the Communities was negotiated and planned by political leaders, and in part the modest goals of the Communities, each of which was considered (at the time) little more than a conventional international organization. It was only later, as membership of the EEC and then the EU involved bigger political commitments and significant changes to national law and policy, and generated more public debate, that national referendums began to appear more regularly on the political calendar. Even so, of today's 28 member states, referendums on joining the EEC/EU have been held in only 16, all but two of which joined after 1995.

Referendum: A form of direct democracy (otherwise known as a plebiscite, a ballot question, or a proposition), in which the affected electorate is asked to vote on whether or not to accept a specific proposal.

The first four membership referendums were held in 1972 in France, Denmark, Ireland and Norway. The French vote was unique in the sense that it asked not whether the French wanted to be part of the EC but whether they favoured the enlargement of the Community to include Britain, Denmark, Ireland and Norway. With 60% turnout, 68% voted in favour. For Denmark, Ireland and Norway, meanwhile, it was a simple question of whether or not to accept membership of the EEC. In the Irish and Danish cases, there was little controversy, high turnout and strong support for joining (83% and 63% respectively). But in Norway there was a debate generated by concerns over fishing, the environment and national sovereignty. In the event, just over 53% voted against Community membership, as a result of which Prime Minister Trygve Bratteli resigned from office. Norway was again accepted for EU membership in 1994, again put the issue to a national vote (in November of that year) and again opted to stay out, this time by the slightly smaller figure of just over 52%.

In 1975, Britain held a referendum that was not only unusual in its timing and its objectives, but was the first national referendum in British history. There had been no vote before Britain joined the EEC on 1 January 1973, on terms negotiated by the Conservative government of Edward Heath. But when a new Labour government won power in 1974 under Harold Wilson, a split emerged within the government, at which point the vote was called. Most senior members of the government and the opposition were in favour, while those opposed came mainly from the left, the far right and the Scottish and Welsh nationalist movements. On referendum day in June, 64% turned out and more than 67% voted Yes (see Broad and Geiger, 1996). This should perhaps have put the matter to rest, but the debate over Britain's membership of the EU has never entirely gone away. Mainly to address a split within his party over EU membership, Prime Minister David Cameron promised a new referendum should his party win an outright majority at the 2015 general election.

In 1982 there was another vote on whether or not to stay in the EEC, this time in a region of a member state, resulting in the first and so far only defection from the EEC/EU. The vote was held in Greenland, a sparsely populated autonomous region of Denmark whose 32,000 residents had voted heavily against Danish membership of the EEC in 1972. Following home rule in 1979 and the election in 1981 of an anti-European government, a decision was taken to hold a referendum, the major issue being protection of fishing rights. The 1982 vote resulted in 54% opting to leave the Community, which Greenland eventually did three years later. In 2008, Greenland voted for self-rule in another referendum, opening the possibility of independence, but during the fallout from the 2007–10 global financial crisis, which hit neighbouring Iceland particularly hard, there was speculation that Greenland might apply to rejoin the EU.

The rising political pressure to put EU membership to a national vote resulted in national referendums in all 3 countries that joined in 1995 (Austria, Finland and Sweden), and in 9 of the 12 countries that joined in 2004–07 (the exceptions being Bulgaria, Cyprus and Romania). For the 1995 applicants, the results ranged from 52% to 67% in favour, while for the 2004–07 applicants, they were in the range of 54% in favour (Malta) to 92% in favour (Slovakia), with turnout rates ranging between 46% in Hungary and 91% in Malta.

In connection with only one other membership issue – adoption of the euro – have national referendums been held, and here the significance has been

Table **16.1** **National referendums on EEC/EU issues**

Year	Country	Issue	Outcome
1972	France	Enlarging the EEC	Yes
	Ireland	Join EEC	Yes
	Norway	Join EEC	No
	Denmark	Join EEC	Yes
1975	UK	Continued membership of EEC	Yes
1982	Greenland	Continued membership of EEC	No
1986	Denmark	Single European Act	Yes
1987	Ireland	Single European Act	Yes
1989	Italy	Mandate for Spinelli treaty	Yes
1992	Denmark I	Maastricht treaty	No
	Ireland	Maastricht treaty	Yes
	France	Maastricht treaty	Yes
	Switzerland	Join European Economic Area	No
1993	Denmark II	Maastricht treaty	Yes
1994	Austria	Join EU	Yes
	Finland	Join EU	Yes
	Sweden	Join EU	Yes
	Norway	Join EU	No
1998	Ireland	Treaty of Amsterdam	Yes
	Denmark	Treaty of Amsterdam	Yes
2000	Denmark	Adopt euro	No
2001	Ireland I	Treaty of Nice	No
	Switzerland	Negotiate EU membership	No
2002	Ireland II	Treaty of Nice	Yes
2003	Malta	Join EU	Yes
	Slovenia	Join EU	Yes
	Hungary	Join EU	Yes
	Lithuania	Join EU	Yes
	Slovakia	Join EU	Yes
	Poland	Join EU	Yes
	Czech Republic	Join EU	Yes
	Estonia	Join EU	Yes
	Latvia	Join EU	Yes
	Sweden	Adopt euro	No
2005	Spain	Constitutional treaty	Yes
	France	Constitutional treaty	No
	Netherlands	Constitutional treaty	No
	Switzerland	Join Schengen Agreement	Yes
	Luxembourg	Constitutional treaty	Yes
2008	Ireland I	Treaty of Lisbon	No
2009	Switzerland	Freedom of worker movement to Bulgaria and Romania	Yes
	Ireland II	Treaty of Lisbon	Yes
2012	Croatia	Join EU	Yes

less with those countries that have held votes than with the large number that have not. Only in two countries – Denmark and Sweden – were referendums held, and in both cases the result was negative (53% opposed in Denmark and

58% opposed in Sweden). Discussions were held in several other member states about the political desirability of a vote, but pro-euro governments often feared the outcome. The Blair administration was in favour of Britain joining the euro and regularly spoke of the possibilities of a referendum, but opinion polls found British opposition running high and the vote was indefinitely delayed. In the Netherlands there was also hostility to the euro, but no referendum; this led to speculation that at least one reason why Dutch voters rejected the European constitution in 2005 was because they had been denied a vote on the euro (Aarts and van der Kolk, 2006).

Adoption of a new treaty

As with membership of the EEC, it was long assumed by most leaders of the member states that no public votes were needed on the adoption of new treaties, ostensibly because they were amendments only to the terms of membership of an international organization. But again, as the impact and reach of the EU expanded, the stakes were raised and public opinion on the treaties took on a new significance.

The first treaty vote was taken in February 1986 in Denmark on the Single European Act. Since the terms of the treaty were relatively uncontroversial, it was accepted by more than 65% of voters, and nearly 70% of voters in a referendum in Ireland in 1987. But then came the Maastricht treaty, containing more controversial proposals about foreign and monetary policy, and this time three member states put the treaty to a vote and it fell to Denmark in June 1992 to become the first EEC/EU member state ever to reject a treaty in a referendum. Ireland and France followed with votes in favour, clearing the way for Denmark to achieve another first: negotiating opt-outs from a treaty and putting it to a second national vote; this it did in May 1993 when a sizeable majority voted Yes.

The Treaty of Amsterdam was again relatively uncontroversial and was put to a national referendum only in Ireland and Denmark, passing by 62% and 55%. Much the same relative peace was expected with the Treaty of Nice, but the Irish Supreme Court had ruled in 1987 that changes to the terms of EU membership required an amendment to the Irish constitution, and all such amendments required a referendum. Expecting no problems, the Irish government did little to promote Nice, and was shocked when voters rejected it in a June 2001 referendum (with just 34% turnout). A second attempt was made in October 2002 after a more organized government information campaign, and this time Nice was approved by a large majority.

Undoubtedly the most important public referendums on a treaty were those held in 2005 on the proposed European constitutional treaty. The stakes had been raised, because, for the first time, ratification by all member states was required in order for the treaty to enter into force. Plans were made in 10 of the 25 member states to hold such referendums, and this time there were much stronger doubts that it would pass every test, the popular assumption being that the spoiler would be Britain, where hostility was clear and substantial. But it was to be two of the Community's founding members – France and the Netherlands – which were to reject the constitution in votes held within days of each other in May and June. With no renegotiation or opt-outs available, the effect of the votes was to stop a treaty dead in its tracks for the first time. Ireland captured the headlines again in 2009 when voters rejected the Treaty of Lisbon. Once again the Irish government was obliged to negotiate written assurances, and in an October 2009 revote, the treaty was approved.

The rules on referendums vary from one state to another, with two key distinctions. The first of these is between referendums that are mandatory (usually required under the terms of a national constitution) and those that are facultative, that is, they can be initiated by a political leader or public demand. In some EU member states, such as Denmark and Ireland, changes to the national constitution require a referendum, but Ireland is the only member state where a new EU treaty requires a constitutional amendment and therefore a referendum. (Non-member Switzerland has a requirement that a referendum must be held on joining an international organization if at least 50,000 people or eight cantons support a petition in favour.) There has been no acknowledgement in Denmark that new treaties need changes to the constitution, so its referendums have been facultative rather than mandatory.

The second distinction is between referendums that are binding (mandatory referendums are almost always binding) and those that are advisory or consultative, and so, by definition, non-binding. The Netherlands offers a curious example of the distinction: the law does not allow for referendums, but between 2002 and 2005 there was a Temporary Referendum Law on the statute books, allowing for non-binding referendums on laws passed by the House of Representatives. The law had lapsed by the time the May 2005 referendum was held on the EU constitutional treaty, the way for which was paved by another temporary law, allowing for the first national referendum (on any topic) in Dutch history (see Nijeboer, 2005).

Illustration 16.2 The 2005 French referendum

French newspaper headlines on 30 May 2005 declare the result of the referendum in which voters rejected the proposed EU constitutional treaty.

As a means of allowing citizens input into decision-making, referendums have their advantages and disadvantages. The main advantage is that they are a form of direct democracy that engages the electorate directly with key political issues. They can also encourage intensive debate about those issues that can help offset some of the problems of voter apathy that have plagued elections. The prospect of a British referendum, for example, was enough to generate a new debate in the UK on the pros and cons of EU membership in 2013–14. Finally, they can be a way of bypassing an impasse in government; if government itself is undecided over what action to take, it can defer the issue to the electorate.

On the other side of the ledger, however, referendums have many disadvantages:

- The fact that so many are either facultative and/or non-binding raises the question of why they should be held in the first place.
- Even though voters are usually asked to vote Yes or No on a contained proposition, the issues and debates behind the proposition are often too complex to be reduced to a single statement. The wording of the proposition can raise problems, potentially defining the issue too narrowly or not defining it narrowly enough and offering governments a means of wriggling out of an unfavourable result. There was a fuss in Britain in 2013, for example, over the wording of the proposed new referendum on membership of the EU. It would have asked 'Do you think the UK should be a member of the European Union?', but was criticized because some potential voters were unaware that Britain was already a member.
- Referendums have been criticized as a means of bypassing representative democracy, potentially handing decision-making to the most motivated and best-informed groups in a society, and opening the way for voters to be influenced by propaganda and expensive advertising campaigns.
- Referendums can be used to defer public debate on an issue, with political leaders claiming that knotty questions should be delayed until the holding of a referendum that may never actually happen.

One problem with referendums that has been particularly obvious in the case of the EU has been the tendency of some member states to repeat their votes until the voters 'get it right'. This happened with the double vote in Denmark on Maastricht, and again with the double votes in Ireland on Nice and Lisbon. To be sure, the initial negative votes left governments with no option but to think again about the content of the treaties, and the terms for Denmark and Ireland were amended slightly in order to placate opponents. But why arrange for voters who had initially said No to vote again following the negotiation of opt-outs and the preparation of better planned government information programmes? And what would have happened if any of the second votes had also been negative? Would the treaties affected have died, or would the other member states have gone ahead without the state that voted No?

There are questions, too, about the importance and political significance of Europe's referendums. As with EP elections, there is evidence to suggest that the results are often driven less by attitudes towards the EU and more by prevailing levels of support for governing and opposition parties at home. In the case of the Maastricht treaty votes, for example, support was high in France but voters used the referendum to punish the unpopular Mitterrand government, while in Denmark the Yes vote was in large part a function of the popularity of the country's new social democratic government (Franklin et al., 1994). Much also depends on what kind of job political parties and interest groups do in mobilizing supporters for their positions. In votes on new treaties, a critical problem has been the complexity of the treaties and the failure of many voters to read the treaties or understand the issues involved. This makes them more vulnerable to manipulation, and also plays into the hands of usually better organized and more motivated opponents. But there is also evidence to suggest that voter opinions are better developed in states that have had referendums, because more effort is usually made to debate and explain the issues than is the case with EP elections (Christin and Hug, 2002).

In spite of the many concerns about referendums, they have become increasingly common in the EU. Several member states have had a long history of local referendums that have now apparently expanded into new support for national votes, several states have broken the habits of centuries by holding their first national referendums, and public support for votes on new EU treaties has grown. As resistance to European integration has expanded, so the arguments that legislative votes on new treaties are enough has come to ring increasingly hollow. The challenge now, though, is to develop a more methodical and consistent approach to organizing referendums and deciding how to respond to the results.

Summary

- Direct elections to the European Parliament have been held every five years since 1979, using proportional representation (PR).

- Among the consequences of PR is the return of numerous political parties to power, resulting in a tradition of coalition governments in most EU states.

- Since the introduction of direct elections to the EP in 1979, turnout has fallen from a high of 62 per cent to a low of just under 43 per cent in 2014. Among the explanations for this trend is the difference between first-order and second-order elections.

- While turnout at EP elections has fallen, support for unconventional forms of political participation has grown.

- Voters in some states have been offered national referendums, although there is no consistency on when and where they will be held. In terms of referendums, Europe has become the single most voted-on issue in the world.

- The subject of most referendums has been membership of the EEC/EU or the euro, or approval of a new treaty.

- Denmark and Ireland have had the most referendums on European issues, and only seven EU member states (Belgium, Bulgaria, Cyprus, Germany, Greece, Portugal and Romania) have had none.

- A distinction must be made between referendums that are mandatory or facultative (initiated by public or political demand), and between those that are binding and non-binding.

- The outcome of EP elections and national referendums is often influenced by the popularity of governing and opposition parties in different member states.

Key terms and concepts

Citizen initiative

Coalition government

First-order and second-order elections

Proportional representation

Referendum

Further reading

Déloye, Yves, and Michael Bruter (eds) (2007) *Encyclopaedia of European Elections* (Basingstoke: Palgrave Macmillan). Useful source of reference on matters relating to European elections.

Lodge, Juliet (ed.) (2001, 2005) *The 1999 Elections to the European Parliament*, *The 2004 Elections to the European Parliament* (Basingstoke: Palgrave Macmillan). Valuable surveys of two recent EP elections.

Mendez, Fernando, Mario Mendez and Vasiliki Triga (2014) *Referendums and the European Union: A Comparative Inquiry* (Cambridge: Cambridge University Press). Hobolt, Sara Binzer (2009) *Europe in Question: Referendums on European Integration* (Oxford University Press). Two contributions to the growing academic literature on referendums on EU issues.

17 Public Opinion

In an ideal democratic world, the values, views and concerns of citizens would be routinely on the minds of elected leaders, who are, after all, the representatives of those citizens. But there are at least two flaws with this proposition. First, it is difficult always to know what citizens want, either because they may not know themselves or because of the pitfalls in measuring public opinion. Second, opinion is divided on almost every public issue, leaving elected officials to decide whether to side with the majority, be concerned only with those who elected them, or do what they think is best.

These are problems at the national and local level within the member states, but they are magnified at the EU level by the mixed feelings of most Europeans about the exercise of integration, coupled with their often low levels of knowledge about the structure and work of the EU. Attitudes can be summed up as follows: mainly supportive, sometimes hostile, occasionally indifferent and often badly informed. Most Europeans do not know what to make of the EU, they neither understand how it works nor fully understand its implications, and their opinions about European integration could at best be described as soft; neither strongly opposing nor strongly supporting what is being done in their name.

This chapter looks at public opinion in the EU as it relates to integration and an understanding of what 'Europe' represents. It focuses on euroscepticism (hostility to integration or the direction being taken by the European project), the knowledge deficit (the gap between the responsibilities of the EU and what Europeans know and understand about how it works) and Europeanism (the values that Europeans have in common, and that often exist independently of the experience of regional integration).

- How is the balance of public opinion on European integration best explained?
- What are the political implications of euroscepticism?
- Given the knowledge deficit, how far can we be sure about public opinion on European integration?
- Why do so few Europeans understand the structure and effects of the EU, and what can be done about this?
- Is Europeanism a useful analytical concept?

Attitudes towards integration

Overall, European public opinion has long been equivocal about the EU and the process of integration, although opinions have hardened in the wake of the euro zone crisis. At one end of the spectrum, there are those Europeans who embrace it with enthusiasm, and are disappointed that it has not gone further and moved more quickly towards the achievement of a federal United States of Europe. In the middle are those who favour integration but are uncomfortable with many aspects of the EU itself, and support reform of its institutions and policies. At the other end of the spectrum, there are those who think that integration has gone too far and that withdrawal of their country from the EU would be no bad thing. We have a good idea of the trends because of the results of the Commission-sponsored Eurobarometer polling service, which has been carrying out biannual surveys of opinion in the member states since 1974.

The most marked trend of recent years is that enthusiasm for the EU has tailed off in the wake of the euro zone crisis. In 2007, those who had a positive image of the EU outnumbered those with a negative image by 52:15, but by 2013 the negatives and the positives were almost equal at 30:29 (see Figure 17.1). At the same time, though, in 20 out of the 28 member states in 2013, most people were neutral, and the proportion of neutral opinions has been gaining ground as Europeans consider the contrasting views of those who believe that the EU's problems can be solved and those who do not. In 11 countries, the number with negative opinions was greater than those with positive opinions in 2013, while positives outweighed negatives in 17 other countries (Luxembourg being the

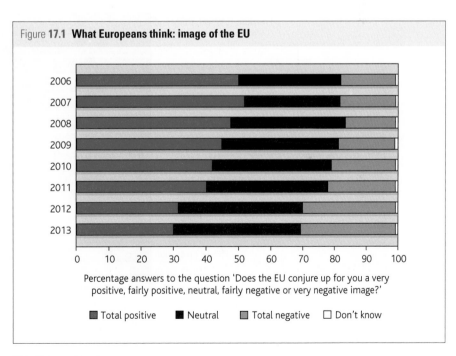

Figure **17.1** **What Europeans think: image of the EU**

Percentage answers to the question 'Does the EU conjure up for you a very positive, fairly positive, neutral, fairly negative or very negative image?'

■ Total positive   ■ Neutral   ▨ Total negative   ☐ Don't know

Eurobarometer: The EU's public opinion polling service, which carries out two major surveys every year, along with 'flash' surveys on more discrete issues.

Note: Spring cycles only.

Source: Eurobarometer 80, Autumn 2013.

exception with a 40:40 positive/negative ratio). The highest positive (49%) was in Bulgaria, the lowest positive (16%) was in Greece, while the highest negative (54%) was in Cyprus and Greece and the lowest negative (10%) was in Poland, Lithuania and Estonia.

Fligstein (2008) argues that attitudes towards integration are driven primarily by association and identity. Hence, business owners, managers, professionals, white-collar workers, the educated and the young have benefited most from integration, have had more to do with their counterparts in other societies, and so think of themselves more as Europeans. On the other hand, older, poorer, less educated and blue-collar Europeans have benefited less, fear the effects of integration on national sovereignty, worry that its pro-business orientation will overwhelm national welfare states, and retain a stronger sense of national identity. Meanwhile, a third group of mainly middle-class Europeans see the EU in mostly positive terms but could go either way.

When asked what the EU means to them personally, most respondents unsurprisingly opt for the practical changes brought by the single market and the availability of the euro (see Figure 17.2). About 20–25% of respondents identify the more nebulous role of integration in promoting peace and democracy, while 24–27% associate the EU with more bureaucracy and wasted money. The latter is a problem with which the EC/EU has long had to wrestle, the media interest in cases of fraud, excessive agricultural spending and expense claims by European officials

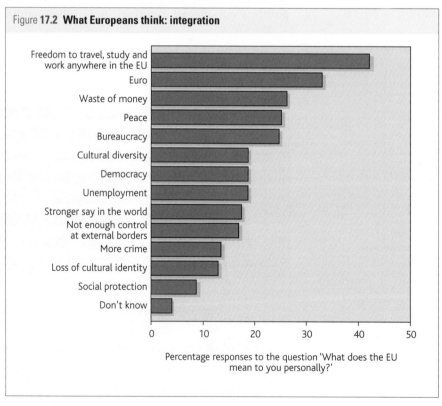

Figure **17.2 What Europeans think: integration**

Percentage responses to the question 'What does the EU mean to you personally?'

Source: Eurobarometer 80, Autumn 2013.

(see Chapter 18)

contrasting with the reality that the EU budget is actually quite small (see Chapter 18). Most Europeans (62%) agree that the EU has made it easier to do business in Europe and that the EU helps tackle global threats and challenges (55%), but most also blame the EU for austerity in Europe (63%) and believe that the EU needs to send a clearer message about itself (81%) (Eurobarometer 80, Autumn 2013).

There has been less study of the reasons why Europeans support the EU than why they do not, presumably because support is taken as the benchmark for understanding the process of integration; Europe has, after all, been working to cooperate rather than disintegrate. We do not even have a label to describe supporters of integration; they may be eurobelievers, euroenthusiasts, federalists, or europhiles. By contrast, hostility to integration has attracted much new attention in recent years on the back of negative votes in national referendums and controversy over the writing of new treaties, such that the phenomenon of euroscepticism has been the subject of growing study and public debate.

When integration was a relatively quiet and modest exercise, as it was until the early 1980s, euroscepticism was so marginal as to be barely measurable, certainly in the public arena. Efforts to complete the single market in the 1980s and 90s were met with generally positive responses, or at least an absence of significant opposition. But as the speed and breadth of integration picked up during the debates over Maastricht, and the process began to reach into more parts of European life, so euroscepticism entered its era of growth. The year 1992 was a watershed, with the Danish vote against Maastricht in June and the crisis in the Exchange Rate Mechanism in September, the first revealing that the public could be encouraged to vote against a European initiative, and the second being a reminder of how far European economies had become invested in the process of integration. Euroscepticism began to play a greater role in domestic politics – with the rise of political parties opposed to European integration, and splits within mainstream parties between Europeans and anti-Europeans – and in

Concept

Euroscepticism

Opposition to the process of European integration, or doubts about the direction in which it is moving, based mainly on concerns about the loss of state sovereignty and the undemocratic or elitist manner in which decisions on integration have been taken. There are many shades of eurosceptic opinion: some eurosceptics argue that integration should go no further, others that the process should either be reformed or reversed, and some that their home state should leave the EU altogether.

Illustration **17.1**
Euroscepticism
Eurosceptic MEPs call on the EU to respect the outcome of the negative Irish vote on the Lisbon treaty in June 2008.

European politics, where it influenced thinking on treaty reforms, enlargement and new policy initiatives.

The arguments put forward by eurosceptics vary by member state, and issue, ideology and time, but they include the following:

- The EU is on its way to becoming a federalized European superstate at the expense of the self-determination of its member states.
- The EU institutions are undemocratic, elitist, bureaucratic, inefficient and insufficiently accountable to the citizens of the member states.
- The EU is promoting policies that are unpopular with the political left (it puts too much emphasis on free markets) and the political right (it puts too much power in the hands of workers).
- Too many decisions are taken by national leaders without reference to their citizens, who are too often denied national referendums on such crucial developments as treaty revisions.
- Attempts to build common policies do not take enough account of national differences; this is true of the Common Foreign and Security Policy, for example, which is seen to threaten the neutrality of member states such as Ireland and Finland.
- The expansion of the European single market has meant more immigration within the EU, and while much of it has long gone unnoticed and unremarked, there has been growing resistance to immigrants of different races and religions, and charges of the abuse of welfare systems.

Euroscepticism first came to prominence in Britain in the 1980s (see below), but it has since spread more widely. As this has happened, so it has become clear that it is far from monolithic, and is less a well-defined ideology than a set of related positions based on opposition to European integration. For Taggart and Szczerbiak (2001), for example, there is a difference between its soft and hard forms: the former is based on qualified opposition to the direction being taken by the EU and a further expansion of its powers, while the latter (which has attracted more attention) implies rejection of the project of European political and economic integration. Kopecký and Mudde (2002) make even finer distinctions, their study of euroscepticism in east central Europe helping them identify four shades of opinion that distinguish between diffuse opposition to the core principle of European integration and specific opposition to the way the EU is evolving (see Figure 17.3).

The long-term significance of euroscepticism is hard to determine. It has certainly grown in breadth and depth since the 1990s, and has been a factor in the calculations of governments as they consider new steps in the process of integration. It has been most politically significant in the case of political parties founded mainly on opposition to their country's membership of the EU, such as the People's Movement in Denmark, the Party for Freedom in the Netherlands, and the UK Independence Party in Britain. For all these parties, however, the freer immigration allowed by the EU is at least as important as any wider concerns about the effects of integration. Criticism of the EU has also been on the agenda of more broad-based parties that resist integration in its current form, such as the Democratic Socialists and the Free Democrats in Germany, the Greens in Portugal and the Netherlands, the British Conservative Party, and several communist parties.

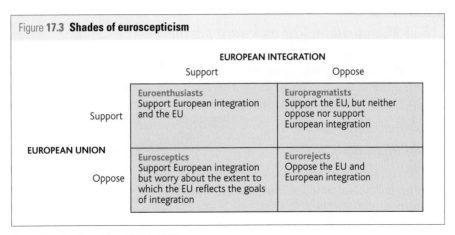

Figure **17.3** **Shades of euroscepticism**

Source: Based on Kopecký and Mudde, 2002.

It is also important to note that public doubts are directed not just at the EU but also at politics and government more generally. Eurobarometer polls have shown that there has been less trust in national government than in the EU, and levels of trust and faith in both have fallen in tandem (see Figure 17.4). And the crisis of confidence in government is not unique to Europe; while polls in 2013 indicated that 49% of Europeans felt that the EU was headed in the wrong direction, and 56% felt that their country was headed in the wrong direction, 58% of Americans felt their country was headed in the wrong direction (Eurobarometer 79, Spring 2013; Miller, 2013). It has been easy and tempting for Europeans to point the finger of blame for their political and economic problems at the EU, but most appear more ready to look closer to home and blame their own governments.

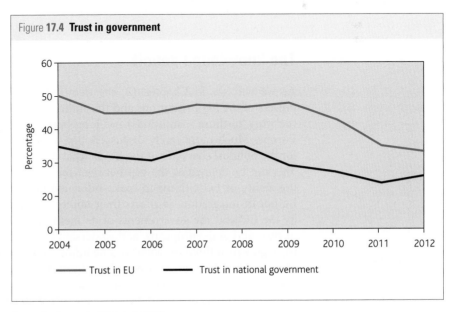

Figure **17.4** **Trust in government**

Source: Eurobarometer 78, Autumn 2012.

Focus on... *Britain: The awkward partner?*

Britain has developed a reputation for being the most eurosceptic of all EU member states, but it has also become a prime example of the adage 'give a dog a bad name and hang him'. In other words, it has been difficult for Britain to shake off its reputation, even if it has not always been entirely deserved.

The story begins even before the creation of the EEC, when Britain opted not to join. Then it changed its mind, but was turned down twice for membership by Charles de Gaulle. Then, in 1975, two years after joining, it became the first and so far only member state to hold a referendum on continued membership. The term *eurosceptism* first began to appear in the British media in the mid-1980s (Harmsen and Spiering, 2005), when Britain resisted numerous EU initiatives ranging from the Schengen Agreement to adoption of the euro, and earned itself the label 'awkward partner' (George, 1990). Then came the 2013 decision of the Cameron government to promise a national referendum on UK membership of the EU, although he was motivated at least as much by an effort to deal with disagreements in his party as to responding to wide public demand for a vote.

The uniqueness of British attitudes is exemplified by a 2013 Eurobarometer poll, which asked people throughout the EU whether they thought their country could better face the future outside the EU. Britain was the only EU member state where those who agreed outnumbered those who disagreed (by 53 to 36%). The EU average was almost exactly the opposite (33% agree, 56% disagree), and even the bruised and battered Greeks felt the future was better in than out, by a factor of 26% to 58% (Eurobarometer 79, Spring 2013). And yet polls taken in the UK by the Ipsos MORI polling service since the late 1970s have found opinion on British membership to be highly changeable: in 1979, 60% were in favour of leaving compared to 32% who wanted to stay in, but by 1989 the proportions had almost exactly reversed, and in the nearly 30 polls taken by Ipsos MORI (www.ipsos-mori.com) between 1990 and 2014, 24 found more people in favour of remaining a member than leaving.

The discussion about euroscepticism in Britain ignores the many occasions when the UK has not just cooperated but provided leadership on European issues, particularly in the realms of foreign, trade and defence policy. It also tends to overlook the low levels of knowledge in Britain about the EU; polls routinely find that most Britons admit to their failure to understand how it works, raising the question of how to interpret British euroscepticism when so few Britons appear able to make informed judgements about the EU (see McCormick, 2014).

The knowledge deficit

As we will see in Chapter 18, the democratic deficit (the gap between the powers of the EU institutions and the ability of EU citizens directly to influence the work of those institutions) has long been at the heart of the debate about Europe. Much more rarely discussed, but with equally important implications for the political character of the EU, is what we might call the knowledge deficit. This can be defined as the gap between the powers of the EU institutions and the ability of EU citizens to make informed judgements about the exercise of European integration. It affects their ability to understand the decisions taken by the EU and the governments of its member states, sort through the claims of pro- and anti-Europeans, and understand how to make use of the channels through which those decisions can be influenced. This is by no means a problem unique to the EU, and observers have been bemoaning the effects of the uninformed populace since the time of the ancient Greeks. But the unique structure of the EU ensures that the deficit has effects that go far beyond those found in its individual member states.

Knowledge deficit: The gap between the way the EU works and the familiarity of ordinary Europeans with its structure and processes.

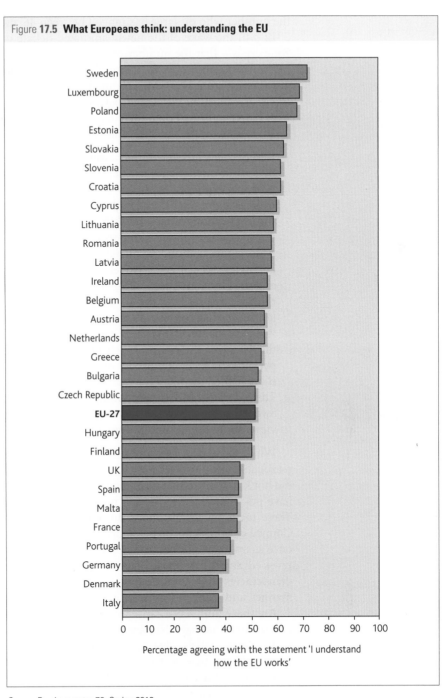

Figure **17.5 What Europeans think: understanding the EU**

Percentage agreeing with the statement 'I understand how the EU works'

Source: Eurobarometer 79, Spring 2013.

The size and reach of the deficit is clearly reflected in the results of recent Eurobarometer surveys. Since the early 2000s, Eurobarometer has been asking Europeans whether or not they agree with the statement 'I understand how the EU works'. The number who agree has ranged between 40 and 46 per cent, while the number who disagree has ranged between 46 and 52 per cent. It was only in 2012 – in the wake of the newly animated debate over the EU during the euro zone crisis – that the number of people who thought they understood how the EU worked outnumbered the number who did not (Eurobarometer 79, Spring 2013) (see Figure 17.5). Men claimed to be better informed than women, higher levels of education correlated with better knowledge, and younger Europeans were better informed than their seniors.

By member state, the 2013 poll had several interesting results:

- Respondents in some of the newer member states considered themselves better informed than those of older member states, a difference that is probably explained by the novelty of membership, which has meant fresher debates about the EU and higher levels of attention paid in national media to the implications of membership. However, the euro zone crisis has ensured revived debates about membership right across the EU.
- Among the six founding members, only the citizens of the three Benelux countries still claimed relatively high levels of knowledge, while the French and the Germans – long at the heart of integration, and German interest renewed as a result of the debate about saving the euro – were surprisingly low on the list, below even eurosceptic Britain.
- It is perhaps surprising that Greece, Portugal and Italy were not higher up the list, given their central roles in the fallout from the euro zone crisis. Or perhaps the sheer complexity of the crisis left many people in these countries more baffled than before.
- The considerable disparity among Scandinavian states is interesting, from Sweden at the top to Denmark near the bottom, given the overlap in their views about the EU and the euro.

While these data measure how much people *think* they know (and we can reasonably ask ourselves how they were able to decide how much they knew or did not know, given that most did not know much), other more specific questions have put knowledge to the test by measuring how much people *actually* know. These focus on details about the European Parliament, the presidency of the Council of Ministers, the EU budget and other issues (see Figure 17.6). The results once again paint a rather dismal picture, although they fit with what studies have revealed about low levels of political knowledge among the citizens of liberal democracies in general, few of whom keep up with politics in any sustained manner, and many of whom are actively repulsed by politics and politicians.

Are these numbers a cause for concern? There is a school of thought in political science that says No, arguing that voters can use 'information shortcuts' such as party labels, elite endorsements, or cues from trusted sources to help them make political decisions and thus give themselves the capacity for reasoned choice (see Sniderman et al., 1991; Page and Shapiro, 1992; Popkin, 1994). But while such shortcuts may be helpful at the national level, at the European level the dynamic is somewhat different.

First, the absence of an informed citizenry encourages and perpetuates the kind of elitism that has long been the chief concern of critics of the EU. If Europeans fail to understand and engage in the work of the EU, and depend on cues from political leaders and the media, then decision-making will inevitably be left in the hands of national leaders, bureaucrats, big business and interest groups.

Elitism: The view that decision-making is focused in the hands of elites, in the case of the EU meaning elected officials, bureaucrats, big business and interest groups.

Figure **17.6** **What Europeans think: misconceptions about the EU**

In polls taken between 2005 and 2013 ...

62%	of respondents knew that the EU had 28 member states (2013)
54%	knew that MEPs were directly elected (2013)
50%	knew that a different member state held the presidency of the Council of Ministers every six months (2008)
36%	knew that the EU had an official anthem (2005)
34%	had never heard of the Council of Ministers (2010)
28%	considered themselves 'very well' or 'fairly well' informed about European political affairs (2007)
27%	thought that agricultural spending was the biggest item on the EU budget (regional spending overtook it several years before) (2007)
27%	thought that the biggest item on the EU budget was administrative costs (they actually accounted for just 5%) (2007)
23%	was the average estimate among Britons of the size of the UK contribution to the EU budget as a percentage of gross national income (true figure was 0.2% (2009)
16%	had a strong interest in politics (2013)

Sources: Eurobarometer 63, September 2005, 78–9; Eurobarometer 66, September 2007, 152–60; Eurobarometer 67, November 2007, 125, 131; Eurobarometer 69, November 2008, 71; Flash Eurobarometer, 2009; Eurobarometer 73, Spring 2010; Eurobarometer 80, Autumn 2013.

When the EEC was more obviously an international organization, negotiations on the terms of integration took place among national government representatives in smoke-filled rooms. As the reach of integration expanded in the 1980s and 90s, so more ordinary Europeans demanded the right to be heard. Yet, there was still a high degree of political manipulation at work, exemplified in the manner in which several governments refused to put the constitutional treaty to a national referendum, and then sidestepped public opinion by repackaging most of the failed constitution as the Treaty of Lisbon.

Second, the effects of the knowledge deficit are not contained within national borders, but several times have had effects across the entire EU. The May 2005 vote in France on the constitutional treaty was a case in point. At the time of the referendum, 74% of French citizens had either heard of the treaty but knew 'very little' about its contents, or had not heard of it at all (Eurobarometer 63, 2005, p. 138). And yet 69% of voters turned out, of whom just under 55% rejected the treaty, resulting not just in its failure in France but throughout the EU. There has been speculation that the result of the vote was not only a reflection of dissatisfaction with the treaty and the direction being taken by European integration, but also hostility to the incumbent Chirac administration and the widening gap between political leaders and citizens in France (Ivaldi, 2006).

Third, ignorance encourages detachment, in the sense that Europeans are less likely to understand what is at stake in EU decision-making, less likely to understand what options they have available to make their views heard, and less likely to make use of elections, referendums or public debates in order to influence politics at the level of the EU. The European Parliament is the institution that suffers most from this dilemma; it is the only directly elected EU institution, and yet more than half of EU citizens apparently do not realize that it is directly elected, and turnout at EP elections (as we saw in Chapter 16) has fallen steadily.

Fourth, their failure to arm themselves with independent information makes Europeans more susceptible to the appeals of pro- and anti-Europeans, who will often use scare tactics, misinformation, or a selective use of facts to state their case and characterize the opportunities offered or the threats posed by integration. This problem has worsened as more people have turned away from mainstream sources of political news to internet sites that cater to their more particular interests and reinforce their biases and predispositions. These trends undermine the quality of the debate about the EU, and there is also a danger that this problem will translate into the success of candidates for office with the same limited views as voters. A knowledgeable and demanding electorate is more likely to elect knowledgeable candidates because they will be better placed to assess the competence of those running for office.

Ireland presents an example of the dilemma. In June 2001, Irish voters stopped the Treaty of Nice in its tracks by voting against adoption (then changed their minds in a 2002 vote), and in June 2008 stopped the Treaty of Lisbon in its tracks with a negative vote (once again changing their minds in a 2009 vote). It is interesting that two-thirds of Irish residents felt at the time of the first Lisbon vote that membership of the EU had been good for their country, and yet only 40% felt that they understood how it worked. What, then, can we make of the referendum results? At least part of the problem was low voter turnout: just 35% in 2001, rising to 48% in 2002, 53% in 2008, and 58% in 2009. Analysis suggests that while some of those who voted No in 2008 were motivated by genuine and well-thought-out opposition, some were motivated either by confusion about the terms of Lisbon, fears about loss of sovereignty, and misplaced fears that Lisbon posed a threat to Ireland's neutrality or might mean the loss of its special low capital tax status.

Why is it that so few Europeans understand the EU, and what can be done to close the knowledge deficit? The core source of the problem is the simple challenge of getting to grips with the rules and procedures of the EU, which is not only a unique entity in organizational terms but regularly changes its own operational rules. It would help if there was a (preferably brief) constitution to which Europeans could refer for clarification of those rules, but instead they have been offered a series of treaties, each of which has amended those that came before, and most of which have contained rules that have even occasionally baffled the experts.

Europeanism

Studies of public opinion on European integration rarely venture much further than asking how people feel about the wisdom of the EU and the place of their member state within the EU. Less frequently discussed has been the broader and more fundamental question of how far Europeans agree (or disagree) on core political, economic and social values. In other words, behind the debate over Europe, how much evidence is there that the balance of European public opinion

Concept

Europeanism

The political, economic and social values that Europeans have in common, are most clearly supported and promoted by Europeans, and give distinctive qualities and personality to the European experience. The view that there might be such values has long been obscured by nationalism, war, conflict and divisions over the merits of integration. Among ordinary Europeans, however, there has been a growing confluence of opinion on universal ideas such as democracy and free markets, as well as more specific issues such as welfare, the definition of the family, attitudes towards work and leisure, capital punishment, the place of force in international relations, and the role of religion in public life.

is moving in the same direction? Is there a growing sense that Europeans think along similar lines and have similar values? While many may have their doubts about integration, most agree not just on the basic principles of democracy and capitalism, but much more besides. As a result, we can identify the phenomenon of **Europeanism**, or the political, economic and social values that Europeans have in common, which help strengthen the sense of identity discussed in Chapter 3. This may not always be entirely obvious at first, but when European public opinion is compared with that in other parts of the world, the distinctions start to become clearer.

The study of Europeanist ideas was given a boost by public opposition to the US-led invasion of Iraq, reflected in the massive anti-war demonstrations held on 15 February 2003 in almost every major European city, from London to Berlin, Paris, Rome, Dublin and Madrid (see Chapter 7). Inspired by what they saw, the philosophers Jürgen Habermas and Jacques Derrida wrote an article for *Frankfurter Allgemeine Zeitung*, in which they described 15 February as marking the birth of a 'European **public sphere**', and argued that the opportunity had been created for the construction of a 'core Europe' that might become a counterweight to the international influence of the US. Looking to explain what Europe represented, they listed several features of what they described as a common European 'political mentality', including secularization, trust in the 'organizational capacities of the state', welfarism, and a preference for multilateralism and a peaceful means to the resolution of international problems (Habermas and Derrida, 2003).

This was an interesting start to the discussion about what Europeans might have in common, but it was limited in its perspective, and overlooked the growing number of studies of the core political, economic and social ideas and goals on which Europeans agree – much of it, ironically, written by American observers of Europe. In his book *The European Dream*, Rifkin (2004, p. 3) contrasts the American emphasis on personal material advancement with the European concern with broader human welfare, noting how Europeans give preference to

> community relationships over individual autonomy, cultural diversity over assimilation … sustainable development over unlimited material growth, deep play over unrelenting toil, universal human rights and the rights of nature over property rights, and global cooperation over the unilateral exercise of power.

Sifting through the data and the analyses, it is possible to identify a substantial set of issues on which Europeans generally agree, and where European public opinion is distinctive, although it is important to warn here of the dangers inherent in generalization; there are few rules and many exceptions.

First, Europeans have an instinctive preference for collective ideas and the welfare state. They understand that social divisions will occur in spite of efforts to address them, but where Americans (for example) emphasize self-reliance and are uncomfortable with large public programmes, Europeans generally support the role of the state as an economic manager and a guarantor of societal welfare. They welcome and encourage individual endeavour, but they also believe that the community is responsible for working to ensure that economic and social handicaps are minimized. They are more ready to criticize capitalism as the

Public sphere: A communicative space within which the members of a community, such as a state, or the EU, can talk with one another about shared

source of many social ills, they believe that individual rights extend to education, healthcare and social security, and they believe that equality of results is more important than equality of opportunity (Prestowitz, 2003, pp. 236–7).

Along these lines, most Europeans, although they might not be familiar with the term, have an instinctive sympathy for communitarianism. This has been defined as a preference for collective ideas over individual independence (Selznick, 2002, p. 4), or a balance 'between community and autonomy, between the common good and liberty, between individual rights and social responsibilities' (Etzioni, 1995, p. x). British Prime Minister Tony Blair summed up communitarian ideas when he argued that in contrast to the 'crude individualism' of Britain in the 1980s, by the 1990s there was more of a focus on addressing problems collectively, and the view that 'It's up to me' was being replaced by 'It's up to us' (Blair, 1998). Most Europeans (unlike Americans) would argue that society can sometimes be a better judge of what is good for individuals rather than vice versa, and there may sometimes be a reason for the state limiting individual rights for the greater good of the community (anti-smoking laws being one example that comes to mind). Critics respond by arguing that this attitude courts the danger of encouraging authoritarianism.

Second, we saw in Chapter 3 that Europeans are changing their views about political identification. They agree that the state has an important role to play in ordering society, but as for what defines their identity, they are increasingly torn between nation, state and Europe, which in turn is encouraging them to rethink their views about patriotism. Although the modern state was born in Europe, it is now being remodelled there more actively than probably anywhere else in the world, squeezed as it is between a revival of identification with nations and the growing reach of Europe. When asked what they are, most Europeans will still call themselves French or Dutch or Latvian or Hungarian, but among those who are members of national minorities, national identity is increasingly important, and a small but growing minority think of themselves first and foremost as Europeans (see Figure 3.1).

Europeans, more than is true of many other parts of the world, except diverse societies such as India and China, have a tradition of multiculturalism. Complex patterns of immigration and invasion dating back centuries have exposed them to different cultures and people speaking different languages, and they have regularly adopted and integrated values from the new groups with which they have come into contact. This has happened so often that it is sometimes difficult to be sure what constitutes a feature of the home culture and what does not, raising challenging questions about the meaning of national identity. There is a limit to European tolerance, however, and it does not always extend to religion or race; the arrival in Europe of new ethnic, racial and religious groups in the postwar era has had the effect of heightening the racism and religious tensions that have long been part of the European experience. But it is important to remember that multiculturalism is not the same thing as multiracialism; when German Chancellor Angela Merkel declared in October 2010 that her country's efforts to create a multicultural society had 'utterly failed' (*The Guardian*, 2010), she was referring to the pressures arising from growing numbers of Muslim and non-European immigrants.

As associations with the state and the nation have been redefined, so more Europeans have turned to the idea that some values and ideas might be universal,

Communitarianism: The view that individual rights should be balanced with those of the community, and that community interests can sometimes outweigh those of individuals.

Multiculturalism: The recognition and promotion of multiple different cultures, without promoting the interests or values of a dominant culture. Contrasts with attempts at assimilation and cultural integration, or the 'melting pot' philosophy.

and that all Europeans, certainly, and possibly even all humans, may belong to a single moral community above and beyond state boundaries or national identities. In this sense, Europeans have championed cosmopolitanism, or the idea that local and global concerns cannot be divorced, and that rather than Europe or the world being separate from the community or state in which each of us lives, the importance of the universal trumps that of the local. The study of this idea is still in its early stages (see Rumford, 2007; Beck and Grande, 2007), much of the literature is heavily theoretical, and not everyone agrees with such trends (see Robertson and Krossa, 2012), but evidence of European cosmopolitanism can be found, for example, in European attitudes towards international affairs, which are generally more inclusive and less exceptionalist than those found in the US.

Third, if there is one quality that unites and distinguishes European attitudes and values more clearly than any other, it is secularism. Religion is growing almost everywhere in the world except Europe, where its role in political and social life has been declining: church attendance has fallen, public expressions of faith have become more unusual, agnosticism and atheism are more openly and widely admitted, the role of religion in political and public life has been marginalized, and Europeans are turning away from organized religion. This is particularly true of western, northern and non-Catholic Europe, where large numbers do not consider themselves affiliated with a religion (see Figure 17.7) and even larger numbers say that religion does not play an important role in their lives.

Finally, European views about interstate relations have undergone a metamorphosis since the end of the Second World War. Where the larger European

Cosmopolitanism: The view that all humans belong to a single community based on a shared morality, and they should rise above more narrow identities based on race, religion, nationality or state.

Secularism: The belief that government should exist independently from religion, and political or social organizations should not be based on religious beliefs.

Illustration **17.2 Secular Europe**

The historical role of Christianity in European public life is symbolized by St Peter's Basilica in Vatican City, Rome, but the growing hold of secularism means that tourists routinely outnumber worshippers in all Europe's great cathedrals.

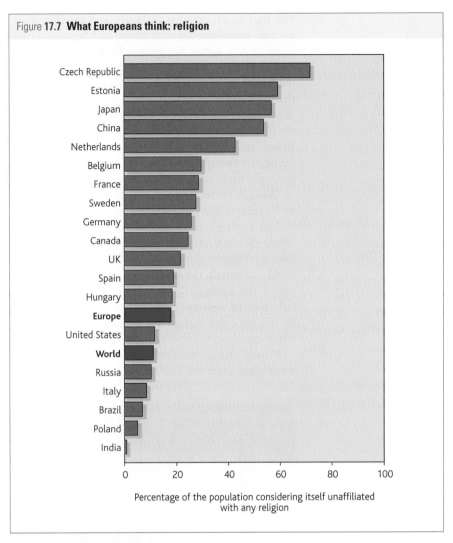

Figure **17.7 What Europeans think: religion**

Source: Pew Research Center, 2012.

states were once engaged in competition for power and influence that frequently dragged in smaller states and led to regional conflict and war, the more popular – if perhaps idealistic – view today is that disputes should be settled peacefully wherever possible, military power should only be used as a residual safeguard and its role should be limited to peacekeeping rather than peacemaking, and state interests should be set aside in the interests of international cooperation and the pursuit of problem-solving through multilateralism (see Chapter 24 for more discussion). European aversion to military force has gone so far that US Defence Secretary Robert Gates was moved in a February 2010 speech to talk of a crisis in NATO because of a failure by European governments to invest in weapons and equipment. The achievement of peace in Europe after 'ages of ruinous warfare' had been a great achievement, he argued, but the trend had now 'gone too far', and might lead to a perception of weakness among hostile states (Dempsey, 2010).

Summary

- Polls find that positive views about the EU have tailed off in the wake of the euro zone crisis. At the same time, opinion is mainly soft, meaning that most people neither strongly oppose nor strongly support what it is being done in their name.

- Particularly since the early 1990s, there has been a growth in levels of euroscepticism, but there are many different shades of opinion, varying by time and place.

- Polls reveal the existence of a European knowledge deficit: levels of knowledge about the EU among Europeans are generally low.

- Political ignorance is not unusual and is found to varying degrees throughout the democratic world.

- While domestic governments can work around the knowledge deficit, at the level of the EU this becomes a problem because it encourages elitism and a detachment from the process of integration, and makes the public more susceptible to the appeals of pro- and anti-Europeans.

- Closing the knowledge deficit is difficult because many Europeans are not interested in public affairs, and most identify more closely with their home states and take a closer interest in domestic politics.

- The debate about Europe has overlooked the broader question of how far Europeans agree (or disagree) on core political, economic and social values.

- Most Europeans agree not just on universal ideas such as democracy and free markets, but also subscribe to concepts such as communitarianism, multiculturalism, cosmopolitanism and secularism, and agree on a wide range of specific issues such as the definition of the family, attitudes towards work and leisure, capital punishment and the role of military force.

Key terms and concepts

Communitarianism

Cosmopolitanism

Elitism

Eurobarometer

Europeanism

Euroscepticism

Knowledge deficit

Multiculturalism

Public sphere

Secularism

Further reading

Fossum, John Erik, and Philip Schlesinger (eds) (2007) *The European Union and the Public Sphere: A Communicative Space in the Making?* (Abingdon: Routledge). Edited collection of studies of the prospects for a European public sphere.

McCormick, John (2010) *Europeanism* (Oxford: Oxford University Press). The last section of this chapter is drawn from arguments made in this book, where more detail can be found on the supporting data and analysis.

Taggart, Paul, and Aleks Szczerbiak (eds) (2008) *Opposing Europe? The Comparative Party Politics of Euroscepticism*, vols 1 and 2 (Oxford: Oxford University Press). Most thorough study yet of euroscepticism.

3 POLICIES

Part 3 focuses on public policy at the EU level: how it is made and the effects it has had. Chapter 18 explains the process by which policy is made and implemented, and reviews the dynamics of policy at the EU level. Chapters 19–25 look in turn at the major areas of policy in which the EU institutions are active and on which the process of integration has had the most telling effect. The most important of these has been economic policy, which has been felt most keenly in the building of the single market and the development of competition policy. Chapter 20 looks at the ups and downs in the story of the euro, and at the key role played by the idea of a single currency in completing the European single market.

Chapters 21–23 look at policy activities in the fields of agriculture and the environment, working and living conditions, workers' rights, education, and justice and home affairs (a collective term for matters related to asylum, immigration, police and judicial cooperation, and terrorism). Chapters 24–25 assess the EU as a global actor, first reviewing the nature of foreign, security, and trade policy, and then looking at how EU relations with particular parts of the world (the US, the neighbourhood, China, and the developing world) have evolved.

18 Public Policy in the EU

Preview

So far in this book we have looked at the history, principles and political character, institutions and processes of the EU, and how it relates to those who live under its jurisdiction. In Part 3 we examine what the EU has meant in terms of the policies it has pursued. We will see where the EU has been most active, what influences bear on the policy process and key policy-makers, and what practical difference integration has made to the lives of Europeans and the place of Europe in the world.

Public policy can be defined as whatever governments do (or avoid doing) to address the needs and problems of society. It takes the form of public statements, government programmes, laws and actions, as well as inertia and avoidance. If it was limited to the formal powers of government and its published objectives, it might be relatively easy to understand and measure, but government and governance are also influenced by informal activities, opportunism, the ebb and flow of political and public interest in policy issues, and simply responding to needs and problems as they present themselves.

Understanding the policy process at the national level is not easy, because of unresolved debates about the personality of government institutions, and the many pressures that come to bear on the process. At the European level, the challenges are compounded by the failure of political scientists to agree on the character and powers of the EU institutions, the debates about how those institutions relate to the governments of the member states, and the competing influences of intergovernmentalism and supranationalism. Matters are further complicated by changes in the rules, membership, powers, priorities and policy agenda of the EU.

Key issues

- What are the legal sources of EU policy?
- Is incremental change desirable and/or inevitable, or does it stifle creative policy-making?
- What are the costs and benefits of differentiated integration?
- Is there a European democratic deficit, and, if so, does it matter?
- Should EU institutions be given more of their own budgetary resources and thus greater policy freedom?

Concept

Concept

Public policy

The actions taken (or avoided) by governments as they address the needs of society. Policy takes the form of platforms, programmes, public statements and laws, but is often also driven by crises and opportunities. Its content is influenced by values and ideology, and its development and implementation in the EU is driven by a complex and ever-changing balance between EU institutions, state and local governments, independent agencies, interest groups, the media, public opinion, and the international policy environment.

The legal basis of policy

Public policy is a collective term for the actions of government. It describes their approaches to the problems and needs of the societies they govern and the actions they take (or avoid taking) to address those problems and needs. When parties or candidates run for office, or administrators are appointed to manage public programmes, they will have a shopping list of issues they plan to address, the list and the nature of their actions being guided by their ideology and their thoughts about the responsibilities of government. But their plans will rarely come to fruition as they anticipated; they may be diverted by other more urgent problems jostling for attention, or find that their proposals lack adequate political support or funding, or that implementing their policies is more difficult than they anticipated. But whatever the outcome, the courses of action they follow or avoid are collectively and individually understood as their policies. These policies become the defining qualities of governments and their leaders, the reference points by which they are assessed, and the key deciding factor in whether or not they will be returned to another term in office.

Although there is no European 'government' as such, as we have seen, EU institutions are active in designing and implementing approaches to the problems and needs of Europeans in areas ranging from agriculture to competition, trade, the environment, regional and social policy. We know this because the treaties outline their responsibilities, and the institutions publish statements, agendas, action programmes and policy papers that spell out their goals, interests, positions and opinions. But having an agenda or a platform is one thing; having the authority to act is quite another, and to pin down the policy responsibilities of the EU, we must first look at its rules. These are found in three main places.

Primary rules

The primary rules are found in the treaties, meaning not just the major agreements such as Rome, Maastricht and Lisbon, but also the more minor housekeeping treaties and the treaties of accession signed by incoming member states. As we saw in Chapter 8, these collectively function as something like the constitution of the EU, outlining its general goals and organization, giving insight into the relative powers and responsibilities of the EU institutions and the member states, and providing the framework on which the development of EU law and policy is based. But the treaties – like most state constitutions – contain ambiguities, and often lack the detail needed to allow us to be certain about how powers and responsibilities are defined or should be implemented. We saw in Chapter 9 how competence in some areas (including competition, trade and monetary policy in the euro zone) lies almost exclusively with the EU institutions, but how in all other cases there is a division of responsibilities between the EU institutions and the member states.

Secondary rules

Secondary rules consist of all the laws adopted by the EU, and related judgments handed down by the European Court of Justice, all of them growing out of the framework provided by the treaties. EU law gives substance to the treaties by converting general goals into more focused and measurable objectives, while ECJ judgments have helped offset some of the ambiguities in the treaties and EU law. Another source of secondary rules is the body of international agreements signed by the EU. Until Lisbon, the EU had no legal personality and so could not enter into legal agreements with third parties (only the European Community could do that), but it now has a legal personality (Article 47) and so can sign agreements with international organizations or non-EU states, although only in policy areas where it has competence.

Tertiary rules

Described as tertiary rules because they are not legally binding, these include recommendations and opinions issued by the EU, as well as the action programmes, strategies and declarations of the EU institutions. They also include Green Papers and White Papers published by the Commission. The former are exploratory policy documents that make suggestions and invite feedback, while the latter often follow Green Papers and outline proposals for new EU laws and policies. Recent Green Papers have dealt with reform of the Common Fisheries Policy, the management of bio-waste, a tobacco-free Europe, diplomatic protection for EU citizens in third countries, public access to EU documents, and mental health. Recent White Papers have included proposals for an EU climate change policy, an EU communication policy (designed to improve the way in which the Commission projects the EU to its citizens), and a European space policy.

These, then, are the formal sources of EU policy. But government and governance contain heavy doses of informality and unpredictability, neatly summed up in the apocryphal comment attributed to British Prime Minister Harold Macmillan in response to a question from a journalist about what might blow his government off course: 'Events, dear boy, events'. Leaders must always expect to have to deal with emergencies and change their policies accordingly. A prime example was offered in April 2010 when a volcano in Iceland erupted, producing clouds of ash that covered most of northern Europe and prompting a decision to close the airspace over most of the EU and cancel thousands of scheduled flights, leaving hundreds of thousands of passengers stranded. Questions were raised after the event about how far the EU was ready to deal with major disruptions to air travel, and there were complaints that the Commission and national transport ministers had been too slow to act, and that air traffic control in Europe was too fragmented. The result included calls to accelerate a pre-existing plan (Single European Sky) to replace the 28 separate air traffic zones with nine 'airspace blocks', upgrade and harmonize air traffic control systems across Europe, and reduce the number of air traffic control centres. These changes might eventually lead to the transfer of air traffic control powers away from the member states to the EU.

The policy cycle

Understanding public policy is as much an art as a craft, and while numerous models of the process have been proposed (institutional, rational, incremental,

Green Papers and White Papers: Documents published by the EU that test the waters by making suggestions for new policies, the latter being more detailed and specific than the former.

elite, public choice and so on), none has won general support. But everyone agrees that policy-making is a complex process, and that the EU case has many similarities with national policy systems. In other words, says Richardson (2006), it is 'ugly but familiar'. The usual way of trying to understand policy is to see it in terms of a cycle; while this imposes unrealistic simplicity and logic on a process that is anything but (see Young, 2014), it offers us a guide through the maze. There are five stages in that cycle (see Figure 18.1).

Agenda-setting

New laws and policies cannot be adopted without agreement that a need or a problem exists, which in turn means a focus on agenda-setting, or placing the issue on the public agenda. The content of that agenda will be driven by numerous forces and pressures, including economic and social conditions, political leadership, the competing perspectives of political parties and governments, the causes and effects of problems, changing levels of public interest, and the competing subagendas of the actors involved in EU decision-making. Some issues are perpetual – like taxes and employment – because they affect most people most of the time, while others are more transient and will come and go according to changing levels of urgency and public interest.

The European Council sets the broad agenda by looking at strategic issues relating to the direction of European integration. The Commission is then charged with working to turn general goals into more specific plans of action. Formally, both are influenced and limited by treaty obligations, the pressures to harmonize national laws and policies in the interests of integration, and legislative pressures that spark new laws out of requirements or assumptions built into existing laws. Informally, they will be influenced by policy evolution (the redefinition of policy responses in light of changing levels of support and under-

Agenda-setting: The process by which the list of problems and issues that require a public response is developed and agreed.

Policy evolution: The process by which the goals of public policy change according to new political and economic pressures, improved understanding, and new levels of public support and interest.

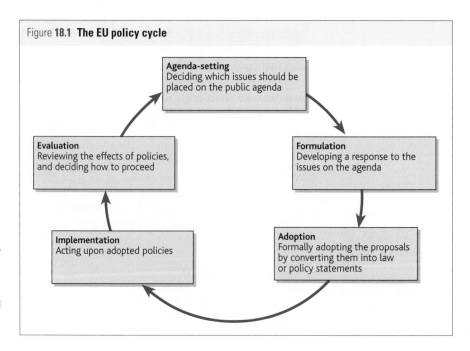

Figure **18.1 The EU policy cycle**

Agenda-setting
Deciding which issues should be placed on the public agenda

Formulation
Developing a response to the issues on the agenda

Adoption
Formally adopting the proposals by converting them into law or policy statements

Implementation
Acting upon adopted policies

Evaluation
Reviewing the effects of policies, and deciding how to proceed

standing), demands and pressures from other EU institutions (including efforts by the European Parliament to encourage the Commission to launch new initiatives), political and public opinion in the member states, the need to respond to emergencies and crises (such as the global financial and euro zone crises), or the obligations of international law.

Formulation

Assuming that there is agreement on the existence of a problem or a need, a response must be developed. This will involve launching studies, drawing up new laws, publishing plans of action, announcing new policy initiatives, or making changes to the EU treaties. In most cases, it will also involve adjustments to spending, which presents its own set of challenges. Conversely, policy-makers may be unable to decide how to respond, or may drag their feet, swayed by the sheer complexity of a problem, doubts about its cause and the best response, or the lack of political and public agreement or support. This has long been a problem with climate change, for example; supporters of action argue that the science is clear, the problem is pressing, and immediate action is needed, while opponents argue that the science is inconclusive, action may cause undesirable economic or social side effects, and there is no point in wealthy industrialized countries taking action without China, India and other newly industrializing powers going along.

Responsibility for policy formulation at the European level lies mainly with the Commission, because of its monopoly over the process of drafting proposals for new laws and policies. But the Commission does not work in a vacuum, and engages with numerous external actors in the design of law and policy, and has its choices limited by the extent of its authority (see Figure 18.2). A phenomenon it has championed since the early 1990s is the open method of coordination. Endorsed by the European Council in 2000, this contrasts with the 'hard' setting of binding legal norms by basing policy-making on a 'soft' combination of cooperation, reciprocal learning and the voluntary participation of member states (see Heidenreich and Bischoff, 2008). It is used mainly in policy areas such as healthcare, education and pensions where the EU has limited competence, and has also been at the heart of the efforts since 1997 to promote a European Employment Strategy (see Rhodes, 2010).

Adoption

Once a new law or policy has been drafted, it must be formally adopted (or rejected). The focus here is on the Council of Ministers and the European Parliament, and their role under the ordinary legislative procedure as the joint institutions of decision. Once again, though, they do not work in a vacuum; the Council will be driven by the opinions of member state governments, and Parliament cannot ignore the views of voters (see Figure 18.2). The member state holding the presidency of the Council of Ministers also plays a role, because it wants to make sure that as much business as possible is successfully concluded during its term. This in turn depends on the resources the presidency is prepared to bring to bear, the negotiating styles of the representatives of each member state, the backlog of unfinished business the presidency inherits from its predecessor, and the prevailing political climate.

Open method of coordination:
A procedure by which EU member states are encouraged to cooperate and agree on voluntary action in policy areas where the EU institutions have limited formal competence.

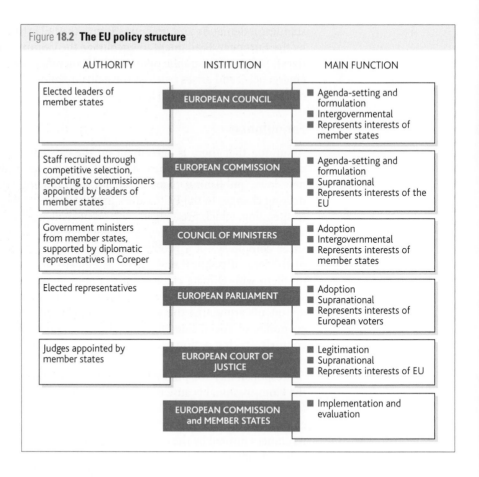

Figure **18.2 The EU policy structure**

AUTHORITY	INSTITUTION	MAIN FUNCTION
Elected leaders of member states	EUROPEAN COUNCIL	■ Agenda-setting and formulation ■ Intergovernmental ■ Represents interests of member states
Staff recruited through competitive selection, reporting to commissioners appointed by leaders of member states	EUROPEAN COMMISSION	■ Agenda-setting and formulation ■ Supranational ■ Represents interests of the EU
Government ministers from member states, supported by diplomatic representatives in Coreper	COUNCIL OF MINISTERS	■ Adoption ■ Intergovernmental ■ Represents interests of member states
Elected representatives	EUROPEAN PARLIAMENT	■ Adoption ■ Supranational ■ Represents interests of European voters
Judges appointed by member states	EUROPEAN COURT OF JUSTICE	■ Legitimation ■ Supranational ■ Represents interests of EU
	EUROPEAN COMMISSION and MEMBER STATES	■ Implementation and evaluation

Implementation

It is tempting to assume that once a new law or policy has been adopted, it will be translated into practical change on the ground in relatively short and painless order. But even at this late stage, there may be political or bureaucratic resistance, and policies can be reinterpreted and redefined (Knill, 2006). Unanticipated problems may arise, including a lack of political agreement or will, difficulties within the institutions responsible for implementation, resistance from the subjects of policy (people, corporations, public agencies and governments), bureaucratic lethargy or inefficiency, inadequate funding, a redefinition of priorities as a result of changed circumstances or new data, and conflicting interpretations of the content and goals of policies.

The Commission is responsible for overseeing implementation, but it must work through national bureaucracies, whose efficiency and commitment varies from one member state to another, and one national department to another. Because the Commission has neither the staff nor the resources to follow progress on every piece of legislation, it relies heavily on individuals and interest groups to keep an eye on their home governments and draw public attention to any foot-dragging, as well as on the European Court of Justice to issue favourable judgments where the Commission decides to take legal action against a member

Illustration **18.1**

The policy-makers

European Parliament President Martin Schulz (*third from left*) meets members of the Latvian parliament in Riga at the end of 2014 in preparation for Latvia taking over the presidency of the Council of Ministers. The EP and the Council play a critical role in the EU policy-making process.

state. The quality of implementation (and policy-making in general) has also been helped by the creation of the specialized agencies reviewed in Chapter 14, which generate data and are in a strong position to monitor the effects of policy.

Evaluation

Continuing to think systematically (which is not always a reflection of reality in the policy world), the final stage in the policy cycle involves deciding whether or not a law or policy has worked. If the root causes of a problem are clear, the problem is relatively contained and visible, targets and dates were included in the policy response, and independent assessments are available (a series of big 'ifs'), then the link between cause and effect might be measurable. But in most cases, it is impossible to be certain of the causes of a problem, or which actions result in which consequences. Take, for example, attempts to reform EU economic performance under the failed Lisbon Strategy of 2000, which was replaced in 2010 by the Europe 2020 strategy (see Chapter 19). The core problem (sluggish economic growth) was fairly clear, but opinion was divided on the causes (was it too much regulation, too few efforts to open up the marketplace, or too little investment in research and development?), why the Lisbon Strategy failed, and how far those failures might be addressed under the Europe 2020 strategy.

The most immediate responsibility for evaluation lies with the member states and the Commission, but the European Parliament, the member states, interest groups, the media and ordinary Europeans will often want their say. And, given that success has a thousand fathers while failure is an orphan, and government institutions will rarely admit their mistakes for fear of losing funding and influence, evaluation is far from a value-neutral process. As a result, the final decision on whether laws and policies should be continued, adjusted or abandoned is more often about changes in levels of political support and limits on spending as it is a well-considered assessment of how a particular policy option has worked out. Since 2002 the Commission has been pursuing a Better Regulation initiative designed to simplify and improve law-making by better assessing the impact of regulations, reducing red tape, and looking more closely at alternatives to regulation.

The characteristics of EU policy

All policy systems, whether at the local, state or international level, have their own distinctive characteristics. These are based on a combination of the powers and responsibilities of the institutions involved, and the political, economic and social environment in the communities for which the policies are being developed. The clues to such qualities can be found in a combination of the formal and the informal.

Formally, policy is driven by institutional rules: what the policy actors are allowed to do and not allowed to do, according to the existing body of constitutions (or treaties), laws and policies. It will also be influenced by the relative powers of the institutions involved, and their different bases of power (the Commission is a supranational bureaucracy, the Council of Ministers is driven by national interests, the EP represents the voters and so on). Informally, policy is driven by circumstances, changing needs and opportunities, crises, and the balance of pressures brought to bear by all the parties interested in policy, including (in the case of the EU) the member states, the EU institutions, interest groups, corporations, political parties, foreign governments, and ordinary citizens. With these thoughts in mind, we can identify at least six main features of the EU policy process.

Compromise and bargaining

Democratic politics is driven by compromise, or the need to blend multiple competing opinions into a decision on a course of action. No one will ever have entirely their own way, because policy-making demands discussion and the striking of bargains, and the parties involved will bring their own priorities, preferences, perspectives and biases to the table. This is particularly true of the coalition governments found in most EU states, where participating parties will routinely be forced into compromises, and federal systems such as Austria, Belgium and Germany, where powers are divided between national and subnational government. In the case of the EU, where power is not always clearly defined and the 'government' is effectively a coalition of member states, the challenges of achieving compromise are that much greater.

Political games

Politics is all about struggles for power and influence, with each of the actors involved trying to press its views on the others and win maximum advantage. In many senses, it is a game, or even a sport, with individuals or teams vying against one another for victory. Peters (1992, pp. 106–7) describes three sets of interconnected games – those between the member states, the EU institutions and the directorates-general within the Commission – but there are many more, including those played by groups of member states pursuing shared goals, interest groups within the member states playing off the EU institutions against their own national governments, political groups within the European Parliament, and the EU and the member states as they try to define their changing relative positions in the international system.

Incrementalism

Policy-making rarely involves dramatic departures, which is why (in describing the actions of leaders) *brave* and *radical* are often seen as codewords for *risky* and *foolhardy*. Instead, policy is usually based on incrementalism, where new initiatives build on what came before, the only distinction being just how much of a change of direction is involved. (The American scholar Charles Lindblom (1959) put it differently when he argued that much policy-making was simply a matter of 'muddling through'.) Political leaders routinely promise change and new approaches when running for office, but they inherit pre-existing laws and policies, and while they may amend or overturn them, or let them fade away through inattention, they will usually take a cautious approach to change. This is certainly true of the EU system of governance, whose intergovernmental qualities mean that member states and EU institutions can rarely take the initiative without wide conferral. So long does it sometimes take to reach agreement that the EU policy process is often accused of inertia.

Another dimension of incrementalism is path dependence, or the idea that policy decisions on new problems will be influenced to some extent by decisions taken in the past. The Commission faces a particular form of such dependence, in the sense that many 'new' EU laws are not really all that new, but are simply a recasting of existing legislation, or so-called 'daughter directives' designed to add more specific goals to earlier framework directives. For example, a 2000 framework directive on water quality outlined the general need to improve water quality; subsequent daughter directives went into more detail on how this would happen.

Differentiated integration

Ideally, all the partners in a shared enterprise will move ahead at the same pace and in the same direction. But while this is usually true of states (although in federations, the partners will sometimes adopt different policies in areas where they have authority), it is not always true of the EU, which has seen many instances of differentiated integration: different levels of integration in terms of the extent of centralization and the number of countries taking part (Leuffen et al., 2012). This takes different forms:

- Integration à la carte: instances where some countries do not participate at all in a given initiative, as in the case of participation in the euro and the Schengen Agreement.
- Multi-speed integration: policies where a country wants to take part but is not yet considered ready, as in the case of delayed membership of the euro for eastern European states.
- Derogation: an arrangement by which a member state is excused from implementing part of a law or a treaty, is allowed to apply it differently, or given longer to achieve implementation, as in the case of Cyprus, Malta and several eastern European countries being given extensions to meet some of the targets on free movement of people, goods and services.

Incrementalism: A method of developing policy through small and often unplanned changes rather than more radical or wholesale change.

Path dependence: Making decisions on the basis of what has gone before, even though circumstances and understanding may have changed.

Differentiated integration: Instances of EU policies (notably monetary policy) that do not apply equally to all the member states.

Derogation: A partial repeal or abrogation of a law, allowing an EU member state to apply a law differently, or giving it longer to meet a deadline.

Understanding Integration... *Spillover*

Spillover is the best known element of neofunctionalist theory, so much so that Saurugger (2013, p. 39) considers it 'the key driving force behind all integration processes'. As we saw in Chapter 1, it describes the process in which integration leads to knock-on effects, or, in American military parlance, 'mission creep', where a project goes beyond its original goals as new needs and opportunities arise. As Wildavsky (1979, p. 62) once put it, policy can become its own cause, in the sense that the actions of organizations can often lead to ever larger numbers of unanticipated consequences.

Haas (1968) originally saw it as a functional economic phenomenon, applying to the manner in which integration in one economic sector would create pressures for further integration within that sector and related areas. But technical spillover implied that disparities in standards would cause states to rise (or sink) to the level of the state with the tightest (or loosest) regulations, and political spillover assumed that once different functional sectors were integrated, interest groups (such as corporate lobbies and labour unions) would switch from targeting national governments to

trying to target the EU institutions, which will encourage them in an attempt to win new powers for themselves.

Spillover is a process that continues today, perhaps most notably as a result of the fallout from the euro zone crisis, which has seen the authority of the European Central Bank expand, and work underway towards the development of a European banking union, both of which have needed political support. Much less often discussed has been the related concept of 'spillback', an idea proposed by Lindberg and Scheingold (1970, p. 135). They were specifically referring to 'a situation in which there is a withdrawal from a set of specific obligations. Rules are no longer regularly enforced or obeyed. The scope of Community action and its institutional capacities decrease.' If spillback is an expansion of policy interest and authority, then spillback implies a contraction sparked by political resistance to integration. This has been a theme in the story of the EEC/EU dating back to the mid-1960s, and very much a factor today in the thinking of euroscepticism.

Leuffen et al. (2012) argue that differentiated integration is likely become a persistent feature of EU politics, such that in order to understand it, we need to understand the level of policy centralization, the functional scope of integration, and its territorial reach.

Elitism and the democratic deficit

The EU has long been criticized as elitist, with too many decisions being taken by unaccountable European bureaucrats and the leaders of the member states, without sufficient reference to public opinion. The use of national referendums, the growing powers of the European Parliament, and the rise of interest group lobbying have all helped make the policy process more open, but the democratic deficit (the lack of institutional openness and direct accountability in EU institutions) remains a problem and a topic of debate. This led to the quip that if the European Community applied for membership of itself, it would not be admitted on the grounds that it did not conform to the democratic principles outlined in the Treaty of Rome (Hansard, vol. 181, col. 1089, 29 November 1990).

How far the deficit exists, however, and how much it poses a problem, depends on how we understand the EU (see below). Although its critics often describe the EU with terms such as 'elitist', 'secretive' and 'remote', and while

Democratic deficit: The gap between the powers of the EU institutions and the ability of European citizens to influence the decisions they take.

Debating... *Does the democratic deficit matter?*

YES

Other than through the European Parliament, European citizens as a whole have no direct representation in the meeting rooms and corridors of the EU institutions, many of whose meetings are not open to the public.

If the EU is to be taken more seriously by its citizens, and its work better understood, then they must have a better idea of their stakes in the process of integration. This is less likely to happen so long as they are not given more direct influence over the membership and decisions of the EU institutions.

As long as European leaders feel that they have only limited direct accountability to the European citizenry as a whole, rather than their own national constituencies, they will continue to be driven by national rather than European interests, are likely to continue to often disagree over key issues, and the EU will have less credibility and influence as a global actor.

NO

The EU is a confederation, which means it is a union of states in which the governments of the states work together to make decisions, representing the interests of their citizens. There is no need for direct representation of citizens within the EU institutions.

The interests of European voters are adequately represented in the European Parliament, whose powers over law-making offset and balance the Council of Ministers. The EP can also place pressure on the Commission to launch policy initiatives.

The governments of the member states are elected, and they either send representatives to the EU institutions (European Council, Council of Ministers) or appoint the leaders of those institutions (European Commission, European Court of Justice). So EU citizens have direct and indirect representation.

Public interests are also represented through the work of the European Court of Justice and the European Court of Human Rights, national referendums (several of which have resulted in changes to policy goals), the work of interest groups, the work of the European ombudsman, and the (as yet untested) option of citizens' initiatives.

the lack of democratic accountability was once considered to be a 'crisis of legitimacy' (Franklin, 1996, p. 197), others are not so sure. Moravcsik (2002) argues that concern for the deficit is misplaced, because the EU institutions are constrained by constitutional checks and balances, including 'narrow mandates, fiscal limits, super–majoritarian and concurrent voting requirements and separation of powers'. On balance, he concludes, 'EU policy-making is, in nearly all cases, clean, transparent, effective and politically responsive to the demands of European citizens.' Follesdal and Hix (2006) disagree, arguing that opposition to the leadership elites and policy status quos is an essential feature of the practice of democracy, political competition is an essential vehicle for opinion formation, and what is missing from the EU is an electoral contest for political leadership at the European level.

The EU budget

There are few influences on the public policy process quite as important as the budget. Most government action costs money, and the impact of policies will often depend on where funds are raised (particularly the balance between taxes and borrowing), the kinds of activities that are taxed, the different levels of taxation, where funds are spent, the efficiency of spending, and the relative amounts spent on different activities. Take, for example, the Common Agricultural Policy (CAP): for decades, more Community funds were spent on agricultural subsidies than on any other area of policy (the CAP share was as high as 75 per cent of Community spending in the late 1970s). This not only had important consequences for European farming and the relative influence of farming and non-farming communities, but also limited the amount that could be spent on other activities, such as regional development.

There are two major defining features of the EU budget:

1 *It is surprisingly small.* In spite of popular misconceptions about copious EU spending, the budget in 2015 was just over €135 billion, based on a limit of 1.02 per cent of the combined gross national income (GNI) of the 28 member states. This worked out at 72 euro cents per person per day in the EU, and was slightly less than the amount budgeted that year for just one government department in just one EU member state: Britain's Department of Work and Pensions.
2 *It must be balanced.* There is no EU debt, so the EU is spared the problems that normally accompany debts (such as interest payments). In this regard, the EU stands in contrast to many of its member states, which have long carried national budget deficits, most of which were made worse by increased borrowing and spending during the 2007–10 global financial crisis.

In spite of its modesty and relative orderliness, the EU budget has long been at the heart of political conflict, much of it driven by the core question of monetary independence: How much should the EU depend on national contributions from the member states (which give the states leverage over the European institutions) and how far should the EU be allowed to have its own resources (independent sources of revenue, which would give the European institutions greater freedom of action)? (For a survey of EU budgetary battles, see Laffan and Lindner, 2014, pp. 214ff.) To this debate have been added questions over the relative role of EU institutions in the budgetary process, and problems generated by efforts in some member states to give as little as possible while taking back as much as possible.

The European Coal and Steel Community had its own (very limited) income, raised by a levy on producers. With the creation of the EEC, the budgetary structure shifted to national contributions, which were calculated roughly on the basis of size, so that France, Germany and Italy each contributed 28% of the EEC budget, Belgium and the Netherlands just under 8% each, and Luxembourg 0.2%. The first major political battle broke out in 1965 when the Commission and Parliament both tried to win more control over the budget but came up against Charles de Gaulle's concerns about national sovereignty and protecting French farmers, sparking the 1965 empty chair crisis (see Chapter 5). But the pressures for reform did not go away, and agreements reached between 1970 and 1975 led to a switch to revenues raised from own resources: customs duties, agricultural levies, sugar contributions, a fixed-rate portion of value added tax (VAT) receipts, and a fixed-rate levy on GNI.

National contributions: The typical method for funding international organizations, based on financial contributions by their member states. In the case of the EU, these are calculated according to gross national income.

Own resources: Independent sources of income for the EU, generated mainly out of policy areas controlled by the EU rather than the member states.

The new structure created several dilemmas: two-thirds of spending went on agricultural subsidies (which grew as European farmers produced more), revenue from customs duties fell in tandem with reductions in the EC's external tariffs, revenue from agricultural levies fell as the EC became more self-sufficient in food production, and income from VAT slowed because consumption was falling as a percentage of the EC's gross domestic product (Shackleton, 1990, pp. 10–11). At the same time, several member states were unwilling to raise the limit on the EC's own resources, and the EC could not make up any shortfalls by running a deficit or borrowing. Matters were brought to a head in the early 1980s by one of the most well-known political conflicts in the history of the EC: the campaign by British Prime Minister Margaret Thatcher to renegotiate British contributions to the EC budget.

With its relatively small farming sector and relatively large import bill, the UK paid more into the EC budget through tariffs and received less back than most other member states. A 1970 agreement reflecting the interests of the six founder states (Laffan and Lindner, 2014, p. 215) had fixed the budgetary rules before Britain became a member, but few could have anticipated Thatcher's position. She saw the CAP as a wasteful distortion of free markets, based on a Franco-German compromise, and an example of profligate spending that flew in the face of her attempts to cut public spending at home. Determined to shake things up, she demanded change at her first European Council meeting in June 1979 (in a statement wrongly but colourfully quoted as 'I want my money back'), but it would be June 1984 before a settlement was reached that won a rebate for Britain while also marking a step forward in reforming EC spending on agriculture (Dinan, 2014, pp. 187–9, 193–6).

With the EC on the brink of insolvency, it was decided to raise the ceiling on own resources to 1.4 per cent of VAT, and more reforms agreed by the Euro-

Illustration **18.2 Thatcher demands her money back**

Meetings of the European Council in the early 1980s had to wrestle with demands by Margaret Thatcher (*centre*) for a renegotiation of British contributions to the EC budget.

pean Council in February 1988 resulted in a shift away from annual (and often politically bruising) debates about the budget to the more orderly agreement of multi-annual financial frameworks (MFFs) that make spending more predictable and keep it within agreed limits; the current MFF runs from 2014 to 2020. Decision-making follows roughly the same path as EU law, with the proposed budget being developed by the Commission, debated and amended by the Council of Ministers and Parliament, and then implemented by the Commission under the watchful eyes of the Court of Auditors. Behind this simplified outline, there is intensive bargaining and thousands of management decisions are taken involving EU institutions and every layer of government in the member states from the national to the local.

In the current MFF, revenues come from three main sources (see Figure 18.3):

1 Nearly 74% from member states according to national levels of economic productivity (up from 43% of revenues in 2003). Each member state makes a contribution that is roughly in proportion to its GNI.
2 Revenues from VAT account for just over 13%, down from 38% in 2003.
3 12% from duties collected on imports from non-member states under the common external tariff, and agricultural levies.

In terms of where the funds are spent, the EU once broke spending down by policy area, so that in 2006, for example, nearly 47% of spending went on agriculture, 30% on the structural funds, nearly 9% on 'internal policies', 5% on external actions and 6% on administration. Since then, the listing has been changed to shift the focus to policy goals. EU expenses (like those of almost all budgets) consist of a combination of mandatory payments to which it is committed, for example agricultural subsidies, and discretionary payments where there is more flexibility, such as spending on regional or energy policy. In 2015, spending was broken down as follows (see Figure 18.3):

- 45.6% (€61.7 billion) went to 'smart and inclusive growth', about two-thirds going to economic, social and territorial cohesion (see Chapter 22), and the

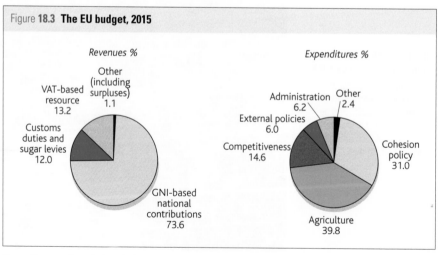

Figure **18.3 The EU budget, 2015**

Source: European Commission, 2013.

rest to competitiveness for jobs and growth, meaning mainly research and development, trans-European energy and transport networks, and education. The proportion of EU spending on cohesion has almost tripled since the mid-1970s.

- Nearly 41% (€55 billion) was set aside for 'sustainable growth', the bulk of which (97%) was spending on agricultural policy.
- 6.2% (nearly €8.4 billion) was spent on administration, including salaries and pensions for EU staff, buildings and infrastructure. Just under half of that went to the European Commission. One of the most common misconceptions about the EU among ordinary Europeans is that spending in this area is much higher than it is.
- Just under 6% (just over €8 billion) was spent on activities promoting 'Global Europe', including development aid, spending under the Common Foreign and Security Policy and the European Neighbourhood Policy.
- 1.5% (about €2 billion) was spent on 'security and citizenship', the former term including police cooperation, drug control, crime prevention and asylum policies, and the latter including culture, identity, health, consumer safety and civil protection.
- The balance of 0.4% was set aside for 'special instruments', including the European Global Adjustment Fund (all figures from European Commission, 2013).

Most notably, the share of spending on cohesion that went to the 12 newest members of the EU crossed the 50% barrier for the first time in 2010 (much of it in the form of agricultural spending). The budget was also impacted by the European Economic Recovery Plan, a stimulus package put together in response to the global financial crisis and involving a transfer of EU spending into infrastructure projects.

Summary

- Public policy describes whatever governments do (or avoid doing) to address society's needs. It takes the form of platforms, programmes, public statements and laws, but is often also driven by crises, emergencies and opportunities.

- Formally, policy-making in the EU is driven by primary rules found in the treaties, secondary rules in the form of laws adopted by the EU and judgments handed down by the European Court of Justice, and tertiary 'rules' in the form of action programmes, strategies, declarations and other activities.

- Informally, there are numerous influences on policy, and many models have been developed to help understand the system.

- One approach is to see policy as a cycle, beginning with the setting of agendas and moving through formulation, adoption, implementation and evaluation.

- EU policy, like all democratic policy-making, is driven by bargaining and the search for compromise, political games among interested parties, elitism, and incremental rather than radical change.

- Policy-making in the EU also has several unique features, including differentiated integration, spillover and the democratic deficit. But opinion on the significance of the latter is divided.

- The EU budget is small, yet it has been the subject of repeated political squabbles over the years. These have abated since a 1988 agreement to replace annual budgets with multi-year budget packages.

- Most revenues come from national contributions from the member states, and most spending goes to regional development and agriculture.

Key terms and concepts

Agenda-setting

Democratic deficit

Derogation

Differentiated integration

Green Papers and White Papers

Incrementalism

National contributions

Open method of coordination

Own resources

Path dependence

Policy evolution

Public policy

Further reading

Buonanno, Laurie, and Neill Nugent (2013) *Policies and Policy Processes of the European Union* (Basingstoke: Palgrave Macmillan). Wide-ranging, thorough study of public policy in the EU, looking at key policy actors, features of the policy process, and specific areas of policy.

Lindner, Johannes (2006) *Conflict and Change in EU Budgetary Politics* (Abingdon: Routledge). One of the more recent of the surprisingly few full-length studies of the EU budget.

Wallace, Helen, Mark A. Pollack and Alasdair R. Young (eds) (2014) *Policy-Making in the European Union*, 7th edn (Oxford: Oxford University Press). Edited collection, focusing on specific policy areas, including agriculture, the single market, competition and social policy.

19 Economic Policy

Preview

European integration has long focused on economic matters. The core goal of the Treaty of Rome was the construction of a single market, while the Single European Act and the Maastricht treaty were (respectively) attempts to complete the single market and prepare for a single currency. Many of the deepest European political struggles have been about subsidies to agriculture, building common trade and competition policies, dealing with unemployment and labour immobility, and (more recently) responding to the global financial crisis and the troubles of the euro zone.

Economic integration was intended to generate wealth and opportunity in order to help Europe recover from the ravages of war, while also building enough ties of mutual interest and dependence to make future war unthinkable. In this sense, it succeeded: Europe today is more peaceful and prosperous than at any time in its history, and the EU is the world's biggest and wealthiest capitalist marketplace, the biggest trading power, market for corporate mergers and acquisitions and source of foreign direct investment. Meanwhile, the euro, in spite of its recent woes, has become one of the world's three leading international currencies.

But many problems remain. These include persistent unemployment, slow economic growth, too little progress on the liberalization of labour markets, the impact of a declining and ageing population, EU dependence on imported oil and natural gas, and claims that Europe's economic possibilities have sometimes been more rhetorical than real. An attempt under the 2000 Lisbon Strategy to make the EU the world's most competitive and dynamic economy within ten years fell flat, forcing an extension to 2020, with critics charging that too few member state governments were prepared to make the necessary reforms.

Key issues

- What are the implications of pooling more responsibility over fiscal policy in the hands of the EU institutions?
- What are the costs and benefits of economic liberalization?
- What are the remaining political, legal, economic and social barriers to the completion of the single market?
- Is the rise of large European corporations as impressive as it sounds?
- Has the pooling of authority over competition policy been good for Europe and Europeans?

The outlines and limits of economic policy

Economic policy is routinely at the top of the public policy agenda in every free-market system, and is often the deciding factor in determining which governments are elected to office and how they fare in public opinion. Yet the dynamics and principles of economic policy are poorly understood, even by professional economists; Laurence J. Peter (author of *The Peter Principle*) defines an economist as an expert who will know tomorrow why the things he predicted yesterday didn't happen today. If economists truly understood how economies functioned, they would be able to predict, correct for and explain downturns in the marketplace. But the 2007–10 global financial crisis caught most unawares, and there has been little agreement on the causes or effects of the crisis in the euro zone, or the future prospects for the euro. As for ordinary Europeans, they react instinctively to problems such as unemployment, inflation and higher taxes, but are rarely equipped to place them in a wider context.

Broadly defined, economic policy deals with the production, distribution and consumption of goods and services. Although it deals mainly with matters relating to money, markets, production, supply, costs and efficiency, it has implications for almost every other sector of policy. It can have an effect on environmental quality, crime rates, education, national security, public health, tourism, scientific research, land use, transport, housing, and every kind of public service. More specifically, it can be divided into four key subfields: fiscal, monetary, competition and trade policy (see Figure 19.1).

Fiscal policy is concerned with budgets: how government raises revenues, how it spends that money, and what effect this has on deficits, taxes and the broader fortunes of the economy. Governments raise revenues mainly through taxation, borrowing (by issuing bonds, for example), drawing on reserves, or selling assets such as land or licences to minerals. Governments can take one of three main stances on fiscal policy: an expansionary stance means that spending exceeds revenue (which has the effect of building debt), a neutral stance keeps spending

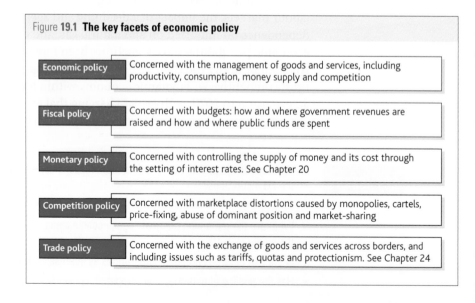

Figure **19.1 The key facets of economic policy**

Economic policy	Concerned with the management of goods and services, including productivity, consumption, money supply and competition
Fiscal policy	Concerned with budgets: how and where government revenues are raised and how and where public funds are spent
Monetary policy	Concerned with controlling the supply of money and its cost through the setting of interest rates. See Chapter 20
Competition policy	Concerned with marketplace distortions caused by monopolies, cartels, price-fixing, abuse of dominant position and market-sharing
Trade policy	Concerned with the exchange of goods and services across borders, and including issues such as tariffs, quotas and protectionism. See Chapter 24

and revenue in balance, and a contractionary stance means that revenue exceeds spending. Fiscal policy is ultimately concerned with how governments use the balance between income and spending to manipulate the economy, for example by encouraging growth and creating jobs. Keynesian economists argue that increased spending and lowered tax rates are the best ways to stimulate demand, while classical economists argue that budget deficits increase demand for credit in the financial markets, lowering demand.

For its part, monetary policy (see Chapter 20) is also concerned with the growth and stability of an economy, but from the perspective of money supply: how government controls the value of a currency and deals with problems such as inflation by raising or lowering interest rates (the cost at which money can be borrowed). Policy can again be expansionary or contractionary, depending on the supply of money; the former involves lowering interest rates during a recession in an effort to encourage job creation, while the latter involves reducing the money supply or taking on inflation by raising interest rates. Where fiscal policy tends to be managed by executives in national systems of government, monetary policy is usually managed by central banks, often with independent powers.

One of the structural problems faced by the EU, which became all too clear with the breaking of the euro zone crisis in 2009–10, was that while the European Central Bank (ECB) had a high degree of control over monetary policy in the euro zone, the EU institutions have had little direct control over fiscal policy. And because the EU budget must be balanced, the Commission cannot use revenues and spending to help it deal with EU-wide economic problems. In other words, responsibility for fiscal and monetary policy – on which there is usually a high degree of coordination at the national level – has been divided at the EU level, with fiscal policy resting with the member states, monetary policy divided between the ECB and the central banks of states outside the euro zone, and the one obvious coordinating body (the European Commission) left with few powers beyond its limited options as a mediator and confidence builder. The euro crisis underlined the importance of EU leaders working more closely together on core economic issues and giving financial markets a better idea of who is in charge.

The single market

The building of a single European market – an area within which there is free movement of people, money, goods and services – has long been at the top of the EEC/EU agenda, has absorbed more political energy than any other item on that agenda, and has been one of the few EU programmes on which supporters and opponents of integration have been able to agree. It has also probably meant more in real, practical terms to Europeans than almost anything else the EU has achieved (except perhaps adoption of the euro), and Eurobarometer polls have found that when asked what the EU means to them personally, most people identify the freedom to travel, study and work anywhere in the EU. Certainly, the single market has had a more easily measurable effect on their personal choices than, say, policies on foreign relations, agriculture, cohesion, or the environment. At the same time, the pressures of spillover have moved the EU in often unexpected directions, the fashioning of policy on the single market often providing a classic example of muddling through.

Concept

Customs union

An arrangement under which all tariffs, duties and other restrictions on trade among participating countries are removed, and a common external tariff is agreed so that all goods coming into the union from third parties are subject to the same costs. Theoretically, it leads to more trade among members of the union, because costs are lower than those on imported goods subject to tariffs. The European customs union was declared complete in 1968, but routine customs checks at internal borders remained until 1993.

Concept

Economic liberalization

The process of opening up markets through reduced regulation and a removal of other restrictions on competition. There is an ongoing debate about how much regulation is enough, the absence of enough financial regulation being one of the causes of the 2007–10 global financial crisis. Within the EU, leaders and parties are divided over the extent to which the state should manage the economy, and the long-held desire to protect national corporations and control the movement of migrants has taken a long time to diminish.

The single market project was founded on economic priorities and has had its greatest impact on policies in the areas of trade, competition and employment. It was the core goal of the Treaty of Rome, but although there was progress in the 1960s and 70s, it was uneven; tariffs and trade quotas ended in 1968 with completion of the customs union, but non-tariff barriers remained a problem, many of them being neither immediately obvious nor visible; they included discriminatory regulations and taxes, efforts by governments to protect national industries, border controls that increased transport costs, and limits on bidding for public contracts (Neal, 2007, p. 129). The 1985 Commission White Paper on the single market (Commission of the European Communities, 1985) identified three main sets of barriers that needed to be removed:

- *Physical barriers:* in the form of internal customs and border checks, which required that almost everyone had to travel with a passport and sometimes even a visa, and demanded additional paperwork for the movement of goods across borders. These checks were the most visible and obvious reminders of Europe's internal economic divisions.
- *Technical barriers:* created by concerns about safety, health, environmental and consumer protection, different requirements for educational and professional qualifications, and problems as routine as different electrical currents and designs for electrical plugs. As many as 100,000 different technical regulations and standards may have been in place in the member states before 1986 (Neal, 2007, p. 131).
- *Fiscal barriers:* in the form mainly of indirect taxation that caused distortions of competition and artificial price differences. Notable examples included excise duties on petroleum products, tobacco and alcohol, and different rates of value added tax (VAT, a consumption tax assessed on the value added to goods and services as they move through the production process). As late as 2002, duties on beer varied from a low of 12 cents per litre in Germany and Spain to a high of €1.16 in Britain and €1.74 in Finland (European Commission, 2002).

It was clear in the 1970s and 80s that the EEC's national economies were too fragmented, European corporations were losing ground to their American and Japanese competitors, there were mounting trade deficits, levels of inflation and unemployment were too high, and the European marketplace was unable to generate enough new jobs. This led to the coining in 1985 of the term 'Eurosclerosis', which was borrowed to also describe the lack of political leadership. New ideas and approaches now converged to spark the 'relaunch' of Europe contained in the Single European Act (SEA).

But while economic liberalization has been at the heart of work on the single market, all has not been well. The market for services has opened up more slowly than the market for goods, for example, and breaking down national markets in financial services and transport has been relatively slow; although it is easier for consumers to use credit and debit cards in other countries and transfer money across borders, restrictions remain. Barriers also continue to be created by national tax systems and the slowness with which the market for postal services has been opened up, although the latter is increasingly a moot point, given the rise of the internet and email.

The failures were reflected in the outcome of a much-trumpeted launch in 2000 of the Lisbon Strategy (see Chapter 7), aimed at making the EU 'the most dynamic and competitive knowledge-based economy in the world' within ten years. But it was already clear by 2004 that governments were not moving quickly enough, the single market programme was showing signs of its age, and there was insufficient political will to deal with too much regulation, too many protections for workers against dismissal, and too few efforts to open up markets. The EU has also fallen behind in research and development, with expenditure as a percentage of GDP stagnant since the mid-1990s, in contrast to high or growing levels of investment in the US, Japan, China and South Korea. And there has been an ongoing tension between two models of economic management, pitting the Anglo-Saxon preference for open markets with the continental or Rhenish preference for government intervention.

As a result, the Lisbon Strategy was transformed into the Europe 2020 strategy, which moved the Lisbon deadline to 2020 and focused on innovation, education, sustainable growth, a low-carbon economy, and job creation. Its goals include jobs for at least 75 per cent of the working-age population, the investment of at least 3 per cent of GDP in research and development, the meeting of targets on climate change, a reduction in levels of poverty, and an increase in the number of Europeans completing their high school education and the number completing a degree or a diploma.

Meanwhile, European economies were hard hit by the global financial crisis, which broke in 2007. European political leaders were quick to blame the US for sparking the crisis by allowing too much credit to be offered to those unable to pay, and not providing enough government regulation of the financial sector. Yet many European financial institutions suffered because they had bought American 'toxic assets'. After some indecision, EU governments generally moved in the same direction as the US, bailing out banks and other financial institutions whose collapse might have posed systemic risks to the EU financial system, working to recapitalize the banking system and protect savers' deposits, raising the minimum guarantee for individual bank deposits, and supporting a stimulus package proposed by the European Commission.

Then came the crisis in the euro zone, which again saw disagreement over what to do. The Greek government had been borrowing heavily since adopting the euro in 2001, building a budget deficit that left it susceptible to the effects of the global financial crisis. With concerns that Greece might default on its debt, or perhaps even leave the euro altogether (or be asked to leave), confidence in the euro fell in 2010, obliging the Greek government to impose unpopular austerity measures, and EU leaders to think about how far they would be prepared to go to rescue troubled national economies. Other EU states were also struggling to keep their budget deficits under control: EU rules set a target of 3%, but Britain, Spain and Ireland were all in the range of 10–12%, and Italy was running at 5%. In the event, it was agreed to offer a combination of euro zone and International Monetary Fund loans as a last resort if Greece was unable to raise loans in the open market (see Chapter 20 for more details).

Europe's regional and national economies have been counted out numerous times over the past few decades, earning the continent a reputation – as *The Economist* lamented in March 2010 – for being one 'whose economy is rigid and sclerotic, whose people are work-shy and welfare-dependent, and whose industrial

Europe 2020 strategy: A long-term economic strategy aimed at job creation, improved educational attainment and sustainable growth.

Global financial crisis: The international financial crisis that broke in 2007, bringing recession to most advanced economies in 2008–10, and challenging the ability of EU leaders to work together on broad economic problems.

base is antiquated and declining'. Europe's particular needs, it went on, included more open labour markets, more limits on public spending, fewer regulations, reforms to welfare and public education, and more incentives to encourage more women into the workplace (*The Economist*, 2010). While the US economy (often praised as a model of openness and innovation by *The Economist*) has also been suffering, and emerging states such as Brazil, India and China emerged relatively unscathed from the global financial crisis, the EU clearly has much work to do to shake off its unfortunate reputation.

Effects of the single market

Eighty years ago, Europe's borders were often rigorously defended for fear of military invasion. Forty years ago, travelling from one European country to another meant producing passports and sometimes even visas, and waiting in lines for customs and immigration checks, with limits on how much in the way of goods and money could be taken from one country to another. Today, customs and immigration checks are almost entirely gone, and there is little to remind road travellers of state borders beyond signs indicating that they are about to leave one country and enter another. Perhaps nothing is more remarkable than driving across the border between Germany and its four immediate western neighbours; where once those borders had deep military and political significance, and France did all it could to protect itself from German invasion, now there are simply signs indicating passage from one state to another.

With some restrictions, today a citizen or legal resident of any EU member state has the right to move across borders and live and work in other member states. They may need to show an identity card or passport, they might have to register with the local authorities, or show that they will not become a burden on the social services of the new country, but they no longer need visas or residence

Illustration **19.1**
The single market
This sign at the border between Germany and Luxembourg symbolizes one of the most remarkable achievements of European integration: the removal of almost all internal border controls among EU member states.

permits, they mainly have the right to be treated the same as a national of the member state, and they can only be expelled on grounds of public policy, public security or public health, and not on economic grounds.

Concerns about the movement of workers from the East to the West following enlargement in 2004–07 led to an agreement that the EU-15 states could temporarily restrict entry of eastern European workers, but on a voluntary basis. Most opted to impose the limits, the most notable exception being the UK, which left its borders open, expecting perhaps no more than 20,000 new arrivals per year after enlargement; it was astonished when it received nearly 450,000 work permit applications from eastern Europe in the period 2004–06 (British Home Office, 2006). The influx gave rise to the creation of the iconic 'Polish plumber' (actually a 2005 invention of French nationalists), representing the influx of cheap labour from the East. But almost all restrictions in the EU-15 have now gone, and by 2008 many of the migrants to Britain had returned home, motivated by recession in the West and improved wages and job opportunities in the East (Pollard et al., 2008). More recent fears that the removal of restrictions on the movement of Bulgarians and Romanians in January 2014 would result in a similar influx of new immigrants came to little.

Not only have the rules on movement across borders changed, but so have the economic and sociological dynamics of migration. Where it was once driven mainly by economic need, with people moving to other countries in search of jobs or better opportunities, and the major flows being from south to north, Europeans are increasingly moving not because they must but because they choose to. Migrants may be looking for a different cultural environment, to be educated in a different country, retiring to warmer parts of the EU, being posted by their employer, or looking for a new start in a new country. And where once it was mainly poorer Europeans who were looking to move, today it is as often students, professionals, managers and retirees.

The binding of the European marketplace has meant not just removing or harmonizing physical, technical and fiscal barriers, but has demanded the building of the infrastructure needed to encourage the flow of people, goods and services. Recognizing this need, in 1990 the Commission adopted an action plan on the building of trans-European networks that would encourage the integration of transport, energy supply and telecommunications systems across the EU. Since then, a list of priority projects has been developed, and changes have come out of a combination of deliberate government policy and incidental economic pressures.

Developments include a Europe-wide transport network based around a set of 30 'priority axes' focused mainly on revitalizing rail transport as a more efficient and environmentally friendly alternative to road and air travel. These axes include:

Trans-European networks: Construction projects aimed at building an integrated European transport, energy supply and telecommunications system.

- the Paris–Brussels–Cologne–Amsterdam–London high-speed rail system
- the Nordic triangle railway/road system
- the so-called 'motorways of the sea' – shipping lanes around the coasts of the EU
- the completion of an inland waterway system from the North Sea to the Black Sea
- a UK/Ireland/Benelux road axis
- high-speed rail links through southwest and eastern Europe.

A European high-speed train network has also been under construction to connect Europe's major cities, with critical links provided by the 1994 opening of the Eurotunnel under the channel between Britain and France, the 1998 opening of a bridge between Sjaelland and Fyn in Denmark, and the 2000 opening of the Øresund Bridge between Denmark and Sweden.

In conjunction with the European Space Agency, the EU is also developing a global navigation satellite system known as Galileo and intended to be an alternative to (although compatible with) the US-operated Global Positioning System (GPS). GPS was developed by the Americans in the 1970s for military purposes (civilian applications came later), and because the US reserves the right to limit its signal strength and even to close public GPS access during times of conflict, there are clear incentives for the EU to develop an alternative. Several non-EU countries have joined the Galileo project, including China, India and South Korea, and there has been talk of Australia, Brazil, Canada, Japan, Mexico, Russia and others joining in the future. The Galileo project was agreed in 2003, but completion has been delayed and the launch of the needed 32 satellites is not now expected to be completed until 2019.

Meanwhile, the pressure for energy supply networks has grown out of plans for a better integrated and interconnected internal market for gas and electricity supply, greater liberalization of that market, and securing the supply of natural gas from Russia. About a quarter of the EU's demand for gas is met by imports from Russia, and much of it comes via pipelines that run through Ukraine. In 2005–06 and again in 2008, disputes broke out when Russia accused Ukraine of falling behind on its payments for gas and diverting some of the gas intended for the EU. When Russia cut the supply, it also meant a reduction in supply to more than a dozen European countries. The disputes accelerated plans to build a supply pipeline direct from Russia to Germany via the Baltic Sea, and another from Russia to the Balkans via the Black Sea. But in the wake of Russian aggression in the Ukraine in 2014, much bigger questions have been asked about the strategic concerns tied to reliance on Russia for gas supplies.

The rise of corporate Europe

Before the Second World War, the capitalist world was dominated by European corporations, their successes often based on preferential access to imperial markets. But the postwar years saw European companies losing market share to competition, first from the US and then from Japan. The new multinationals were more dynamic, invested more in research and development, and had the advantage of large and increasingly wealthy home markets. European business, meanwhile, was typically focused on its own home markets, leading to criticisms that it was nationalistic, hierarchical, conservative and driven less by quantity than by quality. (For a view from the early 1970s, see Brooke and Remmers, 1972, Ch. 6.)

European companies were also discouraged from pursuing corporate mergers or takeovers across state borders by capital gains taxes, double taxation on company profits, different legal systems, differences in regulations and standards, and slow progress on building the common market. Among the mergers that took place in the Community in 1966–69, 59% were between or among

Corporate merger:
An arrangement by which two or more independent companies fuse their assets and liabilities so as to create a single new company. This should be distinguished from a takeover, where the companies involved continue to exist as separate legal entities.

Understanding Integration... *International political economy*

Theoretical debates about the EU have increasingly been influenced by the academic discipline of international political economy (IPE), sometimes labelled 'global political economy' (see Smith et al., 2013). A subfield of political science, which combines an interest in economics and international relations, IPE is a relatively new concept (university courses in IPE were not offered until the 1980s), as a result of which its defining boundaries are still not entirely clear; it overlaps with comparative politics, public policy and international relations. There is general agreement, though, that it focuses on the way in which political actors such as states and institutions influence economic interactions and vice versa. It works to overcome the separation between politics and economics, between states and markets, and between domestic and international factors in understanding economics.

Trade, finance, investment, markets, globalization and development are all topics of interest to scholars of IPE, but regionalism is the primary interest as far as studies of integration are concerned. The topics addressed by IPE include the global economic and political pressures that encourage regionalism, comparison

of the purposes and structures of different regional groupings, variations in the levels of institutionalization, the impact of regionalism on identity, and the impact of regional integration on free trade, the nation-state and the international system (Rosamond, 2000, p. 15). The global financial crisis is a good illustration of the relationship that exists between trade, finance and international institutions, and the difficulties that governments face in managing that relationship.

A topic of particular interest to scholars of the EU has been the tension between economic openness and protectionism. The agenda of European integration has long been topped by the single market and free trade, yet economic nationalism has never entirely gone away, and there has been an ongoing debate about the relative gains and losses of states involved in an open trading system. On the one hand, realists argue that states are the key actors in the international system, they compete with one another, and the pursuit of political power and economic wealth are intimately related. On the other hand, liberals argue that all states gain in some fashion from integration, and the role of states in economic affairs should be kept to a minimum.

companies in the same country, 26% were international (and most of those involved US firms), and just 8% involved companies in two or more Community states (European Commission figures quoted by Layton, 1971, p. 3).

With competitiveness and liberalization moving up the EC agenda in the 1980s, the Commission tried to overcome market fragmentation and wean national governments off their focus on often state-owned 'national champions'. Changes to company laws and regulations made cross-border mergers easier, and the dynamics of the single market increased the pressures for European companies to work harder to profit from new opportunities. They were further encouraged by EC programmes aimed at promoting research in information technology and advanced communications. As a result, there was a surge of takeovers and mergers across European borders, such that the European mergers and acquisitions market is now the biggest in the world. Where once European consumers bought most of their goods and services from companies that were either national, American or Japanese, they now see more businesses coming into their local community from other European states, and many of those businesses have identities that are increasingly European or international. Some of the more notable examples of recent merger and acquisition activities include:

- The string of mergers among British, US and Canadian companies since 1989 that created GlaxoSmithKline, the sixth biggest pharmaceuticals company in the world in 2014.
- The rise of the Dutch company ING, which, in 2014, was the biggest commercial and savings bank in the world.
- The rise of the Belgian-Brazilian company Anheuser-Busch InBev (known as AB InBev), which, in 2008, became the biggest brewing company in the world, with a 25 per cent global market share.
- A string of mergers and cooperative ventures in the energy market, revolving around EDF and GDF Suez in France and E.ON and RWE in Germany, which has raised concerns about competition because these corporations are vertically integrated, in the sense that they generate and transmit energy, helping them keep prices high.
- Efforts by Europe's biggest mobile telecom companies, such as Vodafone, Telefónica, Deutsche Telekom and Hutchison Whampoa, to bring about changes in EU rules that would allow more mergers in a market that is currently divided up among more than 100 service providers. They have argued that only with consolidation will they be able to invest in new networks and technologies and compete against their US and Asian rivals.

One of the more dramatic examples of the building of a pan-European corporation with global reach has been the story of Airbus. Where Britain, France, Germany and other European states long had a history of national success in aircraft manufacture, economic pressures and competition from the Americans forced a string of mergers, takeovers and closures after the Second World War. National manufacturers realized the need to cooperate and the result was the

Illustration **19.2 Airbus**

The European single market has helped encourage the rise of European corporate giants such as Airbus, whose biggest foray into the global aviation market has been the construction of the A380 superjumbo.

creation in 1970 of Airbus Industrie. France, Germany and Britain were the major shareholders, joined in 1971 by Spain. The success of Airbus helped force two major US manufacturers (Lockheed and McDonnell Douglas) out of the civilian aircraft market, leaving a virtual global duopoly today for large aircraft between Airbus and Boeing. The European Aeronautic Defence and Space Company (EADS) was created in 2000 as a result of a merger between Aérospatiale of France, DaimlerChrysler Aerospace of Germany, BAE Systems of Britain (which left the consortium in 2006 and failed in 2012 with efforts to re-merge), and CASA of Spain. As well as being the parent company for Airbus, it also develops and markets military aircraft, communications systems, missiles, and – through its 30 per cent share in Arianespace – space rockets and satellites. EADS was renamed the Airbus Group in 2014.

One of the effects of the recent history of mergers, most of which were encouraged by the pressures and opportunities created by the single market, has been the reclamation of some of the dominant global positions once held by European companies, and lost after the Second World War. In 1969, the *Fortune* magazine list of the world's biggest 400 corporations showed that 238 (nearly 60%) were American, while just 108 (27%) were European. By contrast, the 2010 Fortune Global 500 list of the world's 500 biggest corporations (by revenues) showed that 159 (32%) were based in the EU and 139 (28%) were from the US. Thanks to recession and the rise of competition from China, the EU share of the list had fallen by 2013 (see Figure 19.2), but the corporate landscape was still very different from earlier decades. The 25 biggest corporations in the world in 2013 included Royal Dutch Shell, BP, AXA, Total, Volkswagen and ENI. The sheer size and reach of many European companies has helped them benefit from globalization (Hamilton and Quinlan, 2008).

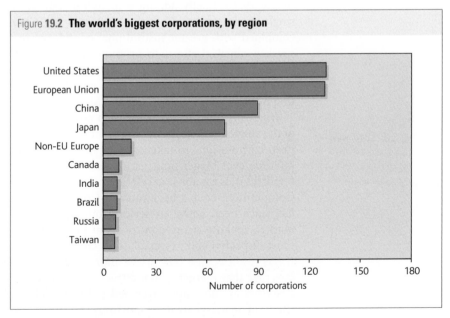

Figure **19.2 The world's biggest corporations, by region**

Source: Fortune magazine data, CNNMoney.com, http://money.cnn.com/magazines/fortune/global500/?iid=G500_fl_header (retrieved April 2014).

Competition policy

Adam Smith, the father of capitalism, once warned that although they seldom met together, people working in the same trade had an inclination to conspire against the public and raise prices. There can never be such a thing as a perfectly free and open market, because there will always be unintentional distortions that give one business or industry advantages over another. But other distortions are more deliberate: a group of businesses may form a cartel to corner and control the market, or reach agreements not to compete with one another. Large companies might try to gain an even larger market share by abusing their dominant position to undermine competitors. A business might monopolize the market altogether, in which case it would be able to raise prices and invest less in product development or good service. And it is not only dominant market share that can lead to distortions; government subsidies, too, can give producers an unfair advantage and lead to skewed patterns of international trade.

Recognizing these problems, the EU – and, more specifically, the European Commission – has long been engaged in efforts to identify and remove barriers to open market competition. For Cini and McGowan (2009, p. 1), its competition policy, while not perfect, has become perhaps the most supranational of all EU policies and something of a flagship for the EU. Unlike many other policy areas, the Commission not only has the power to fine recalcitrant companies, but also has a global reach and can block mergers or impose fines on foreign companies where there are concerns about wider threats to competition.

It took some time for all this to happen, even though the Treaty of Paris included a lengthy outline of the details of ECSC competition policy, the principles of which were carried over in the Treaty of Rome. The Commission focused initially on restrictive practices, then paid more attention to monopoly control in the 1970s, finally adding a focus on state aid and merger controls as the single market took hold in the 1980s and 90s. Changes in the political climate, combined with greater institutional confidence in the European Commission, sparked renewed efforts to promote the liberalization of the single market by preventing abuses such as price-fixing and illegal market-sharing, monitoring state subsidies to corporations, and guarding against abuses of dominant position by bigger companies (Cini and McGowan, 2009; Wilks, 2014).

Ironically, the prospects for such abuses were to grow in large part because of the single market. As we saw earlier in this chapter, it took a while for European corporations to take advantage of the single market, but once they did, building ever bigger multinationals through mergers and acquisitions, so the opportunities for abuse accelerated. The Commission's Directorate-General for Competition, once a backwater of Community administration (Büthe, 2007), has since been active in seeking out and ending attempts to dominate the market, making many controversial decisions but also becoming one of the most respected and powerful of all DGs, enjoying a high degree of discretion. It has also become one of the more well-known DGs, helped by the media coverage that mergers often attract, surrounded by what Wilks (2014, p. 120) describes as sometimes 'frenzied political lobbying' that generates 'theatrical shows of Shakespearean proportions'.

As Harrop (2002) suggests, it is rare to find markets dominated by monopolies, the more common reality being duopolies (where two large corporations have the biggest shares, such as Airbus and Boeing) or oligopolies (where three or more corporations are dominant). The degree of the problems created mounts with the share of the market taken by the biggest corporations, as in the pharmaceuticals, aerospace, motor vehicle and computer markets. Against this background, the three most important aspects of EU competition policy have been the reduction of restrictive practices, the control of mergers, and monitoring the impact of state aid.

Restrictive practices

The Treaty of Rome prohibited business agreements that might interfere with trade between member states by having 'as their object or effect the prevention, restriction, or distortion of competition', and gave the Commission the power to intervene against any abuse of dominant position (Articles 81 and 82). With the completion of the customs union in 1968, cases involving conflict of interest started arriving at the European Court of Justice, which made judgments that helped expand the authority of the Commission, whose caseload grew. It took on IBM in 1980–84 for abuse of dominant position in the computer market, then challenged a wide array of industries for market-sharing agreements, price-fixing, and exclusive purchasing and distribution agreements (Büthe, 2007, pp. 183–4). These are some of the more prominent of its recent decisions:

- In 2001, the Commission imposed an €800 million fine on eight companies accused of running a global cartel aimed at trying to eliminate competition in the market for 12 vitamins.
- In 2003, it charged Japanese electronics company Nintendo with operating an agreement between 1991 and 1998 with seven of its distributors in Europe to maintain high prices for its games consoles and cartridges.
- In 2009, the Commission fined energy giants E.ON and GDF Suez €553 million for a long-standing secret agreement not to compete in the European natural gas market.
- In 2009, a record fine of €1.1 billion was levied on Intel amid charges that it had abused its dominance of the market in computer chips, while Google has been under investigation for similar charges in relation to search engines.

The most notable of the Commission's attempts to deal with allegations of abuse of dominant position relates to Microsoft, which has an estimated 90 per cent share of the global market for computer operating systems. After complaints from competitors that Microsoft was packaging its Media Player brand with Windows and so squeezing out rivals, the Commission ordered Microsoft to offer a version of Windows without Media Player and provide its rivals with information that would allow them to write programs that would work more smoothly on Windows. In March 2004, it imposed a fine of €497 million on Microsoft for abuse of dominant market position.

Microsoft paid the fine and made a version of Windows available without Media Player, but it did not release the necessary information to its rivals. The Commission then imposed a daily fine of €1.5 million on Microsoft, which responded by appealing the original 2004 decision. In 2006, the Commission imposed another fine of €281 million for continued noncompliance. Microsoft finally capitulated in 2007, but the Commission then fined it an additional €899 million in 2008 for failing to comply with the original 2004 ruling, and in 2009 announced that it planned to investigate Microsoft's bundling of its Internet Explorer with Windows.

Mergers

Relatively little was done by the EC in regard to mergers until the effects of the single market began to be more widely felt in the late 1980s, and in 1989 the European Merger Regulation was adopted. If a merger is proposed that exceeds a set sales turnover level, the Commission will investigate and decide whether an opinion is needed. At least in the early years, most mergers were allowed to proceed – only 11 of 140 proposals between 1990 and 1993 were overturned (Harrop, 2002) – but as the number and size of the proposed mergers grew, so did the number of Commission objections. For example:

- The merger in 2003 of pharmaceutical companies Pfizer and Pharmacia was allowed only on condition that they sold or licensed some of their patents, otherwise Pfizer would have controlled large segments of the market.
- A planned 2006 merger between E.ON of Germany and Endesa of Spain was complicated by conditions imposed by the Spanish government designed to create a national champion in the energy sector. The case went to the European Court of Justice, and while E.ON dropped its takeover bid after the Italian company Enel bought a stake in Endesa, Cini and McGowan (2009, p. 153) argue that the case served as warning to any member state that 'might be tempted to prevent flagship companies from falling into foreign hands'.
- In 2007, the proposed takeover by low-cost airline Ryanair of the Irish national airline Aer Lingus was blocked on the grounds that the new airline would have had a near-monopoly of flights in and out of Dublin.

Emphasizing the impact of globalization, the Commission can also block mergers involving companies based outside the EU, as it did most famously in the case of Boeing and McDonnell Douglas in 1997. This move so upset the US government that then Vice President Al Gore threatened a trade war, to which European competition commissioner Karel van Miert responded by threatening heavy fines and the impounding of any Boeing aircraft that entered EU airspace (Cini and McGowan, 2009, p. 158). A compromise was worked out and the merger went ahead, but not so the planned takeover of Honeywell by General Electric in 2001. It was approved by the US government, but the Commission argued that it would have created dominant positions in the markets for the supply of avionics and non-avionics equipment, particularly jet engines. In spite of an angry response from US politicians and media, the takeover was shelved (Reid, 2004, pp. 88–91, 94–105).

State aid

State aid includes subsidies, tax and interest breaks, guarantees, government stakes in companies, grants, contracts and any other agreement or arrangement that gives a company or an industry special advantages. Governments are required to notify the Commission of plans to provide aid, but in most cases the complaints have come from competing firms or other governments (Cini and McGowan, 2009, pp. 170–2). Ironically, the EEC was complicit in one of the most expensive and controversial of all postwar arrangements for state aid: the Common Agricultural Policy.

The provision, measurement and effects of state aid present a different set of challenges to those posed by investigations into restrictive practices and mergers. Unlike mergers and restrictive practices, which usually pit the Commission against private companies, state aid sees the Commission taking on the governments of the member states, making the issue more politically sensitive (Büthe, 2007, p. 189). The issue of state aid has also been vastly complicated by the response of EU governments to the global financial crisis, which included bailouts and assistance to troubled companies, although the Commission did play a moderating role in resisting some of the more extreme suggestions for bailouts.

Summary

- Economic cooperation has long been at the heart of the process of European integration.
- The key elements of economic policy are fiscal and monetary policy, but while member states control the former, they have mainly transferred control of the latter to EU institutions.
- Early progress on the building of the single market was hampered by the persistence of non-tariff barriers, mainly of a physical, technical or fiscal nature.
- While there has been progress since the Single European Act, economic liberalization remains patchy, and the EU was embarrassed by its failure to achieve the goals of the Lisbon Strategy.
- One of the effects of the single market has been an acceleration of corporate mergers and acquisitions across European borders, which has helped European corporations regain some of their prewar global dominance.
- In order to guard against abuse of dominant position, the EU has long had a competition policy focused on the reduction of restrictive practices, the control of mergers, and monitoring the effects of state aid.
- EU competition policy is among the most visible, effective and respected of all policies pursued by the European Commission, and has had implications far beyond the borders of the EU, most notably in the US, where mergers have been blocked and corporations punished for restrictive practices.

Key terms and concepts

Corporate merger

Customs union

Economic liberalization

Europe 2020 strategy

Global financial crisis

Trans-European networks

Further reading

Baldwin, Richard, and Charles Wyplosz (2012) *The Economics of European Integration*, 4th edn (Maidenhead: McGraw-Hill). Introduction to EU economic integration, with separate chapters on related policy areas, ranging from agriculture to trade.

Cini, Michelle, and Lee McGowan (2009) *Competition Policy in the European Union*, 2nd edn (Basingstoke: Palgrave Macmillan). Standard survey of EU competition policy, with chapters on its development, the responsible policy actors and key activities.

El-Agraa, Ali M. (ed.) (2011) *The European Union: Economics and Policies*, 9th edn (Cambridge: Cambridge University Press). Survey of the economic policies of the EU, including chapters on the single market, monetary policy, transport, regional policy, and trade.

20 Inside the Euro Zone

Preview

Although the single market has long been at the top of the agenda of European integration, that market could never be complete and open so long as the member states retained their national currencies: exchange rates fluctuated, costs and profits could never be firmly predicted, and currency conversion meant additional layers of bureaucracy and planning. The creation of a single currency promised to remove all these problems, and would also make European integration felt not just in the pockets and bank accounts of Europeans, but also in global financial markets.

So when the euro was launched in 1999, there were hopes that it would be a major leap forward in the process of integration, offer a visible reminder that Europeans were engaged in a common project, and re-emphasize the strengths of the EU as an international economic actor. But then came the twin blows of the global financial crisis of 2007–10 and the sovereign debt crisis. The latter broke in Greece in 2009 but quickly revealed not just the underlying domestic economic weaknesses of multiple EU member states but also several core design flaws in the euro.

After surviving speculation that some of its members might abandon the euro, and even that the collapse of the euro, and possibly the EU itself, might follow, recovery began. But it did so only after a bitter debate among euro zone members about how best to deal with the crisis and the extension of the authority of the EU institutions to monitor domestic economic policy in the member states. Eighteen EU states now use the euro, and adoption in most of the others is either expected or remains on the political agenda. But questions still remain about the future health and direction of the single currency.

Key issues

- Was moving ahead with the euro a wise choice?
- Would non-euro EU countries be better advised to wait and see, or work more actively to pave the way to joining?
- As the biggest remaining holdout, will Britain benefit or suffer from staying outside the euro zone?
- Could the euro still replace the dollar as the world's leading currency?
- What are the long-term implications of the euro crisis?

Monetary policy

As we saw in Chapter 19, monetary policy is concerned mainly with money supply: the value of a currency, confidence in that currency, and the control of inflation and interest rates. But where such matters are normally managed at a national level, and states have long had a monopoly over the creation and management of currencies, Europeans are now dealing with the world's biggest multinational currency. Because not all EU states have yet adopted the euro and fiscal policy (budgets and taxes) is still mainly controlled by the member states, the euro continues to find itself sailing uncharted waters and faced with policy-making procedures that involve the governments of euro zone states, the European Central Bank (ECB) and the European Commission.

Since its launch in 1999 as an electronic currency, and in 2002 as a cash currency, the euro has changed the daily lives of millions of European consumers and businesses in the euro zone. It has also changed the dynamics of international financial and foreign exchange markets, where it has taken its place alongside the US dollar, the Japanese yen, the British pound and other major international currencies. Its introduction was remarkable, because never before in history had such a large group of sovereign states voluntarily replaced their national currencies with a common currency. Many of those national currencies were deeply entrenched in the histories of their states: the Greek drachma, for example, dated back to classical Greece and more recently to the establishment of the modern Greek state in 1832; the Dutch guilder dated back to the seventeenth century; and the Italian lira dated back to national unification in 1861. The German deutschmark – created in 1948 to replace the Reichsmark – may have been much younger but had become a symbol of West Germany's postwar renaissance, the West German Bundesbank (created in 1957) developing a reputation for independence and helping West Germany to become the region's dominant economy.

Although the creation of the euro was an economic project and the logical partner of the construction of the single market, its significance went further: German Foreign Minister Joschka Fischer (2000) noted that its introduction

> was not only the crowning-point of economic integration, it was also a profoundly political act, because a currency is not just another economic factor but also symbolizes the power of the sovereign who guarantees it.

As well as offering euro zone states a world-class currency that would expand the international financial and political reach of the EU, it also represented the first serious challenge to the global leadership of the US dollar since the latter had displaced the British pound in the 1950s.

As we saw in Chapter 5, stable exchange rates had long been considered an essential prelude to the building of the European single market, most of the early concerns of western European governments being addressed by the Bretton Woods system. Its stabilizing effects through the 1950s and 60s were reflected in the numbers: the British pound remained steady at a value of about $2.80 between 1950 and 1967, while the West German deutschmark ranged modestly between 3.90 and 4.20 to the dollar. Meanwhile, steps were taken towards European monetary cooperation with the signature in 1958 of the European

Monetary Agreement, the convening in 1964 of the Committee of Central Bank Governors, and the 1969 agreement among Community leaders to work towards economic and monetary union. The Werner committee report in 1970 recommended monetary union within ten years, beginning with reduced exchange rate fluctuations, to which end the 'snake in the tunnel' was launched in 1972.

As we also saw in Chapter 5, the viability of the snake was undermined by the 1971 US decision to end convertibility between gold and the US dollar, followed by the energy crises of the 1970s. To complicate matters, there was a philosophical split among EEC governments on how to proceed: 'monetarists' such as Belgium, France and Luxembourg wanted to fix exchange rates as a means to economic convergence, while 'economists' such as the Netherlands and West Germany saw economic convergence leading to the fixing of exchange rates (for details, see Hosli, 2005, pp. 18–21). The monetarist view won out, paving the way for the launch of the European Monetary System (EMS) in 1979, based on an Exchange Rate Mechanism (ERM) intended to encourage exchange rate stability. The EMS encouraged a new focus on monetary policy, paving the way for the introduction of the three-stage Delors plan of 1989, which was confirmed by Maastricht. As we saw in Chapter 6, this set a target of January 1997 for monetary union (later changed to January 1999), and outlined several 'convergence criteria' for states wanting to adopt the currency, including limits on budget deficits, public debt, inflation, interest rates and exchange rate fluctuations.

In 1995 the European Council named the new currency the euro. In 1997 it was decided that 11 member states were ready to begin Stage III of the Delors plan in January 1999, the exceptions being Britain, Denmark and Sweden (which did not want to participate), and Greece (which was not ready). In 1997, at the insistence mainly of Germany, and prompted by concerns about the mixed record of member states in meeting the terms of the convergence criteria, EU leaders signed the Stability and Growth Pact. This obliged them to keep their budget deficits to less than 3 per cent of gross domestic product, placed a 60 per cent limit on government borrowing (Hosli, 2005, pp. 67–9), and allowed the Commission to fine any state in breach of the pact. While supported by most EU leaders in principle, the pact was criticized for being too inflexible, and was described undiplomatically in 2002 by Commission President Romano Prodi as 'stupid'. But the costs of a failure to impose the rules were made only too clear by the case of Greece, which was allowed to adopt the euro in 2001 in spite of its failure to meet the budget deficit target, and went on to so mismanage its economy that in 2009 it set off a debt crisis that rocked the euro to its core.

Stage III of the Delors plan was completed on 1 January 1999 when exchange rates among the participating currencies were permanently locked in place, the ECB took over responsibility for monetary policy in the euro zone, and the euro became available electronically – people could open euro bank accounts, make transfers to other accounts and so on. It became a cash currency in January 2002 when euro coins and banknotes finally replaced national currencies in 12 states (all the EU-15 except Britain, Denmark and Sweden). The euro zone expanded to Slovenia in 2007, Cyprus and Malta in 2008, Slovakia in 2009, Estonia in 2011, Latvia in 2104, and Lithuania in 2015. The euro has also been adopted unofficially in Kosovo and Montenegro, several African countries have pegged their currencies to the euro, and it is increasingly widely accepted in those parts of the world that rely most heavily on European tourism.

Exchange Rate Mechanism (ERM): An arrangement under which member states of the EEC undertook to keep the values of their currencies stable relative to one another.

Stability and Growth Pact: An agreement reached in 1997 by which euro zone governments undertook to control their budget deficits in the interests of currency stability.

Illustration **20.1 The euro**
The creation of the euro was acclaimed by some as one of the most important achievements of integration, from an economic and a political perspective, but was met by others with scepticism bordering on outright opposition.

Following the launch of the euro in 1999, the ERM was transformed from a project to keep EU member states within a band of exchange rate fluctuations to one designed as something of a waiting room to link other EU currencies to the euro. The purpose of this ERM II has been to improve the stability of these currencies and provide a better sense of how potential euro members are faring. Its members are allowed to let their currencies fluctuate within a wide band of ±15 per cent relative to the euro, but can choose to follow narrower bands. Any EU member state can adopt the euro once it has met the convergence criteria and stayed within ERM II for at least two years. With most of its former members now part of the euro club, only Denmark remains within ERM II; it was scheduled to hold a new referendum on euro membership in December 2015, but none of the remaining nine non-euro countries has yet taken the first step of joining ERM II (Alderman, 2014).

The one clear outlier in the debate over the euro has been Britain, where opposition to joining has been clear and constant. British doubts were deeply influenced by the events of Black Wednesday (16 September 1992) when Britain left the ERM following speculation on the pound (see Chapter 6). The Blair government was in favour of joining, but only with a supporting vote in a national referendum that it kept postponing for fear that it would lose. Gordon Brown – then Britain's chancellor of the exchequer (finance minister) – developed his own set of domestic tests of British readiness to join, including convergence between the British and euro zone economies, and the flexibility of business and the workforce. When Brown became prime minister in 2007, he drew unflattering comparisons between growth and unemployment rates in the euro zone and Britain, arguing that domestic policy had helped Britain achieve financial stability and avoid the economic downturn that hit some euro zone states (Buller and Gamble, 2008) (an argument whose ironies became that much clearer as the British economy suffered a downturn during the global financial crisis).

ERM II: A reformed Exchange Rate Mechanism designed to help improve the stability relative to the euro of currencies in EU states outside the euro zone.

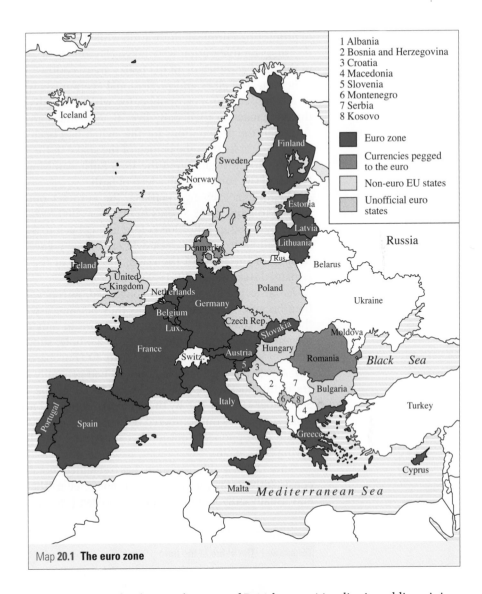

Map **20.1** **The euro zone**

But the most fundamental source of British opposition lies in public opinion: Eurobarometer polls have shown opposition to adoption running at 50–60% (rising to more than 70% in 2014) and support running at about 25–30%. However, national polls have also suggested (at least before the Greek debt crisis) that many Britons might change their mind if the government favoured adoption. The coalition government that took office in May 2010 declared that Britain would not join the euro during its parliamentary term, Prime Minister David Cameron going a step further in 2011 when he said that Britain would 'never' join the euro.

Early responses to the euro

At first, all went well for the euro. Its adoption was driven by political leadership coming mainly out of France and Germany, and had the paradoxical twin effect of promoting European unification while also unleashing new debates about how decisions on integration were taken (Dyson, 2008, p. 3). It also proved to be one of the most complex of all EU policy areas, contrasting the technical opinions of policy-making elites and professional economists with the instinctive reactions of a bemused European public, for which the advent of the euro meant more direct changes in their daily lives than perhaps any other European initiative. Although the preparations for the switch had been carefully made, and can be dated back at least to the launch of the snake in the tunnel in 1972 (but perhaps arguably to the adoption of the 1958 European Monetary Agreement), the final launch of the euro was still a leap of faith.

On foreign exchange markets, the euro set out at a sturdy $1.18, but fell quickly to a low of 82.5 cents in October 2000, regaining ground to a new high of nearly $1.60 in July 2008 before falling back to $1.19 in June 2010 as a result of the fallout from the Greek debt crisis (see Figure 20.1). Since then, and even in spite of the trials of the crisis, the value of the euro against the dollar has remained steady at €1.30–1.40 to the dollar.

As far as public opinion is concerned, Europeans were doubtful at first, but then became more supportive as they became used to the euro. In early 1997 there were majorities in favour of the euro in only eight of the eleven potential member states, and for the EU-15 as a whole, supporters outnumbered opponents by the modest margin of 47 to 40 (Eurobarometer 47, October 1997, p. 28). A year later, favourable opinions had generally strengthened, with supporters outnumbering opponents by 60 to 28 in the EU-15 (Eurobarometer 49, September 1998, p. 45). By the time euro coins and notes went into circulation in 2002, supporters outnumbered opponents by 67 to 25 in the EU-15, and only in Britain did opponents outnumber supporters (by 50 to 31) (Eurobarometer 57, Spring 2002, p. 76).

Since 2006, public opinion has remained notably steady, with a majority consistently in favour, although numbers fell as the euro zone crisis took hold, and usually only about one-third opposed (see Figure 20.2). By member state,

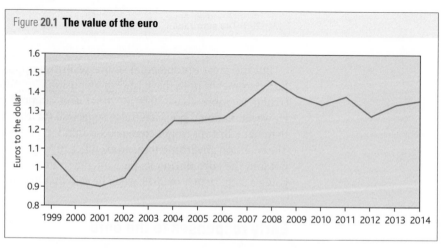

Figure **20.1 The value of the euro**

Note: Exchange rate against US dollar as of the middle of each year.

Source: European Central Bank, www.ecb.int/stats/exchange (retrieved May 2014).

the numbers have been more varied: support in 2014 was strongest in Estonia, Slovenia, Luxembourg, Slovakia, Belgium, the Netherlands, Finland and Germany (all in the range of 75–80% in favour), while opposition was greatest in Sweden, Britain, the Czech Republic and Denmark (all in the range of 66–77% opposed). Even in Greece, with all its problems, supporters of the euro outnumbered opponents by 69 to 29%, and in no euro zone state did opposition outweigh support (Eurobarometer 81, Spring 2014).

The political calculations surrounding the euro – based on a set of often opaquely technical economic and financial considerations – are more complex than the personal calculations of ordinary Europeans, most of whom respond to the euro almost entirely from the perspective of convenience. The most immediate benefit of the euro to consumers is that they can travel to multiple countries without having to exchange currencies or pay fees, and they can more clearly see how prices compare without having to translate them back into their home currency. The existence of the euro has also had an important psychological effect on Europeans, making the foreign seem more familiar, and removing one of the most persistent reminders of the differences among European states. It has also given each euro zone state a more clearly vested interest in the economic welfare of its partners. Finally, the existence of the euro helps businesses, whose transactions are easier to undertake, and who do not have to be concerned about fluctuations in exchange rates.

But there are disadvantages as well, the biggest concern being loss of policy independence. A national currency gives a government (or central banks, at least) a powerful means of managing its economy through adjusting interest rates, which in turn have an effect on inflation and rates of spending and saving. Independent decisions that were once made by the central banks of the euro zone

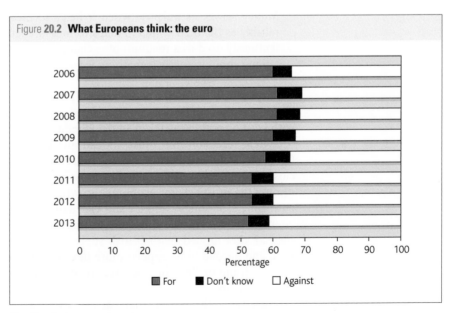

Figure 20.2 **What Europeans think: the euro**

Note: Data for autumn cycles only.

Source: Eurobarometer 81, Spring 2014.

states are now made jointly by those states working within the ECB. And where different countries that had different economic cycles, economic structures and levels of wealth and poverty could once borrow, adjust interest rates and, if necessary, devalue their currencies in response to changed economic circumstances, they must now move in concert with their neighbours. An economic downturn in one (particularly a crisis as dramatic as those that came to Greece and Ireland in 2010) has implications not just for all the other euro states, but even for the global economy.

States adopting the euro must also give up a powerful symbol of national identity and independence. This is true for smaller EU states that have seen their currencies as the last means of exerting some real control over national economies, and is especially true for bigger and wealthier European states with world-class currencies. Consider the case of Germany, where the success of the deutschmark was central to the country's postwar renaissance. Consider also Britain, where national pride explains much of the reticence towards giving up the pound; it is the world's oldest currency still in use (dating back to Anglo-Saxon times), once circulated through much of the British Empire, and was the world's leading international currency for decades. For many Britons, giving up the pound is not just about a loss of economic independence, but would further confirm the decline of Britain's world role. (Some might argue, however, that participation in the euro would actually help increase Britain's global economic influence.)

Crisis strikes the euro zone

Pisani-Ferry (2014, p. 3) argues that currencies should not occupy the centre-stage and that their purpose is to go unnoticed:

> Money serves its purpose when it helps to measure the value of things as reliably as the metric system helps to measure lengths, and when it is unpretentiously used as a medium of exchange and a store of value. If people start talking about it, surely something is going wrong.

Unsurprisingly for such a monumental project, the euro had its teething troubles, the earliest difficulties coming from the challenge that several states faced with keeping within the terms of the Stability and Growth Pact.

When recession hit most industrialized countries in 2002–03, France, Germany, Italy and Portugal either breached the budget deficit limit or came close, and they were soon joined by most other euro zone states, thereby undermining the prospects for economic growth. In November 2003 the two biggest euro zone economies – France and Germany – breached the limits and blocked attempts by EU finance ministers to impose large fines on the two countries. Instead, they argued (with British support) that the rules of the pact were too rigid and needed to be applied more flexibly. By December the pact had all but collapsed, and in 2005 the rules were relaxed in order to make it more achievable and enforceable.

Then came the global financial crisis of 2007–10. The implications of an economic downturn had been anticipated and warned against by some economists, but politics overrode economics, and the recession revealed some of the advantages and disadvantages of monetary union. It particularly showed how far EU states were part of a globalized financial system, where problems in one part could have immediate and sometimes surprising knock-on effects in others. At the same time, the contrasts between Ireland and Iceland gave pause for thought; while the former took some comfort from its membership of the EU and the euro, sharing the costs but also the opportunities, the isolation and vulnerability of Iceland was made clear by a banking crisis in 2008 that sent shockwaves through the Icelandic community and undermined its national currency, the krona. Parties and political leaders that had been lukewarm on EU membership now changed their positions, seeking a haven in European integration, and Iceland lodged its formal application for EU membership in July 2009, although its enthusiasm for the EU has since waned.

After some initial indications of independent national responses to the crisis, EU governments improved their policy coordination. On the monetary front the ECB made interest rate cuts, while calls were made for a complete overhaul of the EU financial system. Then in late 2009 came the most severe test ever faced

---

Focus on... *Explaining the euro crisis, by George Soros*

It is almost impossible to explain the euro zone crisis without causing either bafflement or rebuttal. The needs of the euro were not fully understood from the outset, the rules on membership were often broken, and the ECB was long working with one hand tied behind its back because of the resistance of national governments to give up control over fiscal and tax policy. When the euro's problems began to emerge, the experts differed over how to explain them and what action to take in response. But one of those experts, who has a skill for clarity, is the international financier George Soros (2012), who in early 2012 offered a remarkably clear explanation of the causes of the crisis.

Before the introduction of the euro, Soros argued, poorer EU states such as Greece, Spain and Ireland had to pay more than wealthier members to borrow money, and thus were mainly obliged to live within their means. But the introduction of the euro meant that all euro zone countries could borrow at the same cheaper rate, and banks were quick to lend to the poorer states. While the German economy was doing well, exporting more and becoming more competitive, poorer countries now lived beyond their means, using their new access to cheap credit to buy imports and build houses, while exporting less.

The breaking of the global financial crisis confirmed what many had long known: the economies of the euro zone states were quite different in terms of their structures and possibilities, and lending to one was not the same as lending to another. Once it became clear that poorer euro zone states might have trouble repaying their debts, the interest rates on loans were raised, placing enormous pressure on the banks that had made the loans. Thus, the debt problems of borrower states became intertwined with the problems faced by the banks that had made the loans, which now faced the prospects of insolvency.

It was clearly in German interests to lead a resolution of the problem, because the collapse of the euro would have left it with uncollectable debts and surrounded by countries to which it had exported a great deal, but for which German imports were now much more expensive. The option chosen was to bail out the at-risk euro zone states while demanding austerity (cutbacks in spending) in return. But Soros believes that the authorities did not understand the nature of the euro crisis: they thought of it as a fiscal problem when it was more of a banking and competitiveness problem. And instead of trying to reduce the debt burden by shrinking economies, they should have been trying to grow their way out while working to address the design flaws in the euro. Failing to understand the problem, and unable to see a clear solution, they sought to buy time.

by the euro, and indeed by the EU: the sovereign debt crisis that began in Greece, but which quickly revealed not just that many EU economies were in trouble, but that problems in one promised to have knock-on effects in the others. For Pisani-Ferry (2014), it was the moment when the euro ceased to be boring. Above all, the crisis posed a severe test of the abilities of euro zone leaders to make policy, and threatened to undermine the international credibility of the euro. 'Is Greece's debt trashing the euro?', asked *The New York Times* in February 2010. 'Could Greece kill off the euro?', asked the host of an influential BBC radio news show in May 2010. 'The experiment of a monetary union without political union has failed', argued a commentator in the *Financial Times* in May 2010. 'The EU is thus about to confront a historic choice between integration and disintegration.'

The crisis was a result of a combination of domestic problems in what quickly became known as the PIGS (Portugal, Ireland, Greece and Spain), resistance by Germany to compromise its well-deserved reputation for economic management and success, design flaws in the euro (in particular the inability of the ECB to influence borrowing policies in the member states), and the misfortune of the fallout from the global financial crisis, for which no country was prepared. After months of debate and confused responses to the crisis, with a combination of bailouts and demands for austerity measures, which were in turn followed by complaints that what was needed was growth, not austerity, the euro zone saw the adoption of a stronger Stability and Growth Pact, tighter requirements for balanced budgets, and the creation of new institutions to oversee the European banking sector, securities markets, insurance policyholders and pensions schemes (see Chapter 7).

Opinion on the future of the euro remains divided, the absence of certainty being illustrated by two articles written by American financial experts in 2012. Early in the year, the economist Martin Feldstein (2012) declared unequivocally that 'the euro should now be recognized as an experiment that failed', that its

Illustration **20.2**
The Greek debt crisis
Greek demonstrators protest against austerity measures imposed by their government in the wake of the Greek debt crisis, which posed the most severe challenge yet to the stability of the euro.

failure 'was not an accident or the result of bureaucratic mismanagement but rather the inevitable consequence of imposing a single currency on a very heterogeneous group of countries', and that 'the political goal of creating a harmonious Europe' had also failed. But Feldstein hedged his bets by acknowledging that the euro zone was 'likely to continue with almost all its current members', their challenge now being to change their economic behaviour with balanced budgets and the avoidance of current account deficits.

A few months later, Fred Bergsten (2012) acknowledged the remaining problems of the euro zone, but declared that fears of the collapse of the euro were 'vastly overblown'. The euro zone states had shown that they could and would cooperate to address each stage in the crisis, and had created new institutions and a 'financial firewall to prevent debt problems from spreading'. When the dust had settled, he confidently concluded, the single currency and indeed the entire project of European integration was 'likely not only to survive but to emerge even stronger'.

Debating... *Will the euro thrive?*

YES

The stakes are too great for it not to do so. If the euro struggles, it will undermine the single market and cast unprecedented levels of doubt over the entire exercise of European integration.

The euro zone crisis was at least as much the fault of poor policy choices made by national governments and financial institutions as of problems with the euro itself. The design flaws and the policies pursued by its members have been largely addressed in the wake of the crisis.

Regional integration has always been an exercise in improvisation, driven by frequent crises, but national governments have proved adept at learning from (most of) their mistakes.

The costs for a state opting out of the euro are too great. As well as the immediate expense of converting to a new national currency, there will be numerous longer term costs in the form of reduced investor confidence and currency revaluation.

If the euro is seen as weak, then we have to ask: compared to what? The US dollar remains strong, but US economic policy – with its enormous national debt, trade imbalance and inadequate spending on infrastructure – does not help the dollar, and China is not yet in the position to offer an alternative global currency.

NO

The euro had critical design flaws from the beginning, the most notable being the decision to leave fiscal policy in the hands of the member states. Efforts have been made to fix these problems, but the crisis has shaken the structure of monetary integration, against which must be set the mixed feelings of many Europeans about the euro.

There is still not enough confidence in the ability of euro zone leaders to agree policy or fully understand the implications of the euro's structural faults. The kinds of reforms needed to fully fix the euro are too politically troubling to be accepted by all EU governments and their voters.

The euro zone states continue to have different economic cycles and sometimes different sets of economic policies and priorities, and several suffer high unemployment rates. There can be no 'one-size-fits-all' policies for the euro zone, a problem that is not made easier by the existence of the euro.

A middle-range option is for selected states to leave the euro and the remainder to reformulate themselves as a smaller, deeper and better managed euro zone. So if the old euro zone does not survive in its current form, it might be replaced by a new and sleeker version.

Reserve currency

A reserve currency (or an anchor currency) is a foreign currency held by central banks and other major financial institutions as a means of paying off international debt obligations, or in order to influence domestic exchange rates. Since the 1950s, the US dollar has been the dominant global reserve currency, thanks to a combination of the size and openness of the US marketplace and the pricing of internationally traded commodities in dollars.

The euro as an international currency

Before the shock of the euro zone crisis, speculation had begun to grow in some quarters that the euro had a bright future in store as an international currency, and might pose the first real challenge to the global dominance of the US dollar. For Nobel laureate Robert Mundell (2000, p. 57), the euro promised to 'challenge the status of the dollar and alter the power configuration of the international system'. A 2005 study predicted that if the euro zone continued to expand in size and if US economic policies continued to undermine confidence in the dollar, then the euro could supplant the dollar as the world's leading reserve currency by 2022 (Chinn and Frankel, 2005).

The stability and credibility of a currency depends mainly on three qualities (see Chang, 2009, p. 193):

1 *Its strength as a medium of exchange:* meaning that it can be used to settle international financial transactions.
2 *As a unit of account:* it can be used to invoice foreign trade, anchor exchange rate regimes, or denominate international commodities.
3 *As a store of value:* investors hold deposits and loans in the currency, governments use it as a reserve, and its purchasing power remains reasonably steady over time.

Government and consumer confidence also plays a role: the bigger, wealthier and more open a national economy, the more likely that its currency will circulate internationally, and consumers and businesses will trust and use that currency.

In all senses, the currencies of most advanced capitalist societies are stable and credible, in contrast to those of weaker states whose currencies are often overvalued, have not developed much long-term stability or credibility, and in extreme cases are almost worthless (a problem, for example, that encouraged Zimbabwe in 2009, following years of hyperinflation, to abandon the Zimbabwe dollar and replace it with credible currencies such as the US dollar and the euro). Having a world-leading currency offers many benefits to the state that owns and controls that currency:

- It means political leadership, because the government that controls that currency will inevitably play a major role in international monetary policy decisions, which can be turned to the benefit of its home state.
- Other countries are more likely to hold more of their foreign reserves in that currency, helping it maintain its value.
- There is more chance that key internationally traded commodities such as oil, gold and silver will be denominated in that currency, which means fewer problems for the home state when it comes to buying those commodities; if they are denominated in another currency, the price will fluctuate according to the relative values of the two currencies.
- It makes it easier for a country to run foreign trade deficits, and gives a country the advantage of borrowing in its own currency, making it less hostage to fluctuations in the value of its currency relative to others.

The most telling measure of global monetary influence is the extent to which a currency is used as an anchor or reserve currency, in which governments hold a significant amount of their foreign exchange reserves and products traded in the international marketplace (such as oil and gold) are denominated. During the eighteenth and nineteenth centuries, the British pound was the world's primary reserve currency, its strength underpinned by the size of the British economy and the trade network linking Britain to its empire. But the costs of fighting two world wars, combined with the rise of the US as an economic power, put paid to the dominance of the pound. Underpinned by the size and reach of the US economy and encouraged by the US role as anchor of the Bretton Woods system, during the 1950s the dollar became the world's dominating and most respected currency. Its global leadership continued to be unquestioned until the 1990s, its share of international foreign exchange reserves far exceeding those of the German deutschmark, the British pound, or the Japanese yen.

The launch of the euro changed the nature of the game. Even though two-thirds of international foreign reserves were held in US dollars at the time, the euro took over nearly one-fifth of foreign reserves (thanks mainly to a switch from the deutschmark), since when its share has grown to more than one-quarter (see Figure 20.3). It did this even while holdings in foreign currencies were growing, from $1.4 billion in 1999 to $2.7 billion in 2004, $4.5 billion in 2009, and $6.2 billion in 2013. But after its initial burst of speed, the euro settled onto something of a plateau, holding at about 25 per cent of the share of reserves since 2003, the euro zone crisis having no impact on that share. The role of the dollar continued almost unchanged in spite of the global financial crisis, when the reputation of the US as the home of high-quality and dependable financial assets took a drubbing. It also held despite the rapidly growing US national debt.

Several developments have meanwhile suggested that there is new international interest in seeking an alternative to the US dollar, even if it is not necessarily the euro. Concerns have been driven by the level of influence the US has over inter-

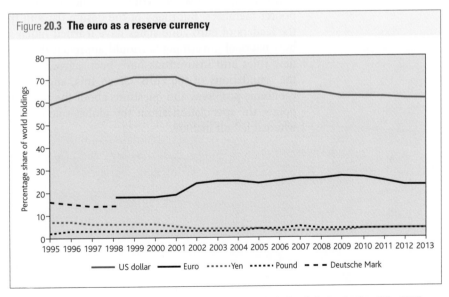

Figure **20.3 The euro as a reserve currency**

Source: International Monetary Fund, www.imf.org/external/np/sta/cofer/eng/index.htm (retrieved May 2014).

national economic policies, but also by the risks that countries such as China are taking in holding large dollar reserves against a background of escalating US debt. Also, as countries trade more with the EU, runs the argument, so they might want to switch more of their foreign reserves into euros. Several countries – including Russia, China and Saudi Arabia – had switched from holding all their foreign reserves in US dollars to using a basket of currencies before the euro zone crisis. There has also been talk in Russia and China of using the Special Drawing Rights made available by the International Monetary Fund since 1969 as an alternative to the US dollar – but these cannot be traded and cannot be used to pay bills. Finally, there has been talk of the development of an Asian currency unit, and even that changes in China might allow the yuan to trade freely on international markets and become a new reserve currency and a lynchpin of world currency markets along with the dollar and the euro (O'Neill, 2010).

Prior to the euro zone crisis, Cohen (2008) argued that the euro suffered several handicaps, the most difficult of which was the lack of clear leadership within the ECB, where decisions are made communally by the Governing Council and the Executive Board, and members may be inclined to think more in terms of national interests than European interests. The president of the ECB had failed to win the same kind of international status and exposure as the chairman of the US Federal Reserve. The failure of the euro to live up to expectations was meanwhile helped by the continuing dominance of the US dollar, helped in turn by the large size and relative stability of the US economy, the established role of the dollar in international markets, and the fact that commodities such as oil and gold are still priced in dollars (Goldberg, 2010).

The euro zone crisis inevitably raised questions about the euro as a global currency, particularly during the more pessimistic days when questions were being asked about countries leaving the euro and its possible collapse. The EU continues to face many economic problems, not least the high unemployment that is a blight on several countries, and the imbalance between its richer and poorer members. But many of the design flaws in the euro have been resolved, the leaders of euro zone states have learned much from the crisis in regard to how national governments should approach their budgets and borrowing, and new rules and institutions have been agreed that are designed to strengthen the foundations of the euro. Given this, and the ongoing concerns about US economic problems and questions about the transparency of Chinese economic policy, the speculation about the global role of the euro is certain to take up where it left off in 2009.

Summary

- The euro was launched in 1999 as an electronic currency, and in 2002 as a cash currency. Its creation was not only an economic act, but also a political act designed to help expand the international financial and political reach of the EU.

- Twelve EU states adopted the euro in 2002, and have since been joined by six more, with expectations that most of the rest (opposition being strongest in Britain, Denmark and Sweden) will eventually follow.

- The euro started out well, with optimistic speculation that it would quickly become a world-class currency. Then came the 2007–10 global financial crisis, when euro zone leaders at first appeared undecided about how to act, before taking ameliorative action. This was followed by the challenge of the sovereign debt crisis that broke in the euro zone in 2009.

- The debt crisis not only revealed the dangers to the euro zone of mismanagement and incompetence in just one member state, but also found euro zone leaders failing to agree on how to respond.

- Immediately on its creation, the euro became the world's second largest reserve currency, leading to speculation that it might pose a serious challenge to the US dollar. But after its share of reserves grew to just over 25 per cent, it appeared to have settled onto something of a plateau, lagging well behind the 60–65 per cent share of the US dollar.

- Questions remain about the long-term prospects of the euro. How will it be impacted by the crisis? Will euro zone leaders learn from their mistakes? How will its weaknesses compare with those of the US, where doubts are growing about the underlying economic stability of the US dollar?

Key terms and concepts

ERM II

Exchange Rate Mechanism

Reserve currency

Stability and Growth Pact

Further reading

Chang, Michelle (2008) *Monetary Integration in the European Union* (Basingstoke: Palgrave Macmillan). Survey of the history behind the euro, monetary policy-making in the EU, and the effects of the euro.

Marsh, David (2011) *The Euro: The Battle for the New Global Currency*, rev. edn (New Haven, CT: Yale University Press). Highly readable study of the history and politics of the euro, based on interviews with an impressive cast of characters.

Pisani-Ferry, Jean (2014) *The Euro Crisis and its Aftermath* (Oxford: Oxford University Press). Story of the fallout from the crisis in the euro zone will continue to evolve, but this is a lively and informative look at how things stood in 2014.

21 Cohesion Policy

Preview

Social and economic inequalities are a fact of life, if for no other reason than because humans have different aspirations and abilities, and economies vary by time and place in the opportunities they provide. Differences in wealth, income and aptitude skew the dynamics of open markets, benefiting some at the cost of others and reducing the free flow of people, money, goods and services. As a result, efforts to remove those differences have long been high on the agenda of European integration.

Cohesion policy is a collective term that describes the efforts made to promote a level economic playing field by creating new opportunities in the poorer parts of the EU: the GDP of the wealthiest EU regions is several times that of the poorest and urban areas are generally wealthier than rural areas, creating disparities that interfere with balanced development. Regional policy tries to address those disparities by investing in job creation and economic growth. Social policy focuses on encouraging free movement of labour, improving living and working conditions, and protecting the rights and benefits of workers. At the core of EU concerns have been the curiously persistent high rates of unemployment in parts of the EU, made worse since 2007 – particularly among younger Europeans – by the effects of the global financial crisis.

Improved social mobility and a more open labour market are, in turn, a function of the portability of educational qualifications. Education policy is still very much the responsibility of the member states, but the Council of Europe and the EU have been behind programmes to establish equivalencies across national borders and encourage Europeans to complete at least part of their education in another member state. Cross-border education also plays a key role in helping build a sense of pan-European identity.

Key issues

- How much can the EU realistically hope to achieve in terms of reducing economic inequalities among its member states?
- Is cohesion better promoted collectively or should there be more emphasis on the use of national resources?
- Is there such a thing as a distinctive European Social Model?
- Why are rates of unemployment as high as they are in parts of the EU but not in others, and what role does integration have in addressing this problem?
- What are the implications of the rise of the Erasmus generation?

The quest for economic equality

Europeans are among the wealthiest people in the world, living mostly in advanced postindustrial societies with diverse economies, a wide array of generous public services, well-developed infrastructure, and a high standard of living when measured by access to education, jobs, housing and disposable income. But economic inequality persists, and levels of income and opportunity vary within EU member states and from one state to another.

Overall, the wealthiest parts of the EU are in the economic heartland running from London to Milan, while the poorest parts are in the eastern, southern and western peripheries. Wealth tends to go hand in hand with education and services, which is partly why Luxembourg – whose economy is based almost entirely on banking and financial services – is one of the wealthiest countries in the world when measured by per capita gross domestic product (GDP). Meanwhile, the tribulations of the EU's marginal areas have different causes: some are depressed agricultural areas; some are declining industrial areas; some are geographically isolated from the opportunities offered by bigger markets; and most suffer lower levels of education and healthcare, as well as underdeveloped infrastructure.

The data illustrate the dimensions of the problem. Using the comparative measure of per capita GDP adjusted to account for purchasing power (how much can be bought with a unit of currency in each member state), Map 21.1 shows that most western European states are at the higher end of the range, and most eastern European states at the lower end. If we express the figure for the whole EU as 100, the per capita GDP of Luxembourg was – at 264 in 2013 – more than five times that of Bulgaria and Romania (47–54), with their larger rural and agricultural populations. The contrasts are even greater when we look at the regions of the member states: while central London in 2013 had a per capita GDP of $81,000 (but was also the most expensive city in the world in which to live) and Brussels was just short of $56,000, Severozapaden in Bulgaria and Nord-Est Romania stood at just $7,200. A related picture is painted by the data for unemployment (see Map 21.2 below).

With such problems in mind, the EU has worked to broaden the provision of economic opportunity. Through what is known as cohesion policy, it tries to strengthen the internal bonds of the European marketplace by supplementing national efforts to reduce regional economic disparities, bringing down the remaining barriers to the single market, and improving the global competitiveness of the EU. In addition to the obvious economic and social benefits of greater opportunity, there is an important psychological element to this: the benefits of integration are made clearer to poorer states benefiting from the new opportunities created by redistribution of wealth, and to richer states capitalizing on the opportunities created by the building of new markets (European Commission, 2007).

The origins of cohesion policy can be traced back to grants made available by the European Coal and Steel Community to help revitalize depressed industrial areas. The Treaty of Rome emphasized the need for the member states to strengthen their economies and 'ensure their harmonious development by reducing the differences existing among the various regions and the backwardness of the less favoured regions'. It also set up a European Social Fund (ESF) designed to help promote worker mobility by supporting retraining and job creation.

Cohesion policy: Policy aimed at redistributing wealth and creating new opportunities in poorer parts of the EU with the goal of closing the income gap.

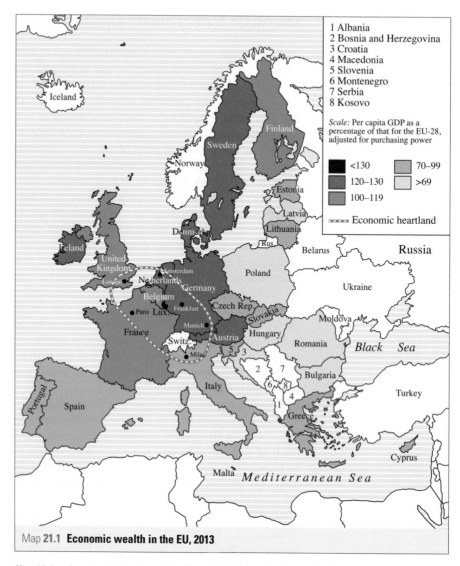

Map **21.1 Economic wealth in the EU, 2013**

Note: Highest figure: Luxembourg, 264, lowest: Bulgaria, 47. Figure for US is 155 and for Japan is 106.

Source: Based on Eurostat figures, http://epp.eurostat.ec.europa.eu (retrieved August 2014).

But because economic disparities among the founding six member states were relatively limited, there was a less than enthusiastic response when in 1969 the Commission proposed a common regional policy, including the creation of a regional development fund.

It was only with the 1973 accession of Britain and Ireland, which widened the economic disparities within the Community, that there was a change of heart. A 1973 Commission-sponsored study (the Thomson Report) argued that regional differences threatened to undermine plans for economic and monetary union, and that they could pose a threat to the common market (Commission of the European Communities, 1973). In response, it was decided to set up the Euro-

Regional policy: Policy aimed at reducing the economic disparities among the regions of the EU, focusing on job creation and economic growth.

pean Regional Development Fund (ERDF) in 1975. Because member states determined which projects would be supported on their home territory, it was more a 'national' policy than a joint European project (Bachtler and Mendez, 2007), and the relatively wealthy regions of richer Community states often received funds when poorer regions in poorer states were in greater obvious need.

The accession of Portugal and Spain in 1986 meant a further widening of regional disparities, added to which there were concerns that the Single European Act (SEA) would result in a greater concentration of wealth in the Community's core economies (McAleavey, 1993, p. 92). These prompted reforms that generated a more genuinely European cohesion policy, with a doubling of spending and more efforts to invest in those parts of the EU most obviously in need. The SEA listed the key goal of strengthening the 'economic and social cohesion' of the Community, since when the term *cohesion* has been used interchangeably with regional and structural policy to describe efforts to bridge economic differences. Another initiative came in 1993 during the negotiations over Maastricht when Spain pushed for the creation of a new Cohesion Fund that would compensate poorer EU states for the costs of tightening their environmental quality standards and investing in improvement of infrastructure.

Eastern enlargement once again changed the nature of the game, bringing in states still suffering from the stultifying effects of decades of Soviet-style central planning and underdevelopment, and further widening the gap between rich and poor parts of the EU. Another round of reforms and adjustments led to the creation of the system that exists today, which is based around five so-called structural funds (see Figure 21.1). Through each, resources are transferred to those parts of the EU most clearly in need of help. Each fund has a different target – whether job creation in inner cities, the retraining of workers, or helping meet the costs of tighter environmental regulation – and eligibility for spending varies according to need.

The EU has also made investments in economic growth through two other funds that, unlike the multi-annual, long-term and strategic qualities of the structural funds, have more focused targets:

- The *Solidarity Fund* (created 2002) supports responses to natural disasters by restoring infrastructure, providing temporary accommodation, funding rescue services, and protecting cultural heritage. By 2014, more than €3.5 billion had been spent from the fund in 23 countries to help alleviate the effects of floods, forest fires, earthquakes, storms and drought.
- The *Globalization Adjustment Fund* (created 2007) helps workers who have lost their jobs as a result of trade liberalization to find new jobs. Most of the help so far has gone to people once employed in the vehicle, mobile phone, furniture, textile and clothing industries. The fund has a budget of €150 million for 2014–20.

In the period 2007–13, a total of nearly €350 billion (or €700 per resident of the EU) was budgeted for the structural funds, and another €325 billion was budgeted for 2014–20. As Figure 21.2 shows, the biggest recipients in per capita and/or absolute terms in 2007–13 were the eastern member states, along with Portugal, Greece and Spain; Estonia received the most in per capita terms (€2,658 per person), while Poland received the most in absolute terms (nearly €67.3 billion, or almost 20 per cent of all structural fund spending). Western

Structural funds: Funds managed by the EU and designed to invest in economic development and job creation in poorer parts of the EU.

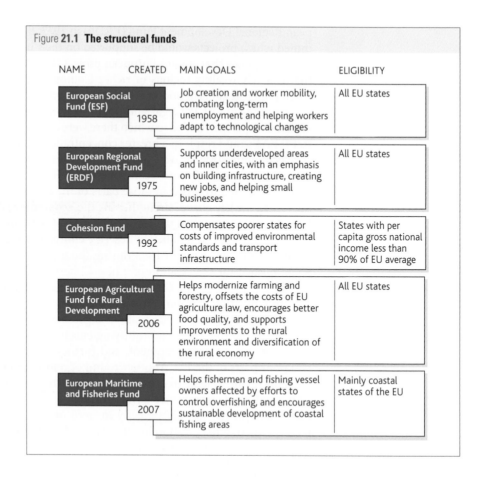

Figure **21.1 The structural funds**

NAME	CREATED	MAIN GOALS	ELIGIBILITY
European Social Fund (ESF)	1958	Job creation and worker mobility, combating long-term unemployment and helping workers adapt to technological changes	All EU states
European Regional Development Fund (ERDF)	1975	Supports underdeveloped areas and inner cities, with an emphasis on building infrastructure, creating new jobs, and helping small businesses	All EU states
Cohesion Fund	1992	Compensates poorer states for costs of improved environmental standards and transport infrastructure	States with per capita gross national income less than 90% of EU average
European Agricultural Fund for Rural Development	2006	Helps modernize farming and forestry, offsets the costs of EU agriculture law, encourages better food quality, and supports improvements to the rural environment and diversification of the rural economy	All EU states
European Maritime and Fisheries Fund	2007	Helps fishermen and fishing vessel owners affected by efforts to control overfishing, and encourages sustainable development of coastal fishing areas	Mainly coastal states of the EU

European states received the least in per capita and absolute terms, the only clear anomalies being Portugal and Greece.

Where once policy priorities were based on dividing the regions of the EU into three categories known as Objectives 1, 2 and 3, they now have different labels but approximately similar goals:

1 The *Convergence Objective* targets regions with a per capita GDP that is less than 75 per cent of the EU average, the goal here being to encourage more investment, new jobs and improved infrastructure. Before eastern enlargement, the Objective 1 regions were mainly on the margins of the EU-15: Greece, southern Italy, Sardinia and Corsica, Spain, Portugal, Ireland, western Scotland, northern Finland and eastern Germany. Except for a few underpopulated areas in Scandinavia, the focus has since moved east, where almost all of eastern Europe now qualifies. The biggest recipients in 2007–13 were Poland, Spain, the Czech Republic, Hungary and Italy. Spending comes out of all three structural funds, and accounts for more than 80 per cent of all EU regional spending.

2 The *Regional Competitiveness and Employment Objective* covers parts of the EU not already covered by the Convergence Objective, and its goal is to make these areas more competitive and more attractive for investment. Funds

come from the ERDF and the ESF, and the biggest recipients in 2007–13 were France, Germany, the UK and Italy.

3 The *Territorial Cooperation Objective* focuses on encouraging cooperation between European regions, and the development of common solutions to the challenges of urban, rural and coastal development. Financed out of the ERDF, it accounted for less than 3 per cent of structural fund spending in 2007–13.

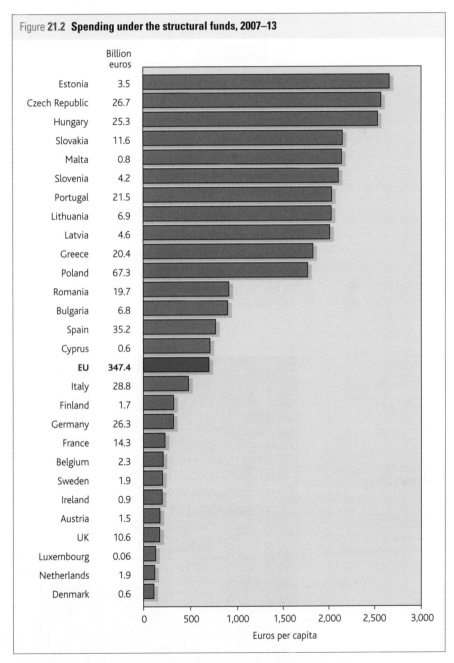

Figure **21.2 Spending under the structural funds, 2007–13**

Sources: Spending totals from European Commission. Per capita figures calculated by author.

Opinion on the effectiveness of spending under the structural funds is divided, mainly because the link between cause and effect in economic matters is difficult to determine. Reducing gaps in wealth and opportunity is as much a function of effective economic policies and changes in the wider economic environment as it is the redistribution of wealth, making it hard to pick out the particular effects of EU spending. In a 2001 review, Pastor (2001, pp. 59–62) argued that EU policy benefited from a clearly defined set of goals and had helped reduce the income gap between rich and poor states, but that there were too many structural funds (creating duplication), policy had tended to generate greater inequalities within poorer states where more prosperous regions had progressed more quickly than less prosperous regions, too big a share of funding had gone to the poorer regions of wealthy states, and while poorer states outperformed richer states during periods of economic growth, they did worse than the EU average during times of recession.

More recently, the effect of the global financial crisis has been to pull EU states in different directions: while the need for more development investment in poorer parts of the EU remains clear, the desire to control spending and budgets has made wealthier governments look more closely at the efficiency of spending patterns. EU funding is intended to complement national spending, but one study (Hagen and Mohl, 2009) suggests that in poorer states in particular it does not result in an increase in national public spending. Questions remain about whether cohesion is better promoted collectively or whether there should be a 'renationalization' of policy through which member states whose GDP is 90 per cent or more of the EU average should use national resources rather than relying on EU assistance, receiving a corresponding reduction in the amount they pay into the EU budget. Unsurprisingly, poorer states oppose this idea, along with the Commission and the European Parliament.

Illustration **21.1**
Cohesion policy

European regional development funds made possible the building of Lisbon's Estação do Oriente as a combined railway/metro/bus station, shopping complex and exhibition site.

Social policy

The quest for economic equality has also meant a debate at the EU level about social policy, covering issues such as improved working and living conditions, and the rights of workers, women and the disabled. The EU's interest in this area is a logical outcome of the postwar histories of welfare promotion in most northern and western European states, and has been part of the single market programme because of the need to ensure equal opportunities and working conditions. At the same time, its efforts have been controversial, pitting supporters in labour unions, the Commission and Parliament against opponents in European business and among conservative political parties. Supporters argue that the opportunities of the single market need to be more equitably spread, while opponents argue that social policy runs the danger of making European companies less competitive in the global market. Questions have also been raised about whether these matters are best dealt with at the national or EU level. The result, concludes Hantrais (2007, pp. 21–2), is that EU activities in the field of social policy have been extended progressively but cautiously.

The Treaty of Rome was based on the hopeful but naive assumption that the single market would help encourage better distribution of resources, allowing the kind of economic growth that would improve life for all European workers. The treaty made provision for the creation of the ESF, but with the political focus in the 1960s on completing the single market and resolving battles over agricultural policy, the movement of workers remained heavily restricted, and market forces failed to address problems such as gender and age discrimination, different wage levels, different levels of unemployment, and improvements in safety and health in the workplace.

The widened economic gap brought on by enlargement in 1973 not only sparked new efforts on regional policy but also pushed social issues back up the agenda (although in a reserved and conditional fashion). In 1974 the first in a series of four-year Social Action Programmes was launched, based on the ambitious goals of achieving full employment, improved living and working conditions, and gender equality. But although there was increased spending under the ESF, with a focus on helping combat long-term unemployment and creating jobs and training schemes for young people, a combination of economic recession and resistance from several Community leaders ensured that words failed to be translated into deeds (Brine, 2002).

Social policy cropped up in the discussions leading up to the SEA, when concerns were raised about worker mobility and social dumping – money, services and businesses moving to those parts of the EU with the lowest wages and social security costs. The Commission tried to focus the attention of national governments on these problems, but further recession ensured more political resistance. In 1987 a new direction was taken when the Belgian presidency of the Council of Ministers suggested that the Community consider developing a charter of basic social rights modelled on Belgium's own new national charter. It also had links with the often overlooked European Social Charter, which was drafted by the Council of Europe, opened for signature in 1961, and addressed many of the same issues.

Hoping to draw more attention to the social consequences of the single market, Commission President Jacques Delors took up the cause of what became

Social policy: Efforts made by the EU to promote equal pay, equal working conditions, gender equality, worker training, and workers' rights.

Social dumping: The process by which businesses cut production costs by moving jobs to countries with weaker labour standards.

| Focus on... *The European Social Model*

There has been much speculation among policy-makers and academics about the qualities and implications of the **European Social Model** (ESM), the features of which (see Giddens, 2006) include support for a developed and interventionist state, a robust welfare system that provides protection for all, efforts to contain inequality, and a key role for unions and related agencies in promoting workers' rights. Tracing its roots back to the postwar economic boom that lasted until the early 1970s, the idea is based on the twin policy goals of sustainable economic growth and improved living and working conditions. It is based, at least in part, on the idea of a contrast with the American model of self-reliance, hard work, and the pursuit of individual prosperity and success. But both 'models' are based, in large part, on mythology and there are troubling questions about their practical realities.

There may have been some uniformity of thinking in the early days of the EEC, but Greece, Portugal and Spain had very different approaches to welfare when they joined the Community, their reliance on family, community and church contrasting with the more universal and tax-funded approaches taken by northern European states. Eastern enlargement later brought in

states still wrestling to move away from the effects of centralized communist government (Hantrais, 2007, pp. 26–7). The contrasting tensions of harmonization and respect for national diversity have since complicated efforts to build a single ESM.

In the early 1990s, the Commission was arguing that while the EU had been unable to achieve many of the goals of the ESM, it could be 'fairly claimed' that nowhere else in the world had so much progress been made (European Commission, 1994). Modernizing the ESM was part of the 2000 Lisbon Strategy to make the EU the most competitive and dynamic knowledge-based economy in the world within a decade. But this target was not met, and those who now question the meaning and prospects of the ESM are easier to find than those who think it is realistic. Marlier et al. (2007) argue that in spite of social spending in the EU, the ESM has been unable to withstand the challenges posed by globalization, and point to the problems posed by high public debts in the member states and the EU's ageing population, high unemployment and low productivity; the ESM, they argue, is unsustainable, and the EU needs to cut social spending and ease business regulation.

European Social Model (ESM):
The notion of a common European approach to social issues, based on an interventionist state, welfare, workers' rights, and efforts to address inequality.

Social Charter: A charter of the social rights of workers, adopted by 11 Community states in 1989 and merged into the treaties by Amsterdam in 1997.

known as the Community Charter of the Fundamental Social Rights of Workers, or, more simply, the Social Charter. But while the moderate conservative West German government was supportive, as were states with socialist governments (such as Greece and Spain), conservative British Prime Minister Margaret Thatcher was enthusiastically opposed. Arguing that it was 'quite inappropriate' for laws on working regulations and welfare benefits to be set at the Community level, she described the document as 'a socialist charter – devised by socialists in the Commission and favoured predominantly by socialist member states' (Thatcher, 1993, p. 750). Undeterred, the other 11 member states adopted the Social Charter at the 1989 Strasbourg summit of the European Council, herald-ing it as the social dimension of the SEA.

The Social Charter brought together all the social policy goals that had been developed by the Community, including the right to freedom of movement, fair remuneration for employment, social protection, freedom of association and collective bargaining, equal treatment, health and safety in the workplace, the protection of children and the handicapped, and a retirement income that allowed a reasonable standard of living. Plans to incorporate the charter into Maastricht were blocked by the government of John Major in Britain, so a compromise was reached whereby it was attached to Maastricht as a protocol (known as the social chapter, and often confused with the Social Charter). Britain was excluded from voting in the Council on social issues, while the other member states formed their own ad hoc Social Community. This example of multi-speed integration ended in 1997 when the new government of Tony Blair committed Britain to the goals of the social protocol, and it was incorporated into the treaties by the Treaty of Amsterdam.

Social policy up to this point was more talk than action, Hantrais (2007, p. 13) arguing that neither the Social Charter nor the social chapter (the Maastricht protocol) signalled 'a strong commitment to social affairs as an objective in its own right, or on a par with economic union'. On specific matters of policy, family issues have been almost entirely excluded, opinion is divided about the impact that EU policy has had on women's rights (particularly equal access to employment), the work of the EU has focused more on awareness-raising than hard policy initiatives, and poverty remains a problem across the EU in spite of the opportunities that were supposed to have been created by the single market.

If one issue has dominated the debate on social policy, it has been the failure of the European marketplace to help reduce the often high rates of unemployment in the EU. Employment levels were high in the 1960s, but then came the recession and energy shocks of the 1970s, causing a steady loss of jobs. By the late 1990s, while the number of unemployed hovered around 5% in the US and 4% in Japan, it ranged from a low of 4–6% in the Netherlands, Britain and Sweden, to 11–12% in Germany, France and Italy, and a high of nearly 19% in Spain (*The Economist*, various issues, late 1998). By 2007 the European figures had improved slightly, but were still not impressive: the euro zone was running at 7.1%, compared to a healthy 4.5% in the US (*The Economist*, various issues, late 1998).

Then came the global financial crisis, which led to job losses throughout the liberal democratic world, a problem made worse by the euro zone crisis. Greece and Spain have suffered the most, their unemployment rates in mid-2014 topping 25% (see Map 21.2). Even more worrying for both countries has been the high levels of unemployment among people aged under 25: the figure in Spain reached a new record of nearly 58% in early 2014, overtaking the Greek figure of nearly 55%. This led to worried speculation about political radicalization and the prospects of a lost generation, and much of the ire of the unemployed was directed at EU austerity measures. In the case of Spain, much of the problem stemmed from the collapse in 2008–10 of the housing market, many of the newly jobless having worked in the construction industry. Job protection also makes it difficult to move workers from one market sector to another.

Why EU rates were so high even before the global financial crisis is debatable, and numerous explanatory factors have been suggested:

1. The large number of European workers (about one-third of the workforce, by some estimates) who lack skills and have few or no formal qualifications, making them less employable.
2. While millions of new jobs have been created in the EU in the past two decades, nearly half have been temporary or part-time jobs, and many are in the service sector. Because men and women new to the job market are filling many of these jobs, their creation has done little to help ease long-term unemployment.

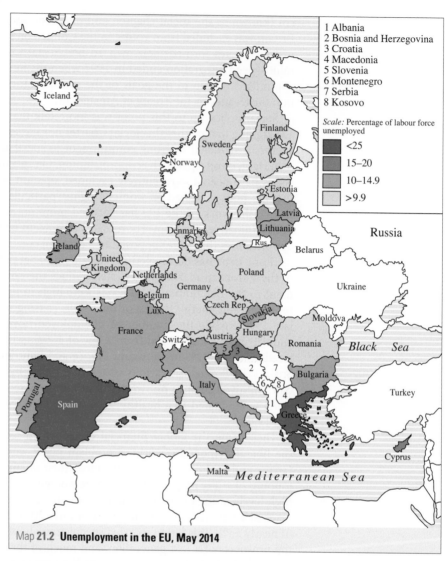

Map **21.2 Unemployment in the EU, May 2014**

Note: Highest figure: Greece, 27.5, lowest: Austria, 4.8. Figure for EU-28: 10.2. Figure for US was 6.3 and for Japan 3.5.

Source: Based on Eurostat figures, http://epp.eurostat.ec.europa.eu (retrieved August 2014).

3 While EU laws have given workers stronger protection against dismissal than is the case in the US, they have also slowed down the creation of new jobs.

4 Short-term trends have made the problem worse, including the erosion of exports and investments in the wake of the global economic crisis, and job cuts in industries that have suffered the effects of the economic downturn.

The Treaty of Amsterdam introduced an employment chapter that left competence for employment policy in the hands of member states but also called on them to develop a coordinated employment strategy. Amsterdam acknowledged that employment was a matter of shared concern for all member states, and set up a system under which information on national employment policies could be shared. It also obliged the EU and the member states to work towards a coordinated strategic approach to employment, and when the European Council met in Luxembourg in November 1997, employment was the sole item on the agenda. The outcome was the launch of a European Employment Strategy (EES, also known as the Luxembourg Process) designed to encourage cooperation on national employment policies through the open method of coordination. Full employment was one of the core goals of the Lisbon Strategy, but a mid-term review of the EES in 2005 was sidelined by growing doubts over the efficacy of the Lisbon Strategy; these were, it later turned out, but a preview of the disorder into which EU economic and employment policies were thrown by the effects of the global financial crisis.

Education policy

It was understood from the early days of the EEC that a true single market demanded an open labour market, but although the Treaty of Rome set the goal of free movement of people, this was subject 'to limitations justified on grounds of public policy, public security or public health'. Because the movement of workers was initially seen in terms of filling economic need, free movement was available only to those who were economically active, and governments discouraged skilled workers from leaving for other countries. As part of the package, education was mentioned in the Treaty of Rome only in connection with the need to develop principles for a common policy on vocational training. It would not be until the era of the SEA in the 1980s, when the issue of free movement moved to the top of the political agenda, that new attention was paid to the importance of educational mobility. Although today there is still no formal EU education policy as such, Walkenhorst (2008) argues that EU initiatives amount to a de facto European policy.

Community activities began in 1987 with the launch of Comett, a programme designed to encourage contacts and exchanges between universities and industry. This was accompanied by Erasmus, named for the sixteenth-century Dutch humanist and priest, and designed to encourage inter-university cooperation. It was followed in 1995 by Socrates, designed to encourage students in higher education to study in different countries, promote cooperation among European universities, and support the recognition of diplomas and courses across borders. This was succeeded in 2000 by Socrates II, which was succeeded in 2007 by the Lifelong Learning Programme. The EU is also interested in education in other parts of the world: Tempus was launched in 1990 to provide support to higher education in eastern Europe (expanding to Central Asia, North Africa and the Middle East), while Erasmus Mundus was launched in 2003 to help bring foreign students and academic staff to Europe and support partnerships between European and non-European universities. In 2014, all the existing EU programmes were brought together under the new Erasmus+, designed to streamline EU policy, to run until 2020, and spend almost €15 billion on education at all levels.

At the heart of EU education policy have been the Lisbon Strategy and the Bologna Process. The Lisbon Strategy gave a boost to the EU's educational activities, with efforts to recycle or update old initiatives and launch new ones, all with the object of helping promote competitiveness, and encouraged in part

Education policy: Policy focused on encouraging cross-border mobility of students and staff, and educational cooperation among the member states.

Bologna Process: An agreement among European states (not limited to the EU) under which requirements for higher education qualifications have been standardized, increasing their transferability.

by the globalization of education (Walkenhorst, 2008). As a result, students and academic staff are more mobile than ever before, encouraged by increased opportunities for study abroad and educational exchanges. The EU is the most popular target for these students, according to UNESCO data: of the approximately 4 million students studying abroad in 2012, almost half were studying in Europe, while 18 per cent were studying in the US. Within the EU, the most popular destinations are Britain, France and Germany (see Figure 21.3).

In 2002 the education ministers of the member states agreed a ten-year work programme based on the open method of coordination. For Walkenhorst (2008), the approach reflects 'a general tendency in EU politics towards more flexibility and away from formal supranational regulation', and has the effect of moving 'the locus of policy coordination away from Brussels to national capitals and EU summits, thereby returning member states to the centre of policy-shaping'. This approach carried over into the Europe 2020 strategy (see Chapter 19), which listed education as one of its five major priorities, and was guided by a strategic framework on education agreed in 2009 based on five benchmarks, including reducing the number of pupils leaving school early, increasing the number of graduates in maths and science, and increasing the participation of adults in lifelong learning.

As for the Bologna Process, the focus here has been on the transferability of educational qualifications across borders. The Commission at first tried plodding through one profession at a time, generating, after years of debate, about 60 separate pieces of Community law dealing with doctors, nurses, dentists, vets, midwives, lawyers, architects and pharmacists (Hantrais, 2007, pp. 55–6). For example, it took 17 years of negotiations to reach agreement on

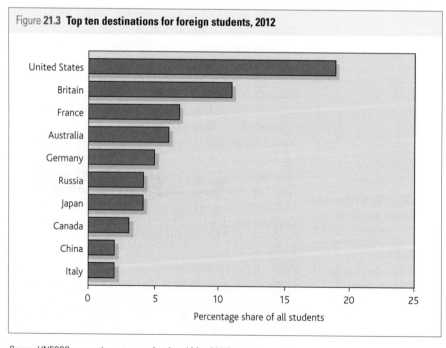

Figure **21.3 Top ten destinations for foreign students, 2012**

Source: UNESCO, www.uis.unesco.org (retrieved May 2014).

standards for architects alone. Mutual recognition has since taken over as the guiding principle, and the only remaining distinction is between the freedom to provide services and the freedom of establishment – any EU national who legally provides services in one state can do so temporarily or occasionally in another without having to apply for recognition of their qualifications, although they may be asked to provide proof of those qualifications, and show language ability. Where someone wants to live and work permanently in another state, they must show proof that their training is at a level equivalent to that required in the new state.

Another problem was created by different ideas in different states about the requirements for higher education: qualifications came in many different guises, with different names, and requiring varying amounts of time and different courses of study. For example, while the equivalent of a bachelor's degree could be earned in Britain and Ireland in three years, on the continent this could take as long as five to eight years. Not only did this place greater pressures on continental students, but there was little agreement among different states on how qualifications from one would be translated or understood in another.

With this dilemma in mind, the Lisbon Recognition Convention was drafted by the Council of Europe and signed in 1997, establishing that university degrees and related qualifications must be recognized by members unless substantial differences can be identified and proven. Two years later, a declaration was signed in Bologna by education ministers from 29 countries proposing a European Higher Education Area, within which university education would be comparable and transferable, and students and academic staff could move freely in order to pursue a job or undertake more study, which would help make European higher education more attractive and internationally competitive.

Although the Bologna Process was born as a means of standardizing credits, it has expanded to make sweeping changes to curricula in Europe. And although it

Illustration **21.2**
Education policy

Thanks to efforts by the Commission to promote educational exchanges, European students now find it easier to study at universities outside their home state and have their qualifications recognized across state borders.

is more a pan-European agreement than an EU initiative, reaching now to nearly 50 countries, it has become a core part of EU education policy. Its major effect has been agreement on three cycles of higher education qualifications, based on comparable numbers of credits under the European Credit Transfer and Accumulation System (ECTS). One year of study equates to 60 ECTS credits, or about 1,500–1,800 hours of study, and university degrees are organized according to the 1-2-3 cycle:

- The first cycle of 180–240 ECTS will usually lead to the award of a bachelor's degree, or equivalent, over three years.
- The second cycle of 90–120 ECTS will usually lead to the award of a master's degree, or equivalent, over two years.
- The third cycle, for which there is no specific ECTS range, will lead to the award of a doctoral degree, over three years.

The ECTS system, which was launched as a six-year pilot programme in 1992 under the EC's Eramus programme, has since evolved from a credit transfer to a credit accumulation system. Although degrees can still retain their different names, most EU member states have switched to a system based on equivalents of the bachelor's degree: so, for example, Italy has converted its four- to six-year *laurea* into a three-year undergraduate *laurea triennale* and a postgraduate *laurea magistrale*, and Austria's *Magister* and *Diplom* have been replaced with a *Bakkalaureus*. The ECTS system has not only encouraged curricular changes in the EU member states, thereby helping build a European higher education area, but has also had an impact internationally: non-European students find it easier and more attractive to study in Europe, and the US has had to pay closer attention to European developments because of the large transatlantic traffic in students (Roper, 2007).

One of the effects of EU policy has been the rise of the Erasmus generation. Erasmus has allowed students and academic staff to study and work in universities outside their home countries, encouraged cooperation between European institutions of higher education, and was later joined by Erasmus Mundus, aimed at helping encourage the globalization of European education. Under Erasmus, about 250,000 European students per year are able to live and study in other European countries for periods of at least three months (see Figure 21.4), encouraging them to learn new languages but also to learn more about the culture of other European countries. Nearly 3 million students had taken advantage of Erasmus by 2013, spearheading the development of a new kind of European: mainly younger, better educated and more cosmopolitan, with a heightened sense of European identity. Members of the Erasmus generation travel, are multilingual, make friends across borders and marry citizens of other European states, and take a more inclusive view of themselves in their political and social environment.

Among the most telling practical and psychological barriers to free movement across borders is language: monolingualism not only discourages migration but also poses a handicap to multinational businesses by making it more difficult to build exports, and stands as a potent reminder to Europeans of their differences, making it more difficult to understand the way other European societies think and work. The EU does not just have its 24 official languages (see Chapter 3), but

Erasmus generation: Students who have participated in the EU's Erasmus educational exchange programme since 1987, and are seen as leaders in the effort to build a sense of European identity.

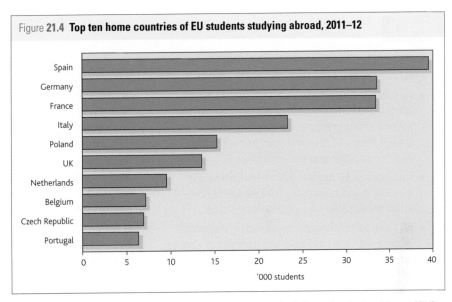

Figure **21.4** **Top ten home countries of EU students studying abroad, 2011–12**

Source: Erasmus+ website, http://ec.europa.eu/programmes/erasmus-plus/index_en.htm (retrieved August 2014).

also many local languages, dozens of dialects, languages spoken by new immigrants from outside Europe, and languages spoken by non-EU European states.

Language training has improved, with almost all secondary school pupils in the EU now required to learn at least one foreign language, and more states requiring two languages, but the record in real language ability is patchy and skills vary substantially from one language to another and from one state to another. English is by far the preferred language of study, being taught to 95% of upper secondary pupils in the EU-27 compared to the 27% learning German, the 26% learning French, and the 19% learning Spanish (Eurostat press release, 26 September 2011). English has become all but a second national language in the Netherlands and the Scandinavian states, and its role as the lingua franca of Europe is being strengthened by its steady rise as the international language of diplomacy, commerce and entertainment. This unfortunately encourages the linguistic laziness of the British and the Irish, and worries the French and increasingly the Germans as they work to stop the infiltration of English words and phrases into their languages.

Summary

- Levels of income and economic opportunity vary within EU member states and from one state to another.

- EU cohesion policy works to strengthen the internal bonds of the European marketplace by supplementing national efforts to reduce economic disparities, mainly through the use of structural funds that redistribute wealth from richer to poorer parts of the EU.

- The effects of EU regional policy have been hard to measure, in part because the links between cause, effect and response are so difficult to measure.

- EU social policy addresses issues such as improved working and living conditions, and the rights of workers, women and the disabled.

- Although the Treaty of Rome referred to the need to improve working conditions and raise the standard of living, most early Community initiatives in this area were more rhetorical than practical.

- The idea of a European Social Model has been more aspirational than actual, although the approaches of northwestern, southern and eastern states have achieved closer uniformity with time.

- One problem that European policy has so far been unable to address has been the persistence of high levels of unemployment in many parts of the EU, a problem made much worse by the effects of the global financial and euro zone crises.

- Initially in the interests of promoting the free movement of workers, since the late 1980s the EU has been increasingly active in efforts to promote mobility in education.

- One of the effects has been the rise of the Erasmus generation, a group of mainly younger, better educated and more cosmopolitan Europeans with a heightened sense of pan-European identity.

Key terms and concepts

Bologna Process

Cohesion policy

Education policy

Erasmus generation

European Social Model

Regional policy

Social Charter

Social dumping

Social policy

Structural funds

Further reading

Baun, Michael, and Dan Marek (2014) *Cohesion Policy in the European Union* (Basingstoke: Palgrave Macmillan). Bachtler, John, Carlos Mendez and Fiona Wishlade (2013) *EU Cohesion Policy and European Integration* (Farnham: Ashgate). Two surveys of cohesion policy, looking at its history, content and the debate over its effects.

Corbett, Anne (2005) *Universities and the Europe of Knowledge* (Basingstoke: Palgrave Macmillan). One of the surprisingly few studies of education policy in the EU, with a focus on its history rather than its results.

Hantrais, Linda (2007) *Social Policy in the European Union*, 3rd edn (Basingstoke: Palgrave Macmillan). Looks at social policy in the EU, its role in setting a European social policy agenda, and its impact on national welfare systems.

22 Managing Resources

Agriculture was long a headline issue in EU politics. It was one of the few policies listed in the Treaty of Rome, and for decades the Common Agricultural Policy (CAP) topped the EC/EU budget. But while spending on agriculture helped encourage greater production, contributing to the end of food shortages and providing essential investments in western Europe's rural communities, it also created several problems: it distorted markets, diverted resources away from other priorities, and created tensions with the EU's trading partners. Attempts to reform agricultural policies were long resisted by western European farmers, but enlargement combined with the pressures of international trade regimes to force changes to agricultural policy, which has since moved down the EU agenda.

The contrasts offered by environmental policy could not be clearer. Environmental issues did not appear on the European policy agenda until the late 1960s, and even then the response was not particularly strategic. It was only as public and political support for environmental management began to build in the late 1970s and early 1980s that environmental policy drew more attention, since when the focus of policy-making in the EU has shifted away from the member states.

The underlying logic has been twofold: different environmental standards stand as a barrier to the single market, and most environmental problems – particularly those relating to air pollution, water pollution and the disposal of waste – are better addressed by states working together rather than in isolation. EU policy has helped transform Europe from a region that was once a policy laggard to one that in many respects has set global standards for environmental management. On the headline problem of climate change, though, while the EU has a well-developed climate change programme, it has failed to have the international impact that many had hoped for.

Key issues

- Why has agriculture traditionally been so prominent a part of the EU policy agenda?
- What does the approach to reforming the CAP say about the nature of policy-making in the EU more generally?
- What is the most effective potential response to dealing with the problem of overfishing?
- What are the costs and benefits of addressing environmental policy needs at the European level rather than at the member state level?
- Has the EU become a global environmental leader? If so, what explains its new role?

Agricultural policy

Agriculture is one of the most fundamental areas of public policy, because without guaranteed supplies of adequate nutrition, much else about our lives is moot. Because agriculture was long ago superseded as the base of liberal democratic economies by industry and services, it contributes little to jobs and wealth, and so is not often a leading political issue; although this is truer today in western European states than in eastern states such as Poland, Romania and Bulgaria, with their relatively large agricultural populations. Yet despite its marginal role in national politics, agricultural policy continues to rank high on the agenda of European integration. The explanation for this lies mainly in the years following the Second World War.

Farming played a key role in western European economies after the war, accounting in 1950 for 12–15% of the GDP of West Germany, France and the Netherlands, and nearly 30% of the GDP of Italy. It was also a large employer, accounting for 44%, 31% and 23% respectively of the workforces of Italy, France and West Germany (see Figure 22.1). The memories of postwar food shortages and rationing were still fresh in the minds of many Europeans, and there were concerns that because food prices fluctuated so much on the international market, and because these fluctuations could have a knock-on effect on inflation (if prices went up) or on jobs and debt (if prices went down), subsidies would be needed to offset the problems and encourage people to stay in the rural areas.

It was against this background that representatives of the six EEC founding states met in Stresa, Italy, in July 1958, and negotiated the details of what would become the Common Agricultural Policy (CAP) of the EEC. They agreed three principles:

- a single market in agricultural produce
- 'Community preference' – a coded term for protectionism aimed at giving Community produce priority over imported produce
- joint financing – the costs of the CAP would be met by the Community rather than by individual member states.

So strong were the interests of the member states that agriculture became one of only five policies listed in the Treaty of Rome – the others being trade, transport, competition and the single market.

The CAP had several goals:

- to increase agricultural productivity, thereby encouraging a 'fair' standard of living for those working in agriculture
- to stabilize markets
- to assure supplies
- to ensure reasonable prices for consumers.

These goals would be achieved mainly through guaranteed minimum prices for EEC farmers, regardless of how much they produced and how much the market could bear. So while much of what the EEC was to achieve on the economic front would be based on encouraging competition and free trade, on the agricultural front it pursued policies that were protectionist, interventionist and anti-market, which insulated a critical economic sector from competitive forces.

Agricultural policy: Policy dealing with the production and distribution of food, with a focus on supply, prices, quality, land use, trade and employment.

Common Agricultural Policy (CAP): One of the oldest and most controversial of EU policies, based at first on a system of price supports for farmers, but later reformed.

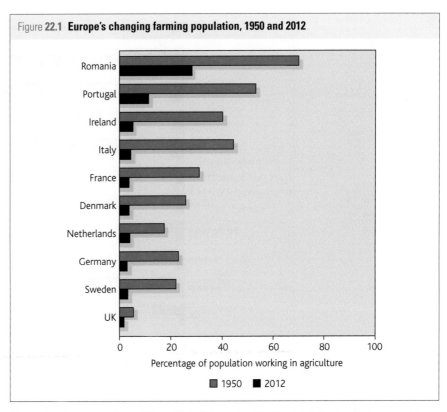

Figure **22.1 Europe's changing farming population, 1950 and 2012**

Percentage of population working in agriculture

■ 1950 ■ 2012

Sources: 1950 figures from Rieger, 2005, p. 163. 2012 figures from World Bank, http://data.worldbank.org (retrieved April 2014).

The long-term result of the CAP was a dramatic growth in agricultural productivity, although much of this might have happened anyway because of technological breakthroughs and greater efficiency. But these achievements came at the cost of soaking up much EEC spending, and drew criticism not just from the member states but also from major trading partners such as the US and the governments of developing countries whose farmers could not compete with EEC prices. By 1990, *The Economist* (1990) spoke for many of the critics of the CAP when it described EU agricultural policy as 'the single most idiotic system of economic mismanagement' ever devised by rich western countries. And the system persisted even as agriculture played a declining role in European economies: down by the year 2000 to less than 3 per cent of GDP in almost every European state except some of those in the east (see Figure 22.2).

How was this system sustained? At the heart of any discussion of the CAP lie the peculiar interests of France, where agriculture was a bigger postwar employer and producer of economic wealth than in any of the EEC six but Italy. Although France was a critical actor in the early agreements on European integration, domestic political and public support was thin, so it had to be shown that integration offered France clear benefits. French farmers enjoyed their own system of national subsidies, which by the late 1950s was helping generate large surpluses, for which export markets were needed. For its part, West Germany

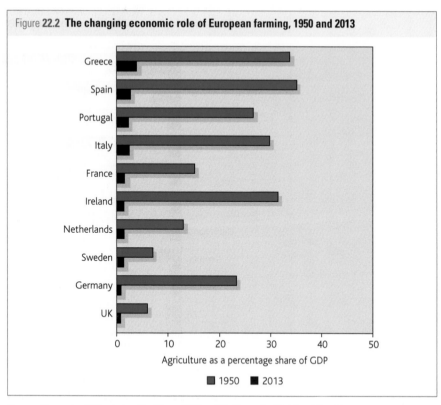

Figure **22.2** **The changing economic role of European farming, 1950 and 2013**

Sources: Figures for 1950 calculated by Rieger, 2005, p. 163. Figures for 2013 from World Bank, www.worldbank. com (retrieved August 2014).

had food shortages, but was importing from countries other than France because prices were lower. The Germans resisted a protectionist CAP, and were more interested in the customs union because of the benefits it promised to German industry, but Charles de Gaulle made progress on the customs union conditional on his having his way with the CAP, and was able to wrest an agreement from the Germans on its key principles in early 1962 (Dinan, 2014, pp. 100–3).

France continued to be the driving force in EU agricultural policy even after the terms of the CAP were agreed. The French farming population fell between 1950 and 2000 from nearly 31% to just 3.4% of the total, while the share of agriculture in GDP fell over the same period from 15% to just over 2%. But French farmers had a strong domestic political role, enhanced by the number of people who live in the rural areas of France (and are thus economically impacted by farming), and by the semi-mythical role that the rural areas have long played in the French national psyche.

More than one-fifth of EU agricultural production continues to come from France, which also takes the biggest share of EU farm spending – about one-sixth in 2010. The French government lobbies the EU on behalf of its farmers, and any threats to their interests are likely to bring French farmers out in organized protests ranging from mass demonstrations to letting cattle loose in local government buildings, blocking highways with tractors, and dumping farm waste on Parisian avenues. But the political influence of farming is declining:

many small farmers live in poverty, thousands leave the land every year to look for other work, and the French farm lobby has been unable to stop reforms to EU agricultural policy.

For its first quarter century, the CAP was a system of agricultural price supports (Burrell, 2009). Every year, representatives of the Commission, the Council of Ministers and farmers unions negotiated three kinds of prices for agricultural products (Grant, 1997, p. 67):

1 A *target price* that they hoped farmers would receive on the open market as a fair return on their investments.
2 A *threshold price* to which EU imports would be raised to ensure that target prices were not undercut.
3 A *guaranteed price* that would be paid as a last resort to take produce off the market if it was not meeting the target price.

For example, the target price for wheat in 1990 was 234 ecus per tonne, the threshold price was 229 ecus, and the guaranteed price was 172 ecus (Swinbank, 2002, p. 166). The costs of this system were borne by the European Agricultural Guidance and Guarantee Fund (EAGGF), which was created in 1962 and rapidly became the single biggest item on the Community budget; by 1970, agriculture was absorbing 75 per cent of Community spending. The Guidance section was used to improve agriculture by investing in new equipment and technology, while the Guarantee section (which accounted for most of the spending) protected markets and prices by buying and storing surplus produce and encouraging agricultural exports.

In some respects, the CAP was a success. Western European agricultural production grew in leaps and bounds; not only did the Community become self-sufficient in almost every product it could grow or produce in its climate, including wheat, barley, wine, meat, vegetables and dairy products, but today's

Illustration **22.1**
Demonstrating French farmers

Agriculture has long been a core public issue in France, such that attempts to reform the Common Agricultural Policy will often spark demonstrations by French farmers.

EU is a global agricultural trading powerhouse. In 2011 it accounted for nearly 38 per cent of the world's agricultural imports and exports, worth $626 billion, although only about a quarter of its trade was with states outside the EU (see Figure 22.3). Duplication was reduced as member states specialized in different products, the CAP helped make most farmers wealthier and their livelihoods more predictable and stable, and the bad old days of food shortages disappeared. But in other respects, the CAP was less successful.

First, spending grew as improvements in agricultural technology helped farmers produce more food from less land, with the result that the supply of commodities such as butter, cereals, beef and sugar exceeded demand. The Community was obliged to buy the surplus, some of which was stored in warehouses, prompting jibes in the media about 'butter mountains' and 'wine lakes' (and jokes about visitors to Brussels stepping off the train and asking for directions to these mountains and lakes). Some of the excess was destroyed or converted, hence wine might be turned into spirits or even into heating fuel, but the rest was sold cheaply outside the Community or given away (dumped) as food aid to poorer countries. This undercut local farmers, distorted the international marketplace, and soured Community relations with the US; even though the latter also subsidized its farmers and engaged in similar dumping. At the same time, the rules of the EAGGF were so convoluted that they were easy to exploit, encouraging farmers and suppliers to inflate their production figures and make fraudulent claims (Laffan, 1997, pp. 207–10).

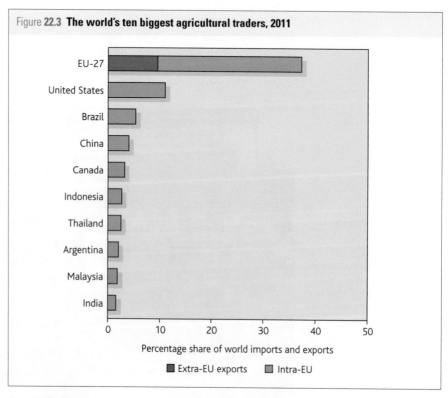

Figure 22.3 **The world's ten biggest agricultural traders, 2011**

Percentage share of world imports and exports

■ Extra-EU exports ■ Intra-EU

Source: WTO, 2014.

As if these problems were not enough, environmentalists complained that the artificially high prices encouraged farmers to increase production by using chemical fertilizers and herbicides, and to cut down hedges and trees and 'reclaim' ecologically important wetlands so as to make their farms bigger and more efficient. The price of food for consumers was inflated, and the sight of excess production and increased spending on the CAP did little to encourage public support for European integration. The CAP also failed to close the income gap between rich and poor farmers: about 70% of spending went to 20% of farms, which were typically the biggest and wealthiest farms in northern Europe, while small farms – accounting for 40% of the Community total and often in the south – received only 8% of funds. Under the circumstances, the case for reform was clear, but most suggestions came up against the resistance of farming lobbies and the governments over which they had the most influence (Dinan and Camhis, 2004).

The first major attempt to reform the CAP came in 1968 with the suggestion – vehemently opposed in France and West Germany – that farms be amalgamated into bigger and more efficient units, and smaller farmers be encouraged to leave the land. The pressure for reform grew, with international criticism generated by the pressures to reduce trade tariffs under the Uruguay Round of negotiations within the General Agreement on Trade and Tariffs. In 1991 agriculture commissioner Ray MacSharry suggested replacing guaranteed prices with a system of direct payments to farmers if prices fell below a certain level, and using the 'set-aside' system to encourage farmers to take land out of production as a condition of receiving CAP funding (Lewis, 1993, p. 337). His proposals (which earned him the nickname 'Mack the Knife' in British tabloids) were accepted in spite of opposition from farmers and their unions.

The pressures for reform continued as the EU began to make plans for eastern enlargement, which promised to increase CAP spending (see Jensen et al., 2009). In 1998, agriculture commissioner Franz Fischler made several new proposals:

- the EU move away from compensating farmers when prices fell below a certain level
- the set-aside scheme be ended
- prices for beef, cereals and milk be cut
- more environmental management conditions be attached to payments to farmers
- more investment in developing the EU's rural areas.

The core idea behind the reforms was 'decoupling' or breaking the link between subsidies and production, and encouraging farmers to produce for the market rather than for EU subsidies. The result of these and other changes would be to leave the CAP 'virtually unrecognizable from the days of old' (Fischler, 2003). The link between subsidies to farmers and the amount they produce has indeed been broken, the prices paid for a wide range of agricultural products have fallen, direct payments for bigger farms have been cut, the CAP has become less trade-distorting and more market-oriented, and the share of EU spending on agriculture has fallen from 75 per cent in 1970 to about 40 per cent today.

Western European farmers were concerned that because so many of their eastern counterparts still worked in agriculture and operated small and relatively unproductive farms, enlargement would soak up most spending under the CAP.

At the same time, it was important to ensure that eastern European governments and their farmers did not feel that they were being treated as second-class citizens. The compromise ultimately agreed (without much enthusiasm) was to allow eastern European farmers a small but growing proportion of agricultural payments. Under a 2000–06 programme designed to help applicant countries prepare for the CAP, €22 billion was invested in eastern European agriculture, a rural development package worth €5.1 billion was made available for 2004–06, and agreement was reached that direct aids would be phased in over ten years, starting at 25 per cent in 2004 and moving up in annual increments of 5 per cent.

In 2008, EU leaders carried out a 'health check' of agricultural policy, and introduced changes that simplified the CAP and allowed it to better respond to changes in the market. Direct payments to farmers have since fallen, funds have been transferred into rural development, and guaranteed prices are now seen mainly as a safety net to be used only when prices are unsustainably low. Reforms continue to be discussed, with an eye to controlling the EU budget while increasing spending in areas outside agriculture. There has been talk of less spending and more regulation, of the imbalance of payments between western and eastern Europe, and the need to compensate farmers for 'public goods' such as land management.

Overall, the CAP today looks very different from the system designed in the 1960s. Then, the focus was on ensuring regular food supplies; today, the focus is on helping farmers survive and compete in European and global markets. 'EU agricultural policy making', argues Burrell (2009), 'can no longer be described as an inward looking process seeking a compromise among different national interests.' Structurally, the main change has been a switch from price supports to direct payments, which now account for most agricultural spending in the EU budget, and overall agricultural spending has fallen as a percentage of total EU spending. There is more of a focus today on quality rather than quantity, driven mainly by changing consumer demands and rising concerns about the state of the environment. CAP payments have conditions attached, linked to food safety, animal health and welfare, sustainable development and the management of rural landscapes. Consumers are helped by more attention being paid to indicating the origin of agricultural produce and encouraging organic production.

Fisheries policy

Although it has not been as controversial or as expensive as agricultural policy, fisheries policy has been the target of an equally sustained programme of political attention, and has been one of the policy areas in which a truly EU-wide approach has been agreed (but with mixed results). (For a survey of EU fisheries policy, see Lequesne, 2004.) Fishing today employs only about 400,000 Europeans, but the EU fishing industry is the world's third biggest (after China and Japan), and the health of that industry has implications for large numbers of Europeans: most EU member states have a coastline (the five exceptions being Austria, the Czech Republic, Hungary, Luxembourg and Slovakia), the EU has the world's largest maritime territory (it has more sea than land), about 60 per cent of the EU population lives within a few kilometres of the sea, and that population accounts for more than 40 per cent of EU gross domestic product.

Understanding Integration... *Multilevel governance*

Multilevel governance (MLG) is an approach to understanding the dynamics of European integration, describing a system in which power is shared among multiple levels of government that interact vertically and horizontally with one another. It has been described as a system of 'overlapping competencies among multiple levels of governments and the interaction of political actors across those levels', and as such is more than a two-level game involving the EU institutions and states, but is instead a set of networks where the structure of policy control is variable across policy areas (Marks et al., 1996, p. 41). How much it is a theory as opposed to descriptive approach, however, remains open to debate.

States are central to the process, but there are a variety of other governmental and nongovernmental actors involved as well, with power relationships understood as existing downwards, upwards and sideways from the member states of the EU. MLG suggests that policy coordination does not just take place vertically among different levels of government in the EU – supranational, national, regional and local – but also horizontally across the member

states. In 2014, the Committee of the Regions adopted a Charter for Multilevel Governance in Europe in an effort to encourage the use of MLG approaches by EU institutions and national and local governments.

Like so many 'new' ideas in the social sciences, it is not all that new, and is reflected, for example, in Donald Puchala's (1975) suggestion that the Community could be seen as 'a multileveled system arranged in political layers from the local to the supranational', with complex organizational linkages binding centre and peripheries, going upwards and downwards, and inwards and outwards.

MLG has become popular as a way of understanding how policy is made in the EU, moving beyond the interactions between the EU institutions and the member states, and offering a more sophisticated approach to understanding integration than that offered by functionalist, neofunctionalist, intergovernmental or institutional approaches. But it has also been applied increasingly to a broader understanding of governance in individual European countries such as Germany and the UK, as well as government systems in Latin America and Asia.

The structure of fishing fleets varies from one member state to another, so, for example, while Greece has by far the biggest fleet in the EU by number of vessels, it ranks low on the list when measured by tonnage. Spain's fleet is third largest by number but is by far the biggest by tonnage (see Figure 22.4).

The main (theoretical) goal of the Common Fisheries Policy (CFP) has been to help support a competitive fishing industry while also preventing overfishing and ensuring sustainability. It does this mainly through:

- conservation
- imposing national quotas (Total Allowable Catches) on the take of Atlantic and North Sea fish
- setting rules on fishing gear and mesh sizes for fishing nets
- requiring accurate reporting of catches and landings
- setting rules on the protection of marine mammals, birds and vulnerable species of fish
- requiring that all EU fishing boats are licensed
- having a fleet management policy that limits the size of EU fishing fleets
- managing the market in order to monitor prices, quality, marketing and competition
- reaching agreements with third countries on access to their fishing grounds.

Common Fisheries Policy (CFP): A joint EU policy aimed at managing fish stocks and regulating the EU fishing industry.

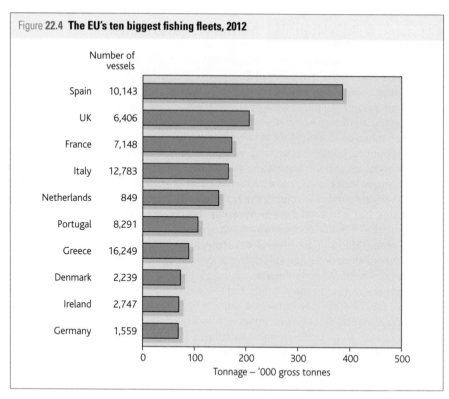

Figure 22.4 **The EU's ten biggest fishing fleets, 2012**

Source: Eurostat, 2013, pp. 216–17.

At the heart of fishing policy has been access to, and management of, resources. Before 1970 each European coastal state had control over its own fishing grounds, but this did not stop the occasional dispute breaking out, such as the famous cod wars of the 1950s and 70s between Britain and Iceland over access to North Sea fisheries. In 1970 it was agreed that Community fishing boats could have access to all national fishing grounds with the exception of those closest to the coast, and a common market for fisheries products was created. In 1976, in line with changes in international law, access to marine resources was expanded from 19 km (12 miles) to 322 km (200 miles) from the coastline, and it was decided to place all national fisheries under Community jurisdiction and develop the CFP, which was finally agreed in 1983. Not all states were happy about opening up their fishing grounds, prompting French patrol boats to fire on Spanish trawlers operating inside the 322-km limit in 1984, and the interception of more than two dozen Spanish trawlers off the coast of Ireland. The Spanish fishing fleet was bigger at the time than the combined EC fleet, and fishing rights were high on the agenda during Spain's negotiations to join the EC.

Reforms came to the CFP in 2002, aimed at placing a greater emphasis on sustainability and minimizing the impact of fishing on marine ecosystems. Problems with enforcement led to the creation in 2005 of the Community Fisheries Control Agency, charged with enforcing the rules and training fisheries inspectors. Another discussion about reform of the CFP in 2009–10 emphasized the problems of fleets that were too large, catches that were unsustainable, and the

Common pool resources

Resources that do not come under the jurisdiction of a single state, authority or government, and are open to unregulated exploitation. They include the air, oceans, rivers, lakes, fisheries, grazing land and groundwater basins. Those motivated by maximum profit and minimum cost will be tempted to extract as much as they can from such resources, leaving the costs to be borne by all other parties interested in the resources. The failure of EU fisheries policy is an example of the difficulties of managing common pool resources.

unprofitability of most fisheries operations. Under the 2014–20 budget package, nearly €6 billion has been set aside for the European Maritime and Fisheries Fund, designed to encourage sustainable fishing and help coastal communities diversify their economies.

The challenges faced by EU fisheries are not unique to Europe; overfishing is a global problem, researchers estimating that as much as one-fifth of the worldwide fish catch is unregulated and illegal, and that overfishing has left major fish stocks depleted. Combined with the effects of pollution, this threatens sustainability and the future of marine ecosystems (see Clover, 2005). Fisheries are a classic example of the dilemma of common pool resources, where a large resource exists that is difficult to effectively manage, and where rational self-interest encourages all those who have access to the resource to extract as much of it as possible, maximizing their benefits at the cost of others. The CFP, then, cannot function in isolation, but must be part of a global regime to manage fisheries. The record so far of the EU on managing its fisheries has not been a good one, and the pressures for reform have been growing.

Environmental policy

In contrast to agricultural policy, which was high on the EEC agenda from the beginning, environmental policy has only crept onto that agenda more recently, a function of changing public and political interest in environmental issues. The environment was not something to which national governments paid much attention in the 1950s, although references in the Treaty of Rome to 'a harmonious development of economic activities, a continuous and balanced expansion, [and] … an accelerated raising of the standard of living' could be interpreted in retrospect as setting the stage for what followed. A few laws were agreed in the early years of the Community dealing with radiation in the workplace and the management of dangerous chemicals, but they were prompted less by concerns for the environment than by the drive to build a single market (Hildebrand, 1993). It was only in the late 1960s and early 1970s that Community governments began to pay much attention to environmental issues, encouraged by heightened public concerns driven by a combination of new scientific understanding, several headline-making environmental disasters (such as oil spills), and growing concerns among the affluent Western middle classes about quality of life issues (McCormick, 1995, Ch. 3).

The landmark United Nations Conference on the Human Environment, held in Stockholm in July 1972, drew wider political and public attention to the problems of the environment for the first time, encouraging governments to create new environmental agencies, develop wide-ranging environmental policies, and pass new laws. Three months later, the EEC heads of government meeting in Paris agreed the need for an environmental policy, and the European Commission adopted its first Environment Action Programme in late 1973. Meanwhile, in an attempt to improve the quality of the data on which policy was based, the European Environment Agency was created in 1993 (see Chapter 14).

The initial focus was on preventive action and the need to guard against different national policies becoming barriers to the single market. The focus later switched to factoring environmental considerations into other policy areas –

Environmental policy: Policy dealing with the management of renewable natural resources, such as air, water, land and forests, and limiting the harmful impact of human activity.

notably agriculture, industry, energy and transport – so that the environment was no longer secondary to the single market (Hildebrand, 1993). But these changes took place outside the treaties, and it was only with enlargement to Greece, Portugal and Spain (none of which had strong environmental standards) that approaches became more formal. The Single European Act (SEA) finally gave a legal basis to Community environmental policy and made environmental protection a component of all EC policies. Most importantly, the SEA began a process by which sustainable development was moved to the heart of European policy. The SEA noted the importance of 'prudent and rational utilization of natural resources', Maastricht called for 'sustainable and non-inflationary growth respecting the environment', and Amsterdam confirmed the need for a 'balanced and sustainable development of economic activities'. Sustainable development is now one of the core policy objectives of the EU, applying to everything it does.

Opinion polls have found that support for action at the EU level is overwhelmingly preferred to action at the member state level. Environmental concerns have also translated into the rise of numerous and often politically influential national public interest groups, the green consumer lifestyle has become thoroughly mainstream since the mid-1990s, and environmental consciousness has translated into support for green politics. Green political parties have had members elected to the European Parliament and the national legislatures of most EU member states, and have been part of coalition governments in Belgium, Finland, France, Germany, Italy and several other countries.

If the breadth and depth of the EU's activities in the environmental field (see Figure 22.5) have not always attracted much attention, in two areas at least there have been exceptions. On chemicals policy the EU has become a world leader, with changes in the way chemicals are tested and recorded at home leading to

Sustainable development:
Development that recognizes natural limits and does not result in permanent and harmful environmental change or natural resource depletion.

Illustration **22.2 Air pollution**

Improving the quality of European air has been a core focus of EU environmental policy, which has helped make scenes such as this increasingly rare on the European landscape.

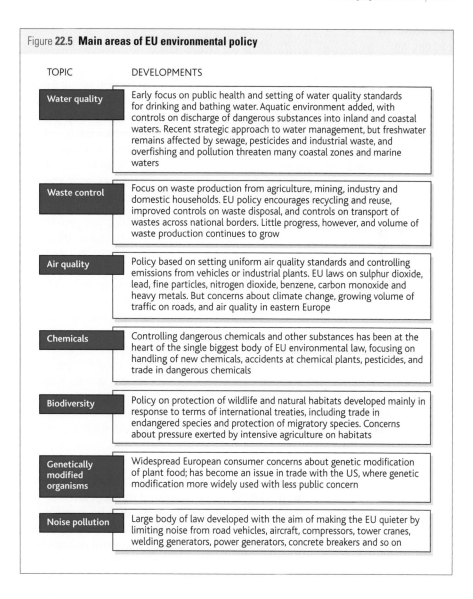

Figure 22.5 **Main areas of EU environmental policy**

TOPIC	DEVELOPMENTS
Water quality	Early focus on public health and setting of water quality standards for drinking and bathing water. Aquatic environment added, with controls on discharge of dangerous substances into inland and coastal waters. Recent strategic approach to water management, but freshwater remains affected by sewage, pesticides and industrial waste, and overfishing and pollution threaten many coastal zones and marine waters
Waste control	Focus on waste production from agriculture, mining, industry and domestic households. EU policy encourages recycling and reuse, improved controls on waste disposal, and controls on transport of wastes across national borders. Little progress, however, and volume of waste production continues to grow
Air quality	Policy based on setting uniform air quality standards and controlling emissions from vehicles or industrial plants. EU laws on sulphur dioxide, lead, fine particles, nitrogen dioxide, benzene, carbon monoxide and heavy metals. But concerns about climate change, growing volume of traffic on roads, and air quality in eastern Europe
Chemicals	Controlling dangerous chemicals and other substances has been at the heart of the single biggest body of EU environmental law, focusing on handling of new chemicals, accidents at chemical plants, pesticides, and trade in dangerous chemicals
Biodiversity	Policy on protection of wildlife and natural habitats developed mainly in response to terms of international treaties, including trade in endangered species and protection of migratory species. Concerns about pressure exerted by intensive agriculture on habitats
Genetically modified organisms	Widespread European consumer concerns about genetic modification of plant food; has become an issue in trade with the US, where genetic modification more widely used with less public concern
Noise pollution	Large body of law developed with the aim of making the EU quieter by limiting noise from road vehicles, aircraft, compressors, tower cranes, welding generators, power generators, concrete breakers and so on

pressures for changes in the US and more generally in the international regime (see below). But undoubtedly the biggest volume of political attention (if not necessarily the most effective policy results) has been drawn by climate change, where the EU is one of the world's four major policy players, along with the US, China and India, and has been at the heart of efforts to achieve international agreement (see Jordan et al., 2010; Wurzel and Connelly, 2010).

The science of the greenhouse effect was established in the nineteenth century, and the problem of climate change was well known to scientists as long ago as the early 1980s, but it has only been since the late 1990s – thanks to increasingly dire warnings of its possible effects – that it has become a headline issue. So firm is its new place on the public policy agenda that it even survived the economic downturns of 2007–10; history has shown that environmental issues tend to rise and fall on the public agenda in inverse relationship to the state of the economy,

---

Focus on... *Europe's leadership on chemicals*

The control and handling of chemicals has long been at the top of the EU environmental agenda, with a large body of laws designed to control the release of new chemicals onto the market, prevent accidents at chemical plants, control the use of pesticides, and regulate trade in dangerous chemicals. The earliest EU chemicals legislation was motivated by the desire to remove obstacles posed to the common market by different sets of national regulations. Later, the desire to protect consumers led to measures to ban or limit the commercialization of dangerous substances and preparations, and there was a focus on efforts to minimize the impact of chemicals on the environment.

All these initiatives were capped in 2006 with the adoption of the REACH (Registration, Evaluation, Authorisation and Restriction of Chemical) regulation, which entered into force in 2007. Prompted by concerns that thousands of new chemical compounds (many of them synthetic) had been placed on the market with little information about their potential threats to human health and the environment, REACH requires that manufacturers and importers gather information

on the properties of the chemicals that are produced or imported and submit that information to the European Chemicals Agency. This manages a database containing information that is made available to consumers and industry, the goal being to make clear any known risks associated with these chemicals. The regulation also encourages manufacturers to develop alternatives to the most dangerous chemicals.

The US government initially lobbied hard against REACH, because US laws on chemicals have traditionally been lax, making bans or restrictions difficult, and manufacturers have been loath to release information for fear of losing competitive advantage. But the US ultimately had to concede not only to its passage, but to the new reality that US chemical manufacturers would have to follow the EU lead or else potentially lose access to the lucrative European market for many of their products (Layton, 2008). Where the US had long been the leader on environmental regulation, with Europeans having to make adjustments, the record on chemicals suggests that the roles may be in the process of being reversed.

---

but this has not applied to climate change. However, placing it on the agenda has been relatively easy compared to the search for viable solutions to the problem (Jordan et al., 2010, p. 3). It has also been argued that much of what the EU has so far achieved has been as a fortuitous result of changes in economic conditions rather than deliberate pollution control policies (Kerr, 2007).

Climate changes as a result of natural causes, but evidence suggests that the warming of the climate has been accelerated by emissions of greenhouse gases such as carbon dioxide (CO_2), which trap more solar radiation, warming the atmosphere, and causing a wide range of climatic and environmental effects. While this is often described as the ultimate global environmental issue, national governments have been reluctant to take unilateral action for fear of losing comparative economic advantage. There is also much residual scepticism about the existence of the problem; while the vast majority of scientists around the world argue that our understanding of the causes and effects of climate change is complete, enough have expressed doubt to offer a way out for those opposed to action. A 2014 poll found that as many as 20–25% of respondents in Germany, Poland and the UK did not agree that climate change was man-made, a view supported by 12–15% of those in France, Italy and Spain and 32% of those in the US (Ipsos MORI, 2014).

The EU both supported and signed the core international agreement – the 1992 UN Framework Convention on Climate Change – and a 1997 protocol to the convention that was signed in Kyoto, Japan, with the goal of giving the convention some substance. In 2000 the Commission launched the European Climate Change Programme, listing measures that could be taken to reduce emissions, including greater use of renewable energy, and in 2002 the EU-15 ratified Kyoto, committing them to cutting CO_2 emissions by 8 per cent on 1990 levels by 2008–12. This would be done with an Emissions Trading Scheme, launched in 2005. Under this arrangement, also known as cap and trade, member states set limits on CO_2 emissions from industrial plants (more than 10,000 are involved), which are given emission allowances. Those that use less than their allowance can sell the balance to companies that are having trouble meeting the limits.

In March 2007, the EU announced a 20-20-20 Strategy aimed at cutting CO_2 emissions by 20% (on 1990 levels) and generating 20% of its energy from renewable sources by 2020. At that point, its emissions were down only 4.3% on 1990 levels, so it appeared to have a long way to go. By 2011, however, EU emissions were down 18.4% and almost every EU member state was in negative territory (see Figure 22.6). Some of the reductions have come in the wake of economic recession, particularly in Spain and Portugal, and gains in the EU were offset by continued foot-dragging in the US and the ongoing growth in emissions in industrializing states such as China (up 172% between 1990 and 2007) and

Emissions Trading Scheme:
A free-market mechanism for reducing greenhouse gases, using emission caps and tradable emission allowances.

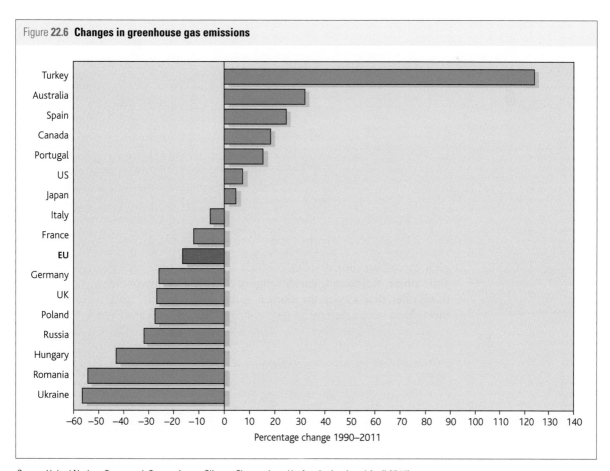

Figure **22.6** **Changes in greenhouse gas emissions**

Percentage change 1990–2011

Source: United Nations Framework Convention on Climate Change, http://unfccc.int (retrieved April 2014).

India (up 125%). But the EU has nonetheless set an example, and by 2010 was accounting for 11% of global CO_2 emissions (7 tonnes per person), while the US accounted for just over 16% (17 tonnes per person) and China 25% (6 tonnes per person) (figures from World Bank, http://data.worldbank.org).

In December 2009, the parties to the Convention on Climate Change and the Kyoto Protocol met in Copenhagen to try and give climate change policy more teeth, but the conference ended in failure. Although an accord was agreed, acknowledging that climate change is one of the greatest challenges facing the world today and that action should be taken to keep temperature increases below 2°C, it was not legally binding, and included no commitments for specific cuts in CO_2 emissions. The EU had entered the negotiations on something of a moral high ground, saying that it would go ahead with its Emissions Trading Scheme whatever was agreed at Copenhagen, but was later criticized for its failure to take a leadership position by increasing its CO_2 reduction commitments and providing the kind of example that many observers felt that the conference needed. In the end, however, it was mainly the failure of the US to make real commitments and China and India to cooperate that led to an absence of agreement.

Summary

- Agriculture has been a far more prominent issue on the EU agenda than it is on the agendas of most economically developed states.

- At the heart of EU activities has been the Common Agricultural Policy, which began as a system of price supports designed to prevent food shortages.

- The CAP encouraged greater production, but also swallowed large amounts of spending, skewed European and global markets, and raised the ire of environmentalists.

- Reforms to the CAP have switched the focus from quantity to quality, breaking the link between payments and the amount farmers produce.

- Fishing employs relatively few people in Europe, but has economic knock-on effects for coastal communities and all EU coastal member states.

- The Common Fisheries Policy was adopted in 1983, focusing on managing fishing fleets and catches, along with the welfare of the marine environment. But overfishing remains a problem in European waters as it does all over the world, and a more effective global regime is clearly needed.

- The environment was a latecomer to the European policy agenda, drawing sustained political and public attention only from the late 1960s.

- EU policy focuses on sustainable development, and EU activities have focused on air and water quality, waste control, chemicals and the protection of biodiversity.

- EU chemicals policy has tightened up controls and management at home and has had global implications by affecting all states that seek access to the European market.

- The EU has set itself ambitious targets on climate change, but has failed to build a global leadership position.

Key terms and concepts

Agricultural policy

Common Agricultural Policy

Common Fisheries Policy

Common pool resources

Emissions Trading Scheme

Environmental policy

Sustainable development

Further reading

Jordan, Andrew, and Camilla Adele (eds) (2013) *Environmental Policy in the European Union: Actors, Institutions and Processes,* 3rd edn (Abingdon: Routledge). Standard study of EU environmental policy, looking at how policy has evolved, the actors involved, and the dynamics of how it is made and implemented.

Jordan, Andrew, Dave Huitema, Harro van Asselt, Tim Rayner and Frans Berkhout (eds) (2010) *Climate Change Policy in the European Union* (Cambridge: Cambridge University Press). Edited collection of this most critical of environmental problems, looking at how policy has evolved and what remains to be done.

Skogstad, Grace, and Amy Verdun (eds) (2010) *The Common Agricultural Policy: Policy Dynamics in a Changing Context* (Abingdon: Routledge). Edited collection of studies of the CAP, including chapters on reforms of the policy, and its impact on trade and the environment.

23 Justice and Home Affairs

Justice and home affairs (JHA) is one of the newer areas of EU policy, describing efforts to develop a coordinated approach to international crime and terrorism, managing immigration, and improving security and the protection of rights through police and judicial cooperation. The pressure for action grew with the final efforts to complete the single market in the late 1980s, which increased the political demand for common internal policies while managing external borders.

The goals of JHA were established by Maastricht; it has at heart been an effort to create an 'area of freedom, security and justice' within the EU, a controversial notion because it has touched on many issues deeply entrenched in national political and judicial systems, and comes up against concerns about the protection of state sovereignty (Lavenex, 2014).

The policies dealt with under JHA combine matters that are internal and external to the EU, including free movement of people within the EU and control of the EU's external borders. Among other things, there have been efforts to standardize the processing of applications for asylum, manage immigration by skilled workers while controlling illegal immigration, develop policies on visas and personal data protection, and encourage cooperation among police forces and judicial authorities in order to control cross-border crime. With time, these efforts have developed more consistency, moving from a loose collection of intergovernmental initiatives to a more coordinated supranational approach. The new dynamic is reflected most clearly in the creation of European arrest and evidence warrants, confirming the trend towards mutual recognition on judicial matters.

Key issues

- Why have EU member states been so resistant to pressures to cooperate on justice and home affairs?
- Does immigration from outside the EU represent a threat or an opportunity?
- Is immigration the only (or best) response to the economic problems posed by Europe's declining and ageing population?
- How far do the self-proclaimed progressive qualities of European society extend, given the sometimes hostile response to non-white and non-Christian immigration?
- Can the threat of terrorism ever be fully expunged?

The evolution of cooperation

As with so many other areas of policy, the need for cooperation on justice and home affairs (JHA) was something to which EU governments turned their attention more by accident than design. When they did so, they moved relatively quickly, and Monar (2001) argues that no other field of endeavour made its way so rapidly or so comprehensively to the centre of the treaties or the top of the EU policy agenda. He notes the importance of several 'laboratories' in which policies were developed early and working practices established – including the Council of Europe, the TREVI group set up to respond to international terrorism, and the Schengen Agreement. He also notes several driving factors behind the development of policy, including transnational challenges such as a sharp rise in the number of asylum applications, the threats posed by Russian organized crime in the 1990s, and the emerging problem of cybercrime.

There was no reference to JHA in the Treaty of Rome, and such cooperation as existed among western European states in the early years of the Community was piecemeal and uncoordinated, lacking either goals or institutional and legal arrangements (Monar, 2001). More active than the Community was the Council of Europe, which addressed issues related to criminal matters and human rights, championed international conventions on extradition and the transfer of sentenced criminals, and hosted meetings that had the effect of encouraging national government ministers dealing with internal affairs to take a more multinational approach to their tasks. But the Community itself took economic integration literally and there was no effort to develop coordinated policies on JHA.

In 1967 the Naples Convention on cooperation between the customs authorities of Community states was signed, although it was not specifically a Community initiative (Hobbing, 2003, p. 8). This provided for the cross-border surveillance of criminal suspects by national police and customs authorities, its key contribution being to encourage exchanges and cooperation between national governments. It was superseded in 1997 by the convention on mutual assistance and cooperation between customs administrations of the EU, otherwise known as Naples II.

In 1971 the Pompidou Group, named for French President Georges Pompidou, was set up to share experience on the combating of drug use and trafficking (it was later incorporated into the Council of Europe). This was followed in 1975 by the creation of the TREVI group (see Chapter 14), set up to coordinate anti-terrorist activities, its mandate expanding after 1985 to include drug trafficking and organized crime. Another impetus for cooperation on JHA came from the 1985 Schengen Agreement, the implementation of which helped begin the process of harmonizing policies on visas, illegal immigration, asylum, extradition and police and judicial cooperation. It also spawned the computerized Schengen Information System, providing police and customs officials with a database of undesirables whose entry into the Schengen area they wished to control. In 1990, the Dublin Convention on asylum was signed by the EC-12 as part of an effort to decide which member state was responsible for reviewing applications for asylum from a third-country national – preventing asylum-seekers from shopping around among member states for the best deal. It was superseded in 2003 by the Dublin Regulation, under which – with some exceptions – asylum-seekers have since had to apply to the member state through which they first enter the EU.

Justice and home affairs (JHA): Policy dealing with issues such as international crime and terrorism, asylum, immigration, and police and judicial cooperation.

Community member states learned from these early exercises in cooperation, so that when the pressures for a more focused and structured approach to policy began to grow in the 1990s, there was already something of a track record in place. But each member state still had its own domestic system of JHA. It was only with the completion of the single market that reform, cooperation and the need for burden-sharing became more pressing. Further need was generated by the activities of Russian criminal gangs in the wake of the collapse of communism, the sharp increase in the number of visa applications in the wake of the Balkan civil wars, and the more inclusive and structured approach to international terrorism sparked by the September 2001 attacks in the US.

The formal inclusion of JHA in the work of the Community arose for the first time in the discussions leading up to Maastricht, when an attempt was made to integrate JHA and the Common Foreign and Security Policy into a single structure. But a difference of opinion emerged among states, cutting to the heart of questions about national sovereignty: security has been central to the definition of state powers since the start of the Westphalian era, and continues to raise challenging questions even today about democracy, civil liberties and the appropriate role of government in the lives of citizens. The messy compromise reached with Maastricht was to make police and judicial cooperation one of the three 'pillars' in the European Union (the others being the European Community and the Common Foreign and Security Policy), which meant that cooperation on JHA matters was intergovernmental and that all decisions had to be unanimous. This did not discourage the rapid growth of cross-border police cooperation, however, with the new European Police Office (Europol, which became fully operational in 1999) helping lead the way.

Constitutional change was brought by the Treaty of Amsterdam. Reflecting the growing dissatisfaction with intergovernmental approaches and a desire to make European integration more relevant for ordinary Europeans, the treaty established 'an area of freedom, security and justice', incorporated Schengen into the *acquis communautaire* (with opt-outs for Britain, Denmark and Ireland), and made asylum, immigration and judicial cooperation EU responsibilities. At the Tampere European Council in October 1999, a programme of action was agreed to address the problems created by free movement across borders, including a list of about 60 initiatives needed to be taken by 2004 on issues such as asylum, immigration and cross-border crime.

The 9/11 attacks in the US forced the hands of EU governments, heightening the urgency of dealing with potential threats arising out of the dismantling of the EU's internal borders; as movement inside the EU became easier, so the need to strengthen external borders became more obvious (see Wolff et al., 2009). In 2004 the European Council adopted the Hague Programme, which listed ten priorities for EU policy, including:

- the strengthening of fundamental rights and citizenship
- a comprehensive response to terrorism
- the development of a balanced approach to dealing with legal and illegal immigration
- the integrated management of the EU's external borders
- the creation of a common asylum procedure
- efforts to better integrate immigrant communities
- the need for a strategic approach to tackling organized crime.

With the passage of the Treaty of Lisbon and the demise of the pillar system, JHA was finally incorporated into the mainstream of EU policy concerns and ceased to be a matter for intergovernmental decision-making. This does not mean, however, that today there is a single European policy in this area. Britain and Ireland, for example, maintain their opt-outs from Schengen, while the picture is complicated by the involvement of non-EU members Iceland, Norway and Switzerland in Schengen and the Dublin Convention. Efforts on the JHA front have reflected all the core notions of spillover, incrementalism and compromise, and overall there has been more of a focus on cooperation rather than harmonization, resulting in a pattern of shared competences involving European, state and substate levels of governance (Lavenex, 2014).

Institutional developments have paralleled those on policy. Europol has grown to be one of the most prominent of the EU's specialized agencies, joined along the way by Eurojust and the European Police College (see Chapter 14 for more details). Specific elements of the JHA agenda are addressed by the European Monitoring Centre for Drugs and Drug Addiction, the European Fundamental Rights Agency, and Frontex, which is responsible for coordination of EU efforts to manage its external borders. Within the Commission, a new directorate-general on JHA was created in 1999, which was later renamed Justice, Liberty and Security, and in 2010 split into two new DGs: the Justice DG is responsible for the development and consolidation of the EU area of freedom, security and justice, while the Home Affairs DG focuses on security and migration. Along the way, JHA has also become central to the agendas of the European Council and the European Parliament.

Asylum and immigration

Migration has long been part of the European demographic landscape, although the issue has taken on new complexity since the Second World War. The scale has also changed: Europe is now home to nearly 70 million migrants, or one-third of the world total, according to UN estimates (see later in this chapter). Where migration flows were once mainly internal to Europe, since the 1950s they have also become an external matter, a new and more difficult dimension added by the arrival of newcomers of different ethnicities and religions. As long as migration was limited to white Christians, it generated relatively little political or social resistance, but as the ranks of immigrants have included more Africans, Middle Easterners, South Asians and Muslims, so racial and religious discrimination have entered the equation; controlling immigration (or, at least, non-white immigration) has become a hot-button issue in the EU (as in the US), generating a more coordinated policy response and also feeding into the rise of right-wing anti-immigrant political parties.

The attraction of life in a wealthy and democratic country – either for the economic opportunities it offers or as a haven from war, persecution or natural disasters at home – is often irresistible to the citizens of states facing hardship, and just as many Latin Americans have sought to move to the US in search of work, so many Russians, Middle Easterners and North Africans have sought to move to the EU. For the wealthy and educated, the challenges are far less than for the poor and the unskilled, who may be welcome as sources of cheap and seasonal labour but are not expected to stay indefinitely.

Asylum – involving efforts by individuals to be admitted to the protection of a country other than their home state, usually for political reasons – has moved up the policy agenda since the 1980s in the wake of a sharp increase in asylum applications. Many of these were generated by the outbreak – following the end of the Cold War – of small wars and ethnic conflicts in which civilians were often targeted. One of the challenges has been to distinguish genuine asylum-seekers from economic migrants, questions about which caused several EU states in the 1990s (in the wake of the Balkan civil wars) to tighten their previously liberal asylum laws.

Asylum-seekers are only a small part of the global refugee problem, but one that matters a great deal to the EU; according to the UN High Commissioner for Refugees (UNHCR), the EU-28 received 65 per cent of the approximately 612,000 asylum claims lodged with industrialized countries in 2013, or about four and a half times as many as those made to the US. Among EU states, Germany, France, Sweden, Britain and Italy accounted for the greatest number of applications, and most asylum-seekers came from the Middle East, Russia, the Balkans and troubled African states, with a notable rise in the number of asylum applications from Syria, Russia and Serbia, and a notable reduction in applications from Iraq (United Nations High Commissioner for Refugees, 2014) (see Figure 23.1).

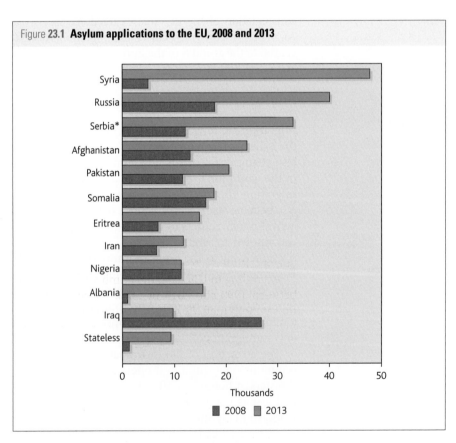

Figure **23.1** **Asylum applications to the EU, 2008 and 2013**

Asylum: An effort by an individual to win residence in a state in order to achieve protection from threats of death, torture or persecution in their home state.

Note: * Mainly from Kosovo.

Source: United Nations High Commissioner for Refugees, 2014.

Immigration

Human populations have never been static, their movements encouraged over the centuries by a changing variety of geographical, economic, political and cultural pressures. At no time have people been so mobile as they are today, encouraged by a combination of 'push factors', including poverty, war, political instability, discrimination, natural disasters, and environmental degradation, and 'pull factors', including labour shortages, strong economies, political and social stability, historical or cultural links, and the presence of large communities from the source country (Europol, 2009). The political response to immigration cuts to the heart of the economic and cultural priorities of states.

All EU member states are signatories to the 1950 Geneva Convention, which commits them to protecting refugees by making sure that they are not returned to a state where they face the risk of death, torture, or other inhuman or degrading treatment. Policy remained focused on the national level until the completion of the single market, at which point there was a clear need for a coordinated approach. But EU policy to date has not gone much further than developing minimum standards and procedures for asylum-seekers, and agreeing how applications should be processed and what kinds of cases merit the granting of asylum.

The Tampere European Council in 1999 supported the idea of moving beyond a loose intergovernmental approach and called for the establishment of a common European asylum system. Lavenex (2001) notes that this thinking was based in part on addressing criticisms of 'fortress Europe', and in part on the hope of avoiding a repeat of the 'embarrassing' European response to the 1999 Kosovo refugee crisis, when more than 800,000 ethnic Albanians fled their homes in the face of attacks by Serb security forces; the EU response was found wanting in policy and structural terms. The EU has been working since 2004 to agree a Common European Asylum System (CEAS), with laws passed aimed at making quicker and fairer asylum decisions, and providing better housing and other conditions for asylum-seekers. The following steps have also been taken:

- 2005: Frontex created.
- 2008: European Refugee Fund opened; helps EU countries receive and resettle refugees and deal with sudden increases in arrivals.
- 2010: European Asylum Support Office opened; helps develop the CEAS and aids EU countries receiving the most asylum applications.

As regards immigration, major changes are taking place in Europe, of an order that Parsons and Smeeding (2006b, p. 1) describe as a 'historic transformation'. Where once Europeans were focused on demographic change within their borders, they are now increasingly focused on the movement of people across borders, with particular concern about inflows of non-Europeans and how to manage those inflows. This is not an issue unique to the EU, because almost all industrialized countries must respond to their magnetic qualities as sources of jobs and opportunities for the residents of poorer and less stable societies. But demographic and economic trends in an already crowded Europe mean that managing numbers poses a particular challenge, and the issue has also become one of critical electoral salience.

According to UN data, the number of international migrants worldwide grew between 1990 and 2013 by 50%, reaching a total of just over 231 million. Of those, more than 72 million (or nearly one-third) were in Europe, where they accounted for just over 10% of the population of the region (United Nations, 2013). These numbers include all those born in another country, whether or not they have adopted the citizenship of their new home state. A different picture is offered by Eurostat data, which include only non-nationals living in the EU; in 2009, there were nearly 32 million, making up 6.4% of the population of the EU. Of these, more than one-third (or 11.9 million) were citizens of another EU member state (Vasileva, 2010).

Luxembourg tops the list with more than 40 per cent of its population foreign-born, a reflection of how its long vibrant economy and liberal immigration laws have attracted workers from many parts of mainly Catholic Europe (the

Illustration 23.1 The EU's external borders
Confidence in the effect of opening up internal EU borders has depended heavily on confidence in protecting its external borders. Here, border guards keep an eye on movements across the Slovak–Ukrainian border.

Portuguese today making up the largest immigrant minority in Luxembourg). Eastern European states sit at the other end of the scale; there was little migration in the region during the Cold War era, and today most of these states are exporters rather than importers of labour (see Figure 23.2). But their situation could change if the record of several western European states is any indication: Greece, Ireland, Italy, Portugal and Spain were all once sources of emigrants, but then economic growth made them a magnet for immigrants coming from as far afield as Albania, Bulgaria, Egypt, Morocco, Poland, Russia, Ukraine and Latin America. This changed with the recession in the wake of the global financial crisis, but it showed what is possible in happy economic times.

National identity of the kind discussed in Chapter 3 has long involved an attitude of 'us' and 'them' in Europe, but the legal and political response to immigration has been far from uniform. European borders were mainly quite open in the decades leading up to the First World War (passports were not required by most travellers), but then few Europeans had either the means or the opportunity to travel to another country, so there were relatively few 'foreigners'. Regulations were tightened before and after the First World War, but it was only with the rise of cheap mass international travel in the 1950s and 60s that immigration moved higher up the policy agenda. Even then, European governments were less concerned about the movements of other Europeans than they were with managing inflows of non-Europeans, such as Algerians to France, Turkish guest workers to Germany, and West Indians and South Asians to Britain.

Policy continued to be made mainly at the national level, but although national policies in the EU have long been restrictive, this has not prevented growing numbers of migrants from making their way into the EU; by 2011, the EU had become the most popular target for legal immigration in the world (see Figure 23.3 below). While legal immigration can be managed, in terms of the numbers allowed to enter, the states from which they come and the jobs they fill, illegal

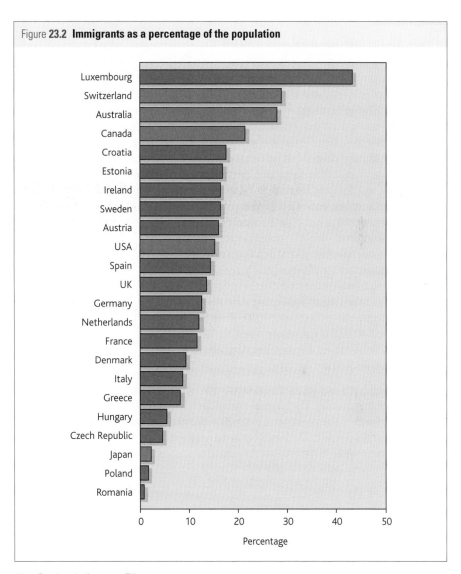

Figure **23.2 Immigrants as a percentage of the population**

Note: Grey bars indicate non-EU states.

Source: UN Department of Economic and Social Affairs, Population Division, 2013b.

immigration poses an entirely different set of challenges. Illegal immigrants have different motives for moving, are usually unskilled, and will sometimes use desperate measures to achieve their goals, risking injury and even death to move to another country. Their efforts overlap with the production of fake identity and travel documents, the trafficking or smuggling of humans, and prostitution, in all of which organized crime is often involved. Once they have reached their target country, illegal immigrants often live on the margins of society, finding it much harder than legal immigrants to adapt and integrate.

By its nature, it is impossible to be sure about the scale of illegal immigration and most statistics are no more than educated guesses. Some estimates place the number of illegal immigrants arriving in the EU each year at about 0.5 million,

Focus on... *France and the Roma*

A relatively small but troubling aspect of European immigration policy captured international media headlines in July 2010 when France expelled more than 1,000 Roma (gypsies), closing down their camps and despatching them to their home states of Bulgaria and Romania. The French government claimed that the camps encouraged the exploitation of children for begging, prostitution and crime, and that living standards in the camps were unacceptable. In fact, domestic political considerations may have been a large part of the equation: President Nicolas Sarkozy had low public approval ratings, and the expulsions may have been part of an attempt to head off growing support for the anti-immigrant National Front. It was by no means the first time that France had taken such action, having closed down camps many times before, and deporting an estimated 10,000 Roma in 2009 alone. About 400,000 of Europe's estimated 10–12 million Roma are thought to live in France, including about 12,000 from Bulgaria and Romania.

The political outcry over the 2010 deportations was immediate and extensive. The European Commission reminded France of the requirements of the 2004 directive on freedom of movement, which establishes the rules for deportation cases, and threatened the possibility of legal proceedings. It also began investigations into whether other EU states were breaking EU rules on the treatment of the Roma. Viviane Reding, the commissioner responsible for justice and fundamental rights, described the deportations as a 'disgrace' and reflected that 'this is a situation I had thought Europe would not have to witness again after the Second World War' (European Commission, 2010). The French action was also condemned by many MEPs, who criticized the French government for targeting the Roma.

However, EU law holds that EU states can deport foreigners considered to be a public security risk or a burden on the welfare system, and while the citizens of Bulgaria and Romania have the right to enter France without a visa, they must have a work or residence permit if they plan to stay for more than three months. Since 2014 they have had full freedom of movement in the EU, like citizens of other EU states. Majority public opinion in France was behind the deportations, which fits with a long history of discrimination against the Roma. But the EU has been criticized for taking too long to develop policies on the Roma, and even critics of French actions admitted that they might finally help concentrate political minds (Peter, 2010).

and estimates of the total number of illegal residents of the EU range as high as 3 million. Frontex reported that just over 140,000 illegal immigrants were found trying to enter the EU in 2008, and another 106,000 in 2009, the decrease being ascribed to a combination of tighter border controls and the global financial crisis. By early 2014, Frontex (2014) was reporting dramatically increased numbers of detections of illegal immigrants (nearly 70,000 in the second quarter alone), which it put down mainly to the growing problems in Syria.

As to where the EU's illegal immigrants come from, Frontex (2014) notes that the nationalities most often detected crossing external EU borders illegally include Albanians, Afghans, Moroccans, Somalis, Iraqis, Tunisians, Nigerians, Eritreans, Palestinians and Algerians, with a sharp increase in the number of Syrians arriving in the wake of the crisis in their country. Most of the illegal immigrants from Africa arrive in Italy, while others enter through Spain and the Canary Islands. Those arriving from the Middle East and South Asia mainly use land routes across Turkey and arrive in Greece, and the western Balkans have become a key transit point for immigrants from all over the world (Europol, 2009). Meanwhile, non-EU eastern European states are a source of illegal immigrants and a point of transit for arrivals from other parts of the world.

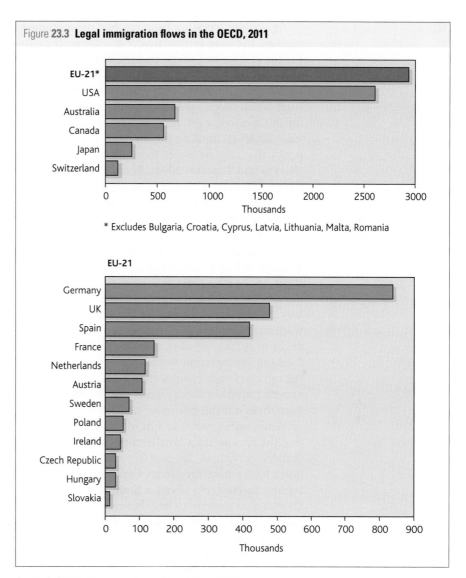

Figure 23.3 **Legal immigration flows in the OECD, 2011**

* Excludes Bulgaria, Croatia, Cyprus, Latvia, Lithuania, Malta, Romania

Source: OECD, http://www.oecd.org (retrieved August 2014).

There was some early talk of the need to coordinate immigration policy across the Community in the 1970s, but it was only with the acceleration of the single market programme in the 1980s that the focus shifted away from states and towards the development of an EU approach (Luedtke, 2006). Even so, rhetoric has long outweighed substantial policy change, and the waters have been muddied by the emotive qualities of the immigration debate, which is regularly sidetracked by myths, stereotypes and discrimination. The Tampere European Council agreed on the need for a common EU policy, arguing that it should be based on a comprehensive approach, with a balance between humanitarian and economic admission, fair treatment for third-country nationals, and the development of agreements with countries of origin.

Agreement has since been reached on contained issues such as family reunification, the long-term status of third-country nationals legally resident in the EU for at least five years, and the status of students and researchers. There has also been work on improving the management of the EU's external borders, and encouraging improved cooperation among police forces and border officials. But there is still no common EU immigration policy. At least part of the explanation for this lies in the extent to which immigration sparks public controversy at the national level, limiting the amount of political support for a harmonized EU policy that may be either more liberal or more restrictive than national policy (Givens and Luedtke, 2004). There is also widespread support for the view that the member states should have the right to decide how many immigrants they will accept, and a belief that Europe already has enough people and the EU should be tightening rather than loosening its borders.

In 2008 a pact on immigration and asylum was adopted, its main goal being to reduce illegal immigration while better managing the arrival in the EU of skilled workers. It had political rather than legal force, and included calls on member states not to offer mass amnesties to illegal immigrants (as Italy and Spain have done in the past), and to remove undocumented foreigners found on their territory. It also cleared the way for the adoption in 2009 of the EU Blue Card, a single work and residence permit designed to mirror the US Green Card by making it easier to attract skilled workers to the EU. But disagreements remain over which forms of immigration to classify as legal (Lavenex, 2010) (for example, should the right to family reunification be extended to children over the age of 12?) and eastern European states argued that the Blue Card should only have been agreed once there was full free movement for citizens of all EU states.

While immigration is a headline issue in Europe, it should not be forgotten that the region has a long history of emigration as well, and there is little sign that the incentives for people to leave are decreasing. Economic problems at home have encouraged many Europeans to head for new opportunities overseas, leading to concerns about a brain drain of professionals and skilled workers. Overall data are hard to find, but recession has recently seen more people leaving Spain, Portugal, Ireland, Slovenia and Cyprus than arriving there, and there are growing concerns about the loss of professionals from Britain, France, Germany and Italy. Where once much of the emigration was from one European country to another, much is now outside the EU, as in the case of Spaniards and Portuguese moving to Latin America (Boudreaux and Prada, 2012).

The debate over immigration has touched on the debate about Europe's ageing and declining population. With the balance between retired and working-age Europeans changing in favour of the former, and concerns that economic growth and the costs of social security cannot be sustained with current trends, the argument has been made that Europe's best hope lies in replenishing numbers through immigration; about 90 per cent of population growth in the EU in recent decades has been met by immigration (Parsons and Smeeding, 2006b, p. 2). But many new immigrants are non-white and non-Christian, posing a severe test of the self-proclaimed progressive qualities of European society. New tensions have been born out of racial and religious intolerance, which in turn has fed into support for right-wing anti-immigrant political parties. They have done particularly well in national elections in Austria (where the Freedom Party

Illustration **23.2 Europe's ageing population**

Immigration from outside the EU has sparked political and social controversy, but some see it as one answer to the problem of Europe's declining and ageing population.

won enough seats to enter a coalition government in 1999), Belgium, Denmark, France, the Netherlands and Sweden, and in local and European elections in several other countries.

Police and judicial cooperation

If immigration is mainly an issue related to the EU's external borders, police and judicial cooperation focuses on how to manage crime, security and migration within the EU. This involves not just improving responses to serious crime, such as drug trafficking, money laundering, child pornography, terrorism and corruption, but also encouraging the mutual recognition of judicial decisions on civil proceedings involving divorce, child custody, bankruptcy and related issues. Civil liberties are also at the heart of this cooperation, including personal data protection, the rights of minorities, the rights of children, the right of free movement, a level playing field for consumers and businesses, and improved harmonization of consumer and contract law.

The work of the Europol and the Judicial Cooperation Unit (Eurojust) was addressed in Chapter 14; the former is a criminal intelligence agency that has eased information exchange among national police forces dealing with serious forms of cross-border crime, while the latter has helped improve investigations and prosecutions involving two or more member states. The EU has also created a **European Judicial Network** responsible for improving judicial cooperation on civil and commercial matters among the member states, complementing the work of Europol and Eurojust. Set up in 1998, it links contact points designated by the member states, drawn from local and state authorities in charge of international judicial cooperation; more than 300 are now in place, managed by a small secretariat within the offices of Eurojust in The Hague.

European Judicial Network: A network of contact points created in 1998 in order to help improve cross-border cooperation within the EU on civil and commercial matters.

One of the most substantial results of European cooperation has been the extension of the principle of mutual recognition to judicial matters, seen most clearly in the agreement of the European arrest warrant, introduced in January 2004. Once issued, it requires a member state to arrest and transfer a suspect or criminal back to the state issuing the warrant within 90 days, and replaces the lengthy extradition process that was once involved in European cross-border criminal actions. It applies only to cases carrying a potential penalty of more than 12 months in jail, or an agreed sentence of at least 4 months, and can be used only for prosecution, not for investigations. It also prevents EU states from refusing to surrender their own nationals, and is based on the idea that EU citizens can be held responsible for their actions wherever they are in the EU. About 14,000 warrants are now issued annually in the EU. One of the early high-profile cases involved a suspect in the July 2005 London bombings, who was arrested in Rome a week after the bombings and extradited to Britain in September; in 2007 he was found guilty of conspiracy to murder and sentenced to 40 years in jail.

Since 2008, the EU has also had a European evidence warrant in place, standardizing methods for obtaining documents, data and other evidence in cross-border cases. Warrants can be issued in the event of criminal proceedings brought before a court in any member state as long as the evidence requested is 'necessary and proportionate' for the proceedings, and it must already exist and be readily available; in other words, the warrant cannot ask police forces in other states to find new evidence. Warrants can either be sent direct to the second state or transmitted via the European Judicial Network. Before the creation of the warrant, it was left to courts or the justice ministry in each member state to decide whether or not to meet a request for evidence; under the terms of the warrant, the grounds for refusal have been greatly limited; for example, it can be refused in cases where immunity exists or national security is potentially harmed. One effect of the new warrant is that fewer cases are likely to collapse for lack of evidence.

The struggle against terrorism

While the push for European police and judicial cooperation has been given new meaning since the 2001 terrorist attacks in the US, terrorism is nothing new to Europeans. They have long had to deal with individuals who feel that the only way to achieve their objectives is to generate fear by attacks on political, military and civilian targets. Terrorism was part of the western European landscape in the 1960s and 70s, with the activities of groups campaigning for recognition of Palestine – one of which was behind the murder of 11 Israeli athletes at the 1972 Munich Olympics – and the disputes in the Basque Country and Northern Ireland, which became particularly violent in the latter after 1968–69. There were also the anti-capitalist activities of the West German Red Army Faction (better known as the Baader-Meinhof gang), which was active mainly between 1970 and 1977, the Red Brigades in Italy (allegedly behind the kidnap and murder in 1978 of former Italian Prime Minister Aldo Moro) and the Armed Revolutionary Nuclei (implicated in a bombing at Bologna railway station in August 1980 that killed 85 people).

European arrest warrant:
A warrant by which member states can request the transfer of suspects or criminals from another member state.

European evidence warrant:
A warrant by which member states can request access to documents and other evidence in cross-border legal cases.

Terrorism: Efforts to achieve political change by creating public fear and insecurity, mainly through attacks on civilian targets.

Illustration **23.3 Terrorism**

A poster in Rome expresses solidarity with Londoners following the July 2005 terrorist bombings. Echoing the well-known headline of a French newspaper after the 9/11 attacks, it declares 'We are all Londoners.'

Agreeing the meaning of the terms *terrorism* and *terrorist* is fraught with difficulty, and no standard definition has yet been agreed under international law. For some, terrorists are criminals and murderers who have chosen to target noncombatants in their efforts to pursue an ideological, political or religious agenda, while for others they are freedom fighters for whom almost any target associated with oppression is legitimate. What they have in common is an effort to generate fear and terror in the hope that this will bring about political change. For Hoffman (2006, p. 41), terrorism is political in its aims and motives, based on the use or threat of violence, designed to have an impact far beyond its immediate target, conducted by an organization with an identifiable chain of command or cell structure, and not perpetrated by a state, although it can be sponsored by a state.

The 2001 attacks in the US may have been directed against US foreign policy, but European states – particularly those like Britain and Spain whose governments had supported the US-led invasion of Iraq – also became the targets of Islamic militants. The threats exemplified by 9/11 were brought much closer to home with a coordinated attack on the Madrid railway system on 11 March 2004 (timed to impact the general election that was held three days later). It resulted in the deaths of 191 people and injuries to nearly 2,000, and was a factor in the defeat of the incumbent conservative government of José María Aznar. On 7 July 2005, a similarly coordinated attack on the London public transport system by suicide bombers resulted in 52 deaths and more than 700 injuries. There have been many other failed or foiled attacks related to Islamic extremism as well, mainly in western European states. These events have fed into growing Islamophobia in Europe, although it must always be stressed that many Muslims are second- or even third-generation Europeans, and that only a small minority are in sympathy with the kind of militancy or extremism that so often captures the headlines.

While the threat of militant Islamic terrorism tends to capture most of the headlines, there are other sources. According to Europol (2014), for example, there were more than 1,300 successful or attempted terrorist attacks in 10 EU member states in 2007–09, only one of which involved Islamic extremists. In the same period, nearly 2,200 individuals were arrested for terrorism-related offences in 18 member states. The greatest number of attacks were planned or carried out by nationalist and separatist movements such as the Basque ETA, the Corsican FLNC and Irish republican splinter groups. Threats were also posed (and attacks often carried out) by left-wing and anarchist groups critical of capitalism, militarism and fascism, right-wing groups mainly targeting racial minorities, and single-issue groups such as animal rights extremists (Europol, 2010). In 2013, there were 152 attacks in five countries, resulting in 7 deaths and 535 arrests. The number of attacks related to left-wing and anarchist terrorism grew, but there were no reports of religiously inspired terrorism (Europol, 2014).

In 2001, just ten days after the US attacks, the European Council adopted a rushed Action Plan on Combating Terrorism, which was revised after the Madrid and London bombings, and has been revised several more times since. Its seven goals included:

- efforts to deepen the international consensus and enhance international efforts to combat terrorism
- reduce the access of terrorists to financial and economic resources
- improve the capacity of EU states to detect and prosecute terrorists and prevent terrorist attacks
- enhance the ability of the EU and its member states to deal with the consequences of a terrorist attack
- address the factors that contributed to support for terrorism.

In 2004 the new post of EU Counter-Terrorism Coordinator was created, but its first holder, Gijs de Vries, former MEP and Dutch deputy interior minister, stepped down in 2007 in protest at his lack of operational powers and the unwillingness of member states to either provide information on their anti-terror activities or give the action plan some substance (Lavenex, 2014). In 2005 a Counter-Terrorism Strategy was agreed, with four goals:

1 *Prevent* people from turning to terrorism by addressing the root causes of radicalization.
2 *Protect* Europeans by reducing Europe's vulnerability to attacks.
3 *Pursue* terrorists across borders and globally.
4 Better prepare European authorities to *respond* to attacks.

Bossong (2008) argues that while the EU agreed an impressive list of anti-terrorism measures after 9/11, the original EU Action Plan did not improve the credibility of the EU's efforts. It was drawn up rapidly, the Commission using it as a window of opportunity to push for large-scale agenda change, but the result was an overload of the EU's decision-making and implementation capacity. By making several controversial proposals and setting tight deadlines for agreeing them, it heightened doubts about the legitimacy and appropriateness of EU efforts, and ultimately raised troubling questions about the right balance between security and liberty.

Following the London bombings, the Council of Ministers decided that all anti-terrorism measures agreed to that point should be adopted immediately. These included:

- the European arrest and evidence warrants discussed earlier
- the strengthening of Schengen and visa information systems
- the inclusion of barometric details on passports, and eventually in visas
- efforts to combat terrorist financing, including tighter controls on money laundering
- efforts to discourage the recruitment of terrorists – a policy given new urgency by the discovery that three of the London bombers were British nationals
- new controls over the trade, storage and transport of explosives.

Summary

- It was only with efforts to complete the single market in the late 1980s and early 1990s that the pressures grew to coordinate policy on asylum, immigration, cross-border crime, and managing the EU's external borders. Policy initiatives were intergovernmental at first, and justice and home affairs was eventually incorporated into the mainstream of EU policy concerns by the Treaty of Lisbon.

- Immigration has long been part of the European demographic landscape, but it has been complicated by the rising numbers of migrants from outside Europe.

- The EU receives more applications for asylum than any other part of the world, but policy has not progressed much beyond agreeing standards and procedures.

- Europe is the most popular target for legal immigration in the world. Illegal immigration has been a rising problem for the EU since the end of the Cold War.

- Immigration may be the only viable response to problems arising from Europe's ageing and declining population, but the new racial and religious diversity of immigrants has sparked controversial anti-immigrant sentiment.

- Police and judicial cooperation has been encouraged by Europol, Eurojust and the European Judicial Network, spawning the introduction of European arrest and evidence warrants.

- Terrorism has long been a problem in Europe, but efforts to take an EU-wide approach were accelerated by the 9/11 attacks in the US and the 2004/05 bombings in Madrid and London.

- The vast majority of successful or attempted terrorist attacks in the EU in recent years have involved not Islamic extremists, but nationalist and separatist movements, left-wing and anarchist groups, right-wing racist groups, and single-issue groups.

Key terms and concepts

Asylum

European arrest warrant

European evidence warrant

European Judicial Network

Immigration

Justice and home affairs

Terrorism

Further reading

Boswell, Christina, and Andrew Geddes (2011) *Migration and Mobility in the European Union* (Basingstoke: Palgrave Macmillan). Study of the patterns of migration within the EU since the end of the Cold War, and EU migration and asylum policies.

Friedrichs, Jorg (2008) *Fighting Terrorism and Drugs: Europe and International Police Cooperation* (Abingdon: Routledge). Review of the EU approach to cooperating in the face of threats posed by terrorism and the drug trade.

Von Hippel, Karin (ed.) (2005) *Europe Confronts Terrorism* (Basingstoke: Palgrave Macmillan). Review of the EU response to 9/11, with country case studies and chapters on transatlantic cooperation.

24 The EU as a Global Actor

The great powers of the nineteenth century were European and exerted global influence mainly through their empires and trading interests. But the toll of two world wars left behind a relatively tame and introspective Europe, and the EEC in its early years was too focused on internal challenges to think much about its global role; western Europe mainly followed the lead of the US, while its eastern states were dominated by the Soviet Union, and a few holdouts tried to remain neutral.

By the 1970s, the logic of Community members working together on a wider range of foreign policy issues was becoming clearer, but it was only with the end of the Cold War that all began to change: Eastern Europe was freed from Soviet control, the borders of the European marketplace expanded, and enlargement took the EU first to the Russian border and then into the former Soviet Union. There was also a change in the nature of security issues, which became more regional in nature, dominated by new problems such as international terrorism and cybersecurity, which contrasted the soft power preferences of the Europeans with the hard power abilities of the US.

This chapter begins with a discussion of the nature of the EU as a global actor, placing it within our changing understanding of power. It then looks at the EU record in foreign, security, defence and trade policy, setting the scene for the assessment in Chapter 25 of developments in EU relations with different parts of the world. Opinion is divided on the global role of the EU, some arguing that it is still weak and unconvincing and others that it plays a critical role in addressing many of the challenges we now face.

- Do the EU's relative military weaknesses matter in the age of globalization?
- How do realism and idealism compare when it comes to explaining the global role of the EU?
- Has Europe achieved Kant's state of perpetual peace?
- What stops the EU being considered a major global actor in the same vein as the US or China?
- Why is the EU's trade power so often overlooked in discussions about its global role, while so much attention is focused on its lack of combined military power?

Understanding the global role of the EU

Until the First World War, the international system was dominated by Europe's great powers, Britain, France, Germany and Russia, which were distinguished by four key qualities (Levy, 1983, pp. 16–18):

- they had large militaries and the ability to project power beyond their borders
- their interests were continental or even global in scope
- they were willing to defend their interests aggressively
- their status was acknowledged by other powers.

No other states had such far-reaching influence and interests, the great powers of the future – the US, China, India and Japan – being either marginalized, isolated or under colonial control.

But the two world wars brought a close to the age of the great European powers, which had been replaced by the late 1940s with the new tensions of the Cold War between the United States and the Soviet Union. By virtue of the size, destructive abilities and global reach of their militaries, based on large nuclear arsenals, the US and the USSR earned a new label: superpower. The US also became an economic and even a cultural superpower, its resources giving it an unprecedented level of global political influence. In this new bipolar system, most other states either sided with the Americans or the Soviets, or tried (usually without much success) to remain nonaligned.

With the break-up of the Soviet Union in December 1991, many commentators began to argue that the world had entered a new unipolar era, in which the US was the only superpower, unchallenged on the military front and also perhaps on the economic and political fronts. Some even described it as a 'hyperpower' (Védrine and Moïsi, 2001, p. 2), a global hegemon, and a new kind of global empire (Ferguson, 2004). But even as this new analysis was getting into its stride, there was talk of the emergence of new global powers in the form of the BRIC states: Brazil, Russia, India and China (O'Neill, 2001). There were suggestions that the unipolar system was being replaced by a multipolar system: the US would remain pre-eminent but would face new competition from China and India. Some even suggested that a mix of domestic problems and foreign competition might be early signs of the decline of America (Mason, 2008).

Overlooked in much of this debate was the European Union. There were a few suggestions that it had great power potential (see Haseler, 2004; Reid, 2004; Leonard, 2005; McCormick, 2007), but they drew little academic and media attention, in spite of the growing EU economic presence. There were several possible reasons for this:

- Great power is still popularly equated with military power, and since the EU has neither a combined military nor a clear common defence policy, or, at least, a policy based on the idea of maintaining a large military with global reach, few consider it a superpower in the same league as the US or the old USSR.
- Great power is still popularly associated with states, the assumption being that only states have the ability to achieve global influence – mainly because only states maintain militaries. Taken individually, even the larger EU states have only a modest international reach, while the EU itself, say the doubters, is not sufficiently coordinated to express its collective power at a global level.

Superpower: An actor that has the ability to project power globally and enjoys a high level of autonomy and self-sufficiency in international relations (Fox, 1944, pp. 20–1).

Bipolar system: An arrangement in international relations in which power is divided, shared and controlled by two dominant actors.

Multipolar system: An arrangement in international relations in which power is divided, shared and controlled by more than two dominant actors.

- Power is more impressive when it is expressed visibly, and nothing is more visible than the sight of massive American ordinance raining down on a rogue regime, or American aircraft carriers being despatched for a show of force. The EU has little to match this kind of raw power, its influence being subtle and latent rather than obvious and assertive.
- Critics point to the regular failure of the EU to provide leadership. They quote its military embarrassments in the Balkans in the 1990s, the often public disagreements among its leaders – prime examples being the divisions over Iraq in 2003 and Ukraine in 2014 – and evidence that the US is taken more seriously by problem states such as North Korea, Iran or Israel.

Yet there is reason to question the efficacy and reach of American power, and to take a closer look at the reach of the EU. The US military did not prevail in Vietnam (and struggled in Afghanistan), militaries are expensive in human and financial terms, they may create new threats by encouraging the building of large militaries by states that themselves feel threatened, and they have little to offer the resolution of problems such as terrorism, poverty, cyberattacks or climate change. Meanwhile, the limits of American economic power were reflected in the US role in sparking the global financial crisis and its inability to respond unilaterally to that crisis.

As for claims that China and India are great powers, these overlook several troubling facts:

- neither state has the ability to commit its military all over the world
- both countries are still remarkably poor – the per capita gross national income of the US in 2013 was more than eight times greater than that of China and nearly 35 times greater than that of India (see Table 0.1)
- their political influence is still mainly regional rather than global
- neither has a world-class currency
- the global reach of their corporations is still quite modest
- China's human rights record and lack of economic transparency limit its global influence
- India must deal with massive poverty and pressing domestic social and religious divisions before it will be able to have much global influence.

As we saw in Chapter 19, the evidence of the EU's economic power is compelling, in spite of the region's many problems (which have their parallels in the US). As a military actor, however, the EU does not measure up so well. If the military forces of the 28 member states are added together, they are substantial (see later in this chapter), and individual EU states – particularly Britain and France – have been active in military operations in different parts of the world since 1945. But the EU projects nothing like the kind of power or presence that the US can project. But does this matter? It does if we still believe that security threats can only be met with force, but perhaps this is no longer true. It may be that we are entering a new era of multipolarity based not on military but economic power, and in which the EU may act as a new kind of international actor, based less on power (a term suggesting a desire to encourage others to change) than on influence (a term suggesting a desire to provide an example). There are four key qualities to the EU as a new model of global power.

First, it has mainly rejected the realist argument that states pursue self-interest in an anarchic international system, with little trust in long-term cooperation

Understanding Integration... *Liberalism*

Liberalism can be defined as the idea that international cooperation is possible and desirable, war and anarchy are not inevitable, and states should work to build domestic values into their foreign policies by promoting democracy abroad. In contrast to realist ideas about interstate rivalry and an anarchic world system, liberals argue that there are many opportunities for cooperation and all areas of policy can be brought into the equation. It traces its roots back to the idealist philosophy that was a product mainly of the First World War, suffered reduced credibility in the years leading up to the Second World War (although it is reflected in the work of David Mitrany), and was supplanted during the Cold War by realism.

While it should by all rights take its place alongside realism in debates about European integration, liberalism is surprisingly rarely discussed; Wiener and Diez (2009) and Saurugger (2013), for example, provide wide-ranging surveys of theoretical approaches to European integration with no more than passing mentions of it. Its

fundamental problem, perhaps, is that it is too idealistic and is driven primarily by a view of things as they should be (the ideal). By contrast, realism is focused more on pragmatic ideas about things as they are (the reality), and on national interests that are easier to list than values, even if they are not always easy to quantify.

Liberalism emphasizes the importance of international organizations and international law in understanding and driving the relations among states, and points to the lessons of democratic peace theory, which suggests that democracies are unlikely to go to war with one another. There has always been an element of self-interest in European integration, to be sure, but there has always been a strong tradition of cooperation and moving beyond hard realities to define aspirational goals. Neoliberalism takes the argument further by suggesting that international institutions can influence the behaviour of states by encouraging rules-based behaviour or promoting shared values.

or alliances (see Chapter 1), and instead more clearly reflects the arguments of liberalism. This is a view of international relations that emphasizes the possibilities of peace through international cooperation and the role of international law.

Second, Europeans have a preference for multilateralism over unilateralism. If the latter is understood as a willingness by a state to go it alone and rely on its own resources to achieve change, then multilateralism means a belief in approaching problems in concert and cooperation with other states. Europeans have long been used to forming political and security coalitions, with decades of experience of working together to agree new laws and policies, and making efforts to be inclusive (although they do not always succeed). In 2003, the European Commission (2003) declared that supporting multilateral cooperation is 'a basic principle' of EU foreign policy, and the EU should consider itself a 'driving force' in pursuing UN initiatives on sustainable development, poverty reduction and international security.

Third, the EU is more interested in the use of civilian power rather than military power. This is an idea suggested as early as 1972 by François Duchêne (1972, pp. 43, 47), when he argued that the lack of military power was not the handicap that it once was, and western Europe might become 'the first major area of the Old World where the age-old process of war and indirect violence could be translated into something more in tune with the twentieth-century citizen's notion of civilized politics'. The EU-28 may have a large military establishment and many EU states have actively engaged in military actions over the past few decades, but most Europeans instinctively prefer the peaceful resolution of prob-

Liberalism: A theory of international relations based on the interdependence of states and international organizations, and the possibilities of cooperation to promote change.

Multilateralism: A belief that problems should be addressed by states working together, perhaps through international organizations, rather than in isolation.

Concept

Perpetual peace
The conditions needed to end state-sponsored violence and achieve a lasting peace. The idea traces its intellectual heritage to Jeremy Bentham with his *Plan for an Universal and Perpetual Peace* published in 1789, which was followed six years later by Immanuel Kant's *Thoughts on Perpetual Peace*. Among Kant's conditions, the most relevant to understanding the EU is that of living under a league of peace in which the partners seek to end all wars forever. Kant's ideas were directed at achieving world peace rather than regional peace in Europe, but the EU has arguably come closest to fulfilling those ideas.

lems. Europe's global power today is expressed more through trade, investment and the reach of European multinational corporations than through conflict and the reach of European militaries.

Finally, and perhaps most importantly, the EU may be a compelling case of the possibilities of Immanuel Kant's notion of perpetual peace. Writing in 1795, Kant argued that the natural state of humans living side by side was one of war (open hostilities or the threat of war) rather than peace, and outlined the necessary conditions for the achievement of a lasting peace (see discussion in Bohman and Lutz-Bachmann, 1997):

■ No peace treaties should be signed that hold out prospects for future war.
■ No states should come under the dominion of others.
■ Standing armies should be abolished.
■ National debts should not be built with a view to war.
■ No states should interfere with the governments of other states.
■ States should not permit acts of hostility during war that would undermine confidence in the subsequent peace.
■ State constitutions should be republican, that is, based on freedom and equality for all, and respect for the rule of law.
■ States should live under a league of peace (seeking to end all wars forever) as distinct from a treaty of peace (seeking to end only one war).
■ Peaceful strangers should not be treated as enemies.

The EU record in almost all these qualities (except the abolition of standing armies) has been strong. The natural state of today's Europe is one of peace rather than war, and while the EU faces the external (and to some extent internal) threat of terrorism, its member states no longer threaten one another, nor does the EU pose a threat to others. The Nobel committee certainly seemed to be thinking along these lines when it awarded the EU the Nobel Peace Prize in 2012, a decision that – as we saw in Chapter 7 – had many critics.

Foreign policy

In its early years, European integration focused almost entirely on economic cooperation and was inward-looking to the point of almost entirely excluding attention to the place of the EEC in the world. Not only were large militaries distrusted because of their role in Europe's historical squabbles, but the focus during the 1950s and 60s was on rebuilding economies rather than militaries. Besides, the West was under the military shield of the Americans, and the East under that of the Soviets, so other than contributing to NATO and Warsaw Pact forces, the military initiative had been mainly taken out of European hands.

But as the reach of integration expanded in the 1960s, it became clear that the EEC needed to think more actively about its place in the world, and a modest first step was taken in 1970 with agreement of European Political Cooperation, an informal process that brought Community foreign ministers together at regular meetings to discuss international issues. With the Single European Act, member states were committed to 'endeavour jointly to formulate and implement a European foreign policy'. But rather than developing a single overall foreign policy – or even a set of common targeted policies – the Community remained

Foreign policy: Policy governing the relations between a state and other states, dealing with issues such as security, trade, immigration and economic relations.

what Groux and Manin (1985) called a mixed system, or one in which national and common policies coexisted.

The tumultuous changes arising from the end of the Cold War in the late 1980s and early 1990s found the Community unprepared to respond to major foreign policy challenges, but the thinking of its leaders was given new focus. Under Maastricht, the EU agreed to 'define and implement' a Common Foreign and Security Policy (CFSP), with the goals of strengthening the security of the EU, promoting peace and international security in accordance with the principles of the UN Charter, promoting international cooperation, and promoting democracy, the rule of law and respect for human rights. Member states were expected to do nothing that would run counter to EU interests, to inform and consult each other on matters of shared interest, and coordinate their actions in international forums. The CFSP also created three organizational tools:

1 *Common strategies* have been agreed where member states have important interests in common, as in their dealings with Russia, Ukraine, Myanmar and the Mediterranean.
2 *Joint actions* bring states together on issues such as support for the Middle East peace process, observing elections in Russia and South Africa, and sending a naval force to discourage piracy off the coast of Somalia.
3 *Common positions* have been agreed on approaches to the Balkans, the Middle East, Myanmar, Zimbabwe, and the International Criminal Court, and policy issues such as arms exports, biological weapons and terrorism.

But there remains a lack of policy focus and leadership, and there are differences of opinion among the member states. Some have their own national agendas, for example Britain and France have special interests in their former colonies, while Austria, Finland, Ireland and Sweden remain formally neutral, in word if not necessarily in deed, and there has long been a fundamental strategic division between Atlanticists, who favour close ties with the US – among them Britain, the Netherlands, Portugal and several eastern European states, and Europeanists, led by France and Germany, who want greater EU policy independence.

Institutionally, outsiders dealing with the EU have been faced with the problem, neatly summed up in the apocryphal question credited to former US Secretary of State Henry Kissinger: 'Who do I call if I want to speak to Europe?' Of all the EU institutions, the one best placed to represent EU interests was the Commission, but in the 1990s it divided the world up among four different commissioners, only establishing more focus in 1999 when a single commissioner for external relations was created. But the waters were muddied when a new position – the High Representative (HR) for the CFSP – was created within the Council of Ministers. The HR was intended to be the EU voice on foreign affairs, the first office-holder being Javier Solana, former secretary-general of NATO, who served two terms between 1999 and 2009. Matters were further complicated by the habit of rotating the presidency of the Council of Ministers among member states, obliging foreign governments to deal with a new set of policy leaders every six months.

Lisbon brought more change by combining the posts of HR and external relations commissioner into a single High Representative of the Union for Foreign Affairs and Security Policy. Appointed by the European Council (using

Mixed system: An arrangement in which state policies and common multi-state policies coexist, as was long the case with the example of EU foreign policy.

Common Foreign and Security Policy (CSFP): An attempt made under the Maastricht treaty to develop common foreign policy principles and positions among EU states.

Atlanticists and Europeanists: The division of opinion between those who continue to support close security ties with the US and those favouring greater European policy independence.

a qualified majority) and confirmed by the president of the Commission, the new HR is charged under Lisbon with 'conducting' the CFSP and ensuring the consistency of the EU's external action. Where the old HR was combined with the post of secretary-general of the Council of Ministers, the new HR not only chairs the Foreign Affairs Council but is also a vice-president of the European Commission, and heads the 5,000-member European External Action Service, a combined foreign ministry and diplomatic corps that began work in 2010. Catherine Ashton was appointed as the first HR in 2009, and was succeeded in 2014 by Federica Mogherini.

But while the existence of a redefined HR gives new focus to EU foreign policy, the coexistence of the president of the Commission and the president of the European Council (not to mention commissioners responsible for enlargement, development, trade and international cooperation) still leaves the waters muddied. Kissinger's apocryphal question has not been clearly answered, and this does not help strengthen the place of the EU in the international system.

Just how far the EU has travelled along the path to a common foreign policy is debatable. It has made much progress since the 1970s, on agreeing common positions and improving its institutional machinery. But another more fundamental question remains: How much have the states with which the EU interacts noticed or cared? The US is still the world's biggest national economy, controls the world's leading international currency, and has by far the largest military; for these reasons alone, its voice is much louder and is listened to more intently when it comes to resolving international economic problems or dealing with the world's hottest trouble spots, from Iran to Ukraine, Libya, Afghanistan, North Korea, Israel–Palestine and Somalia. The EU has a growing presence on economic issues, underpinned by the size of the European marketplace, its dominating position in global trade, and the visibility of the euro. But great power is still defined by most people in military terms, and as long as there is no joint EU military, or until we rethink how we understand power and influence in the world, the impact of the EU is likely to be constrained.

Federica Mogherini

Federica Mogherini (1973–), the incumbent foreign minister of Italy, was the second person appointed to the redesigned post of High Representative of the Union for Foreign Affairs and Security Policy. She began her involvement in politics as a member of the Italian Communist Youth Federation, and in 2001 joined the National Council of the Democrats of the Left. In 2008 she was elected to the Italian parliament as a member of the new Democratic Party, and was appointed foreign minister in February 2014 by Prime Minister Matteo Renzi. She became High Representative in November 2014, replacing Catherine Ashton, whose five-year term had ended. She had more foreign policy experience than Ashton, and had the advantage of taking over a position that was much better defined than it had been when Ashton entered office, but there had been concerns about her pro-Russian sentiments. Like Ashton, she continues to face the twin challenge of making the EU voice heard on the global stage, and working with member states that still want to assert their independence in foreign policy.

Security and defence policy

The EU is a more impressive military force than most people realize. If the budgets, the numbers of uniformed personnel and the armaments of the 28 member states are combined, the EU has the second biggest military in the world after that of the US. Its combined defence budget – while still far short of that of the US – is greater than that of Russia, China, India and Brazil combined, it has nuclear weapons (in Britain and France), nearly 1.9 million active personnel, nearly 3,500 combat aircraft, and more non-nuclear submarines and surface naval combat vessels than the US (aircraft carriers excepted) (see International Institute for Strategic Studies, 2013).

But, as a security actor, the EU is still in its 'early infancy' (Howorth, 2014, p. 3). Although several defence agreements were signed or discussed during the Cold War, western European security fell squarely under the remit of the North Atlantic Treaty Organization (NATO). A different track might have been followed after 1955, when the Western European Union (WEU) was created in the wake of the collapse of the European Defence Community. But the WEU was always marginalized and was eventually wound up in 2011. Its most lasting contribution was the agreement reached in 1992 among its foreign and defence ministers – meeting at the Hotel Petersberg, near Bonn – on the Petersberg tasks. Assuming that the WEU might become the European arm of NATO or the military wing of the EU, the ministers agreed that military units of WEU states, acting under the authority of the WEU, could include humanitarian, rescue, peacekeeping and

Petersberg tasks: The priorities – humanitarian, rescue, peacekeeping and other crisis management operations – set in 1992 by the Western European Union, and later adopted by the EU.

Illustration **24.1 Security policy**
A German naval vessel participating in Operation Atalanta, designed to help protect shipping from the threat of piracy off the coast of Somalia.

other crisis management operations, including peacemaking. These tasks were incorporated into the goals of the EU by the 1997 Treaty of Amsterdam.

The end of the Cold War meant the beginning of a change in the political relationship between the US and the EU: the limits of EU military abilities were revealed in the 1990–91 Gulf War and the crises in the Balkans, while its desire to reduce its reliance on the US has grown (Jones, 2007). Howorth (2014, p. 4) argues that the birth of the EU as a security actor can be dated from a December 1998 meeting in St Malo, France, between Tony Blair – who, as the still new prime minister of Britain, wanted to see his country play a more central role in EU defence matters – and French President Jacques Chirac. The resulting declaration argued that the EU should be in a position to play 'its full role on the international stage', and should have 'the capacity for autonomous action, backed up by credible military forces, the means to decide to use them, and the readiness to do so'. European security policy had now taken on a new significance.

France and Germany had already taken the initiative to set up a joint military force outside formal EC/EU structures when they created Eurocorps in 1992 (see Chapter 14). In 1996, a NATO ministerial meeting agreed that the WEU would be responsible for the development of a European Security and Defence Identity (ESDI); this would allow European NATO members to act independently where NATO did not wish to, and would be run politically by the WEU. But the ESDI turned out to be a false start, and encouraged by the idea that the EU should take responsibility for the development of a European policy outside NATO, in 1999 it was replaced by the European Security and Defence Policy (ESDP). This set the 'headline goal' of the EU states as being able to deploy a 60,000-member Rapid Reaction Force into the field at 60 days' notice and being able to sustain it for at least one year. Organizational committees and a military staff were set up, and the ESDP was given new impetus by the 9/11 attacks in the US and the realization that international terrorism constituted a new kind of threat that would not quickly go away.

In December 2003, the European Council adopted the European Security Strategy, the first ever joint declaration by EU member states of their strategic goals. The strategy declared that the EU was 'inevitably a global player' and 'should be ready to share in the responsibility for global security'. It listed the key threats facing the EU as terrorism, weapons of mass destruction, regional conflicts, failing states and organized crime. Having found that the Rapid Reaction Force idea was too ambitious, in May 2004 EU defence ministers agreed to the formation of as many as 15 'battle groups' made up of 1,500 personnel each, and capable of being deployed at 15 days' notice and sustained for between 30 and 120 days. Also in 2004, a European Defence Agency was created within which national defence ministers meet to promote planning and research in the interests of the ESDP.

In spite of the many doubts and questions that surround EU aspirations on security and defence policy, it has achieved more on security cooperation than most people think, driven by a desire to decrease its reliance on the US (Jones, 2007). For example:

■ It deployed peacekeeping troops in 2003 in Macedonia (Operation Concordia) and in the Democratic Republic of Congo (Operation Artemis).
■ It took over peacekeeping operations from NATO in Bosnia in 2004.

Security policy: Policy dealing with national defence, with identifying and offsetting military and other threats to national interests.

European Security and Defence Policy (ESDP): A critical step in the development of a European security policy outside NATO, based on the Petersberg tasks and the maintenance of 'battle groups' capable of short-notice military action.

European Security Strategy: The first comprehensive outline of the EU's security priorities, identifying threats and outlining key objectives

- It has had police and other missions in Afghanistan, the Central African Republic, Chad, Georgia, Guinea-Bissau, Indonesia, Kosovo, Mali, Macedonia, Palestine and Sudan.
- In 2008 the EU launched Operation Atalanta in the Indian Ocean, aimed at combating piracy off the coast of Somalia.
- At the beginning of 2010, EU personnel accounted for nearly 40 per cent of the forces in Afghanistan, and a significant number of those in Kosovo and Lebanon.
- Britain and France provided much of the lead in the 2011 military intervention in Libya that resulted in the overthrow of Muammar Gaddafi.
- Individual EU states have engaged in military operations such as Britain's mission in Sierra Leone in 2000 (establishing order after a UN force had failed) and France's contributions to peacekeeping in Haiti, Côte d'Ivoire and Lebanon.
- The EU has imposed sanctions against more than two dozen countries, including:
  - trade and travel bans on Belarus
  - arms embargoes on Côte d'Ivoire, Eritrea and Iraq
  - the freezing of funds of leaders in Egypt, Sudan and Zimbabwe
  - restrictions on travel from Iran and Liberia
  - wide-ranging bans on trade with North Korea, Somalia and Syria.
- In 2014 it took the lead on imposing targeted sanctions on Russian leaders in the wake of the crisis in Ukraine.

Debating... *Does the EU need a common military?*

YES

Whatever we say and think about economic power, military power is still regarded as the trump card in international relations. The EU may be the world's wealthiest marketplace and its biggest trading power, but until it can back up its global presence with a combined military and a common defence policy, it will not be able to defend itself effectively from security threats, or to exert much influence over responses to security problems in other parts of the world.

Whatever hopes more idealistic Europeans may have about soft approaches to dealing with international problems, militaries will always be needed as a last resort to deal with security threats.

Without a common military, the EU will have to continue relying either on its individual member states or the US. Either way, its freedom of independent action will be limited as a result.

NO

Military competition has often been a source of Europe's most difficult internal tensions.

The maintenance of large militaries is financially expensive and draws resources away from other needs, such as education, healthcare, the alleviation of poverty, and the building and maintenance of infrastructure.

History is replete with examples of military power failing to achieve its objectives, and even causing problems by creating a threat to which other actors must respond by building their own militaries.

The EU member states have shown that they cannot agree on military matters, so it is best to leave them the freedom to go their own way, and to come together on an ad hoc basis as needed.

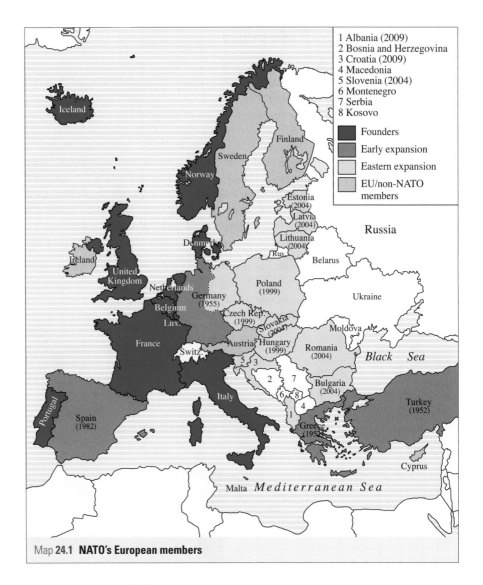

1 Albania (2009)
2 Bosnia and Herzegovina
3 Croatia (2009)
4 Macedonia
5 Slovenia (2004)
6 Montenegro
7 Serbia
8 Kosovo

Founders
Early expansion
Eastern expansion
EU/non-NATO members

Map **24.1 NATO's European members**

Howorth notes (2014, p. 115) that after stagnating between 1989 and 1999, EU security and defence policy has come a long way in a few short years; but he also concludes that the EU 'still has a long way to go before it can overcome all its shortcomings and emerge as a fully credible coordinated military actor able to carry out the full range of Petersberg tasks'. British Foreign Secretary David Miliband (2007) was critical during a speech in November 2007 when he noted that: 'It's frankly embarrassing … when European nations – with almost two million men and women under arms – are only able, at a stretch, to deploy around one hundred thousand at any one time.' Yet questions remain about what the EU *should* be able to achieve: its heritage as a civilian power remains strong, it does not aspire to become a major military actor on a par with the US, and the nature of security threats has changed in recent years. Meanwhile, the question of how far it should develop policy independence from the US and how far it should continue to be driven by the needs of NATO remains unanswered.

Trade policy

While questions linger about the global impact of the EU's foreign and security policies, on matters of trade there are few remaining doubts: the EU is the world's largest trading power (a trading hyperpower, even) and trade has become the EU's 'most powerful external policy domain' (Orbie, 2008). At its core has been the Common Commercial Policy (CCP), in place since the Treaty of Rome. Intended formally to contribute 'to the harmonious development of world trade, the progressive abolition of restrictions on international trade, and the lowering of customs barriers', the CCP was in fact designed to protect the EU's trading interests. Although a comprehensive EU trade policy took many years to develop, the CCP early helped establish strong EU positions on global trade negotiations, and underpinned the growing global presence of the EU as a trading powerhouse. The data make a compelling case:

- The EU is the world's wealthiest marketplace, with a population of more than half a billion predominantly middle-class consumers with plenty of disposable income.
- It accounts for nearly a quarter of global economic output, its combined GDP being bigger than that of the US, more than twice that of China, and nearly 10 times bigger than that of India (see Figure 24.1).
- The EU accounts for approximately one-sixth of trade in merchandise and about a quarter of trade in commercial services (see Table 24.1).

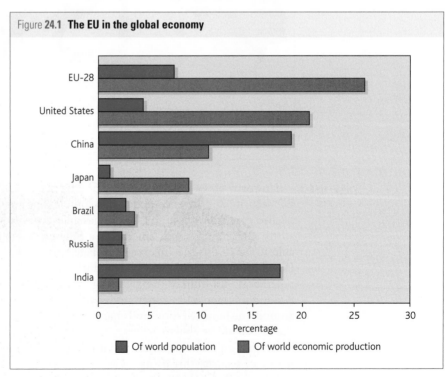

Figure **24.1** **The EU in the global economy**

Of world population Of world economic production

Common Commercial Policy (CCP): The common trade policy of the EU, included in the Treaty of Rome and under which the EU has effectively used its power to deal and negotiate with third parties on trade issues.

Sources: Population figures for 2010 from UN Population Division, www.esa.un.org/esa/population. Economic figures for 2011 from World Development Indicators database, www.worldbank.com (all figures retrieved April 2013).

Table **24.1** **The world's five biggest trading powers**

| | Percentage share | | | |
| | Merchandise | | Commercial services | |
	Imports	Exports	Imports	Exports
EU-27	15.4	14.7	20.2	25.0
United States	12.6	8.4	10.0	14.4
China	9.8	11.1	6.7	4.3
Japan	4.8	4.3	4.2	3.2
Brazil, Russia, India	5.7	5.8	7.5	5.5
Other	51.7	55.7	51.4	47.6

Source: Trade figures for 2012 (excluding data for intra-EU trade) from World Trade Organization, www.wto.org (retrieved April 2014).

- The euro (in spite of its recent problems) sits alongside the US dollar and the Japanese yen as one of the three most important currencies in the world. The Chinese and the Indians have nothing to compare.
- It has long been the biggest source and target of foreign direct investment in the world, although its share has fallen dramatically in the wake of the global financial and euro zone crises; in 2007 it accounted for about two-thirds of investment flows into and out of OECD member states, but its shares of inflows and outflows were down to 40 per cent and 28 per cent, respectively, by 2012 (OECD figures, www.oecd.org/statistics).
- As we saw in Chapter 19, it is the biggest market in the world for mergers and acquisitions and the global presence of European multinationals has grown accordingly in strength and reach.

The most obvious developments on the trade front have been closest to home, where most of the barriers that once divided EU states have disappeared. As late

Illustration **24.2** **Trade policy**

Two of the key players in global trade negotiations, Michael Froman, US trade representative, and Cecilia Malmström, then EU trade commissioner. The two were meeting in Washington DC in 2014 to take stock of progress in negotiations on the Transatlantic Trade and Investment Partnership.

as the 1960s and 70s, it was relatively unusual to find items for sale (or services on offer) in western European states that were not domestically produced, grown or generated, and consumers were supplied mainly by domestic corporations or the big US multinationals such as Ford, Kodak, IBM and Esso. As the single market encouraged mergers and acquisitions across European borders and opened up domestic trading opportunities, so European consumers saw more products and services coming from neighbouring states. The result is that about two-thirds of all EU trade is now generated within the EU. From this base, the EU has in turn become a global trading power, selling goods and services around the world, and being a market to which foreign countries and corporations want access.

The role of the EU as a trading power is reflected in the number of times it has been involved in cases brought before the World Trade Organization (WTO). Since the creation of the WTO with its dispute resolution process in 1995, any member state that has a trade dispute with another can take their case to the WTO, which will investigate and issue a judgement that is binding on the parties involved. Given that the EU and the US are the world's two biggest trading powers, it is not surprising that they have brought more cases before the WTO than any other members (see Figure 24.2). In many instances, the disputes have

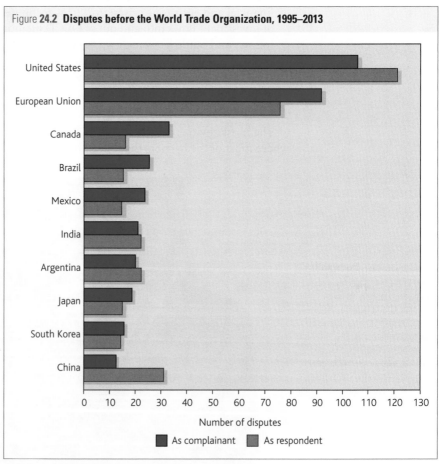

Figure **24.2 Disputes before the World Trade Organization, 1995–2013**

Source: World Trade Organization, www.wto.org (retrieved April 2014).

been between the EU and the US, who have tussled over hormone-treated beef, agricultural imports from Latin America, tariffs on steel imports, and subsidies to aircraft manufacturers. The EU has even gone beyond issues dealing with trade in goods and moved into areas outside its legal competence, including intellectual property rights, trade in services, and the tax regimes of third countries (Billiet, 2005).

The EU has not always had its way on trade negotiations, to be sure, and Meunier (2005) finds a mismatch between the institutional unity of the EU on trade issues and its external bargaining power. But the statistics make a compelling case, and whatever doubts there may be about the internal economic policies of the EU (see Chapter 19), its global economic presence is uncontested. We may never be able to do without military power to deal with the most serious international security problems, but in a world of globalization, new technology, new patterns of migration and greater market freedom, control of the means of production is more important than control of the means of destruction. On the trade front at least, the EU is in a commanding position.

Summary

- Understanding the global role of the EU depends on how we understand power in the international system, long conventionally associated with military power and states.

- Talk of a Cold War bipolar system was briefly replaced after the collapse of the Soviet Union by talk of a unipolar system based on US hegemony, but this has since been replaced with talk of a multipolar system bringing in new powers such as China and India, but curiously often overlooking the EU.

- Depending on how we understand the international system, there is evidence of the EU emerging as a new kind of power based on idealist principles, with a preference for the use of multilateralism, civilian power and soft rather than hard instruments of influence.

- The EU's Common Foreign and Security Policy has been less a common policy than a means to setting shared positions, and it has suffered from a lack of leadership and focus.

- The EU is a more impressive military power than most people realize, but it has made only limited progress along the path to a common security policy.

- Questions remain about what the EU *should* be able to achieve in security policy, how far it should develop policy independence from the US, and how much it should continue to be driven by the needs of NATO.

- Buoyed by the size of the single market and the near-completion of a Common Commercial Policy, the EU has become a trading superpower.

- Its trading power is reflected in the number of disputes in which it has been involved within the World Trade Organization.

Key terms and concepts

Atlanticists

Bipolar system

Common Commercial Policy

Common Foreign and Security Policy

European Security and Defence Policy

European Security Strategy

Europeanists

Foreign policy

Liberalism

Mixed system

Multilateralism

Multipolar system

Perpetual peace

Petersberg tasks

Power

Security policy

Superpower

Further reading

Howorth, Jolyon (2014) *Security and Defence Policy in the European Union*, 2nd edn (Basingstoke: Palgrave Macmillan). Overview of the trials and tribulations of the EU in this critical policy area.

Keukeleire, Stephan, and Tom Delreaux (2014) *The Foreign Policy of the European Union*, 2nd edn (Basingstoke: Palgrave Macmillan). Hill, Christopher, and Michael Smith (eds) (2011) *International Relations and the European Union*, 2nd edn (Oxford: Oxford University Press). Orbie, Jan (ed.) (2008) *Europe's Global Role: External Policies of the European Union* (Aldershot: Ashgate). Three of the numerous published studies on the foreign policies of the EU.

Young, Alasdair, and John Peterson (2014) *Parochial Global Europe: 21st Century Trade Politics* (Oxford: Oxford University Press). In contrast to the extensive publishing on EU foreign policy, one of the few full-length studies of its trade policy, using the evidence it finds to draw conclusions about the personality of the EU as a global actor.

25 The EU and the World

Preview

hapter 24 looked at how the EU's foreign, security and trade policies have shaped its role as a global actor. This chapter examines those policies more closely by looking at the EU's relations with different parts of the world. We begin with an assessment of the most important political and economic relationship in the world, between the EU and the US. This has not always been an easy relationship, the differences that lurked under the surface during the Cold War having become more visible since the collapse of the Soviet Union removed the one project that the two most clearly had in common.

The chapter then looks at the EU's relations with its immediate neighbours: the Mediterranean, the Middle East and Russia. Beyond the inner rim of potential future members of the EU, there is a 'circle of friends' consisting of countries that have no realistic prospect of EU membership, but with which the EU is building close political and economic ties. Particularly important is Russia, by far the biggest of its neighbours but the one over whom the most troubling questions continue to linger, particularly in the wake of the crisis in Ukraine.

Further afield, there are fascinating developments in the EU's relations with China, for many the most convincing candidate for the world's next superpower. Ties between the two have improved, yet uncertainties remain and the EU is wary about China's human rights record and foreign policy. Finally, Europe's former African, Caribbean and Pacific colonies have long played a part in the definition of the EU's global interests, and the EU has become the biggest source of official development assistance in the world. But the jury is still out on the efficacy of development policy.

Key issues

- Can (or do) Europeans and Americans see the world in the same way?
- What does European integration have to offer its near neighbours as a means to the promotion of capitalism and democracy?
- How are the driving forces behind EU relations with Russia and China different, and what are the likely results?
- What impact is the tripartite relationship between the EU, the US and China likely to have on international politics and economics?
- Which holds out better prospects for developing countries: fair trade or official development aid?

The EU and the US

The bilateral relationship between the US and the EU is the most important (and the most thoroughly studied) in the world. The two actors are economic superpowers, between them accounting for nearly half of global economic production, nearly one-third of global trade in services, and about a quarter of global trade in merchandise. They also control the two key international currencies, the dollar and the euro, and, as homes to most of the world's largest multinational corporations, they dominate international commerce, controlling millions of jobs around the world and being the major sources (and targets) of foreign direct investment, as well as being among each other's biggest trading partners. They also maintain the biggest and most powerful military forces in the world, between them accounting for 75 per cent of global spending on defence. Finally, this combination of economic and military power translates into global political influence; the US and the EU dominate the world's major international organizations, and what one says and does matters not only to the other but to much of the rest of the world.

In spite of this, the transatlantic relationship has not always been an easy one (see Lundestad, 2003; McGuire and Smith, 2008, Ch. 1). Before the Second World War, Americans kept their distance, wary of being drawn into European conflicts and critical of European colonialism. Meanwhile, Europeans kept a worried eye on rising American political, economic and cultural influence. After the Second World War, western Europeans fell into an often reluctant subservience to American leadership; they had little choice but to rely on American economic investments and security guarantees, and while their governments might have privately railed against US policy, in public they mainly went along, recognizing the importance of the Atlantic Alliance.

The US has always been a supporter of European integration, and it is unlikely that the EEC would have been created or have evolved into today's EU without that support. It made critical early contributions through the Marshall Plan and by providing a security umbrella in the form of NATO, but its generosity was not entirely charitable: peace and economic reconstruction in western Europe suited American interests, reinforcing the region's abilities to resist and offset Soviet influence, building an important market for American exports, and establishing western Europe as a critical political and economic partner of the US.

While there were deliberate US policies that helped pave the way for European integration, the US also contributed unconsciously in two other ways. First, it pursued policies that helped unite Europeans either in support of US policy or in opposition (but mainly the latter). Their opposition to the war in Vietnam (which peaked in 1965–75) strained the Alliance, while the unilateral decision of the US in 1971 to end dollar convertibility with gold brought political and economic strain. The transatlantic gap in Middle East policy became clear in 1973 as western European governments parted company with the US over military assistance to Israel during the Yom Kippur War. The litany of differences grew: West German policy towards East Germany, US policy in Central America, the 1979 Soviet invasion of Afghanistan, and the deployment by the Reagan administration of nuclear weapons in Europe.

Second, American policy has often helped the EU identify its weaknesses. It was competition from US corporations in the 1960s that helped western

Atlantic Alliance: The military and political alliance between the US and Europe, founded on NATO.

Europeans realize how little progress they were making on rebuilding their own industries, the US decision on the dollar and gold led to exchange rate volatility that helped set the groundwork for monetary union, and then came the serial security embarrassments of the 1990s: the 1990–91 Gulf War, the outbreak of fighting in the Balkans in 1991, and the crisis in Kosovo in 1999. These revealed just how much EU governments still disagreed among themselves on foreign policy and showed how poorly prepared the EU was to deal with major international security problems.

Formal attempts by the two sides to build links have had mixed results. In November 1990 the Transatlantic Declaration committed them to regular high-level contacts and called for cooperation in policy areas such as combating terrorism, drug trafficking and international crime (Commission of the European Communities, 1990). In 1995 the New Transatlantic Agenda committed them to work together on promoting peace and democracy around the world. Under the 1995 Transatlantic Business Dialogue, European and American business leaders began meeting at regular conferences, the 1998 launch of the Transatlantic Economic Partnership was designed to encourage more discussions on trade issues, and discussions are currently underway on the Transatlantic Trade and Investment Partnership, an effort to reach a wide-ranging trade agreement; the US is the EU's major trade partner (see Table 25.1).

But behind the diplomatic smiles, the nature of the game has changed since the end of the Cold War. The one truly common transatlantic project – opposing and outwitting the Soviets – is gone, since when the two sides have been more forthright in their differences of opinion. They have cooperated on numerous key security problems and are united in their efforts to address international terrorism, but they have disagreed on approaches towards Cuba, Iran, Iraq and Libya (Haass, 1999), and the US has been disappointed by the inability or unwillingness of the Europeans always to take their share of responsibility for international security. They have also had fallouts over trade and have often taken each other before the WTO for the resolution of disputes. Public support for common EU foreign policies has grown and is particularly strong on the question of policy independence from the US, favoured by almost four out of five Europeans (see Figure 25.1).

The September 2001 terrorist attacks in the US should have brought the two sides together, but ended up driving them apart. There was an initial outpouring of political and public sympathy in the EU and a hope among European leaders that both sides could work together on a response. But while they agreed on the

Table **25.1 The EU's five biggest external trading partners, 2012**

	% Share exports to		*% Share imports from*
United States	17.3	China	16.2
China	8.5	Russia	11.9
Switzerland	8.0	United States	11.5
Russia	7.3	Switzerland	5.9
Turkey	4.3	Norway	5.6

Source: World Trade Organization, www.wto.org (retrieved April 2014).

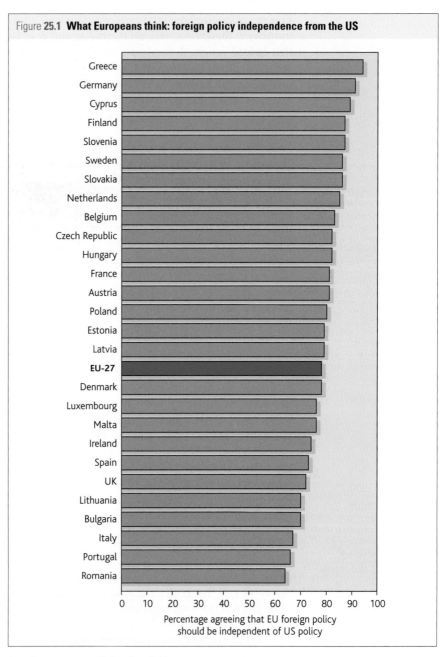

Figure 25.1 **What Europeans think: foreign policy independence from the US**

Percentage agreeing that EU foreign policy
should be independent of US policy

Note: No more recent polls have been held.

Source: Eurobarometer 68, May 2008.

threats posed by terrorism and the invasion of Afghanistan, Europeans were
shocked when the administration of President George W. Bush adopted a bellig-
erent tone of unilateralism, arguing that states were either for or against the US
in the war on terrorism, and rejecting multilateralism in favour of the right of

Illustration **25.1**
Transatlantic relations
The US–EU bilateral relationship is the most important in the world, but the two sides have not always agreed. Here, President Obama meets EU leaders at the G20 summit in Australia. Seated with him are French President François Hollande, British Prime Minister David Cameron, German Chancellor Angela Merkel and European Commission President Jean-Claude Juncker.

the US to act alone. Americans and Europeans also disagreed over the causes of terrorism: Bush argued that terrorists 'hated America' and were envious of its democratic principles, while Europeans preferred to look at the root causes of militant resentment, including the Arab–Israeli problem and the stationing of US troops in Saudi Arabia.

When the Bush administration started making plans for an invasion of Iraq in 2002, the tensions between the US and the EU broke into the open. Led by France and Germany, several European governments openly opposed and criticized US policy, while American critics of the EU accused it of dithering and raised the spectre of 1930s-style appeasement. US Defence Secretary Donald Rumsfeld dismissed Germany and France as 'old Europe', arguing that the centre of gravity in NATO Europe had shifted eastwards to its new members. Europeans responded by using unflattering Wild West metaphors to describe President Bush. In a 2003 poll, 53 per cent of Europeans ranked the US as a threat to world peace on a par with North Korea and Iran (Flash Eurobarometer, 2003, p. 78).

The fallout over Iraq sparked a flood of academic and media analyses of the state of the transatlantic relationship (see, for example, Kagan, 2003; Mowle, 2004; Kopstein and Steinmo, 2008). Optimists argued that it was a short-term squabble and that both sides would overcome their differences because it was in their interests to work together. Pessimists argued that the rift was inevitable, was indicative of deeper problems, and that the relationship could never be the same again. But Iraq showed that the Europeans were willing to be more assertive, and were more aware of how they differed from the Americans on issues as diverse as climate change, the Middle East peace process, and the International Criminal Court – the US is not a state party to the treaty establishing the court, which was championed by the EU and has been signed by all its member states.

Most Europeans welcomed the election of President Barack Obama in 2008, hoping that it would lead to better relations and new US foreign policies with which they could agree. The Obama administration at first showed limited interest in the EU, the president even opting to miss a US–EU summit in 2010, leading to concerns that he was paying more attention to China than Europe (Erlanger, 2010). But then the two sides cooperated on four critical security issues:

1　When a civil war broke out in Libya in 2011, several EU states worked with the US on enforcing a no-fly zone and providing military logistical support to rebels.
2　When a civil war broke out in Syria in 2011, the EU joined with the US in leading the condemnation of the Assad regime.
3　When a 2013 decision by the government of Ukraine to back away from an association agreement with the EU sparked a revolution and the intervention of Russia, the EU took the lead in bolstering the Ukrainian government and punishing Russia with sanctions.
4　When an international response to the threats posed by the rise of the extremist group Islamic State (also known as ISIS) in Iraq was formulated in September 2014, EU states worked closely with the Obama administration.

What are the prospects for continued strong relations between the EU and the US? On the one hand, both parties agree on the general goals of promoting democracy, free markets, human rights and the rule of law. They can, when it suits them, usually set aside their differences to address pressing international problems. They are also deeply invested in each other economically, as reflected in their trade relationship, their mutual flows of foreign direct investment, and the manner in which economic problems in one quickly spill over into the other. On the other hand, both sides are ambitious and assertive, and have different styles and values on a wide range of issues:

- Europeans take a more liberal position than Americans on a host of social issues, including abortion, capital punishment, same-sex marriage and euthanasia.
- Europeans are more willing to support the role of government in providing education, healthcare and welfare. Whereas most Americans feel that it is more important for government to provide them with the freedom to pursue other goals, most Europeans feel that it is more important for government to guarantee that no one is in need (see, for example, discussion in Russell, 2006, pp. 48–9).
- On security policy, Europeans (as we saw in Chapter 24) favour the use of soft power and peacekeeping, while Americans have fewer concerns about hard power.

Americans and Europeans are bound tightly by history, culture, politics and economic principles, but they have long kept their distance from one another, and the rise of a more assertive Europe suggests that – assuming Europeans can build the necessary level of agreement on foreign policy – the transatlantic relationship, while never static in the past, is likely to undergo further substantial change in the future. One multi-author study (Kopstein and Steinmo, 2008, p. 4) agrees on the many differences between the two sides, leaving open only the question of where they will lead; while Europeans and Americans may be growing apart in many respects, they may also find enough common ground to continue to work together. (For more about transatlantic differences, see McCormick, 2007, Chs 6 and 7; for more about similarities, see Baldwin, 2009.)

Looking to the neighbourhood

We saw in Chapters 5–7 how enlargement has influenced developments in new member states of the EU and changed the character of the EU itself. We also saw in Chapter 9 that as many as 16 countries have prospects of eventually becoming members of the EU, if we extend the definition of Europe to include the Caucasus and Turkey. Just outside that ring of potential future members is another group of states that sit on the EU's borders, which do not qualify for membership as the terms are currently defined, yet mainly want a strong bond with the EU, and who the EU is willing to court in the interests of creating a 'circle of friends'. This circle takes in most of North Africa and the Middle East, along with the rather different challenge of how to deal with Russia.

November 1995 saw the launch of the Euro-Mediterranean Partnership – otherwise known as the Barcelona Process – with the goal of strengthening political, economic and social ties between the EU and all North African and Middle Eastern states bordering the Mediterranean; these included Algeria, Egypt, Israel, Jordan, the Palestinian Authority, Turkey and – until they joined the EU – Cyprus and Malta. The programme included goals such as agreeing shared values, promoting democracy, developing policies that complemented those of the US in the Mediterranean, and establishing a free trade area in the Middle East by 2010. Although the partnership encouraged economic and cultural ties, it was tripped up by the lack of progress on the Middle East peace process, concerns among some partner countries about the dominant role of the EU, and the focus on the Mediterranean being distracted by the inclusion of the many EU states that do not border the Mediterranean.

In 2008, on an initiative mainly from French President Nicolas Sarkozy, the Barcelona Process evolved into the Union for the Mediterranean. This was originally to have focused only on Mediterranean states (but would have used EU funds), to have included a Mediterranean Investment Bank, and was proposed (in the case of Turkey) as an alternative to membership of the EU. But in the face of criticism from other EU states, it was expanded to include all EU states, and was portrayed to Turkey as a stepping stone to EU membership rather than an alternative. It has many of the same policy goals as the Barcelona Process, an institutional headquarters in Barcelona, a rotating co-presidency (one EU state and one non-EU state), and consists of 43 members: the 28 EU member states along with 15 neighbouring states (see Map 25.1).

Meanwhile, the European Neighbourhood Policy (ENP) was adopted in 2004 with the goal of avoiding the emergence of dividing lines between an enlarged EU and its immediate neighbours, promoting a relationship that the EU describes as 'privileged'. It targets 16 of those neighbours and is based on developing action plans with each of these countries intended to define how relations between the parties will develop and the interests they share. The EU agenda includes plans to encourage democracy, human rights, the rule of law, market economics and good governance in the ENP countries, and cooperation on measures against terrorism.

Although discussions about the EU's relationship with its neighbours is often couched in terms of rather dry and technical projects and programmes, it has a bigger and wider significance; in a world where debates about how to promote peace and democracy never end, the European soft power model has come to

Barcelona Process: A programme aimed at strengthening ties between the EU and most of its North African and Middle Eastern neighbours.

Union for the Mediterranean: A project by which the Barcelona Process was relaunched in 2008, with a focus on security cooperation, immigration, the environment, transport and education.

European Neighbourhood Policy (ENP): A policy aimed at encouraging democracy and capitalism in the eastern European and North African neighbours of the EU.

offer a contrast to the American hard power model. Arguably, the promise of access to the European marketplace has become the single most effective means for the promotion of democracy and capitalism. This is partly why Mark Leonard (2005, pp. 56, 103–4) believes that 'Europe will run the 21st century'. He argues that it has a transformative power, which:

> comes from its ability to reward reformers and withhold benefits from laggards, [and it functions as] a club with rules and benefits to hand out. By couching their relations in terms of creating a neighbourhood club .... [Europeans] can create the incentives to drive reform without being imperial.

The EU's relationship with the Middle East has long been difficult, made worse in recent decades by tensions with Iran, Iraq and Israel. Europe's interests in achieving Middle East peace are far greater than those of the US, the major foreign player in the region, for at least four major reasons:

1 The EU (which has few domestic oil supplies, unlike the US) relies on the Middle East for about 40 per cent of its oil needs, about twice as big a proportion as the US.
2 The EU has a bigger trading relationship with many Middle Eastern countries than the US.
3 Europe attracts many more immigrants from the Middle East than the US.
4 Europe faces a more immediate threat from Islamic militancy and terrorism than the US, being home to a far greater number of Muslims, having to live more immediately with the prospect of home-grown terrorism, and being easier to reach should Iran ever develop nuclear weapons and the ability to use them. Despite this, the EU has so far played only a supporting role to the US, benefiting (or suffering, depending on your point of view) from the US political-military role in the region while often being critical of US policy (Nitze and Hadar, 2009).

Few problems have been more central to the EU's Middle Eastern policy (and yet, oddly, less closely studied) than Israel. Where Israeli–western European relations were generally strong in the 1950s, they have soured since the 1967 Six Day War and the Israeli occupation of the West Bank and Gaza that has persisted ever since. The Community fell out with the US on arms supplies to Israel during the 1973 Yom Kippur War, Greece and Spain did not establish diplomatic relations with Israel until the 1980s, and the EU has made the creation of a Palestinian homeland a condition of Middle Eastern peace. Perhaps most (in)famously, the 2003 Flash Eurobarometer poll in the EU-15 placed Israel at the top of a list of countries regarded as a threat to world peace, above Iran, North Korea and Iraq. More recently, the EU has been highly critical of Israeli attacks on Lebanon and the Gaza Strip, and is more openly critical than the US of the building of Israeli settlements in the occupied territories of the West Bank, particularly in East Jerusalem.

But how much EU opinion matters to Israel is debatable. The US has long been the political champion of Israel and its major supplier of military aid. The Israeli lobby in Washington DC is strong, and Israeli leaders generally care far more what the US has to say than what the EU has to say. European criticism of Israeli policy has spawned analyses suggesting that anti-Semitism is alive and well

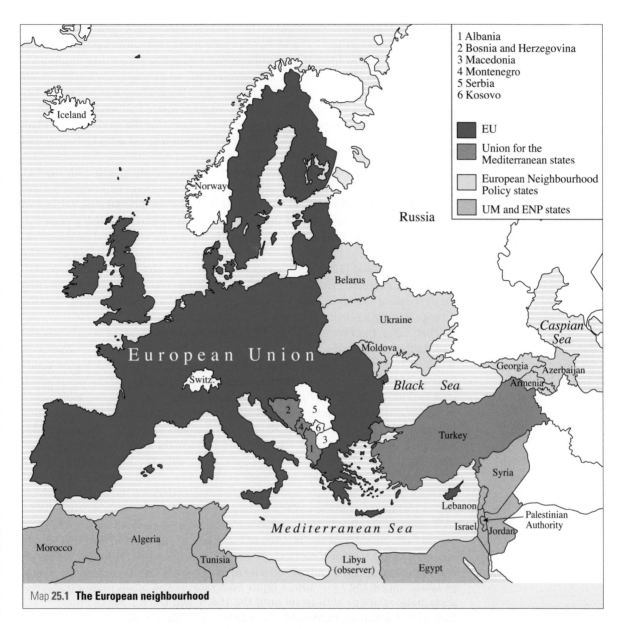

1 Albania
2 Bosnia and Herzegovina
3 Macedonia
4 Montenegro
5 Serbia
6 Kosovo

EU

Union for the
Mediterranean states

European Neighbourhood
Policy states

UM and ENP states

Map **25.1** **The European neighbourhood**

in many parts of Europe. Meanwhile, Israel criticizes what it regards as the EU's pro-Arab policies in the Middle East, while many Europeans abhor the militarism that influences Israeli policy and the strong role played by religious fundamentalism in Israeli justifications for continued occupation of Palestinian territory. At the same time, Israel is heavily dependent on the European market for its exports, and so cannot afford to allow relations to deteriorate too much. In short, it is at best a love–hate relationship. (For more details, see Pardo and Peters, 2009.)

Troubles also loom to the east, where the EU–Russia relationship has blown hot and cold since the end of the Cold War (Antonenko and Pinnick, 2005). At first relations were positive, with Russia seeking the kind of respectability and economic opportunities that the EU could offer, while the EU sought Russian support for eastern enlargement. In 1997 a Partnership and Cooperation Agreement between the EU and Russia came into effect, aimed at encouraging cooperation, establishing the conditions for a possible future free trade area, and expressing EU hopes for 'a stable, democratic and prosperous Russia, firmly anchored in a united Europe free of new dividing lines'. There was talk in the late 1990s of building a Common European Economic Space that would give Russia new access to the European single market in return for the necessary changes in Russian law, and in 2003 the Putin administration sided with Germany and France in opposing the US-led invasion of Iraq.

But then Russia began to worry about its economic imbalance with the EU, and looked askance at the applications for EU membership from three former Soviet republics – Estonia, Latvia and Lithuania. The EU became critical of the authoritarian tendencies of the Putin administration and Russian policy in Chechnya. The two sides disagreed over climate change and illegal immigration from Russia, while tensions grew as NATO membership expanded into the former Soviet bloc (12 former Soviet or eastern bloc states are now members), and Russia expressed displeasure with the leading role of the EU in criticizing the fraudulent October 2004 Ukrainian presidential elections, feeding into the Orange Revolution that led to a new vote in December.

Then came the events of 2013–14 in Ukraine, at the heart of which was the question of whether the country wanted to ally itself with the EU or Russia. A revolt was sparked in December 2013 by the decision of President Viktor Yanukovych not to sign an association agreement with the EU. When Yanukovych later fled to Russia, an interim government took over, and separatists took power in Crimea, which was annexed by Russia in March 2014. The EU immediately imposed targeted sanctions on Russia, pro-Russian separatists declared independence in parts of eastern Ukraine, and in June the new Ukrainian government signed the delayed association agreement with the EU. Matters further deteriorated when a Malaysia Airlines aircraft was shot down over rebel-held territory in Ukraine in July, and questions remained about the extent to which Russia was involved in the eastern Ukrainian uprising.

Today the EU–Russia relationship remains tense. Both sides need each other but do not entirely trust the motives of the other. At the heart of the tensions are economic considerations, particularly energy: the EU relies on Russia for about one-fifth of its oil needs and one-quarter of its gas needs. For its part, Russia is only too aware that the EU not only accounts for 70 per cent of its exports but is also the biggest source of foreign investment in Russian industry and infrastructure.

The EU and China: new discoveries

The Western world has a new fascination with the rising global role of China, whose large population and rapidly transforming economy have led many to conclude that China will soon be (if it is not already) a superpower. But this depends on how we define a superpower (see Chapter 24), and it also rather overlooks China's overall poverty, its lack of a currency with global credibility or a military with global reach, and its poor record on human rights. None of this has been enough to stand in the way of a growing speculative literature on the global role of China, and another more specifically on EU–Chinese relations, assessing the bilateral links between these two economic giants from multiple angles (see, for example, Shambaugh et al., 2008; Casarini, 2009; Ross et al., 2010; Vogt, 2012). China is now the EU's second biggest export market (after the US) and the biggest source of its imports.

Despite this, the EU–China relationship is not yet well understood. For centuries Europe and China have had trade links that have impacted both sides, yet their physical distance from each other has led to a high degree of mutual misunderstanding (Yahuda, 2008), and it is only since the mid-1990s that there have been efforts to build closer relations between the two. Even today the story is not a simple one, being complicated by questions about China's long-term plans and the dynamics of the tripartite relationship between the EU, the US and China. The latter promises not only to change the nature of the international system, but will also inevitably impact the way other states, such as Japan, India and Russia, relate to China (Kerr and Fei, 2007).

Ties between China and the Community were established in 1975 with the first visit to China by a European commissioner. A trade agreement was signed in 1978, an agreement on trade and economic cooperation in 1985, and the Commission opened a Delegation in Beijing in 1988. Relations soured following the June 1989 crackdown in Tiananmen Square, which resulted in the imposition of Community sanctions on China. Within three years relations were back on a stronger footing, although an arms embargo remained in place. A series of EU–China summits were held between 1998 and 2002, supported by policy papers from the Commission that included reference to 'a maturing partnership' between the two sides. An agreement was signed in 2003 bringing China into the Galileo navigation satellite programme (much to the chagrin of the US), and numerous China–EU meetings addressed issues such as human rights, maritime transport, technology, climate change and intellectual property.

The EU has remained critical of China's poor human rights record, and there have been disagreements on climate change and other issues, but where the two sides had once rarely spoken to each other at the diplomatic level, joint meetings have become almost routine. The strengthening of ties has been helped by the removal of the restrictions of the Cold War, the fact that Taiwan is not an issue in Europe as it is in the US (where there is an active Taiwan lobby), Europe (unlike the US) has no military presence in East Asia, the clearly shared commercial and economic interests of the two actors, and the role of the Commission in developing policy proposals that have 'offered a benign view of China's rise and identified a range of areas for collaboration' (Shambaugh et al., 2008, pp. 304–5).

For Casarini (2009, p. 15), the EU–China relationship has gone through three phases: a period of constructive engagement from the mid-1990s, moving to a strategic partnership between the two sides in 2003–05 (marked by cooperation on technology, notably space and satellite navigation), followed more recently by 'pragmatic restraint' in light of US concerns about how the relationship has been evolving. Along the way, Casarini argues, the EU has been unable to define a clear position on China, and its leaders have been unable to agree what kind of power China has become. The result has, in turn, been a challenge to the emergence of the EU as a global actor. Much depends on how the implications of new Chinese power in the world are understood, and the political impact of critics of China's human rights record and military aspirations. Unlike the Europe–US relationship, where communication has always been strong (even if the two do not always

Development policy

Since the end of the colonial era, there has been political and moral pressure on wealthy industrialized states to provide aid to developing countries, many of which were once colonized by the major European powers. The effects of this aid have been controversial; critics charge that it has been targeted for the wrong uses, it has created dependence rather than independence, and too little has been made available. Meanwhile, the leaders of many developing countries have been accused of failing to ensure the equitable distribution of that aid, lining their own pockets, and spending on non-essential showcase projects such as new airports and conference centres rather than schools and hospitals.

agree) and where neither actor has much reason to worry about threats posed by the other, the Europe–China relationship is influenced by questions and doubts about the implications of rapid economic change in China and what China's new wealth and commercial demands will mean for international relations.

The EU and development cooperation

The age of European imperialism is long dead, but its effects are still felt in the heritage of political and economic ties between EU states and former European colonies. Existing colonies were given associate membership of the EEC when it was created in 1958, and former French colonies that are now overseas departments of France – French Guiana, Guadeloupe, Martinique and Réunion – are integrated into the EU. For others, EU development policy has had three main components (Bourdet et al., 2007, pp. 1–3):

1 Trade agreements with different groups of countries aimed at helping them boost exports and economic growth.
2 Official development assistance (ODA) in the form of grants and technical aid.
3 Policies aimed at specific economic sectors with the goal of helping boost long-term development.

But despite the long history of EU development policy, it has (like trade policy) been remarkably little studied and the relative role of the member states and the European Commission is not yet well understood (Carbone, 2007), nor are the overall effects of EU policy on helping address global poverty and underdevelopment.

Under the Africa Caribbean Pacific (ACP) programme (see Table 25.2 for a list of all 80 countries), trade agreements have been signed with selected former colonies, mainly those of Belgium, Britain, France and Portugal. These began with the 1963 and 1969 Yaoundé Conventions (named for the capital of Cameroon, where they were signed), by which 18 former colonies of the original 6 EEC member states were given preferential access to Community markets. In return, the 18 states allowed the Community limited duty-free or quota-free access to their markets. With Britain joining the EEC in 1973, many former British colonies were added to the equation, so the Lomé Convention (named for the capital of Togo) was signed in 1975, raising the number of ACP states to 46, and offering them the opportunity of duty-free exports to the Community. An insurance fund called Stabex was also set up to compensate these states for declines in the value of 50 specified agricultural exports, including coffee, tea and cocoa, and a fund called Sysmin was created to help mineral-producing ACP countries diversify their economies.

A second Lomé Convention was signed in 1980, increasing EEC aid and investment spending. Lomé III (1985–90) shifted the focus to self-sufficiency and food security, while Lomé IV (1990–2000) added a structural adjustment element to ACP aid by encouraging economic diversification in the ACP states rather than simply providing project aid. It also banned exports of toxic wastes between the EU and ACP countries, and included clauses aimed at promoting human rights and protecting tropical forests in ACP countries. But while these agreements may have generated closer commercial ties between the EU and the

Africa Caribbean Pacific (ACP): A programme under which 80 former colonies of EU member states have been targeted for preferential trade agreements.

Table **25.2** **The Africa Caribbean Pacific states**

AFRICA (49)		
Angola	Mauritania	Dominican Republic
Benin	Mauritius	Grenada
Botswana	Mozambique	Guyana
Burkina Faso	Namibia	Haiti
Burundi	Niger	Jamaica
Cameroon	Nigeria	St. Kitts and Nevis
Cape Verde	Rwanda	St. Lucia
Central African Republic	São Tomé and Principe	St. Vincent and the Grenadines
Chad	Senegal	Suriname
Comoros	Seychelles	Trinidad and Tobago
Congo (Republic of)	Sierra Leone	
Congo (Democratic Republic of)	Somalia	**PACIFIC (15)**
Djibouti	South Africa	Cook Islands
Equatorial Guinea	South Sudan	Fiji
Eritrea	Sudan	Kiribati
Ethiopia	Swaziland	Marshall Islands
Gabon	Tanzania	Micronesia
Gambia	Togo	Nauru
Ghana	Uganda	Niue
Guinea	Zambia	Palau
Guinea Bissau	Zimbabwe	Papua New Guinea
Ivory Coast		Samoa
Kenya	**CARIBBEAN (16)**	Solomon Islands
Lesotho	Antigua and Barbuda	Timor-Leste
Liberia	Bahamas	Tonga
Madagascar	Barbados	Tuvalu
Malawi	Belize	Vanuatu
Mali	Cuba	
	Dominica	

ACP states and encouraged an increase in ACP exports to Europe, there were many problems as well. Economic growth in most ACP states was sluggish, imports to the EU from the ACP grew more slowly than those from other parts of the world, development aid funds took too long to be disbursed, not enough attention was paid to the environmental implications of the focus on cash crops for export, and the programme did not much change the EU–ACP relationship.

In 1996 an intensive review of the ACP programme was launched (see Holland, 2000), and negotiations opened in 1998 between the EU and the ACP states aimed at replacing the Lomé Convention with a more flexible structure based around a series of interregional free trade agreements between groups of ACP countries and the EU. The result was the Cotonou Agreement (named for the capital of Benin), which was signed in 2000 to cover a period of 20 years. In spite of the changes it brought, critics are still not impressed, charging that it is less innovative than it might have been and EU development aid policy today is less the model that it once was, and has become more symbolic (Arts and Dickson, 2004).

The second element of EU development policy has been official development assistance (ODA), for which the EU has collectively become the biggest source in the world: its member states in 2012 accounted for 51 per cent of the total

Illustration **25.2**
Development policy

An outbreak of Ebola in West Africa in 2014 prompted a joint partnership between the EU and Unicef, the UN's children's rights and emergency relief programme.

of nearly $127 billion given by the 29 members of the Development Assistance Committee (DAC) of the OECD (see Figure 25.2). Although the US gives by far the most ODA in absolute terms from a single country, the EU states have the advantage in relative terms; the UN General Assembly in 1970 set a target for donor countries of 0.7 per cent of gross national income (GNI), which has to date been met by only five countries in the world: Luxembourg, Sweden, Denmark, the Netherlands and non-EU member Norway.

Donor countries in 2005 made a commitment to increase their assistance, the EU members of the DAC pledging to reach a collective total of 0.56 per cent of GNI by 2010. But they fell short, some having made little general progress towards that target, and several in 2009–12 feeling the pressures arising out of the global financial and euro zone crises; almost all European DAC countries have cut spending, particularly Italy and Spain. It should be noted that private flows of aid are sometimes much greater than official flows; hence France spent twice as much on private aid as on official aid in 2011, and Germany, the Netherlands and the UK about equally as much on private and official aid (but Sweden spent 15 times as much on official aid as on private aid). But private aid is less coordinated and is not an expression of official government policy.

EU states work multilaterally and bilaterally on overseas aid. Much of their collective ODA is channelled through the European Development Fund (EDF), which was set up under the Treaty of Rome to provide technical and financial assistance to former or existing colonies of the original six EEC member states. It is funded directly by the member states rather than coming under the EU general budget, and is managed by its own committee operating according to its own set of rules. It is organized in five-year packages, the amount in each having risen steadily to the nearly €32 billion budgeted under the 11th EDF (2014–20). At the same time, each member state has its own bilateral development policies, but this parallel existence of 28 policies has prevented the EU from agreeing focused development goals, and has undermined the EU's international influence. This is

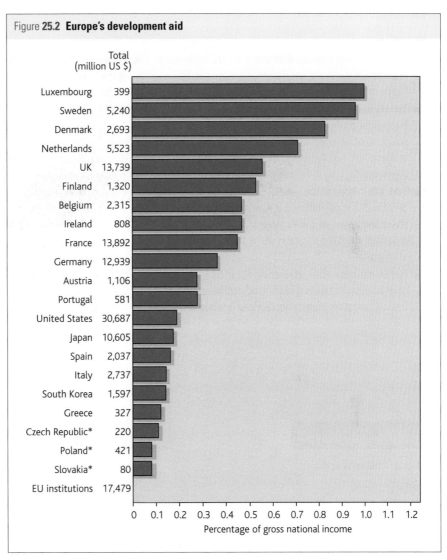

Figure **25.2 Europe's development aid**

Note: Figures are for 2012 for Development Assistance Committee (DAC) of OECD, except * non-DAC members.

Source: OECD, www.oecd.org (retrieved April 2014).

changing, though, as the Commission in particular has set targets and standards (Orbie and Versluys, 2008).

Although the amounts spent by the EU on development are impressive, money is not everything. The real impact of aid depends on how resources are used and how well they are used. ODA is widely criticized for taking a 'band aid' approach to development problems, being invested in the wrong kinds of activities, and breeding dependence rather than independence (see discussion in Lancaster, 2006; Riddell, 2007). There is also the argument that fair trade can do more to help with development than aid, and many questions have been raised about how much political influence aid provides and what role it plays in promoting better governance.

Summary

- The relationship between the EU and the US is the most important in the world, yet it has not always been a happy one.
- The US has provided direct support to European integration, as well as indirect support by pursuing policies that have united the Europeans in support or opposition, and by helping the EU identify its weaknesses.
- Both sides agree on the general goals of promoting democracy and capitalism, but they have different styles and values on a wide range of issues, raising questions about the trajectory of the transatlantic relationship.
- The EU has been active in reaching out to its neighbours, with the goal of creating a 'circle of friends', and promoting democracy and free markets in the region.

- The Barcelona Process had the goal of strengthening political, economic and social ties between the EU and all non-EU Mediterranean states, and was relaunched in 2008 as the Union for the Mediterranean.
- The European Neighbourhood Policy has the goal of avoiding the emergence of dividing lines between an enlarged EU and its immediate neighbours.
- The EU relationship with the Middle East has been troubled, while that with Russia has blown hot and cold, in spite of the fact that both need each other. New tensions have been created by events in Ukraine.
- The EU–China relationship has undergone much change in recent decades, although it is not yet fully understood.
- Their shared history has placed Africa, the Caribbean and the Pacific at the top of the EU development policy agenda. But the jury is still out on the effects of that policy.

Key terms and concepts

Africa Caribbean Pacific

Atlantic Alliance

Barcelona Process

Development policy

European Neighbourhood Policy

Union for the Mediterranean

Further reading

Holland, Martin, and Mathew Doidge (2012) *Development Policy of the European Union* (Basingstoke: Palgrave Macmillan). Useful survey of the history and goals of EU development policy, including chapters with a focus on Asia and Latin America.

Hanhimäki, Jussi, Benedikt Schoenborn and Barbara Zanchetta (2012) *Transatlantic Relations since 1945* (Abingdon: Routledge). Kopstein, Jeffrey, and Sven Steinmo (eds) (2008) *Growing Apart? America and Europe in the Twenty-First Century* (New York: Cambridge University Press). Two assessments of the history, character and prospects of the transatlantic relationship.

Vogt, Roland (ed.) (2012) *Europe and China: Strategic Partners or Rivals?* (Hong Kong: University of Hong Kong Press). Challenges the idea of 'constructive engagement' between the EU and China, and argues that relations are complex and constantly changing, and driven by numerous actors with different interests.

Conclusions:
Where now for the EU?

This has been a book about the politics and policies of the European Union. Its purpose has been to explain how the EU works, where it came from, how it evolved, the context within which it has functioned, how it makes decisions, and its impact on Europe and Europeans. In this book, we have:

- Looked at the underlying theoretical explanations of European integration, and have seen how the EU has evolved from being primarily an international organization to becoming a political system in its own right, with qualities that sit somewhere on a spectrum between intergovernmental and supranational, and between federal and confederal.
- Reviewed the personality and character of Europe and its inhabitants, attempting to pin down the region's geographical and cultural limits, understand what the terms *Europe* and *European* mean, and identify the norms and values that make the EU and its inhabitants distinctive.
- Surveyed the colourful and controversial history of the EU, tracing events from the signature of the Treaty of Paris in April 1951 through to today's EU, containing 28 member states and more than 500 million people, with other European states considering the prospects of membership.
- Examined the structure and work of the major European institutions, seeking to understand how they function relative to each other and the member states, and reviewing what their work has meant for the decisions taken by Europe's national leaders and the lives of ordinary Europeans.
- Assessed the impact of integration on policies in fields as diverse as agriculture, asylum, commerce, competition, corporate mergers and acquisitions, defence, economic development, education, employment, the environment, fisheries, foreign affairs, immigration, monetary affairs, police and judicial cooperation, security, the single market, trade, and workers' rights.

The book began with the assertion that the story of European integration has been one of an ongoing tension between success and failure, between swagger and humility, and between optimism and pessimism. We have seen how European integration has often been a story of muddling through and responding to crises rather than pursuing well-considered strategic initiatives. We have seen how Europeans and their political leaders have often been carried along on a tidal surge of political and economic pressures that they have neither always anticipated nor entirely understood. Opinion is divided on the cumulative results.

On the one hand, supporters of integration point out that Europe has enjoyed the longest spell of generalized peace in its recorded history, and the EU has become the world's wealthiest marketplace, biggest trading power, biggest market for corporate mergers and acquisitions, and biggest source of and target for foreign direct investment. They also argue that the EU has helped promote a new sense of European identity, encouraged greater policy efficiency by reducing duplication and contradictory goals, transformed the global role of Europe, and given birth to a new model of power that relies on civilian rather than military means to project itself.

On the other hand, critics charge that integration has undermined national sovereignty, often proceeded in the face of public hostility, lacked sufficient accountability or transparency, failed to take enough account of the differences within European society, and created a new level of elitist and technocratic government above the level of the member states. Many oppose efforts to build a federal Europe, others believe in integration but argue that the EU is in urgent need of reform, and yet others seek the end of the membership of their country in the EU.

Against this contradictory background, what can we now expect of the EU? Making predictions is always difficult, not least because so many of us see only what we want to see and ignore or dismiss evidence that disproves our preferences. Many of us are also the captives of history, routinely projecting the future on the basis of the past. But while an observer contemplating the new European Coal and Steel Community in 1952 might have made some brave forecasts about its likely long-term effects, it is unlikely that they could have foreseen the end of centuries of on-again, off-again war and conflict in Europe, the dismantling of Europe's borders, the abolition of many of its currencies, the advent of a new Europe less constrained by state structures, the upheavals that would transform European society, and the revolutions in international trade and communications that would fundamentally alter the global connections among states and people alike.

Given today's rapid pace of political, economic, social and technological change, the ongoing controversy about the implications of European integration, and the problem of the number of people who either know little about how the EU works or do not fully grasp what it means, forecasting the future for Europe is even more difficult now than it was in 1952. Undaunted, I will end this book with some general thoughts on how the process of integration may unfold, and what the future might hold for Europe and the European Union.

First, the effects of European integration will not be easily undone. The EU will always have its champions and its critics, but even if the treaties and their accompanying laws could all be magically revoked tomorrow, and all the EU institutions closed down and their staff sent home, the ties that have bound Europeans and their states since 1945 would not only remain but would continue to tighten through an invisible hand of political, economic and social cooperation. But rumours of the death of the EU are greatly exaggerated; the institutions of the EU will continue to function, new laws will continue to be made, the treaties will continue to be fine-tuned, and the attempt to agree a constitution for Europe will almost certainly be revisited, later rather than sooner.

Second, the process of integration will continue to be marked by crisis and controversy. Europe's leaders will continue to be obliged to react to events at least as often as they are able to concentrate on making long-term plans, ordinary Europeans will continue to be puzzled by the EU and divided over its merits, and the process of integration will continue to be periodically described as dead or dying. Partly in response, the rules of the EU will continue to change, driven by the key priority of making the EU institutions more transparent and accountable. The result will be a quite different variation on the theme of federation than any we have yet seen; it may even stop at confederation. But there will be no clearly discernible end-state; as with all polities that have ever existed, the EU will continue indefinitely to be a work in progress. Only the pace of change will alter and, hopefully, the quality of the debate about the nature and effects of such change.

Third, the membership of the EU will continue to grow for the foreseeable future. There are more than a dozen potential future members waiting on the sidelines, the borders of a few existing members could change as the pressures of separatist movements grow, and it is unlikely (although not impossible) that any existing members will opt to leave the EU. As a result, the internal dynamics of the EU will change; the days of Franco-German dominance have gone, the effects of eastern enlargement are still being played out, and future realignments will continue to add new priorities to the mix of European integration, obliging changes of perspective, new policy initiatives and some hard thinking about how best to manage the related demands of widening and deepening. The multi-speed option will remain on the table, but Europeans will continue to find themselves subject to the same sets of political, economic and social pressures, and will continue to move in the same broad direction, with or without the EU.

Fourth, the reach of the European state will continue its steady decline. The Westphalian system may have been born in Europe, but in no other part of the world has its retreat been more evident than in Europe. There have been many causes behind that retreat, but regional integration has been a key part of the mix, represented most forcefully in Europe by the pressures of the single market, but also by the thinking of Europeans. Just as more of them have more actively contemplated their European identity, so more have also rediscovered their national identities, and the state has found itself squeezed between the two. In spite of the rearguard actions fought in the name of intergovernmentalism, the supranational qualities of Europe will continue to grow and the role of the state in European public and political life will continue to decline.

Fifth, the EU will continue to force a reappraisal of the dynamics of the international system. The era of the great European powers is long gone, as is the bipolar era of the Cold War, while the unipolar era of American hegemony is increasingly difficult to discern through the fog of change brought by globalization and the rise of China and India. The EU is routinely overlooked in discussions about the great new powers of the future (or even of the present), and yet as we better understand the increasing advantages of economic and normative power over military power, and as we rethink the nature of the connections among societies, so more people will likely come to appreciate better the impact of the EU on global politics and economics. In one field particularly – the declining value of the military as a primary tool of statecraft – the EU will continue to lead the way, even if its efforts are not always conscious, deliberate, or always entirely understood. Wealthy democratic states do not go to war with one another, and in no other part of the world has this idea taken a firmer grip than in Europe; that grip will continue to tighten, and the EU will continue to be the leading champion of the use of soft power.

Finally, the EU will continue to face major challenges, and many of these will force European governments and societies into a fundamental rethinking of some long-cherished assumptions. The EU will continue to need to adjust to the flaws in its rules and policies, not all of which have been entirely predictable, and many of which have only been revealed by crisis. The EU will also have to continue working on more effective responses to the problems of unsustainable growth, underperforming economies, climate change, unemployment and underemployment, terrorism, poverty, and social exclusion. More generally, the EU will have to address the critical effects of demographic change: Europeans are living longer and getting older, they are having fewer children, and they are witnessing new patterns of immigration, resulting in greater racial, cultural and religious diversity.

Whatever happens, the EU deserves closer and better informed attention. It is a human construct, and like all such constructs it is imperfect, and always will be. The real test it has always faced, and will long continue to face, is to address its imperfections. Winston Churchill once famously argued that democracy was the worst form of government, except for all the rest. The EU may be imperfect, but it might also be argued that in terms of what history suggests about how Europeans might otherwise manage themselves, it is far better than a return to the era of nationalism and competition for power among states.

Bibliography

Aarts, Kees, and Henk van der Kolk (2006) 'Understanding the Dutch "No": The Euro, the East and the Elite', *PS: Political Science & Politics*, 37:2, pp. 243–6.

Acheson, Dean (1969) *Present at the Creation: My Years in the State Department* (New York: W.W. Norton).

Alderman, Liz (2014) 'As Latvia adopts euro, future growth is slowing', *The New York Times*, 1 January.

Alessi, Christopher (2012) 'The Role of the European Central Bank', 12 September, at Council on Foreign Relations. Available at www.cfr.org/world/role-european-central-bank/p28989.

Almond, Gabriel A. (1966) 'Political Theory and Political Science', *American Political Science Review*, 60:4, pp. 869–79.

Almond, Gabriel A., Russell J. Dalton and G. Bingham Powell (eds) (2002) *European Politics Today*, 2nd edn (New York: Longman).

Alter, Karen J. (2009) *The European Court's Political Power: Selected Essays* (Oxford: Oxford University Press).

Anderson, Benedict (2006) *Imagined Communities: Reflections on the Origins and Spread of Nationalism* (London: Verso).

Anderson, Scott (1992) 'Western Europe and the Gulf War', in Reinhardt Rummel (ed.) *Toward Political Union: Planning a Common Foreign and Security Policy in the European Community* (Boulder, CO: Westview Press).

Antonenko, Oksana, and Kathryn Pinnick (eds) (2005) *Russia and the European Union* (Abingdon: Routledge).

Armstrong, Kenneth A., and Simon J. Bulmer (1998) *The Governance of the Single European Market* (Manchester: Manchester University Press).

Arnull, Anthony (2008) *The European Union and its Court of Justice*, 2nd edn (Oxford: Oxford University Press).

Arts, Karin, and Anna K. Dickson (2004) *EU Development Cooperation: From Model to Symbol* (Manchester: Manchester University Press).

Arvanitopoulos, Constantine (ed.) (2010) *Reforming Europe: The Role of the Centre-Right* (New York: Springer).

Aspinwall, Mark, and Justin Greenwood (1998) 'Conceptualising Collective Action in the European Union: An Introduction', in Justin Greenwood and Mark Aspinwall (eds) *Collective Action in the European Union* (London: Routledge).

Bachtler, John, and Carlos Mendez (2007) 'Who Governs EU Cohesion Policy? Deconstructing the Reforms of the Structural Funds', *Journal of Common Market Studies*, 45:3, pp. 535–64.

Bachtler, John, Carlos Mendez and Fiona Wishlade (2013) *EU Cohesion Policy and European Integration* (Farnham: Ashgate).

Baldwin, Peter (2009) *The Narcissism of Minor Differences: How America and Europe Are Alike* (Oxford: Oxford University Press).

Baldwin, Richard, and Charles Wyplosz (2012) *The Economics of European Integration*, 4th edn (Maidenhead: McGraw-Hill).

Balibar, Ötienne (2004) *We, the People of Europe? Reflections on Transnational Citizenship* (Princeton, NJ: Princeton University Press).

Balme, Richard, and Didier Chabanet (2008) *European Governance and Democracy: Power and Protest in the EU* (Lanham, MD: Rowman & Littlefield).

Bardi, Luciano (2002) 'Transnational Trends: The Evolution of the European Party System', in Bernard Steunenberg and Jacques Thomassen (eds) *The European Parliament: Moving Toward Democracy in the EU* (Lanham, MD: Rowman & Littlefield).

Barnet, Richard J. (1983) *The Alliance: America, Europe, Japan; Makers of the Post-war World* (New York: Simon & Schuster).

Bartolini, Stefano (2012) 'The Strange Case of Europarties', in Erol Külahci (ed.) *The Domestic Party Politics of Europeanisation: Actors, Patterns and Systems* (Colchester: ECPR Press).

Bauer, Michael W. (ed.) (2008) *Reforming the European Commission* (London: Routledge).

Baun, Michael, and Dan Marek (2014) *Cohesion Policy in the European Union* (Basingstoke: Palgrave Macmillan).

Beck, Ulrich, and Edgar Grande (2007) *Cosmopolitan Europe* (Cambridge: Polity Press).

Bergsten, C. Fred (2012) 'Why the Euro Will Survive: Completing the Continent's Half-Built House', *Foreign Affairs*, 91:5, pp. 16–22.

Bergström, Carl Fredrik (2005) *Comitology: Delegation of Power in the European Union and the Committee System* (Oxford: Oxford University Press).

Bernstein, Barton J. (1980) 'The Cuban Missile Crisis: Trading the Jupiters in Turkey?', *Political Science Quarterly*, 95:1, pp. 97–125.

Billiet, Stijn (2005) 'The EC and WTO Dispute Settlement: The Initiation of Trade Disputes by the EC', *European Foreign Affairs Review*, 10:2, pp. 197–214.

Birch, Anthony (1966) 'Approaches to the Study of Federalism', *Political Studies*, 14:1, 15–33.

Black, Jeremy (2000) *Modern British History since 1900* (Basingstoke: Macmillan).

Blair, Tony (1998) Speech to the Labour Party Conference, Blackpool. Available at www.britishpoliticalspeech.org/speech-archive.htm?speech=202.

Blankart, Charles B. (2007) 'The European Union: Confederation, Federation or Association of Compound States?', *Constitutional Political Economy*, 18:2, pp. 99–106.

Bohman, James, and Matthias Lutz-Bachmann (eds) (1997) *Perpetual Peace: Essays on Kant's Cosmopolitan Ideal* (Boston, MA: MIT Press).

Borrás, Susana, Charalampos Koutalakis and Frank Wendler (2007) 'European Agencies and Input Legitimacy: EFSA, EMeA and EPO in the Post-Delegation Phase', *Journal of European Integration*, 29:5, pp. 583–600.

Börzel, Tanja (2005) 'What can Federalism Teach us about the European Union? The German Experience', *Regional and Federal Studies*, 15:2, pp. 245–57.

Bossong, Raphael (2008) 'The Action Plan on Combating Terrorism: A Flawed Instrument of EU Security Governance', *Journal of Common Market Studies*, 46:1, pp. 27–48.

Boswell, Christina, and Andrew Geddes (2011) *Migration and Mobility in the European Union* (Basingstoke: Palgrave Macmillan).

Boudreaux, Richard, and Paulo Prada (2012) 'Exodus of workers from continent reverses old patterns', *Wall Street Journal*, 14 January.

Bourdet, Yves, Joakim Gullstrand and Karin Olofsdotter (eds) (2007) *The European Union and Developing Countries: Trade, Aid and Growth in an Integrating World* (Cheltenham: Edward Elgar).

Breslin, Shaun, Richard Higgott and Ben Rosamond (2002) 'Regions in Comparative Perspective', in Shaun Breslin, Christopher W. Hughes, Nicola Phillips and Ben Rosamond (eds) *New Regionalisms in the Global Political Economy: Theories and Cases* (Abingdon: Routledge).

Briand, Aristide (1997) 'Memorandum on the Organization of a Regime of a European Federal Union Addressed to Twenty-six Governments of Europe', in Trevor Salmon and Sir William Nicoll (eds) *Building European Union: A Documentary History and Analysis* (Manchester: Manchester University Press).

Brine, Jacqueline (2002) *The European Social Fund and the EU: Flexibility, Growth, Stability* (London: Continuum).

British Home Office (2006) *Accession Monitoring Report May 2006–June 2006*, published online 22 August.

Broad, Roger, and Tim Geiger (eds) (1996) 'The 1975 British Referendum on Europe', *Contemporary British History*, 10:3, pp. 82–105.

Brooke, Michael Z., and H. Lee Remmers (eds) (1972) *The Multinational Company in Europe: Some Key Problems* (London: Longman).

Brown, L. Neville, and Tom Kennedy (2000) *The Court of Justice of the European Communities*, 5th edn (London: Sweet & Maxwell).

Brunkhorst, Hauke (2004) 'A Polity without a State? European Constitutionalism between Evolution and Revolution', in Erik Oddvar Eriksen, John Erik Fossum and Agustín José Menéndez (eds) *Developing a Constitution for Europe* (London: Routledge).

Buchanan, Allen (1991) *Secession: The Morality of Political Divorce from Fort Sumter to Lithuania and Quebec* (Boulder, CO: Westview).

Buller, Jim, and Andrew Gamble (2008) 'Britain: The Political Economy of Retrenchment', in Kenneth Dyson (ed.) *The Euro at 10: Europeanization, Power, and Convergence* (Oxford: Oxford University Press).

Bulmer, Simon, and Christian Lequesne (eds) (2005) 'Introduction', *The Member States of the European Union* (Oxford: Oxford University Press).

Buonanno, Laurie, and Neill Nugent (2013) *Policies and Policy Processes of the European Union* (Basingstoke: Palgrave Macmillan).

Burgess, Michael (1996) 'Introduction: Federalism and Building the European Union', *Publius*, 26:4, pp. 1–15.

Burgess, Michael (2000) *Federalism and European Union: The Building of Europe, 1950–2000* (London: Routledge).

Burgess, Michael (2006) *Comparative Federalism: Theory and Practice* (London: Routledge).

Burgess, Michael (2009) 'Federalism', in Antje Wiener and Thomas Diez (eds) *European Integration Theory*, 2nd edn (Oxford: Oxford University Press).

Burrell, Alison (2009) 'The CAP: Looking Back, Looking Ahead', *Journal of European Integration*, 31:3, pp. 271–89.

Burrows, Noreen, and Rosa Greaves (2007) *The Advocate General and EC Law* (Oxford: Oxford University Press).

Büthe, Tim (2007) 'The Politics of Competition and Institutional Change in the European Union: The First Fifty Years', in Sophie Meunier and Kathleen R. McNamara (eds) *The State of the European Union*, vol. 8 (Oxford: Oxford University Press).

Camilleri, Joseph A., and Jim Falk (1992) *The End of Sovereignty?* (Aldershot: Edward Elgar).

Carbone, Maurizio (2007) *The European Union and International Development: The Politics of Foreign Aid* (Abingdon: Routledge).

Carubba, Clifford J. (2001) 'The Electoral Connection in European Union Politics', *Journal of Politics*, 63:1, pp. 141–58.

Casarini, Nicola (2009) *Remaking Global Order: The Evolution of Europe–China Relations and its Implications for East Asia and the United States* (Oxford: Oxford University Press).

Cerutti, Furio, and Sonia Lucarelli (eds) (2008) *The Search for a European Identity* (Abingdon: Routledge).

Chang, Michelle (2009) *Monetary Integration in the European Union* (Basingstoke: Palgrave Macmillan).

Checkel, Jeffrey T., and Peter J. Katzenstein (eds) (2009) *European Identity* (Cambridge: Cambridge University Press).

Chinn, Menzie, and Jeffery Frankel (2005) 'Will the Euro Eventually Surpass the Dollar as the Leading International Reserve Currency?', National Bureau of Economic Research Working Paper 11510.

Christiansen, Thomas (2006) 'The Council of Ministers: Facilitating Interaction and Developing Actorness in the EU', in Jeremy Richardson (ed.) *European Union: Power and Policy-Making*, 3rd edn (New York: Routledge).

Christiansen, Thomas, and Christine Reh (2009) *Constitutionalizing the European Union* (Basingstoke: Palgrave Macmillan).

Christiansen, Thomas, and Simon Duke (eds) (2015) *The Maastricht Treaty: Second Thoughts after 20 Years* (Abingdon: Routledge).

Christin, Thomas, and Simon Hug (2002) 'Referendums and Citizen Support for European Integration', *Comparative Political Studies*, 35:5, pp. 586–617.

Churchill, Winston (1946) Speech at Westminster College, Fulton, Missouri (March), at The Churchill Centre, www.winstonchurchill.org.

Cini, Michelle (2007) *From Integration to Integrity: Administrative Ethics and Reform in the European Commission* (Manchester: Manchester University Press).

Cini, Michelle, and Lee McGowan (2009) *Competition Policy in the European Union,* 2nd edn (Basingstoke: Palgrave Macmillan).

Clark, Alan (1993) *Diaries* (London: Farrar, Straus & Giroux).

Clover, Charles (2005) *The End of the Line: How Overfishing is Changing the World and What We Eat* (London: Ebury Press).

Coen, David, and Jeremy Richardson (eds) (2009) *Lobbying the European Union: Institutions, Actors, and Issues* (Oxford: Oxford University Press,).

Cohen, Benjamin, J. (2008) 'The Euro in a Global Context: Challenges and Capacities', in Kenneth Dyson (ed) *The Euro at 10: Europeanization, Power, and Convergence* (Oxford: Oxford University Press).

Collins, Ken, and David Earnshaw (1993) 'The Implementation and Enforcement of European Community Environment Legislation', in David Judge (ed.) *A Green Dimension for the European Community* (London: Frank Cass).

Commission of the European Communities (1970) 'Economic and Monetary Union in the Community' (the Werner Report) *Bulletin of the European Communities,* Supplement 11.

Commission of the European Communities (1973) *Report on the Regional Problems of the Enlarged Community* (the Thomson Report) COM(73)550 (Brussels: CEC).

Commission of the European Communities (1985) *Completing the Internal Market: The White Paper* (the Cockfield Report) COM(85)310 final (Brussels: CEC).

Commission of the European Communities (1989) *Report of the Committee for the Study of Economic and Monetary Union* (Luxembourg: Office of Official Publications).

Commission of the European Communities (1990) *Transatlantic Declaration on EC–US Relations,* 23 November (Brussels: European Commission).

Conant, Lisa (2002) *Justice Contained: Law and Politics in the European Union* (Ithaca: Cornell University Press).

Corbett, Anne (2005) *Universities and the Europe of Knowledge* (Basingstoke: Palgrave Macmillan).

Corbett, Richard, Francis Jacobs and Michael Shackleton (2011) *The European Parliament,* 8th edn (London: John Harper).

Costello, Cathryn (2005) 'Ireland's Nice Referenda', *European Constitutional Law Review,* 1:3, pp. 357– 82.

Criddle, Byron (1993) 'The French Referendum on the Maastricht Treaty, September 1992', *Parliamentary Affairs,* 46:2, pp. 228–39.

Crystal, David (2003) *English as a Global Language,* 2nd edn (Cambridge: Cambridge University Press).

Defarges, Philippe Moreau (1988) 'Twelve Years of European Council History (1974–1986): The Crystallizing Forum', in Jean-Marc Hoscheit and Wolfgang Wessels (eds) *The European Council 1974–1986: Evaluation and Prospects* (Maastricht: European Institute of Public Administration).

De Haan, Jakob, and Helge Berger (eds) (2010) *The European Central Bank at Ten* (Heidelberg: Springer).

Dehousse, Renaud (2002) *Misfits: EU Law and the Transformation of European Governance.* Working Paper No. 2/02, Jean Monnet Center for International and Regional Economic Law and Justice, New York University School of Law.

Delors, Jacques (1991) 'European Integration and Security', *Survival,* 33:2, pp. 99–109.

Déloye, Yves, and Michael Bruter (eds) (2007) *Encyclopaedia of European Elections* (Basingstoke: Palgrave Macmillan).

Dempsey, Judy (2010) 'Shaping policy by playing safe', *The New York Times,* 3 March.

De Rougemont, Denis (1966) *The Idea of Europe* (London: Macmillan).

Deutsch, Karl W., Sidney A. Burrell, Robert A. Kann et al. (1957) *Political Community and* the North Atlantic Area: International Organization in the Light of Historical Experience (Princeton, NJ, Princeton University Press).

De Vreese, Claes H, and Holli A. Semetko (2004) *Political Campaigning in Referendums: Framing the Referendum Issue* (Abingdon: Routledge).

Dimitrakopoulos, Dionyssis (2004) *The Changing European Commission* (Manchester: Manchester University Press).

Dinan, Desmond (2010) *Ever Closer Union: An Introduction to European Integration*, 4th edn (Basingstoke: Palgrave Macmillan).

Dinan, Desmond (2014) *Europe Recast: A History of European Union*, 2nd edn (Basingstoke: Palgrave Macmillan).

Dinan, Desmond, and Marios Camhis (2004) 'The Common Agricultural Policy and Cohesion', in Maria Green Cowles and Desmond Dinan (eds) *Developments in the European Union 2* (Basingstoke: Palgrave Macmillan).

Drake, Helen (2000) *Jacques Delors: Perspectives on a European Leader* (London: Routledge).

Duchêne, François (1972) 'Europe's Role in World Peace', in Richard Mayne (ed.) *Europe Tomorrow: Sixteen Europeans Look Ahead* (London: Fontana).

Duff, Andrew (2008) *True Guide to the Treaty of Lisbon* (Brussels: Alliance of Liberals and Democrats for Europe).

Dunkerley, David, Lesley Hodgson, Stanislaw Konopacki, Tony Spybey and Andrew Thompson (2002) *Changing Europe: Identities, Nations and Citizens* (Abingdon: Routledge).

Dyson, Kenneth (2008) 'Introduction', in *The Euro at 10: Europeanization, Power, and Convergence* (Oxford: Oxford University Press).

Dyson, Kenneth, and Kevin Featherstone (1999) *The Road to Maastricht: Negotiating Economic and Monetary Union* (Oxford: Oxford University Press).

Economist, The (1990) 'Europe's farm farce: the latest quarrel over reforming Europe's farm trade has missed the point', 29 September.

Economist, The (1991) 'War in Europe', 6 July.

Economist, The (2005) 'France after the referendum: It's Chirac, stupid', 2 June, www.economist.com/node/4033317.

Economist, The (2010) 'Germany: Europe's engine', 11 March, www.economist.com/node/15663362.

Eichengreen, Barry (2007) *The European Economy Since 1945: Coordinated Capitalism and Beyond* (Princeton: Princeton University Press).

Eilstrup-Sangiovanni, Mette (2006) *Debates on European Integration* (Basingstoke: Palgrave Macmillan).

El-Agraa, Ali M. (ed.) (2011) *The European Union: Economics and Policies*, 9th edn (Cambridge: Cambridge University Press).

Elgström, Ole (2003) 'Introduction', in Ole Elgström (ed.) *European Union Council Presidencies: A Comparative Perspective* (London: Routledge).

Eriksen, Erik Oddvar, John Erik Fossum and Agustín José Menéndez (eds) (2004) 'Introduction', *Developing a Constitution for Europe* (London: Routledge).

Erlanger, Steven (2010) 'Europe feels snubbed by Obama', *Wall Street Journal*, 2 February.

Etzioni, Amitai (1995) *The Spirit of Community: Rights, Responsibilities and the Communitarian Agenda* (London: Fontana Press).

EU Insight (2008) *Lobbying in the EU: An Overview* (Washington DC: Delegation of the European Commission to the United States).

European Commission (1994) 'European Social Policy: A Way Forward for the Union'. White Paper COM(94) 333 final

European Commission (2002) *Update on the Internal Market: Scoreboard No. 10* (Luxembourg: Publications Office of the European Union).

European Commission (2003) Communication to the Council and the European Parliament, of 10 September, 'The European Union and the United Nations: The Choice of Multilateralism', COM(2003) 526 final.

European Commission (2007) *Growing Regions, Growing Europe: Fourth Report on Economic and Social Cohesion* (Luxembourg: Publications Office of the European Union).

European Commission (2008) *European Agencies: The Way Forward* (Luxembourg: Publications Office of the European Union).

European Commission (2010) 'Statement on the latest developments on the Roma situation', press release, 14 September, http://europa.eu/rapid/press-release_SPEECH-10-428_en.htm.

European Commission (2011) *28th Annual Report on Monitoring the Application of EU Law*, Brussels, COM(2011) 588 final.

European Commission (2013) *Multiannual Financial Framework 2014–2020 and EU Budget 2014: The Figures* (Luxembourg: Publications Office of the European Union).

Europol (2009) 'Facilitated Illegal Immigration into the European Union'. Available at www.europol.europa.eu/publications (retrieved September 2010).

Europol (2010) *EU Terrorism Situation and Trend Report 2009* (The Hague: Europol).

Europol (2014) *EU Terrorism Situation and Trend Report 2014* (The Hague: Europol).

Eurostat (2010) *Household Structure in the EU: 2010 Edition* (Luxembourg: Publications Office of the European Union).

Eurostat (2013) *Agriculture, Forestry and Fishery Statistics 2013 Edition* (Luxembourg: Publications Office of the European Union).

Farrell, David M., and Roger Scully (2007) *Representing Europe's Citizens? Electoral Institutions and the Failure of Parliamentary Representation* (Oxford: Oxford University Press).

Farrell, Mary, Björn Hettne and Luk van Langenhove (eds) (2005) *Global Politics of Regionalism: Theory and Practice* (London: Pluto Press).

Favell, Adrian (2008) *Eurostars and Eurocities: Free Movement and Mobility in an Integrating Europe* (Oxford: Blackwell).

Fawcett, Louise, and Andrew Hurrell (eds) (1992) *Regionalism in World Politics: Regional Organization and International Order* (Oxford: Oxford University Press).

Featherstone, Kevin (2003) 'Introduction: In the Name of "Europe"', in Kevin Featherstone and Claudio M. Radaelli (eds) *The Politics of Europeanization* (Oxford: Oxford University Press).

Featherstone, Kevin, and Claudio M. Radaelli (eds) (2003) *The Politics of Europeanization* (Oxford: Oxford University Press).

Feldstein, Martin (2012) 'The Failure of the Euro: The Little Currency that Couldn't', *Foreign Affairs*, 91:1, pp. 105–16.

Fenby, Jonathan (2010) *The General: Charles de Gaulle and the France he Saved* (London: Simon & Schuster).

Ferguson, Niall (2004) *Colossus: The Price of America's Empire* (New York: Penguin).

Fischer, Joschka (2000) 'From Confederacy to Federation: Thoughts on the Finality of European Integration', speech given at Humboldt University, Berlin, 12 May.

Fischler, Franz (2003) Speech before First European Parliamentary Symposium on Agriculture, Brussels, 16 October.

Flash Eurobarometer (2009) *Attitudes towards the EU in the United Kingdom*, July (European Commission).

Flash Eurobarometer (2003) *Iraq and Peace in the World*, Full Report, No. 151, October (European Commission).

Fligstein, Neil (2008) *Euroclash: The EU, European Identity, and the Future of Europe* (Oxford: Oxford University Press).

Follesdal, Andreas, and Simon Hix (2006) 'Why There is a Democratic Deficit in the EU: A Response to Majone and Moravcsik', *Journal of Common Market Studies*, 44:3, pp. 533–62.

Foret, François, and Yann-Sven Rittelmeyer (eds) (2014) *The European Council and European Governance: The Commanding Heights of the EU* (Abingdon: Routledge).

Forsyth, Murray (1981) *Unions of States: The Theory and Practice of Confederation* (Leicester: Leicester University Press).

Fossum, John Erik, and Philip Schlesinger (eds) (2007) *The European Union and the Public Sphere: A Communicative Space in the Making?* (Abingdon: Routledge).

Fox, W.T.R. (1944) *The Super-Powers: The United States, Britain and the Soviet Union – Their Responsibility for Peace* (New York: Harcourt Brace).

Franklin, Mark (1996) 'European Elections and the European Voter', in Jeremy Richardson (ed.) *European Union: Power and Policy-Making* (London: Routledge).

Franklin, Mark (2005) *Voter Turnout and the Dynamics of Electoral Competition in Established Democracies since 1945* (Cambridge: Cambridge University Press).

Franklin, Mark (2006) 'European Elections and the European Voter', in Jeremy Richardson (ed.) *European Union: Power and Policy-Making*, 3rd edn (Abingdon: Routledge).

Franklin, Mark, Michael Marsh and Christopher Wlezien (1994) 'Attitudes toward Europe and Referendum Votes: A Response to Siune and Svensson', *Electoral Studies*, 13:2, pp. 117–21.

Friedrichs, Jorg (2008) *Fighting Terrorism and Drugs: Europe and International Police Cooperation* (Abingdon: Routledge).

Frontex (2014) *Annual Risk Analysis 2014*, frontex.europa.eu/assets/.../Risk_Analysis/Annual_Risk_Analysis_2014, retrieved 12/12/14.

Gabel, Matthew J. (1998) 'The Endurance of Supranational Governance: A Consociational Interpretation of the European Union', *Comparative Politics*, 30:4, pp. 463–75.

Georgakakis, Didier (2004) 'Was it Really Just Poor Communication? A Socio-political Reading of the Santer Commission's Resignation', in Andy Smith (ed.) *Politics and the European Commission: Actors, Interdependence, Legitimacy* (London: Routledge).

George, Stephen (1990) *An Awkward Partner: Britain in the European Community* (Oxford: Oxford University Press).

Géradin, Damien, Rodolphe Muñoz and Nicolas Petit (eds) (2005) *Regulation Through Agencies in the EU: A New Paradigm of European Governance* (London: Edward Elgar).

Giddens, Anthony (2006) *Europe in the Global Age* (Cambridge: Polity Press).

Giddings, Philip, Roy Gregory and Anthea Harris (2002) 'The European Union Ombudsman', in Alex Warleigh (ed.) *Understanding European Union Institutions* (London: Routledge).

Giersch, Herbert (1985) *Eurosclerosis* (Kiel: Institut für Weltwirtschaft).

Gilbert, Mark (2003) *Surpassing Realism: The Politics of European Integration since 1945* (Lanham, MD: Rowman & Littlefield).

Gillingham, John (1991) *Coal, Steel, and the Rebirth of Europe, 1945–55* (New York: Cambridge University Press).

Gillingham, John (2003) *European Integration 1950–2003: Superstate or New Market Economy?* (Cambridge: Cambridge University Press).

Givens, Terri, and Adam Luedtke (2004) 'The Politics of European Union Immigration Policy: Institutions, Salience, and Harmonization', *Policy Studies Journal*, 32:1, pp. 145–65.

Goldberg, Linda S. (2010) 'Is the International Role of the Dollar Changing?', *Current Issues in Economics and Finance*, 16:1, pp. 1–7.

Goldhaber, Michael D. (2007) *A People's History of the European Court of Human Rights* (Piscataway, NJ: Rutgers University Press).

Gorst, Anthony, and Lewis Johnman (1997) *The Suez Crisis* (London: Routledge).

Grant, Wyn (1997) *The Common Agricultural Policy* (Basingstoke: Macmillan).

Graziano, Paolo, and Maarten P. Vink (eds) (2007) *Europeanization: New Research Agendas* (Basingstoke: Palgrave Macmillan).

Greer, Steven (2006) *The European Convention on Human Rights: Achievements, Problems and Prospects* (Cambridge: Cambridge University Press).

Griffiths, Richard T. (2000) *Europe's First Constitution: The European Political Community, 1952–1954* (London: Kogan Page).

Groux, Jean, and Philippe Manin (1985) *The European Communities in the International Order* (Brussels: Commission of the European Communities).

Guardian, The (2010) Angela Merkel: German multiculturalism has 'utterly failed', 17 October, www.theguardian.com/world/2010/oct/17/angela-merkel-german-multiculturalism-failed, retrieved 12/12/14.

Guild, Elspeth (1997) 'The Legal Framework of Citizenship of the European Union', in David Cesarani and Mary Fulbrook (eds) *Citizenship, Nationality, and Migration in Europe* (London: Routledge).

Haas, Ernst B. (1958) *The Uniting of Europe: Political, Social, and Economic Forces, 1950–1957* (Stanford: Stanford University Press).

Haas, Ernst B. (1964) 'Technocracy, Pluralism and the New Europe', in Stephen R. Graubard (ed.) *A New Europe?* (Boston: Houghton Mifflin).

Haas, Ernst B. (1968) 'Foreword', *The Uniting of Europe: Political, Social, and Economic Forces, 1950–1957*, 2nd edn (Stanford: Stanford University Press).

Haas, Ernst B. (1970) 'The Study of Regional Integration: Reflections on the Joy and Anguish of Pretheorizing', *International Organization*, 24, pp. 607–46.

Haas, Ernst B. (1975) *The Obsolescence of Regional Integration Theory* (Berkeley: Institute of International Studies, University of California).

Haas, Ernst B., and Philippe C. Schmitter (1964) 'Economics and Differential Patterns of Political Integration: Projections about Unity in Latin America', *International Organization*, 18:4, pp. 705–37.

Haass, Richard (ed.) (1999) *Transatlantic Tensions: The United States, Europe, and Problem Countries* (Washington DC: Brookings Institution).

Habermas, Jürgen (2004) 'Why Europe Needs a Constitution', in Erik Oddvar Eriksen, John Erik Fossum and Augustín José Menéndez (eds) *Developing a Constitution for Europe* (London: Routledge).

Habermas, Jürgen, and Jacques Derrida (2003) 'February 15, or What Binds Europe Together: Plea for a Common Foreign Policy, Beginning in Core Europe', *Frankfurter Allgemeine Zeitung*, 31 May. Reproduced in Daniel Levy, Max Pensky and John Torpey (eds) (2005) *Old Europe, New Europe, Core Europe* (London: Verso).

Hagen, Tobias, and Philipp Mohl (2009) 'How does EU Cohesion Policy Work? Evaluating its Effects on Fiscal Outcome Variables'. Discussion paper 09–051, Centre for European Economic Research, Mannheim.

Haltern, Ulrich (2003) 'Pathos and Patina: The Failure and Promise of Constitutionalism in the European Imagination', *European Law Journal*, 9:11, pp. 14–44.

Hamilton, Daniel S., and Joseph P. Quinlan (2008) *Globalization and Europe: Prospering in the New Whirled Order* (Baltimore: Center for Transatlantic Relations).

Hanhimäki, Jussi, Benedikt Schoenborn and Barbara Zanchetta (2012) *Transatlantic Relations since 1945* (Abingdon: Routledge).

Hanley, David (2007) *Beyond the Nation State: Parties in the Era of European Integration* (Basingstoke: Palgrave Macmillan).

Hantrais, Linda (2007) *Social Policy in the European Union*, 3rd edn (Basingstoke: Palgrave Macmillan).

Harmsen, Robert, and Menno Spiering (2005) 'Introduction: Euroscepticism and the Evolution of European Political Debate', in Robert Harmsen and Menno Spiering (eds) *Euroscepticism: Party Politics, National Identity and European Integration* (Amsterdam: Rodopi).

Harrop, Jeffrey (2002) 'Competition Policy', in Jackie Gower (ed.) *The European Union Handbook*, 2nd edn (Chicago: Fitzroy Dearborn).

Hartley, Emma (2006) *Did David Hasselhof End the Cold War? 50 Facts You Need to Know: Europe* (Cambridge: Icon Books).

Hartley, T.C. (2010) *The Foundations of European Union Law*, 7th edn (Oxford: Oxford University Press).

Haseler, Stephen (2004) *Super-State: The New Europe and its Challenge to America* (London: I.B. Taurus).

Hayes-Renshaw, Fiona, and Helen Wallace (2006) *The Council of Ministers*, 2nd edn (Basingstoke: Palgrave Macmillan).

Hayes-Renshaw, Fiona, Christian Lequesne and Pedro Mayor Lopez (1989) 'The Permanent Representations of the Member States of the European Communities', *Journal of Common Market Studies*, 28:2, pp. 119–37.

Heater, Derek (1992) *The Idea of European Unity* (New York: St Martin's Press).

Heater, Derek (2004) *Citizenship: The Civic Ideal in World History, Politics and Education*, 3rd edn (Manchester: Manchester University Press).

Heath, Anthony, Iain McLean, Bridget Taylor and John Curticel (1999) 'Between First and Second Order: A Comparison of Voting Behaviour in European and Local Elections in Britain', *European Journal of Political Research*, 35:3, pp. 389–414.

Heidenreich, Martin, and Gabriele Bischoff (2008) 'The Open Method of Co-ordination:

A Way to the Europeanization of Social and Employment Policies?', *Journal of Common Market Studies*, 46:3, pp. 497–532.

Hildebrand, Philipp M. (1993) 'The European Community's Environmental Policy, 1957 to 1992: From Incidental Measures to an International Regime?' in David Judge (ed.) *A Green Dimension for the European Community: Political Issues and Processes* (London: Frank Cass).

Hill, Christopher, and Michael Smith (eds) (2011) *International Relations and the European Union,* 2nd edn (Oxford: Oxford University Press).

Hitchcock, William I. (2004) *The Struggle for Europe: The Turbulent History of a Divided Continent* (New York: Anchor Books).

Hix, Simon (1994) 'The Study of the European Community: The Challenge to Comparative Politics', *West European Politics*, 17:1, pp. 1–30.

Hix, Simon (2008) *What's Wrong with the European Union and How to Fix It* (Cambridge: Polity Press).

Hix, Simon, and Christopher Lord (1997) *Political Parties in the European Union* (New York: St Martin's Press).

Hix, Simon, and Bjørn Hoyland (2011) *The Political System of the European Union*, 3rd edn (Basingstoke: Palgrave Macmillan).

Hix, Simon, Abdul G. Noury and Gerard Roland (2007) *Democratic Politics in the European Parliament* (Cambridge: Cambridge University Press).

Hobbing, Peter (2003) 'Management of External EU Borders: Enlargement and the European Border Guard Issue'. Paper presented at the Workshop 'Managing International and Inter-Agency Cooperation at the Border', Geneva, 13–15 March. Available at www.dcaf.ch/border/bs_genevaconf_030313Hobbing.pdf.

Hobolt, Sara Binzer (2009) *Europe in Question: Referendums on European Integration* (Oxford: Oxford University Press).

Hodson, Dermot (2010) 'Economic and Monetary Union', in Helen Wallace, Mark A. Pollack and Alasdair R. Young (eds) *Policy-Making in the European Union*, 6th edn (Oxford: Oxford University Press).

Hoffman, Bruce (2006) *Inside Terrorism*, 2nd edn (New York: Columbia University Press).

Hoffmann, Stanley (1965) 'The European Process at Atlantic Crosspurposes', *Journal of Common Market Studies*, 3:2, pp. 85–101.

Hoffmann, Stanley (1966) 'Obstinate or Obsolete? The Fate of the Nation State and the Case of Western Europe', *Daedelus*, 95:3, pp. 862–915.

Hoffmann, Stanley (1982) 'Reflections on the Nation-State in Western Europe Today', *Journal of Common Market Studies*, 21:1/2, pp. 21–37.

Holland, Martin (2000) 'Resisting Reform or Risking Revival? Renegotiating the Lomé Convention', in Maria Green Cowles and Michael Smith (eds) *The State of the European Union: Risks, Reform, Resistance, and Revival* (Oxford: Oxford University Press).

Holland, Martin, and Mathew Doidge (2012) *Development Policy of the European Union* (Basingstoke: Palgrave Macmillan).

Hooghe, Liesbet, and Gary Marks (2001) *Multi-Level Governance and European Integration* (Lanham, MD: Rowman & Littlefield).

Hosli, Madeleine O. (2005) *The Euro: A Concise Introduction to European Monetary Integration* (Boulder, CO: Lynne Rienner).

Hourani, Albert (1989) 'Conclusions', in William Roger Louis and Roger Owen (eds) *Suez 1956: The Crisis and Its Consequences* (Oxford: Clarendon Press).

House of Commons Library (2010) 'How much legislation comes from Europe?', Research Paper 10/62, 13 October.

Howorth, Jolyon (2014) *Security and Defence Policy in the European Union*, 2nd edn (Basingstoke: Palgrave Macmillan).

International Institute for Strategic Studies (2013) *The Military Balance 2013* (London: Routledge).

Ionescu, Ghita (1975) *Centripetal Politics: Government and the New Centres of Power* (London: Hart-Davis McGibbon).

Ipsos MORI (2014) *Global Trends 2014: Navigating the New*, www.ipsosglobaltrends.com.

Ivaldi, Gilles (2006) 'Beyond France's 2005 Referendum on the European Constitutional Treaty', *West European Politics*, 29:1, pp. 47–69.

Jacobs, Francis (2006) 'The Role of the European Court of Justice in the Protection of the Environment', *Journal of Environmental Law*, 18:2, pp. 185–205.

Jagland, Thorbjørn (2012) *Award Ceremony Speech*, 10 December. Available at www.nobelprize.org/nobel_prizes/peace/laureates/2012/presentation-speech.html, retrieved 12/12/14.

James, Robert Rhodes (ed.) (1974) *Winston S. Churchill: His Complete Speeches, 1897–1963*: vol. III, *1943–49* (London: Chelsea House).

Jenkins, Roy (1989) *European Diary, 1977–1981* (London: Collins).

Jensen, Maria Skovager, Kim Martin Lind and Henrik Zobbe (2009) 'Enlargement of the European Union and Agricultural Policy Reform', *Journal of European Integration*, 31:3, pp. 329–48.

Jones, Seth G. (2007) *The Rise of European Security Cooperation* (Cambridge: Cambridge University Press).

Jordan, Andrew, and Camilla Adele (eds) (2013) *Environmental Policy in the European Union: Actors, Institutions and Processes,* 3rd edn (Abingdon: Routledge).

Jordan, Andrew, Dave Huitema, Harro van Asselt and Frans Berkhout (eds) (2010) *Climate Change Policy in the European Union: Confronting the Dilemmas of Mitigation and Adaptation?* (Cambridge: Cambridge University Press).

Judge, David, and David Earnshaw (2008) *The European Parliament,* 2nd edn (Basingstoke: Palgrave Macmillan).

Judt, Tony (2005) *Postwar: A History of Europe since 1945* (New York: Penguin).

Kagan, Robert (2003) *Of Paradise and Power: America and Europe in the New World Order* (New York: Knopf).

Kant, Immanuel ([1795] 2009) *Perpetual Peace: A Philosophical Essay* (London: Penguin).

Kassim, Hussein (2006) 'The Secretariat General of the European Commission', in David Spence (ed.) *The European Commission*, 3rd edn (London: John Harper).

Kaunert, Christian, Sarah Leonard and John Occhipinti (eds) (2014) *Justice and Home Affairs Agencies in the European Union* (Abingdon: Routledge).

Keleman, R. Daniel (2006) 'Shaming the Shameless? The Constitutionalization of the European Union', *Journal of European Public Policy*, 13:8, pp. 1302–7.

Keohane, Robert O., and Stanley Hoffmann (1990) 'Conclusions: Community Politics and Institutional Change', in William Wallace (ed.) *The Dynamics of European Integration* (London: Royal Institute for International Affairs).

Kerr, David, and Liu Fei (eds) (2007) *The International Politics of EU-China Relations* (Oxford: Oxford University Press).

Kerr, Richard A. (2007) 'Global Warming: How Urgent is Climate Change?' *Science*, 318:5854, pp. 1230–1.

Keukeleire, Stephan, and Tom Delreaux (2014) *The Foreign Policy of the European Union,* 2nd edn (Basingstoke: Palgrave Macmillan).

Knill, Christoph (2006) 'Implementation', in Jeremy Richardson (ed.) *European Union: Power and Policy-Making* (Abingdon: Routledge).

Knutsen, Torbjorn L. (1997) *A History of International Relations Theory*, 2nd edn (Manchester: Manchester University Press).

Kopecký, Petr, and Cas Mudde (2002) 'The Two Sides of Euroscepticism: Party Positions on European Integration in East Central Europe', *European Union Politics*, 3:3, pp. 297–326.

Kopstein, Jeffrey and Sven Steinmo (eds) (2008) *Growing Apart? America and Europe in the Twenty-First Century* (New York: Cambridge University Press).

Kowalski, Krzysztof (2009) Lecture on the History and Origins of the EU Flag, Indiana University, September.

Kyle, Keith (2003) *Suez: Britain's End of Empire in the Middle East* (London: I.B. Taurus).

Ladrech, Robert (1994) 'Europeanization of Domestic Politics and Institutions: The Case of France', *Journal of Common Market Studies*, 32:1, pp. 69–88.

Laffan, Brigid (1997) *The Finances of the European Union* (Basingstoke: Macmillan).

Laffan, Brigid, and Alexander Stubb (2003) 'Member States', in Elizabeth Bomberg and Alexander Stubb (eds) *The European Union: How Does it Work?* (Oxford: Oxford University Press).

Laffan, Brigid, and Johannes Lindner (2014) 'The Budget: Who Gets What, When and How?', in Helen Wallace, Mark A. Pollack and Alasdair R. Young (eds) *Policy-Making in the European Union*, 7th edn (Oxford: Oxford University Press).

Lancaster, Carol (2006) *Foreign Aid: Diplomacy, Development, Domestic Politics* (Chicago: University of Chicago Press).

Landman, Todd (2008) *Issues and Methods in Comparative Politics: An Introduction*, 3rd edn (New York: Routledge).

Lasok, K.P.E. (2007) *European Court Practice and Procedure*, 3rd edn (Haywards Heath: Tottel).

Lasswell, Harold D. (1968) 'The Future of the Comparative Method', *Comparative Politics*, 1:1, pp. 3–18.

Laursen, Finn (ed.) (2003) *Comparative Regional Integration: Theoretical Perspectives* (Aldershot: Ashgate).

Lavenex, Sandra (2001) 'The Europeanisation of Refugee Policies: Normative Challenges and Institutional Legacies', *Journal of Common Market Studies*, 39:5, pp. 851–74.

Lavenex, Sandra (2014) 'Justice and Home Affairs', in Helen Wallace, Mark A. Pollack and Alasdair R. Young (eds) *Policy-Making in the European Union*, 7th edn (Oxford: Oxford University Press).

Layton, Christopher (1971) *Cross-Frontier Mergers in Europe* (Bath: Bath University Press).

Layton, Lyndsey (2008) 'Chemical law has global impact', *Washington Post*, 12 June.

Leonard, Mark (2005) *Why Europe will Run the 21st Century* (London: Fourth Estate).

Lequesne, Christian (2004) *The Politics of Fisheries in the European Union* (Manchester: Manchester University Press).

Leuffen, Dirk, Berthold Rittberger and Frank Schimmelfennig (eds) (2012) *Differentiated Integration: Explaining Variation in the European Union* (Basingstoke: Palgrave Macmillan).

Levy, Jack S. (1983) *War in the Modern Great Power System, 1495–1975* (Lexington, KY: University Press of Kentucky).

Lewis, David P. (1993) *The Road to Europe: History, Institutions and Prospects of European Integration 1945–1993* (New York: Peter Lang).

Lightfoot, Simon (2005) *Europeanizing Social Democracy? The Rise of the Party of European Socialists* (London: Routledge).

Lijphart, Arend (1971) 'Comparative Politics and the Comparative Method', *American Political Science Review*, 65:3, pp. 682–93.

Lijphart, Arend (1977) *Democracy in Plural Societies: A Comparative Exploration* (New Haven, CT: Yale University Press).

Lijphart, Arend (1999) *Patterns of Democracy* (New Haven, CT: Yale University Press).

Lim, Timothy C. (2006) *Doing Comparative Politics* (Boulder, CO: Lynne Rienner).

Lindberg, Bjorn, Anne Rasmussen and Andreas Warntjen (eds) (2010) *The Role of Political Parties in the European Union* (London: Routledge).

Lindberg, Leon N. (1963) *The Political Dynamics of European Economic Integration* (Stanford: Stanford University Press).

Lindberg, Leon N. and Stuart A. Scheingold (1970) *Europe's Would-be Polity: Patterns of Change in the European Community* (Englewood Cliffs, NJ: Prentice Hall).

Lindblom, Charles (1959) 'The Science of "Muddling Through"', *Public Administration Review*, 19:2, pp. 79–88.

Lindner, Johannes (2006) *Conflict and Change in EU Budgetary Politics* (Abingdon: Routledge).

Lipset, Seymour Martin (1990) *Continental Divide: The Values and Institutions of the United States and Canada* (London: Routledge).

Lister, Frederick K. (1996) *The European Union, the United Nations, and the Revival of Confederal Governance* (Westport, CT: Greenwood).

Lodge, Juliet (ed.) (2001) *The 1999 Elections to the European Parliament* (Basingstoke: Palgrave Macmillan).

Lodge, Juliet (ed.) (2005) *The 2004 Elections to the European Parliament* (Basingstoke: Palgrave Macmillan).

Luedtke, Adam (2006) 'The European Union Dimension: Supranational Integration, Free Movement of Persons, and Immigration Politics', in Craig Parsons and Timothy M. Smeeding (eds) *Immigration and the Transformation of Europe* (Cambridge: Cambridge University Press).

Lundestad, Geir (2003) *The United States and Western Europe since 1945* (Oxford: Oxford University Press).

Maas, Willem (2007) *Creating European Citizens* (Lanham, MD: Rowman & Littlefield).

McAleavey, P. (1993) 'The Politics of European Regional Development Policy: Additionality in the Scottish Coalfields', *Regional Politics and Policy*, 3:2, pp. 88–107.

McCormick, John (1995) *The Global Environmental Movement* (London: John Wiley).

McCormick, John (1996) *The European Union: Politics and Policies* (Boulder, CO: Westview).

McCormick, John (2007) *The European Superpower* (Basingstoke: Palgrave Macmillan).

McCormick, John (2010) *Europeanism* (Oxford: Oxford University Press).

McCormick, John (2014) 'Voting on Europe: The Potential Pitfalls of a British Referendum', *Political Quarterly*, 85:2, pp. 212–19.

McGrath, Conor (2005) *Lobbying in Washington, London, and Brussels: The Persuasive Communication of Political Issues* (New York: Edwin Mellen Press).

McGuire, Steven, and Michael Smith (2008) *The European Union and the United States* (Basingstoke: Palgrave Macmillan).

McKay, David (2001) *Designing Europe: Comparative Lessons from the Federal Experience* (Oxford: Oxford University Press).

Macmillan, Harold (1971) *Riding the Storm 1956–59* (New York: Harper & Row).

MacMullen, Andrew (2000) 'European Commissioners: National Routes to a European Elite', in Neill Nugent (ed.) *At the Heart of the Union: Studies of the European Commission*, 2nd edn (New York: St Martin's Press).

Mair, Peter (2006) 'Political Parties and Party Systems', in Paolo Graziano and Maarten Vink (eds) *Europeanization: New Research Agendas* (Basingstoke: Palgrave Macmillan).

Majone, Giandomenico (1997) 'The New European Agencies: Regulation by Information', *Journal of European Public Policy*, 4:2, pp. 262–75.

Majone, Giandomenico (2006) 'Federation, Confederation, and Mixed Government: An EU-US Comparison', in Anand Menon and Martin Schain (eds) *Comparative Federalism: The European Union and the United States in Comparative Perspective* (Oxford: Oxford University Press).

Mangold, Peter (2006) *The Almost Impossible Ally: Harold Macmillan and Charles de Gaulle* (London: I.B. Taurus).

Marks, Gary (1993) 'Structural Policy and Multi-level Governance in the EC', in Alan Cafruny and Glenda Rosenthal (eds) *The State of the European Community*, vol. 2 (Boulder, CO: Lynne Rienner).

Marks, Gary, Carole J. Wilson and Leonard Ray (2002) 'National Political Parties and European Integration', *American Journal of Political Science*, 46:3, pp. 585–94.

Marks, Gary, Fritz W. Scharpf, Philippe C. Schmitter and Wolfgang Streeck (1996) *Governance in the European Union* (London: Sage).

Marks, Sally (2003) *The Illusion of Peace: International Relations in Europe, 1918–23*, 2nd edn (Basingstoke: Palgrave Macmillan).

Marlier, Eric, A.B. Atkinson, Bea Cantillon and Brian Nolan (2007) *The EU and Social Inclusion: Facing the Challenges* (Bristol: Policy Press).

Marr, Andrew (2009) 'David Miliband backs Tony Blair for EU president', *The Guardian*, 25 October.

Marsh, David (2011) *The Euro: The Battle for the New Global Currency*, rev. edn (New Haven, CT: Yale University Press).

Marshall, George C. (1947) Speech at Harvard University, June, at George C. Marshall Foundation, http://marshallfoundation.org.

Mason, David S. (2008) *The End of the American Century* (Lanham, MD: Rowman & Littlefield).

Mattli, Walter (1999) *The Logic of Regional Integration: Europe and Beyond* (Cambridge: Cambridge University Press).

Mazey, Sonia, and Jeremy Richardson (2003) 'Interest Groups and the Brussels Bureaucracy', in Jack Hayward and Anand Menon (eds) *Governing Europe* (Oxford: Oxford University Press).

Mazey, Sonia, and Jeremy Richardson (2006) 'Interest Groups and EU Policy-Making', in Jeremy Richardson (ed.) *European Union: Power and Policy-Making*, 3rd edn (Abingdon: Routledge).

Mendez, Fernando, Mario Mendez and Vasiliki Triga (2014) *Referendums and the European Union: A Comparative Inquiry* (Cambridge: Cambridge University Press).

Meunier, Sophie (2005) *Trading Voices: The European Union in International Commercial Negotiations* (Princeton: Princeton University Press).

Meunier, Sophie, and Kathleen R. McNamara (eds) (2007) *Making History: European Integration and Institutional Change at Fifty* (Oxford: Oxford University Press).

Miliband, David (2007) Speech at the College of Europe, Bruges, 15 November, www.coleurop. be/events/909.

Miller, Zeke J. (2013) 'TIME POLL: Americans believe country heading in wrong direction', *Time*, 16 June.

Millett, Timothy (1990) *The Court of First Instance of the European Communities* (London: Butterworth).

Milward, Alan S. (1984) *The Reconstruction of Western Europe 1945–51* (Berkeley: University of California Press).

Minahan, James B. (2000) *One Europe, Many Nations: A Historical Dictionary of European National Groups* (Westport, CT: Greenwood).

Mitrany, David (1966) *A Working Peace System* (Chicago: Quadrangle).

Mitrany, David (1970) 'The Functional Approach to World Organisation', in Carol A. Cosgrove and Kenneth J. Twitchett (eds) *The New International Actors: The UN and the EEC* (London: Macmillan).

Monar, Jörg (2001) 'The Dynamics of Justice and Home Affairs: Laboratories, Driving Factors and Costs', *Journal of Common Market Studies*, 39:4, pp. 747–64.

Monnet, Jean (1978) *Memoirs* (Garden City, NY: Doubleday).

Moravcsik, Andrew (1993) 'Preferences and Power in the European Community: A Liberal Intergovernmentalist Approach', *Journal of Common Market Studies*, 31:4, pp. 473–524.

Moravcsik, Andrew (1998) *The Choice for Europe* (Ithaca, NY: Cornell University Press).

Moravcsik, Andrew (2001) 'Federalism in the European Union: Rhetoric and Reality', in Kalypso Nicolaidis and Robert Howse (eds) *The Federal Vision: Legitimacy and Levels of Governance in the United States and the European Union* (Oxford: Oxford University Press).

Moravcsik, Andrew (2002) 'In Defence of the "Democratic Deficit": Reassessing Legitimacy in the European Union', *Journal of Common Market Studies*, 40:4, pp. 603–24.

Moravcsik, Andrew (2007) 'The European Constitutional Settlement', in Sophie Meunier and Kathleen R. McNamara (eds) *Making History: European Integration and Institutional Change at Fifty* (Oxford: Oxford University Press).

Morgan, Annette (1976) *From Summit to Council: Evolution in the EEC* (London: Chatham House).

Morgan, Iwan W., and Philip J. Davies (eds) (2008) *The Federal Nation: Perspectives on American Federalism* (Basingstoke: Palgrave Macmillan).

Mowle, Thomas S. (2004) *Allies at Odds? The United States and the European Union* (Basingstoke: Palgrave Macmillan).

Müller, Wolfgang C., and Kaare Strøm (eds) (2003) *Coalition Governments in Western Europe* (Oxford: Oxford University Press).

Mulvey, Stephen (2007) 'Poles in war of words over voting', *BBC News Online*, 21 June, http:// news.bbc.co.uk/1/hi/world/europe/6227834.stm, retrieved 12/12/14.

Mundell, Robert (2000) 'The Euro and the Stability of the International Monetary System', in Robert Mundell and Armand Clesse (eds) *The Euro as a Stabilizer in the International Economic System* (Dordrecht: Kluwer).

Neal, Larry (2007) *The Economics of Europe and the European Union* (Cambridge: Cambridge University Press).

Neuhold, Christine, and Pierpaolo Sttembri (2007) 'The Role of European Parliament Committees in the EU Policy-Making Process', in Thomas Christiansen and Torbjörn Larsson (eds) *The Role of Committees in the Policy-Process of the European Union* (Cheltenham: Edward Elgar).

Nijeboer, Arjen (2005) 'The Dutch Referendum', *European Constitutional Law Review*, 1:3, pp. 393–405.

Nitze, William, and Leon Hadar (2009) 'EU could bring peace to Middle East', *The Guardian*, 4 December.

Nugent, Neill (2001) *The European Commission* (Basingstoke: Palgrave Macmillan).

Nugent, Neill (2004) *European Union Enlargement* (Basingstoke: Palgrave Macmillan).

Nye, Joseph S. (1970) 'Comparing Common Markets: A Revised Neofunctionalist Model', *International Organization*, 24:4, pp. 796–835.

Occhipinti, John D. (2003) *The Politics of EU Police Cooperation: Toward a European FBI?* (Boulder, CO: Lynne Rienner).

Ohmae, Kenichi (1995) *The End of the Nation State: The Rise of Regional Economies* (New York: The Free Press).

Ohmae, Kenichi (2005) *The Next Global Stage: Challenges and Opportunities in our Borderless World* (Upper Saddle River, NJ: Wharton School Publishing).

Olsen, Johan P. (2002) 'The Many Faces of Europeanization', *Journal of Common Market Studies*, 40:5, pp. 921–52.

O'Neill, Jim (2001) 'Building Better Global Economic BRICs'. Global Economics Paper No: 66, Goldman Sachs, 30 November.

O'Neill, Jim (2010) 'A Twenty-first Century International Monetary System: Two Scenarios', in Paola Subacchi and John Driffill (eds) *Beyond the Dollar: Rethinking the International Monetary System* (London: Chatham House).

Orbie, Jan (2008) 'The European Union's Role in World Trade: Harnessing Globalisation?', in Jan Orbie (ed.) *Europe's Global Role: External Policies of the European Union* (Aldershot: Ashgate).

Orbie, Jan, and Helen Versluys (2008) 'The European Union's International Development Policy: Leading and Benevolent?', in Jan Orbie (ed.) *Europe's Global Role: External Policies of the European Union* (Aldershot: Ashgate).

Padoa-Schioppa, Tommaso (2000) *The Road to Monetary Union in Europe: The Emperor, the Kings, and the Genies* (Oxford: Oxford University Press).

Page, Benjamin I., and Robert Y. Shapiro (1992) *The Rational Public: Fifty Years of Trends in Americans' Policy Preferences* (Chicago: University of Chicago Press).

Page, Edward C. (2003) 'Europeanization and the Persistence of Administrative Systems', in Jack Hayward and Anand Menon (eds) *Governing Europe* (Oxford: Oxford University Press).

Palayret, Jean-Marie, Helen Wallace and Pascaline Wynand (eds) (2006) *Visions, Votes and Vetoes: The Empty Chair Crisis and the Luxembourg Compromise Forty Years On* (Brussels: Peter Lang).

Palmer, Michael, and John Lambert (eds) (1968) *European Unity: A Survey of European Organizations* (London: George Allen & Unwin).

Pan, Christoph, and Beate Sibylle Pfeil (2004) *National Minorities in Europe* (West Lafayette, IN: Purdue University Press).

Panayi, Panikos (2000) *An Ethnic History of Europe Since 1945: Nations, States and Minorities* (Harlow: Longman).

Pardo, Sharon, and Joel Peters (2009) *Uneasy Neighbors: Israel and the European Union* (Lanham, MD: Lexington Books).

Parsons, Craig, and Timothy M. Smeeding (eds) (2006a) *Immigration and the Transformation of Europe* (Cambridge: Cambridge University Press).

Parsons, Craig, and Timothy M. Smeeding (2006b) 'What's Unique about Immigration in Europe?', in Craig Parsons and Timothy M. Smeeding (eds) *Immigration and the Transformation of Europe* (Cambridge: Cambridge University Press).

Pastor, Robert A. (2001) *Toward a North American Community: Lessons from the Old World for the New* (Washington DC: Institute for International Economics).

Pearce, David, and Francois-Carlos Bovagnet (2005) 'The Demographic Situation in the European Union', *Population Trends*, No. 119 (London: ONS).

Pedler, Robin (2002) *European Union Lobbying: Changes in the Arena* (Basingstoke: Palgrave Macmillan).

Persson, Mats (2012) 'The EU: Quick to Regulate, Slow to Adapt', in Hubert Zimmermann and Andreas Dür (eds) *Key Controversies in European Integration* (Basingstoke: Palgrave Macmillan).

Peter, Laurence (2009) 'Profile: EU Commission Chief Barroso', *BBC News Online*, 8 July.

Peter, Laurence (2010) 'Delays Bedevil EU Help for Roma', *BBC News Online*, 16 September.

Peters, B. Guy (1992) 'Bureaucratic Politics and the Institutions of the European Community', in Alberta Sbragia (ed.) *Euro-Politics: Institutions and Policymaking in the 'New' European Community* (Washington DC: Brookings Institution).

Peters, B. Guy, and Jon Pierre (2004) 'Multi-level Governance and Democracy: A Faustian Bargain?', in Ian Bache and Matthew Flinders (eds) *Multi-Level Governance* (Oxford: Oxford University Press).

Peterson, John, and Mark A. Pollack (eds) (2003) *Europe, America, Bush: Transatlantic Relations in the Twenty-First Century* (London: Routledge).

Pew Research Center (2012) *The Global Religious Landscape: A Report on the Size and Distribution of the World's Major Religious Groups as of 2010.* Pew Forum on Religion & Public Life (Washington DC: Pew Research Center).

Philip, Alan Butt (1985) *Pressure Groups in the European Community* (London: University Association for Contemporary European Studies).

Pienning, Christopher (2001) 'The EP Since 1994: Making its Mark on the World Stage', in Juliet Lodge (ed.) *The 1999 Elections to the European Parliament* (Basingstoke: Palgrave Macmillan).

Pijpers, Alfred (1998) 'Intergovernmental Conferences' entry, in Desmond Dinan (ed.) *Encyclopedia of the European Union* (Basingstoke: Macmillan).

Pinder, John (1991) *European Community: The Building of a Union* (Oxford: Oxford University Press).

Piris, Jean-Claude (2006) *The Constitution for Europe: A Legal Analysis* (Cambridge: Cambridge University Press).

Pisani-Ferry, Jean (2014) *The Euro Crisis and its Aftermath* (Oxford: Oxford University Press).

Pollard, Naomi, Maria Latorre and Dhananjayan Sriskandarajah (2008) *Floodgates or Turnstiles? Post-EU Enlargement Migration Flows to (and from) the UK* (London: IPPR).

Popkin, Samuel (1994) *The Reasoning Voter: Communication and Persuasion in Presidential Campaigns* (Chicago: University of Chicago Press).

Prestowitz, Clyde (2003) *Rogue Nation: American Unilateralism and the Failure of Good Intentions* (New York: Basic Books).

Puchala, Donald J. (1975) 'Domestic Politics and Regional Harmonization in the European Communities', *World Politics*, 27:4, pp. 496–520.

Raz, Joseph (1998) 'On the Authority and Interpretation of Constitutions: Some Preliminaries', in Larry Alexander (ed.) *Constitutionalism: Philosophical Foundations* (Cambridge: Cambridge University Press).

Reid, T.R. (2004) *The United States of Europe: The New Superpower and the End of American Supremacy* (New York: Penguin).

Reiff, Karlheinz, and Hermann Schmitt (1980) 'Nine Second-Order National Elections: A Conceptual Framework for the Analysis of European Election Results', *European Journal of Political Research*, 8:1, pp. 3–44.

Renan, Ernest (1882) 'What is a Nation?' Speech at the Sorbonne in March, translated by and quoted in Timothy Baycroft, *Nationalism in Europe 1789–1945* (Cambridge: Cambridge University Press, 1998).

Rhodes, Martin (2010) 'Employment Policy: Between Efficacy and Experimentation', in Helen Wallace, Mark A. Pollack and Alasdair R. Young (eds) *Policy-Making in the European Union*, 6th edn (Oxford: Oxford University Press).

Richardson, Jeremy (2006) 'Policy-making in the EU: Interests, Ideas and Garbage Cans of Primeval Soup', in Jeremy Richardson (ed.) *European Union: Power and Policy-Making*, 3rd edn (Abingdon: Routledge).

Riddell, Roger (2007) *Does Foreign Aid Really Work?* (New York: Oxford University Press).

Rieger, Elmar (2005) 'Agricultural Policy: Constrained Reforms', in Helen Wallace, William Wallace and Mark A. Pollack (eds) *Policy-Making in the European Union*, 5th edn (Oxford: Oxford University Press).

Rifkin, Jeremy (2004) *The European Dream: How Europe's Vision of the Future is Quietly Eclipsing the American Dream* (New York: Jeremy Tarcher/Penguin).

Ringe, Nils (2009) *Who Decides, and How? Preferences, Uncertainty, and Policy Choice in the European Parliament* (Oxford: Oxford University Press).

Rittberger, Berthold (2005) *Building Europe's Parliament: Democratic Representation beyond the Nation-State* (Oxford: Oxford University Press).

Robertson, Roland, and Sophie Krossa (eds) (2012) *European Cosmopolitanism in Question* (Basingstoke: Palgrave Macmillan).

Robyn, Richard (ed.) (2005) *The Changing Face of European Identity* (Abingdon: Routledge).

Roper, Steven (2007) 'European Education Reform and its Impact on Curriculum and Admissions: Implications of the Bologna Process on United States Education', *Journal of Political Science Education*, 3:1, pp. 51–60.

Rosamond, Ben (2000) *Theories of European Integration* (Basingstoke: Macmillan).

Rosamond, Ben (2013) 'Theorizing the European Union after Integration Theory', in Michelle Cini and Nieves Pérez-Solórzano Borragán (eds) *European Union Politics*, 4th edn (Oxford: Oxford University Press).

Ross, Robert, Øystein Tunsjø and Zhang Tuosheng (eds) (2010) *US–China–EU Relations* (Abingdon: Routledge).

Ruggie, John Gerard, Peter J. Katzenstein, Robert O. Keohane and Philippe C. Schmitter (2005) 'Transformations in World Politics: The Intellectual Contribution of Ernst B. Haas', *Annual Review of Political Science*, 8, pp. 271–96.

Rüland, Jürgen, Heiner Hänggi and Ralf Roloff (eds) (2008) *Interregionalism and International Relations: A Stepping Stone to Global Governance?* (Abingdon: Routledge).

Rumford, Chris (2007) 'Introduction', *Cosmopolitanism and Europe* (Liverpool: Liverpool University Press).

Russell, James W. (2006) *Double Standard: Social Policy in Europe and the United States* (Lanham, MD: Rowman & Littlefield).

Salmon, Trevor, and Sir William Nicoll (eds) (1997) *Building European Union: A Documentary History and Analysis* (Manchester: Manchester University Press).

Saurugger, Sabine (2013) *Theoretical Approaches to European Integration* (Basingstoke: Palgrave Macmillan).

Sbragia, Alberta (1992) 'Introduction' and 'Thinking about the European Future: The Uses of Comparison', in Alberta Sbragia (ed.) *Euro-Politics: Institutions and Policymaking in the 'New' European Community* (Washington DC: Brookings Institution).

Schimmelfennig, Frank, and Ulrich Sedelmeier (eds) (2005) *The Europeanization of Central and Eastern Europe* (Ithaca, NY: Cornell University Press).

Scully, Roger (2005) *Becoming Europeans? Attitudes, Behaviour, and Socialization in the European Parliament* (Oxford: Oxford University Press).

Selznick, Philip (2002) *The Communitarian Persuasion* (Baltimore, MD: Johns Hopkins University Press).

Shackleton, Michael (1990) *Financing the European Community* (New York: Council on Foreign Relations Press).

Shambaugh, David, Eberhard Sandschneider and Zhou Hong (eds) (2008) *China-Europe Relations: Perceptions, Policies and Prospects* (Abingdon: Routledge).

Shapiro, Martin (1992) 'The European Court of Justice', in Alberta Sbragia (ed.) *Euro-Politics: Institutions and Policymaking in the 'New' European Community* (Washington DC: Brookings Institution).

Simpson, A.W. Brian (2001) *Human Rights and the End of Empire: Britain and the Genesis of the European Convention* (Oxford: Oxford University Press).

Skogstad, Grace, and Amy Verdun (eds) (2010) *The Common Agricultural Policy: Policy Dynamics in a Changing Context* (Abingdon: Routledge).

Skouris, Vassilios (2004) Interview with the *Financial Times* (London) 30 June, www.open-europe.org.uk.

Smith, Andy (ed.) (2004) *Politics and the European Commission: Actors, Interdependence, Legitimacy* (London: Routledge).

Smith, Graham (1999) *The Post-Soviet States: Mapping the Politics of Transition* (London: Edward Arnold).

Smith, Michael (2006) 'The Commission and External Relations', in David Spence (ed.) *The European Commission*, 3rd edn (London: John Harper).

Smith, Roy, Imad El-Anis and Christopher Farrands (2013) *International Political Economy in the 21st Century: Contemporary Issues and Analyses* (Abingdon: Routledge).

Sniderman, Paul M., Richard A. Brody and Philp E. Tetlock (1991) *Reasoning and Choice: Explorations in Political Psychology* (New York: Cambridge University Press).

Snyder, Francis (2003) 'The Unfinished Constitution of the European Union: Principles, Processes and Culture', in J.H.H. Weiler and Marlene Wind (eds) *European Constitutionalism Beyond the State* (Cambridge: Cambridge University Press).

Snyder, Jack (2004) 'One World, Rival Theories', *Foreign Policy*, 145, pp. 53–62

Sørensen, Georg (2004) *The Transformation of the State: Beyond the Myth of Retreat* (Basingstoke: Palgrave Macmillan).

Sørensen, Georg (2006) 'The Transformation of the State', in Colin Hay, Michael Lister and David Marsh (eds) *The State: Theories and Issues* (Basingstoke: Palgrave Macmillan).

Soros, George (2012) Remarks at the Festival of Economics, Trento, Italy, 2 June. Available at www.georgesoros.com/interviews-speeches/entry/remarks_at_the_festival_of_economics_trento_italy, retrieved 12/12/14.

Spaak, Paul-Henri (1971) *The Continuing Battle: Memoirs of a European 1933–66* (Boston: Little, Brown).

Spence, David (2006a) 'The President, the College and the Cabinets', in David Spence (ed.) *The European Commission*, 3rd edn (London: John Harper).

Spence, David (2006b) 'The Directorates-General and the Services: Structures, Functions and Procedures', in David Spence (ed.) *The European Commission*, 3rd edn (London: John Harper).

Spero, Joan E., and Jeffrey A. Hart (2003) *The Politics of International Economic Relations* (Belmont, CA: Wadsworth).

Spinelli, Altiero (1972) 'The Growth of the European Movement since the Second World War', in Michael Hodges (ed.) *Europe Integration: Selected Readings* (Harmondsworth: Penguin).

Stirk, Peter M.R., and David Weigall (eds) (1999) *The Origins and Development of European Integration: A Reader and Commentary* (New York: Pinter).

Swinbank, Alan (2002) 'The Common Agricultural Policy', in Jackie Gower (ed.) *The European Union Handbook*, 2nd edn (London: Fitzroy Dearborn).

Taggart, Paul, and Aleks Szczerbiak (2001) 'Parties, Positions and Europe: Euroscepticism in the Candidate States of Central and Eastern Europe'. Paper presented at the Annual Meeting of the Political Studies Association, Manchester, April.

Taggart, Paul, and Aleks Szczerbiak (eds) (2008) *Opposing Europe? The Comparative Party Politics of Euroscepticism*, vols 1 and 2 (Oxford: Oxford University Press).

Taylor, Simon (2009) 'Party deals give Buzek clear run to presidency', *European Voice*, 8 July.

Thatcher, Margaret (1993) *The Downing Street Years* (New York: HarperCollins).

Thomassen, Jacques (2005) 'Introduction', in Jacques Thomassen (ed.) *The European Voter: A Comparative Study of Modern Democracies* (Oxford: Oxford University Press).

Trigg, Roger (2001) *Understanding Social Science*, 2nd edn (Oxford: Blackwell).

Truman, Harry S. (1947) Speech to US Congress, March, at Harry S. Truman Library and Museum, www.trumanlibrary.org.

Tsoukalis, Loukas (2003) 'Monetary Policy and the Euro', in Jack Hayward and Anand Menon (eds) *Governing Europe* (Oxford: Oxford University Press).

Tushnet, Mark V. (2000) *Taking the Constitution Away From the Courts* (Princeton: Princeton University Press).

UN Department of Economic and Social Affairs, Population Division (2013a) *World Population Prospects: The 2012 Revision* (New York: UN).

UN Department of Economic and Social Affairs, Population Division (2013b) *Trends in International Migrant Stock: The 2013 Revision* (United Nations database, POP/DB/MIG/Stock/Rev.2013).

United Nations High Commissioner for Refugees (2014) *Asylum Trends 2013*, www.unhcr.org/5329b15a9.html, retrieved April 2014.

Urwin, Derek W. (1995) *The Community of Europe*, 2nd edn (London: Longman).

Van der Eijk, Cees, and Mark N. Franklin (eds) (1996) *Choosing Europe? The European Electorate and National Politics in the Face of Union* (Ann Arbor, MI: University of Michigan Press).

Van Dormael, Armand (1978) *Bretton Woods: Birth of a Monetary System* (New York: Holmes & Meier).

Van Eekelen, Willem (1990) 'WEU and the Gulf Crisis', *Survival*, 32:6, pp. 519–32.

Vasileva, Katya (2010) 'Foreigners living in the EU are diverse and largely younger than the nationals of the EU Member States', *Eurostat Statistics in Focus*, 45/2010 (Brussels: Eurostat).

Védrine, Hubert, with Dominique Moïsi (2001) *France in an Age of Globalization* (Washington DC: Brookings Institution).

Vogt, Roland (ed.) (2012) *Europe and China: Strategic Partners or Rivals?* (Hong Kong: University of Hong Kong Press).

Von Hippel, Karin (ed.) (2005) *Europe Confronts Terrorism* (Basingstoke: Palgrave Macmillan).

Von Coudenhove-Kalergi, Richard N. (1926) *Pan-Europa* (New York: A.A. Knopf).

Walkenhorst, Heiko (2008) 'Explaining Change in EU Education Policy', *Journal of European Public Policy*, 15:4, pp. 567–87.

Wallace, Anthony (2004) 'Completing the Single Market: The Lisbon Strategy', in Maria Green Cowles and Desmond Dinan (eds) *Developments in the European Union 2* (Basingstoke: Palgrave Macmillan).

Wallace, Helen, Mark A. Pollack and Alasdair R. Young (eds) (2014) *Policy-Making in the European Union*, 7th edn (Oxford: Oxford University Press).

Wallace, William (1983) 'Less than a Federation, More than a Regime: The Community as a Political System', in Helen Wallace, William Wallace and Carole Webb (eds) *Policy-Making in the European Community*, 2nd edn (Chichester: Wiley).

Wallace, William (2005) 'Foreign and Security Policy', in Helen Wallace, William Wallace and Mark A. Pollack (eds) *Policy-Making in the European Union*, 5th edn (Oxford: Oxford University Press).

Walt, Stephen M. (1998) 'One World, Many Theories', *Foreign Policy* 110, pp. 29–32, 34–46.

Ward, Ian (1996) *A Critical Introduction to European Law* (London: Butterworth).

Watts, Ronald J. (2008) *Comparing Federal Systems*, 3rd edn (Montreal: Institute of Intergovernmental Relations).

Weigall, David, and Peter Stirk (eds) (1992) *The Origins and Development of the European Community* (Leicester: Leicester University Press).

Werts, Jan (2008) *The European Council* (London: John Harper).

Westlake, Martin, and David Galloway (eds) (2004) *The Council of the European Union*, 3rd edn (London: John Harper).

WEU (Western European Union) (1964) *Political Union of Europe* (Paris: WEU).

Wexler, Immanuel (1983) *The Marshall Plan Revisited: The European Recovery Program in Economic Perspective* (Westport, CT: Greenwood Press).

Whitaker, Richard (2010) *The European Parliament's Committees* (Abingdon: Routledge).

White, Brian (2001) *Understanding European Foreign Policy* (Basingstoke: Palgrave Macmillan).

Wiener, Antje, and Thomas Diez (eds) (2009) *European Integration Theory*, 2nd edn (Oxford: Oxford University Press).

Wildavsky, Aaron (1979) *Speaking Truth to Power* (New York: John Wiley).

Wilks, Stephen (2014) 'Competition Policy', in Helen Wallace, Mark A. Pollack, and Alasdair R. Young (eds) *Policy-Making in the European Union*, 7th edn (Oxford: Oxford University Press).

Windrow, Martin (2004) *The Last Valley: Dien Bien Phu and the French Defeat in Vietnam* (London: Weidenfeld & Nicolson).

Wolff, Sarah, Nicole Wichmann and Gregory Mounier (eds) (2009) *The External Dimension of Justice and Home Affairs: A Different Security Agenda for the European Union?* (Abingdon: Routledge).

WTO (World Trade Organization) (2012) *International Trade Statistics 2012*, www.wto.org/english/res_e/statis_e/its2012_e/its12_toc_e.htm, retrieved 12/12/14.

Wurzel, Rüdiger, and James Connelly (eds) (2010) *The European Union as a Leader in International Climate Change Politics* (Abingdon: Routledge).

Yahuda, Michael (2008) 'The Sino-European Encounter: Historical Influences on Contemporary Encounters', in David Shambaugh, Eberhard Sandschneider and Zhou Hong (eds) *China–Europe Relations: Perceptions, Policies and Prospects* (Abingdon: Routledge).

Young, Alasdair R. (2014) 'The European Policy Process in Comparative Perspective', in Helen Wallace, Mark A. Pollack and Alasdair R. Young (eds) *Policy-Making in the European Union*, 7th edn (Oxford: Oxford University Press).

Young, Alasdair, and John Peterson (2014) *Parochial Global Europe: 21st Century Trade Politics* (Oxford: Oxford University Press).

Zeff, Eleanor, and Ellen Pirro (eds) (2015) *The European Union and the Member States*, 3rd edn (Boulder, CO: Lynne Rienner).

Zibold, Franziska (2013) 'Briefing: Lobbying the EU Institutions'. Library of the European Parliament, 18 July.

Zimmerman, Joseph F. (2008) *Contemporary American Federalism: The Growth of National Power* (Albany, NY: State University of New York Press).

Zurcher, Arnold J. (1958) *The Struggle to Unite Europe 1940–58* (New York: New York University Press).

Index

Notes: key entries (usually with definitions) indicated in **bold**; entries for countries are limited to major references to those countries.